BRITISH GALLANTRY AWARDS

PLATE 1

Top, left to right: Indian Order of Merit (Military Division), 2nd Class, 1837–1912;
Albert Medal (in bronze, land services); Sea Gallantry Medal in Silver (Edward VII issue, second type).
Centre, left to right: Edward Medal (in bronze, George V issue, first type);
King's Commendation for Brave Conduct (original plastic badge);
Military Medal (George V issue, second type).
Bottom, left to right: Air Force Medal (George VI issue, first type);
Colonial Police Medal for Gallantry (George VI issue, second type);
Distinguished Service Cross (Elizabeth II issue).

BRITISH GALLANTRY AWARDS

P. E. ABBOTT

J. M. A. TAMPLIN

NIMROD DIX & CO · LONDON

Copyright 1981 Nimrod Dix & Co

Published in Great Britain by
Nimrod Dix & Co, 17 Piccadilly Arcade
London SW1

Picton Publishing ISBN 0 902633 74 0

Photography by R. J. Scarlett
Photoset in AM Times Roman
by Chippenham Typesetting, Bath Road, Chippenham, Wiltshire
Colour separations by Format Graphics, Bristol
Text paper supplied by Howard Smith Papers, Bristol
Bound by Western Book Company, Maesteg
Designed and printed in Great Britain by Picton Print
Citadel Works, Bath Road, Chippenham, Wiltshire

List of Contents

Note to the Illustrations

In order to avoid repetition, the following notes are intended to amplify the text in regard to certain awards:

George V second type The crowned effigy of the King was introduced for a number of medals issued after 1st January 1931 although in some cases, which are noted in the text, issues were made in 1930.

George VI second type By a Royal Proclamation of 22nd June 1948 the King's style and titles were altered as a result of his ceasing to be Emperor of India.

Elizabeth II second type By a Royal Proclamation of 28th May 1953 the Queen's titles were altered so as to reflect more clearly constitutional changes which had taken place in the Commonwealth.

It is important to note however that changes in the last two mentioned above were not always immediately reflected in the actual issues made and, where possible, we have given examples of this in the text.

The illustration of the Indian Order of Merit (Civil Division), 1939–47, appears by gracious permission of Her Majesty The Queen. Reproductions of copyright photographs in all other cases appear through the kind offices of Messrs. J. B. Hayward and Son and R. J. Scarlett, except for those in Chapters 8 (Fig.F), 11 (Figs.A and B), 13 (Figs.A and B), 16 (Fig.D), 18 (Figs.A, B, D, E and G to J), 19 (Fig.B), 24 (Figs.A to C and E to H), 26, 36 (Figs.A and C), 37 (Fig.F), 40 (Figs.A and B), 42 (Figs.B, C, E and H to J), 43 (Fig.B) and 44. For these we are grateful to, *inter alios*, J. W. Enticknap Esq., Guinness Superlatives Ltd., Leith Air Ltd., Spink and Son Ltd. and Sotheby Parke Bernet and Co. We are also indebted to the following for making various items available to us for photographing: The Deputy Master and Comptroller of the Royal Mint, Doctor I. M. Dawson, Stanley Gibbons Ltd., S. King Esq., S.G.M., M. S. Leahy Esq., B. A. Seaby Ltd., Spink and Son Ltd., D. Stanley Esq. and E. G. Ursual Esq.

Index to Ribbon Chart

NOTE: The dates of currency given below are amplified in the chapters dealing with individual awards. In selecting ribbons for the chart, official issues have been used where these could be identified; in other cases specimens nearest to the correct colour and quality have been included. For the order of wearing, see Appendix 4.

1. Victoria Cross (Navy, 1856–1918)
2. Victoria Cross (Army from 1856; all Services from 1918; emblem from 1916/1917)
3. New Zealand Cross
4. George Cross (1¼-inches wide in 1940; 1½-inches from 1941)
5. Distinguished Service Order with standard rosette denoting award of bar
6. Indian Order of Merit (Military Division)
7. Royal Red Cross, 1st and 2nd Classes
8. Conspicuous/Distinguished Service Cross
9. Military Cross
10. Distinguished Flying Cross (1918/1919)
11. Distinguished Flying Cross (from 1919)
12. Air Force Cross (1918/1919)
13. Air Force Cross (from 1919)
14. Albert Medal 1st Class for Saving Life at Sea (1867–1917) and Albert Medal in Gold (1917–1949)
15. Albert Medal 1st Class for Saving Life on Land (1877–1917) and Albert Medal in Gold (1917–1949)
16. Albert Medal 2nd Class for Saving Life at Sea (1867–1904; also used for the 1st Class 1866/1867)
17. Albert Medal 2nd Class for Saving Life on Land (1877–1904)
18. Albert Medal 2nd Class for Saving Life at Sea (1904–1917) and Albert Medal (1917–1971)
19. Albert Medal 2nd Class for Saving Life on Land (1904–1917) and Albert Medal (1917–1971)
20. Distinguished Conduct Medal
21. Conspicuous Gallantry Medal (until 1921)
22. Conspicuous Gallantry Medal (from 1921)
23. Conspicuous Gallantry Medal (Flying)
24. George Medal
25. King's Police Medal (for Gallantry or Distinguished Service, 1909–1916)
26. King's Police Medal (for Gallantry or Distinguished Service, 1916–1933)
27. King's Police (and, later, King's Police and Fire Services) Medal, for Gallantry (1933–1954), and Queen's Police Medal, for Gallantry (from 1954)
28. Queen's Fire Service Medal, for Gallantry
29. Edward Medals
30. Distinguished Conduct Medal (for Royal West African Frontier Force and King's African Rifles)
31. Indian Distinguished Service Medal
32. Burma Gallantry Medal
33. King's/Queen's Medals for Bravery (Union of South Africa)
34. Distinguished Service Medal
35. Military Medal
36. Distinguished Flying Medal (1918/1919)
37. Distinguished Flying Medal (from 1919)
38. Air Force Medal (1918/1919)
39. Air Force Medal (from 1919)
40. Constabulary Medal (Ireland); (from 1872; light blue, 1842–1872)
41. Sea Gallantry Medal (from 1904) and Sea Gallantry Medal (Foreign Services) (from 1922)

PLATE 2

1

2

3

7

8

9

13

14

15

19

20

21

25

26

27

31

32

33

37

38

39

43

44

45

49

50

51

55

56

4

5

6

10

11

12

16

17

18

22

23

24

28

29

30

34

35

36

40

41

42

46

47

48

52

53

54

57

58

Foreword to the First Edition

During recent years interest in medal collecting has increased considerably and, since no detailed study of British gallantry awards has yet appeared, we have sought to remedy the omission by the present work. Even in this relatively limited field we have had to be selective and therefore, except for an occasional passing reference, we have omitted those awards which are:

1. given only to foreigners, *i.e.* the Board of Trade "Foreign Services" Medals, and the King's Medal for Courage in the Cause of Freedom,

2. peculiar to the Defence and Police Forces of South Africa but instituted before the creation of the Republic; and those instituted by certain Commonwealth countries after becoming independent, *e.g.* the Ceylon Police Medal[1] for Gallantry, the Uganda Services Medal, etc., and

3. given by private bodies, *e.g.* the Royal Humane Society, the Royal National Life-boat Institution, etc.

For the same reason we have not dealt with awards which are not primarily for gallantry but which have been so awarded, *e.g.* the military Meritorious Service Medal, the African Police Medal for Meritorious Service, the Kaisar-i-Hind Medal, etc. Similarly we have excluded the Order of Burma[2] of which no awards for gallantry seem to have been made.

As far as possible each award has been described separately, and in full. Although this has led to some repetition we hope this will save the reader time in finding the information he needs. Also, with this in mind, we have arranged the awards alphabetically rather than in order of precedence, or of institution. While this has had the effect of placing the Victoria Cross last it has, at least, the merit of making reference simpler. For those to whom the order of precedence is important we have included Appendix Four which gives the detail.

The awards are considered under five main headings, *i.e.* Origin and Development; Description; Verifications and Citations; Numbers Awarded; and Illustrative Award. In the first of these we have quoted fully the instituting Warrants or Orders but have only summarised amendments and such other authorities as are relevant. In regard to authorities, we have drawn widely upon Army Orders, even in cases of awards which are not peculiar to the Army, because these have been readily accessible to us and provide a close dating to many of the changes which have taken place. For "Numbers Awarded" we have used those secondary sources which seemed to us to be accurate, as well as having undertaken many tedious "counts" in the *London Gazette* itself[3]. The latter have brought to light some awards which do not appear in the Gazette indices. Despite this, we cannot claim that our figures are completely accurate[4] except possibly for the rarer awards; but at least they can be taken as a reasonable guide. Our research has been taken up to and including the Gazettes for 1969; since the Gazette indices are not published until almost a year after the last Gazette for any one year we have had to rely on searching the unindexed Gazettes for the later awards. For the "Illustrative Award" it would have been tempting to describe some of the more spectacular groups which are known. We have however rejected this solution because such groups would complicate and not necessarily illustrate the text. The awards we have used for this purpose have been specially chosen, as far as possible, to show the practical application of the text. Where we have quoted details of recipients these are, generally, as they appeared at the time that the particular award was made. To do otherwise would introduce much biographical matter unnecessary for our purpose, although the "Illustrative Award", by its very nature, contains supplementary matter.

1. Which replaced the Colonial Police Medal in that country.

2. Instituted by Royal Warrant on 10th May 1940 (see the *London Gazette* of 4th September 1940) and extended to gallantry by Royal Warrant on 11th September 1945 (see the *London Gazette* of 18th September 1945). At least 24 awards for good service were made (see *The Burma Gazette* of 4th January and 14th June 1941; 2nd June 1942; 5th January 1946; 4th January and 14th June 1947).

3. Where awards have been published in and paged for January as a Supplement to a December Gazette, we have counted them in the awards for January.

4. In particular, honorary awards to foreigners were rarely gazetted.

We have encountered difficulties in dating actual issues. While the date of an award can usually be found by reference to the appropriate authority, the actual piece issued may be of an earlier or later pattern. Thus not all the Distinguished Conduct Medals awarded for the South African War of 1899–1902 or those awarded after 1948 bear the expected obverse, a possible explanation being that existing stocks were used up before issues of the new obverse were made. The Distinguished Service Order presents another difficulty. On 24th July 1902 the cypher on the reverse of the badge was altered by Royal Warrant although the final design was not approved by the King until 5th November following. The last awards for the South African War were gazetted on 31st October 1902 (the corresponding nominations being dated 22nd August 1902), yet all save one of such issues that we have seen have had the Victorian cypher. Because of these difficulties we have drawn only tentative conclusions and deal with such apparent inconsistencies as we have found in the appropriate text. In passing, it is perhaps worthwhile mentioning that certain decorations are dated, either fully[5] or with the year alone[6]. In cases of the latter, gazetting may have occurred in a later year than that given on the decoration.

We have given the question of detail much thought, particularly in regard to naming. To give too little might not serve to expose forgeries, while to give too much might facilitate the making of them, and so we have tried to strike a balance between these two extremes. Anyone buying a rare decoration should seek expert advice first. For "Copies and Fakes" we have used "copy" to describe a replica, and "fake" to mean a copy or Mint specimen which has been fraudulently named. A further pitfall lies in replacements. Some replacements have been issued (and not marked as such) which are difficult to detect readily from the original issue, although occasionally a different type of fitting is used to connect the suspender with the piece. While such replacements are quite genuine, they are not much valued by collectors.

Although we have tried hard to avoid errors, it is unlikely that a work of this nature can be free from them, and we should be grateful for any corrections which can be supported by reference to a genuine piece, or to an official source.

Finally, we wish to record here out debt to Mr. F. K. Mason, of Guinness Superlatives Ltd., whose careful editing of our text and many helpful suggestions have been invaluable to us.

5. *E.g.* the V.C. (date of act), G.C. (date of gazetting).

6. *E.g.* Some issues of the D.S.C., M.C., A.F.C., etc.

The Royal United Service Institution,
Whitehall,
London, S.W.1
November 1970

P. E. Abbott
J. M. A. Tamplin

Foreword to the Second Edition

Since this book was first published in 1971 much additional information has become available, principally in the Public Record Office, which has enabled us to expand many Chapters. This, however, has not been our only source. Through the kindness of old friends, and of many new ones, we have been introduced to fresh material for which we are grateful. We have also taken the opportunity of making a number of minor (and mercifully few) corrections to the original text.

From these sources our second edition springs. The original text has been revised substantially, and expanded by about a third. In this connection we gratefully acknowledge the kindness of Mr J. B. Hayward for permitting us to reproduce in Chapter 12 the "Historical Note" to Abbott's *Recipients of the Distinguished Conduct Medal, 1855–1909*. We have, moreover, modified our original plan by adding ten new Chapters although, for various reasons, we have been unable to include material on awards instituted since 1945 for certain Commonwealth countries (of which those for Australia are among the more recent). The new Chapters are those concerning the African Police Medal; the Allied Subjects' Medal; the King's Medal for Courage in the Cause of Freedom; the four Meritorious Service Medals; the Queen's Gallantry Medal (instituted in 1974); the Royal Red Cross; and the Sea Gallantry Medal (Foreign Services). This has, led us, *inter alia*, to renumber and slightly alter the order of the original Chapters (which remain in alphabetical order); to provide 51 additional illustrations; and to introduce references to more than 300 further recipients so that the total of such references in the text is now slightly over 1,000. Otherwise we have followed the format of the first edition. Where, in "Verifications and Citations", we have referred to the periods covered by certain classes of document in the Public Record Office it will be appreciated that the references to such periods will become out of date as, with the passage of time, more recent documents become available for public inspection. As to "Numbers Awarded" we have carried the figures, where appropriate, up to and including the *London Gazettes* of 1979.

Elsewhere we acknowledge our debt to those who have helped us with our researches. Here, however, we think it appropriate to record our gratitude to Mr D. B. Picton-Phillips and the Staff of Picton Print for making the transition from manuscript to print so painless, and to Mrs C. M. G. Abbott for her patient proof-reading.

The Royal United Service Institution,   P. E. Abbott
Whitehall,   J. M. A. Tamplin
London,
SW1A 2ET
November 1980

Acknowledgements

Crown Copyright material in the India Office Records transcribed in this book appears by permission of the Secretary of State for Foreign and Commonwealth Affairs, while that extracted from records in the Public Record Office, from the *London Gazette* and from other official publications appears by permission of the Controller of Her Majesty's Stationery Office. For permission to use other copyright material we wish to express our gratitude to:

The Editor, *The Devonshire and Dorset Regimental Journal* for an extract from the obituary of W. G. Hand.

Gale and Polden Ltd., for extracts from *The History of the 19th King George's Own Lancers, 1858–1921* by General Sir Havelock Hudson, G.C.B., K.C.I.E.; *The History of the Lancashire Fusiliers, 1914–1918* by J. C. Latter; and *The King's African Rifles* by H. Moyse-Bartlett.

Gieves Ltd., for an extract from *Gallant Deeds* by W. H. D. Boyle.

The Hutchinson Publishing Group Ltd., for an extract from *Deeds that Thrill the Empire*.

Macmillan and Co. Ltd., for extracts from *The History of the Zulu Rebellion, 1906* by J. Stuart.

The New Zealand Government Printer for the biographical details of recipients of the New Zealand Cross which appear in *An Encyclopaedia of New Zealand*.

The Police Review Publishing Co. Ltd., for the citations of Chief Inspector L. Elwell and Police Constable S. H. Jackson.

John Sherratt and Son Ltd., for an extract from *The Lancashire Fusiliers, Salford Brigade (15th, 16th, 19th, 20th and 21st Lancashire Fusiliers)* by C. A. Montague Barlow.

Spink and Son Ltd., for the figures extracted from *The Indian Distinguished Service Medal* by H. Bullock and *Gallantry Awards* by C. J. Kendall-Wingate which appeared in the *Numismatic Circular* for October 1955 and March and September 1960 respectively.

We owe much to friends and correspondents who have provided information not otherwise accessible to us and to those who, often at considerable inconvenience to themselves, have lent us actual awards for examination. Without their help much of this book would not have been possible and we gratefully record our indebtedness to:

P. G. W. Annis, Esq., The National Maritime Museum
R. Atkins, Esq.
R. F. Barden, Esq., of A. H. Baldwin and Sons Ltd.
D. J. Callaghan, Esq., of Hancocks and Co. Ltd.
R. Carnot, Esq., The Royal Mint
The Secretary, The Central Chancery of the Orders of Knighthood
Captain W. W. F. Chatterton-Dickson, R.N.
The Librarian, The Foreign and Commonwealth Office
L. Cripwell, Esq.
D. J. Croll, Esq.
Doctor I. M. Dawson
The late W. P. Dawson, Esq.
Captain K. J. Douglas-Morris, R.N.
Dunlop India Ltd.
A. J. Farrington, Esq., India Office Library and Records
Major A. F. Flatow, T.D.
Garrard and Co. Ltd., The Crown Jewellers
D. G. Glover, Esq.
R. F. Gowans, Esq.
D. C. Hall, Esq.
G. L. Hancock Dore, Esq., of Hancocks and Co. Ltd.

G. W. Harris, Esq.
J. B. Hayward, Esq., of J. B. Hayward and Son
J. H. Hine, Esq., of B. A. Seaby Ltd.
The Director, The Imperial War Museum
Professor R. W. Irwin
R. H. James, Esq.
Major E. Jessup, The Royal Lincolnshire Regiment Museum
E. C. Joslin, Esq., of Spink and Son Ltd.
Miss J. Kenworthy
The late D. W. King, Esq., O.B.E., F.L.A.
S. King Esq., S.G.M.
The late Brigadier H. B. Latham
M. S. Leahy, Esq.
The Librarian and Staff, Ministry of Defence Library, Whitehall, London
J. P. Loffet, Esq.
Canon W. M. Lummis, M.C.
C. A. Lusted, Esq.
The late A. R. McWhirter, Esq.
The Maharajdhiraja Bahadur Sir Uday Chand Mahtab of Burdwan, K.C.I.E.
The Ministry of Defence (Army Department, M.S.3.)
The Ministry of Defence (Air Force Department, S.10.j.Air)
Doctor Felix Mechanik
Doctor F. K. Mitchell
Donald R. Morris, Esq.
The Director, The National Archives of India
The Director, The National Library of Ireland
M. R. Naxton, Esq., of Sotheby Parke Bernet & Co.
The New Zealand High Commissioner, London
H. C. Pownall, Esq., Q.C.
A. A. Purves, Esq., F.R.N.S.
R. Rogers, Esq., The Royal Mint
G. S. Roots, Esq.
Squadron Leader J. Routledge, R.A.F.
The late Commander W. B. Rowbotham, R.N.
The Director-General and Staff, The Royal United Service Institution
Major J. D. Sainsbury, T.D.
R. J. Scarlett, Esq.
The Secretary to the Prime Minister, Republic of South Africa
J. E. Shepherd, Esq., Q.P.M., lately Head Constable, Royal Ulster Constabulary
Colonel J. M. Slabber, lately Military Attaché, South African Embassy, London
W. I. Smith, Esq., Public Archives of Canada
D. Stanley, Esq.
The late Captain G. T. Stagg, F.R.N.Z.S., R.N.Z.A.
C. H. Stewart, Esq., Departmental Library, Department of National Defence, Canada
A. H. Strutt, Esq.
Major C. E. C. Townsend, T.D.
The late H. Y. Usher, Esq.
Lieutenant-Colonel D. D. Vigors, Royal Artillery
The late W. Whitten, Esq., The Department of Trade
W. Y. Wilkin, Esq.
R. C. Witte, Esq.

Bibliography

Abbott, P. E. – *Recipients of the Distinguished Conduct Medal 1855–1909*, 1975
Admiralty – *Uniform Regulations for Officers, Petty Officers and Seamen of the Fleet*, 1879
Admiralty Fleet Orders (as quoted in the text)
Annual Register, The (as quoted in the text)
Anon. – *Deeds that Thrill the Empire*; Standard Art Book Company, c.1917.
Army Council Instructions (as quoted in the text)
Army Orders (as quoted in the text)
Barlow, C. A. Montague – *The Lancashire Fusiliers, Salford Brigade (15th, 16th, 19th, 20th and 21st Lancashire Fusiliers)*, 1919
Bisset, I. – *The George Cross*, 1961
Bles, G. (Publisher) – *Naval Honours and Awards 1939–1940*, 1942
Boyle, W. H. D. – *Gallant Deeds*, 1919
Burma Gazette, The (as quoted in the text)
Cape Government Gazette, The (as quoted in the text)
Chaldecott, O. A. – *The 10th Baluch Regiment*, 1935
Connolly, T. W. J. – *History of the Royal Sappers and Miners*, 1857
Cowan, J. – *The New Zealand Wars*, 1923, reprinted 1956
Crook, M. J. – *The Evolution of the Victoria Cross*, 1975
De la Bère, Sir Ivan – *The Queen's Orders of Chivalry*, 1964
Downes, W. D. – *With the Nigerians in German East Africa*, 1919
Fevyer, W. H. – *The George Medal*, 1980
Gibbs, H. R. K. – *Historical Record of the 6th Gurkha Rifles*, 1955
Gordon, Major L. L. – *British Orders and Awards*, 1959, revised 1968
Gordon Roe, F. – *The Bronze Cross*, 1945
Government of India, Central Publications Branch – *List of Honors awarded to the Indian Army, August 1914–August 1921*, 1931, (reprinted 1978 by J. B. Hayward & Son as *Honours and Awards Indian Army 1914–1921*)
Guinness Book of Records, The (as quoted in the text)
Hansard (Parliamentary Debates) (as quoted in the text)
Hayward, J. B., & Son – *Naval and Air Force Honours and Awards*, 1975
Haywood, A., and Clarke, F. A. S. – *The History of the Royal West African Frontier Force*, 1964
H.M.S.O. – *Annual Report of the Deputy Master and Comptroller of the Royal Mint* (as quoted in the text)
H.M.S.O. – *Catalogue of the Coins, Tokens, Medals, Dies and Seals in the Museum of the Royal Mint* by W. J. Hocking, 1910
H.M.S.O. – *Dress Regulations for the Army* (as quoted in the text)
H.M.S.O. – *Queen's Regulations for the Army* (as quoted in the text)
H.M.S.O. – *Statistics of the Military Effort of the British Empire during the Great War, 1914–1920*, 1922
Hudson, Sir Havelock, – *The History of the 19th King George's Own Lancers, 1858–1921*, 1937
Hypher, P. P. – *Deeds of Valor performed by Indian Officers and Soldiers during the period from 1860 to 1925*, 1927
Hypher, P. P. – *Deeds of Valour of the Indian Soldier which won the Indian Order of Merit during the period from 1837 to 1859*, 1925
India, The Gazette of (as quoted in the text)
Irwin, R. W. – *War Medals and Decorations of Canada*, 1969
Jocelyn, A. – *Awards of Honour*, 1957
Johnson, R. M. – *29th Divisional Artillery War Record and Honours Book, 1914–1918*, 1921
Jones, H. A. – *The War in the Air; being the Story of the part played in the Great War by the Royal Air Force*, 1937
Joslin, E. C. – *The Standard Catalogue of British Orders, Decorations and Medals*, 1969 (and subsequent editions)
Kincaid-Smith, M. – *The 25th Division in France and Flanders* (no date)
Latter, L. C. – *The History of the Lancashire Fusiliers, 1914–1918*, 1949

Leslie, J. H. – *An Historical Roll with Portraits of those Women of the British Empire to whom the Military Medal has been awarded during the Great War, 1914–1918, for "Bravery and Devotion under Fire"*, 1920

London Gazette, The (as quoted in the text)

Masters, D. – *In Peril on the Sea*, 1960

Mayo, J. H. – *Medals and Decorations of the British Army and Navy*, 1897

Merewether, J. W. B., and Smith, F. – *The Indian Corps in France*, c.1918

Milford-Haven, Admiral the Marquess of – *British Naval Medals*, 1919

Military Historical Society, The Bulletin of the (as quoted in the text)

Montgomery, Sir A. – *The Story of the Fourth Army*, c.1920

Moyse-Bartlett, H. – *The King's African Rifles*, 1956

Natal Government Gazette, The (as quoted in the text)

Navy and Army Gazette (Publishers) – *South African War, 1899–1902 – Mentioned in Despatches*, 1902

Navy List, The (as quoted in the text)

New Zealand Gazette, The (as quoted in the text)

Norman, C. B. – *Battle Honours of the British Army*, 1911

O'Moore Creagh, Sir, and Humphris, Miss E. M. – *The V.C. and D.S.O.*, c.1924

Orders and Medals Research Society, The Journal of the (as quoted in the text)

Parry, D. H. – *Britain's Roll of Glory* (editions of 1895, 1898, 1899 and 1906); republished as *The V.C., Its Heroes and Their Valour*, 1913

Petrie, F. Loraine – *History of the Norfolk Regiment 1685–1918*, c.1930

Pickford, Major P. – *War Record of the 1/4th Battalion Oxfordshire & Buckinghamshire Light Infantry*, 1919

Police Chronicle, The (as quoted in the text)

Police Review, The (as quoted in the text)

Purves, A. A. – *Collecting Medals and Decorations*, 1978

Royal United Service Institution, Journal of the – The Conspicuous Gallantry Medal by Commander W. B. Rowbotham (May 1954)

Royal United Service Institution, Journal of the – Origin of the Medal "For Distinguished Conduct in the Field" by Brigadier H. B. Latham (August 1953)

Rudolf, R. de M. – *Short Histories of the Territorial Regiments of the British Army*, c.1905

Sainsbury, Major J. D. – *For Gallantry in the Performance of Military Duty*, 1980

Shakespear, L. W. – *History of the 2nd King Edward's Own Ghoorkhas*, c.1924

Shores, C. and Williams, C. – *Aces High: The Fighter Aces of the British Commonwealth Air Forces in World War II*, 1966

Smyth, Sir John, – *The Story of the Victoria Cross, 1856–1963*, 1963

Smyth, Sir John, – *The Story of the George Cross*, 1968

Snowden Gamble, C. F. – *The Story of a North Sea Air Station*, 1928; republished 1967

Society for Army Historical Research, The Journal of the (as quoted in the text)

Sparrow, G., and MacBean-Ross, J. M. – *On Four Fronts with the Royal Naval Division*, 1918

Spink and Son Ltd., Numismatic Circular – *Gallantry Awards* by C. J. Kendall-Wingate (March and September 1960)

Spink and Son Ltd., Numismatic Circular – *The Indian Distinguished Service Medal* by Brigadier H. Bullock (October 1950)

Stewart, R. – *The Victoria Cross*, c.1928

Stirling, J. – *The Colonials in South Africa, 1899–1902*, 1907

Stuart, J. – *The History of the Zulu Rebellion, 1906*, 1913

Superintendent of Government Printing, Calcutta – *Reports on the Administration of the Mints at Calcutta and Bombay* (as quoted in the text)

Tancred, G. – *Historical Record of Medals and Honorary Distinctions*, 1891

Taprell-Dorling, H. – *Ribbons and Medals*, various editions commencing 1916

Turner, J. F. – *V.C.'s of the Royal Navy*, 1956

Turner, J. F. – *V.C.'s of the Air*, 1960

Turner, J. F. – *V.C.'s of the Army, 1939–51*, 1962

Union of South Africa Government Gazette, The (as quoted in the text)

War Office – *A Review of new Orders, Decorations and gallantry medals instituted by His Majesty during the War 1914–1920*, November 1920

Whitaker's Almanack (as quoted in the text)

Wilkins, P. A. – *History of the Victoria Cross*, 1904

Willcocks, J. – *With the Indians in France*, 1920

Wilson, Sir Arnold, and McEwen, J. H. F. – *Gallantry*, 1939

PLATE 3

*The Distinguished Service Order
(Victoria issue in gold).*

The Albert Medal in Gold (sea services).

The New Zealand Cross.

*The Royal Red Cross
(Edward VII issue).*

*The Ìndian Order of Merit (Civil Division),
1939–47.*

*The Royal Red Cross, 2nd Class
(George VI issue).*

Notes on Replacement Issues, and on Recent Copies

Replacement issues In general, replacement issues have the characteristics existing at the time the replacement was made. While it is does not follow necessarily that the characteristics of the original and of the replacement issues differ, they are more likely to do so when a considerable period has elapsed between issue and replacement. Such differences may be evidenced by a later style of naming; by a greater economy of details given with the naming; or, perhaps more obviously, by a difference in the piece itself e.g. the presence of a fixed suspender where a swivel suspender would be expected, or of a later type suspender. However, great care must be exercised before a medal is stigmatised as a replacement on the grounds of characteristics alone. Comparatively recently the practice was introduced of identifying a replacement issue by adding the word REPLACEMENT or, somewhat curiously, DUPLICATE or even TRIPLICATE, in parentheses to it. This practice has since been modified to the use of the single letter R which, in the case of circular medals, is placed as high as possible on the edge according to whether the medal has a fixed or swivel suspender.

Recent copies Since 1972 copies of a number of orders, decorations and medals have appeared on the market. Most, but far from all, are marked with the word COPY. In general, they are of the correct size with good definition. Where the genuine medal is silver, the copy is made of a soft base metal and has a poor finish. Reference to this Note is made in the text to those awards thus copied.

Note on Posthumous Awards for the Forces

In 1979 the Queen approved the proposal that the following awards, in addition to the Victoria Cross and Mention in Despatches, may be awarded posthumously:

    Royal Red Cross, 1st Class (R.R.C.)
    Distinguished Service Cross (D.S.C.)
    Military Cross (M.C.)
    Distinguished Flying Cross (D.F.C.)
    Air Force Cross (A.F.C.)
    Royal Red Cross, 2nd Class (A.R.R.C.)
    Distinguished Conduct Medal (D.C.M.)
    Conspicuous Gallantry Medal (C.G.M.)
    Distinguished Service Medal (D.S.M.)
    Military Medal (M.M.)
    Distinguished Flying Medal (D.F.M.)
    Air Force Medal (A.F.M.)

Posthumous awards of the R.R.C., A.F.C., A.R.R.C. and A.F.M. are to be permitted only in cases of gallantry. Since the Distinguished Service Order cannot be awarded posthumously, the D.S.C. and M.C. may be awarded posthumously to officers above the rank of commander or major, as the case may be. In this connection it should be noted that eligibility for the D.F.C. already extends to all commissioned ranks. Amendments to the relevant Royal Warrants have yet to be made.

Chapter 1

The African Police Medal for Meritorious Service

ORIGIN AND DEVELOPMENT

On 11th June 1914 the Secretary of State for the Colonies wrote to the Governors and Residents of the Colonies and Protectorates in East and West Africa inviting comments on a proposal to institute a medal for non-European police officers and men of those territories[1]. At that time the only medal available to such officers and men was the King's Police Medal (q.v.) which was awarded on a very restricted scale. Moreover, special medals for distinguished conduct, meritorious service, and long service and good conduct were already available to men of the West African Frontier Force and the King's African Rifles and it was evidently necessary to make somewhat similar provision for the African police. The proposal found the requisite support and, in consequence, on 14th July 1915 the African Police Medal for Meritorious Service was instituted by Royal Warrant[2] to reward distinguished service, or long and meritorious service, in the following terms:

Fig. A: The African Police Medal for Meritorious Service, obverse, George V issue, first type.

> "WHEREAS WE have taken into Our Royal consideration the meritorious services rendered by members of the Police Forces in Our East and West African Colonies and Protectorates, other than those of European descent;
>
> AND WHEREAS We are desirous of distinguishing such meritorious services by some mark of Our Royal favour;
>
> WE do by these Presents for Us, Our heirs and successors, institute and create a new Medal to be awarded to non-commissioned officers and men (other than those of European descent) of the Police Forces in East and West Africa, who shall specially distinguish themselves on any occasion or who may have rendered long and meritorious service.
>
> 2. The Medal shall be of silver and shall be designated and styled "The African Police Medal for Meritorious Service".
>
> 3. The obverse of the Medal shall bear Our effigy and the reverse shall contain a Tudor Crown surmounted by a lion in the centre, encircled by palm branches, with the circumscription "For Meritorious Service in the Police, Africa." The ribbon shall be yellow with two red stripes.
>
> 4. The name and rank of the recipient, together with the name of the Force of which he is a member, shall be inscribed on the rim.
>
> 5. The Medal shall be awarded by the Governor or other officer for the time being Administering the Government of the territory to which the Force may belong, on the recommendation of the Commandant of the Force, subject to the approval of one of Our Principal Secretaries of State.
>
> 6. Except in cases of conspicuous zeal and gallantry the Medal shall only be granted after not less than fifteen years' service marked by exceptional ability and merit, and the recipient must in every case have borne an exemplary character.
>
> 7. The names of the recipients of the Medal shall be published in the Government Gazette of the territories concerned.
>
> 8. If any person to whom the Medal is awarded be guilty of any crime or disgraceful conduct he may be deprived of it by the Governor or Officer Administering the Government with the assent of one of Our Principal Secretaries of State.
>
> GIVEN at Our Court at Saint James's this Twenty-sixth day of July, One thousand Nine hundred and Fifteen, in the Sixth Year of Our Reign.
>
> By His Majesty's Command,
> A. BONAR LAW."

1. See, for example, P.R.O. CO 523/46.
2. Which was published in most of the Gazettes of the territories concerned, e.g. *The Nigeria Gazette* of 9th December 1915.

1

Fig.B: *The African Police Medal for Meritorious Service, obverse, George V issue, second type.*

Fig.C: *The African Police Medal for Meritorious Service, obverse, George VI issue.*

By a Royal Warrant of 10th May 1932 eligibility was extended to non-European policemen of the British South Africa Police[3]. After a relatively short existence of almost 24 years the African Police Medal was discontinued and replaced by the Colonial Police Medal (q.v.) by virtue of clause 9 of the Royal Warrant of 10th May 1938 which instituted the latter medal.

In the order of wearing published in the *London Gazette* the African Police Medal is first shown on 22nd April 1941 where it follows the Royal Naval Volunteer Reserve Long Service and Good Conduct Medal and the Board of Trade Rocket Apparatus Volunteer Long Service Medal. In *LG*, 11th February 1947 it is shown following the Indian Meritorious Service Medal and the Transjordan Frontier Force Long Service and Good Conduct Medal. In *LG*, 12th July 1949 it follows the former medal. In *LG*, 27th July 1951 the Police Long Service and Good Conduct Medal is placed between it and the Indian Meritorious Service Medal, and in *LG*, 15th May 1954 it reaches its final position following the Police Long Service and Good Conduct Medal and the Fire Brigade Long Service and Good Conduct Medal.

DESCRIPTION

Ribbon Yellow, edged on either side with a red stripe, one inch wide.

Suspension By a non-swivelling ring.

Obverse There are three types of obverse as follows:
1. George V first type (Fig.A).
2. George V second type (Fig.B). The first issues of this type with the altered inscription were made from the Royal Mint on 1st May 1931[4].
3. George VI (Fig.C). The first issue of this type was made on 25th January 1938[5].

Reverse (Fig.D). This design was selected from a number prepared by Mr E. B. Burley, the Assistant Librarian at the Colonial Office[6].

Naming Usually engraved in seriffed capital letters with rank, name and force; sometimes these details are preceded by the man's force number.

Copies and Fakes None has been seen.

VERIFICATIONS AND CITATIONS

In most cases awards were published in the Gazette of the territory concerned. In the case of awards for meritorious service the notification appears as a bare announcement of the award. In the case of awards for gallantry, announcements range from a brief account of the circumstances to, more rarely, a full citation. It is by no means certain, however, that some awards which, from the bare announcement, appear to be for meritorious service were not in fact for gallantry. Occasionally details of awards for both gallantry and meritorious service (as well as some which were not gazetted) are mentioned in the annual Police Report of the appropriate territory. Since awards had to be approved by the Secretary of State announcement usually followed approval by several months. Similarly, immediately following approval by the Secretary of State the Colonial Office placed an order for the medal and its engraving with the Royal Mint. In consequence the entry in the Mint register of medals ordered also precedes announcement. The recommendations for some awards are preserved in the P.R.O. series CO 523 (Chief Clerk's correspondence) and in the correspondence of the various territories. However, although reference to the correspondence may be found in the appropriate register, this does not indicate that the actual correspondence has survived.

NUMBERS AWARDED

The following table has been compiled from announcements in the various Gazettes and annual Police Reports, supplemented by information in the Royal

3. See *The Colony of Southern Rhodesia Government Gazette* of 29th July 1932.

4. See order no.880 in the Mint register of medals ordered, P.R.O. MINT 16/4. These were almost certainly in respect of medals for Nigeria (3) and Uganda (5).

5. *Ibid*, order no.689. This was almost certainly for Inspector Edward Akapo Mensah, Southern Provinces Police, Nigeria (*Nigeria Gazeette* 24th March 1938). Between 1927 and 1930 details to be engraved on the medal are frequently recorded in the register; thereafter they rarely appear.

6. See P.R.O. CO 523/46.

Fig.D: The African Police Medal for Meritorious Service, reverse.

Mint register referred to above. Where awards for gallantry have been identified these are shown in parentheses and are included in the overall figures.

	1915 –1930		1931 –1937		1938		Total	
Gambia	3		—		—		3	
Gold Coast	19	(2)	16		—		35	(2)
Kenya	84	(9)	21		8	(2)	113	(11)
Nigeria	37	(22)	16		1		54	(22)
Nyasaland	6		1		—		7	
Sierra Leone	1		—		—		1	
Somaliland	2		—		—		2	
Southern Rhodesia	—		6	(1)	—		6	(1)
Tanganyika	3	(1)	9		—		12	(1)
Uganda	45	(2)	21		1		67	(2)
Zanzibar	22		9		—		31	
Totals	222	(36)	99	(1)	10	(2)	331	(39)

ILLUSTRATIVE AWARD

On 5th July 1917 the Acting Governor of British East Africa wrote to the Secretary of State for the Colonies recommending Corporal Ajoga Adol, East African Police, for the African Police Medal as follows[7]:

"On 22nd April this man who was then a 1st Grade Constable, but who has since been promoted to Corporal, was left in charge of a camp at Turkana with 19 Constables of the East African Police. The camp was attacked by a party of Abyssinians and Swahilis, estimated at twenty rifles, and after an engagement in which one Abyssinian was killed and one Police Constable wounded the raiders were driven off leaving a certain amount of property in their flight. The District Commissioner reports that Constable Ajoga Adol handled his men well and showed initiative in dealing with the situation and in my opinion his behaviour is deserving of special recognition."

The award was approved by the Secretary of State on 16th August 1917, and on the 21st of that month a medal was ordered from the Royal Mint which was ready for despatch on 14th September[8]. Notice of the award appeared in *The Official Gazette of the East Africa Protectorate* on 4th January 1918 as follows:

"HIS EXCELLENCY the Acting Governor has been pleased to award the African Police Medal for Meritorious Service to No.4176, Corporal Ajoga Adol, East Africa Police for initiative and judgement in repelling, in Turkana District, an attack by an armed party on a Camp of which he had been left in charge."

7. See P.R.O. CO 523/51 (Chief Clerk's correspondence).

8. See P.R.O. MINT 16/4 (register of medals ordered, order no.741 of 1917).

Chapter 2

The Air Force Cross

ORIGIN AND DEVELOPMENT

Shortly before the formation of the Royal Air Force on 1st April 1918 a committee was constituted to advise the King whether a special decoration was needed for the new Service, and whether there should be a uniform colour for the ribbon of the Victoria Cross in substitution for the different ribbons (navy, blue; army, red) then worn with that decoration. The committee consisted of:

Colonel Sir Douglas Dawson, Comptroller, Lord Chamberlain's Department (Chairman),

Rear-Admiral A. F. Everett, Naval Secretary to the First Sea Lord,

Lieutenant-General Sir Francis Davies, Military Secretary to the Secretary of State for War,

Rear-Admiral Mark (E. F.) Kerr, representing the Service about to be formed[1],

H. Farnham Burke, Norroy King of Arms.

In a draft report[2], which was approved by the Board of Admiralty on 21st March 1918, the committee recommended that there should be only one colour for the V.C. ribbon and that it should be red; that a decoration should be instituted for officers and warrant officers of the air force, corresponding to the Distinguished Service Cross and to the Military Cross in the other two Services; and that the naval Conspicuous Gallantry Medal and the Distinguished Service Medal, and the army Meritorious Service Medal and Long Service and Good Conduct Medal should be extended to the new Service. Eventually, however, only the first recommendation was accepted in its entirety and, in so far as gallantry was concerned, a range of four flying awards was devised. In a letter of 6th May 1918 from Sir Frederick Ponsonby, Keeper of the Privy Purse, to Commodore Sir Geoffrey Paine at the Air Ministry, the King approved the proposal that the new decorations should be "brought out" on his birthday[3]. Accordingly, this was done and a notice to the effect that the Distinguished Flying Cross, the Air Force Cross, the Distinguished Flying Medal and the Air Force Medal had been instituted appeared in the *London Gazette* of 3rd June 1918. The first awards of all four appeared in the same *Gazette*. Curiously enough, it was not until 17th December 1918 that the King signified in writing his approval of the Royal Warrant instituting the four awards[4] and it was not until 5th December 1919 that the Warrant was published in the *Gazette*[5]. The preamble and the clauses dealing with the Air Force Cross were as follows:

> "Whereas We are desirous of signifying Our appreciation of acts of valour, courage and devotion to duty performed by Officers and Men in Our Air Force and in the Air Forces of Our Self-governing Dominions beyond the Seas, We do hereby, for Us, Our heirs and successors, institute and create two decorations to be designated the Distinguished Flying Cross and the Air Force Cross, and two Medals, to be designated the Distinguished Flying Medal and the Air Force Medal, and We do hereby direct that the following regulations shall be made governing the said Decorations and Medals:—

> Fifthly, it is ordained that the Air Force Cross shall be granted only to such Officers and Warrant Officers of Our said Forces as shall be recommended to Us for an act or acts of valour, courage or devotion to duty whilst flying though not in active operations against the enemy.

> Sixthly, it is ordained that the Air Force Cross shall be silver and shall consist of a

1. Soon to become a Major-General in the R.A.F. According to *Who's Who* Kerr wrote the memorandum of 10th October 1917 which persuaded the Cabinet to form the R.A.F.

2. See P.R.O. ADM 116/1744.

3. See P.R.O. AIR 2/59.

4. See P.R.O. AIR 30/2.

5. The first two amending Warrants (see *post*) also appeared in this *Gazette*.

Fig.A: The Air Force Cross, obverse, George V issue.

Fig.B: The Air Force Cross, obverse, George VI issue, first type.

thunderbolt in the form of a cross, the arms conjoined by wings, the base bar terminating with a bomb surmounted by another cross composed of aeroplane propellers, the four ends enscribed with the letters G.V.R.I. In the centre a roundel thereon a representation of Hermes mounted on a hawk in flight bestowing a wreath. On the reverse the Royal Cypher above the date 1918. The whole ensigned by an Imperial Crown and attached to the clasp and ribbon by two sprigs of laurel.

Seventhly, it is ordained that the Air Force Cross shall be worn on the left breast pendant from a ribbon one inch and a quarter in width, which shall be in colour red and white in alternate horizontal stripes of one-eighth of an inch in depth.

Eighthly, it is ordained that the award of the Air Force Cross shall entitle the recipient to have the initials A.F.C. appended to his name.

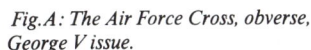

Seventeenthly, it is ordained that Foreign Officers and gradings of an equivalent rank to those above mentioned who have been associated in Military operations with Our Army or Our Indian, Dominion or Colonial Military Forces, shall be eligible for the award of the Distinguished Flying Cross, the Air Force Cross, the Distinguished Flying Medal, and the Air Force Medal.

Eighteenthly, it is ordained that in cases where Officers, Warrant Officers, and Men who have been awarded one of the above decorations or medals shall be recommended for a further act of valour, courage or devotion to duty, he shall be awarded a bar to be attached to the ribbon by which the decoration or medal is suspended, and for every additional such act an additional bar may be awarded.

Nineteenthly, it is ordained that the names of those upon whom We may be pleased to confer the above decorations and medals shall be published in the *London Gazette*, and that a Register thereof shall be kept in the Office of Our Secretary of State for the Royal Air Force.

Twentiethly, it is ordained that any person whom by an especial Warrant under Our Royal Sign Manual We declare to have forfeited the above decorations, medals and bars shall return the same to the Office of Our Secretary of State for the Royal Air Force, and that his name shall be erased from the Register of those upon whom the said decorations, medals and bars shall have been conferred.

Lastly, We reserve to Ourself, Our heirs and successors full power of annulling, altering, abrogating, augmenting, interpreting, or dispensing with these Regulations or any part thereof by a notification under Our Royal Sign Manual.

Given at Our Court at St. James's under Our Sign Manual this third day of June, in the ninth year of Our Reign and in the year of Our Lord one thousand nine hundred and eighteen.

By the Sovereign's Command,
WILLIAM WEIR."

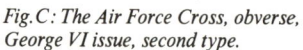

Fig.C: *The Air Force Cross, obverse, George VI issue, second type.*

Fig.D: *The Air Force Cross, obverse, Elizabeth II issue.*

Three amending Royal Warrants were made, as follows:

> *24th July 1919*[6] The ribbon was altered to one having "diagonal stripes of one-eighth of an inch in width running at an angle of 45 degrees from left to right".
>
> *27th August 1919*[6] The 5th Clause was amended so that the cross could also be awarded to "individuals not belonging to Our Air Force (whether Naval, Military or Civil) who render distinguished service to Aviation in actual flying"[7].
>
> *20th April 1921*[8] The 20th Clause was amended by providing for forfeiture in certain specified cases including a conviction by the Civil Power[9], provided that the Air Council did not recommend otherwise. Notices of forfeiture or restoration were to be published in the *London Gazette*.

All four Warrants were incorporated into and amended by one dated 31st August 1929[10]. This Warrant provided that the diagonal stripes of the ribbon were to run at an angle of 45 degrees "downwards towards the wearer's left". It also drew the forfeiture clause rather more widely by omitting reference to specific acts of misconduct and by making the power to order forfeiture completely discretionary. This followed a recommendation by the Interdepartmental Rewards Committee that all awards for gallantry, except in cases of extreme infamy, should be regarded as irrevocable; hence it was unnecessary to limit the power, as had been done before, by prescribing particular circumstances. In turn this Warrant was amended as follows:

> *23rd March 1932* The conditions of award were redefined by providing that the A.F.C. was only to be granted "for exceptional valour, courage or devotion to duty whilst flying though not in active operations against the enemy". The extension of eligibility to civilians by the amending Warrant of 27th August 1919 (see above) was omitted[11].
>
> *7th March 1938* The four ends of the cross were to be enscribed "G.VI.R.I.".

These three Warrants were incorporated into and amended by one dated 22nd September 1940. In this Warrant the order of clauses was changed; provision was made for the wearing of a miniature of the cross on certain occasions; and formal authorisation was given for the wearing of a small silver rose[12] on the ribbon, when the ribbon was worn alone, to denote the award of a bar. The following amending Warrants have been made:

> *11th March 1941*[13] The award was extended to equivalent ranks of the Fleet Air Arm of the Royal Navy serving with the air forces of the Crown.
>
> *23rd February 1942* Recommendations in respect of Dominion personnel were to be made by the appropriate Dominion Minster of State.

6. See *LG*, 5th December 1919.

7. In this connection it was awarded to the well-known United States airman Captain Charles A. Lindbergh, Missouri National Guard, "in recognition of the valuable and distinguished service rendered to aviation by his recent flight from New York to Paris" (*LG*, 31st May 1927). See also P.R.O. AIR 2/207 (101335/21)

8. See *LG*, 17th June 1921.

9. Even if a probation order was made.

10. See *LG*, 1st November 1929.

11. The extension of eligibility to civilians seems to have been unpopular in the Service, see P.R.O. AIR 2/513. The proposal that civilians should again be made eligible was considered during the Second World War but rejected, see P.R.O. AIR 2/6199.

12. Specimen rosettes were made by Spink and Son Ltd. which were submitted to the King on 25th June 1918. They were in dull silver for the A.F.C. and A.F.M., and in bright silver for the D.F.C. and D.F.M. The King thought the dull rosettes clearer and, unless it was necessary to have a distinction, that the same type of rosette should be used for all. As a result of this 100 rosettes were ordered from Spink but the records do not show of which type, see P.R.O. AIR 2/148. At all events, later issues seem to have been in bright silver.

13. See *LG*, 18th March 1941.

Fig.F: The Air Force Cross, reverse, George VI issue, first type.

Fig.G: The Air Force Cross, reverse, George VI issue, second type.

Fig.H: The Air Force Cross, reverse, Elizabeth II issue.

(Left) Fig.E: The Air Force Cross, reverse, George V issue.

Fig.I: Bar to the Air Force Cross.

10th November 1942[14] The designation "Air Branch" of the Royal Navy was substituted for "Fleet Air Arm" and the words "Military or Air Force" for "Air Force" thus extending eligibility to the Army, and to members of that Branch serving with the armies or air forces of the Crown.

15th July 1955 Provision was made for the adoption of the award, with its attendant conditions, by Member Countries of the Commonwealth. The arms of the cross were to be enscribed "E.R.II"[15]. The designation "Fleet Air Arm" was resumed.

24th March 1964[16] The functions hitherto performed by the Secretary of State for Air in regard, *inter alia*, to the A.F.C. were to be performed by the Secretary of State for Defence.

27th July 1968 The conditions for eligibility were revised. It was no longer a condition precedent to award that naval officers and warrant officers should be serving with the military or air forces of the Crown. For the first time the Royal Marines were specifically made eligible. In the case of those Commonwealth countries of which Her Majesty was not Queen eligibility was restricted to members of their armed forces who had been associated in operations with those of the Crown.

DESCRIPTION

Ribbon Originally 1¼ inches wide of red and white alternate horizontal stripes ⅛ inch in depth[17]; from 24th July 1919 similar stripes running at an angle of 45 degrees from left to right.

Suspension By a straight silver bar, ornamented with sprigs of laurel, connected to the cross by a silver link.

Obverse There have been four types as follows:

1. George V (Fig.A) The cross was designed by the Liverpool sculptor, E. Carter Preston[18]; until about 1921 the crosses were made by John Pinches Ltd. of London, and thereafter by the Royal Mint.
2. George VI first type (Fig.B) Cypher changed to "GRI VI"[19].
3. George VI second type (Fig.C) Cypher changed to "GR VI"[20].
4. Elizbeth II (Fig.D) Cypher changed to "ER II". Although this change was not embodied in a Royal Warrant until 1955 (see above), the change probably took place in 1953[21].

Reverse Plain, except for the design in the centre. A reverse matrix "ERI" for King Edward VIII was made but not used[22]. Four types of centre design have been issued as follows:

14. See *LG*, 15th January 1943.

15. This was first issued about 1953.

16. See Army Order No.22 of March 1964.

17. Apparently manufactured by George Kenning and Son, 1–4, Little Britain, London E.C.1., see P.R.O. AIR 2/148.

18. See P.R.O. AIR 2/69.

19. *Annual Report of the Deputy Master and Comptroller of the Royal Mint (1938)*, p.45.

20. *Ibid (1948)*, p.22.

21. *Ibid (1953)*, p.33.

22. *Ibid (1935/36)*, p.53.

1. George V (Fig.E). This was also designed by E. Carter Preston.
2. George VI first type (Fig.F). This was a remodelled version of the previous reverse[23].
3. George VI second type (Fig.G). Cypher changed to "G VI R"[24].
4. Elizabeth II (Fig.H). Cypher changed to "E II R"[25].

Awards made during the Second World War and thereafter have the year of the award engraved on the lower limb of the cross, although a 1939 issue has been seen in which the year appears to have been impressed, and in rather smaller figures than the later awards.

Bar (Fig.I). This has remained constant, and is of the "slip-on" type. Awards made during the Second World War and after have the year engraved on the reverse.

Naming The cross was issued unnamed. However, specimens are often found named (by recipients, next-of-kin, etc.) on the plain surface of the reverse.

Copies and Fakes On some copies the designer's initials, which appear distinctly at 7 o' clock on the edge of the obverse roundel, are omitted, while on the reverse of the George V copy the "G" of the Imperial Cypher is tilted instead of being nearly vertical as it should be. Moreover, "mule" copies exist in which the obverse of a George VI issue has been married to the reverse of a George V issue. In addition, the purported year of award has been found engraved on the upper arm of the reverse instead of the lower arm. Purves (see Bibliography) illustrates a George V copy. Copy bars have a somewhat larger and cruder eagle and a narrower slide at the back. For recent copies see the Note on p.xx.

VERIFICATIONS AND CITATIONS

All awards, except some to foreigners, are given in the *London Gazette*, and appear under the heading "Air Force Cross" in the appropriate "State Intelligence" section of the quarterly indices. In January 1942 the indices were altered, and names appear under a consolidated alphabetical list headed "Honours, Decorations and Medals". Page references continue to be given in the "State Intelligence" section. Awards have, however, been found indexed under the wrong heading, or omitted from the index entirely. There are no citations for any awards from 1918 to the end of 1939, although some, made in the 1920s and 1930s, have reference to the nature of the services rendered. There are no citations for the period 1940 to 1945. Between 1946 and 1979, of the 2,385 awards gazetted, 78 have citations. However, details of many awards are preserved in the Public Record Office in the series AIR 1 which contains some of the recommendations for 1918/19[26]; in AIR 30 (submissions to the King 1918–1946), where a number of unpublished citations are to be found; and in AIR 2 (Code 30) which contains the the original recommendations made during the Second World War[27].

NUMBERS AWARDED

1918–1939 A total of 838 awards, with 12 first bars and three second bars were gazetted between 3rd June 1918 and 31st December 1939. These can be summarised as follows:

			Crosses	First Bars	Second Bars
1918–1919	...	...	679[28]	2	—
1920–1937	...	...	111[29]	10	3
1938–1939	...	...	48	—	—
	Totals:		838	12	3

Those awarded second bars were:

LG for second bar

Squadron Leader W. R. Read, M.C.,
D.F.C., A.F.C.   ...   . 2nd January 1922

23. *Ibid (1937)*, p.53 and (1938), p.45.
24. *Ibid (1948)*, p.22.
25. *Ibid (1953)*, p.33.
26. See the Honours and Awards files in AIR 1/1157; 1160; 1169; 1476; 1479 and 1526.
27. See, for instance, AIR 2/8771; 8886; 8891; 9019; 9061 etc. The numerical sequence of the AIR 2 references does not reflect the strict chronology of the various files and it is necessary to consult the whole Index to the Code when searching.
28. One of which was subsequently cancelled in *LG*, 25th January 1921.
29. For details of the 14 awards gazetted to civilians between 1920 and 1931 see *The Journal of the Orders and Medals Research Society*, Vol. 17, p.172 *et seq*.

Flight Lieutenant P. W. S. Bulman,
   M.C., A.F.C.   ...   .   3rd June 1922
Wing Commander T. A. Langford-
   Sainsbury, A.F.C.   ...   .   11th May 1937

Honorary awards to foreign officers appeared in the Air Minstry Lists of 19th July and 10th December 1919, and in the British Army of the Black Sea List of 20th May 1919. A summary of these awards is as follows:

France	8	
Greece	4	
Italy	5	
USA	9	(including 7 to U.S. Navy – 6 for the airship flight from Newfoundland to England via The Azores, and 1 for the airship flight from East Fortune to Long Island)
Total:	26	

1940–1945 Wingate (see Bibliography) gives the following figures for the period 1918 to January 1959:

	First	*Second*
Crosses	*Bars*	*Bars*
4,329	121	11

By subtracting the figures given above for 1918 to 1939, and those included below between 1946 and January 1959, the following would seem to be the totals for 1940 to 1945:

	First	*Second*
Crosses	*Bars*	*Bars*
2,001	26	1

The second bar was awarded to Wing Commander H. J. Wilson, A.F.C., in *LG*, 8th June 1944.

Honorary awards were made to foreign officers as follows:

Belgium	5
Czechoslovakia ...	7
Egypt	2
France	6
Greece	1
Netherlands	2
Norway	4
Poland	18
USA	13
Total:	58

1946–1979 In this period the following awards were gazetted:

		First	*Second*	
	Crosses	*Bars*	*Bars*	
1946–1947	557[30]	10	—	1 each to Royal Navy and Royal Artillery.
1948–1952 ...	411	20	1	9 to Royal Navy; 1 to Royal Artillery; 10 for Berlin Airlift.

30. One was subsequently cancelled in *LG*, 18th June 1946.

| 1953–1979 | ... ... | 1,274 | 105 | 7 | 48 Royal Navy; 6 Royal Australian Navy; 8 Army Air Corps; 5 Australian Army Aviation Corps; 1 each Royal New Zealand Navy (1979), Royal Artillery attached Army Air Corps (1970), Royal Inniskilling Fusiliers (1960), Royal Marines (1970), Royal Corps of Transport (1968), Jamaica Defence Force (1968), Hong Kong Auxiliary Air Force (1965). |

Those awarded second bars were:

	LG for second bar
Wing Commander T. W. Kean, A.F.C.	8th June 1950
Wing Commander A. H. Humphrey, O.B.E., D.F.C., A.F.C.	9th June 1955
Wing Commander M. D. Lyne, A.F.C.	2nd January 1956
Squadron Leader P. D. Thorne, A.F.C.	2nd January 1956
Squadron Leader R. L. Topp, A.F.C. ...	1st January 1958
Wing Commander F. L. Dodd, D.S.O., D.F.C., A.F.C.	12th June 1958
Wing Commander L. G. Press, A.F.C.	1st January 1959
Group Captain H. P. R. Smith, A.F.C., M.A., M.B.	13th June 1959

One honorary award was made to an officer of the United States Air Force in each of the years 1960, 1975 and 1977.

ILLUSTRATIVE AWARD

Flying Officer Jack Stonier was awarded the A.F.C. in the *London Gazette* of 14th June 1945 where the notification appears without citation. The recommendation was, however, submitted with others to the King on 31st May 1945[31] acompanied by the following particulars:

"Since joining the unit[32] Pilot Officer Stonier has completed 25 day meteorological climbs and 10 night climbs. While engaged in a meteorological climb over Cyprus in October, 1944, when he had only slight geographical knowledge of the area, this pilot was caught in an unprecedented storm without warning. Houses were unroofed and aircraft on the ground severely damaged. At 6,000 feet Pilot Officer Stonier lost sight of the Island. 'Control' refused permission to land at base and advised him to make for Limassol. This was not possible. A thunderstorm was sighted and he made for a landing strip at Salamis where he successfully landed. Within ten minutes the wind rose from ten to fifty miles per hour. As the aircraft would have blown away, Pilot Officer Stonier again took off. He turned back to Cyprus as only the reserve tank was left and the aircraft was finally landed safely at base. By his excellent airmanship and resource Pilot Officer Stonier saved his aircraft and enabled the meteorological result to be broadcast to schedule."

31. See P.R.O. AIR 30/186 and AIR 2/8771.
32. No. 1565 Flight R.A.F.

Chapter 3

The Air Force Medal

Fig.A: The Air Force Medal, obverse, George V issue, first type.

Fig.B: The Air Force Medal, obverse, George V issue, second type.

ORIGIN AND DEVELOPMENT

Shortly before the formation of the Royal Air Force on 1st April 1918 a committee was constituted to advise the King whether a special decoration was needed for the new Service, and whether there should be a uniform colour for the ribbon of the Victoria Cross in substitution for the different ribbons (navy, blue; army, red) then worn with that decoration. The committee consisted of:

Colonel Sir Douglas Dawson, Comptroller, Lord Chamberlain's Department (Chairman),

Rear-Admiral A. F. Everett, Naval Secretary to the First Sea Lord,

Lieutenant-General Sir Francis Davies, Military Secretary to the Secretary of State for War,

Rear-Admiral Mark (E. F.) Kerr, representing the Service about to be formed[1],

H. Farnham Burke, Norroy King of Arms.

In a draft report[2], which was approved by the Board of Admiralty on 21st March 1918, the committee recommended that there should be only one colour for the V.C. ribbon and that it should be red; that a decoration should be instituted for officers and warrant officers of the air force, corresponding to the Distinguished Service Cross and to the Military Cross in the other two Services; and that the naval Conspicuous Gallantry Medal and the Distinguished Service Medal, and the army Meritorious Service Medal and Long Service and Good Conduct Medal should be extended to the new Service. Eventually, however, only the first recomendation was accepted in its entirety and, in so far as gallantry was concerned, a range of four flying awards was devised. In a letter of 6th May 1918 from Sir Frederick Ponsonby, Keeper of the Privy Purse, to Commodore Sir Geoffrey Paine at the Air Ministry, the King approved the proposal that the new decorations should be "brought out" on his birthday[3]. Accordingly, this was done and a notice to the effect that the Distinguished Flying Cross, the Air Force Cross, the Distinguished Flying Medal and the Air Force Medal had been instituted appeared in the *London Gazette* of 3rd June 1918. The first awards of all four appeared in the same *Gazette*. Curiously enough, it was not until 17th December 1918 that the King signified in writing his approval of the Royal Warrant instituting the four awards[4] and it was not until 5th December 1919 that the Warrant was published in the *Gazette*[5]. The preamble and the clauses dealing with the Air Force Medal were as follows:

"Whereas We are desirous of signifying Our appreciation of acts of valour, courage and devotion to duty performed by Officers and Men in Our Air Force and in the Air Forces of Our Self-governing Dominions beyond the Seas, We do hereby, for Us, Our heirs and successors, institute and create two decorations to be designated the Distinguished Flying Cross and the Air Force Cross, and two Medals, to be designated the Distinguished Flying Medal and the Air Force Medal, and We do hereby direct that the following regulations shall be made governing the said Decorations and Medals:—

Thirteenthly, it is ordained that the Air Force Medal shall be granted only to such Non-commissioned Officers and Men of Our said Forces as shall be recommended to Us for an act or acts of valour, courage, or devotion to duty performed whilst flying, though not in active operations against the enemy.

Fourteenthly, it is ordained that the Air Force Medal shall be silver and oval-shaped,

1. Soon to become a Major-General in the R.A.F. According to *Who's Who* Kerr wrote the memorandum of 10th October 1917 which persuaded the Cabinet to form the R.A.F.

2. See P.R.O. ADM 116/1744.

3. See P.R.O. AIR 2/59.

4. See P.R.O. AIR 30/2.

5. The first two amending Warrants (see *post*) also appeared in this *Gazette*.

Fig. C: The Air Force Medal, obverse, George VI issue, first type.

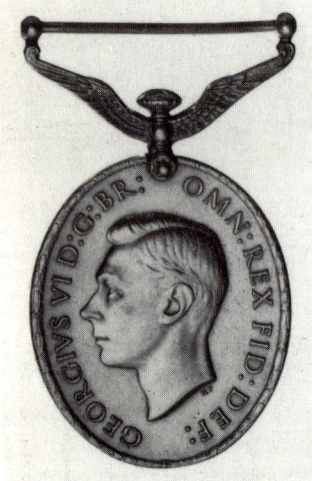

Fig. D: The Air Force Medal, obverse, George VI issue, second type.

bearing Our Effigy on the obverse and on the reverse within a laurel a representation of Hermes mounted on a hawk in flight bestowing a wreath. The whole ensigned by a bomb attached to the clasp and ribbon by two wings.

Fifteenthly, it is ordained that the Air Force Medal shall be worn on the left breast pendant from a ribbon one inch and a quarter in width, which shall be in colour red and white in alternate horizontal stripes of one-sixteenth of an inch in depth.

Sixteenthly, it is ordained that the award of the Air Force Medal shall entitle the recipient to have the initials A.F.M. appended to his name.

Seventeenthly, it is ordained that Foreign Officers and gradings of an equivalent rank to those above mentioned who have been associated in Military operations with Our Army or Our Indian, Dominion or Colonial Military Forces, shall be eligible for the award of the Distinguished Flying Cross, the Air Force Cross, the Distinguished Flying Medal, and the Air Force Medal.

Eighteenthly, it is ordained that in cases where Officers, Warrant Officers, and Men who have been awarded one of the above decorations or medals shall be recommended for a further act of valour, courage or devotion to duty, he shall be awarded a bar to be attached to the ribbon by which the decoration or medal is suspended, and for every additional such act an additional bar may be awarded.

Nineteenthly, it is ordained that the names of those upon whom We may be pleased to confer the above decorations and medals shall be published in the *London Gazette*, and that a Register thereof shall be kept in the Office of Our Secretary for the Royal Air Force.

Twentiethly, it is ordained that any person whom by an especial Warrant under Our Royal Sign Manual We declare to have forfeited the above decorations, medals and bars shall return the same to the Office of Our Secretary of State for the Royal Air Force, and that his name shall be erased from the Register of those upon whom the said decorations, medals and bars shall have been conferred.

Lastly, We reserve to Ourself, Our heirs and successors full power of annulling, altering, abrogating, augmenting, interpreting, or dispensing with these Regulations or any part thereof by a notification under Our Royal Sign Manual.

Given at Our Court at St. James's under Our Sign Manual this third day of June, in the ninth year of Our Reign and in the year of Our Lord one thousand nine hundred and eighteen.

By the Sovereign's Command,
WILLIAM WEIR."

Three amending Royal Warrants were made, as follows:

24th July 1919[6] The ribbon was altered to one having "diagonal stripes of one-sixteenth of an inch in width running at an angle of 45 degrees from left to right".

27th August 1919[6] The 13th Clause was amended so that the medal could also be awarded to "individuals not belonging to Our Air Force (whether Naval, Military or Civil) who render distinguished service to Aviation in actual flying"[7].

20th April 1921[8] The 20th Clause was amended by providing for forfeiture in certain specified cases including a conviction by the Civil Power[9], provided that the Air Council did not recommend otherwise. Notices of forfeiture or restoration were to be published in the *London Gazette*.

All four Warrants were incorporated into and amended by one dated 31st August 1929[10]. This Warrant provided that the diagonal stripes of the ribbon were to run at an angle of 45 degrees " downwards towards the wearer's left". It also drew the forfeiture clause rather more widely by omitting reference to specific acts of misconduct and by making the power to order forfeiture completely discretionary. This followed a recommendation by the Interdepartmental Rewards Committee that all awards for gallantry, except in cases of extreme infamy, should be regarded as irrevocable; hence it was unnecessary to limit the power, as had been done before, by prescribing particular circumstances. In turn this Warrant was amended as follows:

23rd March 1932 The conditions of award were redefined by providing that the A.F.M. was only to be granted " for exceptional valour, courage or devotion to duty whilst flying though not in active operations against the enemy". The extension of

6. See *LG*, 5th December 1919.

7. E.g., it was awarded to Mr. C. Corby, aeroplane rigger (Messrs. Vickers Ltd., Aviation Department), in connection with the experimental flight of a Vickers Vimy aircraft in an attempt to fly from England to South Africa organised by *The Times* newspaper.

8. See *LG*, 17th June 1921.

9. Even if a probation order was made.

10. See *LG*, 1st November 1929.

Fig.E: The Air Force Medal, obverse, Elizabeth II issue.

11. The extension of eligibility to civilians seems to have been unpopular in the Service, see P.R.O. AIR 2/513. The proposal that civilians should again be made eligible was considered during the Second World War but rejected, see P.R.O. AIR 2/6199.

12. Specimen rosettes were made by Spink and Son Ltd. which were submitted to the King on 25th June 1918. They were in dull silver for the A.F.C. and A.F.M., and in bright silver for the D.F.C. and D.F.M. The King thought the dull rosettes clearer and, unless it was necessary to have a distinction, that the same type of rosette should be used for all. As a result of this 100 rosettes were ordered from Spink but the records do not show of which type, see P.R.O. AIR 2/148. At all events, later issues seem to have been of bright silver.

13. See *LG*, 18th March 1941.

14. See *LG*, 15th January 1943.

15. See Army Order No.22 of March 1964.

16. *Annual Report of the Deputy Master and Comptroller of the Royal Mint (1930)*, pp.45 and 46; "The change (to the "crowned head") was, generally speaking, introduced as for issues after the 1st January, 1931, but the following changes actually took place and issues were made in the year under review . . . Air Force Medal, Distinguished Flying Medal"

17. *Ibid* (1938), p.45. However, the award to Flight Sergeant J. Rawlinson, R.A.F. (*LG*, 1st January 1938) is of the previous type.

18. *Ibid* (1949), p.30.

19. See P.R.O. AIR 2/69.

eligibility to civilians by the amending Warrant of 27th August 1919 (see above) was omitted[11].

7th March 1938 The 14th Clause was amended by providing that the reverse of the medal should have the year "1918" added within the wreath of laurel.

These three Warrants were incorporated into and amended by one dated 22nd September 1940. In this Warrant the order of clauses was changed; the obverse of the medal was to bear the effigy of the Sovereign, thus obviating further amendment on the accession of a new Sovereign; and formal authorisation was given for the wearing of a small silver rose[12] on the ribbon, when the ribbon was worn alone, to denote the award of a bar. The following amending Warrants have been made:

11th March 1941[13] The award was extended to equivalent ranks of the Fleet Air Arm of the Royal Navy serving with the air forces of the Crown. A miniature replica of the medal was authorised.

23rd February 1942 Recommendations in respect of Dominion personnel were to be made by the appropriate Dominion Minister of State.

10th November 1942[14] The designation "Air Branch" of the Royal Navy was substituted for "Fleet Air Arm", and the words "Military or Air Force" for "Air Force" thus extending eligibility to the Army, and to members of that Branch serving with the armies or air forces of the Crown.

15th July 1955 Provision was made for the adoption of the award, with its attendant conditions, by Member Countries of the Commonwealth. The designation 'Fleet Air Arm" was resumed.

24th March 1964[15] The functions hitherto performed by the Secretary of State for Air in regard, *inter alia*, to the A.F.M. were to be performed by the Secretary of State for Defence.

27th July 1968 The conditions for eligibility were revised. It was no longer a condition precedent to award that equivalent naval ranks should be serving with the military or air forces of the Crown. For the first time the Royal Marines were specifically made eligible. In the case of those Commonwealth countries of which Her Majesty was not Queen eligibility was restricted to members of their armed forces who had been associated in operations with those of the Crown.

DESCRIPTION

Ribbon Originally 1¼ inches wide of red and white alternate horizontal stripes ¹⁄₁₆ inch in depth; from 24th July 1919, similar stripes running at an angle of 45 degrees from left to right.

Suspension By a straight, non-swivelling, silver suspender fashioned in the form of two wings.

Obverse Five types of obverse are known, as follows:

1. George V first type (Fig.A).
2. George V second type (Fig.B). This was introduced in 1930[16].
3. George VI first type (Fig.C). This was introduced in 1938[17].
4. George VI second type (Fig.D). This was introduced in 1949[18].
5. Elizabeth II (Fig.E). Only issues with the Queen's titles, as altered by the Royal Proclamation of 28th May 1953, have been seen.

Reverse There have been two types of reverse, as follows:

1. George V (Fig.F). This was designed by the Liverpool sculptor E. Carter Preston[19].
2. George VI and Elizabeth II, all issues (Fig.G). The change took place in 1938[17].

Bar (Fig.H). This has remained constant and is of the "slip on" type. Bars awarded from 1954 have the year of award engraved on the reverse.

Naming All awards are issued named. Those for the First World War are impressed in large seriffed capital letters with number, rank, initials, surname and Service

Fig.F: The Air Force Medal, reverse, George V issues.

Fig.G: The Air Force Medal, reverse, George VI and Elizabeth II issues.

Fig.H: Bar to the Air Force Medal.

20. See, for instance, AIR 2/8771; 8886; 8891; 9061 etc. The numerical sequence of the AIR 2 references does not reflect the strict chronology of the various files and it is necessary to consult the whole Index to the Code when searching.

21. Hayward (see Bibliography) lists all awards in the period 1918–1939.

22. F. W. Sherratt, *LG*, 14th May 1920 (engineer, Rolls-Royce Ltd. – successful flight London to Cape Town); C. Corby, *LG*, 12th July 1920 (rigger, Vickers Ltd. – unsuccessful flight London to Cape Town); G. R. Long, *LG* 19th May 1925 (2nd Coxswain – gallantry when airship R.33 broke from mooring mast).

number; in some cases the initials follow the surname. Some 1939 awards are impressed in thin sans-serif capital letters. Those for the Second World War are rather crudely engraved with similar details in sans-serif capital letters. The crudeness is caused largely by the greater roundness of the edge of the medal in later years.

Copies and Fakes For recent copies see the Note on p.xx. Copy bars have a somewhat larger and cruder eagle, and a narrower slide at the back.

VERIFICATIONS AND CITATIONS

All awards, except those to foreigners, are given in the *London Gazette*, and appear under the heading "Air Force Medal" in the "State Intelligence" section of the appropriate quarterly index. Two awards – those to Sergeant A. V. Bax (*London Gazette*, 1st January 1931) and Sergeant L. C. Lambert (*London Gazette*, 1st February 1937) – are omitted from the indices, while that to Sergeant A. H. Ward (*London Gazette*, 8th October 1926) is indexed as "Royal Air Force Medal". In January 1942 the indices were altered, and names appear under a consolidated alphabetical list headed "Honours, Decorations and Medals". Page references continue to be given in the "State Intelligence" section. No citations were gazetted until 1943 when three appeared. The next was not gazetted until 1962 since when a further 18 have been published. However, a number of post–1945 announcements give some indication of the nature of the services for which the medal was awarded eg. the Berlin Airlift, operations in Malaya, Korea, Cyprus etc. Details of many awards are preserved in the Public Record Office series AIR 30 (Submissions to the King 1918–1946) where a number of citations are to be found, and in the series AIR 2 (Code 30) which contains the original recommendations made during the Second World War[20].

NUMBERS AWARDED

	Medals	First Bars	
1918[21]–1919	102	2	
1920–1929	48	3	3 medals to civilians[22]
1930–1937	20	—	
1938–1939	38	—	
1940–1945	259	—	2 to Army Air Corps
1946–1948	51	—	10 for Berlin Airlift
1949–1952	124	—	
1953–1979	209	4	1 New South Wales floods (1955); 2 Cyprus (1956); 1 Royal Artillery for Korea (1956); 5 Royal Navy; 3 Army Air Corps.

Those awarded first bars were:

	LG for first bar
Sergeant J. M. Bennett	26th December 1919
Sergeant W. H. Shiers	26th December 1919
S.M. II W. R. Mayes, D.S.M.	4th June 1921
Flight Sergeant S. J. Heath	4th June 1921
Flight Sergeant G. W. Hunt	19th May 1925
Flight Sergeant G. Aklam	10th June 1954
Acting Flight Sergeant A. W. Card ...	11th June 1960
Flight Sergeant J. W. Allen	21st December 1971
Sergeant J. Donnelly	8th February 1977

An honorary award was made to Chief Mechanic Mate E. S. Rhoads, U.S. Navy, in the Air Ministry List of 19th July 1919 for the airship flight from Newfoundland to England via The Azores.

Further honorary awards were made in the Second World War as follows:

Czechoslovakia	...	3
France	... ...	1
Norway	... ...	1
Poland	... ...	6
USA	... ...	3
Total		14

ILLUSTRATIVE AWARD

Sergeant Alfred Victor Bax was awarded the A.F.M. in the *London Gazette* of 1st January 1931 where the notification appears without citation. The recommendation was, however, submitted to the King on 13th December 1930[23] accompanied by the following particulars:

> "This airman pilot has rendered services of outstanding merit with No.47 (Bomber) Squadron, Middle East Command.
>
> He has taken part in all important flights carried out by this unit in the Sudan, notably those with His Royal Highness The Prince of Wales, in the West African Flight, and also in the anti-locust campaign, when he ably carried out duties usually performed by experienced officers.
>
> On several occasions he has displayed great ability and energy in effecting repairs and resuming flight after forced landings."

23. See P.R.O. AIR 30/84.

Chapter 4

The Albert Medal

ORIGIN AND DEVELOPMENT

The Albert Medal was instituted by a Royal Warrant of 7th March 1866[1]. Only one award was made under this Warrant[2]. By a Royal Warrant of 12th April 1867, First and Second Class decorations were instituted. Since this Warrant recites the original Warrant it is convenient to reproduce both together as follows:

> "WARRANT REVOKING a WARRANT dated 7th March, 1866, instituting A NEW DECORATION be styled "THE ALBERT MEDAL" and instituting in lieu thereof TWO NEW DECORATIONS, to be styled respectively "THE ALBERT MEDAL OF THE FIRST CLASS", and "THE ALBERT MEDAL OF THE SECOND CLASS"
>
> "VICTORIA R.
>
> VICTORIA by the Grace of God, of the United Kingdom of Great Britain and Ireland, Queen, Defender of the Faith, etc.
>
> To all to whom these presents shall come, greeting:
>
> Whereas a Warrant was given under Our Royal Sign Manual, bearing date the 7th day of March, 1866, in the 29th year of Our reign, intituled a "Warrant instituting a new Decoration, to be styled 'The Albert Medal' ", and such Warrant was in the terms following, that is to say:
>
> ' "Victoria R.
>
> ' "Victoria by the Grace of God, of the United Kingdom of Great Britain and Ireland, Queen, Defender of the Faith, etc.
>
> ' "To all to whom these presents shall come, greeting:
>
> ' "Whereas We, taking into Our Royal consideration that great loss of life is sustained by reason of shipwrecks and other perils of the sea; and taking also into consideration the many daring and heroic actions performed by mariners and others to prevent such loss and to save the lives of those who are in danger of perishing by reason of wrecks and perils of the sea; and taking also into consideration the expediency of distinguishing such efforts by some mark of Our Royal favour:
>
> ' "Now for the purpose of attaining an end so desirable as that of rewarding such actions as aforesaid, We have instituted and created, and by these presents for Us, Our Heirs and Successors, institute and create a new Decoration, which we are desirous should be highly prized and eagerly sought after, and are graciously pleased to make, ordain and establish the following Rules and Ordinances for the government of the same, which shall from henceforth be inviolably observed and kept.
>
> ' "First. – It is ordained, that the Distinction shall be styled 'THE ALBERT MEDAL' and shall consist of a gold oval-shaped badge or decoration enamelled in dark blue, with a Monogram composed of the letters V. and A., interlaced with an Anchor erect in gold, surrounded with a Garter in Bronze, inscribed in raised letters of gold 'For Gallantry in Saving Life at Sea,' and surmounted by a representation of the Crown of His Royal Highness the lamented Prince Consort, and suspended from a dark blue riband of five-eighths of an inch in width with two white longitudinal stripes.
>
> ' "Secondly. – It is ordained, that the Medal shall be suspended from the left breast.
>
> ' "Thirdly. – It is ordained, that the names of those upon whom We may be pleased to confer the Decoration shall be published in the *London Gazette*, and a registry thereof kept in the Office of the Board of Trade.
>
> ' "Fourthly. – It is ordained, that any one who, after having received the Medal, again performs an act which, if he had not received such Medal, would have entitled him to it, such further act shall be recorded by a bar attached to the riband by which the Medal is suspended; and for every such additional act an additional bar may be added.

1. See *LG*, 13th March 1866. Wilson and McEwan (see Bibliography) reproduce some of the correspondence in the Royal Archives at Windsor Castle leading to the institution of the award, the policy for selecting early recipients, and its extension to acts ashore.

2. To Samuel Popplestone in *LG*, 12th June 1866. This award was, of course, in gold but the ribbon would have been of the pattern used with the bronze medal instituted the following year.

' "Fifthly. – It is ordained, that the Medal shall only be awarded to those, who after the date of this instrument, have, in saving or endeavouring to save the lives of others from shipwreck or other peril of the sea, endanger their own lives, and that such award shall be made only on a recommendation to Us by the President of the Board of Trade.

' "Sixthly. – In order to make such additional provision as shall effectually preserve pure this most honourable Distinction, it is ordained, that if any person on whom such Distinction is conferred be guilty of any crime or disgraceful conduct which in Our judgment disqualifies him for the said Decoration, his name shall forthwith be erased from the registry of individuals upon whom the said Decoration shall have been conferred by an especial Warrant under Our Royal Sign Manual, and his Medal shall be forfeited. And every person to whom the said Medal is given shall, before receiving the same, enter into an engagement to return the same if his name shall be so erased as aforesaid under this regulation. It is hereby further declared, that We, Our Heirs and Successors, shall be the sole judges of the circumstances demanding such expulsion. Moreover, We shall at all times have power to restore such persons as may at any time have been expelled, to the enjoyment of the Decoration."

'And whereas it has been represented to Us, that mariners and others perform many acts in preventing loss of life from shipwreck and other perils of the sea, that are not of a character sufficiently daring and heroic to bring them under Our Warrant above cited, and are yet worthy of some distinguishing mark of Our Royal favour. And whereas We, taking into Our consideration that it is expedient to reward such mariners and others who perform heroic actions to prevent loss of life from shipwreck and other perils of the sea, are pleased in place of the Decoration created by Our Warrant of the 7th March, 1866, to institute and create two Decorations, which We are desirous should be highly prized and eagerly sought after, and are graciously pleased to make, ordain and establish the following Rules and Ordinances for the government of the same, which shall henceforth be inviolably observed and kept.

'First. – It is ordained, that one of the said two Decorations shall be styled "THE ALBERT MEDAL OF THE FIRST CLASS", and shall consist of a gold oval-shaped Badge or Decoration, enamelled in dark blue, with a Monogram composed of the letters V. and A., interlaced with an Anchor erect in gold, surrounded with a Garter in bronze, inscribed in raised letters of gold "For Gallantry in Saving Life at Sea", and surmounted by a representation of the Crown of His Royal Highness the lamented Prince Consort, and suspended from a dark blue riband of an inch and three eighths in width, with four white longitudinal stripes.

'Secondly. – It is ordained, that the other of the two Distinctions shall be styled "THE ALBERT MEDAL OF THE SECOND CLASS", and shall consist of the like shaped enamelled Badge, save and except in this class it shall be entirely worked in bronze, instead of gold and bronze, and suspended from a dark blue riband of five-eighths of an inch in width, with two white longitudinal stripes.

'It is ordained that each Medal shall be suspended from the left breast.

'Thirdly. – It is ordained, that the names of those upon whom We may be pleased to confer either of these Decorations shall be published in the *London Gazette*, and a registry thereof kept in the Office of the Board of Trade.

'Fourthly. – It is ordained, that anyone who, after having received either of the Medals, again performs an act which, if he had not received such Medal, would have entitled him to it, such further act shall be recorded by a bar attached to the riband by which the Medal is suspended; and for every such additional act an additional bar may be added.

'Fifthly. – It is ordained, that the Medals shall only be awarded to those who, after the date of the said Warrant of the 7th March, 1866, have, in saving or endeavouring to save the lives of others from shipwreck or other peril of the sea, endangered their own lives, and that such award shall be made only on a recommendation to Us by the President of the Board of Trade.

'Sixthly. – It is ordained, that THE ALBERT MEDAL OF THE FIRST CLASS shall be confined to cases of extreme and heroic daring, and that THE ALBERT MEDAL OF THE SECOND CLASS shall be given in cases which, though falling within the cases contemplated by this Warrant, are not sufficiently distinguished to deserve THE ALBERT MEDAL OF THE FIRST CLASS.

Fig.A: The Albert Medal for Saving Life at Sea

3. The preamble to the Warrant mentions "heroic acts performed on land . . . in preventing loss of life from accidents in mines, on railways, and at fires, and other perils on shore".

4. The first awards (4 gold, 21 bronze) for gallantry at the Tynewydd Colliery disaster were made in *LG*, 7th August 1877. This disaster attracted considerable public attention and it was the gallantry of the rescue party which led to the extension to acts of gallantry on land.

5. Royal Warrant, 13th September 1881 (see *LG*, 20th September 1881).

6. Royal Warrant, 12th March 1891 (see *LG*, 27th March 1891).

7. Royal Warrant, 24th March 1904 (see *LG*, 25th March 1904).

8. Royal Warrant, 5th June 1905 (see *LG*, 9th June 1905).

9. The preamble to the 1877 Warrant had limited the awards to "acts performed on land within Our Dominions".

10. Royal Warrant, 28th August 1917 (see *LG*, 31st August 1917).

11. All previous Warrants had been extremely prolix.

12. For the Army this appeared in Army Order No. 271 of September 1918.

13. Royal Warrant, 1st October 1930 (see *LG*, 10th October 1930).

14. No forfeitures have been found in the *London Gazette*.

'Seventhly. – In order to make such additional provision as shall effectually preserve pure this most honourable Distinction, it is ordained that if any person on whom such Distinction is conferred be guilty of any crime or disgraceful conduct which in Our judgment disqualifies him from the said Decorations, his name shall forthwith be erased from the registry of individuals upon whom the said Decoration shall have been conferred by an especial Warrant under Our Royal Sign Manual, and his Medal shall be forfeited. And every person to whom the said Medal is given shall, before receiving the same, enter into an engagement to return the same if his name shall be so erased as aforesaid under this regulation. It is hereby further declared, that We, Our Heirs and Successors, shall be the sole judges of the circumstances demanding such expulsion. Moreover, We shall at all times have power to restore such persons as may at any time have been expelled to the enjoyment of the Decoration.

'Given at Our Court at St. James's this Twelfth day of April, One thousand eight hundred and sixty-seven, in the thirtieth year of Our reign.

By Her Majesty's Command,
'S. H. WALPOLE.'

As a result of the 1867 Warrant, awards of the Sea Gallantry Medal (q.v.) ceased. Although no written decision on the matter can be traced, awards of that medal were resumed in 1876 the standard of gallantry for the silver medal being that which just failed to reach the standard for the Albert Medal.

By a Royal Warrant of 30th April 1877 (see *LG*, 1st May 1877), the 1867 Warrant was extended to acts of gallantry in saving life on land[3]. The First and Second Class medals so instituted were to be similar to those for saving life at sea, except for altered wording in the Garter, the omission of the anchor, and the substitution of crimson for dark blue in the enamelling and ribbon[4].

Recommendations for saving life on land were to be made by the First Lord of the Treasury (i.e. the Prime Minister), and the registry was to be kept in the office of one of the Principal Secretaries of State. In 1881[5] the rules were amended whereby recommendations for all awards were to be made only by the Home Secretary, although preliminary steps and enquiry concerning medals for gallantry at sea were to be made by the President of the Board of Trade. In 1891[6] they were further amended so that, for those serving in the Royal Navy or Royal Marines, preliminary steps and enquiry concerning medals for gallantry at sea were to be made by the Lords Commissioners of the Admiralty, who were also to keep an appropriate registry. The cumulative effect of these Warrants is that three registries are now in existence, being at the Department of Trade (all sea awards to 1891, thereafter civilian sea service only), at the Home Office (land awards), and at the Admiralty (sea service awards to R.N. and R.M. personnel from 1891). In 1904[7] the width of the ribbon of both types of Second Class medal was made the same as that for the First Class medals (i.e. $1\frac{3}{8}$ inches). The following year all preceding Warrants were cancelled and replaced by a new one[8]. The only innovation in the new Warrant was the extension of the award of medals for saving life on land to include acts performed outside the King's Dominions[9]. In 1917 this Warrant was cancelled and replaced by another[10]. The new Warrant provided that both First Class medals were in future to be known as "The Albert Medal in Gold", and the Second Class medals as "The Albert Medal". Other than this no fresh provisions were introduced although opportunity was taken to simplify the wording of the Warrant[11]. Shortly afterwards King George V gave permission for recipients to use the letters "A.M." after their names[12]. In 1930[13] the 7th Clause of the 1917 Warrant (which dealt with forfeiture) was abrogated and a fresh clause substituted. This clause gave a general power to order forfeiture by omitting reference to "crime or disgraceful conduct" (which previously had been conditions precedent to forfeiture), and provided that forfeiture should be authorised by an Order under the Sign Manual and not by Royal Warrant, as before[14]. This followed a recommendation by the Interdepartmental Rewards Committee that all awards for gallantry, except in cases of extreme infamy, should be regarded as irrevocable; hence it was unnecessary to limit the power, as had

18

been done before, by prescribing for particular circumstances. In 1944 an amending Warrant[15] provided that recommendations for award or forfeiture, where appropriate, should be made direct to the Sovereign by Dominion Ministers of State.

The standard of gallantry qualifying for an award has always been very high. On 27th March 1917 a conference was held at the War Office regarding awards of the medal to serving army officers and men[16]. In consequence of the strongly held view of the Home Secretary that the standard of gallantry required for the A.M. was the same as that required for the V.C.[17] it was decided that all military recommendations should be laid before the V.C. Board who would, in suitable cases, forward them to the Home Secretary. Where recommendations were not forwarded, in the case of officers they would be refused[18], but in the case of the men they would be considered by the Military Secretary for award of the Meritorious Service Medal (q.v.) For awards sponsored by the Board of Trade the criterion adopted was that the recipient's risk of death had to be greater than his chances of survival and, in the case of the gold medal, the risk had to be altogether exceptional[19]. However, the institution of the George Cross and the George Medal (q.v.) in 1940 added two further awards to those already available and, in certain cases, it became difficult to decide which was the most appropriate[20]. Accordingly, in November 1949 King George VI gave approval that awards of the gold medal should cease[21], and that in future the bronze medal should only be awarded posthumously[22]. With effect from 14th November 1968 surviving United Kingdom recipients of the Albert Medals were to be entitled to annual gratuities of £100[23], irrespective of whether the medal awarded was in gold or bronze. Gratuities were to be paid to other Commonwealth recipients under local regulations. By 1971, however, it was thought that, since no Albert or Edward Medals had been awarded – except posthumously – since 1948, the general public were no longer as conscious as they were of their significance and status. This had the effect of depriving surviving holders of those medals of the recognition which was their undoubted due[24]. Accordingly, by Royal Warrants of 15th December 1971[25], which came into effect from 21st October of that year, the existing Albert and Edward Medal Warrants were revoked; recipients of the Albert or Edward Medals who were living on that day were deemed to be persons who had been awarded not the Medal, but the George Cross[26]; and accordingly the Medals might[27] be exchanged for the George Cross.

The order of wearing the Albert Medal has varied. Army Order No. 196 of October 1905 showed it as following the Order of St. John and the Conspicuous Service Cross, while Army Order No. 246 of August 1912 placed it after the Constabulary Medal (Ireland) in a group of gallantry awards which, at that time, followed Polar medals. Army Council Instruction No. 754 of July 1918 gives it in its final position following the Order of St. John (see also Appendix 4).

DESCRIPTION (For coloured illustration, see Plate 3)

Medals for Saving Life at Sea (Fig.A) These were designed by Jemmett Browne[28].

Ribbon Gold Medal – dark blue ⅝ inch wide with two white stripes (1866); dark blue 1⅜ inch wide with four white stripes (from 1867).

Bronze Medal – dark blue ⅝ inch wide with two white stripes (1867); dark blue 1⅜ inch wide with two white stripes (from 1904).

Obverse Gold Medal – In gold and bronze.
Bronze Medal – In bronze.

Medals for Saving Life on Land (Fig.B)

Ribbon Gold Medal – crimson 1⅜ inch wide with four white stripes.
Bronze Medal – crimson ⅝ inch wide with two white stripes (1877); crimson 1⅜ inch wide with two white stripes (from 1904).

15. Royal Warrant, 7th October 1944 (see *LG*, 3rd November 1944).

16. What follows is summarised from a note of the meeting preserved in the Ministry of Defence (Army Department).

17. This view does not take into account the two classes of A.M.

18. As a result of refusal a number of appointments were made to the Order of the British Empire, notably in the 1918 Birthday Honours.

19. See the *Board of Trade Journal* of 8th February 1923 at p.160 where the standards are fully discussed.

20. Thus Bombardier W. J. Watkins, Royal Artillery, was awarded the George Medal in *LG*, 22nd January 1941, for saving life at sea when his troopship was torpedoed.

21. The last award of the gold medal was to Sick Berth Attendant A. Fanconi, Royal Navy, in *LG*, 15th May 1945. This seems to have been a land service award; it was posthumous.

22. The effect of this order is summarised at pp.190/191 of the Appendix to the Navy List for December 1950. A similar order was made regarding the Edward Medal (q.v.).

23. Royal Warrant, 24th January 1969 (see *LG*, 7th February 1969). A similar award was made to recipients of the Edward Medals (q.v.).

24. See *Hansard* (House of Commons) for 21st October 1971, column 189.

25. See *LG*, 6th January 1972. There were separate Warrants for each Medal.

26. This is a curious drafting device *cf.* the eleventh clause of the George Cross Warrant.

27. The wording regarding exchanges, unlike that relating to the Empire Gallantry Medal, is permissive. In consequence a few recipients preferred to retain their medals.

28. Who in 1868 was presented with the gold model which had been made from his design, see P.R.O. MT 9/41 (M.6240/68).

Fig.B: The Albert Medal for Saving Life on Land

Obverse Gold Medal – In gold and bronze.
Bronze Medal – In bronze.

Features common to all Medals

Suspension By a ring of the appropriate metal approximately $^{7}/_{16}$ inch in diameter.

Naming on reverse The oval part of the reverse is slightly convex[29]. Some medals are numbered at the bottom of the reverse at the back of the ornament at the foot of the Garter loop. The numbering seems to be consecutive, irrespective of class, but in separate series for sea and land awards, and probably ceased in the late 1870s. The early awards have a small plate fixed to the reverse of the crown giving the maker as

"PHILLIP'S
COCKSPUR ST."

All medals were made by Messrs. Phillips, Brothers and Son until 1902; thereafter they were produced by the Royal Mint[30].

The inscription on the oval portion of the reverse is engraved in horizontal lines in widely differing styles, certain words (e.g. "HIS MAJESTY", the name of the recipient, the date of the act, etc.) being larger than the others. Capital letters are often used throughout, with or without serifs, although some inscriptions employ a mixture of capital and interrupted script lettering. The first and last words of the inscription (i.e. "PRESENTED" or "AWARDED BY", and the date of the act) are usually curved to conform with the shape of the oval back plate. The following variants of the initial wording have been seen:

"PRESENTED IN THE NAME OF HER MAJESTY"
(or "HIS MAJESTY")

"PRESENTED BY HIS MAJESTY"

"AWARDED BY HIS MAJESTY" (or "HER MAJESTY")

"AWARDED BY THE KING" (or "THE QUEEN")

The formula "Presented in the name of" was used on awards which the Sovereign was unable to present personally while "Awarded by" was used almost invariably for posthumous awards.

The inscription also includes the full names[31] and description of the recipient (with rank, Service[32] or unit, and sometimes the Service number, as appropriate); the words "in" (or "for"), "saving" (or "endeavouring to save"), "life"[33]; and usually the place of the act (e.g. "at sea", "in France", "at Ferozepore", etc.). Some posthumous awards include a reference to the recipient having lost his life. Requisitions for awards between 1923 and 1956 from the Home Office, Admiralty, Board of Trade etc, which also give the inscription required are preserved in the Public Record Office[34].

Bar None has been awarded. The Royal Mint records contain no reference to a bar and it is possible that a bar was not designed.

Copies and Fakes. According to the correspondence reproduced in Wilson and McEwen, specimens of the 1866, both 1867 and both 1877 medals were made for Queen Victoria. However, the Warrants disclose no apparent difference between the 1866 and 1867 gold medals, except for the ribbons. Specimens of the gold and bronze medals for land services appeared in the Phillips sale of 1925. Other specimens are known in silver gilt instead of gold. For recent copies see the Note on p.xx.

VERIFICATIONS AND CITATIONS

Almost every award can be verified from the *London Gazette*[35] where the class of award is also given. Commencing mainly in the First World War, awards sponsored by the Admiralty usually specify that the award is for sea services as,

29. The reverse is fitted to the obverse by rivets passing through the side of the decoration at 2, 5 and 7 o'clock.

30. See P.R.O. MINT 20/96 and MT 9/737 (M.13803/02). Messrs. Phillips last account was rendered in respect of two bronze medals (land) for G. Biloca and G. Zammit (*LG*, 18th February 1902). Each had a "new crown specially pierced by hand" and there is a suggestion in the papers that the Home Office did not much like them. At all events the original crown re-appears on subsequent awards. The gold medals were reduced from 22-carat to 18-carat "at the beginning of the 1914/18 War", and the pattern of enamel changed in 1916, see P.R.O. MINT 20/829.

31. Middle names are sometimes represented as initials.

32. In the case of some Army awards before 1914, the *Gazettes* do not give the recipient's regiment, and this detail is omitted from at least some of the medals issued.

33. This phrase is sometimes omitted.

34. In MINT 20/829.

35. But the bronze medals awarded to Chief Stoker J. Sullivan, R.N., (27th August 1913), Petty Officer J. C. S. Hendry, R.N.A.S. (15th April 1915) and Mechanician F. G. Marshall (13th May 1915) do not seem to have been gazetted, although the dates of authorisation given here are those appearing in the Navy List. The citations for all three are given by Wilson and McEwen.

36. The awards to H. Kemp (*LG*, 16th January 1883), E. Nicholls (*LG*, 8th December 1905) and H. H. Wadsworth (*LG*, 18th December 1934) do not appear under the award heading in the indices. Some Edward Medals (q.v.) are wrongly given as Albert Medals in the index for January/March 1918, although they are correctly described in the *Gazette* itself. Conversely, the award to Veladi Sammai (*LG*, 12th May 1925) is wrongly indexed under the Edward Medal.

37. Who give Commander R. B. Cay, R.N., as being awarded the bronze medal for sea service in 1868; in fact, Cay was only given a vellum certificate as Inspecting Commander of Coastguard, Penzance, for services rendered on 6th December 1868. They show George Williams twice as receiving the bronze medal for sea services and wrongly couple him in the first instance with the award to F. Jaggers; Williams' only award appears in *LG*, 6th May 1881. They also omit the gold sea service award to Stoker E. Lynch of H.M.S. *Thrasher* (*LG*, 21st December 1897). A photograph of Lynch taken at the time of investiture appears in *The Navy and Army Illustrated* of 4th March 1898.

38. The Register is under reference BT 97/1, and the album under BT 97/2.

39. The recipients listed in the Register are those given in Chapter 18 of Wilson and McEwen up to and including Shaik Mohiden (*LG*, 31st October 1913), with three from the Admiralty Register, i.e. Seedie Tindal of Stokers Farabani (*LG*, 23rd November 1880), Boatman F. Jaggers (*LG*, 24th January 1882) and Able Seaman J. Barber (*LG*, 20th December 1889). Wilson and McEwen render Mohiden as Muhi-ud-Din.

40. The index to these Returns is to be found under "WRECKS.IV.4" in the "General Alphabetical Index of Bills, Reports, Estimates, Accounts and Papers printed by order of the House of Commons, and the Papers Presented by Command, 1852–1899". Due to a minor alteration in the title of the Returns, those to 1870 are indexed separately.

41. *LG*, 29th July 1887.

42. Incident 15th November 1899; awards *LG*, 14th June 1910.

from 1940, do those sponsored by the Ministry of War Transport (Board of Trade); otherwise it is necessary to refer to the citation itself to determine whether a sea or land award is appropriate. Even this is not always easy to decide as, for instance, where landsmen save life in ships in harbour. Probably the sponsoring Department determines the type of award although, even then, this is complicated by some duplication between the Registers.

Before 1918 the gazetting of some awards shows that the Sovereign, or the Sovereign's representative, has already invested the recipient or next-of-kin. Occasionally, the notice of an award shows that the recipient was unable to attend for investiture and later a notice of the investiture and repeat of the citation may appear. But instances have been found of multiple awards where the investiture of certain recipients only has been gazetted and awards to the remainder merely inferred from the group citation. No doubt all these variations account for the different types of inscription found on actual medals (see above).

From 1866 to December 1941 the names of recipients are indexed under the award heading in the "State Intelligence" section of the appropriate quarterly index[36]. Thereafter this section gives only the pages upon which awards are to be found; these references are sometimes faulty and have made it difficult to assess accurately the actual numbers awarded. Sometimes names are also given in the "Civil Promotions" section of the indices, and from January 1942 they appear in a comprehensive nominal section headed "Honours, Decorations and Medals". Full citations are normally given except for land awards gazetted between February 1883 and February 1902, and for a few Second World War awards, where an abbreviated notice appears. Where citations exist to February 1938 most are reproduced, with some misprints, wrong classes of award and *Gazette* dates, by Wilson and McEwen[37].

The Board of Trade Register for 1886 to 1913 is preserved in the Public Record Office, together with a corresponding album containing photographs of some of the earlier recipients[38]. The Register is a beautifully bound volume, in a special case, with an index at the back[39]. Recipients are entered in order of award, initial details being in illuminated lettering. Complete citations are included, some of which are longer than those given by Wilson and McEwen, and in the *London Gazette*. The earlier entries are accompanied by a copy of the certificate signed by each recipient to the effect, *inter alia*, that he undertakes to return the decoration if so required. The Register also contains copies of a number of Royal Warrants relating to the Albert Medal. The accompanying album contains photographs of 26 of the earlier recipients, most of whom are shown wearing their medals. Other details of awards are contained in the Board's files in the series MT 9, and for awards for services at sea between 1856 and 1876 in the Annual Returns of Wrecks which were ordered to be printed by Parliament[40]. The citations contained in the latter are frequently more detailed than the corresponding versions published in the *London Gazette*, or given by Wilson and McEwen. Many Home Office files relating to awards of the Albert Medal to 1948 are also preserved in the Public Record Office in the series HO 45. In addition to general correspondence dealing with policy, there are files concerning individuals or groups of individuals which contain eye-witness reports, recommendations, etc. In a number of cases the recommendations were not approved.

NUMBERS AWARDED

Although no bars have been awarded it is interesting to note that, according to the *Gazette* announcement[41], Queen Victoria originally approved the award of a bronze medal for saving life at sea to T. A. Whistler, First Mate of the *Ennerdale*. However, in view of a subsequent act of gallantry by him, a gold medal was awarded instead.

A delay of almost 11 years occurred before awards were made to C. Wagner (gold) and A. J. Stewart (bronze)[42]. These men were driver and fireman respectively of an armoured train ambushed during the South African War in which W. S. Churchill was travelling. According to his book *My Early Life*, Churchill was unable to obtain awards for them at the time but did so on becoming Home Secretary in 1910.

The youngest recipients were Anthony Farrer, aged eight, and Dorothy Ashburnham, aged 11, who saved each other's lives when attacked by a cougar in Canada[43]; and David Western, aged 10, who attempted to save the lives of three companions who had fallen through the ice of a frozen lake[44].

In so far as the following table is concerned it is hoped that the figures given are reasonably reliable, although they must be taken as approximate[45]. Several factors have contributed to the difficulty in assessing true numbers. Thus it is sometimes impossible to decide with any degree of certainty whether an award is for sea or land service (see above); in some cases only actual investitures were gazetted and it is necessary to read every citation to determine whether other recipients were involved; because the post-1941 "State Intelligence" section of the *Gazette* indices is unreliable, it is easy to miss an award; and the description given to some recipients makes it difficult to classify them for the purposes of the table. In the table, navy and army awards include those to the corresponding Commonwealth forces and auxiliaries, and Merchant Navy awards are included under the heading "civilian".

			London Gazettes					
			(or year of authorisation where not gazetted[46])					
	1866 –1876	1877[47] –1914	1915 –1919	1920[48] –1939	1940 –1945	1947[49] –1949	1950[50] –1971	Totals
Gold Medals								
Navy	—	2	7	1	3	—	—	13[51]
Army	—	3	12	—	—	—	—	15
R.F.C.	—	—	1	—	—	—	—	1[52]
Civilian – Sea	8	7	2	—	—	—	—	17
Land	—	22	1	1	—	—	—	24
Totals:	8	34	23	2	3	—	—	70
Bronze Medals								
Navy	7	16	46	11	27	4	8	119[53]
Royal Marines	—	1	2	3	—	—	—	6[54]
Army	—	32	83	17	—	—	—	132[55]
R.F.C./R.A.F.	—	—	10	3	—	—	—	13[56]
Civilian – Sea	9	32	16	15	10	2	9	93
Land	—	94	14	13	3	3	8	135[57]
Totals:	16	175	171	62	40	9	25	498

	Summary		
Gold	– Sea	… …	25
	– Land	…	45
Bronze	– Sea	… …	216
	– Land	…	282
Total:			568

ILLUSTRATIVE AWARDS

Services at sea Two awards in gold and three in bronze were made as a result of an incident off the Dogger Bank in 1904 when, during the Russo-Japanese War, the Russian Fleet opened fire on some British fishing vessels which had been mistaken for Japanese warships. An announcement from the Board of Trade dated 13th May 1905, which appeared in the *London Gazette* three days later at p.3515, reads as follows:

43. *LG*, 21st December 1917 (bronze medals).

44. *LG*, 13th August 1948 (bronze medal).

45. For the period 1866–1939 the table given by Wilson and McEwen totals 532 awards of both classes whereas our count for the same period is 490. For the period 1866–1960 Wingate (see Bibliography) gives 76 gold medals (7 sea, 69 land) and 525 bronze (sea and land); our count for the same period is 69 gold medals (24 sea, 45 land) and 490 bronze (sea and land). We are unable to account for the discrepancies between both these sets of figures and ours, unless it is because the authors concerned, in computing the overall figures, failed to take into account the duplication of some names between the three Registers.

46. See footnote 35.

47. No First World War awards were gazetted in 1914.

48. No Second World War awards were gazetted in 1939.

49. No awards were gazetted in 1946.

50. All medals awarded in this period were posthumous, the last being in 1970.

51. Includes five land awards, and awards to R.N.A.S.

52. Land award to Major C. L. N. Newall (later Marshal of the Royal Air Force the Lord Newall, G.C.B., O.M., G.C.M.G., C.B.E., A.M.) in *LG*, 19th May 1916.

53. Includes 13 land awards, and awards to R.N.A.S.

54. Comprising five sea and one land award.

55. Includes 12 sea awards.

56. All land awards.

57. Includes two to merchant seamen.

"The KING was pleased to-day, at Buckingham Palace, to present to William Smith, Mate, and Arthur Rea, Second Engineer, of the steam trawler *Crane* of Hull, Albert Medals of the First Class, and to Charles Beer, Mate, and Harry Smith, Chief Engineer, of the steam trawler *Gull*, of Hull, Albert Medals of the Second Class, conferred upon them by his Majesty's command for gallantry in saving life at sea as detailed below:-

Edwin Costello, Boatswain of the *Gull* was also awarded the Albert Medal of the Second Class, but was unable to be present to receive it.

The steam trawler *Crane* was so badly damaged by the gun fire of the Russian Baltic Fleet in the North Sea on the night of 21st October and the morning of 22nd October last, that she began to sink. The skipper and the third hand of the vessel had been killed, and, with one exception, the surviving members of the crew were all wounded.

The mate, William Smith, was severely wounded while on his way to assist the injured boatswain, and when he found that the skipper was killed, took charge of the sinking vessel. He subsequently signalled for assistance, and when the boat from the steam trawler *Gull* arrived he assisted in putting the wounded and the bodies of the dead into the boat, and was the last to leave the *Crane* just before she sank.

As the Chief Engineer had been wounded and rendered insensible soon after the firing began, the Second Engineer, Arthur Rea (22 years of age), took charge of the engines, and, although the lights had been extinguished, he went into the stokehold to discover the cause of a loud report and an escape of steam. He was knocked down by a shot on his way but went on, and finding the stokehold more than a foot deep in water and steam blowing from the engine side, looked at the gauge glass and pumping additional cold water into the boiler partially drew the fires with the object of averting an explosion. He also set the pumps of the vessel working; and, after reporting that the vessel was sinking went a second time into the engine room and stopped the engines. Although wounded he did not stop working until he left the ship.

In answer to signals of distress from the *Crane*, Charles Beer, Mate, Harry Smith, Chief Engineer, and Edwin Costello, Boatswain, of the steam trawler *Gull*, after the firing, went in a boat to the *Crane* and succeeded with great difficulty in rescuing the wounded from the rapidly sinking vessel, and in bringing away the dead bodies of those who had been killed[58]."

The Board of Trade file dealing with the awards is preserved in the Public Record Office under reference MT 9/769. They include the Submission to the King dated 15th January 1905 accompanied by a statement of services which, in the event, formed the material for the published citation; newspaper reports of the investiture[59]; undertakings signed by each man to return his medal if called upon to do so; and correspondence with the Royal Mint regarding the inscriptions to be engraved on the medals. As to the latter it was found that those originally proposed were inconveniently long for the size of the medal and, accordingly, they were shortened. For Smith and, with adaption, for Rea the final version was "Presented by His Majesty to William Smith, Mate of the trawler *Crane* of Hull, for gallantry and devotion to duty when that vessel was sinking in the North Sea after damage by the gunfire of the Russian Fleet on the 21st–22nd October, 1904"[60] and for Beer and, with adaption for the remainder "Presented by His Majesty to Charles Beer, Mate of the trawler *Gull*, of Hull, for gallantry in rescuing the wounded survivors of the crew of the trawler *Crane* when sinking in the North Sea after damage by the gunfire of the Russian Fleet on the 21st–22nd October, 1904". Despite considerable effort to bring all five men together for the investiture something went wrong in regard to Costello who was then in Ireland and he did not attend the investiture. His medal was presented to him at the Board of Trade on 15th May 1905.

Services on land Lieutenant John Neale, R.N.V.R., was awarded the bronze medal during the First World War. His citation appears in the *London Gazette* of 25th January 1918 at p.1,227 as follows:

"On the 25th August 1916, Lieutenant Neale was conducting certain experiments which involved the projection from a Stokes Mortar of a tube containing flare powder. An accident occurred rendering imminent the explosion of the tube before

58. The version given by Wilson and McEwen differs in minor details.

59. Ie. *The Sports Express* of Hull and *The Hull Daily Mail* for 13th May 1905.

60. Taken from Smith's actual medal. There is a slightly longer version in the file.

leaving the mortar which would almost certainly have resulted in the bursting of the mortar with loss of life to bystanders. Lieutenant Neale, in order to safeguard the lives of the working party, at once attempted to lift the tube from the mortar. It exploded while he was doing so with the result that he was severely injured, but owing to the fact that he had partly withdrawn the tube from the mortar no injury was caused to others."

Wilson and McEwen give two versions of the citation, that under "Land Service Jan. 1915 – Dec. 1919" being rather shorter than that under "Royal Navy and Royal Marines 1868–1938". In neither case is the *London Gazette* entry exactly reproduced. The inscription on the reverse of the actual medal is engraved in upright capital letters (which vary in size according to the line in which they appear) as follows: PRESENTED/BY/HIS MAJESTY/TO/LIEUTENANT/ JOHN NEALE, R.N.V.R/FOR GALLANTRY/IN SAVING LIFE/AT/ CLAREMONT PARK,/ESHER/ON THE/25th AUGUST. 1916.

The Home Office papers dealing with Neale's award are preserved in the Public Record Office under reference HO 45/10889/353040. They contain, *inter alia*, the original recommendation made on behalf of the Minister of Munitions (Winston Churchill); the submission to the King; the draft citation; a copy of the inscription to be engraved on the reverse of the medal; and correspondence leading to the investiture at Buckingham Palace on 6th April 1918.

Chapter 5

The Allied Subjects' Medal

ORIGIN AND DEVELOPMENT

The proposal to recognise the services of Allied subjects who had assisted British prisoners-of-war[1] in the First World War seems to have originated in the Army Council[2]. At all events, on 1st May 1919 the Treasury gave approval for a maximum of £500 to be spent on the provision of gold and silver "medallions" for this purpose, providing that the Foreign Office did not object. Accordingly, the War Office took up the matter with the Foreign Office[3]. In agreeing with the proposal, the Foreign Office suggested that the award should be extended to neutrals, and to British subjects who had worked abroad on behalf of British prisoners since it was desirable to limit the number of appointments to the Order of the British Empire. In reply the War Office accepted the extension to neutrals but not to British subjects, because the latter were "motivated by patriotism as well as humanity" and, moreover, because the value of the proposed award would be depreciated if conferred on a British subject for services which did not merit a British decoration or order. Here, for the time being, the matter was left.

Foreign Office agreement having been obtained, on 12th July 1919 the War Office wrote to the Royal Mint for a suggested design, and for an estimate for 50 gold and 750 medallions. In reply the Mint suggested that the *Transylvania* medal should be used, with a suitably modified reverse[4]. The estimated cost was £478.16.6. The Secretary of State for War (W. S. Churchill) thereupon submitted a proposal to the King that gold and silver medallions should be awarded to Allied and neutral subjects who had rendered assistance to British prisoners-of-war; that in form they should be similar to the *Transylvania* medal; and that the reverse should bear the inscription "A token of gratitude from King George V for services rendered to his subjects 1914–1918". The King's Private Secretary replied that the King thought the proposal "an excellent idea" but that the classical head should appear on the obverse and that a better design might be found for the reverse. Accordingly, following correspondence between the War Office and the Mint, on 7th November 1919 three designs of reverse were submitted to the King: with a wreath similar to that on the *Transylvania* medal; with an ornamental border similar to that on the 1911 Coronation Medal; and with a specially cut laurel spray. The King, however, thought the designs should be submitted to an expert committee and therefore, on 27th November 1919, the War Office sent them to Sir Cecil Harcourt-Smith, Director of the Victoria and Albert Museum. Harcourt-Smith in turn consulted G. F. Hill, Keeper of Coins and Medals at the British Museum, their conclusion being that the designs were of such character that no good purpose would be served by altering them in matter or form. Further correspondence followed between Harcourt-Smith and the War Office, it being agreed eventually that the artist, Edmund Dulac[5], should be invited to submit a design for the reverse. While this was going on the Foreign Office forwarded to the War Office a copy of a despatch from H.M. Ambassador to Belgium. In his despatch the Ambassador urged that the award should be suspended from a ribbon, citing the Continental practice of wearing ribbons in buttonholes, and protesting that medallions were frequently given on the Continent for trivial reasons, eg. by sporting clubs[6]. The War Office made short work of these objections by stating flatly, if inaccurately, that medals were reserved for the Armed Forces but adding that in exceptional cases the award of a British Order might be considered. Here the matter rested although storm clouds were not far below the horizon.

1. Strictly speaking, a person is not a prisoner until captured. It seems that some of the awards eventually made were in respect of servicemen who successfully evaded capture; but the point is academic for our purpose.

2. The majority of what follows is taken from the Public Record Office files WO 32/5571, 5573 and 5574 which contain most of the material. The corresponding Foreign Office documents are scattered over a large number of P.R.O. files and mostly duplicate those on the War Office files. Where they do not, separate Foreign Office references are given.

3. The correspondence was, of course, on behalf of the Army Council on the one hand, and the Secretary of State for Foreign Affairs on the other. For our purposes it is less cumbersome to refer to the Departments themselves except where it is necessary to draw attention to individuals.

4. A medal awarded to certain Italians who assisted in the rescue of British subjects when the transport *Transylvania* was torpedoed near Savone on 4th May 1917.

5. A Frenchman, born in Toulouse in 1882, and living in London.

6. A similar objection was raised by Dame Adelaide Livingstone, Head of the War Office Special Commission regarding the Missing, Brussels.

On 18th June 1920 Harcourt-Smith sent a sketch of Dulac's design to the War Office explaining that it represented "a prisoner sustained by Divine Power, proceeding out of clouds", and that it was based on an idea from Psalm 63, verse 8[7]. The design was sent to Lord Stamfordham, the King's Private Secretary, for submission to the King. In reply, Stamfordham indicated that the design did not appeal to the King who, however, did not feel competent to criticise it from an artistic point of view. Nevertheless, "if the competent authorities consider it in every way suitable, His Majesty would prefer to offer no opinion" and the matter should be proceeded with. Accordingly, Dulac made a cast of his design which was then passed by a committee consisting of Harcourt-Smith and Hill, who the former had originally consulted, and C. J. Holmes of the National Gallery. On 22nd September 1920 the War Office sent a photograph of the cast to the Foreign Office adding that the War Office proposed to issue 99 gold and 550 silver medallions. This produced an explosion. The Foreign Secretary, Lord Curzon, did not like the design and submitted it to the Cabinet who did not like it either. The Cabinet also agreed with Lord Curzon that the medal should be capable of being worn, and the whole matter was therefore brought to the attention of the King. The King agreed that a new design should be prepared for the medal and that it should be suspended by a ribbon. Accordingly, and perhaps not before time, on 28th October 1920 a conference was held at the War Office at which the Foreign Office was represented. The conference concluded that:

1. Dulac should be informed, with regret, that owing to a subsequent Cabinet decision a medal of a different nature was desired and that his design was not now required. The War Office would pay his fee.

2. The same medal should be given to both Allies and neutrals. Claims would have to be admitted of certain persons who were technically or otherwise enemy subjects, especially in view of the extreme danger they ran. British subjects would in no circumstances be eligible.

3. The shape of the medal should be distinguished, in some way, from that of a campaign medal[8]. The example of the 1902 Coronation Medal, which had a wreath round the edge, might be followed. The medal should be attached to the ribbon by a ring.

4. The question of the design of the reverse should be referred to Hill[9]. Because the medal would go to many different nationalities the inscription should be in Latin. The choice of an artist to carry out any suggestions which Hill might make was to be referred to the Adjutant-General's Committee on War Medals.

5. The question of the colour of the ribbon should be referred to the Committee headed by Sir Fredericc Ponsonby[10].

6. In view of the numbers required the medals should be in silver and in bronze.

7. Certain posthumous awards might be made in cases where the persons concerned would, but for their deaths, have been recommended for the M.B.E.[11]

8. The award of a medal was not be withheld by reason of the proposed recipient's already having been rewarded in connection with services other than those on behalf of British prisoners.

9. The War Office recommendations for some 649 awards being known and those of the Foreign Office being in process of collection, no further recommendations should be put forward except those of a very exceptional nature.

A somewhat hazy outline of these proposals was submitted by the War Office to the King on 6th December 1920, the only matter at issue being that Lord Curzon favoured an English inscription on the reverse of the medal. In accepting the Committee's proposals the King indicated that he too preferred an English inscription[12].

It was now necessary to deal with the rejected design and to set matters in train for the preparation of a new one. On 23rd December 1920 the War Office wrote to Harcourt-Smith explaining that it was not possible to accept Dulac's design. This provoked a predictably indignant reply from all three members of that Committee asking, in effect, for the rejection to be reconsidered. Matters were finally laid to

7. "My soul followeth hard after thee; thy right hand upholdeth me."

8. It is difficult to see how such a suggestion ever could have been implemented, short of a lunatic shape.

9. Keeper of Coins and Medals at the British Museum and a member of Harcourt-Smith's Committee.

10. Keeper of the Privy Purse.

11. In fact, posthumous awards were made where otherwise the person concerned would have been recommended for the O.B.E.

12. In the event, there was no inscription on the reverse.

rest by a mollifying letter from the War Office explaining that the decision had been made by the Cabinet, and by the payment of a fee of £50 to Dulac. Also on 23rd December 1920, in accordance with the decision taken at the Conference on 28th October, the War Office wrote to Hill asking if he would suggest a suitable reverse. Since Hill had been a member of Harcourt-Smith's Committee it is not surprising that on 21st February 1921 he replied to the effect that, in all the circumstances, he was unable to help. In the meantime, Treasury approval had been given for expenditure of up to £1500 in view of the increased number of awards, and change in the design contemplated. On 21st March 1921 the War Office again took up the question of design by asking if the King's head should appear on the obverse (and, if so, what the design should be), and whether the reverse should bear an inscription or merely a symbolic design, adding that it proposed to arrange for a limited competition for the Royal Society of British Sculptors. Ponsonby replied to the effect that the classical head should appear on the obverse, and a symbolic deign on the reverse, the King hoping "that the rooted idea of all artists to represent nude figures may be curtailed as much as possible". Treasury permission having been given for the expenditure of £100 on the competition[13], steps were taken to bring the competition to the notice of the Society. On 22nd July 1921 the Adjutant General's Artistic Committee inspected a number of designs for the reverse at the Society's Headquarters and selected that by C. L. J. Doman. The design was then submitted to Lord Curzon, to the Cabinet and finally on 30th August to the King who approved it. On 12th October the War Office accepted a tender from Messrs. Wright and Son of Edgware, Middlesex for the production of 150 silver and 600 bronze medals. The next month specimens were sent to the King for approval, and following this, delivery of the whole order was made to the War Office by 23rd December 1921.

While all the foregoing was in progress, steps were being taken to obtain recommendations. In so far as the War Office was concerned, the majority of these seem to have been put forward by the British Military Intelligence Commission in Brussels. For this purpose a specially printed form[14] in French was used which was to be completed in respect of the person recommended. The wording on the form indicates that it was intended to be completed by the person concerned which suggests that claims were invited. Some of the forms we have seen were completed by applicants, while others were completed on their behalf. Among the information requested was concise details and dates of the assistance rendered to British prisoners; the names of the prisoners and, if possible, their ranks, regiments and private addresses; if the applicant had been arrested as a result of giving assistance, details were required regarding arrest, detention, examination, the sentence and its execution; also required were the names and addresses of persons who could attest to the accuracy of the account given.

By April 1920 the Commission had investigated over 2000 cases[15] and had made the following recommendations:

Honorary appointments to the	
Order of the British Empire ...	36
Gold medallions	89
Silver medallions	480
Letters of thanks	957
No award	574

It will be recalled that at this stage gold and silver medallions were contemplated. However, following the decision to award silver and bronze medals, on 12th November 1920 the Foreign Office forwarded a consolidated list of awards[16], for approval by the King, as follows:

C.B.E.	1
O.B.E.	9
M.B.E.	18
Silver Medals	104

13. Out of the maximum of £1500 allotted.

14. Referred to in the correspondence as a *fiche*.

15. See Foreign Office letter of 20th April 1920 addressed to Lord Derby (Ambassador to France) in FO 372/1505.

16. See FO 372/1523. Although the covering letter says there were 535 recommendations for bronze medals, the copy on WO 32/5573 shows only 534, one having been deleted from p.2 of the list as being duplicated. There is a first draft of the list on FO 372/1756, some alterations evidently having been made to the recommendations of the Military Intelligence Commission. In fact, a further two bronze medals were duplicated (see Foreign Office letter of 6th July 1922 on WO 32/5574) reducing the true total to 532.

27

Bronze Medals	... ...	525
Letters of Thanks	... ...	1055

The King having approved the list, prior to the issue of the insignia of the Order and of the medals, letters were sent to those selected for the awards. In the case of those receiving medals, the text of the letters[17], which were signed by Lord Curzon, read as follows:

"His Britannic Majesty's Government, having learned with high appreciation of the valued services which you have rendered to British Prisoners of War in the course of the Great War desire to express to you their deep sense of gratitude for the self-sacrificing efforts which you so readily made on their behalf.

It accordingly becomes my pleasing duty to address to you this letter of acknowledgement as a testimony of Britain's thanks for the timely help which you gave to our distressed comrades.

I have received the King's commands to inform you that in recognition of the signal services which you have thus given, you have been awarded the (Silver/Bronze) Medal specially instituted by His Majesty as a token of gratitude for such assistance to His Subjects. This Medal will be delivered to you as soon as possible."

In certain cases, where the award of a silver medal was posthumous, the next-of-kin were informed that an appointment to the Order of the British Empire would have been made had such an appointment been possible. In cases where a Letter of Thanks only was approved[18], the last paragraph of the letter quoted above was omitted. In a number of instances recipients replied to the letters, expressing gratitude for the recognition conferred[19].

The main list of awards having been submitted to the King on 12th November 1920, in 1921 and 1922 further awards were made, totalling 30 silver and 42 bronze medals. In March 1922 the medals were sent by the War Office to the Foreign Office, and by the following July the majority had been distributed to recipients through the foreign governments concerned[20]. About the time the medals were delivered to the Foreign Office a Press announcement was agreed between the two Departments, which read as follows[21]:

"ASSISTANCE TO BRITISH SOLDIERS BEHIND THE ENEMY'S LINES. AWARDS TO BELGIAN AND FRENCH NATIONALS.

The King has approved of the issue of a Medal in silver and bronze to those persons of Allied nationality, who, almost always at the risk of their liberty and often at the risk of their lives, rendered assistance to British soldiers behind the enemy's lines. Some of these soldiers were Prisoners of War actually in captivity, others were endeavouring to escape, and yet others, cut off by the German advance, were in hiding and seeking to rejoin their units.

The design of the reverse side of the Medal, which is the work of Mr. C. L. J. Doman, R.B.S., shows a draped female figure representing HUMANITY, standing amid ruins and broken ground, the desolation of war, and offering a cup of water to a recumbent British soldier. On the reverse is the head of His Majesty. The colours of the riband are as follows: centre, a blue stripe, outside of which are two broad yellow stripes, two narrow black stripes, two white stripes of the same width as the centre; the whole being bordered by two broad red stripes.

The list of awards comprises 133 silver medals and 573 bronze medals. In addition to these awards, 28 honorary appointments have been made to the Order of the British Empire in exceptionally deserving cases, while specially prepared letters of thanks have been issued in upwards of 1,000 other instances.

The medals will be distributed through the British Embassies at Brussels and Paris in the near future."

The announcement was not entirely accurate in that awards had been approved not only to Allied subjects[22], but to neutrals and, in one case, to an enemy national. Moreover, the services rewarded included some performed after the Armistice, notably in connection with the repatriation of prisoners, which were not "behind the enemy lines" nor at risk of life or liberty. These inaccuracies may be attributable to the fact that the medal was not instituted by Royal Warrant and

17. There is an example on FO 372/1765.

18. In certain cases these letters were in recognition of the services of groups of persons, eg. in towns, convents etc. and the letters were accordingly addressed to the Mayor, Burgomaster, Mother Superior, as appropriate.

19. See, for instance, FO 372/1764.

20. For various reasons it was decided not to present them publicly under arrangements initiated by Embassies, see Foreign Office letter of 14th March 1921, and annexures thereto, on WO 32/5573.

21. See, for instance, The Times of 7th March 1922.

22. Who, in any case, were not exclusively Belgian and French as implied by the sub-heading (see "Numbers Awarded" below).

Fig.A: The Allied Subjects' Medal, obverse.

Fig.B: The Allied Subjects' Medal, reverse.

23. The matter was considered at the Conference of 28th October 1920 but no proposals were made.

24. Jocelyn (see Bibliography) calls it, slightly more accurately if less elegantly, the "British Prisoners of War Succour Medal".

25. See WO 32/5574.

26. The Foreign Office did not think that naming was necessary, see *ibid*, letter of 8th October 1921.

27. We have adjusted this figure to exclude duplicated names.

28. See FO 372/1523 for the covering letter. A copy of the list is on WO 32/5573. There is a draft list on FO 372/1756.

29. The list contains details of those recommended for honorary appointments to the Order of the British Empire, for silver and bronze medals, and for Letters of Thanks only.

30. See WO 32/5574.

31. In FO 372/1519.

32. E.g. in FO 372/1504 and 1505.

hence the services for which it was to be awarded, and the eligibility of potential recipients, were not precisely defined. Indeed, the medal was never given a name[23]. It is, however, commonly known as "The Allied Subjects' Medal" and, while this is open to objection, there is now little point in seeking to depart from established usage[24].

DESCRIPTION

Ribbon Red, 25mm wide, with light blue (2mm) centre, flanked by stripes of yellow (4mm), black (1.5mm) and white (2mm). In a letter of 6th September 1921 the War Office told the Foreign Office that the ribbon was being chosen by the Army Council and would be submitted to the King[25].

Suspension By a non-swivelling ring of the appropriate metal.

Obverse (Fig.A)

Reverse (Fig.B) Designed by C. L. J. Doman. For a description of the design see the Press announcement quoted above.

Naming The medals were issued unnamed[26].

VERIFICATIONS AND CITATIONS

The names of recipients were not gazetted. The majority of names, totalling 636 medallists[27], are contained in the list submitted to the King on 12th November 1920[28]. This list gives the full names of the person recommended; their address; nationality, where known; and class of award proposed[29]. A further 63 awards were made in a supplementary list of 8th October 1921, being mainly for nationals of neutral countries[30], where only the names, nationality and class are listed. 6 additional awards are annexed to a Foreign Office letter of 6th July 1922, only names and class being given, while similar details regarding one more are to be found in a War Office letter of 4th August 1922[30]. Finally, two awards of the bronze medal are added in manuscript to a typewritten summary which appears on the War Office file[30]; from internal evidence it seems likely that these were added after July 1922.

We have been unable to find any citations as such. Occasionally some details may be found in the Foreign Office files in the Public Record Office by obtaining the appropriate reference against the recipient's name in the official "Index to the Correspondence of the Foreign Office" for the years 1919 to 1922. In addition we have found a list of very brief statements of service for all 28 Danish recipients[31] and a very small number of the Military Intelligence Commission's application forms, mentioned above[32]. In the following examples, we give recipients' names; nationality; type of medal awarded; some indication of the services performed; and the Public Record Office reference:

Father William Peter Azoo; Superior of the Chaldean Cathedral Church, Bagdad; bronze; valuable services to prisoners of the Kut-el-Amara garrison; FO 372/1946.

Doctor Harald Erik Abrahamson; Danish; silver; senior surgeon on s.s. *Russ* during the repatriation of prisoners; FO 372/1519.

Henri Florency Dessene; French; bronze; "for having harboured British soldiers during the war. For doing this he was condemned by the Germans in May 1916 to 10 years hard labour including three in the cells"; FO 372/1763.

Mmes. Eliza Armande Flament and Pauline Alice Cochet (mother and daughter); French; bronze; alleviated the suffering of prisoners in a camp near their farm by giving them food of all sorts, especially bread, and washing their verminous clothing, despite being forbidden to do so by the German commandant. Some of the prisoners were dying of hunger and a post mortem examination on one of them revealed pieces of wood in his stomach. The recommendation for Mme. Flament gives the names of two soldiers who had given her their identity discs as souvenirs; FO 372/1505.

Octave Sepulchre; Belgian; bronze; assisted an aviator to cross the frontier (? into Holland), and was accordingly taken hostage and imprisoned in Germany; FO 372/1504.

Mme. Smits de Savoye; Belgian; silver; "when, after the explosion of the German ammunition depot at Mévergnies in March 1918, British prisoners were given the dangerous task of clearing away, Mme. Smits de Savoye endeavoured by all means to come to their aid. She got in touch with the Dutch Legation who provided her with the main items for distribution (*les principaux objets à distribuer*); with great difficulty she obtained from the occupying authority permission to see the prisoners, and when this authorisation was withdrawn, she succeeded in remaining in constant and secret touch with the prisoners"; FO 372/1764.

Francis Edward Weiner; Belgian; bronze; "kept some prisoners in the cellar of an old Chateau, twenty-five others in a house in Avenue Marnix (Brussels), and an officer was lodged in his own house"; FO 372/1756[33].

NUMBERS AWARDED

In the following table, awards to women are shown in parentheses and are included in the adjoining figure. We have prepared the table from the material contained in WO 32/5574, adjusting for duplicated awards as revealed in the correspondence, and taking into account awards made after submission of the main list to the King on 12th November 1920.

Nationality	Silver Medals		Bronze Medals	
Belgian	60	(27)	307	(118)
Danish	10	(1)	18	(4)
Dutch	15	(6)	6	
French	39	(18)	210	(109)
Georgian	1			
German			1[34]	(1)
Italian			1	
Luxembourgeois			3	(2)
Polish			2	(1)
Swiss			2	
United States			2	(2)
Unidentified[35]	9	(4)	22	(10)
Totals	134[36]	(56)	574	(247)

ILLUSTRATIVE AWARD

Gustave Preux, a Frenchman of St. Quentin, was awarded the bronze medal in the list sent for approval to the King on 12th November 1920. A letter from the Mayor of St. Quentin sent to the Military Intelligence Commission on 26th August 1919[37], sets out the circumstances, as follows:

"It is right that (Gustave Preux) harboured an Irishman named John Hughes from 29th August (1914) to 7th February 1915. He has told us that he did no more than his duty in so acting and claims absolutely nothing for feeding this unfortunate Irishman. That which he does regret is the fatal sequel which came to this soldier. Also, on account of being denounced, M. Preux was imprisoned from 7th February 1915 to 24th November 1918 and taken away to Germany, first to Aix la Chapelle, (then) to Dusseldorf and afterwards to Cassel Wehlinden where he was freed. Unfortunately, the privations to which he was subjected during his captivity, mainly the dampness of the penal establishments, have given him rheumatism in the joints (*rhumatismes articulaires*). At the moment he cannot work and is unable to provide for the needs of his family – his wife aged 54, his three daughters; 21, 19 and 17, and his son aged 14.

M. Preux is well esteemed in the neighbourhood; he has no more than the wages of his two eldest children."

An accompanying Foreign Office letter, addressed to Lord Derby, the Ambassador to France, shows that Preux was sentenced to 15 years hard labour for harbouring Hughes, and that the British Government subsequently paid him 3,000 francs. The letter also mentions that Hughes was shot on 8th March 1915. This man was almost certainly No.10234 Rifleman John Hughes, 2nd Battalion, Royal Irish Rifles[38].

33. These details are taken from an account of the activities of various Belgians published in *The Morning Post* of 4th January 1921, and written by "An Ex-prisoner of War". The Foreign Office file reveals that this was, in fact, Captain Oliver Marlow who had made a number of recommendations which were forwarded through the War Office to the Foreign Office. Becoming impatient with the delay in recognising the persons concerned, Marlow wrote the article in *The Morning Post* and sent a copy, accompanied by a stiff letter, to the Foreign Office. In the event, of the 12 persons recommended by Marlow, only Weiner received a medal; 10 received Letters of Thanks; and in one case no award was made.

34. The recipient's Christian names suggest that she was not German born.

35. Almost all the names are of Belgian or French origin.

36. Including four deceased persons, (1 Belgian and 3 French, one of the latter being a woman) who otherwise would have been given honorary appointments in the Order of the British Empire.

37. See FO 372/1523.

38. See *Soldiers died in the Great War*, Part 67, p.21 (H.M.S.O. 1921). Hughes was born at Crumlin, Co. Antrim and enlisted at Cork.

Chapter 6

The Burma Gallantry Medal

ORIGIN AND DEVELOPMENT

On 1st April 1937 Burma ceased to be part of British India[1], and became a separate territory with a considerable measure of self-government[2]. By Royal Warrants of 10th May 1940 two awards were instituted for certain of the armed forces in Burma, i.e. the Order of Burma, and the Burma Gallantry Medal[3]. The Order of Burma was to be a reward for "long, faithful and honourable service" and, by virtue of the Regulations made for the purposes of the Warrant, would normally only be conferred on Governor's Commissioned Officers on the active list[4]. The Burma Gallantry Medal was to be a reward for "conspicuous gallantry", the Warrant[5] and Regulations made thereunder being as follows:

"GEORGE THE SIXTH, by the Grace of God, of Great Britain, Ireland, and the British Dominions beyond the seas, King, Defender of the Faith, Emperor of India

To all to whom these Presents may come:

GREETING:

Whereas We have taken into Our consideration the means of adequately rewarding acts of gallantry by members of certain of Our Armed Forces in Burma:

Now, We do by these Presents for Us, Our Heirs and Successors, institute a new Decoration and We are pleased to make the following ordinances for its governance.

First – It is ordained that the Decoration shall be named "The Burma Gallantry Medal".

Secondly – It is ordained that the Medal may be conferred by Our Governor of Burma upon Governor's Commissioned Officers, Non-Commissioned Officers and other ranks of the Burma Army, the Burma Frontier Force, the Burma Military Police, the Burma Royal Naval Volunteer Reserve Force and the Burma Auxiliary Air Force, for any act of conspicuous gallantry performed in connection with their duties.

Thirdly – It is ordained that the Decoration shall be a Silver Medal of the same size as a War Medal having therein the Effigy of the Sovereign. On the reverse side a laurel wreath with the words "Burma", "For Gallantry" in relief thereon.

The medal shall be worn on the left breast immediately on the right of all War Medals suspended by a dark green ribbon 1¾ inches wide[6] with a crimson bar in the centre ¼ of an inch wide.

Fourthly – It is ordained that any act of gallantry which is worthy of recognition by the Award of the Burma Gallantry Medal but is performed by one upon whom the decoration has already been conferred, may, at the discretion of Our Governor of Burma be recorded by a bar attached to the riband by which the medal is suspended. For every such additional act an additional Bar may be added and for each such bar awarded a small silver rose shall be added to the riband when worn alone.

Fifthly – It is ordained that Our Governor of Burma may cancel and annul the award of the Medal to any person and that thereupon the said person shall be required to surrender his Insignia, provided that Our Governor may subsequently abrogate any such cancellation and annulment.

Sixthly – It is ordained that it shall be competent for Our Governor of Burma for the time being to make Regulations to carry out the purposes of this Warrant.

Given at Our Court at St. James's the tenth day of May, one thousand nine hundred and forty, in the fourth year of Our Reign.

By His Majesty's Command,
ZETLAND.

1. See section 46(2) of the Government of India Act 1935.

2. See the Government of Burma Act 1935.

3. See the *Burma Gazette* of 13th July 1940, and *LG*, 4th September 1945.

4. For an illustration of, and further details regarding the Order see *The Journal of the Orders and Medals Research Society*, Volume 14, p.61 *et seq.*

5. The wording of the published version is unusually imprecise. Thus "ribbon" is spelt as such in the third clause, but as "riband" (twice) in the fourth clause; the second sentence of the third clause does not have a verb; and in the same clause the stripe to the ribbon is called a "bar".

6. This seems to be a misprint; the only ribbon seen has been 1¼ inches wide.

Regulations relating to the Award of
the Burma Gallantry Medal

1. The Burma Gallantry Medal may be awarded to Governor's Commissioned Officers, Warrant Officers, Other Ranks, enrolled non-combatants and temporary personnel of the Burma Army, including the Burma Army Reserve, the Burma Frontier Force, the Burma Military Police, the Burma Royal Naval Volunteer Reserve Force and the Burma Auxiliary Air Force who have distinguished themselves in peace or on active service by acts of personal bravery.

2. It will be awarded by the Governor on the recommendation of:

    (i) The General Officer Commanding, Burma, in the case of the Burma Army, the Burma Royal Naval Volunteer Reserve Force and the Burma Auxiliary Air Force.

    (ii) The Inspector-General, Burma Frontier Force, in the case of the Burma Frontier Force.

    (iii) The Inspector-General of Police, Burma, in the case of the Burma Military Police.

3. Each recommendation will state the name and rank of the person recommended and particulars of the action for which the grant of the Medal is recommended.

4. The Medal may be awarded to:

    (a) Governor's Commissioned Officers for gallantry not sufficient to justify a recommendation for the V.C. or M.C.

    (b) Burma Other Ranks for gallantry not sufficient to justify a recommendation for the Empire Gallantry Medal.

Awards will be made as soon as possible after the event occasioning the grant.

5. The award of the Burma Gallantry Medal carries with it a Monetary allowance of Rs.5 per mensem payable for life to the recipient, irrespective of rank, unless forfeited for misconduct. An initial award of Rs.5 per mensem will be payable under the same conditions, for each bar to the medal which may be awarded."

On 11th September 1945 amending Warrants were made relating to the Order of Burma and to the Burma Gallantry Medal; both Warrants were to have retrospective effect from 16th March 1945[7]. The Order remained as a reward for long, faithful and honourable service by Governor's Commissioned Officers of the Burma Army, Frontier Force and Military Police but was extended to "acts of conspicuous gallantry" by Governor's Commissioned Officers of the Burma Army and by Warrant Officers of the Burma Royal Naval Volunteer Reserve and of the Burma Volunteer Air Force[8]. The Medal was restricted to non-commissioned officers and other ranks of the Burma Army, Frontier Force, Military Police and Volunteer Air Force and to petty officers and ratings of the Burma Royal Naval Volunteer Reserve. The revised Regulations for the B.G.M. were as follows.

"1. The Burma Gallantry Medal may be awarded to Non-Commissioned Officers and men of the Burma Army, the Burma Army Reserve, the Burma Frontier Force, the Burma Military Police, Petty Officers and Ratings of the Burma Royal Naval Volunteer Reserve and Non-Commissioned Officers and Aircraftsmen of the Burma Volunteer Air Force who have distinguished themselves in peace or on active service by acts of personal bravery or for acts of gallantry not sufficient to justify a recommendation for the Victoria Cross.

2. It will be awarded by the Governor on the recommendation of—

    (i) The General Officer Commanding, Burma, in the case of the Burma Army, the Burma Army Reserve, the Burma Frontier Force and the Burma Military Police.

    (ii) The Formation Commander in which the force or personnel is serving in the case of the Burma Royal Naval Volunteer Reserve.

    (iii) The Formation Commander in which the force or personnel is serving in the case of the Burma Volunteer Air Force.

3. Each recommendation will state the name and rank of the person recommended and particulars of the action for which the grant of the Medal is recommended. Recommendations on Army Form W–3121 will be submitted through normal

7. See the *Burma Gazette* of 8th December 1945 (which also published the revised Regulations consequent on these changes) and *LG*, 18th September 1945. The changes were anticipated by an announcement in the *Burma Gazette Extraordinary* of 12th May 1945.

8. In fact, no awards of the Order of Burma for gallantry were ever made.

Fig.A: The Burma Gallantry Medal, obverse.

Fig.B: The Burma Gallantry Medal. reverse.

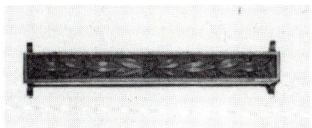

Fig.C: Bar to the Burma Gallantry Medal.

channels to the Governor's Secretary and awards will be made as soon as possible after the event occasioning the grant.

4. The award of the Burma Gallantry Medal carries with it a monetary allowance of Rs.8 per mensem unless forfeited for misconduct. An additional award of Rs.4 per mensem will be payable, under the same conditions, for each Bar to the Medal which may be awarded.

The above allowances will be admissible to individuals awarded the Medal and Bars for acts performed on or after 16th March 1945.

5. The allowances attached to the Medal and Bars will be admissible for two lives, i.e., recipient and widow. The widow will continue to receive the allowance until her remarriage or death. The payment of the allowance will, however, be continued to a widow who remarries her late husband's brother and lives a communal life with the other heirs eligible for a family pension."

The amendment of the Warrants governing the Order and the Medal followed proposals made at a meeting on 14th March 1945 of the Committee on the Grant of Honours, Decorations and Medals in Time of War[9] whereby N.C.O.s and men of the Burma Army and Burma Volunteer Air Force were to be eligible for the M.M., and petty officers and ratings of the Burma Royal Naval Volunteer Reserve for the D.S.M. The status of the B.G.M. was to be raised to that of the I.D.S.M. (which was, by then, regarded as equivalent to the D.C.M.) and the C.G.M. The Order of Burma was to have status equivalent to that of the Military Division of the I.O.M. (which itself had been enhanced by the Royal Warrant of 20th December 1944, see p.163) No awards of the B.G.M. were made to the Burma Royal Naval Volunteer Reserve and only one was made to the Burma Volunteer Air Force[10]. No awards were gazetted after the Burma Independence Act 1947 came into force on 4th January 1948. The B.G.M. is shown only twice in the order of wearing published in the *London Gazette*. In 1941[11] it is shown following the Colonial Police Medal for Gallantry, and in 1947[12] in its enhanced position following the Indian Distinguished Service Medal (see also Appendix 4).

DESCRIPTION

Ribbon Dark green, 1¼ inches wide, with a ¼ inch central crimson stripe.

Suspension By a swivelling scroll bar suspender.

Obverse (Fig.A).

Reverse (Fig.B).

Bar (Fig.C) Silver, with "slip-on" fitting.

Naming A 1944 award has been seen engraved in upright sans-serif capital letters with rank, name and corps; other awards for that year and for 1945 have been found impressed with similar details but with the addition of a regimental or army number.

Copies and Fakes So far none has been seen.

VERIFICATIONS AND CITATIONS

The only details found have been published as follows:

London Gazette The first awards were published in the *Gazette* of 26th March 1942 and the last (all late awards) in that of 28th November 1947. Some corrections were published after the latter date, one being as late as 1951. The "State Intelligence" section of the quarterly indices gives the medal heading and only the pages upon which awards are to be found; the "Honours, Decorations and Medals" section provides a comprehensive nominal list of those who have received awards of all types during the quarter to which the particular index refers, but this section gives only the names and does not specify the award made. Burmese names are indexed under the first name. No citations are given.

9. See P.R.O. AIR 2/6409.
10. To Aircraftman Saw Robert Nyein in *LG*, 21st February 1946.
11. See *LG*, 22nd April 1941.
12. See *LG*, 11th February 1947.

Burma Gazette We have found no indices for the period covered by the award of the B.G.M. However, the *Burma Gazette* entries usually precede those in the *London Gazette*, sometimes by several months, and so the latter can be used to limit the field of search. The last citations appear in 1943 and thereafter only a bare announcement of the award is given.

The only awards appearing in the *Burma Gazette* which do not seem to be repeated in the *London Gazette* are to Havildar Maung Kyaw, 1st Burma Rifles (2nd June 1943); and Jemadar (now Captain) Maung Khin, 1st Burma Rifles (4th January 1947).

Gazette of India Some awards, without citations, appear in the *Gazette of India* and are repeated in Indian Army Orders.

The only award appearing in the *Gazette of India* which does not seem to be repeated in the *London Gazette* is to Jemadar I. C. Chowdhury, Indian Army Medical Corps (10th February 1945, being in substitution for the I.D.S.M. awarded in the *Gazette* of 14th October 1943).

NUMBERS AWARDED

The following summary has been compiled for the awards found in the *London Gazette* supplemented by the three awards appearing in the *Burma Gazette* and the *Gazette of India* which are mentioned above:

	Medals	*First Bars*
Burma Army Intelligence Corps ...	2	–
Burma Army Reserve of Officers ...	1	–
Burma Army Service Corps	3	–
Burma Army Signals	11	1
Burma Auxiliary Force	1	–
Burma Civil Affairs Police	1	–
Burma Frontier Force	7	–
Burma Hospital Corps	1	–
Burma Levies	27	–
Burma Military Police	2	–
Burma Regiment	65	–
Burma Rifles	48	–
Burma Sappers and Miners	1	–
Burma Volunteer Air Force	1	–
Chin Hills Battalion	1	–
Chin Hills Levies	5	–
Chin Rifles	4	–
2nd Gurkha Rifles[13]	1	–
Indian Army Medical Corps	1	–
Northern Kachin Levies	12	1
Western Chin Levies	12	1
Totals:	207	3

The three first bars were awarded to:

	London Gazettes
Jemadar Nawng Seng, Northern Kachin Levies	16th December 1943
	4th January 1945
W.803 Naik Saw Su Po, Burma Army Signals	21st February 1946
	21st February 1946
Levy Leader Van Kul, Western Chin Levies	28th June 1945
	17th January 1946

The medal awarded to 8398 Havildar Lahtaw La, Burma Rifles, appears twice. It was first gazetted on 25th July 1945, the recipient's names being corrected on 9th April 1948, and again, with names as subsequently corrected, on 28th November 1947.

13. To Jemadar Lian Nawn, *LG*, 19th October 1944.

ILLUSTRATIVE AWARD

In the *Burma Gazette Extraordinary* of 18th December 1942, the B.G.M. was awarded to 8316 Rifleman Dum Naw, 3rd Battalion, Burma Rifles[14], whose citation reads as follows:

> "At the crossing of the Sittang River on the 22nd February, 1942, Rifleman Dum Naw assisted Rifleman Saw Saw Maung who had obtained possession of a boat in making three trips to the far side of the Sittang Bridge in the course of which they successfully brought over some 60 men under constant fire. The two Riflemen then proceeded to another part of the far bank of the river and carried across a number of men including some who were badly wounded. The work of rescue ended only when the unit was ordered to withdraw. It was carried out with the utmost gallantry and complete disregard of personal safety."

Rifleman Saw Saw Maung also received the B.G.M. in the same *Gazette Extraordinary*[14], his citation being rather differently worded.

14. The award also appeared in *LG*, 9th March 1943.

35

Chapter 7

The Burma Police Medal

ORIGIN AND DEVELOPMENT

Following the separation of Burma from British India in 1937 the Burma Police Medal was instituted by a Royal Warrant of 14th December 1937[1], as follows:

"GEORGE R.I.

GEORGE THE SIXTH by the Grace of God of Great Britain Ireland and of the British Dominions beyond the Seas King Defender of the Faith Emperor of India.

To all to whom these presents shall come:

GREETING:

Whereas We have taken into Our Royal consideration the good services rendered by Members of the Police Forces and of Fire Brigades within Burma:

And Whereas We are desirous of making further provision for distinguishing meritorious services rendered by them:

We do by these presents for Us, Our Heirs and Successors, institute and create a new Medal to be awarded by Our Governor of Burma for the time being on Our behalf for distinguished conduct.

First: It is ordained that the Medal shall be designated and styled "The Burma Police Medal."

Secondly: It is ordained that the Burma Police Medal shall consist of a circular Medal of bronze with the Effigy of the Sovereign on the obverse, and on the reverse a wreath surmounted by a Crown, and shall bear on the rim the name of the person to whom the Medal is awarded.

Thirdly: It is ordained that the Medal shall be awarded only to those members of a recognised Police Force or of a properly organised Fire Brigade within Burma who have performed services of conspicuous merit.

Fourthly: It is ordained that the names of those to whom this Medal may be awarded shall be published in the *Burma Gazette*, and that a Register of such names shall be kept in the Office of the Secretary to the Governor of Burma.

Fifthly: It is ordained that each Medal shall be suspended from the left breast, and the riband, of an inch and three-eighths in width, shall be dark blue with a narrow silver stripe on either side and a bright blue stripe in the centre.

Sixthly: It is ordained that any distinguished conduct which is worthy of recognition by the award of the Burma Police Medal, but is performed by one upon whom the Decoration has already been conferred, may be recorded by a Bar attached to the riband by which the Medal is suspended; and for every such additional award an additional Bar may be added.

Seventhly: It is ordained that the number of Medals awarded in any one year (excluding Bars) shall not exceed 25.

Eighthly: It is ordained that it shall be competent for Our Governor of Burma for the time being to cancel and annul the award to any person of the above Decoration and that thereupon the name of such person in the Register shall be erased, but that it shall be competent for Our said Governor to restore any Decoration which may have been so forfeited. And every person to whom the said Decoration is awarded shall, before receiving the same, enter into an agreement to return the Medal if his name shall be erased as aforesaid.

Ninthly: It is ordained that it shall be competent for Our Governor of Burma for the time being to make regulations to carry out the purposes of this Our Warrant.

Given at Our Court at St. James's the Fourteenth day of December, One thousand nine hundred and thirty-seven, in the Second year of Our Reign.

By His Majesty's Command,
ZETLAND."

1. See the *Burma Gazette* of 5th February 1938.

36

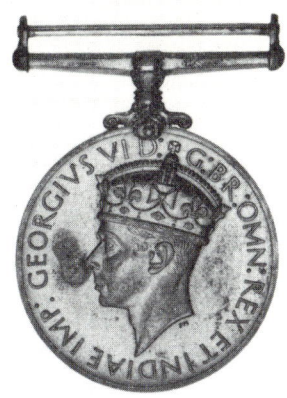

Fig.A: The Burma Police Medal, obverse, George VI issue, first type.

Fig.B: The Burma Police Medal, obverse, George VI issue, second type.

Fig.C: The Burma Police Medal, reverse.

2. See the *Burma Gazette* of 13th September 1947.

3. "... has the standard medal crowned effigy for obverse, and for the reverse a wreath surmounted by a crown, and the inscription BURMA POLICE – FOR DISTINGUISHED CONDUCT". See the *Annual Report of the Deputy Master and Comptroller of the Royal Mint (1938)*, pp.17 and 42.

Only one amending Warrant was made. This was dated 10th July 1947[2] and abrogated the 7th Clause by substituting the following:

> "*Seventhly*: It is ordained that the number of Medals awarded on any ground other than that of conspicuous gallantry shall not in any one year exceed 25."

The Regulations referred to in the 9th Clause were published with the instituting Warrant and were as follows:

> "(*a*) The Medal will be open to all ranks of the Police, civil and military, including the Frontier Force, and to the members of properly organised Fire Brigades in Burma.
>
> (*b*) It will be awarded by the Governor on the recommendation of the Officer in Command of the Police Force or, in the case of members of Fire Brigades, of the Commissioner of the Division.
>
> (*c*) Each recommendation will state the name and rank of the person recommended, the Police Force or Fire Brigade, of which he is or was a member, and particulars of the action or service for which the grant of the Medal is recommended.
>
> (*d*) The Medal will be awarded:
>
> > (i) for conspicuous gallantry. Awards for gallantry will be made as soon as possible after the event occasioning the grant;
> >
> > (ii) for valuable services characterised by resource and devotion to duty, including prolonged service of ability and merit. Such awards will be made once annually on the 1st January from the list of recommendations which should reach the Secretary to the Governor not later than the 15th November in each year.
>
> (*e*) When awarded for gallantry, the Medal will carry a monetary allowance at half the rates sanctioned for the award of the King's Police Medal for gallantry.
>
> (*f*) The number of Medals to be awarded each year will not exceed 25.
>
> (*g*) The Medal shall be worn next to and immediately after the Indian Police Medal.
>
> (*h*) The award of the Medal will not be a bar to the subsequent award of the King's Police Medal."

The Regulations were twice amended by the Governor of Burma. Firstly, in the *Burma Gazette* of 26th November 1938 the following proviso was added to Regulation (*e*):

> "Provided that a Medal awarded to an Officer, already in receipt of an allowance in respect of the award of an Indian Police Medal, will carry a monetary allowance at half the rates sanctioned for a Bar to the King's Police Medal awarded for gallantry to an Officer already in receipt of an allowance."

Secondly, in the *Burma Gazette* of 11th May 1940 when in Regulation (*d*) (ii) "1st October" was substituted for "15th November".

The Burma Police Medal awarded for gallantry is shown only in 1941 and 1947 in the order of wearing published in the *London Gazette*. In both cases it is shown following the Indian Police Medal awarded for gallantry (see also Appendix 4).

DESCRIPTION

Ribbon Dark blue, 1⅜ inches wide, with a narrow silver stripe on either side and a bright blue stripe in the centre.

Suspension By a straight non-swivelling bronze suspender.

Obverse
1. George VI first type (Fig.A).
2. George VI second type (Fig.B). A medal with this obverse was struck but may not have been issued.

Reverse (Fig.C) This remained constant[3]

Bar No bar was awarded.

Naming Engraved in seriffed capital letters with rank, names and force.

Copies and Fakes None has been found. Some Royal Mint specimens are in existence.

VERIFICATIONS, CITATIONS AND NUMBERS AWARDED

Awards of the medal for gallantry, or for meritorious service, are published in the *Burma Gazette*. Both classes of award are accompanied by citations. For the period 1938 to 1948 we have found 53 awards for gallantry and 80 for meritorious service, plus a further eight awards in 1942 which we have been unable to classify. However, during the Second World War the *Gazette* was published for nearly 3½ years in India, on sheets of varying size, which made binding difficult, and we are not sure that we have seen every issue. For this reason our figures must be treated with reserve although it is likely that we have noted most, if not all, of the awards. Five of the gallantry awards were to Europeans[4], and one to a member of the Mandalay Municipal Fire Brigade[5]. No bars were awarded.

ILLUSTRATIVE AWARD

Sub-Inspector of Police Maung Maung, Police Station Officer, Ayadaw Police Station, Lower Chindwin District, was awarded the Burma Police Medal in the *Burma Gazette* of 5th October 1940[6] where his citation reads as follows:

> "Sub-Inspector of Police Maung Maung with the help of one Head Constable and an armed villager distinguished himself by engaging a gang of seven dacoits armed with two guns at Kaingywa Village, Lower Chindwin District, on the night of the 3rd March 1940. When the dacoity occurred the Sub-Inspector of Police and his two companions were sent into the village to a previously selected position within close range of the dacoited house by his Inspector who remained outside the village with the rest of the Police party to cut off the dacoits' retreat.
>
> The Sub-Inspector of Police immediately attacked the dacoits and shot dead two while a third was killed by the Head Constable. A fourth dacoit who fired at the Sub-Inspector of Police while he was re-loading was promptly accounted for by him. The villager wounded a fifth dacoit and the remaining two were wounded by the Police party outside the village, all three being subsequently captured.
>
> Maung Maung displayed conspicuous courage in attacking at short range an armed gang which outnumbered his small party by more than two to one and at the same time coolly controlled his fire so as to avoid causing injury to the inmates of the house and to the other villagers.
>
> The award is made for this act of courage and devotion to duty."

4. To Sub-Inspector P. L. Daly (*Burma Gazette* of 24th May 1941); Assistant Superintendents J. W. Capel (*Burma Gazette* of 1st March 1947), A. W. Pink (*Burma Gazette* of 3rd May 1947), T. M. Spitteler (*Burma Gazette* of 7th June 1947) and C. B. Stanley (*Burma Gazette* of 23rd August 1947).

5. To Fireman Maung Sein Win (*Burma Gazette* of 17th May 1941).

6. At pp. 1,251–2.

Chapter 8

The Colonial Police Medal

ORIGIN AND DEVELOPMENT

The Colonial Police Medal was instituted by a Royal Warrant dated 10th May 1938[1]. The Warrant and the Regulations made thereunder were as follows:

"GEORGE THE SIXTH, by the Grace of God, of Great Britain, Ireland and the British Dominions beyond the Seas King, Defender of the Faith, Emperor of India. To all to whom these presents shall come:

GREETING:

Whereas We have taken into Our Royal consideration the good services which are rendered by members of the Police Forces and of Fire Brigades in Our Colonies and in Territories under Our Protection:

And Whereas We are desirous of rewarding meritorious service rendered by them:

We do by these presents for Us, Our Heirs and Successors institute and create a new Medal to be awarded to members of the aforesaid Police Forces and Fire Brigades for distinguished conduct.

First: It is ordained that the Medal shall be designated and styled "The Colonial Police Medal".

Secondly: It is ordained that the Colonial Police Medal shall consist of a circular medal of silver with the Effigy of the Sovereign on the obverse, and on the reverse an emblematic design with the words "For Gallantry" or "For Meritorious Service", as the case may be. The Medal shall bear on the rim the name and rank of the person to whom it is awarded and the name of the Police Force or Fire Brigade for service in which the award is made.

Thirdly: It is ordained that the Medal shall be awarded only to those members of recognised Police Forces or of properly organised Fire Brigades in Our Colonies and in Territories under Our Protection who have performed services of conspicuous merit, and that such award shall be made only on a recommendation to Us by one of Our Principal Secretaries of State.

Fourthly: It is ordained that the names of those to whom this Medal may be awarded shall be published in the *London Gazette*, and that a Register of such names shall be kept in the Office of Our Principal Secretary of State for the Colonies.

Fifthly: It is ordained that the Medal shall be worn on the left breast suspended from a ribbon one inch and three-eighths in width, of which the central part (one half of an inch in width) shall be dark blue with two green borders, each three-eighths of an inch in width, and two silver stripes, each one-sixteenth of an inch wide, separating the borders from the central part. In the case of awards for gallantry the green borders of the ribbon shall each be centrally divided by a crimson stripe one-sixteenth of an inch in width.

Sixthly: It is ordained that any gallant conduct which is worthy of recognition by the award of the Colonial Police Medal, but is performed by one upon whom the Medal has already been conferred, may be recorded by a Bar attached to the ribbon by which the Medal is suspended. For each such additional award an additional Bar may be added, and for each Bar awarded a small silver rose may be added to the ribbon when worn alone.

Sevently: It is ordained that it shall be competent for Us, Our Heirs and Successors by an Order under Our Sign Manual and on a recommendation to that effect by or through one of Our Principal Secretaries of State to cancel and annul the award to any person of the Colonial Police Medal, and that thereupon the name of such person in the Register shall be erased: Provided that it shall be competent for Us, Our Heirs and Successors to restore the Medal so forfeited when such recommendation has been withdrawn. And every person to whom the said Medal is awarded shall, before

1. It will be noted that clause 9 of the Warrant discontinued the African Police Medal (q.v.)

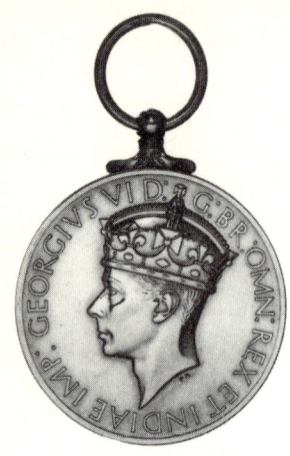

Fig.A: The Colonial Police Medal, obverse, George VI issue, first type.

Fig.B: The Colonial Police Medal, obverse, George VI issue, second type.

receiving the same, enter into an agreement to return the Medal if his name shall be erased as aforesaid.

Eightly: It is ordained that the Medal shall be awarded under such regulations as to grant, forfeiture, restoration and other matters in amplification of these Our rules and ordinances as may be issued from time to time by one of Our Principal Secretaries of State.

Ninthly: It is ordained that as from the date of this Warrant the grant of "The African Police Medal for Meritorious Service", which was instituted and created by His late Majesty King George the Fifth by a Warrant under His Sign Manual dated the twenty-sixth day of July nineteen hundred and fifteen, for award to non-commissioned officers and men (other than those of European descent) of the Police Forces of East and West Africa, shall be discontinued for future service; and the aforesaid Warrant is hereby cancelled.

Lastly: We reserve to Ourself, Our Heirs and Successors full power of annulling, altering, abrogating, augmenting, interpreting or dispensing with these rules and ordinances, or any part thereof, by a notification under Our Sign Manual.

Given at Our Court at St. James's the tenth day of May, one thousand, nine hundred and thirty-eight in the second year of Our Reign.

By His Majesty's Command.
HARLECH.

REGULATIONS

The following Regulations shall be observed in recommending His Majesty to grant the Colonial Police Medal:

(*a*) The Medal shall be open to all ranks of the Police Forces, civil and military, and to all members of properly organised Fire Brigades, in the Colonies and in Territories under His Majesty's Protection (including Mandated Territories).

(*b*) Each recommendation for the Medal shall state the name and rank of the person recommended, the Police Force or Fire Brigade of which he is or was a member, and particulars of the action or service for which the grant of the Medal is recommended.

(*c*) The qualifications for the Medal shall be as follows:

   (i) Conspicuous gallantry.

   (ii) Valuable service characterised by resource and devotion to duty, including prolonged service marked by exceptional ability, merit and exemplary conduct.

(*d*) Any award of the Medal for conspicuous gallantry shall be made as soon as possible after the event occasioning the grant; and all other awards shall be made annually on the occasion of His Majesty's Birthday.

(*e*) The number of Medals to be awarded in any one year, for services other than conspicuous gallantry, shall not exceed one hundred and fifty save and except that in very special circumstances which, in His Majesty's opinion, would justify an exceptional grant, His Majesty may award Medals exceeding that number.

(*f*) The Medal shall be worn next to and immediately after the Burma Police Medal.

(*g*) The award of the Medal will not be a bar to subsequent recommendation for the King's Police Medal.

HARLECH.
10th May, 1938."

In May 1952 Regulation (*d*) was amended by making provision for bi-annual awards (i.e. in the New Year and Birthday Honours Lists[2]), and Regulation (*f*) was amended by providing that the Medal in future was to be worn immediately after the Ceylon Police Medal.

By an amending Warrant of 25th October 1972[3] recipients are entitled to use the postnominal letters "C.P.M." on all occasions when the use of such letters is customary.

2. In fact, some had already appeared in the New Year Honours Lists for 1946, 1950, 1951 and 1952. The 14 awards in 1946 were omitted from the *London Gazette*, but were published in the *Palestine Gazette* of 1st January 1946, p.2, all being awarded to the Palestine Police.

3. See *L.G.*, 14th December 1972.

Fig.C: The Colonial Police Medal, obverse, Elizabeth II issue, first type.

Fig.D: The Colonial Police Medal, obverse, Elizabeth II issue, second type.

Fig.E: The Colonial Police Medal, for Gallantry, reverse; Police issue.

4. I.e., on the award to Constable Timour Mehmet, Cyprus Police (*LG*, 20th August 1957).

5. Adapted from the punch of the existing Long Service Medal. See the *Annual Report of the Deputy Master and Comptroller of the Royal Mint (1939)*, p.29.

DESCRIPTION

Ribbon Green, 1⅜ inches wide, with a dark blue central stripe flanked by silver stripes each ¹⁄₁₆ inch in width. For gallantry awards the green borders are divided by scarlet stripes each ¹⁄₁₆ inch in width.

Suspension By a non-swivelling silver ring, approximately ½ inch in diameter.

Obverse There are four types, as follows:

1. George VI first type (Fig.A).
2. George VI second type (Fig.B).
3. Elizabeth II first type (Fig.C) This type was still in issue as late as 1957[4].
4. Elizabeth II second type (Fig.D).

Reverse There are two types of gallantry reverse, as follows:

1. Police (Fig.E).
2. Fire Brigades[5] (Fig.F).

Bar (Fig.G) Silver, as for the King's Police Medal, laurelled version.

Naming A police issue awarded in 1938 is engraved in large serif capital letters with the abbreviated rank, full names, and title of the Force. Post-War police issues have been seen with similar details engraved in small capital letters without serifs; others have been seen engraved in large capital letters with serifs.

Copies and Fakes None has been seen.

VERIFICATIONS AND CITATIONS

All awards are published in the *London Gazette*. Until the first quarter of 1942, names are given under the heading "Colonial Police Medal" in the "State Intelligence" portion of the quarterly *Gazette* indices. Thereafter this heading gives only the pages upon which awards are to be found, the names being relegated to a comprehensive nominal index headed "Honours, Decorations and Medals". Mistakes have sometimes been found in the page references given under the former heading from 1942 where they may be corrupt, omitted or entered under the wrong heading.

No citations are given. However, awards are re-published, often with citations, in local *Gazettes* (e.g. *The Cyprus Gazette, The Kenya Gazette*, etc.), and in Force Orders. Moreover, local press notices may sometimes provide details.

NUMBERS AWARDED

The following gallantry awards have been gazetted:

London Gazettes		Medals		First bars	
		Police	*Fire*		
1938–1948	...	171	2	...	2
1949–1952	...	103	—	...	1
1953–1979	...	191	15	...	6

The nine first bars, all to policemen, were awarded as follows:

	Police Force	London Gazette
Inspector P. R. Adams ...	Palestine	28th January 1944
Senior Inspector Hisham bin Haji Nawawi	Federation of Malaya	23rd November 1948
Constable Kibelion arap Kori	Kenya	22nd August 1950
Sergeant Edward Angwin Boatswain	Trinidad	13th March 1956
Assistant Inspector Githieya Ndirangu	Kenya	1st February 1957
Assistant Superintendent-D. S. Ross	Tanganyika	2nd May 1958
Assistant Commissioner D. J. G. Rose, M.B.E. ...	British Guiana	10th May 1960

Fig.F: The Colonial Police Medal, for Gallantry, reverse; Fire Brigades issue.

Fig.G: Bar to the Colonial Police Medal, for Gallantry.

Deputy Superintendent C. M.
  Roberts ... ...   St. Vincent   4th May 1962
Staff Sergeant 1st Class
  Tsang Wing ... ...   Hong Kong   6th February 1968

No woman has yet received the medal for gallantry.

The corresponding overall figures for meritorious service awards are:

	Medals	
London Gazettes	Police[6]	Fire
1938–1948 ...	457	5
1949–1952 ...	433	4
1953–1979 ...	2,246	160

ILLUSTRATIVE AWARD

British Constable Kenneth Sindall, Palestine Police, was awarded the Colonial Police Medal for Gallantry in the *London Gazette* of 8th November 1938[7]. No citation appears in the *Gazette* but a copy of the official recommendation was given to Sindall, which is as follows:

> "At 6.15p.m. on 4th August, 1938, the two armoured cars of the Police posts at Majdal Krum and Rameh on the Acre – Safad road were ambushed by some 12 to 14 armed men as they were returning from patrol. They were subjected to a raking fire from men concealed behind a series of large rocks on the foot-hills, some 30 yards from the road.
>
> Both car crews brought their Lewis guns into action. A number of the gang attempted to gain the crest of the hill under cover of the fire from the remainder, but owing to the accurate gunnery from the cars, this was frustrated and they suffered considerable casualties.
>
> Three dead bodies could be seen, and in order to attempt to gain possession of their rifles and S.A.A., B/Sgt. Gander and B/Const. Sindall left their car under cover of Lewis gun fire and made for the foothills, making their way to within a few yards of the bodies. They were here heavily and accurately sniped at by other members of the gang and having emptied their revolvers into two snipers who were within a few yards of them, they were forced to make their way back to the cars.
>
> At this moment, a further party of some 25/30 armed men were seen approaching from the rear and heavy fire was opened on them from this party.
>
> B/Sgt. Gander then ordered both cars to move off and make for the nearest post which they did under heavy fire, from both sides of the road. They sustained no casualties but both cars were hit by bullets and the tyres punctured.
>
> The following morning a large number of live and empty rounds were found on the scene together with ample evidence of casualties sustained.
>
> From reliable information it is believed that a fourth man was killed and some 10 to 12 men were wounded in this engagement.
>
> Constable Sindall has come under notice on three occasions recently for courage and initiative under fire whilst serving on the Frontier, and I consider his conduct on this occasion is deserving of the award of the King's Police Medal for Gallantry."

Sindall also received the General Service Medal with one bar for Palestine. He served in the Army during the Second World War, being commissioned in 1942. He received the 1939–45 Star, the Africa Star with bar for the 8th Army, the Defence and War Medals. In 1946 he was granted a Short Service Commission in the Army and later received the bar for Palestine 1945–48 to his General Service Medal. He transferred to the Regular Army Reserve of Officers in 1955. Sergeant S. J. Gander, who is mentioned in Sindall's citation, received the King's Police Medal for Gallantry for the action described above, and for a further action in the same area on 8th August following[8].

6. Of which five were to women police officers.

7. This was one of the first four awards made. The *Palestine Gazette* of 8th November 1938 also published the award with brief details, as follows: "For gallantry on the 4th August, 1938, during an engagement against armed men on the Acre – Safad road."

8. See *LG*, 28th October 1938.

Chapter 9

The Conspicuous Gallantry Medal

The development and description of the Conspicuous Gallantry Medal falls conveniently into two phases; firstly, the Medal granted in 1855, and secondly, that instituted in 1874.

THE MEDAL OF 1855

ORIGIN AND DEVELOPMENT

This Medal was awarded in the War against Russia, 1854–1856, as the naval counterpart of the Distinguished Conduct Medal (q.v.). The Royal Warrant of 4th December 1854 (which made financial provisions for, and instituted, the D.C.M.) did not apply to the Royal Navy and Royal Marines[1] who were also heavily engaged in the War. Accordingly, an Order in Council of 13th September 1855 sanctioned similar rewards for men of the Royal Navy and Royal Marines, as follows:

13th August 1855
MEDALS AND GRATUITIES FOR
DISTINGUISHED GALLANTRY IN ACTION.

WHEREAS we are humbly of opinion, that the petty officers and seamen of Your Majesty's Navy, and the sergeants, corporals, and privates of Royal Marines, who may serve in the present war, are justly entitled to receive rewards for distinguished gallantry in action, similar to those which have been accorded to the Army by Your Royal Warrant of the 4th December 1854. We do therefore most humbly submit that Your Majesty may be graciously pleased, by Your Order in Council, to authorize us to confer rewards, by the grant of medals and gratuities, on any petty officers, seamen, and Royal Marines, who shall, whilst so serving, particularly distinguish themselves in action with the enemy, the same to be granted on the recommendation of the Commanders-in-Chief of your Majesty's Naval forces, in the proportion of eight petty officers or sergeants and corporals of Royal Marines, and ten seamen or privates of Royal Marines, for every thousand men, and in sums of fifteen pounds to each first class petty officer, or sergeant of Royal Marines; ten pounds to each second class petty officer, or corporal of Royal Marines; and five pounds to each seaman, or private of Royal Marines; and in the event of any smaller number of men being engaged, the medals and gratuities to be granted in like proportion, according to the number actually employed, the amount to be paid out of the vote for sea wages, and not to exceed the sum of four thousand pounds in any one year. We further beg leave to represent to Your Majesty that the Lords of Your Majesty's Treasury have signi-fied to us, by a letter, dated the 10th instant, their concurrence in the same."

On 11th October 1855 the Board of Admiralty decided that the existing Royal Marine M.S.M. should be adapted by substituting the words "CONSPICUOUS GALLANTRY" for "MERITORIOUS SERVICE" which appeared on that medal, and that the ribbon for wear with the new medal should have equal stripes of blue, white and blue[2]. In due course a number of awards of the medal thus adapted were made. On 12th June 1856 the Lords Commissioners of the Admiralty wrote to the Secretary of State for War (Lord Panmure) asking whether previous award of the medal and gratuity would exclude an individual from grant of the V.C. and pension; or whether the V.C. and pension should be given in lieu of the medal; or whether the V.C. and pension might be given in

1. An Order in Council of 8th February 1855 extended the number of Meritorious Service Medals available to sergeants of the Royal Marines by increasing the total amount available for pecuniary awards from £250 to £300 p.a. The additional £50 was used, in conjunction with the M.S.M., to reward R.M. sergeants for gallantry, see the article by Captain K. J. Douglas-Morris, R.N., in the *Journal of the Orders and Medals Research Society*, Vol. 13 (1974), p.201 *et seq.*

2. See P.R.O. ADM 1/5660. For what follows we are indebted to Captain K. J. Douglas-Morris, R.N., who has kindly placed the results of his researches at our disposal.

Fig.A: The Conspicuous Gallantry Medal, obverse, (the Medal of 1855).

Fig.B: The Conspicuous Gallantry Medal, reverse, (the Medal of 1855).

3. See P.R.O. ADM 1/5685.

4. See P.R.O. ADM 139/31.

5. See P.R.O. ADM 12/640.

6. It is not clear why this should have been so unless there has been delay in the Admiralty. Lists of those recommended in both Services were not submitted to the Queen (and then informally) until 15th February 1857.

7. See Lord Lyon's letter of 10th May 1856 in P.R.O. ADM 1/5685 recommending three men (excluding Doran) for the V.C. In the event the three were appointed to the 5th Class of the Legion of Honour. The name John (*sic.*) Doran has been added in pencil to the recommendation and since the ship and date of the action on Doran's medal exactly correspond with the event described above the inference is obvious.

8. His genuine medals, including the V.C., C.G.M. and five others, are illustrated in Messrs. Glendining's catalogue of the W. Phillips collection sold on 17th June 1925.

9. E.g., in Messrs. Glendining's sale of 19th June 1925, Lot 894.

10. *LG*, 20th November 1855, p.4,361.

11. Mentioned in Despatches, *LG*, 8th December 1855, p.4,665.

12. Awarded the Victoria Cross in *LG* of 24th February 1857.

addition to the medal and gratuity. Lord Panmure's reply was to the effect that a man might "change" the medal for the V.C. but he could not be allowed to "bear" both. Such a man would receive the pension although the gratuity would not be recalled[3]. In the event six of the eleven men who received the C.G.M. also received the V.C. for the same act (see below) but in circumstances which are far from clear. From surviving groups of medals it is clear that the C.G.M. was not withdrawn from the man concerned although he was not supposed to wear it.

A comparatively late award of the medal (and gratuity of £15) occurred in the case of James Doran, Boatswain's Mate of *Agamemnon*, who himself had solicited the V.C.[4] Although Doran's self-recommendation was endorsed by Admiral Lord Lyons, Commander-in-Chief in the Mediterranean, it did not reach the Admiralty until 11th January 1857[5] and by the time it was disposed of on 27th February following it was said to be "Too late for grant of Victoria Cross"[6] The event for which Doran's medal was awarded appears to have taken place on 17th October 1854 during the Fleet bombardment of Sebastopol and Fort Constantine. A shell caused *Agamemnon*'s mainsail to catch fire and Doran, with three others, extinguished it[7].

DESCRIPTION

Ribbon 1¼ inches wide with equal stripes of dark blue/white/dark blue.

Suspension By an ornate scroll swivelling suspender.

Obverse (Fig.A) Since the Meritorious Service Medal was used, the date "1848" appeared below the Queen's bust on all issues.

Reverse (Fig.B) As indicated above, the words "MERITORIOUS SERVICE" were removed and the resulting blank engraved "CONSPICUOUS GALLANTRY". The word "FOR" remained in raised letters.

Bar None.

Naming The medals were engraved in serif capitals with the recipient's name, rank, ship and date of the act.

Copies and Fakes Owing to its makeshift nature, this medal has lent itself to faking. A fake to J. Taylor has been seen[8], and un-named specimens have appeared[9].

VERIFICATIONS AND CITATIONS

The recommendations for some of the medals appear in the *London Gazette* in the despatches published therein. Only in the case of Quartermaster W. Rickard, however, can we find the specific mention that "in consideration of the services mentioned in the above Despatches, a Medal and £15 gratuity, for conspicuous gallantry, have been awarded to William Rickard, Quartermaster of Her Majesty's ship *Weser*"[10].

NUMBERS AWARDED

Twelve awards were made to eleven recipients. In the following list the date given is that of the act of gallantry:

D. Barry, Able Seaman, *Cracker*, 14th October 1855, Kinburn, Black Sea.

D. Barry[11], Able Seaman, *Cracker*, 4th–6th November 1855, Sea of Azoff.

G. Belding, Leading Seaman, *Firefly*, 8th August 1855, Gulf of Bothnia.

J. Doran, Boatswain's Mate, *Agamemnon*, 17th October 1854, Fleet bombardment of Sebastopol etc. (see above)

P. Hanlan[11], Able Seaman, *Curlew*, 4th–6th November 1855, Sea of Azoff.

G. Ingoueville, Captain of the Mast, *Arrogant*, 13th July 1855, Viborg, Baltic[12].

T. Kerr[13], Gunner, Royal Marine Artillery, *Vesuvius*, 4th–6th November 1855, Sea of Azoff.

W. Rickard[14], Quartermaster, *Weser*, 11th October 1855, Sea of Azoff[12].

J. Shepheard (otherwise Sheppard or Shepherd), Boatswain's Mate, *St. Jean d'Acre*, 15th July 1855, Naval Brigade at Sebastopol[12].

Fig.C: The Conspicuous Gallantry Medal, obverse, Victoria issue (the Medal of 1874).

Fig.D: The Conspicuous Gallantry Medal, obverse, Edward VII issue.

J. Sullivan, Boatswain's Mate, *Rodney*, 10th April 1855, Naval Brigade at Sebastopol[12].

J. Taylor, Captain of the Forecastle, *London*, 18th June 1855, Naval Brigade at Sebastopol[12].

J. Trewavas[15], Ordinary Seaman, *Agamemnon* (lent to *Beagle*), 3rd July 1855, Straits of Genitchi, Sea of Azoff[12].

The services described in *Hart's Army List* of 1873 for Quartermasters R. Halling and J. Woon of the Royal Marine Light Infantry include in each case reference to the award of the "Medal for Conspicuous Gallantry" for China 1857–59, when serving in the ranks. In addition each received an annuity of £10[16], which would have ceased on appointment to a commission. Since the C.G.M. had been instituted for "the present war" (i.e. that against Russia) and attracted a gratuity only, it seems more likely that they received the Royal Marine M.S.M.

THE MEDAL INSTITUTED IN 1874

ORIGIN AND DEVELOPMENT

At the end of the Ashantee War of 1873–1874, by an Order in Council dated 7th July 1874, the Conspicuous Gallantry Medal was re-instituted as follows:

7th July 1874

CONSPICUOUS GALLANTRY

Medals and Annuities for, to Seamen and Marines.

WHEREAS your Majesty was graciously pleased by your Orders in Council, dated the 8th day of February, 1855[17], and thirteenth day of August, 1855, to establish certain Rewards for such Petty Officers and Seamen of your Majesty's Navy, and Non-commissioned Officers and Privates of your Majesty's Corps of Royal Marines, as distinguished themselves by acts of conspicuous gallantry in action during the Crimean war only; and whereas your Majesty was graciously pleased by your Royal Warrant, dated the thirteenth day of September, 1862, to establish for your Majesty's Army Rewards for distinguished conduct in the field at any time and in any part of the world. And whereas we are humbly of opinion that it would be desirable to extend the provisions of your Majesty's said Warrant of the thirteenth day of September, 1862, to the Petty Officers and Seamen of your Majesty's Navy, and non-commissioned Officers and Privates of your Majesty's Corps of Royal Marines. We do, therefore, beg leave to recommend that your Majesty will be graciously pleased by your Order in Council to establish a Silver Medal, bearing on one side your Majesty's effigy, and on the other side the words "For Conspicuous Gallantry", for such Petty Officers and Seamen of your Majesty's Navy, and Non-commissioned Officers and Privates of your Majesty's Corps of Royal Marines, as may at any time distinguish themselves by acts of pre-eminent bravery in action with the enemy. And we further beg leave to recommend that in the case of Chief and First-class Petty Officers of your Majesty's Navy, and Sergeants of your Majesty's Corps of Royal Marines, an Annuity (not exceeding £20 to each) may be awarded with such Medal at our discretion, and provided that the amount authorized from time to time for such awards by the Lords Commissioners of your Majesty's Treasury is not exceeded.

The Lords Commissioners of your Majesty's Treasury have signified to us their concurrence in this proposal."

Further Orders in Council were issued, as follows:

22nd February 1896 An annuity could be extended to all recipients, whatever their rank or rating when the Medal was awarded, on promotion to chief or 1st class petty officer, or to sergeant, Royal Marines.

20th May 1903 A seaman or marine holding the Medal without annuity could be awarded a gratuity of £20 on completion of service, or on invaliding from the Service, or on promotion to a commission; the same gratuity could be awarded in similar circumstances to a seaman or marine who had received the D.C.M. for service under the War Office, except where such recipient already had the C.G.M. with annuity; a seaman or marine, granted an extra pension for gallantry under Naval Regulations, was not to be precluded from receiving the D.C.M. gratuity.

13. Mentioned in Despatches, *LG*, 8th December 1855, p.4,665.

14. Mentioned in Despatches and awarded the Medal, *LG*, 20th November 1855, pp.4,359–4,361

15. Mentioned in Despatches, *LG*, 23rd July 1855, p.2,824.

16. See the article by Captain Douglas-Morris *op. cit.*

17. This referred to the increased allocation of Meritorious Service Medals, and the accompanying pecuniary awards, to the Royal Marines, mentioned above.

Fig.E: The Conspicuous Gallantry Medal, obverse, George V issue.

Fig.F: The Conspicuous Gallantry Medal, obverse, George VI issue.

Fig.G: The Conspicuous Gallantry Medal, reverse (from 1874).

18. See P.R.O. ADM 116/1744.

19. Thus making provision, *inter alia*, for those engaged in air/sea rescue.

20. The equivalent of chief petty officer and below in the Merchant Navy. No such awards were made.

21. For all these provisions, see Orders in Council of 2nd April 1947, 14th October 1947 and 4th September 1952.

27th June 1916 Seamen or marines promoted to permanent or temporary commissions, other than that of Quartermaster, Royal Marines, could retain the C.G.M. annuity; a bar for subsequent acts of gallantry was to be awarded where appropriate.

In September 1916 the King decided that, for the duration of the War, officers and ratings of the Royal Naval Division and officers and men of the Royal Marines, who were serving in France, should be eligible for military decorations and medals. Following discussion between the Admiralty and the War Office it was agreed, therefore, that if an officer or rating who already held a naval decoration or medal was recommended for a further award, the recommendation should be made through naval channels for a bar to the naval award, and not for a military decoration or medal[18]. This ruling accounts for the award of a bar to the C.G.M. to A. R. Blore, see p.49 below.

According to Rowbotham (see Bibliography), on 5th November 1917 approval was given for recipients to use the post-nominal letters "C.G.M.", and in June 1921 the ribbon of the Medal was changed to one similar to that used on the Naval General Service Medal, 1793–1840 (see below). Further Orders in Council were made, as follows:

23rd July 1931 Forfeiture and restoration of the Medal were to be at the Sovereign's pleasure while annuities were to be forfeited and restored at the discretion of the Admiralty.

10th November 1932 Gratuities could be granted to recipients on discharge before the full term of their active service had expired, although not invalided nor promoted to a commission.

17th April 1940 N.C.O.s and men of the Royal Air Force, serving with the Fleet, were to be eligible.

1st July 1942 N.C.O.s and men of the Army, serving in defensively-equipped Merchant Ships (D.E.M.S.), were to be eligible.

17th September 1942 Persons in the Merchant Navy, of status equivalent to that of Petty Officer or Seaman in the Royal Navy, were to be eligible.

13th January 1943 N.C.O.s and men of the Royal Air Force, serving afloat, yet not with the Fleet, were to be eligible[19].

10th December 1943 Submissions of awards in respect of Dominion personnel were to be made by the appropriate Minister of State for the Dominion.

In so far as pecuniary awards are concerned, the amount of the annuity has varied over the years, and has generally been between £10 and £20 per annum. The specific sum is quoted in the Navy List for awards to 1920 (see below). The annuity continued to be awarded to chief petty officers, petty officers and equivalent ranks in the Royal Marines who were awarded the Medal up to the end of the Second World War, but will not accompany future awards. For Second World War recipients below petty officer[20], or their Royal Marine equivalents, a 6d. per day addition was made to the Service or disablement pension, or a gratuity of £20 was awarded on transfer to the Reserve without pension, or upon appointment to a commission. For future awards these latter provisions have been extended to include chief petty officers, petty officers and their Royal Marine equivalents[21].

To judge by early photographs, no order of wearing for the C.G.M. seems to have been prescribed. In the Admiralty Uniform Regulations of 1879 (see Bibliography), which incorporated the regulations regarding the wearing of medals made on 28th August 1877, British decorations were to precede British medals and, within this arrangement, were to be worn in the order of date of award. No specific mention of the C.G.M. was made and, indeed, it is arguable whether, at any time, it was classified as a decoration or as a medal. In the latter event it might have been worn, like the D.C.M., after the appropriate war medal. Army Order No. 196 of October 1905 shows the C.G.M. then following Jubilee, etc., medals. Army Order No. 246 of August 1912 reversed the relative position of the C.G.M. and D.C.M., showing them in their present positions (see also Appendix 4).

46

Fig.H: Bar to the Conspicuous Gallantry Medal.

DESCRIPTION

Ribbon Originally 1¼ inches wide, with equal stripes of dark blue/white/dark blue. In June 1921 a white ribbon with narrow dark blue edges was introduced to distinguish more clearly the C.G.M. from the D.S.C.

Suspension Victorian issues have either a straight suspender[22] or, for the later issues, a scroll suspender as for the 1855 version of the Medal. The Edward VII[23] and later issues have a straight suspender. George VI awards have swivel suspenders, including one gazetted as late as 1945[24].

Obverse There are four types, as follows:

1. Victoria (Fig.C). On 5th August 1874 the Admiralty placed an order with the Royal Mint for 50 medals, and sent a Meritorious Service Medal as pattern, subject to substituted wording on the reverse. During the next month there was some correspondence between Sir Henry Ponsonby, the Queen's Private Secretary, and the Deputy Master, about the medal (the former being glad to hear that the reverse would have raised letters, and not letters "scratched out" as before). On 5th October 1874 the medals were sent to the Admiralty[25]. An unnamed specimen exists which has for obverse the veiled head of Queen Victoria as on the Ashantee War medal. This specimen has every appearance of being struck officially and it may be a trial pattern. In any event, for many years the Admiralty had an adequate stock remaining from the initial order of 50, and this may well account for awards with the original reverse right up to the death of the Queen.

2. Edward VII (Fig. D) Two awards were made in 1904[26].

3. George V (Fig.E). The King's effigy was prepared by Bertram Mackennal, M.V.O., A.R.A.[27]

4. George VI (Fig.F).

Reverse (Fig.G) This has remained constant.

Bar (Fig.H) The only bar awarded was to A. R. Blore (see below)[28]. Unlike the contemporary D.S.M. bar it was not dated on the back of the slide[29].

Naming Considerable variation in naming occurs. The early issues are generally engraved with the recipient's rank, name, ship and, sometimes, with the place and year of award. Those to the Royal Marines for the Egyptian campaign of 1882 are impressed in upright capitals similar to those on the corresponding campaign medal. Awards for the First World War have impressed lettering, similar to that appearing on the contemporary D.S.M., and the details include the recipient's serial number, name, rank, ship and (for those gazetted from about May 1916) the date of the action. Sometimes the place, e.g. STRAITS OF OTRANTO, is also given. The award to Able Seaman C. Beese (*LG*, 6th May 1927) is impressed with all the foregoing details in small, widely spaced capital letters but with the numerical form of date i.e. "5.9.26." Second World War awards are either engraved, or impressed in small non-serif capitals, with the rank, name and serial number. Some of the earlier of these awards also have the year of the action[30], while others have the name of the ship. Except for those awards gazetted in early 1940, which are engraved, those until early 1944 are impressed, thereafter they are engraved.

Copies and Fakes (see also the Note on p.xx). Proof specimens have been sold at auction[31], and at least one George VI re-issue is known.

VERIFICATIONS AND CITATIONS

No awards appear to have been gazetted between 1874 and 1894 although in some cases recipients are mentioned in the despatches of the admirals commanding the naval forces engaged in certain operations. However, the names of recipients do appear in the Navy Lists of the period (see below). All awards[32] from 1901 are

22. Illustrated, for instance, by Mayo and Milford Haven (see Bibliography).

23. According to the Royal Mint Museum Catalogue by Hocking (see Bibliography).

24. To Petty Officer W. T. W. Scott (*L.G.*, 10th July 1945).

25. See the correspondence in P.R.O. MINT 16/99.

26. To Petty Officer 1st Class J. Murphy and Corporal J. E. Flowers for Somaliland in the *London Gazette* of 6th September 1904. Murphy's medal is impressed in the style of lettering on First World War awards; his serial number and the date and place of the action do not appear.

27. Originally for the Naval L.S. & G.C. medal, see *Annual Report of the Deputy Master and Comptroller of the Royal Mint (1911)*, p.15

28. The pattern is mentioned in the *Annual Report by the Deputy Master and Comptroller of the Royal Mint (1917)*, p.24, following the institution of the bar in 1916 (see above).

29. See the illustration in the *Journal of the Orders and Medals Research Society*, Volume 12, p.39.

30. *E.g.* for the Battle of the River Plate in 1939.

31. *E.g.* Messrs. Glendining's sales of 19th June 1925 (lot 898); 25th June 1940 (lot 111); 4th May 1943 (lot 156); 12th February 1952 (lot 200).

32. Except the award to Lance Sergeant J. E. Preston, R.M.L.I., of the shore detachment of H.M.S. *Orlando*, for gallantry in the Defence of the Legations, Pekin, on 13th July 1900, although his name appears in the Navy List awards. Preston was also awarded the D.C.M. which was gazetted on 25th July 1901 at p.4,916 and where his initials are given as T. E. His medals are in the Royal Marines' Museum, Portsmouth.

gazetted and it is interesting to note that the award to Petty Officer First Class Edward Turner "since deceased"[33] does not appear in the Navy List because of his death. Awards in 1901 and 1904 appear in the section of the *Gazette* headed "Naval Promotions" which follows the "State Intelligence" portion of the indices. All awards from 1914 to 1941 appear under the heading "Conspicuous Gallantry Medal" in the "State Intelligence". In 1942 the indices were altered, names appearing in a comprehensive list headed "Honours, Decorations and Medals" while the medal heading in the "State Intelligence" merely gives the pages upon which awards may be found. References to some of the 1901 and 1904 recipients are to be found in the despatches mentioned above. From 1914 citations accompany the announcement of a very large number of awards. Between January 1875[34] and January 1920 lists of surviving recipients were published in the Navy List, and thereafter in Admiralty Fleet Orders for January and July. Citations or other information regarding awards in both World Wars are to be found in the Public Record Office series ADM 1 (Code 85) and in ADM 116 (Code 85); both series contain a large number of files and it is desirable to know the date of award and, where possible, the action or theatre to which the award relates, before consulting the indices. Details of the awards gazetted in 1901 are in ADM 1/7453 (South Africa) and 7456 (China).

Bles, Boyle and Tancred (see Bibliography) record details of a number of awards. The totals of the awards given by Tancred at p.202 do not entirely agree with Rowbotham. Boyle gives details of the 108 awards made between 1914 and 1919, and Bles those for 1939 and 1940.

NUMBERS AWARDED

Between 1874 and 1946 (when the last award so far was made) a total of 235 awards, with one bar, have been made, in the years as follows:

Years	Royal Navy	Royal Marines	R.N.A.S. and Fleet Air Arm	R.N.R.	R.N.V.R.	Dominion Navies	Totals
1874–75 (Ashantee)	12	10	—	—	—	—	22
1876 (Perak)	3	—	—	—	—	—	3
1881 (S. Africa)	1	—	—	—	—	—	1
1883–85 (Egypt etc.)	3	9	—	—	—	—	12
1889 (Indoni[35])	1	—	—	—	—	—	1
1894 (Benin)	2	—	—	—	—	—	2
1901 (S. Africa and China[36])	9	1	—	—	—	—	10
1904 (Somaliland)	1	1	—	—	—	—	2
1914–19 (W.W.1 and Baltic[37])	60	15	4	16	13	—	108
1927 (Shanghai)	2	—	—	—	—	—	2
1940–46	56	7	2	3	—	4[38]	72
Totals	150	43	6	19	13	4	235

In addition eight honorary awards were made for the Second World War. Of these four were to men to the United States Marine Corps and one to the United States Navy; two to the Royal Norwegian Navy[39]; and one to the French Navy.

33. See the *London Gazette* of 22nd March 1901; Turner's C.G.M., his China 1900 and Naval Long Service and Good Conduct Medals are in the National Maritime Museum.

34. This gives the names of 20 recipients who were awarded the C.G.M. in 1874.

35. Suppression of the slave trade; award to Ship's Corporal John Bray.

36. Only one award was made for South Africa being to Petty Officer Edward Turner, see above.

37. Only one award was made for the Baltic being to Chief Motor Mechanic Hugh Beeley (*LG*, 22nd August 1919).

38. One each to R.C.N.V.R., R.C.N.R., R.A.N.V.R. and S.A.N.F.

39. Including the award to Lief Andreas Larsen who received honorary awards of the D.S.M. in 1942; the C.G.M. and bar to the D.S.M. in 1943; the D.S.C. in 1944; and the D.S.O. in 1946.

One bar to the C.G.M. has been awarded: Leading Seaman A. R. Blore, R.N.V.R., Anson Battalion, was awarded the C.G.M. for services on 4th June 1915 at Cape Helles, Gallipoli[40], and a bar to the C.G.M. as an acting Petty Officer for services on 2nd September 1918 at Prouville, France[41]. Blore also received the M.M. as a Chief Petty Officer[42].

ILLUSTRATIVE AWARD

Chief Petty Officer John Frederick Tadman was awarded the C.G.M. in the *London Gazette* of 20th July 1917 where his citation appears as follows:

> "For conspicuous gallantry in climbing out on the wing of an aeroplane to plug a leak in the radiator. He remained in this position for a period of twenty minutes, thus enabling the aeroplane to return safely to her base."

However, Boyle (see Bibliography) amplifies the citation by the following account:

> "On the 27th May, 1917, at 0905, seaplane S656, piloted by Flight Sub-Lieut. J. E. A. Hoare, R.N., was despatched to search for a German submarine reported off the Scillies. At 0920 he sighted her and altered course to attack. The submarine had reduced her buoyancy on sighting the seaplane, but remained on the surface and opened fire with a machine gun. Four 100lb. bombs were dropped from the seaplane, two direct hits being obtained. The submarine sank by the bow, the seaplane remaining in the vicinity. At 0928 a serious leak in the starboard radiator was noticed and Chief Petty Officer Frederick Tadman climbed out on the wing root and plugged the leak, remaining in this position for the return flight to the Scillies, nearly half an hour. The cause of the leak was a large bullet hole.

> The officer, in making his report said, "Had it not been for C. P. O. Tadman's courage and presence of mind in climbing out on to the wing and partially stopping the leak, there is no doubt that the sea plane would have had to land and, in view of the heavy swell, the chances are that the plane and crew would have been lost."

Flight Sub-Lieutenant J. E. A. Hoare, R.N.A.S., was awarded the Distinguished Service Cross in the *London Gazette* announcing Tadman's award.

40. *LG*, 13th September 1915.
41. *LG*, 29th October 1918; see pp.46 and 47 above for the circumstances leading to award of, and pattern of the bar.
42. *L.G.*, 14th May 1919.

Chapter 10

The Conspicuous Gallantry Medal (Flying)

ORIGIN AND DEVELOPMENT

While the Army had the Distinguished Conduct Medal and Military Medal, and the Navy the Conspicuous Gallantry Medal and Distinguished Service Medal, only the Distinguished Flying Medal[1] was available to "other ranks" of the Army and Royal Air Force as a reward for gallantry during flying duties in action. To make good this deficiency, by a Royal Warrant of 10th November 1942, the Conspicuous Gallantry Medal was extended to Army and Royal Air Force personnel "whilst flying in active operations against the enemy". Although the medal itself is identical with the Naval Conspicuous Gallantry Medal it is provided with a distinctive ribbon and special conditions of award apply. Accordingly it is convenient to treat it as a completely separate award, although the terms of the Warrant are ambiguous on this point. On 15th January 1943 the Warrant was published in the *London Gazette*[2] as follows:

"Air Ministry, 15th January, 1943.
THE CONSPICUOUS GALLANTRY MEDAL
(FLYING).
ROYAL WARRANT.

GEORGE R.I.

GEORGE THE SIXTH, by the Grace of God, of Great Britain, Ireland and the British Dominions beyond the Seas, King, Defender of the Faith, Emperor of India; To all to whom these Presents shall come.   Greeting.

Whereas Her late Majesty Queen Victoria was graciously pleased by Her Order-in-Council dated 7th July, 1874, to establish a medal designated the Conspicuous Gallantry Medal for such petty officers and seamen of the Royal Navy and non-commissioned officers and privates of the Royal Marines as distinguish themselves by acts of conspicuous gallantry in action with the enemy.

And whereas We deem it expedient to provide for the award of the Conspicuous Gallantry Medal to members of Our Military and Air Forces for acts of conspicuous gallantry whilst flying in active operations against the enemy.

Now therefore We do by these Presents for Us, Our Heirs and Successors, ordain that the following regulations shall govern the award of the said medal to members of Our Military and Air Forces:

1. *Description.*
The Conspicuous Gallantry Medal shall be as described in the above-mentioned Order-in-Council, that is to say, it shall be silver and shall bear on the obverse the Royal Effigy and on the reverse the words "For conspicuous gallantry" encircled by a wreath surmounted by a crown.

2. *Ribbon.*
The medal shall be worn on the left breast pendent from a ribbon one inch and a quarter in width which shall be in colour light blue with dark blue marginal stripes one eighth of an inch in width.

3. *Abbreviated title.*
The award of the medal shall entitle the recipient to have the initials C.G.M. appended to his name.

4. *Eligibility.*
(1) The medal shall be granted to such persons as shall be recommended to Us by or through Our Secretary of State for Air (or, in the case of any of Our Dominions the

1. The Distinguished Flying Medal (q.v.) was extended to the Fleet Air Arm by a Royal Warrant of 11th March 1941.

2. At p.331; for the papers leading to the institution of the medal see P.R.O. AIR 2/6278.

Government whereof shall so desire, the appropriate Minister of State for the said Dominion) for acts of conspicuous gallantry whilst flying in active operations against the enemy.

(2) The following shall be eligible for the medal:

(*a*) warrant officers, non-commissioned officers and men of any Military or Air Force raised in Our United Kingdom of Great Britain and Northern Ireland, Our Indian Empire, Burma, any of Our Colonies or a territory under Our protection; or within any other part of Our Dominions Our Government whereof shall so desire or within any territory under Our protection administered by Us in such Government.

(*b*) foreign personnel, of ranks equivalent to those above-mentioned, who have been associated in operations with any of the aforesaid Military or Air Forces.

5. *Bars.*

When an individual who has been awarded the medal shall again be recommended to Us by or through Our Secretary of State for Air (or, in the case of any of Our Dominions the Government whereof shall so desire, the appropriate Minister of State for the said Dominion) for further conspicuous gallantry, he shall be awarded a bar to be attached to the ribbon by which the medal is suspended, and for every additional such recommendation an additional bar may be awarded. For every bar awarded a small silver rose shall be added to the ribbon when worn alone.

6. *Miniatures.*

Reproductions of the medal in miniature, which may be worn on certain occasions by those to whom the medal is awarded, shall be approximately half the size of the medal and sealed patterns of the miniature medal shall be deposited and kept in the Central Chancery of Our Orders of Knighthood.

7. *Gazettement and registration.*

The names of those upon whom We may be pleased to confer the medal shall be published in the London Gazette and a register thereof shall be kept in the Office of Our Secretary of State for Air.

8. *Forfeiture and restoration.*

(1) It shall be competent for Us, Our Heirs and Successors by an Order under Our Sign Manual and on a recommendation by or through Our Secretary of State for Air (or, in the case of any of Our Dominions the Government whereof shall so desire, the appropriate Minister of State for the said Dominion) to cancel and annul the award to any person of the medal and thereupon the name of such person in the register shall be erased; but We, Our Heirs and Successors shall at all times have power to restore any medal which may have been forfeited when such recommendation shall have been withdrawn. (2) The forfeiture shall involve the cessation of any gratuity or pension in lieu thereof to which the possession of the medal might entitle the recipient, but no such forfeiture shall extend to any sum of money which has already been paid. (3) When a forfeited medal shall have been restored, any gratuity or pension in lieu thereof which attaches to it shall also be restored. (4) A notice of forfeiture and of restoration shall in every case be published in the London Gazette.

9. *Annulment, etc., of regulations.*

We reserve to Ourself, Our Heirs and Successors full power of annulling, altering, abrogating, augmenting, interpreting, or dispensing with these regulations or any part thereof by a notification under Our Royal Sign Manual.

Given at Our Court of Saint James's this 10th day of November, 1942, in the sixth year of Our Reign.

By His Majesty's Command.
Archibald Sinclair."

By a Royal Warrant of 24th March 1964[3] the functions hitherto performed by the Secretary of State for Air in regard, *inter alia*, to the C.G.M. (Flying) were transferred to the Secretary of State for Defence.

The C.G.M. (Flying) is worn in the same relative position as the Naval C.G.M. (see Appendix 4).

3. See Army Order No.22 of March 1964.

51

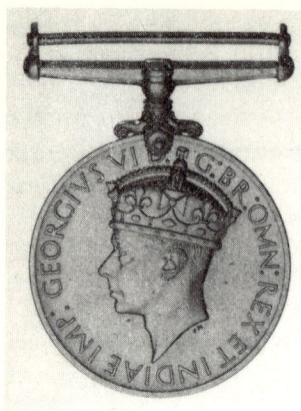

Fig.A: The Conspicuous Gallantry Medal (Flying), obverse; George VI issue.

Fig.B: The Conspicuous Gallantry Medal (Flying), obverse, Elizabeth II issue.

4. This award was misprinted as a D.F.M. in *LG*, 24th September 1943 at p.4,248, but was corrected to a C.G.M. in the reference given above.

5. There are separate files containing the recommendations for immediate and periodic awards. The numerical sequence of the AIR 2 references does not reflect the strict chronology of the various files and it is necessary to consult the whole index to the Code when searching.

6. See *LG*, 16th August 1945, p.4,158. The award was for North West Europe. There is no citation.

7. See *LG*, 10th December 1968, p.13,230. An illustrated article on Coughlan appears in *The Journal of the Orders and Medals Research Society*, Vol.20, p.26. The C.G.M. was awarded "in recognition of his gallantry, skill and devotion to duty, while a helicopter crewman, during rescue operations in Vietnam."

DESCRIPTION

Ribbon Light blue, 1¼ inches wide, with a dark blue marginal stripe ⅛ inch wide.

Suspension By a straight silver suspender; some 1943 awards have been found with a swivel suspender. Other awards made in that year and later have fixed suspenders.

Obverse There are two obverses as follows:
1. George VI (Fig.A) As for the Naval C.G.M. This appeared on all Second World War awards.
2. Elizabeth II (Fig.B) This appeared on the only award made since the end of the Second World War (see below).

Reverse (Fig.C) As for the Naval C.G.M.

Bar None has been awarded.

Naming The number (usually omitted for Warrant Officers), abbreviated rank, initials, name and service are engraved in plain capital letters without serifs.

Copies and Fakes None has been seen. Some re-issues are known.

VERIFICATIONS AND CITATIONS

All awards appear in the *London Gazette*. Names are indexed in a comprehensive quarterly nominal index headed "Honours, Decorations and Medals" while the sub-heading "Conspicuous Gallantry Medal" in the "State Intelligence" portion of the index gives only the pages upon which awards, including those of the Naval C.G.M., are to be found. The indices are not entirely accurate and the page references for the following awards are omitted from the medal sub-heading:

	London Gazette
Bowers, Sergeant D.R.	18th May 1945, p.2,574
Corbin, Warrant Officer H.A.	17th October 1945, p.4,749
Hilton, Sergeant P.A.	29th March 1946, p.1,577
Howe, Sergeant J.A.W.	28th September 1943[4], p.4,308
Larden, Flight Sergeant A.W.J.	24th September 1943, p.4,247
Rees, Flight Sergeant D.	24th September 1943, p.4,247
Robb, Warrant Officer A.	18th May 1945, p.2,574
White, Flight Sergeant T.E.	2nd June 1944, p.2,535

About three-quarters of the total awards gazetted are accompanied by citations. Details of many awards are preserved in the Public Record Office in the series AIR 30 (Submissions to the King 1918–1945) where a number of unpublished citations are to be found, and in the series AIR 2 (Code 30) which contains the original recommendations made during the Second World War[5]. Details of some awards appeared in Press Releases from which extracts were frequently made in local newspapers.

NUMBERS AWARDED

1939–1946 (Second World War) During this period 109 awards were gazetted, a summary of which is as follows:

R.A.F., R.A.F.V.R. and R.Aux.A.F.	82
R.A.A.F.	10
R.C.A.F.	12
R.N.Z.A.F.	4
Glider Pilot Regiment	1 (W.O.2 L. W. Turnbull[6])

In addition, two honorary awards were made, but not gazetted, to the following:

Sergeant Jozef Pialucha, Polish Air Force (approved 22nd August 1944)
Sergeant James J. Reardon, United States Army Air Force (approved 18th January 1945)

1946–1979 During this period only one medal was awarded, this being in 1968 to Corporal J. D. Coughlan, R.A.A.F., for Vietnam[7]. No citation appears.

Fig. C: The Conspicuous Gallantry Medal (Flying), reverse.

ILLUSTRATIVE AWARD

On 19th August 1943 the Group Captain No.5 Group recommended Sergeant G. W. Oliver, R.A.F. of 467 (R.A.A.F.) Squadron for the C.G.M. (Flying) in the following terms[8]:

> "Sergeant Oliver was the Mid-Upper Gunner in a Lancaster aircraft, captained by Warrant Officer Wilson, which was detailed to attack Peenemunde on the night 17/18th August, 1943.
>
> Soon after leaving the target, which was successfully bombed, the aircraft was attacked by an enemy night fighter. The first burst from the fighter wounded the rear gunner, destroyed the hydraulics and put the rear turret out of action. At the same time fire broke out inside the aircraft, setting alight the ammunition.
>
> Sergeant Oliver engaged the enemy aircraft from the very first and continued the engagement despite the heat and smoke from the fire inside the Lancaster, until he was certain the fighter was destroyed. He then informed the captain that fire had broken out. The heat and smoke by this time were intense, but despite this Sergeant Oliver without hesitation attempted to extinguish the fire. Finding himself unable to do this alone he went forward and obtained assistance from the other members of the crew.
>
> By his courage, coolness under fire and prompt action, he undoubtedly saved the lives of the crew and much valuable equipment. Sergeant Oliver has completed twenty-three successful operational sorties, and has proved himself to be an outstanding member of his crew as shown by this display of gallantry of a high order which I consider fully merits the immediate award of the Conspicuous Gallantry Medal."

On 24th August 1943 the Air Officer Commanding the Group endorsed the recommendation "strongly recommended for the immediate award of the C.G.M." On 24th August the Commander-in-Chief of Bomber Command forwarded it to the Air Ministry and the recommendation was submitted, with others but without citation, by the Secretary of State for Air to the King on 30th August 1943[9]. At the same time, Oliver's captain, Warrant Officer W. L. Wilson, R.A.F., was recommended for the D.F.C. Both awards were published in the *London Gazette* of 17th September 1943, p.3,973, where their joint citation appears as follows:

> "One night in August, 1943, these airmen were pilot and mid-upper gunner respectively of an aircraft detailed to attack Peenemunde. The objective was successfully bombed but, shortly afterwards, the aircraft was hit by cannon fire from an enemy fighter. The rear gunner was wounded, his turret rendered useless and ammunition in the aircraft was set alight, while the elevator and rudder trimmers were shot away. In spite of these harassing circumstances, Sergeant Oliver fought the attacker with great determination and succeeded in shooting it down. He then turned his attention towards the fire which was beginning to spread and, with assistance from other members of the crew, succeeded in quelling it. Meanwhile Warrant Officer Wilson coolly and skilfully evaded several fighters and afterwards flew the crippled bomber to base. This pilot displayed superb qualities throughout, while Sergeant Oliver's courageous and skilful efforts proved of the greatest assistance."

Oliver also received the 1939/45 Star; the Air Crew Europe Star with bar "France and Germany", the Italy Star, the Defence Medal, and the War Medal.

8. See P.R.O. AIR 2/4995.
9. See P.R.O. AIR 30/175(169).

Chapter 11

The Constabulary Medal (Ireland)

Fig.A: Badge and Chevrons of the Irish Constabulary.

ORIGIN AND DEVELOPMENT

The Constabulary Medal (Ireland), to use its later title, was instituted in 1842 as a reward for deserving members of the Irish (later Royal Irish) Constabulary. It is interesting to note that the medal was not instituted directly by the Crown[1] and that, in a sense, it was a purely local award[2]. The original intention was that the medal was normally to be awarded only on qualification for a fifth (from 1856, for a fourth) chevron of merit, although it could be awarded for a single act. Moreover, even half chevrons could be awarded, and these could count towards the total required for the medal. In any event, however, chevrons were abolished in 1872 and of the 12 awards of the medal made before that year it seems that only one man (see below) qualified for it by accruing chevrons, the remainder being "single act" awards.

The Regulations regarding both chevrons and the medal, as approved by the Lord Lieutenant of Ireland, were published in a Constabulary Circular of 15th April 1842, prefaced by a somewhat breathless homily by the Inspector-General of Constabulary. The next year further instructions were published in a Circular and it is convenient to consider them both together as follows:

"REWARD OF MERIT

Constabulary Office, Dublin Castle,
15th April, 1842

In promulgating to the Force the following Regulations, the Inspector-General feels it is his duty to remind them of the real objects for which the Reward Fund was originally instituted.

Though a high degree of zeal and exertion for the prevention of crime and the detection and prosecution of Criminals may reasonably be expected from every Member of the Establishment who feels the obligations imposed upon him as a conservator of the Public peace, and as an individual expressly maintained by the Country for the purpose of rendering his best services in bringing to justice those who have offended against its Laws, yet it has gradually become so much the practice for the Men to claim undue merit for the proper performance of these obligations, and to expect for it a mercenary reward, that it seems important to impress upon them that the marks of distinction referred to in the following Rules will only be conferred upon those Head or other Constables, who, in addition to habitual good conduct, shall manifest, in the discharge of particular duties, an extraordinary degree of intelligence, tact or courage.

If, therefore, such distinctions shall be found difficult of attainment, the possession of them will prove proportionately honorable to those to whom they may be awarded, and as all reasonable claims will be brought periodically under the deliberate consideration of a Board, consisting of the Officers at Head Quarters, the Inspector-General confidently trusts that no act really worthy of record, shall ever be allowed to pass unrewarded.

In forming the calculations of the sums to be attached to each badge of merit, the Inspector-General has endeavoured fully to appreciate the growing zeal and efficiency of the Force.

He has accordingly framed them on such a scale as will enable the Government at once to continue to grant out of the Fund undiminished gratuities to the respectable

1. In this it has affinity with the Indian Order of Merit, the Sea Gallantry Medal and the New Zealand Cross (q.v.).

2. Rather like regimental medals for gallantry although the analogy must not be taken too far since the Constabulary Medal had official recognition.

54

Widows and Orphans of such well conducted men as may die in the service, and to provide for an increasing number of men who may aspire to distinction in the performance of arduous Constabulary duty.

REGULATIONS

With a view of increasing the motives to zealous exertion in the discharge of their duties on the part of Members of the Force, His Excellency has been pleased to cancel the existing Rule, which regulates the distribution of Rewards, and to direct the substitution of the following Regulations:

1. No Grant, is henceforward to be made out of the Reward Fund to any man while serving in the Force, except under peculiar circumstances, to which it is unnecessary herein to advert.

2. When any Head or other Constable, or Sub-Constable, shall so distinguish himself, by his zealous, intelligent, and spirited conduct as to be entitled to particular consideration, he will be permitted to wear, as a mark of distinction, a Chevron of Lace on the left fore-arm of his Jacket.

3. When a man already distinguished by four such marks shall merit a fifth Chevron, he will cease to wear these marks, and instead thereof, there will be conferred upon him a Silver Medal, which he will wear suspended by a light blue Ribband on his left breast.

4. For every occasion on which he shall distinguish himself after being in possession of a Medal, he will be allowed to wear a Chevron in addition to the Medal.

5. Should a man's conduct be worthy of consideration, and yet not sufficiently distinguished to entitle him to a Chevron, a record of his meritorious action will be ordered to be made in the General and County Register, on the understanding that two such Records will entitle him to a Chevron.

6. But a man's conduct may be so highly meritorious as to entitle him for a single act to two or more Chevrons, or even a Medal.

7. Every man, on his discharge, will receive from the Reward Fund, if a Head Constable, the sum of £6; and if a Constable or Sub-Constable, the sum of £4 for every Chevron; and if distinguished by a Medal, he will receive instead of the above mentioned sums, the sum, if a Head Constable, of £35, and a Constable or Sub-Constable, the sum of £25, in addition to any pension or gratuity that may be otherwise awarded him; which sum, should the man die in service, will be paid to his Widow or Children, (but to no other relatives) in addition to any other gratuity that may be given them, according to the customs of the Service.

8. The Medal will be regarded as the property of the Public until the man's discharge; when he will be entitled to carry it with him as an honourable testimony of his conduct while in the Public Service.

9. No man can be considered as eligible to wear a Badge of Distinction whose conduct is not marked by morality and general respectability; and a man for misconduct will be liable to the forfeiture of one or more Badges, according to the nature and degree of such offence.

10. Claims for marks of distinction will be forwarded in the usual manner by County Inspectors, and will be recommended to the Inspector-General, on the investigation of a Board, to be held in Dublin, monthly or quarterly, for that purpose.

11. But no man will be entitled to the distinction of a Medal, or be liable to its forfeiture, except under the express sanction of His Excellency the Lord Lieutenant.

12. Sub-Constables with Medals, without regard to their service, will take precedence of all others in their class, in the absence of permanent Acting Constables.

13. The Medals awarded by His Excellency's command, will be delivered by the County Inspectors to those entitled to the distinction, in the presence of their comrades, assembled at the ensuing Assizes, or on any convenient intervening occasion, when a large body of the Force may be brought together.

D. McGregor, Inspector-General."

Fig.B: The Constabulary Medal (Ireland), obverse, early issue.

Fig.C: The Constabulary Medal (Ireland), obverse, later issue.

Fig.D: The Constabulary Medal (Ireland), obverse, final issue.

3. From 1883 Constables became Sergeants, and Sub-Constables became Constables.

"Constabulary Office, Dublin Castle
1st June 1843

CHEVRONS

1. The preparation of the Chevrons referred to in the Reward Regulations, dated 15th April, 1842, not having been completed, (through unforeseen delays) until the present time, it has not been possible, heretofore, to transmit them to those Head and other Constables to whom they have been awarded on the recommendation of the Reward Board. They will now, however, be forwarded without loss of time.

2. The Chevrons are to be worn on the left arm, one inch above the seam of the cuff, the badge being in front.

3. The single Chevron is marked with one blue stripe upon the band; a second, third, and fourth Chevron by as many additional stripes.

4. When an additional Chevron is awarded to a Head or other Constable who is already in possession of one or more, the band is to be returned to Head Quarters, in order that another may be substituted, having an additional stripe.

5. And when the number of Chevrons awarded amounts to the value of a Medal (i.e. five Chevrons) the silver Badge, as well as the band, must be returned to Head Quarters before the Medal can be forwarded.

6. If the band, as forwarded, does not fit the arm of the wearer, the hooks may be adjusted accordingly, but no other alteration is to be made therein, without authority from Head Quarters, on pain of forfeiture of the Chevron, and such other penalty as may be called for. If the band should be, by accident, lost or damaged, representation thereof may be made to Head Quarters, that the propriety of granting another may be considered.

7. In future Reports, Head and other Constables who have received any of the marks of approbation referred to, are to be distinguished by appending the nature of such marks to their names, thus:

Constable   A _____ B _____ ,   (Two Chevrons.)
Head Constable C_____ D _____ ,   (Medal.)

8. County Inspectors will carefully distinguish between a mere expression of approbation from Head Quarters, and a favourable record according to No. 5 of the Reward Regulations. Whenever the latter is intended, it will be expressly mentioned and may be termed, for the sake of brevity, a Half Chevron.

9. In the event of forfeiture of any of the above distinctions, through subsequent misconduct, the party so punished is to be required to return the printed paper which accompanied the mark of distinction, with which it is to be sent up to Head Quarters.

D. McGregor, Inspector-General."

The Regulations seem to have envisaged the award of chevrons to Head Constables, Constables[3] and Sub-Constables only and it is not clear whether this restriction was originally intended to apply to the medal as well. At all events, the first medals awarded were to Sub-Inspectors Joseph Cox and Thomas Trant for gallantry during the "Young Ireland" rising on 29th July 1848. A large number of insurgents had gathered at Bouleigh Common, Co. Tipperary, the first contact having been made by Sub-Inspector Trant and 46 men of the Constabulary who were forced to take refuge in a house. Cox, with a party of 32 men came to the rescue, dispersing the insurgents and capturing the leaders.

It seems that later there was bad blood between Cox and Trant, possibly over this incident. At all events, according to the entry against his name in the Constabulary General Register (see below), Trant was admonished in 1850 for declining to wear the medal awarded him, and the following year incurred the Lord Lieutenant's strong disapprobation "in bringing frivolous and unwarrantable charges" against Cox.

In a Constabulary Circular of 10th May 1856 the medal was to be awarded on qualification for the fourth, instead of the fifth, chevron. First Head Constable John Crowley was the only man to receive the medal under this Regulation. His medal was awarded on 22nd November 1859 for distinguished service, rather than a specific act of bravery[4]. Indeed, he seems to be the only person who qualified for the medal by accruing chevrons, all subsequent awards being for individual acts. By a Royal Warrant of 6th September 1867 the Force was designated "Royal"[5], and on the same day a number of medals[6] were presented in Phoenix Park, Dublin, for gallantry during the Fenian Rising of that year.

In 1872 new Constabulary Standing Rules and Regulations were issued. These discontinued the award of chevrons and specific gratuities for medals and chevrons; changed the colour of the medal ribbon from light blue to light green; and in Section 1267 prescribed that the medal should be awarded as follows:

> ". . . When a member of the Force in the performance of police duty, displays pre-eminent valour and bravery, in addition to any other award[7] he may receive, a silver medal will be conferred on him which is to be suspended by a light green ribbon. Holders of Constabulary Medals will be designated in official reports by the word "medal" after their name or signature."

The medal thus became solely an award for gallantry although it continued to be inscribed "Reward of Merit"[8]. The above paragraph was repeated in subsequent issues of the Regulations until the final issue which was published in 1911.

In 1922 the Force was disbanded and the medal ceased to be awarded. The last serving member of the Royal Ulster Constabulary to hold the medal was 69508 Constable G. H. Buckley who retired from duty on 20th April 1960. Buckley won his medal in June 1920 at Leap, Co. Cork, when, with two comrades, he was ambushed by an armed party of the Irish Republican Army. Two of the ambush party were captured and the remainder driven off with casualties.

Army Order No. 246 of August 1912 showed the Constabulary Medal (Ireland) following immediately after the Polar Medals. In 1921[9] it followed the Air Force Medal and the Indian Distinguished Service Medal and in 1947[10] it was shown in its present position following the former medal (see also Appendix 4).

DESCRIPTION

Chevrons Regulation 2 of the 1842 Circular prescribes lace chevrons, presumably of silver. The colour of the cuff band on which they were worn is not given although Regulation 3 of the 1843 Circular adds that the band is to be striped with blue according to the number of chevrons. By 1867 the chevrons were of silver metal and fixed to a black patent leather band, with a silver badge above. Later still the colour of the band was changed to green. About 1867 the pattern of the badges was changed to that illustrated here (Fig. A), which is $2\frac{1}{4}$ inches by $1\frac{3}{4}$ inches. When worn alone the badge denoted a half-chevron. The back of the badge (when awarded alone as a half-chevron) and the front of the chevron had the recipient's rank and name engraved thereon[11].

Medals

Ribbon $1\frac{1}{4}$ inches wide; light blue until 1872; thereafter light green.

Suspension Originally by a fixed bar suspender[12] (see Fig. B); by 1876 a swivelling silver wire suspender (Fig. C) had been introduced[13].

Obverse The design of the harp varies, the earlier awards having the female figure incorporated (Figs. B and C), while the later awards have the Gaelic harp with a wreath composed entirely of shamrock, and a different-shaped crown (Fig. D). Minor variations also occur due to the use of different dies. Although the title "Royal" was conferred in 1867, this does not appear on a medal issued in 1876[14] and, indeed, for some reason at least one award with the female harp and pre-1867 title was made in 1921[15]. At least two of the 1888 awards had the second type obverse[16].

Reverse (Figs. E and F) The rank, name and date of the award or act[17], are engraved on the reverse; between 1867 and 1876 the place of the act is also

4. See *The Times* of 24th November 1859. In the Constabulary List of 1858 some 323 men were shown as holders of a chevron or half-chevron. Of these quite a number held more than one chevron, while four held three.

5. See *The Dublin Gazette* of 13th September 1867.

6. In all, nine were awarded for the Fenian Rising, but the account of the presentation (see below) does not make it clear whether they were authorised at the same time.

7. Other editions of the Regulations give this as "reward".

8. C.f. the Indian Order of Merit where "valor", "gallantry" or "bravery" are variously enscribed on the badges of the Order.

9. See *LG*, 22nd April 1921.

10. See *LG*, 11th February 1947.

11. The badge and chevrons illustrated here were awarded to 15357 Sub-Constable Patrick Corry who was appointed on 17th September 1851 and resigned on 6th February 1868. According to the Constabulary General Register the badge and chevrons were awarded at the same time, see PRO HO 184/8. Although no date is given it is likely that he received them for his part in the defence of the Barracks at Castlemartyr when attacked by Fenians on 6th March 1867. For this Corry received a Government reward of £15. On resignation he was granted a gratuity of £8 for the chevrons.

12. See the illustrations of Sub-Inspector Burke's medal in *The Irish Sword*, Volume 8, p.7. The reverse of the medal is engraved "Sub-Inspector D. F. Burke – Tallaght – 5–6 March – 1867". The medals awarded to Constables Derivan and Forsythe (see below) also have this type of fixed suspender.

13. *E.g.*, on the medals awarded to Constable M. Nugent and Sub-Constable Jones (see below). However, the medal awarded to Constable F. R. Tuckett in 1921 (see below) has a very small fixed ring suspender connected by a neck to the edge of the piece.

14. The medal awarded to Constable M. Nugent (see below).

15. I.e., the award to 71686 Constable F. R. Tuckett which is dated August 1921 on the reverse.

16. I.e. the awards to Acting Sergeant A. Donohoe and Constable J. Connell (see below).

17. The later practice seems to have been to give the month and year, or only the year, of the act.

Fig.E: The Constabulary Medal (Ireland), reverse, early naming.

given, while from 1888 (in the case of the men) the recipient's Force number appears. Cox's medal (see above) is engraved on the reverse "Presented by His Excellency the Lord Lieutenant to Sub Inspector Cox for his conduct on the 29th of July 1848". The medal awarded to Crowley (see above) has his rank and name on the edge, and on the reverse "Presented by His Excellency the Earl of Carlisle as a reward for distinguished Police Service and Exemplary Conduct, 22nd Novr. 1859"[18].

Bars Bars were first authorised, apparently, in 1920 (see below), but we have been unable to discover the pattern used.

Copies and Fakes None has yet been seen.

VERIFICATIONS AND CITATIONS

Recipients of the medal are given in the Constabulary Lists[19] and individual awards are briefly noted in Constabulary Circulars. Up to and including the List for July 1869 returns of men rewarded since since last publication are given. The rewards concerned include medals, chevrons, badges, grants from the Reward Fund etc., and are frequently accompanied by a short statement of the services. In addition, until including 1859 the Lists give a return, by counties, of all men awarded chevrons. Further details may sometimes be found in newspapers published at the time of the incident, or of the award (e.g. in *The Irish Times*) or in the Constabulary Journal. The Fenian Rising citations, and their source, are given below.

The Constabulary General Register is preserved in the Public Record Office, London[20], and gives personal and service details of all officers and men appointed to the Force from 1st August 1816 to 31st August 1922. Men are registered serially according to their Force numbers which, excluding the Auxiliary Force of 1881–82 and the Auxiliary Division of 1920–22, run from 1 to 83743[21] in 42 volumes, while the officers are registered in four additional volumes. Unless a man's Force number is known in advance it is necessary to consult separate indices to find the appropriate volume of the Register. The entries cover the individual's whole career and, in addition to personal details, include postings, promotions, punishments, injuries, discharge particulars, etc. There is a column for "Rewards, Marks of Distinction or Favourable Records" which usually only gives the type of award[22], the numerical authority and often the date. Occasionally the type of award is omitted and the numerical authority alone gives no clue to the entry intended. Moreover, the meaning of some of the abbreviations used is far from clear.

There are indications that at least the pre-1843 entries have been copied from an earlier Register and the completeness and accuracy of some individual records, particularly the later ones, is open to doubt. The four officers' volumes have a slightly different layout from those of the men although the details given are similar.

NUMBERS AWARDED

No register of medals seems to have survived. We have found 316 recipients of medals in the General Register[23] In four early cases[24], the entry "Medal" in the Register does not seem to indicate the constabulary Medal and therefore we have excluded them. Awards were made in the following years[25]:

Year		
1848 ..	2	(Sub-Inspectors J. Cox and T. Trant, see above)
1859 ..	1	(2164 Head Constable J. Crowley, see above)
1867 ..	9	(Fenian Rising, see below)
1871 ..	1	(8187 Constable C. Supple)
1876 ..	2	(see "Illustrative Award" below)
1888 ..	13	(Lisdoonvarna, see below)
1916 ..	23	(Easter Rising)
1917 ..	1	(District Inspector M. J. Molloy[26])

18. See the illustration in *The Military and Naval Medal Magazine*, edited by Douglas Glendining, for May 1896. Crowley's medal also had the fixed bar suspender.

19. Recipients are listed among holders of campaign and other medals. The last List we have found is for July 1921.

20. Under reference HO 184/1 (et seq.). In what appears to be an isolated case the recommendation for No. 70157 Constable David Kemp for gallantry during the attack on the R.I.C. Barracks at Feakle on 2nd June 1920 is in P.R.O. HO 45/20095 (487728).

21. The last effective appointments were in December 1921, subsequent appointments being notional transfers from the Dublin Metropolitan Police.

22. *E.g.*, "Medal" or "Const(abular)y Medal", "Chev(ron)", "F.R." (Favourable Record – of which there were three classes), etc.

23. 43 awards of the King's Police Medal were gazetted to the Force between 1909 and 1923, 18 of the recipients being officers. For the same period 27 King's Police Medals were gazetted to the Dublin Metropolitan Police, 22 of the recipients being sergeants or constables. Members of the latter Force were not eligible for the Constabulary Medal.

24. I.e., 1174 H. Kerr, 4338 J. Egan, 8834 J. Edwards, and 21390 T. Mannion. According to the Constabulary Lists Egan's only medal was that of the Royal Humane Society.

25. In some cases the act for which the award was made was performed in the previous year.

26. For services in quelling a riot.

Fig.F: The Constabulary Medal (Ireland), reverse, later naming.

1919 .. 20
1920 .. 180[27]
1921 .. 55
1922 .. 9

In addition, the Constabulary Lists for 1920 and 1921 reveal 26 men as recipients for whom there seems to be no corresponding entry in the General Register. Of these, 52148 Head Constable Martin Boyle had the King's Police Medal[28] which is noted in the Register.

Cumulative awards The General Register reveals seven men who received more than one award. These appear either as additional medals, or as bars, to the following recipients:

	First award	*Later award*
68100 Constable P. Martyn	Not given	28th May 1920[29] (bar)
68464 Constable J. Molloy	3rd March 1920	4th November 1920 (medal)
64316 Constable F. Duffy	13th July 1920	19th November 1920 (medal)
67191 Constable W. Willis	27th July 1920	19th November 1920 (medal)
64366 Constable P. Murphy	19th July 1920	12th January 1921 (bar)
69975 Constable T. Holmes	13th July 1920	21st April 1921 (medal)
62117 Sergeant T. R. Kelly	13th July 1920	{ 21st April 1921 (medal) / 15th October 1921 (bar)

In Molloy's case a second medal was prepared but not issued[30]. Possibly Molloy, and all or some of the men recorded as having a second medal, received a bar.

Fenian Rising, 1867 A presentation took place on 6th September 1867 at the Constabulary Depot, Phoenix Park, Dublin, in respect of those who had distinguished themselves against the Fenians. Shortly afterwards the Lord Lieutenant caused a small book to be distributed to every Constabulary Barrack in Ireland. This book gave an account of the presentation, the citations of those decorated, the names of those of the Force who had been rewarded with varying sums of money from a special Parliamentary vote of £2,000, and some reports of the Rising. The nine citations, which are as follows, indicate that only four persons received medals; however, other evidence suggests that the remaining five also received medals for the Fenian Rising, although it is not clear how this came about:

Sub-Inspector Robert Gardiner – "In command at Drogheda, who on the night of the 5th of March, attacked and dispersed a large body of armed Fenian insurgents assembled in that town, taking many prisoners and a considerable quantity of arms and ammunition – a medal"[31].

Sub-Inspector Dominick F. Burke – "In command at Tallaght on the same night, when the Fenian insurgents were defeated, many taken prisoners, and a large quantity of arms and ammunition captured – a medal"[31].

Sub-Inspector Oliver Milling – "... who proceeded on the morning of the 6th of March, from Kilfinane to Kilmallock, with a small body of Constabulary, to the relief of the party attacked by the Fenians in the police barrack, and with them routed the assailants – a medal"[31].

(5042) Head Constable Richard Adams – "In command of the party surrounded by the Fenians, in the barrack of Kilmallock, who sustained the attack during several hours, until relieved by Sub-Inspector Milling – £70 from the Government, and £50 private subscriptions"[32].

(11800) Constable James O'Connell – "In command of the party who bravely defended their barrack at Castlemartyr against a large body of armed Fenians, shooting their leader, and putting the assailants to flight – £20 from the Government, and £15 private subscriptions"[33].

(10814) Constable George Forsythe – "In command at Ardagh, when an armed body of Fenians attacked and fired into the barracks and broke open the door, the Constabulary within returned the fire, wounded one of the assailants, and compelled the whole to fly – a chevron"[33].

(11508) Constable Patrick Derivan[34] – "In command at Emly, when the Constabulary resisted the attack of a large body of armed insurgents, who fired into the barrack and threatened to burn it if not surrendered – a chevron".

27. We have included two awards in this figure which are doubtful, one of which may have been entered in error and the other which is noted in pencil as cancelled.

28. *LG*, 1st January 1919.

29. The numerical reference is undated but corresponds with other entries bearing this date. It is strange that no details are given in the Register of Martyn's initial award and it could be that the entry of a bar is an error, and that the medal only was intended. Alternatively, he may have received both the medal and the bar under the same authority.

30. The medal was sent by the Irish Office to the Home Office for retention as a specimen on 7th March 1923; see P.R.O. HO 45/11593.

31. Also received a Parliamentary reward of £104.

32. Shown as a medallist in Constabulary Lists. The only General Register entry is an "approbation".

33. Shown as a medallist in the General Register (the numerical reference being undated), and in the Constabulary Lists; also received a Parliamentary reward of £34.

34. Given as "Derwan" in the original, and on the chevron, but spelled correctly on the medal.

(10458) Constable Marin Scarry – "In command at Gurtavoher, when the Constabulary repulsed a large body of armed insurgents, who surrounded the barrack, fired into it, and demanded its surrender – a chevron"[33].

(18695) Mounted Constable William Duggan – ". . . who, on the night of the 13th of February, was conveying official despatches, and was called upon, near Glenbeigh, by a large body of insurgents, to stop and deliver up those documents, which he refused to do, but proceeded with courage and fidelity on his journey, when he was fired at, and severely wounded and disabled. The Constable is still suffering from the effects of the wound[35], and was in consequence unable to proceed to Dublin to receive the medal that has been awarded him"[36].

Lisdoonvarna, 1887 During the agitation for Irish land reform an organisation was active in many parts of the country killing and burning out landlords, or "moonlighting" as it was called. On 11th September 1887 a detachment of Constabulary was guarding the house of a Mr. Sexton of Lisdoonvarna when it was attacked by a large body of "moonlighters". Heavy fighting ensued, both inside and outside the house, and the officer in command of the detachment, Head Constable Whelehan, was killed. All the "moonlighters" were eventually arrested[37]. For this episode 13 Constabulary Medals were awarded, of which 12 were presented on 9th January 1888 in Phoenix Park, Dublin, to the following:

41221 Head Constable H. Brady	47167 Constable J. Duignan
34292 Head Constable P. Keenehan	50611 Constable J. Garvey
40005 Acting Sergeant J. Clinton	55215 Constable J. Hall
45872 Acting Sergeant A. Donohoe	49437 Constable C. Huggard
46548 Acting Sergeant M. Langan	49258 Constable P. McDermott
42362 Acting Sergeant E. Stapleton	47724 Constable J. O'Neill

A group photograph, taken at the time, shows the men wearing their medals. The remaining recipient, 48014 Constable J. Connell, was unable to attend the presentation due to wounds, and was pensioned shortly afterwards[38].

ILLUSTRATIVE AWARD

On 30th March 1876 Constable Matthew Nugent and Sub-Constable William Jones were acting as police escort to Mr. Patten S. Brydge, a land agent, of Galtee Castle, Co. Cork[39]. Sometime previously rents had been increased on the property for which Brydge was agent and, in consequence, many of the tenant farmers concerned had been reduced to penury. Brydge had therefore become the object of much local hatred and, following a determined attempt on his life in 1875, it had been necessary to station permanently four members of the Constabulary in an iron "barrack" at his very door. On going out he was invariably armed and acompanied by two members of the Constabulary.

On the day in question, having collected rents at his estate office in Mitchelstown some 6¾ miles away, Brydge began the return journey in a jaunting car accompanied by his steward Patrick O'Loghlen, his coachman John Hyland, and the two officers mentioned above. O'Loghlen and Hyland were unarmed. On reaching the hamlet of Garrylee[40] they were ambushed by three men, one being behind a fence on one side of the road while the others were behind a whitethorn hedge on the opposite side. The man behind the fence, later found to be Thomas Crowe[41], fired a blunderbuss at Brydge and, almost simultaneously, two further shots came from the hedge. The shot fired by Crowe killed Hyland who fell to the ground. Brydge and Nugent were also wounded although it is not clear by whom since the newspaper report of the incident and that of the inquest on Hyland are difficult to reconcile. Hyland was killed by a "pellet"[42] through the heart[43], Nugent sustained various injuries including a serious leg wound, while Brydge received wounds in the face, right hand, arms and legs. Nugent immediately fired at Crowe but missed him, while Jones fired at the men on the other side of the road, and shot the hat off one. Despite his wounds, Nugent jumped down from the car and confronted Crowe who by this time had a loaded horse pistol in his hand. Although his rifle was unloaded, Nugent presented it at Crowe and ordered

35. Duggan was pensioned shortly afterwards, see P.R.O. HO 184/10.

36. Shown as a medallist in the General Register (the numerical reference being undated), and in the Constabulary Lists; also received a Parliamentary reward of £15.

37. Summarised from contemporary newspapers.

38. Connell also received a monetary reward of £15, see P.R.O. HO 184/25. His medal is engraved with the date of the presentation.

39. Our account of the incident and subsequent inquest has been summarised from that given in *The Irish Times* of 3rd April 1876.

40. Spelt "Garryleigh" on the medals awarded to Jones and Nugent.

41. The report of the inquest gives his name as Croghe. He was about 60 years of age and was not a tenant of the estate for which Brydge collected rents, although he had formerly held land there.

42. "Slug" would seem to be a better word. The guns later found at the scene were loaded with pieces of rod iron, lead and wire which, at short range, would be formidable missiles.

43. His spine was fractured, and he had other wounds.

him to surrender. Losing his presence of mind, Crowe dropped the pistol whereupon Nugent closed with him and, after a hard struggle, succeeded in making him prisoner.

In the meanwhile, Jones engaged the other two men. Reloading his rifle he entered the field and fired at them, apparently hitting one who dropped a revolver but picked it up again. After a further exchange of shots the men made off leaving two shot guns behind, and Jones returned to assist Nugent who, as it happened, had by then secured Crowe and was himself coming to help Jones.

The newspaper report contains a barbed comment to the effect that at the moment Hyland was shot, Brydge, although armed to the teeth, never fired a shot but made off as fast as he could with O'Loughlen in the car to make the matter known at Kilbehenny Barracks. However, the report adds, not unfairly, that Brydge had been seriously wounded. The car in which they were ambushed had been perforated at all sides and the rug which Hyland had wrapped around him had 17 shot holes.

The inquest on Hyland concluded at Cork on 1st April, but despite the clear evidence of Jones the jury returned an open verdict. It seems that those who tried Crowe were, however, made of sterner stuff; he was convicted of murder and hanged at Cork on 25th August 1876.

Both Nugent and Jones received the Constabulary Medal for their part in the affair. Nugent's medal has a swivelling wire suspender and the first type obverse; the reverse is engraved "Constable – Matthew Nugent – No. 23363 – Garryleigh – 30th March 1876" in five lines (see Fig. E)[44]. The General Register entry for both awards is dated 3rd April 1876. Nugent was appointed to the Force on 12th May 1858 being then 20 years of age[45]. He was the subject of a favourable notice on 11th July 1859 and, in addition to his medal, received an award of £25 on 7th August 1876. He was discharged on 1st December 1883, receiving an award of £40 from Constabulary funds and a pension of £68 per annum. Jones was appointed to the Force on 6th March 1875 being then 18 years of age[46]. On 14th February 1892 he was discharged with a pension of £25–15–10 per annum.

44. Jones's medal is engraved with similar details.

45. Details from P.R.O. HO 184/13 (No. 23363).

46. Details from P.R.O. HO 184/22 (No. 41016).

Chapter 12

The Distinguished Conduct Medal

ORIGIN AND DEVELOPMENT

Before the Crimean War there was no official gallantry medal for other ranks of the British Army[1] although since 1829 some attempts had been made to reward deserving soldiers[2]. By a Royal Warrant ("R.W.") of 14th November 1829 a gratuity of £15 for sergeants, £7 for corporals[3] and £5 for privates could be awarded on discharge, in addition to pension, to a limited number of men annually. In order to be recommended such men had to have completed 21 years actual service in the infantry, and 24 years in the cavalry[4]. Moreover, they were to be men who "have never been convicted by Court Martial, and must have borne an irreproachable character, or particularly distinguished themselves in the Service". This wording suggests that if a candidate did not satisfy the two criteria for character, he could nevertheless be considered if he had distinguished himself in some way. Unfortunately, no evidence has been found so far to establish whether this was interpreted so as to include gallantry. The Warrant further provided that men were to be recommended for gratuities by Commanding Officers, confirmation being in the hands of the Commander-in-Chief. By a R.W. of the following year[5] the Long Service and Good Conduct Medal ("L.S. & G.C. Medal") was instituted for soldiers who received a gratuity for "meritorious conduct" on discharge. In 1833[6] the provisions regarding gratuities and medals were consolidated, the criteria for length of service and for character remaining unchanged.

In 1845[7] the Meritorious Service Medal ("M.S.M.") was instituted, and the provisions regarding the L.S. & G.C. Medal and accompanying gratuities were amended, as follows:

> *M.S.M.* £2,000[8] was to be available annually for annuities, not exceeding £20 each, to sergeants for "distinguished or meritorious service". Such sergeants[9] were also to receive the M.S.M. Both annuity and medal could be awarded during service, or after discharge with or without pension. Selection was to be made by the Commander-in-Chief for recommendation to the Queen.

> *L.S. & G.C. Medal* The criteria for length of service remained the same[4] while those for conduct were amended so that the men recommended must "have never been convicted by Court Martial, and must have borne an irreproachable character: or, if not coming strictly within these latter conditions, must have particularly distinguished themselves by gallantry and zeal in Our Service". From this it seems clear that "gallantry and zeal" were alternatives to the unblemished conduct otherwise required, but that in any case, long service was a prerequisite. Once the Commander-in-Chief had approved the award of a gratuity on discharge, the man concerned was to receive the Medal which he was to wear throughout the remainder of his service[10].

An Horse Guards' Circular Memorandum of 5th February 1850 provided that no individual could hold both the M.S.M. and the L.S. & G.C. Medal and that a sergeant who was awarded the former would be required to relinquish the latter, if he already had it, together with its attendant gratuity.

Despite the provision regarding "gallantry and zeal"[11] no awards of the L.S. & G.C. Medal have been found so far where this was invoked[12]. There are, however, a number of instances where the M.S.M. was awarded under the 1845 R.W. for what amount to acts of gallantry. Thus Colour-Sergeant James Young, Royal

1. Some Regiments awarded medals, either for long and zealous service or for gallantry, or a combination of both. In general, these were unofficial although that, for instance, of the 5th Fusiliers received recognition in 1832. The Indian Order of Merit for natives of the Honourable East India Company's Armies was instituted in 1837.

2. For officers the Order of the Bath was, of course, open to those of field rank and above, and there were other means of recognition available e.g. brevet promotion.

3. Increased to £10 by the R.W. of 19th December 1845, see *post*.

4. Decreased to 18 years in the infantry, and 21 years in the cavalry by the R.W. of 13th April 1854.

5. R.W. 30th July 1830.

6. R.W. 7th February 1833.

7. R.W. 19th December 1845.

8. Increased to £4,000 by an annual progression of £250 (or such other rate as the Secretary at War deemed expedient) by the R.W. of 4th June 1853.

9. The word "sergeant" included all higher non-commissioned ranks, the description "warrant officer" not then being in existence.

10. By a R.W. of 13th April 1854 the gratuity was to be awarded with the Medal, and was to remain in the Regimental Savings Bank at interest until discharge.

11. In the R.W.s for the Pay etc. of the Army ("P.W.s") between those of 3rd March 1866 and 10th June 1884 the alternative to unblemished conduct was the somewhat forbidding requirement that the man recommended should have "brilliantly distinguished himself by gallantry and zeal" or, in later editions, have "displayed zeal and brilliant gallantry". The P.W. of 15th November 1887 reverted to "zeal and gallantry".

12. For the position regarding the Royal Marines, to whom some Naval L.S. & G.C. Medals and (R.M.) M.S.M.s were given for gallantry, see the articles by Captain K. J. Douglas-Morris, RN, in *The Journal of the Orders and Medals Research Society* for December 1972 and Winter 1974.

Sappers and Miners, was awarded an annuity of £10 and the M.S.M. by an Order of the Board of Ordnance dated 5th February 1847[13] for gallantry in action against the "Emigrant Farmers" in Natal in May and June 1842[14]. The events concerned were the attack on the Boer Camp at Congella, near the settlement at Port Natal (otherwise Durban) on 23rd/24th May and the subsequent siege of the fort at the settlement by the Boers under Andries Pretorious. On 27th February 1847 Armourer-Sergeant Henry Ulyett, 13th Light Infantry, was awarded an annuity of £20 and the M.S.M.[15] for capturing Mahomet Akbar's standard at Jellalabad on 7th April 1842. Subsequently Ulyett was three times convicted by Court Martial, and in 1851 was deprived of both medal and annuity by order of the Secretary-at-War. However, in 1858, following consideration of the similar case of Sergeant J. Grant, 18th Foot (see below), the annuity, and apparently the medal, were restored to Ulyett on the ground that deprivation could be ordered only by sentence of Court Martial[16]. In a Submission of 20th October 1848, which is preserved in the Ministry of Defence (Army Department), the Queen approved of the award of an annuity of £20 and the M.S.M. to Colour Sergeant John Murphy, 91st Foot for "meritorious conduct" when the transport *Abercrombie Robinson* (which was carrying the Reserve Battalion of that Regiment) was wrecked in Table Bay on 28th August 1842, and to Sergeant Luke Dunne, Reserve Battalion 36th Foot who, while in command of 12 men of his Regiment, "successfully resisted an armed party of Peasantry of upwards of 200 Men at Argostoli in the Island of Cephalonia, on 26th September, 1848." In a Submission of 6th November 1860 Sergeant Major Lewis Purnell, 54th Foot received an annuity of £20 and the M.S.M. "as a Reward for Meritorious Service, – more particularly in Canada during the years 1851–1852–1853 and 1854, and at the Wreck of the 'Sarah Sands' on passage to India in November 1857". A further instance may have occurred in the case of Colour-Sergeant Michael Burke, 60th Rifles who, with effect from 1st March 1855 was awarded an annuity of £20 and a "Silver Medal for Meritorious Conduct"[17]. Form 26 of the Muster Rolls of the Depot, 3rd Battalion, 60th Rifles (where Burke later served) shows that the award was made for "capturing one of the Enemy's Standards at Zoormundi[18], E.I., on the 14th Decr. 1849"[19]. Burke is shown as an annuitant in the Army Estimates commencing 1856/57. However, on 16th December 1858 a D.C.M. was ordered for him from the Royal Mint[20] which suggests that, his only active service having been in India before the Mutiny, this was either a replacement for the M.S.M. already issued or that it was for some other service for which he could receive neither annuity nor gratuity under the rules regarding them (see below). In September 1891 Burke's application to commute his annuity was refused; he died on 31st March 1895[21].

Thus on the outbreak of the War with Russia on 28th March 1854 there was no award for corporals and privates which could be made exclusively for gallantry in action, while for sergeants the M.S.M. was of indeterminate status. By 5th November following the Army in the Crimea had not only won the battles of the Alma, of Balaklava and of Inkermann but had already begun the long siege of Sebastopol and the Government was under pressure in the House of Commons, and from the Press, to institute an award which recognised individual acts of gallantry. Accordingly, on 4th December 1854 a R.W. was signed which was designed to meet some objections[22], as far as other ranks were concerned, by modifying the provisions of the 1853 R.W. (M.S.M.) and the 1854 R.W. (L.S. & G.C. Medal), as follows[23].

"VICTORIA R.

WHEREAS by Our Royal Warrant of the 4th June, 1853, We were pleased to extend the Rewards to Serjeants of Our Army for distinguished Service from £2,000 a year to £4,000 a year, by an annual progression at the rate of £250 a year, or such other rate as might be deemed most expedient by Our Secretary at War, AND WHEREAS We deem it expedient to mark Our Sense of the Distinguished, Gallant, and Good Conduct of the Army serving in the East under the command of Field Marshal Lord

13. Due to an oversight the medal was not ordered from the Royal Mint until 13th March 1848, see P.R.O. MINT 16/2.

14. See his discharge documents in P.R.O. WO 97/1152, and Connolly (see Bibliography).

15. Ordered from the Royal Mint on 26th July 1847, see P.R.O. MINT 16/2. It was sent to his Commanding Officer for presentation on 29th November 1847, see the early M.S.M. Register P.R.O. WO 101/1.

16. See P.R.O. WO 43/834; his discharge documents in P.R.O. WO 97/1431; and Major-General Sir Henry Everett's *The History of the Somerset Light Infantry (Prince Albert's), 1685–1914,* (1934). Ulyett's M.S.M. is in the Regimental collection.

17. See his discharge documents in P.R.O. WO 97/1569. 38 M.S.M.s were ordered from the Royal Mint on 8th March 1855, see P.R.O. MINT 16/2 where, however, no names are given.

18. One of four villages on the North West Frontier of India destroyed in operations against refractory tribesmen. Burke was then serving in the 1st Battalion of his Regiment. For further details about him see Volume 3 of *The Annals of the King's Royal Rifle Corps* by Lieutenant-Colonel Lewis Butler (1926).

19. See P.R.O. WO 12/7014 and 7015. Burke's discharge documents show that he was promoted corporal for this act.

20. See P.R.O. MINT 21/6.

21. See the M.S.M. Register, P.R.O. WO 101/6. This Register contains details of some of the early D.C.M. annuitants who survived long enough to be carried forward into it.

22. In addition, a number of deserving Sergeants (one per Regiment) were appointed Cornet or Ensign, see Crimea General Orders 28th December 1854, and *L.G.* 6th February 1855. Their commissions were ante-dated to 5th November 1854.

23. See *L.G.,* 12th December 1854.

Raglan, Our Will and Pleasure is, that one Serjeant in each Regiment of Cavalry and Infantry and of each Battalion of the Foot Guards, and of the Rifle Brigade, serving in the East, in the Crimea or elsewhere, under the command of Field Marshal Lord Raglan, shall be selected by the Commanding Officer and recommended to Us for the grant of an Annuity not exceeding £20, provided that the aggregate of grants now made, and to be made, shall not exceed £4,000 in any one year.

The Annuity so granted is to be at the disposal of such Serjeant, although he may still be in Our Service.

It is also Our Will and Pleasure to extend the provisions of Our Royal Warrant of the 13th April, 1854, and with the special view of marking Our Sense of the Distinguished Service and Gallant Conduct in the Field of Our Army now serving in the East, in the Crimea or elsewhere, under the command of Field Marshal Lord Raglan, to order and direct that the Commanding Officer of each Regiment of Cavalry shall be allowed to recommend one Serjeant, two Corporals, and four Privates, and the Commanding Officer of each Regiment of Infantry and of each Battalion of Foot Guards, and of the Rifle Brigade, shall be allowed to recommend one Serjeant, four Corporals, and ten Privates, to receive a Medal and a Gratuity of:

For a Serjeant	£15
For a Corporal	£10
For a Private	£5

The Gratuity to be placed in the Regimental Savings' Bank, there to remain in deposit at Interest until his Discharge from Our Service, and to be deemed his Personal Property, in conformity with the terms of Our Royal Warrant of 13th April, 1854.

Given at Our Court at St. James's, this fourth day of December, 1854, in the Eighteenth year of Our Reign.

By Her Majesty's Command,
(Signed) Sydney Herbert."

Several features of this Warrant are significant. In the first place, the awards were for one portion of the Army only, i.e. that serving under Lord Raglan's command. In the case of medals with annuity awards were restricted to one per Regiment within the overall sum available, and in the case of medals with gratuity by a fixed number per Regiment allotted by ranks. Moreover, selection for the medal with annuity was to be by the Commanding Officer[24] and not, as in the case of the M.S.M., by the Commander-in-Chief. In due course, the restrictive financial and other provisions of the Warrant were to cause considerable confusion and friction.

In order to give effect to the Warrant, it was promulgated to Commanding Officers by War Office Circular No. 1171 of 14th December 1854 which directed that:

"The Serjeant to be selected for the Annuity of £20, is to be the Individual whom you may consider most deserving of such a Reward, and which when granted is at once to be at his own disposal though he may be still serving.

I am further directed to observe, that in selecting individuals for the Gratuities to be awarded for distinguished Service or Gallant Conduct in the Field, you are not to be fettered in your selection by any consideration as to length of Service, the General Good Conduct of the Individual (and especially in the late operations) being alone the qualification to entitle him to this Reward."

An Horse Guards' letter of 18th December 1854[25], addressed to Lord Raglan in the Crimea, instructed Commanding Officers recommending men for the medal with gratuity "to furnish a Record of Service, specifying therein the date or dates of gallant service performed by the Individual recommended for the honorable distinction[26], also quoting the date of the Warrant authorising the Grant, in order that Soldiers recommended for gallant Acts may have their names recorded distinct from those who may receive a similar decoration for 'Good Conduct & Long Service'[27] under the Royal Warrant of 13th April 1854". The letter also laid down that "applications" for the medal with annuity were to be submitted through the Military Secretary (at the Horse Guards).

24. However, recommendations were submitted to the Queen (see the Submissions in P.R.O. WO 146/1) through the Commander-in-Chief. Those for the medal with gratuity were not, being approved by the Commander-in-Chief himself.

25. Repeated in Crimea General Orders 11th January 1855.

26. The recommendations do not seem to have survived.

27. The majority of names of men of the Cavalry and Infantry are recorded in the L.S. & G.C. Medal Register (P.R.O. WO 102/14) where they are entered in red ink.

28. See the papers of Lord Raglan now in the National Army Museum.

29. See R.A. General Regimental Order of 23rd August 1855.

30. See Connolly, Volume 2 at pp.403, 442 and 443.

31. P.R.O. WO 43/852.

32. It may have been intended that the M.S.M. was to accompany the award of an annuity, and that there was a muddle somewhere. Oddly enough, the D.C.M. awarded with annuity to QMS J. Linford, 63rd Foot, in the Submission of 7th February 1855 (P.R.O. WO 146/1) was exchanged for the M.S.M. on 25th April following (P.R.O. MINT 21/5) but the correspondence leading to this does not seem to have survived.

33. P.R.O. MINT 1/42.

34. See entries in P.R.O. WO 102/14.

35. On 2 July 1855 D.C.M.s for the next-of-kin of the following were sent to the Deputy Secretary-at-War for onward transmission: Lance-Sergeant W. Seggie, 2nd Dragoons; and Sergeant G. Seymour, Corporal W. Bish and Private J. Mercer, all of 95th Foot, see P.R.O. WO 3/535.

36. Calculated from entries in P.R.O. MINT 21/5. L.S. & G.C. medals were issued for Colour Sergeant Peter Andrew Farrell and Private William Mann, both of the 20th Foot, the recommendations having been made in the wrong form. These were recalled and replaced by D.C.M.s, see P.R.O. WO 3/535.

37. 17th Foot (first recommendations 12th March 1855); 18th Foot (first recommendations 24th July 1855); 34th Foot (first recommendations 5th October 1855); and 90th Foot (first medals ordered 23rd June 1856), see P.R.O. WO 102/14 and MINT 21/6.

38. First medals ordered 24th July 1856, see P.R.O. MINT 21/6.

39. For Corporal M. Lynch; medal ordered 12th September 1855, see P.R.O. WO 3/535; £5 gratuity, see P.R.O WO 102/14.

40. 2nd Dragoons (one sergeant less); 20th Foot (one corporal less); 2nd Rifle Brigade (one corporal and five privates less), see P.R.O. WO 102/14.

41. Thus gratuities of £5 each were awarded to Sergeant C. E. Booth and Corporal W. Dowdall, both of the 17th Foot, by a special Horse Guards' authority of July 1859, see P.R.O. WO 102/14. These were the last Crimean gratuity awards made.

Since the Warrant made no mention of awards to the Royal Artillery and the Royal Sappers and Miners, on 27th December the Commander-in-Chief wrote to the Deputy Master General of the Ordnance (the Master General – Lord Raglan – being in the Crimea) drawing his attention to the Warrant and suggesting that the Board of Ordnance might like to issue the rewards "in proportion to the numbers engaged in the Crimea"[28]. The Board was, however, dissolved in May 1855 and the awards for both arms were issued eventually through the Office of the Commander-in-Chief. 64 medals were given to the Royal Artillery (four with annuity; the remainder with varying gratuities)[29] and 16 to the Royal Sappers and Miners (one with annuity; the remainder with varying gratuities)[30].

On 21st December 1854 the Commander-in-Chief wrote to the Secretary-at-War asking whether the medal with gratuity awarded under the Warrant should be the L.S. & G.C. Medal or "... whether Mr. Sydney Herbert proposes to cause a different medal to be struck, illustrative of the Gallantry exhibited"[31]. In the ensuing correspondence it was agreed that the reverse inscription should read "For Distinguished Conduct in the Field" rather than "For Gallant Conduct in Action" since, as the Secretary-at-War pointed out, the medals might be given for some distinguished service not strictly in action. Similarly, the existing L.S. & G.C. Medal obverse (i.e. the trophy and shield type then in use) was thought more suitable than the single word "Crimea" which had been proposed since that word would "probably" appear on the campaign medal about to be issued. Although the Commander-in-Chief's original query had related to medals with gratuity, the fact that some were to be awarded with annuity seems to have been overlooked in the correspondence but, whatever the explanation, in the event, the same medal was given whether an annuity or gratuity was awarded[32]. It was also agreed that a silver suspender should be used in place of the unsatisfactory steel one which had been used on the L.S. & G.C. Medal. A specimen of the new medal was submitted to the Queen on 25th January 1855 and on 2nd February following the War Office placed an order with the Royal Mint saying that "The number required for immediate issue will be about 1,000 ..."[33]. In the meantime recommendations had been coming in from the Crimea and the Royal Mint acted with commendable speed, bulk consignments being sent to the Crimea on 26th March, 3rd April and 14th May[34]. These events were noticed in the Press. Thus under the heading "Medals for Distinguished Service in the Field", *The United Services Gazette* of 31st March 1855 noted "We are glad to announce that these Medals were forwarded to the Crimea this week. It is a very handsome medal with a red ribbon and blue centre", while *The Naval and Military Gazette* of 7th April 1855 mentioned that "The medals for distinguished service in the field were forwarded to the Crimea in the past week. The Medal is silver, with a red ribbon and blue centre. The relatives of those men who have died since their service will receive them"[35]. By 20th December 1855 some 747 medals had been issued[36].

Despite the clear financial restrictions imposed by the 1854 R.W., complications soon arose in the allocation of the pecuniary awards accompanying the medals, and it is convenient therefore to deal separately with those awarded with gratuity, and those awarded with annuity.

Awards with gratuity The R.W. made no provision for allocations to Regiments which arrived subsequently in the Crimea. In fact, awards were made to all Regiments arriving before 31st December 1854 except for the 62nd and for the 89th Foot. Five Regiments, including the latter, arrived during December 1854 and awards were made eventually to four of them[37]. No awards were made to Regiments arriving after that date except for the 72nd Foot which received its full quota[38], and for the 3rd Foot which received only one[39]. Three Regiments did not apply for their full allotment[40] and it seems likely that some of the resulting surplus was allocated elsewhere[41] but the paucity of surviving information makes an exact computation impossible. Matters were complicated further by the sanctioning, in

42. E.g. on 23rd July 1855 to Sergeant T. Murphy, and to Privates J. Eagle and F. Wheatley, VC, all of the 1st Rifle Brigade, and on 5th October 1855 to Corporal G. Lang, 47th Foot, see P.R.O. WO 3/535. In the latter case Lang was given a supernumerary award because his Commanding Officer had thought, contrary to fact, that the medal and £5 gratuity awarded to Lance-Sergeant T. Quinn of the same Regiment were "forfeited" on appointment to Ensign, see *ibid*. In due course Lang seems to have received the gratuity but it is not clear where this came from.

43. E.g. on 8th May 1855 a corporal's gratuity of £10 was awarded to Sergeant T. Halpin, 20th Foot, see P.R.O. WO 102/14.

44. Deduced from entries in P.R.O. WO 102/14 where the 55th Foot are shown as receiving gratuities for two corporals and 14 privates, instead of four corporals and 10 privates. In either case the gratuities would total £90.

45. P.R.O. WO 3/535. A few recommendations were posthumous, a circumstance which, for one reason or another (e.g. evacuation to Scutari), may not have been known at the time.

46. *ibid*.

47. P.R.O. WO 3/536.

48. P.R.O. WO 3/537, letter of 11th September 1856.

49. P.R.O. MINT 21/6, entry No. 517.

50. P.R.O. WO 12/8292 (Muster Roll). It is not clear whether the medal was ever recovered from the elusive Mooney.

51. What appears to be part of the original recommendations for gratuity medals are reproduced in the *Chronology and Book of Days of the 42nd Royal Highlanders, The Black Watch, from 1729 to 1874* with an introduction by "J.W." (Edinburgh: William Elgin and Sons: 1874) as follows: Colour-Sergeant P. White – "Distinguished himself when in the trenches before Sebastopol on several occasions in 1854." Corporals J. McClelland and J. Mumford, Privates A. Bowie, J. Grant, J. Hartley, R. Holmes and J. Miller – "Gallant conduct when employed as sharpshooters before Sebastopol between 17th and 24th October, 1854." Corporals J. Patterson and W. Petrie, Privates C. Christison, D. Haddow, D. Hislop, W. Kerr and D. Logg – "Good and gallant soldiers, and not a day absent from their duty during the operations in the Crimea."

52. P.R.O. WO 3/536.

53. By this date Hospital Sergeant G. Archer, 11th Hussars, and Paymaster Sergeant H. Harvey, 2nd Rifle Brigade, had each received the D.C.M. with gratuity although whether these awards were made for gallantry is impossible to say.

54. P.R.O. WO 3/536.

55. This was John McRoberts who was awarded an annuity of £20 and the M.S.M. under the 1854 Warrant in a Submission of 22nd March 1856.

exceptionally deserving cases, of some supernumerary awards without gratuity[42]; by some gratuities being awarded at a rate lower than that to which the recipient's rank would otherwise have entitled him[43]; and by the total value of a number of gratuities being divided into a greater number of lesser gratuities[44]. Moreover, from the correspondence in the P.R.O. it is clear that some Commanding Officers were in doubt as to the exact interpretation of the R.W. Thus on 9th June 1855 the War Office wrote to the Officer Commanding the 95th Foot to the effect that the D.C.M.s of deceased soldiers belonged to their next-of-kin, and that there was no authority under the R.W. for further medals and gratuities for his Regiment[45]. Similarly on 25th June 1855 the Officer Commanding the 7th Foot was told that all medals and gratuities for his Regiment had been appropriated[46], and the same answer was sent on 8th March 1856 to the General Officer Commanding in the Crimea in reply to a query regarding the 97th Foot[47]. It was, however, the Officer Commanding 77th Foot who really got himself into hot water on this issue. On 2nd June 1856 he recommended 15 men for the medal and varying gratuities. The medals having been issued, it was discovered, apparently when the gratuities were about to be credited to the accounts of the men concerned, that the 77th had already received its quota the previous year. This brought down the wrath of the Commander-in-Chief on the head of the Commanding Officer who was ordered to return the second batch of medals. Although he protested, the Commander-in-Chief was inexorable since otherwise "it would be obviously a gross act of injustice to every other Regiment which has served in the Crimea"[48]. Accordingly, the medals were returned to the Royal Mint on 9th October 1856[49] except that of Private Patrick Mooney who had been discharged on 20th September previously[50]. While no doubt the Commander-in-Chief had good reason for disallowing the awards it may be permissible to wonder why the staff of his own Office had not noticed earlier that the 1856 application was, in effect, a double one. In due course the gratuity fund was exhausted, apparently by July 1859 (see footnote 41), and no further awards were made for the Crimean War. However, the situation regarding annuity awards was different, and awards continued to be made (see below).

Before turning to the matter of annuity awards, some other matters of general application fall to be considered.

Since the original recommendations made by Commanding Officers do not seem to have survived[51] it is impossible to say what standards were applied in selecting men for awards, even in the unlikely event of some sort of uniform standard being achieved. When the inscription on the medal was being considered (see above) it was accepted that the medal could be given for some distinguished service not necessarily in action. Similarly the War Office Circular of 14th December 1854 and the Horse Guards' letter of 18th December 1854, both of which are quoted above, can be read together as meaning that gallantry was more appropriate to awards with gratuity, than to those with annuity. Thus on 30th January 1856 the War Office wrote to the Adjutant-General in the Crimea[52] refusing an award to an Hospital Orderly of the 8th Hussars on the ground that the D.C.M. was "exclusively the Prize of Courage in the Field of Battle", and adding that the man concerned should be recommended for the L.S. & G.C. Medal with gratuity if his length of service was sufficient to make him eligible[53]. The matter was raised again on 17th March 1856 in a Memorandum by the Adjutant-General, Horse Guards, for the Military Secretary[54], regarding the proposed award of a medal with annuity to the Hospital Sergeant of the 2/1st Foot[55]. In this the Adjutant-General suggested that such "noncombatants", eligible for annuities, should receive the M.S.M. under the 1854 R.W. unless recommended for an act of gallantry in which case they should receive the D.C.M. He went on to say:

"The latter part of the Warrant referred to, relating to Medals and Gratuities for Noncommissioned officers and Privates has been invariably interpreted to apply only to 'Distinguished Conduct in the Field', and no noncombatant has accordingly received them, however exemplary may have been the performance of his duties.

66

56. In passing it is worth mentioning that the citations for the following recipients of the French *Médaille Militaire* show that they also received the D.C.M. for gallantry: – Privates C. Quigley (Alma and Inkerman) and J. Smith (Alma), both of the 30th Foot (see Parliamentary Papers, 1856, Vol. 40, p.349); Colour-Sergeant P. Pope and Private J. Dunn, both of the 55th Foot and both for Inkerman (see Parliamentary Papers, 1857, Vol. 9, pp.235/6). Similarly some of the recommendations for the VC in P.R.O. WO 98/2 refer to previous awards of the D.C.M.

57. P.R.O. WO 3/535.

58. P.R.O. MINT 21/6.

59. P.R.O. WO 3/535.

60. P.R.O. WO 3/537.

61. His medal had been sent to the Regiment on 25th July 1856, see P.R.O. WO 3/537. Presumably another medal was issued for Smallie.

62. P.R.O. WO 97/2063.

63. P.R.O. WO 3/510, letters of 16th September and 21st October 1857; see also WO 43/834.

64. He was still shown as an annuitant in the Army Estimates for 1886/87.

65. Thus on 13th April 1855 Quartermaster-Sergeant T. Clifford, 50th Foot, was killed in action and the vacancy was awarded to Quartermaster-Sergeant J. Duncalf of the same Regiment.

66. Thus Sergeant-Major T. Lumsden, 28th Foot, was appointed Quartermaster on 14th December 1855, and the vacancy was awarded to Quartermaster-Sergeant T. McEvoy of the same Regiment.

67. Hence Sergeant-Major P. Callaghan, 13th Foot, Sergeant A. Emmett, 56th Foot, Sergeant-Major J. Jobberns, 39th Foot, and Sergeant J. White, 72nd Foot, each received annuities of £15; while Sergeant D. Shingleton, 30th Foot, and Colour-Sergeant C. Walker, 55th Foot, each received annuities of £10. Thus six annuities of varying sums did duty for what would otherwise be four annuities of £20 each. To make confusion doubly confounded, five sergeants received the M.S.M. with annuities under the 1854 Warrant. These were Hospital Sergeant John McRoberts, 2nd/1st Foot (£20, 22nd March 1856); Sergeant Major George Thomas Carpenter Burgum, 82nd Foot (£15, 20th June 1856); Sergeant Major James Gordon, 92nd Foot (£10, 25th June 1856); Regimental Sergeant Major Charles Hickman, 10th Hussars (£15, 5th July 1856); and Colour Sergeant Samuel Francis, 48th Foot (£15, 7th July 1856).

68. P.R.O. WO 146/1.

The Medals accompanying the Annuities already bestowed on Noncombatant Serjeants and inscribed 'For Distinguished Conduct in the Field' have been, if these arguments are correct, erroneously conferred, and the cases should not be made a precedent."

By the date of the Memorandum seven Hospital Sergeants had received the medal and annuity and no doubt these were the cases which the Adjutant-General recommended should not be made precedents. All in all, it seems likely that the great majority of awards for the Crimea were, however, made for acts of gallantry[56].

As is the way with all soldiers, it was not long before medals began to be lost. Thus on 30th October 1856 replacements were sent to the Crimea for Corporal D. Hourigan and Private W. Mill, both of the 38th Foot, who had lost their medals in the assault on the Redan on 8th September 1855[57], while on 21st May 1857 a replacement was requested for that awarded to Private J. Gipson, 20th Foot, who had been "robbed at Portsmouth"[58]. Difficulties also arose where men committed offences. Thus on 1st August 1855 the War Office wrote to the Officer Commanding the Grenadier Guards in regard to Private J. Bancroft to the effect that once a man had been awarded the D.C.M. it was impossible to deprive him of it, notwithstanding subsequent misconduct[59]. However, authority was given on 8th September 1856[60] for the medal and £5 gratuity for Private J. Nash, 90th Foot, to be awarded to Sergeant J. Smallie of the same Regiment in consequence of Nash's having been convicted of theft. The letter does not show whether Nash was deprived of the awards by a specific sentence of Court Martial[61], nor do his discharge documents make any reference to them[62]. In 1857 Sergeant J. Grant, 18th Foot, was reduced to the ranks by Court Martial. Since he had received both the medal and an annuity of £20 the question of his retaining both awards was raised. However, because the Court did not deprive him of them[63], Grant continued to enjoy the annuity as a private[64].

Crimean awards with annuity Unlike the awards with gratuity which were made from a specially constituted fund and which ceased once the fund was exhausted, those with annuity were made from a continuing fund voted annually to the Army Estimates. In consequence, vacancies caused by death[65] or by appointment to a commission[66] could be filled as they occurred. Moreover, awards were not generally restricted to Regiments which had arrived in the Crimea before 31st December 1854 although, since all the later arriving Regiments did not receive an annuity award, it is difficult to say why this should have been the case unless it was due to some existing M.S.M. annuities falling vacant. All the 1855 annuities, which were the great majority, were for £20 but some of those awarded the following year were for lesser sums which suggests that, as with the gratuity medals, some adjustments were made in order to extend the total sum available to a greater number of recipients than would otherwise have been the case[67]. A curious circumstance arose in the case of Quartermaster-Sergeant J. Linford, 63rd Foot, whose recommendation for the D.C.M. and annuity was submitted to the Queen, with others, on 7th February 1855[68]. On 25th April 1855 the medal was returned by the Horse Guards to the Royal Mint with the request that it should be exchanged for a M.S.M.[69]. No explanation for this is now available although it may be that the original recommendation had not been for gallantry. At all events, Linford was appointed Quartermaster on 28th December 1855 and a D.C.M. and the vacant annuity were awarded then to Colour-Sergeant W. Aherin of the same Regiment[70]. Following the end of the Crimean War D.C.M.s with annuity continued to be awarded to sergeants and above who had served in it, the last award under the 1854 R.W. being in the Submission to the Queen of 17th August 1861 in respect of Colour-Sergeant J. Wilson, 47th Foot[71]. However, two further awards were made (by which time the 1862 R.W. was in force, see below) to Colour-Sergeant W. Mason, 33rd Foot[72] and to Sergeant-Major J. Young, late 62nd Foot[73]. There were two awards for combined service in the Crimea and in

69. P.R.O. MINT 21/5. Sergeant Major John Granger, 42nd Highlanders received an annuity of £20 and both the D.C.M. and M.S.M. as a result of the Submission of 20th July 1855. As the Submission has not survived it cannot be said which medal was intended.

70. Aherin's D.C.M. was ordered on 14th April 1856, see P.R.O. MINT 21/6.

71. P.R.O. WO 145/1.

72. Medal ordered 5th July 1866, see P.R.O. MINT 21/8. Mason was discharged unfit on 28th October 1856 on account of a wound received at the Alma, and joined the Permanent Staff of the North Lincoln Militia, (see P.R.O. WO 97/1498).

73. A.O. No. 186 of April 1889.

China 1860[74], and four which seem to have been for combined service in the Crimea and Indian Mutiny, see below.

The 1854 R.W. having been promulgated, complications soon arose regarding its financial provisions. While no soldier could hold two annuities because both those for the D.C.M. and the M.S.M. were paid from the same fund, it was not clear whether a man holding the D.C.M with gratuity could also hold the M.S.M. with annuity. Moreover, there were cases where a D.C.M. annuitant had been awarded the L.S. & G.C. Medal with gratuity. One such case was Staff-Sergeant G. Marvin, Royal Horse Artillery, who in 1855 was awarded the D.C.M. with an annuity of £20 for his services in the Crimea[75]. The following year he was awarded the L.S. & G.C. Medal with a gratuity of £15[76] and on 1st October 1858 was appointed Quartermaster whereby his annuity lapsed. In consequence, a Royal Artillery General Regimental Order of 23rd December 1858 provided that:

"13. The Secretary of State for War having decided that the Medal and Gratuity for 'Long Service and Good Conduct' cannot be conferred on an individual enjoying an annuity for 'Distinguished Service in the Field', Quartermaster Marvin has relinquished the Medal and Gratuity held by him, and His Royal Highness The General Commanding-in-Chief has approved of the same being distributed as follows, viz.:

A Silver Medal for 'Long Service and Good Conduct', with a Gratuity of 5l. to each of the following Master Gunners, viz.:–

William Swanson, Blackness Castle
David Dawson, Scarborough Castle
John Smith, Greencastle, Lough Foyle."

That the unfortunate Marvin did actually relinquish the L.S. & G.C. Medal (presumably he refunded the gratuity as well) is shown by a photograph of him c.1860 in which it does not appear. In an Horse Guards' Circular Memorandum of 1st June 1859 an attempt was made to clarify the matter of annuities and gratuities, and their accompanying medals, as follows:

"It being desirable that the principles which regulate the grant of annuities and medals to Serjeants who may be already in possession of Medals and Gratuities should be more clearly defined than they are at present, the following rules have been framed by HIS ROYAL HIGHNESS the General Commanding-in-Chief, in concurrence with the Secretary of State for War, for the guidance of the Army generally.

1st. The Medal accompanying the Annuity, and inscribed 'For Meritorious Service' is to be considered as given for Service of the same nature as that accompanying the Gratuity 'For Long Service and Good Conduct'; the former being held by serjeants only, the latter by Non-Commissioned Officers and Privates indifferently.

2ndly. Both Annuity and Gratuity are also given, under special circumstances, accompanied by medals similarly inscribed, 'For Distinguished Conduct in the Field'.

3rdly. When a Serjeant, on becoming an Annuitant receives a Medal denoting by its inscription that it is given for Service similar to that for which he has already received a Medal, he will be required to relinquish the latter Medal with its accompanying Gratuity and to sign a Declaration that he does so voluntarily.

4thly. When, however, the inscription on the Medal granted to a Serjeant together with an Annuity, shows that it is given for Service of a different nature from that for which he already holds a Medal, he will be required to relinquish the Gratuity only, making a like declaration as to its voluntary relinquishment.

5thly. Commanding Officers are at liberty to recommend the reappropriation of a relinquished Gratuity to any other deserving Soldier or Soldiers, provided that they shall have been serving in the year for which the Gratuity was originally awarded and shall have fulfilled the required conditions as to service and character in that year."

74. To Quartermaster-Sergeant D. Reddin, 44th Foot, Submission of 7th January 1861 in P.R.O. WO 146/1, and to Sergeant G. Leach, 31st Foot, Submission of 9th February 1866. The Submission for Leach is not in the P.R.O. series.

75. Royal Artillery General Regimental Order of 23rd August 1855. Marvin was also made a Chevalier of the Legion of Honour, see L.G. 4th August 1856.

76. Royal Artillery General Regimental Order of 17th May 1856.

This Memorandum is defective in that it deals only with those cases where a soldier already had a gratuity before being awarded an annuity, unlike the case of Marvin whose annuity preceded the gratuity. Moreover, it is important to note that paragraph 5 permitted relinquished gratuities to be re-appropriated for the L.S. & G.C. Medal only, and not for the D.C.M. The whole matter was put rather differently in the Queen's Regulations of 1st December 1859 which provided that:

77. This remained the position up to and including the P.W. of 30th May 1899. The P.W. of 26th October 1900 omitted this provision and recipients were permitted to retain but not to wear the L.S. & G.C. Medal. The matter was resolved finally in A.O. No. 250 of November 1902 which permitted the M.S.M. and the L.S. & G.C. Medal to be worn at the same time.

78. A number of such cases are known, one being Quartermaster Sergeant William Wilson, 2nd/16th Foot who was awarded the M.S.M. with an annuity of £20 in the Submission of 12th November 1866. Wilson had been awarded the D.C.M. with a gratuity of £10 for services in the Crimea as a corporal in the 28th Foot. At the time of award of the M.S.M. he also held the L.S. & G.C. Medal which, under the rules then obtaining, would have been relinquished.

79. The Submission of 7th January 1861 (see P.R.O. WO 146/1) in regard to Sergeant-Major R. Lindsay, 53rd Foot, also refers to service in India during 1845–49. This may also be the case in the award to Sergeant G. Gardner, 6th Dragoons late 14th Light Dragoons, whose medal was ordered on 6th October 1862, see P.R.O MINT 21/7, but for whom no Submission survives. Gardner died at Mhow on 20th November 1862 see P.R.O. WO 12/741. His award was probably *vice* Sergeant-Major T. H. Clark, 14th Light Dragoons, who was promoted Quarter-master on 2nd September 1862.

80. I.e. Sergeant-Major W. Handley, 23rd Foot, (medal ordered 7th October 1858; £10 annuity); Sergeant-Major J. Pyle, 71st Foot (medal ordered 26th February 1859; £15 annuity); Sergeant-Major R. Elliott, 2nd Bn. Military Train (medal ordered 28th March 1861; £20 annuity), see P.R.O. MINT 21/6 and 21/7, and Army Estimates. Elliott's service in the Crimea was with the 1st Foot from which he transferred to the Military Train on 1st November 1856, see P.R.O. WO 97/1703. The last such award, which also included services on the North West Frontier of India in 1863, was to Quartermaster-Sergeant J. MacKenzie, 79th Foot (£10 annuity), see the Submission of July 1895 in P.R.O. WO 146/1.

81. Sergeant-Major R. Duncan, 60th Rifles, and Quartermaster-Sergeant M. Walsh, 75th Foot (medals ordered 30th June 1858; both £5 annuity), see P.R.O. MINT 21/6 and Army Estimates. Colour-Sergeant W. Nolan, 64th Foot, Submission of 17th August 1866, (£15 annuity), see P.R.O. WO 146/1.

82. P.R.O. MINT 21/6. Hart was appointed ensign on 10th September 1858.

"A Serjeant on becoming an Annuitant will in all cases be required to relinquish the Gratuity of which he may be in possession, making a declaration in writing that he does so voluntarily. The Medal inscribed for 'Meritorious Service' cannot be held together with that for 'Good Conduct and Long Service'; but the latter must be surrendered on receipt of the former[77]. Neither can two Medals for 'Distinguished Conduct' be held by the same individual, but a Serjeant on becoming an Annuitant must relinquish one of them. An Annuitant may, however, hold the 'Meritorious Service Medal', or that for 'Good Conduct and Long Service', together with the Medal for 'Distinguished Conduct in the Field'."

and went on to repeat paragraph 5 of the Memorandum. Again the Regulations dealt, in terms, only with cases where the gratuity preceded the annuity[78] but, in addition, seemed to permit an M.S.M. annuitant to hold the D.C.M. (without gratuity), or a D.C.M. annuitant to hold the L.S. & G.C. Medal (without gratuity). If this is so, it was of no avail to Marvin since there is no evidence that his L.S. & G.C. Medal was ever restored to him.

Indian Mutiny etc. awards with annuity Although the gratuity awards under the 1854 R.W. were made exclusively for services in the Crimea, this was not the case with annuity awards. It is difficult to say why such awards were sanctioned unless it was because that, being made from the annuity fund, it was a matter of comparative indifference whether the person concerned received the M.S.M. or the D.C.M. Indeed, the 1862 R.W. (see below) specifically made the D.C.M. an alternative to the M.S.M. for sergeants. So far, 18 awards have been found for the Mutiny[79], the annuities being for £10 or £15, with a further four for combined service in the Crimea and Mutiny[80]. The first awards for the Mutiny were made in 1858 and the last, apart from the final award for combined service, was made in 1866[81]. The case of Sergeant-Major J. Hart, 78th Foot, is of interest. A D.C.M. was ordered for him on 28th October 1858 but was returned to the Royal Mint on 22nd October 1859 on the ground that he had been appointed ensign[82]. The reason for this is not clear unless it was that, since he was appointed ensign apparently before the annuity was authorised[83], the award of both the annuity and its accompanying medal were thereby vitiated. There is, however, clear evidence in many cases that a D.C.M. annuitant who was appointed Quartermaster (and thereby ranked as subaltern) retained the D.C.M. despite the lapse of the annuity. The only D.C.M. awarded between 1854 and 1862 for which service in the Crimea or Mutiny was not an element was that to Colour-Sergeant M. Burke, 60th Rifles (see above).

The whole matter of the D.C.M. having become considerably complicated, on 7th November 1861 the Military Secretary to the Commander-in-Chief wrote to the Under-Secretary of State for War[84], as follows:

"Sir – I am directed by the General Commanding in Chief to request that you will inform the Secretary of State for War that His Royal Highness is desirous of drawing his attention to the circumstances under which medals 'For Distinguished Conduct in the Field' were first granted with Annuities and Gratuities under the provision of the Royal Warrant of the 4th December 1854, such marks of distinction being then intended as Rewards for Service in the Crimea.

In reference to such Medals granted with Gratuities, the issue necessarily ceased as soon as the allotted Sums varying from £15, to £5, were awarded to the respective Regiments entitled to them.

With regard to 'Distinguished Conduct Medals' granted with Annuities, on the latter becoming vacant by death or promotion, other Non-Commissioned Officers have succeeded to them who would not be rewarded at an earlier period from the fact of the Fund being appropriated.

In some instances the Serjeants who have recently been rewarded in this manner have had strong claims on account of combined service in the Crimea and India[85], but some cases (as shown in the accompanying copies of letters from Colonel Ewart, 78th Highlanders), are now under consideration in which the service has been confined to India, but yet is of such a distinguished character that it is very desirable to mark it by a Medal of that nature to accompany the Annuity which it is proposed to award to

83. He is shown in the 1859/60 Army Estimates only as a £15 annuitant. The Estimates were, of course, prepared in advance.

84. P.R.O. WO 32/6042.

85. This was not, of course, strictly true, a number of awards having been made from 1858 for service exclusively in India (see above).

one of the four Serjeants named in the margin,★ belonging to a Regiment that bore so important a part in the Operations for the Suppression of the late Mutiny in that Country.

Under the circumstances His Royal Highness is desirous of being informed whether Sir George Lewis is of the opinion that a new Warrant is necessary for the grant of 'Distinguished Conduct Medals' in such cases above alluded to, and would also suggest whether it would not be desirable to authorise the issue of such Medals either with the Annuity or Gratuity, where the conduct of the Soldier is represented to have been of such a nature as to fairly entitle him to that mark of approbation for Service performed in any part of the World.

I have the honor to be,
Sir,
Your obedient Servant,
(Signed) W. F. Forster, Major General.

P.S. I have to request that the four Records of Service, sent herewith, may be returned.

★Colour-Serjeant George Topp, George Bertram, David Christie; Serjeant James Reid."

In the ensuing correspondence[86] (in which a draft R.W. was considered and to which various amendments were suggested), the Secretary of State for War objected that, as then proposed, the award of the D.C.M. without gratuity would make the Commander-in-Chief the sole arbiter of the award; while this was all very well in the case of the L.S. & G.C. Medal where questions of discipline arose, it would not do in the case of an award analogous to the V.C., although given for "less conspicuous gallantry", since it was a military honour over which the Secretary of State should have control[87].

Eventually, after a good deal of muddled argument a compromise was reached whereby the medal was to be retained for the future without pecuniary award except for specially selected sergeants who might also receive an annuity "subject, however, to the conditions and limitations now in force as to the grant of annuities". It was also agreed that annuity awards might be made for past services on the ground that the medal was, in effect, an alternative to the M.S.M.[88] but that awards without gratuity should be for future service only[89]. Before turning to the R.W. resulting from these deliberations it is interesting to note that of the four senior N.C.O.s recommended by the Officer commanding 78th Highlanders, Christie received the D.C.M. with an annuity of £15[90]. Reid was discharged on 4th February 1862 and his documents were endorsed to the effect that he had been recommended for the D.C.M. with annuity[91]. However, although two D.C.M.s were ordered from the Royal Mint on 14th February 1862[92], no names appear in the Mint Register. While it may be that one of these was for Christie, Reid does not appear as an annuitant in the Army Estimates and so the matter is inconclusive as far as he is concerned[93]. Bertram eventually received the M.S.M.[94], as probably did Topp[95].

The terms of a new R.W. having been finally agreed, they were approved by the Queen in the following terms:

"VICTORIA R.

Whereas with a view to reward Distinguished and Meritorious Service, and of promoting Good Conduct in Our Army, We have been pleased to declare that a certain fixed Sum may be granted in Annuities to Serjeants in Our Service, and that the Serjeants selected for the same shall be entitled to receive and wear a Silver Medal, bearing on one side the Royal Effigy, and on the other the words 'For Meritorious Service', the name and rank of the Serjeant being inscribed thereon.

It is Our Royal Will and Pleasure that a Silver Medal, bearing on it the words 'For Distinguished Conduct in the Field', shall, in certain cases where specially recommended, be issued to Serjeants with Annuity, in lieu of the before-mentioned Medal for 'Meritorious Service' with Annuity, subject, however, to the conditions and limitations now in force as to the grant of Annuities.

86. P.R.O. WO 32/6042.

87. This objection was met by incorporating into the resulting R.W. a provision that recommendations were to be aproved by the Secretary of State. All subsequent recommendations were submitted to the Queen.

88. A number of annuity awards for services in the Crimea and Mutiny were later made, see above.

89. Accordingly, recommendations in respect of nine men made by the Officer Commanding 32nd Foot (presumably for services in the Mutiny) were not proceeded with, see P.R.O. WO 32/6042, letter of 6th November 1862. There were others.

90. See his discharge documents in P.R.O. WO 97/1619. The authority is dated 20th January 1862.

91. See P.R.O. WO 97/1621.

92. P.R.O. MINT 21/7.

93. Cases are known of men dying shortly after being awarded an annuity and, in consequence, their names do not appear in the Army Estimates.

94. A.O. No. 138 of April 1888. He received an annuity of £15 from 26th December 1887, and died on 2nd January 1915, see P.R.O. WO 101/2.

95. Annuity of £10 from 1st April 1878; died 27th December 1892, see P.R.O. WO 101/6.

And further, that a like Medal be granted without Annuity or Gratuity to Serjeants, Corporals and Privates of Our Army, where specially recommended by the General Commanding in Chief, and approved by Our Secretary of State for War, for individual acts of Distinguished Conduct in the Field in any part of the World.

Given at Our Court at St. James's, this thirtieth day of September, 1862, in the twenty-sixth year of Our Reign.

By Her Majesty's Command
(Signed) G. C. Lewis."

Horse Guards' Circular Memorandum No. 233 of 25th November 1862 notified the decision, mentioned above, that no retrospective action would be given to the R.W. in so far as D.C.M.s without annuity or gratuity were concerned[96].

The first occasion on which the Sovereign presented the D.C.M. was on 16th May 1874 when Queen Victoria decorated a number of men at Windsor Castle for services in the Ashanti War of 1873/74[97]. It seems that previous presentations had been made, as far as possible, on parade by the Commanding Officer concerned as provided in the 1833 and 1845 R.W.s, and in Queen's Regulations, for the L.S. & G.C. Medal[98].

The first awards to coloured soldiers were made to men of the West India Regiment for services in British Honduras the recommendations for which having been submitted to the Queen on 14th November 1872[99]. Further awards were made to this Regiment for the Ashanti War which followed the next year. A number of awards to soldiers of various native African regiments were subsequently made until the West African Frontier Force, and the King's African Rifles' D.C.M.s were instituted in 1903. These special D.C.M.s continued to be awarded until 1942. The first awards to Europeans of overseas contingents were made to Corporal W. Vinnicombe and Trooper R. Brown, both of the Frontier Light Horse, for services in the Zulu War, a Submission being made to the Queen in September 1879[100]. In 1894 a "Colonial" D.C.M. was instituted[101] which, although the matter is not entirely free from doubt, may have been intended originally for award to locally raised troops operating alone within the territory concerned under a local commander.

A R.W. of 7th February 1881 authorised the award of a bar[102] to the D.C.M., when appropriate, in the following terms:

"VICTORIA R.

Whereas We deem it expedient to amend the Regulations under which Medals are awarded to Serjeants, Corporals and Privates of Our Army for Distinguished Service in the Field;

Our Will and Pleasure is that in cases where Non-Commissioned Officers and Privates, who are in possession of Medals for Distinguished Service, under Articles 1072 and 1073 of Our Warrant of 1st May 1878[103], have been recommended by Our Commander-in-Chief on account of further Distinguished Conduct in the Field, a Bar shall be added to the Distinguished Conduct Medal already conferred.

Given at Our Court at Osborne, this 7th day of February, 1881, in the 44th year of Our Reign.

By Her Majesty's Command.
(signed) Hugh C. E. Childers."

The bar was to bear the date of the act for which it was awarded[104]. Dated bars continued to be issued until September 1916; thereafter the laurelled bar was used. From about May 1881 the practice also began of adding the date of the act, after the description of the recipient, on the edge of the medal and this continued, in general, until early 1900 although there are rare later exceptions.

By the P.W. of 10th June 1884 an additional sum of up to 6d. per day (3d. for "black" soldiers) might be added to the pension of D.C.M. recipients on discharge, subject to recommendation by the Commander-in-Chief and approval by the Secretary of State for War. A R.W. of 26th August 1884 provided that a D.C.M. or M.S.M. annuitant would not be required to surrender a gratuity if he

96. Some later awards were long delayed. Thus Sergeant J. Whelan, Royal Artillery, was awarded the D.C.M. in RA Regimental Order No. 54 of February 1873 for services in Bhootan in 1865, while Acting Bombardiers H. McAndrew, T. Portman and J. Watts, also of the Royal Artillery, received their medals in 1890 (Submission of 10th August) for the Naga Hills Campaign of 1879. Similarly, the Submission of 3rd October 1892 regarding Sergeant C. Williams, Medical Staff Corps, was for the Nile Campaign of 1885.

97. See *The Broad Arrow* and *The Illustrated London News*, both of 23rd May 1874.

98. E.g. four supernumerary awards to the Rifle Brigade were sent to the Crimea on 23rd July 1855 which were to be "presented on the first available public occasion", see P.R.O. WO 3/535.

99. P.R.O. WO 146/1.

100. *Ibid.*

101. R.W. 24th May 1894.

102. Provision for bars had already been included in the instruments instituting the VC (R.W. 29th January 1856), the Albert Medal (R.W. 7th March 1866) and the New Zealand Cross (instituted 10th March 1869); in the case of the last two, no bars were ever awarded.

103. This refers to the P.W.

104. The design had been approved by the Queen, the first orders being placed with the Royal Mint in April 1881, see P.R.O. MINT 16/84.

had held it for 12 months at the date the annuity was awarded. A R.W. of 9th May 1885 continued the award on discharge of the £5 gratuity (£3 for black soldiers) for recipients of the L.S. & G.C. Medal while the P.W. of 15th November 1887 extended these gratuities to recipients of the D.C.M.[105]. Finally, a R.W. of 2nd February 1900 made provision for a £20 gratuity to recipients of the D.C.M. on discharge[106], if they had not been granted an extra pension[107], or an annuity.

Army Order ("A.O.") No. 290 of August 1916 authorised a silver rose emblem for wear on the ribbon, when this was worn alone, to denote the award of a bar to the medal, while by A.O. No. 13 of January 1918 recipients of the D.C.M. (and also the M.M.) were permitted to use the appropriate letters after their names.

By 1920 it was clear that the existing provisions regarding the D.C.M. required amendment and consolidation and accordingly this was done in the R.W. of 6th November 1920[108], as follows:

"GEORGE R.I.

GEORGE THE FIFTH by the Grace of God of the United Kingdom of Great Britain and Ireland, and of the British Dominions beyond the Seas, King, Defender of the Faith, Emperor of India, to all to whom these presents shall come. Greeting:

WHEREAS Her late Majesty Queen Victoria, by a Warrant under her Royal Sign Manual dated 30th September, 1862, did institute and create a silver medal bearing the words 'For Distinguished Conduct in the Field', to be granted to serjeants, corporals and privates of the Regular Army, for individual acts of distinguished conduct in the Field in any part of the world:

AND WHEREAS the rules and ordinances for the governance of the same have been amended from time to time:

AND WHEREAS We deem it expedient that the said Royal Warrant, as well as amendments thereto, which have been heretofore promulgated, or are now to be promulgated, shall be incorporated in a Royal Warrant under Our Sign Manual:

NOW THEREFORE We do hereby declare that the rules and ordinances heretofore in force shall be abrogated, cancelled, and annulled; and We are pleased to make, ordain, and establish the following rules and ordinances in substitution for the same, which shall from henceforth be inviolably observed and kept:

Firstly: – It is ordained that the medal, which shall be of silver, shall be designated 'The Distinguished Conduct Medal', and shall bear on the obverse the Royal Effigy; and on the reverse the words 'For Distinguished Conduct in the Field'.

Secondly: – It is ordained that the Distinguished Conduct Medal may be awarded on the recommendation of a Commander-in-Chief in the Field to Warrant Officers Classes I and II, non-commissioned officers, and men, serving in any of Our Military Forces for distinguished conduct in action in the Field.

Thirdly: – It is ordained that should anyone who has been awarded the Distinguished Conduct Medal be subsequently recommended for such approved act or acts of distinguished conduct in action in the field as would have rendered him eligible for the Medal, had he not already received it, may be awarded a Bar to be attached to the riband by which the Medal is suspended; and that for every additional such act or acts of distinguished conduct an additional Bar may be awarded.

Fourthly: – It is ordained that the Distinguished Conduct Medal shall not confer any individual precedence, but shall entitle the recipient to the addition after his name of the letters 'D.C.M.'.

Fifthly: – It is ordained that the names of those upon whom We may be pleased to confer the Distinguished Conduct Medal shall be published in the *London Gazette*, and that a register thereof shall be kept in the office of our Principal Secretary of State for War.

Sixthly: – It is ordained that the Distinguished Conduct Medal shall be worn before war medals in such order as We may from time to time assign to it, and that it shall be worn on the left breast pendant from a riband of one inch and one quarter in width, which shall be in colour crimson, having in the centre a dark blue stripe of a width equal to the crimson stripes on each side of it.

105. The 1887 P.W. gave the 1885 R.W. as authority for the gratuities. However, the latter only continued the existing L.S. & G.C. gratuities.

106. Extended to include promotion to a commission in the R.W. of 13th January 1902.

107. The word "extra" was omitted from the P.W.s commencing with that of 20th August 1913.

108. See *L.G.*, 19th November 1920.

Seventhly: – It is ordained –

(1) that a Warrant Officer Class I or II, non-commissioned officer, or man, belonging to any of Our Military Forces who has been awarded the Distinguished Conduct Medal shall be paid a gratuity of £20 on promotion to a Commission, on transfer to Our Army Reserve, or on discharge without pension;

(2) that if he is discharged with a pension he shall be eligible for an additional pension of 6d. a day for Europeans, and 3d. a day for non-Europeans, if not already in receipt of such additional pension;

(3) that, if he is awarded a bar or bars to his Distinguished Conduct Medal, and he comes under sub-paragraph (1) above, each bar shall for gratuity purposes be regarded as an original award of the medal. If, however, he comes under sub-paragraph (2) above, no gratuity or further addition to pension shall be issuable in respect of a bar or bars; and

(4) that soldiers of an Allied or Associated Army, of ranks equivalent to those of Our Military Forces specified in the second clause of this Our Royal Warrant, who have been associated in operations with Our Military Forces shall be eligible for the award of the Distinguished Conduct Medal but no pension or gratuity shall accompany such award.

Eighthly: – It is ordained –

(1) that a recipient of the Distinguished Conduct Medal who suffers death by sentence of Court Martial; or, if an officer, is cashiered, dismissed or removed from Our Naval, Military, or Air Forces for misconduct; or if a soldier, sailor, or airman is discharged from Our Naval, Military, or Air Forces with ignominy, or for misconduct, or on account of a conviction by the Civil Power, or for having been sentenced to penal servitude, shall forfeit the Distinguished Conduct Medal (unless otherwise recommended by Our Army Council).

(2) that if a recipient of the Distinguished Conduct Medal is convicted by the Civil Power, or is dealt with under the Probation of Offenders Act, 1907, he shall be liable to a like forfeiture at the discretion of Our Army Council;

(3) that the forfeiture of the Distinguished Conduct Medal shall involve:

(a) the erasure of the recipient's name from the register of persons upon whom the Distinguished Conduct Medal has been conferred; and

(b) the cessation of any pension or gratuity to which the possession of the medal might entitle the recipient, but no such forfeiture shall extend to any sum of money which has already been paid;

(4) that a forfeited Distinguished Conduct Medal and any forfeited annuity, pension or gratuity attaching to it, may be restored to its former holder under regulations approved by Our Army Council:

PROVIDED that We, Our Heirs and Successors, shall at all times have power to restore a forfeited Distinguished Conduct Medal, and with it such pension or gratuity as may have been forfeited;

(5) that a notice of forfeiture and of restoration under this clause shall in every case be published in the *London Gazette*.

Lastly: – We reserve to Ourself, Our Heirs and Successors full power of annulling, altering, abrogating, augmenting, interpreting or dispensing with these Regulations, or any part thereof, by a notification under Our Royal Sign Manual.

Given at Our Court at St. James's this 6th day of November, 1920, in the eleventh year of Our Reign.

By His Majesty's Command.
(signed) W. S. Churchill."

109. In that War a number of awards were made to men of the Army Ordnance Corps and the Army Pay Corps whose opportunity of seeing action, in the nature of things, was limited. The award to First Class Staff Sergeant Major H. A. Yates, Army Pay Department, in *L.G.* 27th September 1901 was cancelled in *L.G.* 11th February 1902 because he had already been awarded the M.S.M.

It is significant that the new Warrant made no reference to any R.W.s before that of 1862 (as, indeed, neither did that Warrant itself) although this is hardly surprising in view of the complications following the institution of the award in 1854. The 1920 R.W. is important, however, in that it provided that the medal was to be awarded for distinguished conduct *in action* in the field. It is by no means certain, for example, that all awards for the South African War of 1899–1902 were made for services in the face of the enemy[109] and no doubt the limiting words of this and subsequent R.W.s were intended to confine the D.C.M. to being an

73

110. Even gallantry does not seem to have been an element in the awards to Company Sergeant Major A. Phipps, Army Service Corps (*L.G.*, 30th June 1915 – "For conspicuous zeal and devotion to duty at all times, and for valuable assistance in connection with the training and discipline of his column.") and to Superintending Clerk C. J. O'Keefe, Royal Engineers (*L.G.*, 21st June 1916 – "For consistent good work in connection with the records of signal units.") A R.W. of 4th October 1916 extended the M.S.M. to all other ranks who had rendered valuable and meritorious service. Awards made under the R.W. did not entitle the recipient to any pecuniary reward. A R.W. of 23rd November 1916 instituted a bar for existing M.S.M. recipients who later performed "an approved act of gallantry, not necessarily on active service, in the performance of military duty or in saving, or attempting to save, the life of an officer or soldier". A R.W. of 3rd January 1917 enlarged the conditions of award of the M.S.M. itself to those who were "duly recommended for the grant in respect of gallant conduct in the performance of military duty otherwise than in action against the enemy, or in saving or attempting to save the life of an officer or soldier, or for devotion to duty in a theatre of war". These conditions lapsed with the R.W. of 7th September 1928 when the M.S.M. reverted to an annuity award. The Albert Medal (for which a very high standard was always required) was, of course, throughout available to both officers and men.

111. The Military Medal was, in any event, restricted to bravery in the field.

112. See P.R.O WO 32/5232 and 32/5400. Despite the restriction to services in action, awards were gazetted on 3rd October 1918 to Sergeant J. Spencer and Corporal A. Bramwell, both of the Royal Welsh Fusiliers, and to Private J. Gray, Cameron Highlanders "in recognition of great devotion to duty and valuable services rendered by them when prisoners of war, during epidemics of Cholera and Typhus Fever, at the Prisoners of War Camp in Gottingen, Germany". The following year the M.S.M. was used to reward similar services, see Chapter 29.

113. Engine Driver G. Pickerill, *L.G.* 19th April 1901; Engine Driver J. Crighton and Fireman C. Sheehan, *L.G.* 31st October 1902; Private E. H. G. Winyard, *L.G.* 27th September 1901 and Supernumerary Officer C. W. Baker, *L.G.* 31st October 1902 (correction in *L.G.* 24th February 1903), both of the St. John Ambulance Brigade.

award only for gallantry in battle. Indeed, during 1915/16 a number of awards had been made for gallant conduct behind the lines in conditions which could not be regarded as under fire[110] and on 1st January 1917 orders were given to all commanders in the field that the D.C.M. (as well as the Distinguished Service Order and the Military Cross[111]) should be restricted, as far as possible, to the "Fighting Services". These were defined as the personnel of brigades, divisions, corps and army troops, together with certain ancillary services associated in battle with these formations. In June/July 1918 the conditions of award of the D.S.O., M.C. and D.C.M. were again considered at a conference at the War Office. The conference recommended that the three decorations concerned should be regarded primarily as distinctions for services in action (including air raids, bombardments etc. producing conditions equivalent to actual combat); and that some emblem should be adopted to distinguish future "immediate" awards of them from awards conferred through the medium of "Honours Gazettes". Only the former recommendation was accepted by the Army Council and it was notified generally on 1st August 1918; in fact, this had little practical result as the instructions of 1st January 1917 had already confined the award of the distinctions concerned largely to services in action[112]. The R.W. also made provision for awards to foreigners. A number of awards had been made during the First World War to interpreters serving with the British Forces in the field, as well as to other foreign soldiers. Except for some awards in 1915 these were not gazetted and no doubt reflected reciprocal arrangements made with the countries concerned, many of whom made their awards available to the British Forces. It is noteworthy that the R.W. made no provision for awards to civilians. What appear to be five such awards were made during the South African War although it is not possible to say if some of the men concerned were enlisted under local or other arrangements[113]. There was at least one similar award in the First World War[114]. The R.W. also made no provision for awards to the Royal Navy and the Royal Air Force, although awards to these services had been made during the First World War[115]. However, it may have been envisaged that the Distinguished Flying Medal and the Air Force Medal (both instituted on 3rd June 1918) would serve the Royal Air Force for the future[116], while similarly the Conspicuous Gallantry Medal and the Distinguished Service Medal would serve the Royal Navy. In the event, however, provision was made many years later for the award of the D.C.M. to members of these Services (see below).

The 1920 R.W. was superseded, in turn, by one dated 5th February 1931[117]. Apart from minor changes in wording, this Warrant provided that the 3d. per day additional pension was payable to Maltese recipients, and widened the forfeiture clause by omitting reference to the various conditions precedent prescribed by the 1920 R.W.; henceforth forfeiture and restoration were to be completely discretionary depending upon a recommendation to the Sovereign by the

114. Driver A. J. Hook, British Red Cross Society (No. 4 Motor Ambulance Convoy), *L.G.* 23rd June 1915. There were also awards to men of the British South Africa Police. Again the question of enlistment arises.

115. In September 1916 the King decided that, for the duration of the War, officers and ratings of the Royal Naval Division and officers and men of the Royal Marines, serving in France, should be eligible for military decorations and medals, see P.R.O. ADM 116/1744.

In consequence, a number of D.C.M.s were awarded to naval ratings, the first being gazetted on 1st January 1917; D.C.M.s were, in fact, already being awarded to men of the Royal Marines for services ashore. Following discussion between the Admiralty and the War Office it was agreed that should an officer or rating already holding a naval decoration be recommended for a further award, the recommendation should be made through naval channels for a bar to it, instead of a military decoration

or medal. For the Royal Air Force the first D.C.M.s were gazetted on 26th June 1918 (Corporal W. Beales and Sergeant E. J. Elton), while for the Royal Flying Corps (which was part of the Army) the first awards were gazetted on 3rd June 1915 (Corporal S. C. Griggs and 2nd Class Air Mechanic J. H. Dollittle).

116. Both awards, however, were restricted to acts "whilst flying".

117. See *L.G.* 20th March 1931.

Fig. A: The Distinguished Conduct Medal, obverse, Victoria issue.

118. Between 1929 and 1931 similar modifications were made regarding other decorations and medals. These followed a recommendation by the Interdepartmental Rewards Committee that all awards for gallantry, except in cases of extreme infamy, should be regarded as irrevocable; hence it was unnecessary to limit the power, as had been done before, by prescribing for particular circumstances.

119. See A.O. No. 144 of August 1939.

120. See A.O. No. 79 of July 1947

121. The first award to the Royal Air Force, ostensibly under the 1931 R.W., had been made to Sergeant D. D. W. Nabarro in *L.G.* 19th January 1943. The 1947 R.W. was evidently to regularise what had already been done. No Naval awards were, in fact, made.

122. See A.O. No. 95 of October 1948.

123. In the case of the Dominions, recommendations could be made by the Officer Commanding Dominion Forces, if the Dominion Government so desired.

124. This had been originally authorised in A.O. No. 290 of August 1916, see above, but until now had not found its place in a R.W.

125. See A.O. No. 67 of October 1961.

126. See A.O. No. 22 of March 1964.

127. On 25th January 1855 Messrs. J. & C. Ratcliff of Coventry contracted to supply the Mint with ribbon at 9½d. per yard, see P.R.O. MINT 21/5 (miscl. 2557).

Secretary of State for War[118]. An amending R.W. of 21st August 1939[119] made provision for the short-lived rank of Warrant Officer Class III while a further amending R.W. of 16th July 1947[120] extended eligibility to naval and air force personnel for distinguished conduct in action on the ground with effect from 4th November 1942[121]. A consolidating Warrant of 11th October 1948[122] re-affirmed the latter provision, and the eligibility of Forces of the Dominions[123], Colonies, Protectorates, Mandated Territories, and the Sudan Defence Force; permitted a silver rose emblem indicating a bar to be worn on the ribbon when it was worn alone[124], and provided that recommendations for forfeiture and restoration could be made, as before, by the Secretary of State for War, or (in future) by the appropriate Minister of State for a Dominion. Unlike the 1920 and 1931 R.W.s, this Warrant did not specify the amounts of the monetary rewards accompanying the medal but merely provided that they should be as prescribed by the Government concerned. An amending R.W. of 30th September 1961[125] took account of certain constitutional changes by making eligible the Forces of "Member Countries of the Commonwealth overseas and the Forces of Our Colonies or Our other Territories or the Territories under Our Protection or Administration . . ." and made corresponding changes in the clauses regarding monetary rewards, and forfeiture and restoration. By a R.W. of 24th March 1964[126] the functions of the Secretary of State for War with regard, *inter alia*, to the D.C.M. were transferred to the Secretary of State for Defence.

To judge by early photographs, no order of wearing for the D.C.M. seems to have been prescribed originally. The earliest mention is in Queen's Regulations for the Army for May 1881 which laid down that it was to be worn immediately after the corresponding campaign medal. A.O. No. 181 of July 1902 gave the D.C.M. precedence of all war medals while A.O. No. 196 of October 1905 showed it following the C.G.M. which, in turn, followed Jubilee etc. medals. A.O. No. 246 of August 1912 showed the C.G.M. following the D.C.M. (See also Appendix 4).

DESCRIPTION

Ribbon Crimson, 1¼ inches wide with a ⅜ inch central blue stripe[127].

Suspension Ornate scroll bar suspender. The claw fitting on the Victorian issue was replaced by a flange and pin on the Edward VII and later issues (including re-issues) which, from about 1926, did not swivel. Recent Elizabeth II issues have a fitting similar to that used, for example, on the Burma Gallantry Medal.

Obverse There are eight obverses as follows:

1. Victorian (Fig.A) This is also common, *inter alia*, to the corresponding L.S. & G.C. medal which was designed and engraved by B. Pistrucci. On certain issues the designer's name appears in the exergue just above the drum, but this seems to be of little significance. A D.C.M. exists which has for obverse Queen Victoria's effigy as it appears on the M.S.M., having no date below the bust. This medal has every appearance of being struck officially and it may have been a trial pattern. However, it is difficult to see why such a striking should have been made since when the initial order was placed with the Royal Mint on 2nd February 1855 (see above) it was made clear that the obverse was to be as for the L.S. & G.C. Medal. The medal referred to here is named in a highly suspect engraved, interrupted and irregular script to Corporal William Finch, Coldstream Guards, who was a Crimean recipient. It could be that the striking is in some way connected with that of the Conspicuous Gallantry Medal of 1874 (q.v.)

2. Edward VII (Fig.B) On 25th September 1902 the King approved that his effigy should appear on the M.S.M. in place of the Queen's head, and on the L.S. & G.C. Medal in place of the trophy of arms. In a letter from the War Office to the Royal Mint of 17th October 1902 the Deputy-Master was informed that the King had further decided that his effigy should be substituted for the trophy (where it appeared) on all medals bearing an

Fig.B: The Distinguished Conduct Medal, obverse, Edward VII issue.

128. See P.R.O. MINT 20/147.

129. The Queen died on 22nd January 1901. No less than 1,333 medals (including two which were subsequently cancelled by the award of bars) were gazetted on 27th September 1901.

130. See the Royal Mint book recording the issue of medals, P.R.O. MINT 16/3.

131. This is the date on which Lord Roberts relinquished command in South Africa. See also the *Schedule of Despatches and Recommendations for South Africa during the Command of Field-Marshal Rt. Hon. F. S. Roberts, K.G., K.P., G.C.B., &c., V.C.* in the Ministry of Defence Library (Central and Army).

132. This probably occurred in the case of Driver N. Harding, 7th Battery R.F.A., whose medal for an act of gallantry on 22nd February 1900 was gazetted on 19th April 1901. According to the *Army and Navy Gazette* of 27th July 1901 the King decorated Harding at Marlborough House two days earlier. It is likely that the medal actually presented had the Victorian obverse although Harding's surviving medal has the Edward VII obverse.

133. Originaly for the Army L.S. & G.C. medal, see *Annual Report of the Deputy Master and Comptroller of the Royal Mint (1911)*, p.15.

134. *Annual Report of the Deputy Master and Comptroller of the Royal Mint (1930)*, p.45.

135. *I.e.,* To Private J. L. Pannell, Queen's Own Royal West Kent Regiment (*L.G.*, 22nd January 1952).

136. *Annual Report of the Deputy Master and Comptroller of the Royal Mint (1953)*, p.33. The medal awarded to Acting Corporal Balbahadur Rana, 2nd Gurkha Rifles, for Malaya (*L.G.*, 8th May 1956) is of this type.

137. See P.R.O. MINT 16/84. The design of the bar was approved by the Queen.

inscription on the reverse, and that the D.C.M., and the Colonial D.C.M., M.S.M. and L.S. & G.C. Medal should be altered accordingly[128]. It is possible that the matter had been under consideration for some time since of the total awards gazetted from the Queen's death[129] to the date of the letter only about 60% had actually been issued from the Royal Mint[130], apparently with the trophy of arms obverse. Whatever the true position is – if, indeed, it is capable of any form of analysis – from surviving medals it is clear that medals with either the Victorian or Edwardian obverse were issued as a result of the *Gazette* of 27th September 1901. However, due to the lack of information regarding the services for which D.C.M.s were awarded in the South African War it is impossible to say whether, in general, the obverse has any significance in relation to the act for which the medal was awarded. A further complication arises in regard to the *Gazette* of 27th September 1901 which says that all the awards notified therein (including appointments to the D.S.O. etc.) are to bear the date 29th November 1900[131] "except where otherwise stated". Although no dates are given for any of the D.C.M.s awarded in that *Gazette* it is known that some were in respect of services rendered after that date. Moreover, cases are known where a lost Victorian issue D.C.M., awarded for the South African War, has been replaced officially by an Edward VII issue[132].

The last D.C.M. awarded before the First World War was gazetted on 21st December 1909 to Colour Sergeant W. King of the Black Watch (attached 1st Battalion, Southern Nigeria Regiment) for services in Southern Nigeria.

3. George V first type (Fig.C) This obverse appears on all awards made between 1914 and 1924. The King's effigy was prepared by Bertram MacKennal, M.V.O., A.R.A.[133].

4. George V second type (Fig. D) No D.C.M.s were awarded between 1925 and 1935 although from about 1930[134] this obverse was used, no doubt initially on official specimens. It was also used on those awarded during the short reign of Edward VIII.

5. George VI first type (Fig. E) This type was issued from about 1939 until several years after the end of the Second World War.

6. George VI second type (Fig.F) By a Royal Proclamation of 22nd June 1948 the King's style and titles were altered. However, the first type continued in issue for some time and, indeed, both types were presented at an investiture in 1952 by H.M. The Queen, each having been gazetted in 1949. An award gazetted in 1952 was of this type[135].

7. Elizabeth II first type (Fig. G) This type dates from about 1953[136].

8. Elizabeth II second type (Fig. H).

Reverse (Fig. I) This has remained constant since the medal was first struck. On issues with the Edward VII obverse, and on those with the George V obverse to about 1917 the rim is stepped, the step being on the inside.

Bars (Fig. J) In 1881 a bar for subsequent acts of gallantry was authorised (see page 71). The bar originally bore, in relief, the date of the act, the first order being placed by the War Office with the Royal Mint in April 1881[137]. Before the First World War only the following awards had been made:

Bar with Victorian D.C.M.	Recipient	Authority and Campaign
SEPTEMBER 1st 1880	Sergeant G. Jacobs, 72nd Foot	Submission to Queen of 20th March 1880; Second Afghan War.

138. A specimen of this bar is known on which the day follows the month.

139. *The History of the Norfolk Regiment* by Petrie (see Bibliography) has a photograph of Crampion wearing the D.C.M. and bar and what appears to be another D.C.M. Crampion was awarded a second D.C.M. in *L.G.*, 27th September 1901, but this was amended to a bar in the *L.G.* quoted above. Both Crampion's D.C.M.s are in the collection of the Royal Norfolk Regiment.

140. Where it is given as a D.C.M; the award was corrected to a bar in Army Order No. 10 of January 1903.

141. See P.R.O. MINT 16/4 (orders for medals 1916–1941). Some of the orders for dated bars in this book (and its predecessor, MINT 16/3) do not relate to known recipients; some are repeated, being required apparently as replacements or specimens; while at least one is for the "African" D.C.M. Some dated bars for the M.M. (see p.225) were ordered on 9th and 28th September 1916 (including two already struck for the D.C.M.) and issues were made on 6th October and 6th November respectively. Further dated bars for the D.C.M. were ordered on 13th and 20th October and 4th November 1916 but, although dies were made as a result of the first of these orders, no issues were made. Due to the conflicting evidence it is impossible to say exactly how many dated bars for the "Imperial" D.C.M. were issued to recipients in the First World War. However, as far as can be ascertained, the total probably was 53 of which two may have been for Sergeant G. Mitchell, Black Watch (see below). Mitchell's first bar was dated "25th SEPTEMBER 1915" and the second, of which there is no record of an order, would (if specially struck) have borne the date "12th APRIL 1916" Sergeant C. Leadbeater, Lincolnshire Regiment (see below) also received two bars but only the first ("13th OCTOBER 1915") was dated. Up to and including *L.G.*, 27th July the award is called a "clasp"; and thereafter a "bar". The laurelled bar is first mentioned in the *Annual Report of the Deputy Master and Comptroller of the Royal Mint* (1917), p.24.

SEPTEMBER 1st 1880	Sergeant R. R. Lauder, 72nd Foot	Submission to Queen of 20th March 1880; Second Afghan War.
28th APRIL 1887	Sergeant T. Healey, Cameron Highlanders	G.O. No. 176 of November 1887; Sudan.
3rd AUGUST 1889[138]	Sergeant T. Healey, Cameron Highlanders	Army Order No. 122 of April 1890; Sudan.
NOVEMBER 21st–24th 1899	Colour Sergeant G.E. Seabright, Royal Marine Artillery	*London Gazette,* 1st May 1900; Sudan.
NOVEMBER 21st–24th 1899	Sergeant F. J. Sears, Royal Marine Artillery	*London Gazette,* 1st May 1900; Sudan.
FEBRUARY 1900	Sergeant Major F. Crookes, Royal Army Medical Corps	*London Gazette,* 19th April 1901; South Africa.
29th MARCH 1900	Private C. Crampion, Norfolk Regiment	*London Gazette,* 31st October 1901; South Africa[139].
JULY 13th 1900	Corporal F. West, Black Watch, late Colour Sergeant, West African Frontier Force	*London Gazette,* 25th April 1902; West Africa[140].
JANUARY 1901	Sergeant G. Smith, Royal Engineers	*London Gazette,* 26th June 1902; South Africa.
Bar with Edward VII D.C.M.		
8th JUNE 1901	Colour Sergeant H.E. Worthing, Rifle Brigade (Acting Sergeant Major, 2nd Mounted Infantry)	*London Gazette,* 11th March 1902; South Africa.
1st JULY 1901	Corporal T. J. May, Royal Engineers	*London Gazette,* 21st April 1903; South Africa.
27th SEPTEMBER 1901	Sergeant Major F.L. Andrews, 9th Lancers	*London Gazette,* 21st April 1903; South Africa.

During the First World War issues of the dated bar continued to be made until 15th September 1916 after which, due to the expense of striking individual bars, the familiar laurelled version (Fig. K) was adopted. The first order for laurelled bars (500) was placed on 4th December 1916[141]. This pattern has remained in use ever since. During the First World War 16 first bars were awarded to earlier D.C.M. recipients; of these 14 were to South African War D.C.M.s and one each to D.C.M.s for Kandia 1898 and Sudan 1898.

Naming This varies with the date of issue and does not necessarily correspond with that current at the time of authorisation of the award. The following notes are merely a general guide, and exceptions can be found in almost every case:

Crimean War and Indian Mutiny awards These are impressed in serif capitals. Regimental numbers are not given and in the cavalry and infantry the ranks of private soldiers are omitted. First names appear in full, or abbreviated, or by initials. The regiment is given sometimes in full but, more frequently, in a wholly or partly abbreviated form. Infantry regiments are usually indicated by the number followed by the abbreviation "REGT.," except where a special designation is appropriate, e.g. "42nd HIGHLANDERS". Occasionally the battalion number is given where the regiment had more than one battalion.

Fig.C: The Distinguished Conduct Medal, obverse, George V issue, first type.

Fig.D: The Distinguished Conduct Medal, obverse, George V issue, second type.

Fig.E: The Distinguished Conduct Medal, obverse, George VI issue, first type.

142. Bombardier A. O. Keating, New Zealand Military Forces, *L.G.*, 22nd July 1943.

Awards made after the Indian Mutiny and before the South African War of 1899–1902 Frequently these follow the style of naming on the associated campaign medal but this is not always so, e.g. for the Abyssinian, Ashanti and Zulu Wars. Some of those for the "Boer" War of 1880–81 (for which no campaign medal was issued) are impressed in sloping capitals. Sometimes, especially with the later issues, the regimental number appears except, apparently, in the cavalry. The rank, including that of private soldiers, is often abbreviated and the first names appear as initials. For numbered infantry regiments the word "FOOT" usually follows the number which is sometimes supplemented by the battalion number where appropriate; after the Cardwell reforms of 1881, an abbreviated regimental designation is given, usually preceded by the battalion number. Most of the medals issued from 1881 onwards had the date of the action added to the edge of the medal (see below).

Awards made from and including the South African War of 1899–1902 to before the First World War These were impressed in plain block capitals, without serifs, although a few issues for South Africa and China were engraved in differing styles. The regimental number almost invariably appears, although it is omitted from some cavalry, corps and colonial awards. The rank is abbreviated in various forms and the first names appear as initials. Where the rank is given wholly in block capitals it is often separated from the first initial by a colon. The regiment is usually abbreviated and the battalion number sometimes appears. For the Royal Artillery, the Battery is not often given on the Victorian issue, except for Militia and Volunteer Artillery, although it sometimes appears on the Edward VII version. Some of the earlier Victorian issues were dated on the edge of the medal (see below).

First World War awards Except for some early issues, these were impressed in plain block capitals with the regimental or equivalent number, rank, initials, surname and unit of the recipient. The battalion number is often given, as are the Royal Artillery Batteries and/or Brigades. The rank and unit are abbreviated. The list of D.C.M.s which appears in the *London Gazette* for 17th December 1914 is followed by a Note requiring all recipients of unnamed medals awarded in that Gazette to send them to the Deputy Director of Ordnance Stores, Woolwich Dockyard, for *engraving*. The medal presented by the King on 5th December 1914 to Corporal A. H. Sutton, R.F.A., appears in the list and is engraved in block capitals with the appropriate particulars, followed by "RICHEBURG. 1914." According to the Royal Mint records, 1,000 D.C.M.s were sent to Woolwich Dockyard between 27th November and 10th December 1914, although it is not known how many were, in fact, engraved rather than impressed. From 1918, where a recipient also had another award, e.g. the M.M., the appropriate letters frequently follow the surname. However this is not always so, especially where the D.C.M. recommendation was submitted before the other award was gazetted.

Later awards Those issued immediately after the First World War conform to the preceding style of naming. Later awards are impressed in smaller block capitals with the Army number, rank, initials, surname and unit of the recipient, usually without battalion number. The rank and unit are abbreviated; sub-units are not given. The naming on some Second World War awards is very faint. Some medals awarded to men serving in or with the Indian Army in the Second World War are engraved in plain block capitals, while one to a New Zealander[142] is impressed with the usual details and the year "1943".

Dated awards The practice of adding the date of the act of gallantry to the edge of the medal, following the particulars of the recipient, seems to have begun with those awards submitted to the Queen from May 1881 and to have ended early in 1901. The operative beginning date appears to have been that of this particular batch of submissions since some D.C.M.s for the Second Afghan War are dated while some, approved before May 1881, are not. Thus the medal given to Bombardier T. Portman, Royal Artillery, for the Naga campaign is dated 22nd November 1879, but the recommendation was not submitted and approved until 30th August 1890. Moreover, two D.C.M.s are in existence which were awarded to Sergeant M. Brooke, Grenadier Guards, for the Sudan campaign of 1898. One is dated while the other, apparently a re-issue, is not. Most, but not all, D.C.M.s are dated in the period under review. Thus undated specimens exist which were awarded to Drummer F. E. Challis, King's Own Scottish Borderers, Colour-

Fig. F: The Distinguished Conduct Medal, obverse, George VI issue, second type.

Fig. G: The Distinguished Conduct Medal, obverse, Elizabeth II issue, first type.

143. In at least two cases medals were dated with the wrong year. Thus on the medal awarded to Conductor S. Reid, Commissariat and Transport Corps (General Order No. 148 of 1887) for services at Hasheen on 20th March 1885 the year is given as 1886, while on that awarded to Lance-Corporal S. Fisher, East Surrey Regiment (*L.G.*, 19th April 1901) for services on the Tugela Heights on 23rd February 1900, the year is given as 1901.

144. For the difficult question of the dating on some First and Second World War awards see "Naming" above.

145. There are fakes named to Private T. Dow, South African Light Horse and Private W. S. Penny, French's Scouts.

146. *E.g.*, the Victorian re-issue to Lance-Corporal W. J. Johnstone, Royal Engineers, has had "Ambigol Wells Sudan" added to the edge of the medal. Another to the same man has instead "DEC. 1885".

147. Under reference WO 102/14.

148. The lists in the Estimates do not differentiate between those annuitants who received the D.C.M., and those who received the M.S.M. There are no lists in the Estimates 1915/19.

Sergeant J. Keeling, Derbyshire Regiment (both for the Tirah Expedition 1897–98) and Colour-Sergeant F. Jenvey, Royal Marine Artillery (for the Sudan campaign 1898), none of which seem to be re-issues. Oddly enough, Jenvey's D.C.M. was not gazetted as it should have been at this time, but appears in Army Order No. 153 of 1899. The dating on the pre-South African War issues, when it does appear, takes the form of the day of the month, followed by the lettered abbreviation of the month, followed by the year in full, e.g. "2nd SEPT: 1898". In some cases, two days or two months are given. The early South African War issues have a numerical form of date, e.g. 2–8–00, although at least one shows the previous form[143]. The last dated awards seem to have been among those gazetted on 19th April 1901, but many gazetted on or before that date are undated[144].

Copies and Fakes Apart from officially made specimens (not all of which have "SPECIMEN" on the edge) at least three types of copy exist. The first is a well made copy of the Edward VII issue which can be detected by the obverse where the details of the hair of the King's beard and of his medals are rougher; the Garter sash ends in a line away from the rim of the medal and does not merge with it; and the further lapel of the coat near the letter "E" does not come down to the rim. There is another variant of this copy on which, in addition to the foregoing features, the tops of the letters to the left of the King's head fade away as they near the rim, particularly "EDVS VII". The lettering on the reverse is out of alignment, especially the "D" in "CONDUCT"; the letter "G" has its horizontal serif extending inwards only instead of both sides; and the overall length of the words is fractionally greater than normal. The suspender and claw are coarser made, and the sides of the claw are flatter. Purves (see Bibliography) illustrates this copy. The naming (in which the faker seems to have favoured Colonial units) looks almost right, but the letters are thinner, rather too widely spaced, and uneven[145].

Copies of the first type George V and George VI issues are also encountered. These also are well made but somewhat larger and thicker than the originals. On the obverse the designer's initials are missing from the base of the bust. The reverse shows the same peculiarities as the Edward VII copy, while the suspender is rather wider and deeper. A few otherwise genuine medals have been re-named unofficially, while some have had unofficial details added to, or partly replacing, the original matter[146]. For recent copies see the Note on p.xx.

VERIFICATION AND CITATIONS

Although it is usually possible to verify an award, difficulties arise with the earlier ones, while citations before the outbreak of the First World War are comparatively rare. However, Abbott (see Bibliography) lists all awards made before the First World War, together with the individual authorities and, where they exist, references to citations contained in official sources. In the following notes, sources for authorities and citations are dealt with together.

Before 1899 There is an official Register of awards made before 1909 and various copies of it are in circulation among collectors. The Register does not list, however, the Crimean awards to the Royal Artillery and Royal Sappers and Miners. It appears to have been compiled from various sources (some of doubtful accuracy) and a few Crimean and Indian Mutiny awards are omitted. The 64 D.C.M.s to the Royal Artillery are to be found in the R.A. Regimental Order of 23rd August 1855 (where the medal is described as being for "Distinguished *Service* in the Field") and these were re-published in Jackson's *Woolwich Journal* of 1st September 1855, p.135. The 16 D.C.M.s awarded to men of the Royal Sappers and Miners are given by Connolly in Vol.2 at pp.403, 443 and 444 and also appear in *The Naval and Military* Gazette of 5th July 1856 at p.421. The names of the men of the cavalry and infantry who received the D.C.M. with gratuity for the Crimea are to be found in the roll of the Long Service and Good Conduct Medal in the Public Record Office[147] which also gives the amount of the gratuity; date of recommendation; and date of issue of the medal. The names of some Crimean annuitants appear among the submissions to the Queen (see *post*), and those of all surviving annuitants in the Army Estimates between those for 1855/56 and 1924/25[148]. Lists of recipients of county infantry regiments, together with some

Fig.H: The Distinguished Conduct Medal, obverse, Elizabeth II issue, second type.

149. In the series MINT 21.

150. In some cases men recommended for the V.C. in the Crimea had already received the D.C.M. and a passing reference to the circumstances of that award may be found among the V.C. recommendations in P.R.O. WO 98/2. This also occurred in the citations for some of those who received the *Al Valore Militare* or the *Medaille Militaire* as well as the D.C.M. for services in the Crimea. The citations for these foreign awards are reproduced, *inter alia,* in Carter's *Medals of the British Army* 1861.

151. In the series WO 97.

152. In the series WO 12. Form 26 of the rolls (introduced in 1860 but not used in India) which lists annuitants, sometimes gives details of the award.

153. R.A. Regimental Orders also show awards authorised between 1873 and 1882 as well as those for the Crimean War mentioned above. The award for Sergeant John Whelan, 7th Battery, 12th Brigade, R.A. for "services rendered before the enemy in Bhootan in 1864–5" was published in R.A. Regimental Order No. 54 of 22nd February 1873, while the D.C.M. Register shows that it was for an action on 30th January 1865 (presumably that at Dewangiri). We can find nothing to account for the delay of eight years between the act and the award. In fact, Whelan was serving with the Bengal Sappers and Miners at the time of the act (see his discharge papers in P.R.O. WO 97/1845). The D.C.M. is inscribed to Royal Artillery but his India General Service Medal to Bengal Sappers and Miners.

154. Under reference WO 146/1. The submission regarding Gunners W. Ball, A. Boddy, W. H. Rabb and Driver E. Lancashire, all of 69th Battery R.F.A., for the action at Itala, Zululand on 26th September 1901 is in WO 32/7473.

155. P.R.O. WO 97/1585.

156. P.R.O. WO 146/1 (10).

citations, are given by Rudolph (see Bibliography) to 1904, but details are not always accurate, some known recipients being omitted and questionable ones added. Other recipients may be found in regimental histories, and in the Royal Mint letter registers in the Public Record Office[149] where orders for medals, often quoting personal particulars of the man are noted. Occasionally a regimental history gives details of the act meriting the medal, but with Crimean awards this is rare since it seems to have been given mostly for general good service in the field rather than an isolated act[150]. Sometimes details may be gleaned from soldiers' documents[151] and from the muster rolls[152] in the Public Record Office.

The first awards published for general information appear in Army General Order No. 61 of June 1885[153]; this practice continued thereafter, "General" Orders becoming "Army" Orders. The first D.C.M.s to be gazetted appear in the *London Gazette* of 15th November 1898, although they are not given in the quarterly index. Occasionally despatches published in the *London Gazette* mention the names of recipients but with little or no detail of the act performed or reference to the medal. The Public Record Office has some of the actual submissions made to the Sovereign[154]. By no means all the actual submissions have survived, and very few citations or descriptions of the act of bravery are given. Most are in manuscript but some of the later ones are typed. A typical submission reads as follows:

Most Humbly submitted to Your Majesty
by His Royal Highness the
Field Marshal Commanding in Chief
with the approval of
The Secretary of State for War

61010
1625
That a Silver Medal for
Distinguished Conduct in the
Field be granted, without Annuity
or Gratuity, to Corporal (now
Sergeant), William Eaton, Royal
Artillery, in recognition of his gallant
conduct at the battles of Abu Klea
and Gubat, during the Sudan Campaign
of 1884–5.

Horse Guards
War Office
6th November 1886

This submission is endorsed "Appd. Victoria R.". Eaton's medal is dated "17 & 19th JAN: 85" on the edge and the award was published in General Order No. 150 of December 1886. Yet a further source is the Regular Soldiers' Documents in the Public Record Office in the series WO 97 (discharges to 1913). Not all the documents of soldiers discharged seem to have been preserved and in any case it is necessary to have some idea of the date of discharge before beginning what might be a long and fruitless search. If the documents can be found, there is usually a brief reference to the medal in the section dealing with special instances of gallant conduct or elsewhere in the documents. Thus those[155] of Colour-Sergeant W. Nolan, 64th Foot, show that he was "severely wounded on 29th July 1857 in side (left arm amputated) on which occasion he distinguished himself in command of a sub-division of grenadiers." The action referred to was near Lucknow and probably gave rise to the award of the D.C.M. with a £15 annuity, the recommendation for which being submitted to the Queen on 17th August 1866[156]. No doubt it was not until then that there was a vacancy in the gratuity fund. Occasionally citations may be found also in the P.R.O. series WO 32, in Code O (AU) (South Africa); Code 50 (M) (recommendations for the V.C.); and Code 50 (S) (D.C.M. 1865–1908).

1900–1909 This period covers from the South African War to the last award made before the First World War. Apparently all awards were gazetted and are to be found in the quarterly indices in the Section headed "Military Promotions" before the sub-section headed "Regiments". The awards are repeated in Army Orders (sometimes with the addition of the regimental number which does not always appear in the Gazette) at a date later than the Gazette entry. Apart from the information derived from regimental histories, few citations are available; however, lists of men mentioned in despatches are gazetted (but not indexed) and some of these give the

Fig.I: The Distinguished Conduct Medal, reverse.

Fig.J: Dated Bar to the Distinguished Conduct Medal.

Fig.K: Laurelled Bar to the Distinguished Conduct Medal.

information upon which the award seems to have been based. But this applies in comparatively few instances and the date of the act mentioned sometimes post-dates the award of the medal. In such cases the "mention" is clearly a second act meriting recognition. Most recipients of the D.C.M. during this period were mentioned in despatches, some on several occasions. There is a supplementary Register covering awards made between 1900 and 1909. It adds little to what is already published but gives details of the disposal of the medal, e.g. "to mother", "SA 8/01", "presented by G.O.C. N.W. District 4/7/03", "died of pneumonia 27/6/01" etc. As far as the Royal Artillery is concerned, the Battery given is not always that in which the man was serving when the act of gallantry was performed. Some Submissions made during this period are available at the Public Record Office (see above).

Later awards During the First World War all medals were gazetted and almost all were accompanied by a citation. Many citations are given in full although later in the War they seem to have been edited since those given in unit histories are often longer than the gazetted versions. There are no citations published for those awards made for services in captivity, or escaping or attempting to escape under the terms of Army Order No. 193 of 1919. The names appear under the main heading of the medal in the "State Intelligence" section of the appropriate index.

Frequently the award and citation are separated and it is then necessary to search in later indices to find the citation. Those for the Easter Rising of 1916 are to be found in the Gazette of 3rd March 1917, although no indication is given as to where the services were performed. In September 1917 the practice began of adding the recipient's home town to the details given, but this ceased after the end of the War – to be resumed in July 1941, although the information even then is not always given. In rare cases during the Second World War the recipient's full address appears.

Awards continued to be indexed under the medal heading until January 1942 when they were consolidated into a comprehensive quarterly nominal list headed "Honours, Decorations and Medals". A medal heading was retained in the "State Intelligence" section which merely lists pages upon which awards are to be found. This last was badly done and references are corrupt or omitted altogether. On occasion, references appear under the wrong medal and this makes the checking of numbers awarded very difficult. The 1942 and later nominal indices, however, seem to be reliable. Almost no citations have appeared since 1922. A few were published after the end of the Second World War but none since 1967.

Many of the original First World War recommendations for men of the R.F.C. and R.A.F. serving in France and Belgium are to be found in the Honours and Awards files in the Public Record Office series AIR 1. Where only the date of award is known it is preferable to search for the recommendation in the files of H.Q. R.F.C./R.A.F. which are arranged according to date; where the formation or unit is known the corresponding files may be consulted first although not all have been preserved.

During the Second World War details of some awards appeared in War Office Press Releases from which extracts were frequently made in local newspapers.

NUMBERS AWARDED

In compiling the following figures recourse has been made to Abbott, Wingate, the official statistics of the First World War (see Bibliography), and the *London Gazette*.

Before the First World War A summary of the awards given by Abbott (excluding bars, for which see above) is as follows:

India and Burma 1845–1908	... 122 (including 2 cancelled; 17 for Mutiny)
Crimea 1854–55	... 826 (including 15 disallowed for 77th Foot, see above, and 3 cancelled)
China 1860	2
New Zealand 1863–65	22
British Honduras 1872	3
Africa 1873–1908	114 (excluding Egypt, South Africa and the Sudan)
South Africa 1878–79	16
Afghanistan 1878–80	61
South Africa 1880–81	20
Egypt and the Sudan 1882–89 ...	135 (including 1 cancelled)

Crete 1898	6	
The Sudan 1898–99	87	
South Africa 1899–1902	2096 (including 4 cancelled and some posthumous)	
China 1900	13	
The Sudan (Ajembio) 1903	1	
Aden 1903–04	1	
Tibet 1903–04	4	
Total	3529 (including 25 disallowed/cancelled; excluding 13 bars to 12 recipients	

First World War The official statistics cover the period from August 1914 to May 1920 and thus include not only the campaigns against the Central Powers during the War proper but also some later campaigns, e.g. that in Russia after 1918.

The figures given are:

	Services in the Field	Services in connection with the War
D.C.M.	24,591	29
– 1st bars	472	—
– 2nd bars	9	—

Those for services in connection with the War include awards for the Easter Rising, air raids and coastal bombardments. These figures are probably suspect in that 10 two-bar medals were in fact gazetted (see below) and that the first bar of the second bar awards are included in the figure for the former. Moreover, for the period 1914–1918 Wingate gives the total as 24,571 medals with 469 first bars and 10 second bars; since these figures do not apparently cover the same period they are difficult to reconcile, but the overall picture is not substantially affected.

The Royal Navy received 72 D.C.M.s (including one with one bar[157] and one with two) for services ashore; the Royal Flying Corps 93; the Australian Flying Corps 1; and the Royal Air Force 5 (all in 1918) and 1 first bar[158].

The recipients of two-bar medals, together with the date of the *London Gazette* awarding the second bar, are as follows:

Company Sergeant Major A. Bonsor	2/2nd London Regiment	18th February 1919
Petty Officer J. G. Cowie, M.M.	Hood Battalion, Royal Naval Volunteer Reserve	18th February 1919
Company Sergeant Major J. P. Dobson, M.M.	9th Battalion, York and Lancaster Regiment	17th April 1919
Lance-Sergeant J. J. Hickman, M.M.	2nd Battalion, Middlesex Regiment	18th February 1919
Sergeant C. Leadbeater	Lincolnshire Regiment	17th September 1917
Sergeant W. Logan	Black Watch	1st May 1918
Sergeant G. Mitchell	Black Watch	20th October 1916
Company Sergeant Major S. Phillips	1st Battalion, Worcestershire Regiment	12th March 1919
Sergeant G. H. Soles	72nd Battalion, Canadian Infantry	18th February 1919
Company Sergeant Major T. E. Woodward	2nd Battalion, Royal Scots Fusiliers	12th March 1919

These, together with that awarded to Sergeant T. Healey in 1890 (see above), total the 11 two-bar medals awarded. Some unofficial lists also give Gunner F. Vercoe, R.G.A. His first bar was gazetted on 30th March 1916 (it was dated "14th FEBRUARY 1916") but a second bar cannot be found in the Gazette indices, and his actual D.C.M. has only one bar.

157. Petty Officer W. Punton, R.N.V.R.; *L.G.*, 28th March 1918.
158. Acting Sergeant F. Johnson, R.A.F.; *L.G.*, 3rd September 1918.

We have traced a number of honorary awards to foreigners for the First World War which were sponsored by the War Office. Some were published in the *London Gazette* of 16th November 1915; thereafter they appeared in printed War Office Lists dated between May 1916 and 4th November 1920. The first four Lists were unnumbered. The remainder were numbered from 3 to 68 of which we have been unable to find nos. 23, 42, 46, 47 and 52. The following summary is therefore incomplete to the extent of any in the missing lists:

Belgium	263	(and 1 first bar)
Czechoslovakia ...	290	
France	1563	(154 in *L.G.*, 16th November 1915)
Greece	36	
Italy	879	
Japan	50	
Montenegro	6	
Portugal	2	
Roumania	132	
Russia	2	
Serbia	97	
USA	117	
Total	3437	

1920–1939 From June 1920 to December 1939 the following 46 D.C.M.s were gazetted:

1920	14	(12 late awards; 1 Mesopotamia; 1 Somaliland)
1921	7	(4 Mesopotamia; 3 North West Frontier)
1922	2	(late awards)
1923	2	(Malabar)
1924	1	(Waziristan)
1936	14	(1 North West Frontier; 13 Palestine)
1937	4	(2 North West Frontier; 2 Waziristan)
1939	2	(North West Frontier and Palestine)

In addition one bar for Mesopotamia was gazetted in 1921. The late awards all seem to have been for the First World War although the Gazette details are not always clear.

Second World War Wingate gives 1,879 D.C.M.s and 19 first bars as being awarded between 1939 and 1945. The Gazette indices, however, reveal only nine first bar awards as follows:

		London Gazette for Bar
Sergeant E. Batchelor	New Zealand Military Forces	21st June 1945
Acting Colour Sergeant G. M. Boyle	Lincolnshire Regiment	22nd June 1944
Company Sergeant Major R. Drapeau	Canadian Infantry Corps	16th November 1944
Lance-Corporal E. B. Hazle	Essex Regiment	3rd August 1944
Sergeant H. F. Hutchinson	Royal Armoured Corps (Hussars)	19th March 1942
Company Sergeant Major P. MacPhillips	Argyll and Sutherland Highlanders	25th April 1941
Warrant Officer 1st Class A. J. Medley	4th Queen's Own Hussars	9th August 1945
Sergeant A.S. Obbard, M.M.	Queen's Own Royal West Kent Regiment	10th May 1945
Regimental Sergeant Major C. J. Rose	Essex Regiment	24th August 1944

All awards gazetted in 1946 appear to be for the Second World War except for one which was for South East Asia. However, in a number of cases the *Gazette* announcement contains no identifying details. Seven D.C.M.s were awarded to men of the Royal Air Force, two to the Royal Australian Air Force and one to the Royal Canadian Air Force; there was none to the Royal Navy. At least two awards were made for services at sea, in each case during the evacuation from Dunkirk. These were to Sergeant J. T. Carr, Royal Artillery, for gallantry when the destroyer HMS *Grafton* was torpedoed[159], and to Corporal L. W. Goddard, Royal Engineers, for the defence of the anti-aircraft ship HMS *Crested Eagle*[160].

107 honorary awards, which were not gazetted, were made as follows:

Belgian Army	11	
Free French Forces	20	
Netherlands Army ...	1	
Norwegian Army ...	9	
Polish Forces	13	(army 12; air force 1)
United States Army	53	

1947–1979 The 153 D.C.M.s gazetted during this period are as follows:

Theatre	London Gazette	Medals
Arabian Peninsula	1959–1976	7
Borneo	1965–1966	4
Kenya	1955	1
Korea	1951–1953	24
Late awards	1947	12
Malaya	1949–1958	49
Near East	1957	1
Northern Ireland	1972–1978	10
Vietnam	1965–1972	45

Of these, 49 were gazetted between 1949 and 1952 inclusive, and 104 between 1953 and 1979. In addition to the above, first bars were awarded as follows:

		London Gazette for Bar
Colour Sergeant Bhaktabahadur Thapa	6th Gurkha Rifles	31st August 1951 (Malaya)
Corporal L. Major	*Royal 22e Regiment* (Canada)	12th February 1952 (Korea)
Sergeant W. J. Rowlinson	Royal Australian Regiment	4th March 1952 (Korea)
Warrant Officer 1st Class E. J. Morrison	Royal Australian Infantry	27th July 1965 (Vietnam)

As with those gazetted during the Second World War, the *Gazette* indices are sometimes defective and hence it is difficult to be certain that all awards have been traced.

ILLUSTRATIVE AWARD

Gunner William Moorhead was awarded the D.C.M. for the action at Ulundi in the Zulu War. In addition, he received the South African Medal with bar "1879". The D.C.M. is named in thin, serif, sloping capital letters "GUNNER, W. MOORHEAD, R.A.", the actual letters being blacked in. The recommendation for the D.C.M., which is now preserved in the Royal Artillery Museum, was submitted to the Queen on 1st June 1880, the formal parts of the text being similar to the submission for Eaton, see above. Because the submission was made before May 1881 the medal is not dated on the edge. The award was published in R.A. Regimental Order No. 68 of 1880 which reads as follows:

> "Her Majesty the Queen has been pleased to approve, on the recommendation of His Royal Highness the Field-Marshal Commanding in Chief, of the grant of a silver medal for distinguished service in the field (without annuity or gratuity) to No. 2348 Gunner William Moorhead, No. 10 Battery, 7th Brigade, Royal Artillery, as a reward for his distinguished conduct at the action of Ulundi, Zululand, on 4th July 1879."

Moorhead's attestation and discharge papers are preserved in the Public Record Office[161] which show that he enlisted on 4th October 1876 (having previously

159. *L.G.*, 27th August 1940.
160. *L.G.*, 26th September 1940. At the time of the evacuation Goddard was serving in the Royal Engineers but he transferred to the Royal Artillery before his award was gazetted. His medal is named as Bombardier, Royal Artillery.
161. P.R.O. WO 97/3495.

served in the Cumberland Militia) and was discharged as medically unfit on 4th September 1883. He served in Natal from 13th March to 15th October 1879 and was severely wounded by a rifle bullet in the right foot at Ulundi[162]. In addition to listing the two medals awarded, under "Special instances of gallant conduct" the following is recorded – "Though severely wounded, refusing to go to Fd. Hospl. and continuing to assist in preparing Cartridges under fire for $\frac{1}{2}$ hour at action of Ulundi". Further reference to Moorhead appears in *The Illustrated London News* of 23rd August 1879[163] which, in turn, quotes a letter published in *The Natal Witness*. Part of that letter reads:

> "The artillery were particularly conspicuous for their cool conduct. At one moment an artilleryman fell dead over the limber of a gun, but no pause was made to pick him up. A gunner of the name of Moorhead attracted special notice. He was wounded in the leg, and rendered incapable of remaining at his gun. He was, however, determined not to remain idle, for when safe inside the square he crawled to where the drums of the Gatling battery were being filled with cartridges, and insisted on helping the sergeant to charge them. The Gatlings, by-the-way, were disappointing, having to cease firing six times during the action."

Moorhead's Battery had come to South Africa from Mauritius and was equipped with Gatling guns. The jamming mentioned above was caused by faulty ammunition.

162. He is reported as severely wounded in *L.G.*, 21st August 1879, p.5,104.
163. At p.182.

Chapter 13

The Distinguished Conduct Medal (Dominion and Colonial Issues)

Fig. A: The Distinguished Conduct Medal (Canada), reverse.

ORIGIN AND DEVELOPMENT

In 1894 a Royal Warrant made provision, *inter alia*, for the award of the D.C.M. to men of Dominion and Colonial Forces in the following terms:

> "VICTORIA R.I.
>
> Whereas it is Our desire to grant Medals for Meritorious Service, for Distinguished Conduct, and for Long Service, under Regulations similar, as far as circumstances permit, to those now existing for Our Regular Forces, to Warrant Officers, Non-commissioned Officers and Men of Our Indian Forces and of Our Colonial Forces.
>
> It is hereby ordained that such Medals shall be issued to Our said Indian and Colonial Forces, under such Regulations as may from time to time be recommended by the Governor-General of India, the Governor-General of the Dominion of Canada, or the Governors of the other Colonies of Our Empire, and approved by Our Secretary of State.
>
> Given at Our Court at Balmoral, this 24th day of May, 1894, in the 57th year of Our Reign.
>
> By Her Majesty's Command,
> H. Campbell Bannerman."

Hitherto the Imperial issue had been used for all D.C.M. awards[1] and, although the wording of the Warrant is vague, the intention seems to have been that special D.C.M.s should be instituted for certain overseas possessions. Indeed, while the matter is not entirely free from doubt, such D.C.M.s may have been intended for local troops operating under a local commander within the territory concerned. The following year the original Warrant was superseded by one dated 31st May. This repeated the wording of the first Warrant but extended the awards to men "of forces raised for Our Service in countries under Our Protection". Apart from those to men of the native African regiments, the only D.C.M. awards which seem to have been made under the Warrants were by the Government of Natal and possibly by that of Canada; but in any case the last two issues had ceased by the outbreak of the First World War[2]. The vast majority of awards to Overseas Contingents in the South African War were of the Imperial issue.

Canada In 1894 and 1895 copies of the Royal Warrants quoted above were sent to the Governor-General. In 1897 the proposed regulations regarding the Canadian Long Service and Good Conduct Medal were approved by the British Government and at the same time specimens of the Canadian D.C.M. and M.S.M. were sent to Canada. They were then approved for issue to the Canadian Permanent Forces[3]. Between 1900 and 1902 there was an exchange of correspondence between the two Governments regarding the regulations for all three medals, the regulations themselves being published in Canadian General Order No. 104 of October 1902. In so far as the D.C.M. is concerned, it was to be awarded as follows:

> "Upon the special recommendation of the Officer Commanding the Militia a silver medal for "Distinguished Conduct in the Field" may be granted to a soldier who has performed service of a distinctly gallant and distinguished nature. Bars may be added on account of further distinguished conduct."

1. *E.g.*, to Trooper R. Brown, Frontier Light Horse (Zulu War, 1879), Native Officer Dambornu, Gold Coast Hausa Constabulary (West Africa, 1888), and many others.

2. In addition, however, specimens were struck for New South Wales, New Zealand, Queensland and Tasmania, and are quoted in the Royal Mint Museum Catalogue (see Bibliography) although we have been unable to find reference to them in the Royal Mint Reports. Effect to the Royal Warrants quoted above was given, for example, in the *New Zealand Gazette* (Notice No. 30 of 1898) but the records show that no awards of the New Zealand D.C.M. were made. In connection with the Warrants it is important to notice that "local" Meritorious Service and Long Service Medals were authorised and of which many variants exist.

3. Canadian Privy Council Minute No. 285.K. of 29th August 1897.

Fig.B: The Distinguished Conduct Medal (Natal), reverse.

4. *Natal Government Gazette.* Notice No.570 of October 1897.

5. *Ibid.* Notice No.583 of October 1908.

6. *Union of South Africa Government Gazette Extraordinary,* No. 596 of October 1914.

7. See P.R.O. CO 534/4 and WO 32/9009.

8. *E.g.,* to Bugler Moma, 1st Battalion, W.A.F.F., and others in *L.G.,* 26th April 1901, p.2,855, and Sergeant Ndermani, 2nd Battalion, K.A.R., and others in *L.G.,* 7th August 1903, p.4,982.

9. *I.e.,* in *L.G.,* 25th August 1905, p.5,831, for operations in North and South Nigeria, 1903–04. According to Haywood and Clarke at p.74, the D.C.M. awarded to Private Musa Katsena, Northern Nigeria Regiment, was a W.A.F.F. issue. However, *L.G.,* 24th January 1905, p.573, where the award appears, does not specify the type of medal. No mention of the first striking of the W.A.F.F. D.C.M. appears in the Royal Mint Reports.

10. There was an Imperial issue to Private Mandelumba, 2nd Battalion, K.A.R., in *L.G.,* 17th February 1904, p.5,776.

11. *L.G.,* 11th February 1941, p.812.

12. As the 7th Battalion, K.A.R., these three men would have been eligible for the K.A.R. D.C.M.

13. No special reverse was struck for this Regiment.

14. *L.G.,* 21st July 1942, p.3,191.

15. *L.G.s,* 24th April 1936, p.1,621, and 22nd April 1941, p.2,286.

16. *L.G.,* 11th February 1947, p.697.

17. Unlike the ribbons of the Colonial Meritorious Service, and Long Service and Good Conduct Medals.

18. It was approved in 1903 for the W.A.F.F., see P.R.O. CO 445/16, and in 1906 for the K.A.R., see P.R.O. CO 534/4.

19. *Annual Report of the Deputy Master and Comptroller of the Royal Mint (1930),* p.45.

20. *Ibid (1907),* p.53. See also P.R.O. CO 534/4.

The Order also made provision for the submission of recommendations, forfeiture and restoration, and the replacement of lost medals; unlike the 1908 Natal Regulations mentioned below, no special reverse was quoted nor were any financial provisions included. The Meritorious Service, and Long Service and Good Conduct Medals were to be for regular soldiers only. So far we have traced only one Canadian D.C.M. with the special reverse; this was awarded for the South African War (see below).

Natal The first Regulations were published in 1897[4] and also made provision for the Meritorious Service, and Long Service and Good Conduct Medals. The Regulations dealt with eligibility, submission of recommendations, forfeiture and restoration, gratuities, etc. Only the Meritorious Service, and Long Service and Good Conduct Medals were to have the name of the Colony on the reverse. Amended Regulations were published in 1908[5], the conditions for the award of the D.C.M. following the wording of the Canadian Regulations quoted above. The name of the Colony was to appear on the reverse of all three medals. A Natal D.C.M. for the South African War exists, and Stuart (see Bibliography) mentions nine for the Zulu Rebellion of 1906 (see below). Consolidated Regulations for the Union Defence Forces were published in 1914[6].

King's African Rifles and (Royal) West African Frontier Force In 1902 Regulations were approved regarding the award of the W.A.F.F. D.C.M., and the following year similar Regulations were approved regarding that of the K.A.R.[7] Prior to this the Imperial version had been issued to African soldiers[8]. Mention of the African D.C.M. (as it became to be called) was made in both the K.A.R. and the W.A.F.F. Provisional Regulations of 1905. The first W.A.F.F. D.C.M.s for which we have been able to find gazettes appear in 1906[9], although evidence in records at the Ministry of Defence (Army Department), see "Numbers Awarded" below, suggests that some were issued in 1903. The first K.A.R. D.C.M.s were awarded in 1907[10] to Chief Native Officer Mbaruk Effendi and Native Officer Mursal Effendi Mahrus, both of the 3rd Battalion.

A large number of awards to both corps was made during the First World War. During the Second World War 11 African D.C.M.s were gazetted in 1941[11] (four to the K.A.R., three to the Somaliland Camel Corps[12] and four to the Northern Rhodesia Regiment[13]), but the following year the same awards were cancelled by the substitution of the Imperial D.C.M.[14] This followed a recommendation by the Honours and Awards Committee that the Imperial D.C.M. should be awarded to the Regiments concerned. King George VI approved this proposal on 18th June 1942. In 1936[15] and 1941[15] the lists published in the *London Gazette* showed the R.W.A.F.F. and K.A.R. D.C.M.s as following the D.S.M. From 1947[16] they are shown following the Edward Medal (see also Appendix 4).

DESCRIPTION

Ribbon According to the Royal Mint Museum Catalogue, except for the K.A.R. and W.A.F.F., the ribbon was as for the Imperial issue[17]. For the K.A.R. and W.A.F.F. it was blue, 1¼ inches wide, with a ³⁄₁₆ inch central light green stripe flanked on either side with similar stripes of maroon[18].

Suspension As for the corresponding Imperial issue.

Obverse As for the corresponding Imperial issue. George V "crowned head" issues for the K.A.R. and R.W.A.F.F. were struck in 1930[19], apparently as specimens, since no awards were made during the currency of this type of obverse.

Reverse
    Canada (Fig.A).
    Natal (Fig.B).
    King's African Rifles (Fig.C) The die for this reverse was made in 1907[20].
    (Royal) West African Frontier Force (Fig.D) The design of this reverse was

21. See P.R.O. CO 445/16.

22. A new die was made, see the *Annual Report of the Deputy Master and Comptroller of the Royal Mint (1928)*, pp.17, 34 and 36.

23. *Annual Report of the Deputy Master and Comptroller of the Royal Mint (1909)*, p.41.

24. *E.g.*, New Zealand (trophy of arms obverse) and Natal (Edward VII obverse) in Messrs. Glendining's sale of 15th June 1925.

25. The Regulations for the Cape D.C.M., M.S.M. and L.S. & G.C. Medals were published in the *Cape Government Gazette* as Notice No.926 of September 1896. Amended Regulations were published in Notice No.792 of June 1906. The Regulations did not mention a special reverse for any of the three medals.

26. *I.e.*, that to Farrier C.D. Mitchell, Transvaal Mounted Rifles.

27. At p.573; D.C.M. awarded to Private Musa Katsena, 1st Battalion, Northern Nigeria Regiment. Haywood and Clarke, however, give this as an African D.C.M.

28. At p.9,673; seven awards to the Southern Nigeria Regiment.

29. And are indexed as such, see *L.G.* 11th February 1941, p.812.

30. *L.G.*, 21st July 1942, p.3,191.

31. D.C.M.s to Sergeant George Williams, Corporal Matukuta and Private Mulandi Wa Mwibi, all of the K.A.R., and to Private Helasi Sempa of the Uganda Police Battalion; bar to C.S.M. Belo Akure, W.A.F.F.

32. Messrs. Glendining's sales of 16th December 1938 and 30th January 1939.

33. *L.G.*, 27th September 1901, and Canadian Militia Order No.248 of 1901. Callaghan also appears in the War Office D.C.M. Register.

approved in 1903[21]. The designation "Royal" was conferred in 1928[22] but no actual awards with this type of reverse seem to have been made. There is a George V "crowned head" specimen of this medal on which the ornaments at the foot of the reverse conform to the curve of the edge of the medal.

Naming

Canada and Natal. No details have been found.

King's African Rifles and (Royal) West African Frontier Force. All issues so far seen are impressed in plain capital letters with the rank, full native names and unit of the recipient. The regimental or equivalent number sometimes appears, and the rank and unit are abbreviated.

Bars The Royal Mint Museum Catalogue mentions a bar "N. NIGERIA 1908" which was awarded to Sergeant Jatto (or Yatto) Yola, Northern Nigeria Regiment[23] (Fig.D). The only other bar of this type was dated "4th NOVEMBER 1914" and awarded to Company Sergeant Major Belo Akure, 2nd Nigeria Regiment, in *The Nigeria Gazette* of 25th November 1915. The remaining bars awarded were of the laurelled type (Fig.E).

Copies and Fakes No copies have been found although a number of specimens have appeared on the market[24]. A Cape of Good Hope issue on which the word "SPECIMEN" still appears, although partly erased, on the edge, is crudely impressed "C. CACTUM. P.O. H.M.S. POWERFUL"[25].

VERIFICATIONS AND CITATIONS

Canada and Natal The South African War awards appear in the *London Gazette* without differentiation from the Imperial issue; Stirling (see Bibliography) lists these awards, as well as providing other useful details, e.g. citations appearing among the mentions in despatches. The Natal awards for the Zulu Rebellion of 1906 appear in the *Natal Government Gazettes* of 26th June 1906 and 10th September 1907. Stuart gives details in the text of all these awards save one[26].

King's African Rifles and (Royal) West African Frontier Force Until 1909 all awards appear in the *London Gazette* and are indexed in the Section headed "Military Promotions" before the sub-section headed "Regiments". Until and including *L.G.*, 24th January 1905[27], the wording of the Gazette notices suggests that awards were of the Imperial issue; the awards are repeated in Army Orders. Thereafter until and including *L.G.*, 21st December 1909[28] when, with one exception, the last notices appear, the W.A.F.F. D.C.M. alone is specified, there being none to the K.A.R. No citations are given although the campaign is noted. However, details may sometimes be found in the published despatches from commanders in the field. These awards are not repeated in Army Orders. Some awards appear, with or without citations, in local Gazettes e.g. *The Nigeria Gazette, The Nyasaland Government Gazette, The Sierra Leone Gazette, The Uganda Gazette* etc. In 1941 eleven African D.C.M.s were gazetted[29], but the following year, the African D.C.M. having been abolished, these awards were cancelled[30] by the substitution of the Imperial D.C.M. Moyse-Bartlett mentions a few awards in the text while Haywood and Clarke give rather more. However, neither give the full tally, and those given by Haywood and Clarke are not indexed. Downes (see Bibliography) gives a number of W.A.F.F. citations for the campaign in German East Africa. Many First World War awards appear, usually without citations, in General Routine Orders by the Commander-in-Chief, East African Force. *The Times* of 11th May 1917, at p.3, on what seems to be an isolated occasion, gives citations for five typical awards[31], but does not give the source.

NUMBERS AWARDED

Canada A Canadian D.C.M. with "trophy of arms" obverse, named to Corporal T. Callaghan, 2nd Canadian Mounted Rifles, appeared twice at auction in London[32]. This was for services in the South African War[33] but without the

Queen's and King's South Africa medals to which Callaghan was also entitled. Callaghan was discharged on 30th December 1900, being then commissioned into Howard's Scouts[34]. This D.C.M. may have been one of a batch with the special reverse which was used up before recourse was made to the Imperial issue; or it may have been a local replacement, or even a fraudulently named specimen. Irwin (see Bibliography) states that the Canadian D.C.M. was only issued as a specimen. Sixteen D.C.M.s were awarded to men of the Canadian Forces for services in the South African War[35].

Natal A Natal D.C.M. with the "trophy of arms" obverse, named to Trooper F. C. Farmer, Natal Carbineers, appeared once at auction in London[36]. This was also for services in the South African War[37] but no campaign medals accompanied it. Its origin may lie in circumstances similar to those suggested for Callaghan, mentioned above. Stuart (see Bibliography) gives nine for the Zulu Rebellion of 1906, as follows[38].

Squadron Sergeant Major W. Calverley	Zululand Mounted Rifles
Trooper W. Deeley	Zululand Mounted Rifles
Trooper O. L. M. Folker	Natal Police
Sergeant C. W. Guest	Natal Police
Trooper W. C. Holmes	Royston's Horse
Trooper W. Johnson	Zululand Mounted Rifles
Farrier Sergeant C. D. Mitchell	Transvaal Mounted Rifles
Trooper G. W. Oliver	Zululand Mounted Rifles
Sergeant S. Titlestad	Zululand Mounted Rifles

King's African Rifles From information provided by the Ministry of Defence (Army Department) we calculate that approximately 195 medals and eight first bars were awarded between 1906 and 1925. Two of these medals were awarded in 1906 (see above), the remainder being awarded after 1911, for the most part during the First World War. The decision in 1942 to replace the African D.C.M. by the Imperial D.C.M. has been referred to above.

(Royal) West African Frontier Force According to the Royal Mint Report of 1909[39] a bar was awarded to Sergeant Jatto (or Yatto) Yola, Northern Nigeria Regiment[40]. From the Ministry of Defence information mentioned above we calculate that approximately 57 medals and one first bar (Jatto Yola) were awarded between 1903 and 1910, while a further 167 medals, seven first bars, and one second bar[41], were awarded between 1911 and 1924. The majority of the latter were for the First World War. Haywood and Clarke give 13 D.C.M.s for the Second World War which, however, would all have been of the Imperial issue in conformity with the 1942 decision mentioned above.

ILLUSTRATIVE AWARD

Corporal Stima, 1st King's African Rifles, was awarded the African D.C.M.[42] in the *Nyasaland Government Gazette* of 29th April 1916, at p.86, where his citation appears as follows:

> "For conspicuous gallantry and tenacity at the action of Kasoa on 9th September, 1914, in handling a Maxim after Mr. Merriman, N.V.R., who was in charge, had been mortally wounded."

Stima received a bar to his D.C.M.[43] in the *Nyasaland Government Gazette* of 30th June 1917, at p.160, where his citation appears as follows:

> "These two men[44] at Tandala on the 19th February, 1917, were the sole survivors of two Maxim teams with a Company of K.A.R. which was attacked by four hundred enemy. They did their utmost to destroy the guns under heavy rifle and maxim fire. Cpl. Stima eventually brought in the lock and feed-block of one gun, Pte. Saiti being wounded in the head. Their action was a magnificent example of devotion to duty without consideration of personal danger and was beyond all praise."

34. Canadian Militia Order No.15 of 1901.

35. See the *Journal of the Orders and Medals Research Society,* December 1967, note 15; March 1968, note 19; and June 1968, p.26.

36. Messrs. Glendining's sale of 12th October 1949.

37. *L.G.,* 19th April 1901. It was for "conspicuous gallantry in rescuing Lieutenant Mackay, who was wounded, under heavy fire" at Colenso; see General Buller's Despatch of 30th March 1900, published in *L.G.,* 8th February 1901.

38. None of these names appear in the War Office D.C.M. Register.

39. *Annual Report of the Deputy Master and Comptroller of the Royal Mint (1909),* p.41.

40. His first award appears in *L.G.,* 25th August 1905, p.5,831, as a W.A.F.F. issue, being repeated in the *Northern Nigeria Gazette* of 31st October 1905, p.107. His second award appears as another medal in the latter Gazette of 31st March 1909, p.53.

41. To Company Sergeant Major Samanu (or Sumanu), 3rd Nigeria Regiment in G.R.O. No.549 of 17th June 1918, and the *Nigeria Gazette* of 10th October 1918, p.395.

42. The award arose from a recommendation contained in a despatch by the Governor-General of Nyasaland regarding the operations of the Nyasaland Field Force. The despatch was published in *L.G.,* 3rd August 1916, the recommendation appearing at p.7,653. The recommendation, in which Stima's rank is given as lance-corporal, is similar to the citation quoted above except that Merriman's name is not given, and a further sentence is added – "The latter (i.e. Merriman) specially requested that this act of gallantry should be rewarded".

43. The award also appeared, without citation, in East African Force General Routine Order No.536 of 20th May 1917.

44. *I.e.,* Stima, whose rank is given as lance-corporal, and Private Saiti, who was awarded the K.A.R. D.C.M. in the same announcement.

Moyse-Bartlett deals with the action near Tandala thus:

> "When daylight came Wintgens[45] brought his machine guns into play, and concentrated his attack on Masters'[46] two machine guns, which were posted on a small hill covering the right flank. By mid-afternoon this hill had fallen to a bayonet charge, and half the K.A.R. had become casualties. Though unable to bring away the guns, Corporal Stima and Private Saidi (*sic*), the sole survivors of the detachment, remained to disable them before withdrawing."

In addition to the above awards, Stima was twice mentioned in despatches[47]. His D.C.M. is of the normal K.A.R. issue, the bar being of the laurelled type. The medal is impressed in the usual capital letters with his number, rank (given as corporal), name, battalion and regiment. Stima also received the Ashanti War Medal 1900; the Africa General Service Medal with bars Somaliland 1902–04, Jidballi, and Nyasaland 1915; the 1914/15 Star; the British War and Victory Medals; and the K.A.R. Long Service and Good Conduct Medal of the George V "crowned head" issue[48]. Varying spellings of his name appear on the medals.

45. Captain (Hauptmann) Wintgens, the German force commander.

46. Captain A. C. Masters, commanding a half-company of 1st K.A.R., sent in advance of a column reinforcing Tandala.

47. *L.G.s,* 7th March 1918, p.2,888 (lance-corporal) and 5th June 1919, p.7,261 (sergeant).

48. The award appeared in the *Nyasaland Government Gazette* of 31st August 1932, p.152. The crowned head issue was introduced in 1930, see the *Annual Report of the Deputy Master and Comptroller of the Royal Mint (1930),* p.41.

Fig.D: The Distinguished Conduct Medal (West African Frontier Force), reverse, with dated bar.

Fig.E: Laurelled Bar to the Distinguished Conduct Medal (King's African Rifles and West African Frontier Force).

Chapter 14

The Distinguished Flying Cross

ORIGIN AND DEVELOPMENT

Shortly before the formation of the Royal Air Force on 1st April 1918 a committee was constituted to advise the King whether a special decoration was needed for the new Service, and whether there should be a uniform colour for the ribbon of the Victoria Cross in substitution for the different ribbons (navy, blue; army, red) then worn with that decoration. The committee consisted of:

Colonel Sir Douglas Dawson, Comptroller, Lord Chamberlain's Department (Chairman),
Rear-Admiral A. F. Everett, Naval Secretary to the First Sea Lord,
Lieutenant-General Sir Francis Davies, Military Secretary to the Secretary of State for War,
Rear-Admiral Mark (E.F.) Kerr, representing the Service about to be formed[1],
H. Farnham Burke, Norroy King of Arms.

In a draft report[2], which was approved by the Board of Admiralty on 21st March 1918, the committee recommended that there should be only one colour for the V.C. ribbon and that it should be red; that a decoration should be instituted for officers and warrant officers of the air force, corresponding to the Distinguished Service Cross and to the Military Cross in the other two Services; and that the naval Conspicuous Gallantry Medal and the Distinguished Service Medal, and the army Meritorious Service Medal and Long Service and Good Conduct Medal should be extended to the new Service. Eventually, however, only the first recommendation was accepted in its entirety and, in so far as gallantry was concerned, a range of four flying awards was devised. In a letter of 6th May 1918 from Sir Frederick Ponsonby, Keeper of the Privy Purse, to Commodore Sir Geoffrey Paine at the Air Ministry, the King approved the proposal that the new decorations should be "brought out" on his birthday[3]. Accordingly, this was done and a notice to the effect that the Distinguished Flying Cross, the Air Force Cross, the Distinguished Flying Medal and the Air Force Medal had been instituted appeared in the *London Gazette* of 3rd June 1918. The first awards of all four appeared in the same *Gazette*. Curiously enough, it was not until 17th December 1918 that the King signified in writing his approval of the Royal Warrant instituting the four awards[4] and it was not until 5th December 1919 that the Warrant was published in the *Gazette*[5]. The preamble and clauses dealing with the Distinguished Flying Cross were as follows:

> "Whereas We are desirous of signifying Our appreciation of acts of valour, courage and devotion to duty performed by Officers and Men in Our Air Force and in the Air Forces of Our Self-governing Dominions beyond the Seas, We do hereby, for Us, Our heirs and successors, institute and create two decorations to be designated the Distinguished Flying Cross and the Air Force Cross, and two Medals, to be designated the Distinguished Flying Medal and the Air Force Medal, and We do hereby direct that the following regulations shall be made governing the said Decorations and Medals:

> Firstly, it is ordained that the Distinguished Flying Cross shall be granted only to such Officers and Warrant Officers of Our said Forces as shall be recommended to Us for an act or acts of valour, courage or devotion to duty performed whilst flying in active operations against the enemy.

1. Soon to become a Major-General in the R.A.F. According to *Who's Who* Kerr wrote the memorandum of 10th October 1917 which persuaded the Cabinet to form the R.A.F.

2. See P.R.O. ADM 116/1744.

3. See P.R.O. AIR 2/59.

4. See P.R.O. AIR 30/2.

5. The first amending Warrant (see *post*) also appeared in this *Gazette*.

Secondly, it is ordained that the Distinguished Flying Cross shall be silver and shall consist of a Cross flory terminated in the horizontal and base bars with bombs, the upper bar terminating with a rose, surmounted by another cross composed of aeroplane propellers charged in the centre with a roundel within a wreath of laurels a rose winged ensigned by an Imperial Crown thereon the letters R.A.F. On the reverse the Royal Cypher above the date 1918. The whole attached to the clasp and ribbon by two sprigs of laurel.

Thirdly, it is ordained that the Distinguished Flying Cross shall be worn on the left breast pendant from a ribbon one inch and a quarter in width, which shall be in colour violet and white in alternate horizontal stripes of one-eighth of an inch in depth.

Fourthly, it is ordained that the award of the Distinguished Flying Cross shall entitle the recipient to have the initials D.F.C. appended to his name.

Seventeenthly, it is ordained that Foreign Officers and gradings of an equivalent rank to those above mentioned who have been associated in Military operations with Our Army or Our Indian, Dominion or Colonial Military Forces, shall be eligible for the award of the Distinguished Flying Cross, the Air Force Cross, the Distinguished Flying Medal, and the Air Force Medal.

Eighteenthly, it is ordained that in cases where Officers, Warrant Officers, and Men who have been awarded one of the above decorations or medals shall be recommended for a further act of valour, courage or devotion to duty, he shall be awarded a bar to be attached to the ribbon by which the decoration or medal is suspended, and for every additional such act an additional bar may be awarded.

Nineteenthly, it is ordained that the names of those upon whom We may be pleased to confer the above decorations and medals shall be published in the *London Gazette*, and that a Register thereof shall be kept in the Office of Our Secretary of State for the Royal Air Force.

Twentiethly, it is ordained that any person whom by an especial Warrant under Our Royal Sign Manual We declare to have forfeited the above decorations, medals and bars shall return the same to the Office of Our Secretary of State for the Royal Air Force, and that his name shall be erased from the Register of those upon whom the said decorations, medals and bars shall have been conferred.

Lastly, We reserve to Ourself, Our heirs and successors full power of annulling, altering, abrogating, augmenting, interpreting, or dispensing with these Regulations or any part thereof by a notification under Our Royal Sign Manual.

Given at Our Court at St. James's under Our Sign Manual this third day of June, in the ninth year of Our Reign and in the year of Our Lord one thousand nine hundred and eighteen.

By the Sovereign's Command,
WILLIAM WEIR."

The provisions regarding the D.F.C. were amended by Warrant as follows:

24th July 1919[6] The ribbon was altered to one having "diagonal stripes of one-eighth of an inch in width running at an angle of 45 degrees from left to right".

20th April 1921[7] The 20th Clause was amended by providing for forfeiture in certain specified cases including a conviction by the Civil Power[8], provided that the Air Council did not recommend otherwise. Notices of forfeiture or restoration were to be published in the *London Gazette*.

These three Warrants, together with one of 27th August 1919[9] (which applied only to the Air Force Cross and the Air Force Medal) were incorporated into and amended by one dated 31st August 1929[10]. This Warrant provided that the diagonal stripes of the ribbon were to run at an angle of 45 degrees "downwards towards the wearer's left". It also drew the forfeiture clause rather more widely by omitting reference to specific acts of misconduct and by making the power to order forfeiture completely discretionary. This followed a recommendation by the

6. See *L.G.*, 5th December 1919.
7. See *L.G.*, 17th June 1921.
8. Even if a probation order was made.
9. See *L.G.*, 5th December 1919.
10. See *L.G.*, 1st November 1929.

Interdepartmental Rewards Committee that all awards for gallantry, except in cases of extreme infamy, should be regarded as irrevocable; hence it was unnecessary to limit the power, as had been done before, by prescribing particular circumstances. An amending Warrant of 23rd March 1932 redefined the conditions of award by providing that the D.F.C. was only to be granted "for exceptional valour, courage or devotion to duty whilst flying in active operations against the enemy". These two Warrants, together with those portions of the 1932 Warrant which dealt with the A.F.C. and A.F.M. and the Warrant of 7th March 1938 which dealt with the A.F.C., D.F.M. and A.F.M., were incorporated into and amended by one of 22nd September 1940. In this Warrant the order of clauses was changed; provision was made for the wearing of a miniature of the cross on certain occasions; and formal authorisation was given to the wearing of a small silver rose[11] on the ribbon, when the ribbon was worn alone, to denote the award of a bar. The following amending Warrants have been made:

11th March 1941[12] The award was extended to equivalent ranks of the Fleet Air Arm of the Royal Navy serving with the air forces of the Crown.

23rd February 1942 Recommendations in respect of Dominion personnel were to be made by the appropriate Dominion Minister of State.

10th November 1942[13] The designation "Air Branch" of the Royal Navy was substituted for "Fleet Air Arm", and the words "Military or Air Force" for "Air Force" thus extending eligibility to the Army, and to members of that Branch serving with the armies or air forces of the Crown.

15th July 1955 Provision was made for the adoption of the award, with its attendant conditions, by Member Countries of the Commonwealth. The designation "Fleet Air Arm" was resumed.

24th March 1964[14] The functions hitherto performed by the Secretary of State for Air in regard, *inter alia,* to the D.F.C. were to be performed by the Secretary of State for Defence.

27th July 1968 The conditions for eligibility were revised. For the first time the Royal Marines were specifically made eligible. In the case of those Commonwealth countries of which Her Majesty was not Queen eligibility was restricted to members of their armed forces who had been associated in operations with those of the Crown.

DESCRIPTION

Ribbon Originally 1¼ inches wide of violet and white alternate horizontal stripes ⅛ inch in depth[15]. From 24th July 1919, similar stripes running at an angle of 45 degrees from left to right.

Suspension By a straight silver bar, ornamented with sprigs of laurel, connected to the cross by a silver link.

Obverse (Fig.A) This has remained constant. The cross was designed by the Liverpool sculptor, E. Carter Preston[16]. Until about 1921 crosses were made by John Pinches Ltd, of London, and thereafter at the Royal Mint.

Reverse Plain, except for the design in the centre. A reverse matrix "E R I" for King Edward VIII was made but not used[17]. Four types of centre design have been issued as follows:

1. George V (Fig.B). This was also designed by E. Carter Preston.
2. George VI first type (Fig.C). This was a remodelled version of the previous reverse[18].
3. George VI second type (Fig.D). Cypher changed to "G VI R"[19].
4. Elizabeth II (Fig.E). Cypher changed to "E II R"[20].

Awards made during and after the Second World War have the year of the award engraved on the lower limb. A 1939 award has been seen engraved in this fashion[21].

11. Specimen rosettes were made by Spink and Son Ltd. and were submitted to the King on 25th June 1918. They were in dull silver for the A.F.C. and A.F.M., and in bright silver for the D.F.C. and D.F.M. The King thought the dull rosettes clearer and, unless it was necessary to have a distinction, that the same rosette should be used for all. As a result 100 rosettes were ordered from Spink but the records do not show of which type, see P.R.O. AIR 2/148. At all events, subsequent issues seem to have been in bright silver.

12. See *L.G.,* 18th March 1941.

13. See *L.G.,* 15th January 1943.

14. See Army Order No.22 of March 1964.

15. Apparently manufactured by George Kenning and Son, 1-4 Little Britain, London E.C.1, see P.R.O. AIR 2/148.

16. See P.R.O. AIR 2/69.

17. *Annual Report of the Deputy Master and Comptroller of the Royal Mint (1935/36)*, p.53.

18. *Ibid* (1937), p.53 and (1938), p.45.

19. *Ibid* (1948), p.22.

20. *Ibid* (1953), p.33.

21. To Flight Lieutenant I. W. Braye, R.A.F. (*L.G.,* 17th October 1939, for Waziristan).

Fig.A: The Distinguished Flying Cross, obverse.   *Fig.B: The Distinguished Flying Cross, reverse, George V issue.*

Bar (Fig.F) This has remained constant, and is of the "slip-on" type. Awards made during the Second World War and after have the year of the award engraved on the reverse.

Naming The cross was issued unnamed. However, specimens are often found named (by recipients, next-of-kin, etc.) on the plain surface of the reverse.

Copies and Fakes A number of these exist. On one, the most obvious fault is that the "A" in "R.A.F." on the obverse rises beyond the top of the rose petal whereas on the genuine issue it merely reaches it. On most genuine crosses the designer's initials "E.C.P." appear very faintly at 5 o'clock on the outer edge of the centre circle. They do not appear on some genuine crosses dated "1944", nor do they appear on copies except occasionally as a blur where the copy has been made from a genuine issue. On the reverse the most prominent feature on one copy of the George V issue is that the "G" of the Imperial cypher is at a pronounced angle instead of being nearly vertical; on the George VI second type copy the numerals "VI" are small and set too far apart, while on the Elizabeth II copy the figure "8" is too large in relation to the other figures. Purves (see Bibliography) illustrates a George V copy, while various additional copies are illustrated in *Hayward's Gazette* for April 1975 and February 1979. For other copies see the Note on p.xx. The copy bar has a somewhat larger and cruder eagle, with a narrower slide at the back.

VERIFICATIONS AND CITATIONS

All awards, except those to foreigners, appear in the *London Gazette*, and are given under the heading "Distinguished Flying Cross" in the "State Intelligence" section of the quarterly indices. In January 1942 the indices were altered, and names appear under a consolidated alphabetical list headed "Honours, Decorations and Medals". Page references continue to be given in the "State Intelligence" section. Awards have, however, been found indexed under the wrong heading, or omitted from the index entirely.

Citations are given for a number of awards gazetted between 1918 and 1939 and are noted under "Numbers Awarded" below. In this period the theatre of operations is also given for all awards commencing with the *Gazette* of 12th July 1920, and for some earlier ones e.g. France, North Russia etc. The majority of awards gazetted between 1940 and 1945 do not have citations. Of the 651 awards gazetted between 1946 and 1968, 17 have citations; thereafter none has appeared.

Fig.C: The Distinguished Flying Cross, reverse, George VI issue, first type.

Fig.D: The Distinguished Flying Cross, reverse, George VI issue, second type.

Fig.E: The Distinguished Flying Cross, reverse, Elizabeth II issue.

Fig.F: Bar to the Distinguished Flying Cross.

22. See the Honours and Awards files in this series. Where only the date of award is known it is preferable to search for the recommendation in the files of HQ R.F.C./R.A.F. which are arranged according to date; where the formation or unit is known the corresponding files may be consulted first although not all have been preserved.

23. There are separate files containing the recommendations for immediate and periodic awards. The numerical sequence of the AIR 2 references does not reflect the strict chronology of the various files and it is necessary to consult the whole index to the Code when searching.

All awards gazetted since 1949 give the theatre of operations except those for 1969 which are apparently for Vietnam. Details of many awards are preserved in the Public Record Office in the series AIR 1 which contains the First World War recommendations for members of the R.F.C. and R.A.F. serving in France and Belgium[22]; in AIR 30 (Submissions to the King 1918–1946); and in AIR 2 (Code 30) which contains the original recommendations made during the Second World War[23]. During the Second World War details of some awards appeared in Press Releases from which extracts were often made in local newspapers.

NUMBERS AWARDED

1918–1939 A total of 1,217 crosses, 88 first bars and 7 second bars were gazetted in this period a summary of which is as follows:

		D.F.C.	First Bars	Second Bars	
1918	...	572	38	1	First World War; citations for all except 44 crosses; some citations appear in later L.G.s.
1919	...	507	31	2	Crosses: 31 Russia, 3 Baltic; first bars: 6 Russia, 1 Baltic; remainder First World War; citations for 208 crosses, 17 first bars and 1 second bar.
1920	...	32	6	1	Crosses: 16 Russia, 4 Baltic, 4 Afghanistan, 4 Kurdistan, 2 Somaliland, 1 Waziristan, 1 Albu Kemal; first bars: 2 Russia, 1 Afghanistan, 1 Somaliland, 2 Waziristan; second bar: Afghanistan; citations for 9 crosses.
1921	...	16	5	1	Crosses: 12 Mesoptamia, 4 Waziristan; first bars: 4 Mesoptamia, 1 Waziristan; second bar: Mesopotamia; citations for all.
1922	...	9	5	—	Crosses: 4 Iraq, 2 Kurdistan, 2 Waziristan, 1 Somaliland; first bars: 2 Iraq, 2 Kurdistan, 1 Waziristan.
1924	...	16	—	—	6 Iraq, 6 Kurdistan, 4 Waziristan; 1 citation.
1925	...	5	—	—	Waziristan.
1926	...	3	—	—	2 Iraq; 1 Aden.
1929	...	3	—	1	Crosses: 1 Iraq, 1 Aden, 1 Nuer Country; second bar: Iraq.
1931	...	5	3	—	Crosses: 1 Iraq, 3 North West Frontier, 1 Sudan; first bars: North West Frontier.
1932	...	2	—	—	North West Frontier; Northern Kurdistan.
1933		5	—	1	Crosses: 1 Northern Kurdistan, 1 North West Frontier, 3 Chitral Reliefs; second bar: North West Frontier.
1935	...	2	—	—	Aden; North West Frontier.
1936	...	7	—	—	3 North West Frontier; 4 Palestine.
1937	...	5	—	—	Waziristan.
1938	...	9	—	—	5 Waziristan, 4 Palestine.
1939	...	19	—	—	1 Aden, 8 Palestine, 3 Waziristan, 7 Second World War (the last all with citations).

Those awarded second bars were: *London Gazette for*
                                    Second Bar

Lieutenant (temporary Captain) A. H.
    Cobby, D.F.C.   ...   . 21st September 1918

Captain R. M. Smith, M.C. (and bar),
    D.F.C.   ...   . 8th February 1919

Lieutenant (acting Captain) W. H.
    Longton, D.F.C., A.F.C.   ...   ... 3rd June 1919

Flight Lieutenant R. Halley, D.F.C.,
    A.F.C.   ...   . 12th July 1920 (Afghanistan)

Flying Officer J. W. B. Grigson, D.S.O.,
    D.F.C.   ...   . 28th October 1921 (Mesopotamia)

Squadron Leader H. A. Whistler,
    D.S.O., D.F.C.   ...   . 15th March 1929 (Iraq)

Squadron Leader S. B. Harris, D.F.C.,
    A.F.C.   ...   . 8th September 1933
                                         (North West Frontier of India)

Honorary awards to foreign officers appeared in the Air Ministry Lists of 19th July and 10th December 1919, and in the British Army of the Black Sea List of 20th May 1919. A summary of these awards is as follows:

Belgium	2
France	7
Greece	2
Italy	4
Slavo-British Aviation Corps ...	10 (and a first bar)
USA	21
Total:	46

The D.F.C. was also awarded to King Albert of the Belgians who on many occasions during the War was flown over the lines in a British aircraft to reconnoitre enemy positions[24].

1939–1945 The figures given by Wingate are as follows:

D.F.C.s   20,354
– First bars   1,550
– Second bars   42

The Guinness Book of Records (see Bibliography) states that 21,281 awards, including bars, were made in the period 1939–1945. Eighty seven crosses and two first bars were awarded to officers of the Royal Artillery engaged in flying duties during 1944 and 1945.

The following honorary awards to foreign officers were made:

	Crosses	First Bars	Second Bars
Belgium	59	5	1
Brazil	6	—	—
Czechoslovakia ...	56	1	—
Denmark	4	—	—
France	201	6	—
Greece	15	—	—
Netherlands	43	1	—
Norway	80	13	1
Poland	192	5	1
USA	264	3	—
USSR	4	—	—
Yugoslavia	3	—	—
Totals	927	34	3

24. See P.R.O. AIR 2/207
(101335/21).

1946–1979 In this period the following 678 crosses, 42 first bars and 5 second bars were gazetted:

		D.F.C.	First Bars	Second Bars	
1946	...	361	15	2	1 each to Royal Australian Navy and Australian Military Forces; 7 and 1 first bar to Royal Artillery; 1 to Glider Pilot Regiment[25]
1947	...	11	—	—	5 to Royal Artillery.
1948	...	—	1	—	Aden
1949	...	3	1	—	Crosses for Malaya; bar for Yangtse
1950	...	4	—	—	Malaya
1951	...	22	5	—	5 and 1 bar for Malaya; 15 and 4 bars for Korea; 2 to Royal Artillery and dated 1945.
1952	...	36	4	1	9 including 3 Royal Artillery, 1 first and 1 second bar, for Malaya; 27 (3 citations) including 4 Royal Artillery, 1 Royal Scots and 1 South Lancashire Regiment, 3 first bars, for Korea.
1953	...	35	4	—	5 and 3 bars for Malaya; 30 (3 citations) including 6 Royal Artillery, 1 The Buffs and 1 Royal Canadian Artillery, 1 bar, for Korea.
1954	...	25	2	1	15 including 4 Royal Navy, 1 Royal Signals, 1 first and 1 second bar for Malaya; 8 including 2 Royal Artillery, 1 first bar, for Korea; 2 for Kenya.
1955	...	18	—	1	16 including 2 Royal Navy, 3 Royal Artillery for Malaya; 2 and 1 second bar, for Kenya.
1956	...	14	1	—	13 including 2 Royal Artillery, 1 bar, for Malaya; 1 for Kenya.
1957	...	13	2	—	12 (1 citation) including 1 Royal Navy, 1 Royal Artillery, 2 bars, for Malaya; 1 for Aden.
1958	...	19	3	—	16 (2 citations) including 1 Royal Artillery and 1 Royal Engineers for Malaya; 3 and 3 bars for Aden.
1959	...	12	1	—	8 (2 citations) including 2 Royal Artillery for Malaya; 4 for Aden; 1 bar for Oman.
1960	...	2	—	—	Malaya (1 citation); 1 Royal Artillery.
1964	...	1	—	—	Borneo
1965	...	6	1	—	5 for Borneo; 1 for Radfan; bar for Vietnam.
1966	...	8	1	—	5 for Borneo; 2 (citations) to Royal Tank Regiment and Army Air Corps for Aden; 1 and 1 bar for Vietnam.
1967	...	6	—	—	1 South Arabian Federation (citation); 5 Vietnam.
1968	...	8	1	—	1 (citation) for Aden; 1 (citation) to Royal Corps of Transport for Southern Arabia; 6 including 1 each to Royal Australian Artillery, Royal Australian Infantry and Royal Australian Electrical and Mechanical Engineers, 1 bar, for Vietnam.
1969	...	22	—	—	Vietnam including 1 each to Royal Australian Navy and Australian Staff Corps.

25. All apparently for the Second World War although in some cases the Gazette announcement contains no identifying details.

1970	...	13	—	—	Vietnam including 1 each to Australian Aviation Corps and Royal New Zealand Armoured Corps.
1971	...	30	—	—	Vietnam including 5 to Royal Australian Navy, 4 to Australian Army Aviation Corps.
1972	...	8	—	—	Vietnam including 2 to Australian Army Aviation Corps and 1 to Royal New Zealand Regiment.
1975	...	1	—	—	Northern Ireland; Army Air Corps.

Those awarded second bars were:

London Gazette for
Second Bar

Acting Squadron Leader J. Berry, D.F.C.	12th February 1946
Flight Lieutenant M. D. Seale, D.F.C.	5th March 1946
Squadron Leader W. G. G. D. Smith, D.S.O., D.F.C.	29th August 1952 (Malaya)
Wing Commander N. T. Quinn, D.F.C.	22nd June 1954 (Malaya)
Wing Commander C. G. St. D. Jeffries, D.F.C.	22nd March 1955 (Kenya)

In addition 8 honorary crosses and 2 first bars were awarded to officers of the United States Air Force for services in Korea. The bars were awarded to Colonels R. A. Berg and L. R. Chase whose crosses were awarded in the Second World War.

ILLUSTRATIVE AWARD

On 19th April 1942 the Group Captain commanding R.A.F. Tangmere recommended Acting Squadron Leader Rhys Henry Thomas, R.A.F.V.R., of 129 (Mysore) Squadron R.A.F. for the D.F.C. in the following terms[26]:

> "S/Ldr. Thomas has now completed over 400 hours' operational flying. He was posted to No.129 Squadron on 22nd June 1941, as Flight Commander of "B" Flight. Previous to this he had been with No.266 Squadron for nearly a year during which time he had fought through the Battle of Britain taking part in some 92 operational flights. He has been commanding No.129 Squadron since the 3rd January, 1942, and on 6 occasions, in the absence of the Wing Leader, he himself has led the Wing. During the time he has been either a Flight Commander or a Squadron Commander his unit has destroyed 17 enemy aircraft, probably destroyed 4, for the loss of 9 pilots. Although he himself has not been credited with any enemy aircraft destroyed, I consider him a Squadron Commander of outstanding merit, who can always be relied upon to carry out the particular role which is allotted to his Squadron with sound judgement and careful planning."

On 4th May the Air Officer Commanding 11 Group endorsed the recommendation as follows:

> "Since the above report, this Officer has been leading the Wing on several occasions, and has done exceedingly well. I recommend him for the immediate award of the Distinguished Flying Cross."

On 7th May the Air Officer Commanding-in-Chief, Fighter Command, approved the recommendation which was submitted with others by the Secretary of State for Air to the King[27] on 20th May accompanied by the following citation:

> "The officer is a squadron commander of outstanding merit. He has participated in a large number of sorties against the enemy with success. During the period he has acted as flight or squadron commander, his unit destroyed at least 17 hostile aircraft. Squadron Leader Thomas has at all times displayed great skill, sound judgement and reliability."

26. See P.R.O. AIR 2/8466.
27. See P.R.O. AIR 30/170(68).

This citation was repeated when the award was published in the *London Gazette* of 22nd May 1942. On 21st August Thomas was recommended for the D.S.O.[28]; the recommendation was submitted to the King on 7th September[29]; and the resulting award was published, with a long citation, in the *London Gazette* of 11th September 1942. Further details of Thomas's career are given by Shores and Williams (see Bibliography). He joined the R.A.F. in 1939 and, after serving in various Squadrons, he was promoted to command No.129 Squadron. His personal score of enemy aircraft at the end of the Second World War was five. In addition to the two decorations mentioned above, Thomas also received the 1939–45 Star with bar "Battle of Britain", the Air Crew Europe Star with bar "France and Germany", and the Defence and War Medals.

28. See P.R.O. AIR 2/4900.
29. See P.R.O. AIR 30/170(154).

Chapter 15

The Distinguished Flying Medal

Fig.A: The Distinguished Flying Medal, obverse, George V issue, first type.

ORIGIN AND DEVELOPMENT

Shortly before the formation of the Royal Air Force on 1st April 1918 a committee was constituted to advise the King whether a special decoration was needed for the new Service, and whether there should be a uniform colour for the ribbon of the Victoria Cross in substitution for the different ribbons (navy, blue; army, red) then worn with that decoration. The committee consisted of:

Colonel Sir Douglas Dawson, Comptroller, Lord Chamberlain's Department (Chairman),

Rear-Admiral A. F. Everett, Naval Secretary to the First Sea Lord,

Lieutenant-General Sir Francis Davies, Military Secretary to the Secretary of State for War

Rear-Admiral Mark (E.F.) Kerr, representing the Service about to be formed[1],

H. Farnham Burke, Norroy King of Arms.

In a draft report[2], which was approved by the Board of Admiralty on 21st March 1918, the committee recommended that there should be only one colour for the V.C. ribbon and that it should be red; that a decoration should be instituted for officers and warrant officers of the air force corresponding to the Distinguished Service Cross and to the Military Cross in the other two Services; and that the naval Conspicuous Gallantry Medal and the Distinguished Service Medal, and the army Meritorious Service Medal and Long Service and Good Conduct Medal should be extended to the new Service. Eventually, however, only the first recommendation was accepted in its entirety and, in so far as gallantry was concerned, a range of four flying awards was devised. In a letter of 6th May 1918 from Sir Frederick Ponsonby, Keeper of the Privy Purse, to Commodore Sir Geoffrey Paine at the Air Ministry, the King approved the proposal that the new decorations should be "brought out" on his birthday[3]. Accordingly, this was done and a notice to the effect that the Distinguished Flying Cross, the Air Force Cross, the Distinguished Flying Medal and the Air Force Medal had been instituted appeared in the *London Gazette* of 3rd June 1918. The first awards of all four appeared in the same *Gazette*. Curiously enough, it was not until 17th December 1918 that the King signified in writing his approval of the Royal Warrant instituting the four awards[4] and it was not until 5th December 1919 that the Warrant was published in the *Gazette*[5]. The preamble and the clauses dealing with the Distinguished Flying Medal were as follows:

> "Whereas We are desirous of signifying Our appreciation of acts of valour, courage and devotion to duty performed by Officers and Men in Our Air Force and in the Air Forces of Our Self-governing Dominons beyond the Seas, We do hereby, for Us, Our heirs and successors, institute and create two decorations to be designated the Distinguished Flying Cross and the Air Force Cross, and two Medals, to be designated the Distinguished Flying Medal and the Air Force Medal, and We do hereby direct that the following regulations shall be made governing the said Decorations and Medals:

1. Soon to become a Major-General in the R.A.F. According to *Who's Who* Kerr wrote the memorandum of 10th October 1917 which persuaded the Cabinet to form the R.A.F.

2. See P.R.O. ADM 116/1744.

3. See P.R.O. AIR 2/59.

4. See P.R.O. AIR 30/2.

5. The first amending Warrant also appeared in this *Gazette*.

Ninthly, it is ordained that the Distinguished Flying Medal shall be granted only to such Non-commissioned Officers and Men of Our said Forces as shall be recommended to Us for an act or acts of valour, courage or devotion to duty performed whilst flying in active operations against the enemy.

Tenthly, it is ordained that the Distinguished Flying Medal shall be in silver and oval-shaped, bearing Our Effigy on the obverse and on the reverse within a wreath of laurel a representation of Athena Nike seated on an aeroplane, a hawk rising from her right arm above the words "for Courage". The whole ensigned by a bomb attached to the clasp and ribbon by two wings.

Eleventhly, it is ordained that the Distinguished Flying Medal shall be worn on the left breast pendant from a ribbon of one inch and a quarter in width, which shall be in colour violet and white in alternate horizontal stripes of one-sixteenth of an inch in depth.

Twelfthly, it is ordained that the award of the Distinguished Flying Medal shall entitle the recipient to have the initials D.F.M. appended to his name.

Seventeenthly, it is ordained that Foreign Officers and gradings of an equivalent rank to those above mentioned who have been associated in Military operations with Our Army or Our Indian, Dominion or Colonial Military Forces, shall be eligible for the award of the Distinguished Flying Cross, the Air Force Cross, the Distinguished Flying Medal, and the Air Force Medal.

Eighteenthly, it is ordained that in cases where Officers, Warrant Officers, and Men who have been awarded one of the above decorations or medals shall be recommended for a further act of valour, courage or devotion to duty, he shall be awarded a bar to be attached to the ribbon by which the decoration or medal is suspended, and for every additional such act an additional bar may be awarded.

Nineteenthly, it is ordained that the names of those upon whom We may be pleased to confer the above decorations and medals shall be published in the *London Gazette,* and that a Register thereof shall be kept in the Office of Our Secretary of State for the Royal Air Force.

Twentiethly, it is ordained that any person whom by an especial Warrant under Our Royal Sign Manual We declare to have forfeited the above decorations, medals and bars shall return the same to the Office of Our Secretary of State for the Royal Air Force, and that his name shall be erased from the Register of those upon whom the said decorations, medals and bars shall have been conferred.

Lastly, We reserve to Ourself, Our heirs and successors full power of annulling, altering, abrogating, augmenting, interpreting, or dispensing with these Regulations or any part thereof by a notification under Our Royal Sign Manual.

Given at Our Court at St. James's under Our Sign Manual this third day of June, in the ninth year of Our Reign and in the year of Our Lord one thousand, nine hundred and eighteen.

By the Sovereign's Command,
WILLIAM WEIR."

The provisions regarding the D.F.M. were amended by Warrant as follows:

24th July 1919[6] The ribbon was altered to one having "diagonal stripes of one-sixteenth of an inch in width running at an angle of 45 degrees from left to right".
20th April 1921[7] The 20th Clause was amended by providing for forfeiture in certain specified cases including a conviction by the Civil Power [8], provided that the Air Council did not recommend otherwise. Notices of forfeiture or restoration were to be published in the *London Gazette.*

These three Warrants, together with one of 27th August 1919[9] (which applied only to the Air Force Cross and the Air Force Medal) were incorporated into and amended by one dated 31st August 1929[10]. This Warrant provided that the diagonal stripes of the ribbon were to run at an angle of 45 degrees "downwards towards the wearer's left". It also drew the forfeiture clause rather more widely by omitting reference to specific acts of misconduct and making the power to order forfeiture completely discretionary. This followed a recommendation by the Interdepartmental Rewards Committee that all awards for gallantry, except in

6. See *L.G.*, 5th December 1919.
7. See *L.G.*, 17th June 1921.
8. Even if a probation order was made.
9. See *L.G.*, 5th December 1919.
10. See *L.G.*, 1st November 1929.

Fig.B: The Distinguished Flying Medal, obverse, George V issue, second type.

cases of extreme infamy, should be regarded as irrevocable; hence it was unnecessary to limit the power, as had been done before, by prescribing particular circumstances. The 1929 Warrant was amended twice as follows:

23rd March 1932 The conditions of award were redefined by providing that the D.F.M. was only to be granted "for exceptional valour, courage or devotion to duty whilst flying in active operations against the enemy".

7th March 1938 The 10th Clause was amended by providing that the reverse of the medal should have the year "1918" added within the wreath of laurel.

These three Warrants were incorporated into and amended by one of 22nd September 1940. In this Warrant the order of clauses was changed; the obverse of the medal was to bear "the Effigy of the Sovereign", thus obviating further amendment on the accession of a new Sovereign; and formal authorisation was given to the wearing of a small silver rose[11] on the ribbon, when the ribbon was worn alone, to denote the award of a bar. The following amending Warrants have been made:

11th March 1941[12] The award was extended to equivalent ranks of the Fleet Air Arm of the Royal Navy serving with the air forces of the Crown. A miniature replica of the medal was authorised.

23rd February 1942 Recommendations in respect of Dominion personnel were to be made by the appropriate Dominion Minister of State.

10th November 1942[13] The designation "Air Branch " of the Royal Navy was substituted for "Fleet Air Arm", and the words "Military or Air Force" for "Air Force" thus extending eligibility to the Army, and to members of that Branch serving with the armies or air forces of the Crown.

15th July 1955 Provision was made for the adoption of the award, with its attendant conditions, by Member Countries of the Commonwealth. The designation "Fleet Air Arm" was resumed.

24th March 1964[14] The functions hiterto performed by the Secretary of State for Air in regard, *inter alia*, to the D.F.M. were to be performed by the Secretary of State for Defence.

27th July 1968 The conditions for eligibility were revised. For the first time the Royal Marines were specifically made eligible. In the case of those Commonwealth countries of which Her Majesty was not Queen eligibility was restricted to members of their armed forces associated in operations with those of the Crown.

DESCRIPTION

Ribbon Originally $1\frac{1}{4}$ inches wide of violet and white alternate horizontal stripes $\frac{1}{16}$ inch in depth; from 24th July 1919, similar stripes running at an angle of 45 degrees from left to right.

Suspension By a straight non-swivelling silver suspender fashioned in the form of two wings.

Obverse Five types are known as follows:
1. George V first type (Fig.A).
2. George V second type (Fig.B). This was introduced in 1930[15].
3. George VI first type (Fig.C). This was introduced in 1938[16].
4. George VI second type (Fig.D). This was introduced in 1949[17].
5. Elizabeth II (Fig.E). Only issues with the Queen's titles, as altered by the Royal Proclamation of 28th May 1953, have been seen. One of these was awarded to Flight Sergeant J. M. Reilly, R.A.F.[18].

Reverse There have been two types as follows:
1. George V (Fig.F). This was designed by the Liverpool sculptor E. Carter Preston[19].
2. George VI and Elizabeth II, all issues (Fig. G). The change took place in 1938[16].

11. Specimen rosettes were made by Spink and Son Ltd. and were submitted to the King on 25th June 1918. They were in dull silver for the A.F.C. and A.F.M., and in bright silver for the D.F.C. and D.F.M. The King thought the dull rosettes clearer and, unless it was necessary to have a distinction, that the same rosette should be used for all. As a result 100 rosettes were ordered from Spink but the records do not show of which type, see P.R.O. AIR 2/148. At all events, subsequent issues seem to have been in bright silver.

12. See *L.G.*, 18th March 1941.

13. See *L.G.*, 15th January 1943.

14. See Army Order No. 22 of March 1964.

15. *Annual Report of the Deputy Master and Comptroller of the Royal Mint (1930)*, pp.45 and 46 – "The change (to the "crowned head") was, generally speaking, introduced for issues after the 1st January, 1931, but the following changes actually took place and issues were made in the year under review . . . Air Force Medal, Distinguished Flying Medal".

16. *Ibid (1938)*, p.45.

17. *Ibid (1949)*, p.30. The award for Malaya to Flight Sergeant N. Grove, R.A.F. (*L.G.*, 6th March 1953) is of this type.

18. *L.G.*, 24th April 1953.

19. See P.R.O. AIR 2/69.

Fig. C: The Distinguished Flying Medal, obverse, George VI issue, first type.

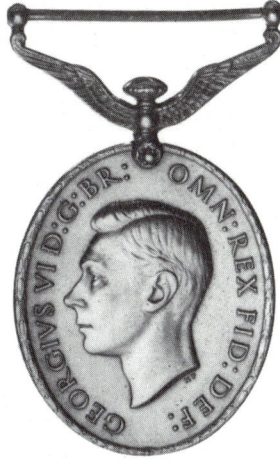

Fig. D: The Distinguished Flying Medal, obverse, George VI issue, second type.

20. See the Honours and Awards files in this series. Where only the date of award is known it is preferable to search for the recommendation in the files of HQ R.F.C./R.A.F. which are arranged according to date; where the formation or unit is known the corresponding files may be consulted first although not all have been preserved.

21. There are separate files containing the recommendations for immediate and periodic awards. The numerical sequence of the AIR 2 references does not reflect the strict chronology of the various files and it is necessary to consult the whole index to the Code when searching.

22. Hayward (see Bibliography) lists the awards in this period.

Bar (Fig.H) This has remained constant and is of the "slip-on" type. Awards made since 1939 have the year of the award engraved on the reverse.

Naming All awards are issued named. Those for the First World War are impressed in large serif capital letters with the Service number, rank, initials, surname and Service; in a number of cases the initials follow the surname. Those for the Second World War and after are engraved rather more crudely with similar details but without serifs. The crudeness is largely caused by the greater roundness of the edge of the medal in later years.

Copies and Fakes A very poor copy, made in France, is known. It is thinner than the official issue and the detail is inferior throughout. A poorly made George VI first type cast copy also exists which has a dull, pitted surface. For recent copies see also the Note on p.xx. Copy bars have a somewhat larger and cruder eagle, with a narrower slide at the back.

VERIFICATIONS AND CITATIONS

All awards, except those to foreigners, are given in the *London Gazette*, and appear under the heading "Distinguished Flying Medal" in the "State Intelligence" section of the appropriate quarterly index. In January 1942 the indices were altered, and names appear under a consolidated alphabetical list headed "Honours, Decorations and Medals". Page references continue to be given in the "State Intelligence" section. Between 1918 and 1939, 54 awards are accompanied by citations out of 187 awards made in this period. A number of citations were gazetted during the Second World War. Between 1946 and 1979, 138 awards were made of which only 10 have citations, as follows:

	London Gazette
Sergeant R. A. Strawbridge	30th May 1952 (Korea)
Sergeant D. H. Rose, B.E.M. ...	3rd December 1957 (Malaya)
Corporal S. Lidster, R.A.S.C.	4th February 1958 (Malaya)
Staff Sergeant K. A. Mead, Army Air Corps	1st July 1958 (Malaya)
Staff Sergeant R. W. Bowles, Army Air Corps	9th December 1958 (Malaya)
Sergeant B. A. Horsey, Royal Artillery, attached Army Air Corps	16th June 1959 (Malaya)
Sergeant W. A. Patrick, Parachute Regiment, attached Army Air Corps	14th June 1960 (Malaya)
Corporal (acting Sergeant) M. R. Nichols, R.E.M.E., attached Army Air Corps	21st August 1964 (Borneo)
Sergeant N. Bailey, Royal Artillery, attached Army Air Corps	20th December 1966 (Aden)
Sergeant W. Pollard, Royal Artillery ...	1st August 1967 (Aden)

All awards gazetted since 1949 give the theatre of operations except for those for 1969 which are apparently for Vietnam. Details of many awards are preserved in the Public Record Office in the series AIR 1 which contains the First World War recommendations for members of the R.F.C. and R.A.F. serving in France and Belgium[20]; in AIR 30 (Submissions to the King 1918–1946); and in AIR 2 (Code 30) which contains the original recommendations made during the Second World War[21]. Details of some awards made in the Second World War appear in Press Releases from which extracts were frequently made in local newspapers.

NUMBERS AWARDED

1918–1939[22] During this period 184 medals and 4 first bars were gazetted as follows:

Fig. E: The Distinguished Flying Medal, obverse, Elizabeth II issue.

Fig. F: The Distinguished Flying Medal, reverse, George V issues.

		Medals	First bars	
1918	...	45	1	(First World War; all with citations)
1919	...	59	1	(First World War except 2 medals for Russia; 8 citations)
1920	...	4	—	(Kurdistan)
1921	...	7	—	(1 Waziristan; 6 Mesopotamia)
1922	...	6	—	(5 Iraq, 1 Somaliland)
1924	...	10	—	(1 Waziristan, 3 Iraq, 6 Kurdistan)
1925	...	5	—	(Waziristan)
1926	...	5	—	(1 Aden, 3 Iraq, 1 Kurdistan)
1929	...	4	—	(1 Aden, 3 Iraq)
1931	...	6	—	(North West Frontier)
1932	...	1	—	(Kurdistan)
1933	...	5	1	(medals 3 Chitral Reliefs; 2 Kurdistan; bar North West Frontier)
1934	...	1	—	(Upper Mohmands)
1935	...	1	—	(North West Frontier)
1936	...	4	—	(3 North West Frontier, 1 Palestine)
1937	...	4	—	(Waziristan)
1938	...	8	—	(3 Waziristan, 5 Palestine)
1939	...	9	1	(medals 1 Aden, 2 Waziristan, 5 Palestine, 1 Second World War with citation; bar Palestine)

Those awarded first bars were:

	London Gazettes	
	Medal	*Bar*
Sergeant Observer A. Newland	21st September 1918 (First World War)	3rd December 1918 (First World War)
Sergeant Mechanic J. Chapman, D.S.M.	21st September 1918 (First World War)	3rd June 1919 (First World War)
Corporal R. W. Ellis	26th June 1931 (North West Frontier)	8th September 1933 (North West Frontier)
Sergeant J. Coggins	22nd November 1938 (Palestine)	14th April 1939 (Palestine)

Four honorary awards were made to foreigners (3 Belgian, 1 French) in the Air Ministry List of 10th December 1919. One of these is named "No. 243 Flight Warrant Officer Charles Delloye, Aviation Belge." The remainder were to Sergeant Major (1) Joseph Vuylsteke, Scout Pilot and Flight Warrant Officer Leon Pirlot, Pilot, both *Aviation Belge;* and Sergeant Pilot Andre Emile Louis Verdier, *Aviation Française* (Salonika).

1940–1945 Wingate (see Bibliography) gives the following figures for "1939–1945":

Medals	...	...	...	6,637
– First bars	...	...		60
– Second bar	...	...		1

The second bar was awarded to Flight Sergeant D. E. Kingaby, R.A.F.V.R. (later D.S.O. and A.F.C. also), in *London Gazette*, 11th November 1941. Between 1943 and 1945, 34 medals and one first bar[23] were awarded to soldiers (and a further six for the Second World War in 1946, see below); of these the award to Lance-Bombardier J. D. Gibbs, Royal Artillery, is probably unique[24]. Gibbs was rear observer in an artillery observation aircraft flying over Boulogne in September 1944. His pilot was wounded and temporarily lost consciousness. Gibbs grasped the control column and kept the aircraft in level flight while rendering first aid to the pilot. When the pilot regained consciousness he was able to operate the control column with his left hand. However, it was necessary for Gibbs to manipulate the throttle under the directions of the pilot. He did this so skilfully that the aircraft was landed safely.

23. To Staff Sergeant H. N. Andrews, Army Air Corps (*L. G.*, 15th February 1945) for North West Europe.

24. *L. G.*, 1st February 1945.

Fig. G: The Distinguished Flying Medal, reverse, George VI and Elizabeth II issues.

Fig. H: Bar to the Distinguished Flying Medal.

The following honorary awards to foreign airmen were made:

	Medals	First Bars
Belgium	1	—
Czechoslovakia	14	1
France	33	—
Netherlands	7	—
Norway	6	—
Poland	66	1
USA	39	—
USSR	4	—
Totals	170	2

1946–1979 In this period the following 138 awards were gazetted:

1946[25]	...	47[26] (1 to R.A.S.C.; 5 to Glider Pilot Regiment for Arnhem)
1947	...	4 (late awards for Second World War)
1949	...	1 (Aden)
1950	...	1 (Malaya)
1951	...	6 (3 each Malaya and Korea)
1952	...	16 (14 for Korea, including 1 to K.R.R.C.; 2 for Malaya)
1953	...	17 (8 for Korea including 1 to Glider Pilot Regiment; 9 for Malaya)
1954	...	9 (3 for Korea; 6 for Malaya, including 1 to Royal Engineers and 1 to R.A.S.C.)
1955	...	4 (3 for Malaya, including 1 to Royal Navy and 1 to R.A.S.C.; 1 for Kenya)
1956	...	3 (all for Malaya, including 1 to R.A.S.C.)
1957	...	6 (all for Malaya, including 2 to R.A.S.C. and 1 to Oxford and Bucks LI)[27]
1958	...	4 (all for Malaya, including 1 to R.A.S.C. and 2 to Army Air Corps)
1959	...	5 (3 for Malaya, including 1 to Royal Artillery; 1 for Oman; 1 for Arabian Peninsula)
1960	...	2 (both for Malaya)
1964	...	1 (to R.E.M.E.[28] for Borneo)
1966	...	1 (to Royal Artillery[28] for Aden)
1967	...	1 (to Royal Artillery for Aden)
1969	...	4 (Vietnam)
1971	...	6 (Vietnam)

An honorary award was made in 1955 to Airman 2nd Class T. C. McFadzen, United States Air Force, for services in Korea.

ILLUSTRATIVE AWARD

On 3rd July 1918 the major commanding 205 Squadron R.A.F., in a minute addressed to the officer commanding the 22nd Wing[29], recommended Sergeant (Observer) William Jones for the D.F.M. in the following terms:

"On 2nd inst. he acted as Leading Observer of two raids of 14 machines each, attacking Rosieres Station and Dump, and despite heavy and embarassing anti-aircraft fire succeeded in obtaining direct hits on both occasions.

On the 1st inst. as leading Observer on a raid on dumps between Bray and Chuignolles, he obtained a direct hit on an ammunition train, causing enormous explosions, which spread and carried on for several hours, resulting in several thousand tons of ammunition being blown up.

This N.C.O. Observer has on many previous occasions distinguished himself on bombing raids in spite of attacks by E.A. (i.e. enemy aircraft) and by anti-aircraft fire, and is a most conscientious and accurate bomb dropper at all times.

He did a great amount of valuable work in the heavy fighting in March and April. In addition to his skill as a bomb dropper, he has destroyed or brought down completely out of control six enemy machines. Up to date he has flown in 105 successful bombing raids."

25. All awards gazetted in this year appear to be for the Second World War although in some cases the *Gazette* announcement contains no identifying details.

26. Excluding the award for Normandy to Staff Sergeant E. J. Baker, Army Air Corps, which was first gazetted on 19th October 1944 and repeated with the addition of "since deceased" in *L.G.*, 14th November 1946.

27. Attached Glider Pilot Regiment.

28. Attached Army Air Corps.

29. See P.R.O. AIR 1/1599 (204/83/40)

This recommendation found its way to H.Q. 5th Brigade R.A.F. where it was edited and forwarded by the brigade commander on 5th July 1918 on Army Form 3121/4[30] as follows:

> "For conspicuous courage and determination in bombing enemy dumps and aerodromes, often in the face of strong hostile opposition and intense anti-aircraft fire.
>
> On July 1st, 1918, while on a Bombing Raid on the Dumps between Bray and Chuignolles, he obtained a direct hit on an ammunition train, causing an enormous explosion, which spreading lasted for several hours, destroying large quantities of munitions.
>
> On July 2nd, 1918, he carried out two successful raids, in each dropping his bombs with effect on his objectives, the Station and Dump at Rosieres.
>
> He has taken part in One hundred and five successful Bombing Raids, and has destroyed, or brought down, six hostile machines."

On 17th September 1918 the recommendation was submitted to the King in the form of a galley proof which became the *London Gazette* of 21st September 1918[31]. By this time the citation had been further edited as follows:

> "He has taken part in 105 successful bombing raids and has shown conspicuous courage and determination often in the face of strong opposition and intense anti-aircraft fire. He has destroyed or brought down out of control six hostile machines."

30. The form used for recommending awards, see P.R.O. AIR 1/1033 (204/5/1434).

31. See P.R.O. AIR 30/34 (9).

Chapter 16

The Distinguished (formerly Conspicuous) Service Cross

ORIGIN AND DEVELOPMENT

The Conspicuous Service Cross, later to become the Distinguished Service Cross[1], was instituted in June 1901 as the result of a Memorial from the Lords Commissioners of the Admiralty, addressed to the King, as follows[2]:

"At the Court at St. James's
The 15th day of June, 1901.

Present:

The KING'S Most Excellent Majesty in Council.

WHEREAS there was this day read at the Board a Memorial from the Right Honourable the Lords Commissioners of the Admiralty, dated the 14th day of June, 1901, in the words following, viz.:

'Whereas we are of opinion that there should exist some means of recognising Distinguished Service before the Enemy on the part of Warrant Officers or Subordinate Officers of Your Majesty's Fleet, who by reason of not holding a Commission in the Royal Navy, are not eligible for appointment to any existing Order or Decoration.

We beg leave to recommend that Your Majesty will be graciously pleased by Your Order in Council to institute a Decoration to be designated the Conspicuous Service Cross, and to consist of a Silver Cross, with the reverse side plain, but having on the obverse side in the centre Your Majesty's Imperial and Royal Cypher, E.R.I., surmounted by the Imperial Crown.

We would beg leave to recommend to Your Majesty that this Decoration be awarded for meritorious or distinguished services before the Enemy performed by Warrant Officers, or Acting Warrant Officers, or by subordinate Officers of Your Majesty's Fleet: and that no person shall be nominated thereto unless his services shall have been marked by the especial mention of his name in despatches by the Admiral or Senior Naval or Military Officer Commanding the Squadron or detached Force.

The award of this Decoration to carry with it the right to have the letters C.S.C. appended to the Officer's name.

We would submit further that the names of those upon whom Your Majesty may be pleased to confer this Decoration shall be published in the *London Gazette*, and a registry thereof kept in the Office of the Lords Commissioners of the Admiralty.'

His Majesty, having taken the said Memorial into consideration, was pleased, by and with the advice of His Privy Council, to approve of what is therein proposed. And the Right Honourable the Lords Commissioners of the Admiralty are to give the necessary directions herein accordingly.

A. W. FITZROY."

From the preamble to the Memorial it will be seen that the intention was to institute a decoration for certain naval officers who, by reason of their not being commissioned, were ineligible for appointment to, *inter alia*, the D.S.O. Indeed, for this reason, the C.S.C. was given some affinity with the D.S.O. in that it was to be awarded for meritorious or distinguished services in action; mention in despatches was a condition precedent to award; and the Cross itself was made to resemble the D.S.O. in outline. With the outbreak of the First World War a need arose to reward officers below the rank of lieutenant-commander whose services did not reach the standard required for appointment to the D.S.O.[3] Accordingly, by an Order in Council of 14th October 1914 the Cross was re-designated "The

1. In 1914, on the extension of eligibility to commissioned officers below the rank of Lieutenant-Commander.

2. First published in the Navy List of October 1901.

3. A similar need arose in the Army, see Chapter 32, The Military Cross.

Fig.A: The Conspicuous Service Cross, obverse.

Fig.B: The Distinguished Service Cross, obverse, George V issue.

4. Captains and subalterns of the Royal Marines were, by implication, included.

5. Thus obviating further Orders in Council on the accession of future Sovereigns.

6. See *L.G.*, 23rd December 1939.

7. The original of this Order is in P.R.O. ADM 1/1186.

8. Thus making provision, *inter alia*, for those serving in air/sea rescue.

9. See Army Order No. 196 of October 1905.

10. See Army Order No. 246 of August 1912.

11. See Army Council Instruction No. 754 of July 1918.

12. This is the width given in the Royal Mint Museum catalogue (see Bibliography).

Distinguished Service Cross" and was to bear the initials (*sic.*) of King George V instead of those of the late King; eligibility was extended to officers below the rank of lieutenant-commander[4]; and recipients were entitled to use the letters "D.S.C." after their names. Subsequently, further Orders in Council made provision for the Cross, as follows:

2nd March 1915 – foreign officers of equivalent rank who had been associated in naval or military operations with Naval Forces were to be eligible for the honorary award of the D.S.C.

7th September 1916 – a Bar was to be awarded to those who performed subsequent acts of service before the enemy; officers of the Royal Indian Marine were to be equally eligible with officers of the Royal Navy for the Cross.

20th February 1924 – a miniature decoration, half the size of the ordinary badge, was approved and a sealed pattern was to be deposited with and kept in the Central Chancery of the Orders of Knighthood; officers already in possession of miniatures might retain and wear them.

The foregoing were consolidated into an Order in Council of 19th May 1931 which extended eligibility to officers of the Merchant Navy and Fishing Fleets who rendered services in circumstances considered by the Admiralty to merit the award; made provision for forfeiture and restoration at the Sovereign's pleasure; and provided that the Cross was to bear on the obverse the Imperial and Royal Cypher[5], surmounted by the Imperial Crown. Further Orders in Council were made, as follows:

20th December 1939[6] – officers of the Fleet of the rank, or equivalent rank, of Commander and Lieutenant-Commander were to be eligible, and foreign naval officers of corresponding rank were to be similarly eligible for an honorary award.

17th April 1940 – officers and warrant officers of the Royal Air Force, serving with the Fleet, were to be eligible.

5th November 1942 – officers and warrant officers of the Army, serving in defensively-equipped Merchant Ships (D.E.M.S.) were to be eligible[7].

13th January 1943 – officers and warrant officers of the Royal Air Force, serving afloat, yet not with the Fleet, were to be eligible[8].

10th December 1943 – submissions for awards in respect of Dominion personnel were to be made by the Minister of State for the Dominion concerned.

The relative order of wearing the Cross has varied. In 1905[9] the C.S.C. was shown following the Order of St. John, and in 1912[10] following the C.G.M. However, in 1918[11] it was shown in its present position (see also Appendix 4).

DESCRIPTION

Ribbon 1.375 inches wide[12], with equal stripes of dark blue, white and dark blue.

Suspension By a hall-marked silver ring, approximately ¾ inch in diameter, passing through a smaller ring fixed to the top of the Cross. The C.S.C. ring was slightly smaller.

Obverse There have been five types of obverse, as follows:

1. Edward VII (Fig.A).
2. George V (Fig.B).
3. George VI first type (Fig.C).
4. George VI second type (Fig.D). The cypher "G VI R" probably was introduced in 1949 following the change in the King's style and titles which took place in the previous year.
5. Elizabeth II (Fig.E).

Reverse Until about 1940 this was plain, but thereafter had the year of the award engraved on or at the top of the lower arm. The C.S.C. has pronounced rounded unbevelled edges while the D.S.C. has a bevelled edge, similar to the obverse. The Crosses are hall-marked. From 1954, when they were first made

Fig.C: The Distinguished Service Cross, obverse, George VI issue, first type.

Fig.D: The Distinguished Service Cross, obverse, George VI issue, second type.

13. For further details regarding the use of a maker's mark by the Royal Mint, see P.R.O. MINT 20/877.

14. 29 awards to French officers were published in *L.G.*, 23rd December 1915.

15. See *L.G.*, 23rd February 1940.

16. See, for example, the Honours and Awards files in AIR 1/1032; 1033; 1152; 1479; 1515; 1598 and 1599.

at the Royal Mint, the maker's mark is the initials of the Deputy Master[13]. With the C.S.C. the marks appear on the edge, and with the D.S.C. at the bottom of the lower arm.

Bar (Fig.F) The bar is silver, with a "slip-on" fitting, and the design has remained constant. With issues before about 1940 the back of the slide, which is wider than the bar itself, is plain, but thereafter has the year of the award engraved upon it.

Naming The Cross is issued unnamed although the reverse is sometimes found unofficially engraved with varying details of the recipient.

Copies and Fakes Two types of George V copy exist, neither of which is hall-marked. One is thin and poorly finished. The other is almost as thick as the genuine Cross but the bevelling on the arms is shallow, particularly on the reverse, while the suspender ring is of comparatively narrow gauge and the join clearly visible. For recent copies see the Note on p.xx.

VERIFICATIONS AND CITATIONS

1901–1913 The names of recipients are to be found under the heading "Conspicuous Service Cross" in the Naval Promotions section of the quarterly *London Gazette* indices. No citations are given. However, all recipients were mentioned in despatches at least once and some details can be gleaned from these sources. Lists of awards also appear quarterly in the Navy List commencing with the List for October 1901.

1914 onwards All awards, except for some to foreigners[14], are published in the *London Gazette*. Until the last quarter of 1941, names are given under the heading "Distinguished Service Cross" in the "State Intelligence" section of the Gazette indices. Thereafter this heading gives only the pages upon which awards are to be found, the names being relegated to a comprehensive nominal index headed "Honours, Decorations and Medals". Errors have been found under the former heading after 1941 where page numbers are sometimes corrupt, omitted, or put under the wrong heading. No errors have been found in the nominal indices. There are some citations for First World War awards. Where there is no citation some details may occasionally be found in the despatch for the operation giving rise to the award. For the Second World War and after the only citations to be found are for the action with the *Admiral Graf Spee*[15]; however, the *Gazette* notices frequently mention the operation and/or vessel concerned which provides a useful basis for searching in other sources. Lists of awards continued to be published in the Navy List until 1920, and thereafter were published in the January and July Admiralty Fleet Orders. The Navy List also gave the names of foreign officers upon whom the D.S.C. had been conferred in the First World War. Bles (see Bibliography) gives awards for 1939–1940. Citations or other information regarding awards in both World Wars are to be found in the Public Record Office series ADM 1 (Code 85) and ADM 116 (Code 85); both contain a large number of files (although by no means all the original files have survived) and it is advisable to know the date of award and, where possible the theatre for which it was made, before consulting the indices. Some First World War recommendations for members of the Royal Naval Air Service serving in France and Belgium are in the series AIR 1[16].

NUMBERS AWARDED

1901–1913 Only eight awards of the C.S.C. were made, all being Edward VII issues to the Royal Navy, as follows:

		London Gazette
Midshipman T. C. Armstrong	... ...	2nd July 1901 (South Africa)
Midshipman C. A. E. Huddart	... ...	2nd July 1901 (South Africa; killed in action)

Fig.E: The Distinguished Service Cross, obverse, Elizabeth II issue.

Fig.F: Bar to the Distinguished Service Cross.

17. Apparently including bars and 153 awards to foreign officers. There were a further 23 initial awards, three first bars and one second bar gazetted in 1920.

18. *E.g.*, in Russia.

19. According to the Navy List for January 1920, officers of the following Navies received honorary awards: Belgian 1; French 85; Italian 61; Japanese 3; and Russian 1. Not all these awards seem to have been gazetted. There may be others which we have not traced.

20. *L.G.*, 13th September 1915.

21. *L.G.*, 15th February 1919.

22. These awards were accompanied by citations of varying length.

23. This award is omitted from the *L.G.* index.

24. See *The Times* of 20th March 1919, p.9.

25. His other awards were gazetted as follows: D.S.C., 11th November 1919 (Kronstadt Harbour); first bar, 23rd May 1944 (invasion of the Italian mainland); second bar, 27th March 1945 (invasion of the South of France). Only the D.S.C. is accompanied by a citation.

26. Awards of the D.S.M. to members of the R.A.F. were for a wider variety of services.

27. All the *L.G.* announcements, except that for Coates, are accompanied by citations.

28. See also P.R.O. ADM 1/14578.

Midshipman R. B. C. Hutchinson	... 2nd July 1901 (South Africa)
Gunner E. E. Lowe	... 2nd July 1901 (South Africa)
Gunner G. Mascull	... 26th June 1902 (China)
Midshipman A. G. Onslow	... 6th September 1904 (Somaliland)
Midshipman T. F. J. L. Wardle	... 2nd July 1901 (South Africa)
Gunner J. Wright	... 2nd July 1901 (China and South Africa)

Photograph portraits of Armstrong, Lowe, Wardle and Wright appear in *The Navy and Army Illustrated* for 24th August 1901.

First World War Wingate (see Bibliography) for "1914–1918" gives 1,983 crosses with 91 first bars and 10 second bars, while Wilson and McEwen (see Bibliography) for "1914–1919" give 1,786 awards[17]. However, our count of the Gazette entries for 1914–20 (which include campaigns usually associated with the War but ending after 11th November 1918[18]) reveals only 1,694 crosses[19]. The D.S.C. awarded in 1915[20] to Lieutenant W. P. Mark-Wardlaw, R.N., was replaced by the D.S.O. in 1919[21]. The recipients of second bars were as follows:

	London Gazette for second bar
Staff Paymaster W. R. Ashton, R.N.R.	... 17th November 1917
Lieutenant W. B. Chilton, R.N.R.	... 22nd January 1919
Flight Commander R. J. O. Compston, R.N.A.S.	... 16th March 1918[22]
Flight Sub-Lieutenant R. F. L. Dickey, R.N.A.S.	... 30th November 1917
Flight Lieutenant J. S. T. Fall, R.N.A.S.	... 19th December 1917[22]
Flight Commander T. D. Hallam, R.N.A.S. ...	... 19th December 1917
Flight Commander T. F. le Mesurier, R.A.F. ...	... 21st June 1918
Acting Flight Commander R. P. Minifie, R.N.A.S.	... 17th April 1918
Flight Commander J. G. Struthers, R.N.A.S. ...	... 22nd February 1918
Sub-Lieutenant S. P. R. White, R.N.R.	... 2nd November 1917[23]

In 1919 the D.S.C. was conferred upon the Port of Dunkirk[24].

Between the Wars Only seven awards were gazetted as follows:

	London Gazette
Midshipman N. V. Dickinson, R.N.	... 14th January 1921 (theatre not given)
Lieutenant P. W. Gretton, R.N. ...	... 6th November 1936 (Palestine)
Lieutenant F. J. C. Halahan, R.N.	... 3rd June 1929 (China)[22]
Mr. J. W. Hurst, O.B.E., Admiralty Pilot	... 2nd December 1938 (China).[22]
Acting Sub-Lieutenant W. J. Melrose, R.N.	... 14th January 1921 (theatre not given)
Lieutenant J. Peterson, R.N.	... 6th May 1927 (China)[22]
Captain A. C. Thomson, Mercantile Marine	... 6th May 1927 (China)[22]

Second World War Wingate gives 4,524 crosses, 434 first bars, 44 second bars and one third bar. The first awards, of which there were 18, appeared in the *London Gazette* of 23rd December 1939. The recipient of the third bar was Temporary Acting Commander N. E. Morley, R.N.V.R., whose third bar was gazetted on 12th June 1945 for minesweeping operations in the Gulf of Corinth[25]. Three oficers of the Maritime Royal Artillery received crosses as follows:

	London Gazette
Lieutenant N. M. Bryant	... 11th December 1945
Lieutenant H. L. Haw	... 11th December 1945
Lieutenant C. E. Wilkinson	... 8th December 1942

as did eight of the R.A.F. all of whom were engaged in air/sea rescue[26]:

	London Gazette[27]
Flying Officer B. W. Ahearn ...	... 12th June 1945
Flight Lieutenant G. F. L. Coates ...	1st January 1942
Squadron Leader E. A. Haines	20th February 1945
Flight Lieutenant D. A. Jones	...: 24th March 1944
Flight Lieutenant J. F. Lang	14th January 1944[28]

Flying Officer G. Lockwood ... ... 20th February 1945
Flying Officer J. Rogers ... ... 1st September 1944
Flight Lieutenant E. R. H. Watson ... 20th February 1945

Honorary awards were made to foreign officers as follows:

	D.S.C.	1st bar	2nd bar
Belgium	2	—	—
Denmark	1	—	—
France	35	3	1
Greece	13	1	—
Netherlands	41	2	—
Norway[29]	62	3	1
Poland	24	3	—
U.S.A.	46	—	—
U.S.S.R.	4	—	—
Totals	228	12	2

All awards gazetted in 1946 were for the Second World War.

1947–1979 In this period the following awards were gazetted:

Year	Crosses	First Bars	Second Bars	
1947 ...	3	1	—	(1 D.S.C. for Sumatra 1946; remainder for Palestine; all R.N.)
1949 ...	3	1	—	(all for Yangtse; 1 D.S.C. to R.A.F.; remainder R.N.)
1951 ...	6	4	1	(all for Korea; D.S.C.: 5 R.N., 1 R.C.N.; first bars: 3 R.N., 1R.C.N.; second bar R.N.)
1952 ...	42	7	1	(all for Korea; D.S.C.: 24 R.N., 3 R.M., 7 R.A.N., 5 R.C.N., 3 R.N.Z.N.; first bars: 6 R.N., 1 R.A.N.; second bar, R.A.N.)
1953 ...	17	3	3	(all for Korea; D.S.C.: 12 R.N., 3 R.A.N., 2 R.C.N.; first bars: 2 R.N., 1 R.N.Z.N.; second bars, R.N.)
1954 ...	4	—	—	(all for Korea; 1 each to R.N., R.A.N., R.C.N. and R.N.Z.N.)
1957 ...	5	2	—	(all for Near East; 2 D.S.C.s to R.A.F.; remainder R.N.)
1963 ...	1	—	—	(to R.N. for Brunei)
1965 ...	4	—	—	(one each to R.N. and R.A.N. for Malacca and Singapore Straits, 2 to R.N. for Borneo)
1966 ...	1	—	—	(to R.N.Z.N. for East and West Malaysia)
1968 ...	2	—	—	(to R.A.N. for Vietnam)
1969 ...	4	—	—	(to R.A.N. for Vietnam)
1971 ...	3	—	—	(to R.A.N. for Vietnam)

The R.A.F. awards were to:

	London Gazette
Flight Lieutenant M. E. Fearnley	1st November 1949 (Yangtse, H.M.S. *Amethyst*)
Squadron Leader D. C. L. Kearns, A.F.C.	13th June 1957 (Near East, October – December 1956)
Flying Officer R. C. Olding	13th June 1957 (Near East, October – December 1956)

Eight honorary awards were made in 1955 to officers of the United States Navy for services during the Korean War.

ILLUSTRATIVE AWARD

Gunner R. W. Clare, R.N., of H.M.S. *Grenade* was awarded the D.S.C. in the *London Gazette* of 27th August 1940 for services in the withdrawal of the Allied

29. Including 18 to officers of the Royal Norwegian Army. For those to Lieutenant L. Larsen, and 2nd Lieutenants C. Fougner and E. Johansen, see P.R.O. ADM 1/14340.

Armies from the beaches of Dunkirk. His ship was a destroyer which was lost as a result of bomb damage on her second trip to Dunkirk. Clare's recommendation for the award is in P.R.O. ADM 116/4504, and reads as follows:

"Acted with great coolness and courage, taking complete control of after end of ship when burning and sinking. Closed and flooded magazines at correct moment thereby minimising disaster. Example of gallantry under fire."

In addition to the D.S.C. (which is dated "1940" on the reverse), Clare received the Naval General Service Medal with bar "Palestine 1936–39"; the 1939/45 Star; the Atlantic Star; the Africa Star with bar "North Africa 1942–43"; the Pacific Star; and the War Medal.

Chapter 17

The Distinguished Service Medal

Fig.A: The Distinguished Service Medal, obverse, George V issue, first type.

ORIGIN AND DEVELOPMENT

The Distinguished Service Medal was instituted in October 1914 as the result of a Memorial from the Lords Commissioners of the Admiralty, addressed to the King, as follows:[1]

"At the Court at Buckingham Palace,
The 14th day of October, 1914.

Present:

The KING'S Most Excellent Majesty in Council.

WHEREAS there was this day read at the Board a Memorial from the Right Honourable the Lords Commissioners of the Admiralty, dated the 14th day of October, 1914, in the words following, viz.:

'WHEREAS Her late Majesty Queen Victoria was graciously pleased, by Her Order in Council dated the 7th July, 1874, to establish a Silver Medal, known as the Conspicuous Gallantry Medal, for such Chief Petty Officers, Petty Officers and Men of the Royal Navy, and Non-Commissioned Officers and Men of the Royal Marines, as might at any time distinguish themselves by acts of pre-eminent bravery in action with the enemy:

And whereas we are of opinion that it would be desirable to establish a Medal which could be awarded in the numerous instances of courageous service in war by Chief Petty Officers, Petty Officers and Men of Your Majesty's Navy, and by Non-Commissioned Officers and Men of Your Majesty's Corps of Royal Marines, and all other persons holding corresponding positions in Your Majesty's Service afloat, in cases where the award of the Conspicuous Gallantry Medal would be inappropriate:

We beg leave humbly to recommend that Your Majesty may be graciously pleased by Your Order in Council to establish a medal, to be called the Distinguished Service Medal, for such of the above classes of Your Majesty's Navy as may at any time show themselves to the fore in action, and set an example of bravery and resource under fire but without performing acts of such pre-eminent bravery as would render them eligible for the Conspicuous Gallantry Medal.'

HIS MAJESTY, having taken the said Memorial into consideration, was pleased, by and with the advice of his Privy Council, to approve of what is therein proposed. And the Right Honourable the Lords Commissioners of the Admiralty are to give the necessary directions herein accordingly.

ALMERIC FITZROY."

From the penultimate paragraph of the Order it will be seen that among the conditions precedent of award were that it should arise from circumstances "in action" and "under fire". In May and June 1918 some doubt was expressed at the Admiralty as to whether a number of recent awards had come strictly within these terms of the Order. Accordingly it was decided that future recommendations for the medal would be confined to those for services in the presence of the enemy, including the known presence of mines[2]. In the proposals for the Naval M.S.M.[3] (*q.v.*), that medal, and not the D.S.M., was to be regarded as the appropriate award in cases of minesweeping on known minefields and minelaying in enemy waters, but where the service was of a particularly hazardous nature the D.S.M. would be given. Subject to the latter exception, the D.S.M. for service at sea would be restricted to cases where the man had distinguished himself in action between

1. First published in the Navy List of January 1915.
2. See P.R.O. ADM 116/1744.
3. See the letter of 11th October 1918 from the Admiralty to the War Office in P.R.O. WO 32/4968.

Fig.B: The Distinguished Service Medal, obverse, George VI issue, first type.

his own vessel and a hostile ship, submarine or aircraft. It should be noted that the terms of the Order did not preclude awards for services ashore and, indeed, a number of such awards were made in both World Wars[4]. Additional Orders in Council made provision for the D.S.M. as follows:

> *27th June 1916* – a Bar was to be awarded to those who again performed such service as merited the award of the Medal, had they already not received it.

> *23rd July 1931* – forfeiture and restoration of the Medal were to be at the Sovereign's pleasure while forfeiture and restoration of the accompanying monetary awards, either wholly or in part, were to be at the discretion of the Admiralty.

> *17th April 1940* – N.C.O.s and men of the Royal Air Force, serving with the Fleet, were to be eligible.

> *1st July 1942* – N.C.O.s and men of the Army, serving in defensively-equipped Merchant Ships (D.E.M.S.) were to be eligible.

> *17th September 1942* – persons in the Merchant Navy, of status equivalent to that of Petty Officer or Seaman in the Royal Navy, were to be eligible.

> *13th January 1943* – N.C.O.s and men of the Royal Air Force, serving afloat yet not with the Fleet, were to be eligible[5].

> *10th December 1943* – submissions for awards in respect of Dominion personnel were to be made by the appropriate Minister of State for the Dominion.

> *14th October 1947* – certain monetary benefits were to be given to recipients awarded the Medal after 2nd September 1939.

In the order of wearing, the Distinguished Service Medal now follows the Union of South Africa King's (Queen's) Medal for Bravery, in silver (see also Appendix 4).

DESCRIPTION

Ribbon Dark blue, 1¼ inches wide, with two white stripes, each approximately ³⁄₁₆ inch wide in the centre.

Suspension By a straight suspender. In 1941 the swivelling suspender was replaced by a fixed one[6] but issues of the former continued until early the next year[7].

Obverse Five obverses are known, as follows:

1. George V (Fig.A) The King's effigy was prepared by Bertram Mackennal, M.V.O., A.R.A.[8] The Royal Mint Report for 1930[9] mentions the introduction of a "crowned head" obverse. However, the medal awarded to D. Jones in *L.G.*, 18th December 1936 (see below) has the original obverse and it may be that the crowned head obverse was never issued.

2. George VI first type (Fig.B). This was introduced in 1938[10].

3. George VI second type (Fig.C). This was probably introduced in 1949[11] following the change in the King's style and titles which took place the previous year.

4. Elizabeth II first type (Fig.D). This was probably introduced in 1953 and was being issued as late as 1957[12].

5. Elizabeth II second type (Fig.E).

Reverse (Fig.F) This has remained constant.

Bar (Fig.G) This was authorised by the Order in Council of 27th June 1916 (see above). On 28th August 1916 the Admiralty ordered a clasp from the Royal Mint bearing the date "27th MAY 1916"[13]. This was delivered to the Mint Office for despatch on 29th September 1916. By the date of the order only one bar had been awarded, being that to Leading Seaman A. Button in *L.G.*, 14th July 1916. The remaining bars gazetted in 1916 were to Leading Seaman I. Overton in *L.G.*, 6th September 1916[14] and to Chief Writer S. G. White in *L.G.*, 15th September 1916. A bar bearing the date "31 MAY–1 JUNE 1916", apparently for White, was ordered on 20th September 1916 and delivered on 6th October 1916. It appears, however, that the pattern of the bar was under discussion because on 23rd October 1916 the King approved a coloured sketch

4. In the First World War awards were made for services, *inter alia*, in Belgium, Gallipoli and France. The award to Telgraphist H. Monks in *L.G.*, 14th November 1944 was for services ashore on D-day with a Combined Operations Bombardment Unit. For another award for services ashore in the Second World War see footnote 38.

5. Thus making provisions, *inter alia*, for services in air/sea rescue.

6. *Annual Report of the Deputy Master and Comptroller of the Royal Mint (1941)*, p.99.

7. The award to Yeoman of Signals E. T. Himbury (*L.G.*, 1st January 1942) swivels; that to Able Seaman H. H. Farley (*L.G.*, 28th April 1942) does not.

8. Originally for the Naval L.S. & G.C. medal, see *Annual Report of the Deputy Master and Comptroller of the Royal Mint (1911)*, p.15.

9. *Annual Report of the Deputy Master and Comptroller of the Royal Mint* (1930), p.41.

10. *Ibid* (1938) p.45.

11. The award to Acting Petty Officer L. Frank (*L.G.*, 1st November 1949, Yangtse) is of this type; but see under "Naming" *post*.

12. The award to Leading Seaman T. Dyer (*L.G.*, 13th June 1957, Near East) is of this type.

13. See the Royal Mint register of medals ordered between 1916 and 1941 in P.R.O. MINT 16/4.

14. Overton's bar is known. It is of the laurelled pattern with 30.MAY 1915 on the back of the slide.

Fig. C: The Distinguished Service Medal, obverse, George VI issue, second type.

Fig. D: The Distinguished Service Medal, obverse, Elizabeth II issue, first type.

15. See P.R.O. MINT 20/586.

16. The laurelled bar is first mentioned in the *Annual Report of the Deputy Master and Comptroller of the Royal Mint* (1917), p.24.

17. The medal issued to Leading Seaman B. G. E. Shepherd, R.N.R., is also impressed with the date "SEPT.1942". Shepherd's award was announced in *L.G.*, 16th February 1943.

18. *I.e.*, the awards to Acting Petty Officer L. Frank and Leading Seaman T. Dyer, mentioned above. Another D.S.M. to Frank also exists which has the first type George VI obverse, a swivel suspender, and impressed naming. It is not known which of these medals is the re-issue.

19. We have found some awards to foreign ratings published in 1915.

20. These, however, appeared in the *Gazette of India*.

of the laurelled bar, shown on a D.S.M. ribbon, which had the date "24th MAY 1916" on the back of the slide[15]. On 16th November 1916 the Admiralty sent the sketch to the Mint saying that it had been approved by the King for the D.S.C., C.G.M. and D.S.M. and asking for dies to be prepared. The C.G.M. and D.S.M. bars were to have the date of the act engraved on the back of the slide. On 28th November 1916 the Mint sent a specimen bar to the Admiralty which, after some discussion regarding the side pieces, was approved on 20th January 1917, the Admiralty having agreed earlier to be responsible for the engraving of dates, as it had already arranged for the engraving of medals. During the course of the discussions the Admiralty informed the Mint that it had been decided to adopt a different bar for the D.S.C. which would be manufactured by Messrs. Garrard, who already made the Cross. On 10th February 1917 the Admiralty ordered 20 bars of the approved pattern from the Mint[16]. Most First World War bars of this pattern have the date of the action engraved or impressed on the back of the slide, e.g. "8.AUGUST.1917." Those for the Second World War are undated.

Naming First World War issues are impressed in large serif capital letters with the Service number, initials, surname, rating, and often with the name of the ship. Sometimes the type of operation (e.g. anti-submarine) or location (e.g. "St. George's Channel"), and, for those gazetted from about May 1916, the date follow. The 1921 award to J. Alderman (see below) follows the First World War style of naming. The 1927 award to F. H. Image (see below) is impressed with these details in small, widely spaced, non-serif capital letters but with the numerical form of date i.e. "5.9.26.", while that to D. Jones (see also below) is impressed in rather more closely spaced capital letters and with "PALESTINE 1936." Until early 1944 Second World War issues are usually similarly impressed with number, initials, surname, rank and sometimes the Service e.g. R.N.R., R.A.F. etc; many awards made before early 1942 give the name of the ship[17]. From early 1944 the naming changed to engraved, non-serif capital letters in varying styles with rank, initials, surname and number; men of the Maritime R.A. are thus described. Post-War awards are engraved with similar details in thin non-serif capital letters[18].

Copies and Fakes See the Note on p.xx.

VERIFICATIONS AND CITATIONS

All awards, except for some to foreigners[19] and members of the Royal Indian Navy[20], are published in the *London Gazette*. Until the last quarter of 1941, names are given under the heading "Distinguished Service Medal" in the "State Intelligence" section of the Gazette indices. Thereafter, this heading gives only the pages upon which awards are to be found, the names being relegated to a comprehensive nominal index headed "Honours, Decorations and Medals". Errors have been found under the former heading after 1941 where page numbers are sometimes corrupt or omitted altogether. No errors have been found in the nominal indices.

There are some citations for First World War awards. Where there are no citations details may sometimes be found in the despatch for the operation giving rise to the award. Thereafter there are very few citations although the notices frequently mention the operation and/or the vessel concerned which provide a useful basis for searching in other sources. From January 1915 until January 1920 lists of awards were published quarterly in the Navy List; thereafter they were published in the January and July Admiralty Fleet Orders. The Navy List also contained the names of foreigners upon whom the D.S.M. had been conferred. Bles (see Bibliography) gives awards for 1939–1940.

Citations or other information regarding awards in both World Wars are to be found in the Public Record Office series ADM 1(Code 85) and ADM 116(Code 85); both series contain a large number of files and it is desirable to know the date

Fig.E: The Distinguished Service Medal, obverse, Elizabeth II issue, second type.

of award and, where possible, the action or theatre for which it was made, before consulting the indices. Some First World War recommendations for men of the R.N.A.S. serving in France and Belgium are contained in the Honours and Awards files in AIR 1/1152 and 1479.

NUMBERS AWARDED

First World War Wingate (see Bibliography) for "1914–18" gives 5,519 medals, 67 first bars and two second bars, while Wilson and McEwen (see Bibliography) for the period to January 1920 give 5,513 awards which includes the same number of bars. However, our count of the Gazette entries for 1914–1920 (which include campaigns usually associated with the War but ending after 11th November 1918[21]), reveals only 4,052 medals[22] but the same number of bars as given by Wingate. The two second bars were awarded to:

	London Gazette for second bar
Deckhand L. Findlay, R.N.R.	29th August 1917
Chief Engine Room Artificer 1st Class J. Paterson, R.N.	12th December 1919

One case is known of the award of two D.S.M.s to the same man. The *Gazette* of 12th May 1917 announced the award of the medal to Seaman James Moar, Mercantile Marine; this was in respect of services in the Mediterranean Sea on 16th February 1917. During the Second World War Moar was awarded a second medal as a Boatswain, Merchant Navy, for services rendered on passage to North Russia, the award being announced in the *Gazette* of 6th August 1943[23]. The award of the second medal is explicable only on grounds of inadvertence, a bar to the first medal being the appropriate award[24].

Between the Wars 10 awards were gazetted as follows:

	London Gazette and Theatre
Signalman J. Alderman	14th January 1921 (theatre not given)
Ordinary Seaman J. Baldock	6th May 1927 (China)
Petty Officer W. T. Bourne	6th May 1927 (China)[25]
Able Seaman F. H. Image	6th May 1927 (China)
Marine D. Jones, R.M.	18th December 1936 (Palestine)
Able Seaman W. Kell	6th May 1927 (China)
Able Seaman G. Mellors	14th January 1921 (theatre not given)
Leading Seaman W. A. Richards	6th November 1936 (Palestine)
Stoker Petty Officer J. Shorter	6th November 1936 (Palestine)
Officer's Steward Yueng Chung Kaig ...	2nd December 1938 (China)[25]

Second World War Wingate gives 7,132 medals (of which 174 were to foreign ratings), 153 first bars, four second bars and one third bar. Apparently he includes recipients of second and third bar awards among those of the first bar, and the recipient of the third bar among those of the second. The recipients of second bars were:

	London Gazette for second bar
Temporary Acting Petty Officer W. Kelly[26]	13th June 1944
Acting Chief Petty Officer A. J. Mallett[27]	4th September 1945
Chief Petty Officer T. A. Topley[28]	8th September 1942

The third bar was awarded to Temporary Petty Officer W. H. Kelly in the *London Gazette* of 13th June 1944[29]. The *London Gazette* of 16th August 1940 published a long list of awards including 14 to personnel of H.M. Transports, Hospital Carriers and Tugs; five to the Merchant Navy; three to civilian crews of motor boats and yachts; and awards to:

21. *E.g.*, in Russia.

22. Of which 52 were to ratings of the French Navy, and one to a rating of the Imperial Russian Navy. The discrepancy of 1,461 between our figures and Wingate's might be accounted for by additional awards to foreigners which we have not traced.

23. He also received the B.E.M. (Civil Division) in the Birthday Honours announced in *L.G.*, 12th June 1941.

24. See p.227 for the award of two M.M.s under similar circumstances.

25. These awards are accompanied by citations.

26. D.S.M., *L.G.*, 14th September 1943; first bar, *L.G.*, 22nd February 1944.

27. D.S.M., *L.G.*, 1st January 1940; first bar, *L.G.*, 22nd December 1942.

28. D.S.M., *L.G.*, 1st January 1940; first bar (given as another D.S.M.), *L.G.*, 7th June 1940.

29. D.S.M., *L.G.*, 7th April 1942; first bar, *L.G.*, 30th July 1942; second bar, *L.G.*, 22nd February 1944. Wingate probably includes Kelly's second bar in the four second bars he gives.

Fig. F: The Distinguished Service Medal, reverse.

Fig. G: Bar to the Distinguished Service Medal.

30. Their names are listed in Volume 16 of the *Journal of the Orders and Medals Research Society* at p.28.

31. See P.R.O. ADM 1/14361.

32. Sergeant G. R. I. Parker received the D.S.M. (*L.G.,* 1st January 1942) for services in air/sea rescue. Subsequently he was commissioned and received the D.F.C. (*L.G.,* 24th November 1944), a bar to the D.F.C. (*L.G.,* 23rd March 1945) and the A.F.C. (*L.G.,* 10th June 1948)

33. See also P.R.O. ADM 1/14578.

34. O'Neill was a member of the R.A.F. Regiment on passage to Malta in June 1942, see P.R.O. ADM 1/14338.

35. See also P.R.O. ADM 1/12368.

36. Including Sergeants P. E. Islaas and H. Munthe-Kaas of the Royal Norwegian Army.

37. For this man's other awards see p.48 ante.

38. To Able Seaman Saw Aaron for "bravery in numerous ambushes and small actions behind the Japanese lines between 1943 and 1945." This is an example of a D.S.M. being awarded for services ashore.

Sub Officer A. J. May, London Fire Brigade, of the Fire Float *Massey Shaw*, and Canteen Manager A. Harris, H.M.S. *Albury*.

Between 1942 and 1945, 51 N.C.O.s and men of the Royal Artillery[30] received the D.S.M. for services in defensively equipped Merchant Ships under the Order in Council of 1st July 1942. Hitherto soldiers serving in those ships had been awarded the B.E.M. (Civil Division) although one had been awarded the G.C. (see p.142) and another the M.M. (see p.228). In 1943 an honorary award of the D.S.M. (which was not gazetted) was made for secret services to Sergeant P. E. Islaas, Royal Norwegian Army[31]. Between 1942 and 1946, 23 N.C.O.s and men of the R.A.F.[30] received the D.S.M. for services with the Fleet under the Order in Council of 17th April 1940, or otherwise afloat (e.g. air/sea rescue[32], anti-minelaying, convoys etc.) under the Order in Council of 13th January 1943. Of these citations appear in the *London Gazette* for the following:

	London Gazette
Flight Sergeant A. Docherty	1st December 1944
Flight Sergeant J. N. F. Edwards, B.E.M.[33]	14th January 1944
Corporal T. H. Mould	2nd July 1943
Aircraftman I. R. O'Neill[34]	6th July 1943
Corporal E. R. Parham	1st September 1944
Leading Aircraftman A. P. White ...	28th April 1944
Aircraftman S. G. Whitlock[35]	24th November 1942

Honorary awards were made to foreigners as follows:

	D.S.M.	*1st bar*	
France	38	1	
Greece	12	—	
Netherlands	44	—	
Norway[36]	41	1	(L. A. Larsen[37])
Poland	26	—	
U.S.A.	16	—	
U.S.S.R.	5	—	
Totals	182	2	

All awards gazetted in 1946 were for the Second World War.

1947–1979 In this period the following awards were gazetted:

Year	Medals	First Bars	Remarks
1947 ...	7	—	(1 D.S.M. to Burma R.N.V.R. for Second World War[38], remainder to R.N. for Palestine)
1949 ...	7	—	(all for Yangtse; 6 R.N., 1 R.M.)
1951	4	1	(all for Korea; D.S.M., 3 R.N., 1 R.C.N.; bar to R.N.)
1952 ...	18	—	(all for Korea; 11 R.N., 2 R.M., 2 R.A.N., 1 R.C.N., 2 R.N.Z.N.)
1953 ...	10	—	(all for Korea; 8 R.N., 1 R.M., 1 R.C.N.)
1957 ...	2	—	(to R.N. for Near East)
1963 ...	1	—	(to R.N. for Brunei)
1965 ...	1	—	(to R.N. for Borneo)
1966 ...	1	—	(to R.N.Z.N. for East and West Malaysia)
1968 ...	2	—	(to R.A.N. for Vietnam)
1969 ...	1	—	(to R.A.N., for Vietnam)
1971 ...	1	—	(to R.A.N. for Vietnam)

The first bar was awarded to Yeoman of Signals D. R. J. Clare in the *London Gazette* of 2nd February 1951. In 1955 seven honorary awards were made to members of the United States forces for services during the Korean War (six United States Navy and one United States Air Force (Corporal C. W. Poole)).

ILLUSTRATIVE AWARD

Chief Stoker George H. Sturdy and Stoker Petty Officer Alfred Britton, both of H.M.S. *Laurel,* were each awarded the D.S.M. for the action off Heligoland on 28th August 1914. Their awards appear in the *London Gazette* of 23rd October 1914[39], and their citation in Commodore R. Y. Tyrwhitt's despatch of 26th September 1914 which was published in the *London Gazette* of 23rd October 1914[40]. This reads as follows:

> ". . . who both showed great coolness in putting out a fire near the centre gun after an explosion had occurred there; several lyddite shells were lying in the immediate vicinity."

An artist's representation of the incident, together with a note of the citation appears in Volume 4 of *Deeds that Thrill the Empire* (see Bibliography). However, only Britton is shown in the illustration and mentioned in the caption.

39. At p.8,502. The awards are repeated at p.8,510.

40. At p.8,499. It was repeated at p.8,507.

Chapter 18

The Distinguished Service Order

Fig.A: The Distinguished Service Order, obverse, Victoria issue.

ORIGIN AND DEVELOPMENT

A number of campaigns of varying sizes followed the Indian Mutiny and it was eventually realised that no adequate means existed of recognising the services of junior officers. The Victoria Cross was, of course, reserved for acts of outstanding gallantry while the C.B. could not be awarded to officers below the equivalent rank of major who, in any case, had first to be mentioned in despatches. On rare occasions the Royal Navy had recognised the services of junior officers by accelerated promotion, while in the Army a more widely-used system of brevet promotion obtained. The latter gave rise to inconvenience and even embarrassment as, for instance, where an officer promoted by brevet could be senior to his own commanding officer. Accordingly, various proposals were considered[1] and in 1886 (see *London Gazette*, 9th November 1886) the D.S.O. was instituted by Royal Warrant in the following terms:

"VICTORIA R.I.

Whereas We have taken into Our Royal consideration that the means of adequately rewarding the distinguished services of officers in Our naval and military services, who have been honourably mentioned in Despatches, are limited; now for the purposes of attaining an end so desirable as that of rewarding individual instances of meritorious or distinguished service in war, We have instituted and created, and by these presents, for Us, Our heirs and successors, do institute and create a new naval and military order of distinction, to be designated as hereinafter described, which We are desirous should be highly prized by the officers of Our naval and military services, and We are graciously pleased to make, ordain and establish the following rules and ordinances for the government of the same, which shall henceforth be inviolably observed and kept—

Firstly: It is ordained that this order shall henceforth be styled and designated the "Distinguished Service Order".

Secondly: It is ordained that the order shall consist of the Sovereign, and of such members or companions as We, Our heirs or successors, shall appoint.

Thirdly: It is ordained that We, Our heirs and successors, Kings and Queens regnant of the United Kingdom of Great Britain and Ireland, Emperors and Empresses of India are, and for ever shall be, Sovereigns of this order.

Fourthly: It is ordained that no person shall be eligible for this distinction who doth not actually hold, at the time of his nomination, a Commission in Our navy, in Our land forces or marines, or Our Indian or Colonial naval or military forces, or a Commission in one of the Departments of Our navy or army, the holder of which is entitled to honorary or relative navy or army rank, nor shall any person be nominated, unless his services shall have been marked by the especial mention of his name by the Admiral or senior naval officer commanding a squadron or detached naval force, or by the commander-in-chief of the forces in the field, in Despatches, for meritorious or distinguished service in the field, or before the enemy.

Fifthly: It is ordained that foreign officers who have been associated in naval and military operations with Our forces shall be eligible to be honorary members of this order.

Sixthly: It is ordained that when We, Our heirs and successors, shall be pleased to appoint any person to be a member of this order, such appointment shall be made by Warrant under Our Sign Manual, and countersigned by one of Our Principal Secretaries of State.

1. These are given at length by Wilson and McEwen (see Bibliography).

Seventhly: It is ordained that the decoration of the order shall be and shall be worn as is hereinafter set forth.

Eighthly: It is ordained that an officer shall be appointed to this order, that is to say, a Secretary and Registrar.

Ninthly: It is ordained that the Secretary and Registrar of this order shall be appointed by Us, Our heirs and successors, and shall have the custody of the archives of the order. He shall attend to the service of the order and shall execute such directions as he may receive from Our Principal Secretary of State for War.

Tenthly: It is ordained that this order shall rank next to and immediately after Our order of the Indian Empire, and that the companions thereof shall, in all places and assemblies whatsoever, have place and precedency next to and immediately after the companions of Our said order of the Indian Empire, and shall rank among themselves according to the dates of their respective nominations.

Eleventhly: It is ordained that the badge of the order, which shall consist of a gold cross, enamelled white, edged gold, having on one side thereof in the centre, within a wreath of laurel, enamelled green, the Imperial Crown in gold, upon a red enamelled ground, and on the reverse, within a similar wreath and on a similar red ground, Our Imperial and Royal Cypher, V.R.I., shall be suspended from the left breast by a red riband edged blue, of one inch in width.

Twelfthly: It is ordained that the names of those upon whom We may be pleased to confer the decoration shall be published in the *London Gazette*, and a registry thereof kept in the office of Our Secretary of State for War.

Lastly: We reserve to Ourself, Our heirs and successors, full power of annulling, altering, abrogating, augmenting, interpreting or dispensing with these regulations, or any part thereof, by a notification under the Sign Manual of the Sovereign of the order.

Given at Our Court at Balmoral, this sixth day of September, in the fiftieth year of Our reign, and in the year of Our Lord, one thousand eight hundred and eighty-six.

By Her Majesty's Command,
W. H. SMITH."

An amending Royal Warrant of 24th July 1902 provided that the D.S.O. would rank after the Royal Victorian Order, and altered the cypher on the reverse of the badge from V.R.I. to E.R.I. A further amending Warrant of 2nd July 1903 (see *London Gazette*, 14th July 1903) placed it immediately after the 4th Class of the Royal Victorian Order, while one of 15th October 1903 (see *London Gazette*, 20th October 1903) changed the cypher to E.R. VII. A bar or bars for subsequent acts of gallantry was instituted by a Warrant of 23rd August 1916 (see *London Gazette*, 26th August 1916), the first such awards being notified in the *London Gazette* of 26th September 1916[2], and in Army Order No. 290 of August 1916 a silver rose emblem was authorised to denote the award of a bar when the ribbon alone was worn.

Because the wording of the original Warrant had provided that the D.S.O. was to be awarded for meritorious or distinguished service in war, a number of appointments had been made between 1914 and 1916 under circumstances which could not be regarded as under fire. A strong feeling had arisen both in the Army and elsewhere that the D.S.O. should be restricted to services performed in action and it is noteworthy that the Warrant instituting the bar had specified that it was to be awarded for gallantry. Accordingly, on 1st January 1917 orders were given to all commanders in the field that the D.S.O. (as well as the M.C. and D.C.M.) should as far as possible be restricted to the "Fighting Services", i.e. the fighting personnel of brigades, divisions, corps and army troops, together with certain ancillary services associated in battle with these formations. During September 1917 proposals were under consideration as to whether there should be classes of the D.S.O. and M.C., Class I to be for the "Fighting Services", and Class II for the "non-Fighting Services", each to be distinguished by a different ribbon, or emblem worn on the ribbon. These proposals were not supported by the Army Council and no further action was taken at that stage. They were reconsidered at a

2. To Lieutenant Albert Ball (later V.C., D.S.O. and two bars, M.C.) R.F.C., and Major A. A. Goschen, R.F.A.

conference at the War Office in June and July 1918. The conference recommended that the D.S.O., M.C. and D.C.M. should be regarded primarily as distinctions for services in action with the enemy (including air raids, bombardments etc. producing conditions equivalent to actual combat); and that some emblem should be adopted to distinguish future "immediate" awards of those decorations from awards conferred through the medium of "Honours Gazettes". Only the former recommendation was accepted by the Army Council and notified generally on 1st August 1918; in fact this had little practical result as the instructions of 1st January 1917 had already largely confined the award of the distinctions concerned to services in action[3].

A revised Royal Warrant had, however, been approved on 1st April 1918 (see *London Gazette*, 12th July 1918). Except for the provision relating to the bar, the new Warrant made no specific mention of gallantry. It repeated much of the original and amending Warrants; extended the award to the Royal Air Force; gave precedence immediately after Commanders of the Order of the British Empire; and made detailed provisions for forfeiture and restoration. The cypher on the reverse of the badge was merely described as the "Royal Cypher". On 5th February 1931 (see *London Gazette*, 20th March 1931) the conditions for the award were finally resolved by an amending Warrant which laid down that the D.S.O. was to be given only for "distinguished services under fire or under conditions equivalent to service in actual combat with the enemy". This Warrant also widened the power to order forfeiture and restoration (such notifications were to be published in the *London Gazette*), and authorised a half-size miniature badge for wear on certain occasions. The widening of the power to order forfeiture followed a recommendation by the Interdepartmental Rewards Committee that all awards for gallantry, except in cases of extreme infamy, should be regarded as irrevocable; hence it was unnecessary to limit the power, as had been done before, by prescribing for particular circumstances. An amending Warrant of 11th January 1938 provided that the reverse of the badge should bear the "Royal and Imperial Cypher".

On 8th March 1943 a revised Warrant was approved[4] which incorporated the previous amendments and extended eligibility to officers of the Merchant Navy[5] and Home Guard (and similar forces); removed the original condition precedent that the recipient had to be mentioned in despatches[6]; and made provision for the procedure in the case of Dominion recommendations. This Warrant was, in turn, replaced by one of 11th September 1961[7] which, although making no basic alterations, was necessitated by constitutional changes in the Commonwealth. This Warrant omits "Imperial" from the description of the crown on the obverse and of the cypher on the reverse of the badge and, strangely enough, mentions for the first time that rosettes are to be worn on the ribbon, when worn alone, to denote bars, although they had been authorised in 1916 (see above).

By a Royal Warrant of 24th March 1964 (see Army Order No. 22 of March 1964) the functions performed by the Secretary of State for War in regard to the D.S.O. were transferred, *inter alia*, to the Secretary of State for Defence.

Traditionally, Companions have been permitted to use the letters "D.S.O." after their names and it is interesting to find that this has often been officially added to the inscription on some campaign medals given subsequently to the award. However, it is not done consistently. For instance, it does not appear on First World War campaign medals except in the case of the 1914 or 1914/15 Star where the award was made before the First World War. Nor does it always appear on later campaign medals, being no doubt dependent upon how or when the medal rolls were compiled.

3. See P.R.O. WO 32/5232 and 5400.

4. It was to take effect from 31st August 1942.

5. The first awards appear in *L.G.*, 8th September 1942, to the following Masters: Captains D. R. MacFarlane, F. N. Riley and R. Wren. A total of 14 such awards were made in the Second World War. A number of awards to Mercantile Marine officers holding commissions in the Royal Naval Reserve were made in the First World War.

6. Even before this condition was removed it does not seem to follow that the "mention" and subsequent nomination were necessarily proximate. Thus H. A. Young, Royal Artillery, was mentioned as a captain in the First World War (*L.G.*, 12th January 1920). He was awarded the D.S.O. as a lieutenant-colonel in the Second World War (*L.G.*, 11th July 1940) but his only "mention" was in the First World War.

7. See Army Order No. 66 of October 1961.

Fig.B: The Distinguished Service Order, obverse, Victoria and Edward VII issues.

8. The correspondence leading to the approval of the design of the badge is given by Wilson and McEwen (see Bibliography).

9. See the *Journal of the Society for Army Historical Research*, Museum Supplement No. 47 (June 1961) where crowns and coronets on military appointments are discussed in detail.

10. The Royal Warrant of 11th September 1961 calls it the "Royal Crown". In previous Warrants it was called the "Imperial Crown".

11. All five designs are now in the Ministry of Defence Library (Central and Army).

12. i.e. the awards to Lieutenant-Colonel C. Rawnsley (*L.G.*, 31st October 1902) and Lieutenant H. F. P. Percival (*L.G.*, 26th June 1902), both of the Army Service Corps. Replacements for Rawnsley's Queen's and King's South Africa medals were issued on 20th June 1913 (see P.R.O. WO 100/212 and 349) and it may be that a replacement D.S.O. was issued at the same time. There is no indication in the rolls that Percival's South Africa medals were replaced. His D.S.O. was presented by the King on 18th December 1902, almost six weeks after the Edward VII cypher was approved and it could be that his was one of the first issued with that cypher; alternatively, it could be a replacement. Rawnsley's Edward VII D.S.O. is in the Royal Corps of Transport Central Medal Collection at Aldershot.

13. To Major G. Mac K. Heriot, Royal Marine Light Infantry.

14. *Annual Report of the Deputy Master and Comptroller of the Royal Mint (1938)*, p.43. See also the Royal Warrant of 11th January 1938 mentioned above and P.R.O. WO 32/10550. This followed a recommendation by the "Committee of 1937 on the alteration of the Insignia of Orders and the alteration of Decorations and Medals with the Change of Reign" that the Royal and Imperial Cypher should be substituted for the Royal Cypher which appeared on the badge of the last two reigns.

DESCRIPTION[8] (For coloured illustration see Plate 3)

Ribbon Red, 1 inch wide, with narrow blue borders. The ribbons actually in production all seem to be slightly wider than the official size.

Brooch bar (Fig.A) This flat laurelled bar has a plain raised border, and is fitted with a pin and catch at the back. Frequently the pin and catch are removed to facilitate mounting on a medal brooch. Victorian issues of the badge have rather narrower and thinner brooch and suspender bars, with much narrower raised borders. The brooch and suspender bars issued from about 1916 have leaves of rather coarser design.

Suspension By a small swivelling ring to a laurelled suspender which is similar to the brooch bar, but without pin and catch. From 1938 the year of award is engraved on the back of it, two figures of which appear on either side of the swivel barrel.

Issues in gold Before about 1890 the badge was made of gold; thereafter it has been made of silver gilt although the laurels and centre pieces of both obverse and reverse remain of 16-carat gold. The gold badges were slightly smaller and thinner than the later Victorian issues but weigh (together with the suspender bar) about 0.86 ounces Troy as against 0.73 ounces for the silver gilt version. The gold and earlier Victorian silver gilt badges have a crown with rather flatter arches, and the cypher is fractionally smaller. Taking 1889 as the last year in which gold badges were issued, about 153 awards would have been made.

Obverse Disregarding minor variations in manufacture, there are four main representations of the crown[9], as follows:

1. Victorian (Fig.A) The crown with flatter arches appeared on the gold and earlier silver gilt badges.

2. Victorian and Edward VII (Fig.B) In May 1901, following the death of Queen Victoria, a new representation of the crown was approved. The new crown, however, appeared on most awards with the Victorian and Edwardian reverses gazetted after that date.

3. George V, George VI and Elizabeth II (Fig.C) The 1901 crown continued to be represented on the badge although it was made slightly larger than before[10]. In both World Wars a number of different strikings appeared, no doubt due to the large numbers needed.

Reverse There are six types of reverse, as follows:

1. Victorian (Fig.D) This corresponds with obverses 1 and 2, details of which are given above.

2. Edward VII (Fig.E) On 13th October 1902 three designs (one obverse, two reverses) were submitted to the King. The reverse designs consisted of the entwined letters "ERI" and "VII", one with crown and the other without, the construction of the cypher being different in each case. Two further reverse designs were submitted on 5th November following, of which that illustrated here was approved, the other design being similar but without crown[11]. Despite the Royal Warrant of 24th July 1902 it seems that no ERI cypher was issued although we have seen a photograph of a specimen which, however, does not correspond with any of the designs submitted. Messrs. Garrard, the Crown Jewellers, who manufacture the badge, have no record of such a reverse. With two exceptions[12], all awards seen for the South African War have the Victorian cypher. Seventy-eight D.S.O.s were gazetted between 1903 and 1908, there being none between 1909 and 1910.

3. George V (Fig.F) The first D.S.O.[13] of the new reign was gazetted on 19th June 1911 and this may have been of the George V issue. No Edward VIII issues seem to have been made.

4. George VI first type (Fig.G) This cypher was first struck in 1938[14] and continued in issue until about 1948.

Fig.C: The Distinguished Service Order, obverse, George V, George VI and Elizabeth II issues.

Fig.D: The Distinguished Service Order, reverse, Victoria issue.

Fig.E: The Distinguished Service Order, reverse, Edward VII issue.

5. George VI second type (Fig.H) This cypher was in use from about 1949 until 1952, during which period 63 awards were gazetted.

6. Elizabeth II (Fig.I) This cypher was first struck about 1953 and is still in use. Unlike the obverse, the crown is the St. Edward crown.

Bar (Fig.J) The first bars issued seem to have been similar in design to the brooch and suspender bars, but this may have been a temporary expedient being shortly replaced by the type illustrated here. From about 1938 the year of the award has been engraved on the back of the slide in rather smaller figures than those appearing on the suspender bar.

Naming The badges are issued unnamed although occasionally brooch or suspender bars are found with details unofficially engraved on them.

Copies Several copies of varying quality exist, details of which are as follows:

1. George V. There are several variants. In general the crowns are poorly cut or made very small. The cyphers are fractionally larger than normal and the arches of the crown above the cypher not fully voided. In regard to the markings made on the metal plates to which the red enamel is keyed and upon which the crowns and cyphers are mounted, some copies have radial instead of concentric markings. These copies have radial markings only and it is important to note that some genuine George V badges, as well as the Victorian and Edward VII versions, have both concentric and radial markings on the same plate, the latter usually being in the form of a star. With copies, the red plates are poorly enamelled and the gilt is generally thin and lighter coloured. Similarly, the enamel of the laurels is dull and some copies do not have the berries picked out in red. The whole badge is rather flatter and, on occasion, the arms are narrower. Some copies do not have the securing pin running diagonally through the centre of the cross, which is found on all genuine issues.

2. George VI first type. The laurels are pale green and the gilt is poor. The arms of the cross are rather narrow and the whole badge is somewhat flat. The crowns and the cypher are badly cut and the year of award is omitted from the back of the suspender bar although, of course this can be added fraudulently. The cypher is too thick and the crown above not voided.

3. George VI second type. In addition to poor enamelling and gilding, the cypher is rather larger than it should be and the crown above is not voided. The seam where the front and back halves of the badge are joined can just be seen below the gilt.

4. Elizabeth II. This is a very dangerous copy. It has much the same characteristics as the George VI first type copy except that the gilt and enamel are rather better and it is of almost exactly the right size.

The copy second award bar has no holes at the back of the slide for stitching it to the ribbon.

VERIFICATIONS AND CITATIONS

All awards can be verified from the *London Gazette*. From 1886 to June 1940 the names are indexed in the Gazette under the award heading in the "State Intelligence" portion of the appropriate quarterly index. Thereafter this section gives only the pages upon which awards are to be found; sometimes the references are corrupt, or refer to a different type of award, or sometimes are omitted altogether. From 1886 to December 1900 and from 1914 to December 1941 names are also given in the "Civil Promotions" (later "Civil Appointments and Promotions") section of the indices. From January 1942 they appear in a comprehensive section headed "Honours, Decorations and Medals". Before 1914 no citations, as such, are available although from time to time an explanatory sentence is added to the Gazette entry. Occasionally the appropriate despatch will give details of the services performed since, until 1943, a condition precedent to the award was that

Fig.F: The Distinguished Service Order, reverse, George V issue.

Fig.G: The Distinguished Service Order, reverse, George VI issue, first type.

the officer concerned should have been so mentioned. Some South African War despatches are particularly useful in this respect. During the First World War a large number of "periodic" appointments were made which carry no citation; very rarely, some details may be found in unit or formation histories. Where citations are given in the Gazette these are sometimes separated from the award and it is then necessary to search in later indices to find the reference to the citation. Since 1921 very few citations have been published in the *London Gazette*, except for some for the Royal Navy and Royal Air Force, and a number for recent operations, e.g. in Aden and Vietnam. No citations have been published since 1968.

O'Moore Creagh (see Bibliography) gives many useful biographical details and provides much information not otherwise readily available. Until 1921 Companions and Honorary Companions are listed in Burke's *Peerage* where serial numbers are assigned to the names of the former. However, these numbers are misleading in that, in certain cases, the same number is repeated with the addition of a differently lettered suffix. Until the early 1930s brief biographical details appear in the editions of Debrett which contain the "Companionage". From October 1888 to October 1908 names of surviving recipients appear in the Quarterly Army Lists together with the date of award (which usually corresponds with the date of the *L.G.*[15]). Names also appear in the Supplement[16] to the Monthly Army Lists between April 1900 and April 1920, and in the Navy Lists to January 1920.

For naval awards some citations or other information regarding awards in both World Wars are to be found in the Public Record Office series ADM 1 (Code 85) and ADM 116 (Code 85); both series contain a large number of files and it is desirable to know the date of award and, where possible, the action or theatre for which it was made, before consulting the indices. The Honours and Awards files in AIR 1 contain many of the First World War recommendations for officers of the R.N.A.S., R.F.C. and R.A.F. serving in France and Belgium. Where only the date of award is known it is preferable to search for the recommendation in the files of HQ R.F.C./R.A.F. which are arranged according to date; where the unit or formation is known the corresponding files may be consulted first although not all have been preserved. For other flying awards details may be found in AIR 30 (Submissions to the King 1918–1946) and in AIR 2 (Code 30) which contains the original recommendations made during the Second World War. Here there are separate files for immediate and periodic awards; however, the numerical sequence of the AIR 2 references does not reflect the strict chronology of the files and it is necessary to consult the whole Index to the Code when searching. Details of some Second World War awards appeared in Press Releases from which extracts frequently found their way into local newspapers.

NUMBERS AWARDED

The Monarch is the Sovereign of the Order, and Queen Victoria received her insignia at the hands of the Secretary of State, see the *London Gazette*, 26th November 1886.

1886–1914 Excluding the Sovereign and two cases in which appointments would have been made had the officer concerned survived[17], 1,732 appointments were gazetted in respect of services performed before the First World War as follows:

1886	...	42	(Burma 12; Egypt (Ginnis)30)
1887	...	67	(Burma 64 (6 R.N.); Soudan 3 (Sarras 2))
1888	...	13	(Burma 10; W. Africa 3 (1 R.N.))
1889	...	30	(Burma 10; Egypt (Toski) 8; Hazara 8; Sikkim 2; W. Africa 2)
1890	...	12	(Chin-Lushai 10 (1 R. Indian Marine); Egypt (Toski) 1; W. Africa 1)
1891	...	20	(Burma (1886-9) 5; Chin-Lushai 1; E. Africa (Witu) 1 (R.N.); Egypt (1885) 3 (1 R.N.); Hazara (1888) 1; Hazara (1891) 4; N. Eastern

15. Awards in *L.G.*, 27th September 1901 were to bear the date 29th November 1900 (except where stated). The latter date is given in the Army Lists.

16. Published in January, April, July and October.

17. Honorary Major General A. G. Huyshe, C.B. (*L.G.*, 26th November 1886 – action at Ginnis, Egypt) and Brevet Major Prince Christian of Schleswig-Holstein, King's Royal Rifle Corps (*L.G.*, 19th April 1901 – South Africa)

Fig.H: The Distinguished Service Order, reverse, George VI issue, second type.

Fig.I: The Distinguished Service Order, reverse, Elizabeth II issue.

Fig.J: Bar to the Distinguished Service Order.

18. Including the honorary award to Count R.Z. dal Verme attached 2nd King's Own Yorkshire Light Infantry in *L.G.*, 27th September 1901 which is not mentioned by O'Moore Creagh and the award to Captain H. N. Schofield, R.F.A. which was changed to the V.C. see p.289 below, but excluding Prince Christian mentioned above.

19. Including the award to Lieutenant H. A. Carter, Indian Army, which was changed to the V.C., see p.289 below.

20. To Lieutenant W. Ll. Jones, Middlesex Regiment, in *L.G.*, 4th August 1914.

21. British Army and W. India Regiment 925, R.N. 3, R.M.L.I. 3; Australia – naval 1, military 62; Canada 20; Indian Army 14; New Zealand 10; South Africa and Rhodesia – naval 1, military 130.

Frontier 1; Samana 2; Soudan (1884 and 1891) 2. *Note*: No indication is given on the services leading to the 13 appointments announced in *L.G.*, 30th May 1891. However, it is possible to deduce them with reasonable accuracy from the biographical details given by O'Moore-Creagh)

1892	...	8	(Burma 4; Hunza 1; W. Africa 3)
1893	...	6	(Burma and Chin Hills 1; Chilas (N.W.F.) 1; Juba River (W. Africa) 1 (R.N.); W. Africa 3 (R.N.))
1894	...	13	(Benin River (W. Africa) 3 (R.N.); Burma and Chin Hills 3; Gambia (W. Africa) 6 (2 R.N.); W. Africa 1)
1895	...	18	(Chin Hills 2; Chitral 9; Waziristan 6; W. and Central Africa 1)
1896	...	37	(Benin River 1894 (W. Africa) 4; Chitral 16; Egypt and Soudan 14 (1 R.N.); Uganda 3)
1897	...	17	(Benin (1897) 5 (4 R.N.); E. Africa 2; Niger (1897) (West Africa) 1; N.W.F. (Maizar 1897) 1; Rhodesia 7; W. Africa 1)
1898	...	84	(Dawkita (W. Africa) 1 (R.N.); Egypt and Soudan (1898) 41 (2 R.N.); Kandia (Crete) 1 (R.N.); Mashonaland 1; N.W.F. (Maizar 1897) 1; N.W.F. (1897/8) 35; Soudan (1897) 2 (1 R.N.); Uganda 2)
1899	...	34	(Egypt and Soudan (1898) 3; Kandia (Crete) 4; N.W.F. (1897/8) 6; Uganda 11; W. Africa 10)
1900	...	20	(China 5 (R.N.); Sierra Leone 8; South Africa 5 (2 R.N., 1 Victorian Navy, 1 Natal Naval Volunteers); Uganda 1; W. Africa 1)
1901	...	888	(Ashanti 16; China 17 (1 R. Indian Marine); South Africa 855[18] (1 R.N.)
1902	...	337	(Aro (W. Africa) 11; Ashanti 1; Lango (Uganda) 2; N. Nigeria 3; Somaliland 2; South Africa 307; Uganda 1; Waziristan 10)
1903	...	10	(China 3 (1 R. Indian Marine); N. Nigeria 3; Somaliland 1; South Africa (1899/02) 1; Waziristan 2)
1904	...	27	(N. Nigeria 1; S. Nigeria 2; Somaliland 14[19] (1 R.N. and 1 R. Indian Marine); South Africa (1899/02) 1; Tibet 9)
1905	...	13	(Aden (1903/4) 4; Nigeria 9)
1906	...	5	(Kissi 1905 (W. Africa) 1; N. Nigeria 1; S. Nigeria 3)
1907	...	6	(Kalahari Desert 1; Natal 2; N. Nigeria 3)
1908	...	17	(E. Africa 2; N. Nigeria 1; N.W.F. 13; S. Nigeria 1)
1911	...	1	(Persian Gulf)
1912	...	6	(Abor 1911/12 (N.W.F.) 5; Soudan 1)
1914	...	1	(E. Africa[20])

Many of these awards were made in relation to a campaign rather than to an isolated incident. In certain cases (for example, some small expeditions in Africa and the disturbances in 1898 in Crete) no campaign medal accompanied the award.

The total number of awards for South Africa 1899/02 is 1,169[21] (including 5 to naval officers). Both the official statistics which give 1,143 (apparently excluding the naval awards) and Norman (see Bibliography) who gives 1,088, are wrong.

It is interesting to note that in the period up to the outbreak of the First World War the following three officers had also received the D.C.M.:

	D.C.M.	*D.S.O.*
Caulfield, A. M. *alias*, in the ranks, Frederick Williams	Lance-Corporal, 66th Foot; for Maiwand (submission of 1st February 1881)	Lieutenant, Northumberland Fusiliers; for Burma (*L.G.*, 25th November 1887)
Boyd, G. F.	Sergeant, Devonshire Regiment; for South Africa (*L.G.*, 27th September 1901)	Lieutenant, East Yorkshire Regiment; for South Africa (*L.G.*, 31st October 1902)
Holman, R. C.	Sergeant Major, N.S.W. Mounted Infantry; for South Africa (*L.G.*, 27th September 1901)	Captain, N.S.W. Mounted Rifles; for South Africa (*L.G.*, 31st October 1902)

First World War The official statistics cover the period from 1914 to May 1920, and thus extend beyond the campaigns against the Central Powers. The figures given, which seem to be for War Office awards only although some to the Royal Naval Division are included, are as follows:

	Services in the Field	Services in connection with the War
D.S.O.	8,981	21
– First bars ...	708	1
– Second bars ...	71	—
– Third bars ...	7	—

Those for services in connection with the War include awards for the Easter Rising, air raids, coastal bombardments, etc. During the same period Admiralty and Air Ministry[22] awards were as follows:

	Admiralty	Air Ministry
D.S.O	826	53
– First bars ...	52	7
– Second bars ...	4	1

At least six officers received the D.S.O. in substitution for an earlier award, as follows:

	Original award and London Gazette	London Gazette substituting D.S.O.
Captain R. D. Anderson, East African Transport Corps	M.C. 4th May 1917	22nd June 1918
Major S. T. Grigg, M.C., West Yorkshire Regiment	O.B.E. 18th November 1918	19th December 1918
Acting Captain A. Mac G. MacDonald, Seaforth Highlanders	M.C. 19th November 1917	22nd April 1918
Lieutenant W. P. Mark-Wardlaw, Royal Navy	D.S.C. 13th September 1915	15th February 1919
Temporary Captain H. C. Pemberton, Lancashire Fusiliers	M.C. 2nd April 1919	27th June 1919
Temporary Captain A. Witham, Royal Field Artillery	M.C. 18th February 1918	1st May 1918

The recipients of third bars were:

	London Gazette for Third Bar
Temporary Commander A. W. Buckle, R.N.V.R., Anson Battalion, Royal Naval Division	8th March 1919
Temporary Brigadier-General W. D. Croft, 27th Infantry Brigade	15th February 1919
Temporary Lieutenant-Colonel W. R. A. Dawson, Queen's Own Royal West Kent Regiment	8th March 1919
Acting Lieutenant-Colonel R. S. Knox, Royal Inniskilling Fusiliers	8th March 1919
Temporary Brigadier-General F. W. Lumsden, V.C., Royal Marine Artillery	22nd April 1918
Temporary Lieutenant-Colonel A. N. S. Jackson, North Lancashire Regiment attached King's Royal Rifle Corps	2nd December 1918

22. The first Air Ministry awards were gazetted on 3rd June 1918.

Temporary Brigadier-General E. A.
  Wood, General List ... ... 12th December 1919

Thirty five officers received one or more bars to a pre-War award.

We have traced a number of honorary appointments of foreign officers sponsored by the Admiralty, the War Office and the Air Ministry between 1915 and 1920. The only Admiralty awards we have found were published in *L.G.*, 23rd December 1915 although it seems likely that other awards were made which were not gazetted. Some War Office awards were published in *L.G.*, 16th November 1915; thereafter they appeared in printed lists dated between May 1916 and 4th November 1920. The first four lists were unnumbered, the remainder being numbered from 3 to 68 of which we have been unable to trace nos. 23, 42, 46, 47 and 52. The Air Ministry lists were dated 19th July and 10th December 1919. The following summary, in which all are War Office awards except where noted, is therefore incomplete to the extent of some probable Admiralty awards and any in the missing War Office lists:

Arab Army ...	6	
Belgium	134	(including 1 Air Ministry award)
China	2	
Czechoslovakia	20	
France	678	(including 10 Admiralty and 13 Air Ministry awards)
Greece	43	
Italy	251	
Japan	21	
Montenegro ...	1	
Portugal	21	
Rumania	29	
Russia	1	
Serbia	38	
Slavo-British Aviation Corps	1	(Air Ministry)
USA	83	
Total	1329	

1920–1939 From June 1920 to December 1939 the following 162 D.S.O.s were gazetted:

1920	...	36	(15 Afghan War 1919; 1 Black Sea; 2 Burma; 2 Mesopotamia; 6 services in or escaping from captivity; 3 Somaliland; 3 South Russia; 4 Waziristan)
1921	...	21	(2 Asia Minor 1920; 12 Mesopotamia/Iraq; 1 Palestine; 1 South Persia; 5 Waziristan)
1922	...	6	(Waziristan)
1923	...	2	(Razmak and Waziristan)
1924	...	5	(1 Kurdistan; 4 Waziristan)
1925	...	7	(1 Khartoum; 6 Waziristan)
1926	...	1	(Kurdistan)
1928	...	2	(Iraq)
1931	...	1	(Iraq)
1932	...	7	(4 Burma; 3 North West Frontier)
1933	...	2	(1 Chitral; 1 Northern Kurdistan)
1934	...	3	(North West Frontier)
1935	...	2	(North West Frontier)
1936	...	6	(3 Palestine; 3 North West Frontier)
1937	...	20	(1 North West Frontier; 19 Waziristan)
1938	...	17	(1 North West Frontier; 4 Palestine; 10 Waziristan; 2 Yangtse, December 1937)
1939	...	24	(9 Palestine; 1 "recent operations" (? Palestine); 14 Second World War)

In addition the following 16 first bars were gazetted:

1920	...	2	(Afghan War 1919 and Waziristan)

1921 ... 4 (1 Asia Minor 1920; 2 Mesopotamia; 1 "minor operations in the Indian Empire and adjacent territories")
1931 ... 1 (North West Frontier)
1932 ... 3 (North West Frontier)
1933 ... 2 (Northern Kurdistan)
1937 ... 2 (Waziristan)
1938 ... 1 (Waziristan)
1939 ... 1 (Aden)

Second World War Wingate gives a useful analysis for the period 1939–1945 which may be adapted as follows:

		D.S.O.	1st Bar	2nd Bar	3rd Bar
Navy	Royal Navy	618	110	21	3
	Royal Marines	34	3	1	—
	Merchant Navy	14	—	—	—
	Royal Indian Navy	2	—	—	—
	Royal Australian Navy	14	1	—	—
	Royal Canadian Navy	7	—	—	—
	Royal New Zealand Navy	4	—	—	—
	Honorary	80	2	—	—
Army	British Army	1,745	203	18	2
	Indian Army	235	38	5	—
	Colonial Forces	2	—	—	—
	Australian Military Forces	180	24	—	—
	Canadian Army	349	17	2	—
	New Zealand Military Forces[23]	112	14	2	1
	South African Military Forces	63	6	1	—
	Honorary	296	5	—	—
Air Force	Royal Air Force	870	62	8	2
	Royal Indian Air Force	1	2	—	—
	Royal Australian Air Force	69	3	—	—
	Royal Canadian Air Force	69	4	1	—
	Royal New Zealand Air Force	44	3	—	—
	South African Air Force	34	—	—	—
	Honorary	38	—	—	—
	Totals:	4,880	497	59	8

The eight third bar awards were as follows:

	London Gazette for Third Bar
Acting Air Vice-Marshal Sir Basil E. Embry, Royal Air Force	20th July 1945
Lieutenant-General Sir Bernard E. Freyberg, V.C., New Zealand Military Forces	5th July 1945
Commander E. A. Gibbs, Royal Navy	6th July 1943
Temporary Lieutenant-Colonel R. B. Mayne, Special Air Service	11th October 1945
Captain R. G. Onslow, Royal Navy ...	31st October 1944
Temporary Lieutenant-Colonel A. S. Pearson, Army Air Corps	1st February 1945
Wing Commander J. B. Tait, Royal Air Force	9th January 1945
Captain F. J. Walker, Royal Navy ...	13th June 1944

1946 All awards gazetted in this year appear to be for the Second World War except for 13 D.S.O.s and 2 first bars for South East Asia. However, in a number of cases the *Gazette* announcement contains no identifying details.

1947–1979 A summary of the awards gazetted during this period is as follows:

23. The O.B.E. awarded to Lieutenant-Colonel F. W. Voelcker, M.C. in *L.G.*, 7th December 1944 for services in the South West Pacific was replaced by the D.S.O. in *L.G.*, 7th February 1946.

128

Theatre	London Gazettes	D.S.O.s	1st Bar	2nd Bar	3rd Bar
Arabian Peninsula	1958–1976	6	1	—	—
Borneo	1964–1966	3	—	1	—
Brunei 1964		1	—	—	—
Congo	1961–1962	2	—	—	—
Cyprus 1957		1	1	1	—
Kenya 1955		1	—	—	—
Korea	1950–1954	74	7	3	1
Late awards	1947–1948	39	4	—	—
Malaya	1949–1958	26	3	—	—
Near East 1957		3	2	—	—
Northern Ireland	1972–1973	5	—	—	—
Palestine 1948		2	1	—	—
South East Asia 1947		2	—	—	—
Vietnam	1965–1972	37	—	—	—
Yangtse 1949		2	1	—	—
	Totals:	204	20	5	1

Of these, 63 D.S.O.s together with six first bars and two second bars were gazetted between 1949 and 1952 inclusive, and 98 D.S.O.s together with 9 first bars, three second bars and one third bar between 1953 and 1979 inclusive. The third bar was awarded to Temporary Brigadier D. A. Kendrew, late Infantry, in London Gazette, 8th December 1953.

1886–1953 For this period Wingate gives a total of 16,476 initial awards, with 1,268 first bars, 132 second bars and 17 third bars. However, it seems that these figures should be corrected to 133 second bars and 16 third bars.

ILLUSTRATIVE AWARD

On 27th December 1944 the Commander, Pathfinder Force (No. 8 Group) recommended Acting Wing Commander D. T. Witt of 635 Squadron R.A.F. for the D.S.O. in the following terms[24]:

> "On 25.10.44 this officer was captain of an aircraft detailed to carry out blind marking on the heavily defended target of Essen. On 30.10.44 he was again detailed for a similar role on Cologne, and on 2.11.44 on Dusseldorf. It was absolutely imperative that, irrespective of the odds, this officer should fly his aircraft with absolute precision in order to mark accurately.
>
> On each of these three occasions his aircraft was engaged and hit by heavy and accurate flak which made his job extremely difficult, and on one occasion his aircraft hard to handle. Disregarding these heavy odds on each of these occasions, this officer pressed home his attacks with the utmost determination and with excellent results. His handling of the aircraft and total disregard of his personal safety in these circumstances set a rare example which has seldom been surpassed.
>
> This officer has now completed 100 operational sorties against the enemy's most heavily defended objectives, including Hamburg, Kiel, Stuttgart, Duisburg and Berlin.
>
> As a captain and pilot he has pressed home his attacks with the utmost determination and vigour. No defences have proved too formidable, and any task, however arduous, allotted to him has been carried out in a cheerful, cool and confident manner. As flight commander his leadership, co-operation and strong sense of duty have been an inspiration to all and of the utmost value to his Squadron.
>
> I strongly recommend him for the award of the Distinguished Service Order."

On 8th January 1945 the Commander-in-Chief, Bomber Command approved the recommendation which was submitted, with others and without citation, by the Secretary of State for Air to the King on 18th January 1945[25]. The award was published in the London Gazette of 16th February 1945 at p.929 with the following citation:

24. See P.R.O. AIR 2/9044.
25. See P.R.O. AIR 30/186 (15).

"As a pilot of aircraft this officer participated in 100 sorties, many of them against the most heavily defended targets. His last 3 missions were against Essen, Cologne and Dusseldorf respectively. On each of these occasions he pressed home his attacks with the greatest determination in the face of intense anti-aircraft fire to obtain good results. He has displayed the highest standard of skill and bravery, setting an example of a high order."

Witt also received the D.F.C.[26] and the D.F.M.[27]. In addition, he had the 1939/45 Star, the Air Crew Europe Star with bar "France and Germany", the Africa Star, the Defence and War Medals, the General Service Medal (Army and R.A.F.) with bar "Malaya", and Queen Elizabeth II's Coronation Medal. The D.S.O. is of the first type George VI issue with the date "1945" engraved on the reverse of the suspender bar. Witt's decorations are not given after his name on the General Service Medal.

26. See *L.G.*, 5th August 1941 at p.4, 516: P.R.O. AIR 2/9541 (recommendation) and AIR 30/163 (92) (submission).

27. See *L.G.*, 22nd October 1940 at p.6, 137; P.R.O. AIR 2/9467 (recommendation) and AIR 30/157 (129) (submission).

Chapter 19

The Edward Medal

Fig. A: The Edward Medal, obverse, Edward VII issue.

ORIGIN AND DEVELOPMENT

Prior to July 1907 the Albert Medal (q.v.) was the only official award available for saving life in mines[1]. Since that medal was sparingly granted it was thought desirable that there should be some further distinction which would cover the type of act which had hitherto gone unrecognised. Accordingly, the suggestion was made by Sir Henry Cunynghame of the Home Office, who took a great interest in mining questions, that such acts should be rewarded by silver and bronze medals and that the conditions of award should be similar to those for the Sea Gallantry Medal (q.v.): namely, that life should be risked but that it should not be necessary that the probability of death should exceed the chance of survival[2] (which was the formidable standard for the Albert Medal). A leading colliery owner, Mr A. Hewlett, offered to subscribe a sum of up to £600 to defray the cost of establishing the medal, and to bear the preliminary cost of design. The original intention had been to restrict the medal to acts performed in mines and quarries in the United Kingdom. However, when the proposal was announced an article appeared in the Press urging its extension to the whole of the Empire. An Australian gentleman, Mr A. G. Wise, who happened to be in the United Kingdom at the time, took up the suggestion which was brought to the attention of the Home Secretary, Mr H. J. Gladstone, who gave it his whole-hearted support. The main difficulty was to find the additional money. Accordingly, Mr Wise approached one of his Australian friends, Sir Malcolm McEacharn, who undertook to provide the £400 which it was estimated would be required. The matter was put to the King who, at first, expressed some doubt as to the necessity for two Classes. Eventually, however, he approved the scheme, and the suggestion that the medal should be called "The Edward Medal". In due course the medal was instituted by a Royal Warrant of 13th July 1907[3] in the following terms:

"EDWARD, R. & I.

EDWARD THE SEVENTH, by the Grace of God, of the United Kingdom of Great Britain and Ireland and of the British Dominions beyond the Seas King, Defender of the Faith, Emperor of India, to all to whom these Presents shall come, Greeting!

Whereas We are desirous of distinguishing by some mark of Our Royal Favour the many heroic acts performed by Miners and Quarrymen and others who endanger their own lives in saving or endeavouring to save the lives of others from perils in Mines and Quarries within Our Dominions and in territories under Our Protection or Jurisdiction, We do by these Presents for Us, Our Heirs, and Successors institute and create a new Medal to be awarded for such acts of gallantry:

Firstly. – It is ordained that the Medal shall be of two classes which shall be designated and styled "The Edward Medal of the First Class" and "The Edward Medal of the Second Class".

Secondly. – It is ordained that the Edward Medal of the First Class shall consist of a circular Medal of Silver with Our Effigy on the obverse, and on the reverse a design representing the rescue of a miner with the inscription "for courage".

Thirdly. – It is ordained that the Edward Medal of the Second Class shall consist of a Circular Medal of Bronze of a similar design.

Fourthly. – It is ordained that the Medals shall only be awarded to those of Our Faithful Subjects and others who, in saving or endeavouring to save the lives of others from perils in Mines and Quarries within Our Dominions and in territories under Our Protection or Jurisdiction, have endangered their own lives, and that such award shall be made only on a recommendation to Us by Our Principal Secretary of State for the Home Department.

1. The preamble to the Royal Warrant of 30th April 1877, extending the Albert Medal to land services, had particularised "heroic acts performed . . . in preventing loss of life from accidents in mines . . . and other perils on shore . . ." among the reasons for the extension.

2. See P.R.O. HO 45/13628 from which the above is summarised.

3. See *L.G.*, 18th October 1907.

Fig.B: The Edward Medal, obverse, George V issue, first type.

Fig.C: The Edward Medal, obverse, George V issue, second type.

Fig.D: The Edward Medal, obverse, George VI issue, first type.

4. To G. H. Lamb, see *L.G.*, 21st February 1908.

5. In fact, during the whole period of the existence of the medal there have been slightly more than two awards for services in mines for every one in industry.

6. The King's Police Medal (q.v.), which was also available to members of recognised fire brigades, was instituted on 7th July 1909.

7. See *L.G.*, 3rd December 1909.

Fifthly. – It is ordained that the names of those upon whom We may be pleased to confer either of these Decorations shall be published in the *London Gazette*, and that a Register thereof shall be kept in the Office of Our Principal Secretary of State for the Home Department.

Sixthly. – It is ordained that each Medal shall be suspended from the left breast and the riband, of an inch and three-eighths in width, shall be dark blue with a narrow yellow stripe on either side: Provided that when the Medal is awarded to a woman it shall be worn on the left shoulder, suspended from a riband of the same width and colour, fashioned into a bow.

Seventhly. – It is ordained that any act of gallantry which is worthy of recognition by the award of the Edward Medal, but is performed by one upon whom the Decoration has already been conferred may, on a recommendation to Us by Our Principal Secretary of State for the Home Department, be recorded by a Bar attached to the riband by which the Medal is suspended; and for every such additional act an additional Bar may be added.

Eighthly. – In order to make such provision as shall effectually preserve pure these most honourable Decorations, it is ordained that if any person, on whom either of such Decorations is conferred be guilty of any crime or disgraceful conduct which, in Our judgment, disqualifies him for the same, his name shall, by an especial Warrant under Our Royal Sign Manual be forthwith erased from the Register of those upon whom the said Decoration shall have been conferred and his Medal shall be forfeited. And every person to whom the said Medal is given shall before receiving the same, enter into an agreement to return the same, if his name shall be so erased as aforesaid under this regulation. It is hereby further declared, that We, Our Heirs and Successors, shall be the sole judges of the circumstances demanding such forfeiture. Moreover, We shall at all times have power to regrant a Medal to any person whose Medal may at any time have been forfeited.

Given at Our Court at Saint James's, the thirteenth day of July, one thousand nine hundred and seven, in the seventh year of Our Reign.

By His Majesty's Command.
H. J. GLADSTONE."

In order that a uniform standard should be maintained it was decided that overseas recommendations should be submitted to the King through the Home Secretary. The King expressed the wish that the medal should not be awarded for rash and injudicious acts however gallant they might be. In October 1907 the King asked whether there was any practical means of recognising the gallantry of a miner who had lost his life in a fire in a mine in Canada. No provision for posthumous awards had been made in the Warrant but, after various precedents had been considered, it was decided to recommend a posthumous award in this case. The King approved the recommendation and the award was made[4] which became the precedent for future posthumous awards.

When the proposal for the Edward Medal was first put forward it was suggested that it should also be awarded for acts arising in factories and workshops, as well as for those in mines and quarries. However, Mr Hewlett desired that the medal for which he had provided the money should be confined to mines and quarries although he had no objection to the financing by others of a medal for other acts. As it seemed desirable to complete the scope of the medal by extending it to other industrial pursuits some well-known industrialists (Sir Hugh Bell, Lord Airdale, Mr David Colville, Mr R. A. Hadfield and Sir William Lewis) were approached privately and each agreed to subscribe £100 to defray the cost if the King agreed to the extension. It was pointed out that, in general, industrial occupations do not attract such great risks as are to be found in mining, and hence the number of medals required would be smaller[5]. Policemen and members of fire brigades would not be eligible because a special medal for them was under consideration[6]. Accordingly, the proposal was approved by the King and by a Royal Warrant of 1st December 1909[7] the scope of the original Warrant was extended to include heroism in industry, for which a medal with a different reverse was prescribed. The operative part of this Warrant was as follows:

Fig.E: The Edward Medal, obverse, George VI issue, second type.

Fig.F: The Edward Medal, obverse, Elizabeth II issue, first type.

8. Until then no such awards had been made. In fact, the bronze medal awarded to Ben Littler Jones for an act of gallantry, performed with William Williams at the Llysfaen Quarry, Caernarvonshire, on 21st May 1938 (*L.G.*, 9th September 1938) has the mines reverse. The medal also bears the date of the act on the edge.

9. It was arguable whether the wording of the 1909 Warrant restricted awards to persons who were themselves employed in industry. However, this was not too narrowly interpreted and three awards were made to soldiers under the Warrant, see below and P.R.O. HO 45/10722/249623. The wording of the 1917 Warrant was slightly altered to avoid this difficulty.

10. See *L.G.*, 10th October 1930.

11. No forfeitures have been found in the *London Gazette*.

12. See *L.G.*, 9th March 1937.

13. A similar order was made regarding the Albert Medal (q.v.). The last silver medal was awarded to Frank Bradley in *L.G.*, 1st November 1949 (mining incident).

14. Royal Warrant of 24th January 1969 (see *L.G.*, 7th February 1969). A similar award was made to recipients of the Albert Medals (q.v.).

"Whereas We, by a Warrant under Our Royal Sign Manual, bearing date the thirteenth day of July, one thousand nine hundred and seven, in the seventh year of Our Reign, did institute and create a new Medal to be entitled the Edward Medal, to be awarded for heroic acts performed by Miners and Quarrymen and others, who endanger their own lives in saving or endeavouring to save the lives of others from perils in Mines and Quarries within Our Dominions, and Territories under Our protection and jurisdiction:

And whereas We are desirous of extending the scope of this decoration:

It is ordained that the Edward Medal of the First Class and the Edward Medal of the Second Class shall be awarded to those of Our faithful subjects who in course of Industrial Employment endanger their own lives in saving or endeavouring to save the lives of others from perils incurred in connection with such Industrial Employment in these Our Dominions, and in Territories under Our protection or jurisdiction, and such awards shall be made only on a recommendation to Us by Our Principal Secretary of State for the Home Department.

Where the said Medal is granted otherwise than for acts performed in Mines, the Medal shall bear Our effigy on the obverse, and on the reverse a suitable design, with the words "For Courage".

Given at Our Court at Sandringham, the first day of December, one thousand nine hundred and nine, in the ninth year of Our Reign.

By His Majesty's Command.
H. J. GLADSTONE."

The apparent effect of this extending Warrant was to prescribe the industrial reverse for acts of gallantry in quarries[8] instead of the mining reverse as hitherto; and, by widening the scope of the award, to include acts previously rewarded by the Albert Medal, e.g. gallantry by railwaymen and dock workers.

A Royal Warrant of 28th August 1917 (see *London Gazette* of 31st August 1917) consolidated the two previous Warrants. The new Warrant differed little from its predecessors except that the operative part did not particularise acts of gallantry in mines but made the medal available generally for acts of gallantry in industry[9] which, of course, included mines. Nor did the Warrant mention the different reverses but merely provided that the medal would have a reverse of suitable design. This more general wording made no practical difference since both types of reverse continued to be issued. The Warrant also provided that in future the First Class medal was to be known as "The Edward Medal in Silver", and the Second Class medal as "The Edward Medal". By a Royal Warrant of 1st October 1930[10] the forfeiture clause of the 1917 Warrant was abrogated and a fresh clause substituted. This enlarged the power available by omitting reference to "crime or disgraceful conduct" (which previously had been conditions precedent to forfeiture), and provided that forfeiture should be authorised by an Order under the Sign Manual and not by Royal Warrant as before[11]. The enlarging of the power to order forfeiture followed a recommendation by the Interdepartmental Rewards Committee that all awards for gallantry, except in cases of extreme infamy, should be regarded as irrevocable; hence it was unnecessary to limit the power, as had been done before, by prescribing for particular circumstances. By a Royal Warrant of 1st March 1937[12] the 1917 Warrant was further amended by a provision that the obverse should bear the effigy of the Sovereign. The 1917 Warrant had provided that the obverse should bear "Our Effigy" (i.e. that of King George V) although, in fact, George V issues had commenced with the new reign (see also footnote 22).

With the institution in 1940 of the George Cross and the George Medal two further awards were added to those already available and, in certain cases, it became difficult to decide which was the most appropriate. Accordingly, in November 1949 King George VI gave approval that awards of the silver medal should cease, and that in future the bronze medal should only be awarded posthumously[13]. With effect from 14th November 1968 surviving United Kingdom recipients of the Edward Medals were to be entitled to annual gratuities of £100[14], irrespective of whether the medal awarded was in silver or bronze.

15. See *Hansard* (House of Commons) for 21st October 1971, column 189.

16. See *L.G.*, 6th January 1972. There were separate Warrants for each Medal.

17. This is a curious drafting device in comparison with the eleventh clause of the George Cross Warrant.

18. The wording regarding exchanges, unlike that relating to the Empire Gallantry Medal, is permissive.

19. *L.G.*, 22nd November 1929, p.7,529.

20. *L.G.*, 22nd April 1941, p.2,286.

21. *L.G.*, 11th February 1947, p.697.

22. *Annual Report of the Deputy Master and Comptroller of the Royal Mint (1911)*, p.50. However, the medal awarded to F. Smith (industry, bronze), gazetted on 14th February 1911, has the Edward VII obverse. On the death of King Edward VII the question arose as to whether the late King's effigy should continue to appear on the medal in view of its name. After considering various precedents King George V decided that his own effigy should appear on it.

23. *Annual Report of the Deputy Master and Comptroller of the Royal Mint (1931)*, p.43.

24. *Ibid* (1937), p.39.

25. i.e. to R. Mallinson in *L.G.*, 31st March 1953.

26. These were her maiden names. She was the wife of Captain Robert Falcon Scott, C.V.O., R.N., the famous explorer, and was later created Lady Scott in recognition of her husband's services.

27. *Annual Report of the Deputy Master and Comptroller of the Royal Mint (1912)*, p.15. However, the silver medal awarded to Harry Parsons in *L.G.*, 17th December 1912, had the original reverse, and it may be that all or only some of the 20 industrial medals (three silver and 17 bronze) awarded during that year also bore the original reverse. Surprisingly, the bronze medal awarded to A. E. Stroud in *L.G.*, 27th May 1913, for an act of gallantry as a guard on the East Indian Railway, has the mines reverse. This was apparently due to an error made at the Home Office, see the relevant order in the Royal Mint register of medals ordered in P.R.O. MINT 16/3.

28. *E.g.*, the bronze medal (mines) to David Noel Booker (*L.G.*, 3rd February 1938) has "14th MAY, 1937", while the bronze medal (industry) to Wilfred Beasley (*L.G.*, 11th March 1947) has "HIGH SPEED ALLOYS Ltd WIDNES, 16th NOV. 1946". The lettering on Beasley's medal is rather small and the inscription occupies the whole visible edge of the medal.

Gratuities were to be paid to other Commonwealth recipients under local regulations. By 1971, however, it was thought that, since no Albert or Edward Medals had been awarded – except posthumously – since 1948, the general public were no longer as conscious as they were of their significance and status. This had the effect of depriving surviving holders of those medals of the recognition which was their undoubted due[15]. Accordingly, by Royal Warrants of 15th December 1971[16], which came into effect from 21st October of that year, the existing Albert and Edward Medal Warrants were revoked; recipients of the Albert or Edward Medals who were living on that day were deemed to be persons who had been awarded not the Medal, but the George Cross[17]; and accordingly the Medals might[18] be exchanged for the George Cross.

The order of wearing the Edward Medal has varied. In Army Order No. 246 of August 1912 it was shown following the Indian Order of Merit (Civil) in a group of gallantry awards which, at that time, followed Polar medals. In 1929[19] it was shown in a similar group which followed the Air Force Medal; in 1941[20] between the George Medal and the Indian Distinguished Service Medal; and in 1947[21] after the George Medal and the King's Police Medal for Gallantry (see also Appendix 4).

DESCRIPTION

Ribbon Dark blue, 1⅜ inch wide, with narrow yellow borders.

Suspension By an oval ring of the appropriate metal, approximately ⁹⁄₁₆ inch at its widest, on a small mounting. On some issues the mounting is fixed to the piece by a claw, and on others it is fixed directly to the edge of the medal. On most issues the ring swivels. A 1947 award has been seen with a fixed suspender while on a 1953 award the ring swivels.

Obverse There are seven types of obverse as follows:

1. Edward VII (Fig.A) This was designed by G. W. de Saulles.
2. George V first type (Fig.B) This was introduced in 1911[22].
3. George V second type (Fig.C) This was introduced in 1931[23].
4. George VI (Fig.D) This was introduced in 1937[24].
5. George VI second type (Fig.E) This probably appeared on the eight awards made in 1949. No awards were made between 1950 and 1952. At least one award of this type was made in 1953[25].
6 and 7. Elizabeth II first and second types (Figs. F and G).

Reverse (Mines) (Fig.H) This was designed by W. Reynolds-Stephens.

Reverse (Industry) There are two reverses, as follows:

1. 1910–1911 (Fig.I) The original reverse was designed by Kathleen Bruce[26].
2. 1912 to 1971 (Fig.J) This reverse was introduced in 1912 after a design by Gilbert Bayes[27].

Bar Only two bars were awarded both being to silver medals awarded for services in mines (see below). The design of the bars was similar to that of the dated bar for the King's Police Medal. In the case of J. H. Thorne the bar was dated "11th MAY 1910", and in the case of G. H. Silkstone "19th NOVEMBER 1910".

Naming The full names of the recipient are engraved in upright serif capital letters around the edge of the medal. By at least 1938 the date of the act, and sometimes the place, were added to the details on the edge[28].

Copies and Fakes For recent copies see the Note on p.xx. A number of Royal Mint specimens were struck, some of which were presented to those who had financed the institution and extension of the medal.

Fig. G: The Edward Medal, obverse, Elizabeth II issue, second type.

VERIFICATIONS AND CITATIONS

All awards can be verified in the *London Gazette* where the class of award is given[29]. Some of the early notices show that the Sovereign invested the recipient or next-of-kin. From 1908 to December 1941 the names of recipients are indexed under the award heading in the "State Intelligence" section of the appropriate quarterly index. However, bronze medals to the following, although gazetted, are omitted from the indices:

	London Gazettes
Benton, H. … … … … … …	10th August 1909 (mines)
Bywater, C. … … … … … …	9th December 1913 (industry)
Edwards, G. … … … … … …	5th July 1912 (mines)
Gale, G. … … … … … …	22nd March 1918 (industry)
Graham, I. … … … … … …	22nd July 1910 (mines)
Graham, J. … … … … … …	22nd July 1910 (mines)
Holliday, A. … … … … … …	25th July 1913 (industry)
Morris, A. E. … … … … …	4th July 1924 (mines)
Pickersgill, H. … … … … …	25th April 1911 (mines)
Rothery, J. … … … … … …	22nd July 1910 (mines)
Vinters, T. … … … … … …	9th December 1913 (industry)
Wagstaff, T. … … … … …	25th July 1913 (industry)
Welsby, J. … … … … … …	28th July 1908 (mines)

Moreover, bronze medals awarded to the following in *London Gazette*, 22nd January 1918, are wrongly indexed under the Albert Medal[30]:

Ashley, Corporal C.	Harris, Acting Sergeant C. T.
Booth, W.	Jeffells, W.
Dugdale, Bombardier B.	Morrison, A.
Edwards, Acting Bombardier A. F.	Stebbings, Lieutenant J. M.

From January 1942 the "State Intelligence" section gives only the pages upon which awards are to be found, but the names appear in a comprehensive nominal section headed "Honours, Decorations and Medals". Full citations are usually given except principally for some awards made during the First World War where details were omitted for security reasons[31]. Where citations exist to December 1938 they are reproduced, with some misprints and wrong classes of award, by Wilson and McEwen. Many Home Office files relating to awards of the medal to 1949 are preserved in the Public Record Office in the series HO 45. In addition to general correspondence dealing with policy, there are files concerning individuals or groups of individuals containing eye-witness reports, recommendations (not all of which were approved), correspondence regarding presentations, undertakings to return the medal if forfeited, etc. The Colonial Office series also contains similar documents, either in the Chief Clerk's correspondence (CO 523), or in that for individual Colonies.

NUMBERS AWARDED

In the following table we include medals for acts by mine workers above ground, and by quarrymen, among the mining awards.

London	Mines		Industry		
Gazettes	Silver	Bronze	Silver	Bronze	Totals
1908–1910	29[32]	78	2	5	114
1911	2[33]	35	1	11[34]	49
1912–1930	31	134	19[35]	114	298[36]
1931–1936	4	37	2	12	55
1937–1948	10	23	1	19	53[37]

29. Except in the case of the medal awarded to J. Welsby (miner) which was presented to his widow. The Gazette does not specify the class (*L.G.*, 28th July 1908) but Wilson and McEwen (see Bibliography) give it as 2nd Class.

30. Conversely, the bronze Albert Medal awarded to Veladi Sammai (*L.G.*, 12th May 1925) is wrongly indexed under the Edward Medal.

31. No citation is given in the case of the bronze medal awarded to G. H. Frank for services in an industrial disaster (*L.G.*, 3rd June 1931) but full details are given by Wilson and McEwen.

32. And a bar to J. H. Thorne in *L.G.*, 22nd July 1910, the medal itself being awarded in *L.G.*, 28th July 1908.

33. And a bar to G. H. Silkstone in *L.G.*, 25th April 1911, the medal itself being awarded in *L.G.*, 22nd July 1910. Silkstone died in South Africa.

34. The medal awarded to F. Smith in *L.G.*, 14th February 1911, has the Edward VII obverse.

35. For awards in 1912 and 1913 see footnote 27.

36. Includes 117 awards between 1915 and 1919. 9 were made to officers and men of the Army for incidents in explosives factories-Sergeant J. Burt and Private D. McPolland, both of The Scottish Rifles (*L.G.*, 27th June 1916); Private J. Wiltshire, 59th Company Royal Defence Corps, later 1/5th Battalion, The Buffs (*L.G.*, 16th March 1917); Lieutenant J. M. Stebbings, Corporal C. Ashley, Bombardier B. Dugdale, all R.F.A., Acting Bombardier A. F. Edwards, R.G.A. (invested with the G.C. 13th February 1972), and Acting Sergeant C. T. Harris, R.E. (*L.G.*, 22nd January 1918); Lieutenant A. H. Bristowe, Oxfordshire and Buckinghamshire Light Infantry (*L.G.*, 21st January 1919). Burt received a silver medal, and the remainder received bronze medals.

37. Includes 25 awards between 1940 and 1946.

Fig.H: The Edward Medal, (Mines), reverse.

Fig.I: The Edward Medal (Industry), reverse, first type.

| London Gazettes | Mines | | Industry | | |
	Silver	Bronze	Silver	Bronze	Totals
1949–1952	1	5	—	2	8
1953–1971	—	6	—	1	7[38]
Totals:	77	318	25	163	584

Summary Silver: Mines ... 77 } 102
Industry ... 25
Bronze: Mines ... 318 } 482
Industry ... 164

ILLUSTRATIVE AWARDS

Silver medals George Shearer Christie (Manager, No. 7 and No. 10 Colliery, Cowdenbeath), James Erskine (Manager, Dalbeith Colliery), David Baird (Master Sinker), Andrew Scott (Sinker), Edward McCafferty (Shaftsman) and John Boyle (Sinker) were awarded the Edward Medal in silver for gallantry on 20th January 1917 at No. 7 Colliery, Cowdenbeath, which was owned by the Fife Coal Company Ltd. Notification of the awards appeared in the *London Gazette* of 17th July 1917 at p.7,125 with the following citation:

> "On the 20th January, 1917, at about 10a.m., while operations were being conducted for the widening of a shaft at the Cowdenbeath Colliery, Fife, a portion of the side of the shaft collapsed, throwing a workman named Newton down the mine to a scaffold about 90 feet below.
>
> Scott, McCafferty and Baird at once descended in a large bucket or kettle to attempt a rescue. The whole of the shaft below the point at which the fall had occurred was in a highly dangerous condition: stones and rubbish were continually falling, and there was constant danger of a further collapse. Newton was found, alive and conscious, buried beneath about 12 feet of debris and pinned by some fallen timber. The men worked continuously from 10.45a.m. until 7p.m. They were joined at 11a.m. by Christie, and at 1.30p.m. by Baird[39], both of whom remained at work with the others until 7p.m. During the whole of this period all five men were in serious danger.
>
> At 12.45 Boyle descended in the kettle with two other men. While the kettle was descending a fall occurred, killing one of his companions and injuring another. Boyle drew the kettle to the side of the shaft until the fall was over, and then took the kettle again to the surface. He subsequently remained in charge of the kettle, exposed to constant danger, until 7p.m.
>
> At 7p.m., after 9 hours' continuous and highly dangerous labour, the rescue party was relieved by other men. Unfortunately, Newton died at 8.30p.m. Attempts to recover his body were then postponed until the shaft could be worked with greater safety."

Accounts of the incident; the inquiry into the death of the two men at which the jury commended all those who had taken part in the attempted rescue; the presentation of Carnegie Hero Fund awards; and of the investiture appeared in the local Press[40]. The investiture of all six men took place at Buckingham Palace on 20th October 1917. Erskine's medal has the mines reverse and is engraved in capital letters "JAMES ERSKINE".

The Home Office file concerning the awards is preserved in the Public Record Office under reference HO 45/10840/335770. They include, *inter alia*, the official report into the incident; the submission to the King; correspondence leading to the investiture; and undertakings, signed by the recipients, to return the medals should their names be erased from the register.

Bronze Medals Thomas Wagstaff and Allan Holliday were awarded the Edward Medal in bronze for gallantry on 20th February 1913 at the Burton Brewery Company's Works, Burton-on-Trent. Notification of the awards appeared in the *London Gazette* of 25th July 1913 at p.5,322[41] with the following citation:

38. All posthumous. Only one award was gazetted between 1960 and 1971; this was in 1968. The bronze medal (mines) awarded to R. Mallinson in *L.G.*, 31st March 1953 has the George VI second type obverse. Three other medals were awarded in that year.

39. A misprint for Erskine. This was never corrected in the *Gazette* but, according to the Home Office file mentioned above, correction was made before the citation was read out at the investiture.

40. All in 1917. *West Fife Echo* for 24th January and 24th October; *Cowdenbeath & Lochgelly Times & Advertiser* for 24th January, 28th February, 25th July; *Dunfermline Press* for 14th April. The Carnegie Hero Fund awarded £20 and a honorary certificate to each of the six men; sums of £15 and £10 with honorary certificates to others concerned in the incident; and a medallion to Henry Rowan, J.P., the Company's agent at Cowdenbeath. The Company also made awards of medallions and watches to those concerned.

41. Both names are omitted from the index.

First: It is ordained that the Decoration shall be designated and styled "The George Cross".

Secondly: It is ordained that the Decoration shall consist of a plain cross with four equal limbs, the cross having in the centre a circular medallion bearing a design showing St. George and the Dragon, that the inscription "For Gallantry" shall appear round this medallion, and in the angle of each limb of the cross the Royal cypher "G.VI" forming a circle concentric with the medallion, that the reverse of the Cross shall be plain and bear the name of the recipient and the date of the award, that the Cross shall be suspended by a ring from a bar adorned with laurel leaves, and that the whole shall be in silver.

Thirdly: It is ordained that the persons eligible for the Decoration of the Cross shall be

(1) Our faithful subjects and persons under Our protection in civil life, male and female, of Our United Kingdom of Great Britain and Northern Ireland, India, Burma, Our Colonies, and of Territories under Our Suzerainty, Protection or Jurisdiction,

(2) Persons of any rank in the Naval, Military or Air Forces of Our United Kingdom of Great Britain and Northern Ireland, of India, of Burma, of Our Colonies, and of Territories under Our Suzerainty, Protection or Jurisdiction, including the Home Guard and in India members of Frontier Corps and Military Police and members of Indian States' Forces and in Burma members of the Burma Frontier Force and Military Police, and including also the military Nursing Services and Women's Auxiliary Services,

(3) Our faithful subjects and persons under Our protection in civil life, male and female, within, and members of the Naval, Military or Air Forces belonging to, any other part of Our Dominions, Our Government whereof has signified its desire that the Cross should be awarded under the provisions of this Our Warrant, and any Territory being administered by Us in such Government.

The Cross is intended primarily for civilians and award in Our military services is to be confined to actions for which purely military Honours are not normally granted.

Fourthly: It is ordained that awards shall be made only on a recommendation to Us, for civilians by Our Prime Minister and First Lord of the Treasury, and for Officers and members of Our Naval, Military or Air Forces, as described in the previous Clause of this Our Warrant, only on a recommendation by Our First Lord of the Admiralty, Our Secretary of State for War or Our Secretary of State for Air, as the case may be.

Fifthly: It is ordained that the Cross shall be awarded only for acts of the greatest heroism or of the most conspicuous courage in circumstances of extreme danger, and that the Cross may be awarded posthumously.

Sixthly: It is ordained that every recommendation for the award of the Cross shall be submitted with such description and conclusive proof as the circumstances of the case will allow, and attestation of the act as the Minister or Ministers concerned may think requisite.

Seventhly: It is ordained that the Cross shall be worn by recipients on the left breast suspended from a ribbon one and a quarter inches in width, of dark blue, that it shall be worn immediately after the Victoria Cross and in front of the Insignia of all British Orders of Chivalry, and that on those occasions when only the ribbon is worn, a replica in silver of the Cross in miniature shall be affixed to the centre of the ribbon.

Provided that when the Cross is worn by a woman, it may be worn on the left shoulder, suspended from a ribbon of the same width and colour, fashioned into a bow.

Eighthly: It is ordained that the award of the George Cross shall entitle the recipient on all occasions when the use of such letters is customary, to have placed after his or her names the letters "G.C.".

Ninthly: It is ordained that an action which is worthy of recognition by the award of the Cross, but is performed by one upon whom the Decoration has been conferred, may be recorded by the award of a Bar to be attached to the ribbon by which the Cross is suspended, that for each such additional award an additional Bar shall be added, and that for each Bar awarded a replica in silver of the Cross in miniature, in addition to the emblem already worn, shall be added to the ribbon when worn alone.

Tenthly: It is ordained that the names of all those upon or on account of whom We may be pleased to confer or present the Cross, or a Bar to the Cross, shall be published in the *London Gazette*, and that a Register of such names shall be kept in the Central Chancery of the Orders of Knighthood.

Eleventhly: It is ordained that from the date of this Our Warrant, the grant of the Medal of the Order of the British Empire, for Gallantry, which was instituted and created by His late Majesty King George the Fifth, shall cease, and a recipient of that Medal, living at the date of this Our Warrant, shall return it to the Central Chancery of the Orders of Knighthood and become instead a holder of the George Cross: provided that there shall be a similar change in relation to any posthumous grant of the Medal of the Order of the British Empire, for Gallantry, made since the commencement of the present war.

Twelfthly: It is ordained that reproductions of the Cross, known as a Miniature Cross, which may be worn on certain ocasions by those to whom the Decoration is awarded shall be half the size of the George Cross.

Thirteenthly: It is ordained that it shall be competent for Us, our Heirs and Successors by an Order under Our Sign Manual and on a recommendation to that effect by or through Our Prime Minister and First Lord of the Treasury, Our First Lord of the Admiralty, Our Secretary of State for War, or Our Secretary of State for Air, as the case may be, to cancel and annul the award to any person of the George Cross and that thereupon the name of such person in the Register shall be erased: provided that it shall be competent for Us, Our Heirs and Successors to restore the Decoration so forfeited when such recommendation has been withdrawn.

Lastly: We reserve to Ourself, our Heirs Successors, full power of annulling, altering, abrogating, augmenting, interpreting, or dispensing with these rules and ordinances, or any part thereof, by a notification under Our Sign Manual.

Given at Our Court at St. James's, the twenty-fourth of September, one thousand nine hundred and forty, in the fourth year of Our Reign.

By His Majesty's Command,
Winston S. Churchill."

By a Royal Warrant dated 8th May 1941[9], and published in the *London Gazette* of 24th June 1941, the 7th Clause was amended so that the width of the ribbon was now to be $1\frac{1}{2}$ inches wide and not $1\frac{1}{4}$ inches as formerly.

There have been three further Royal Warrants. The first, dated 17th October 1942, and published in the *London Gazette* of 3rd November 1942, amended the 3rd, 4th and 13th Clauses so that condominion awards, and direct submissions in the case of any of the Dominions, were now permitted. The second, dated 9th April 1964 and published in the *London Gazette* of 26th May 1964, amended these same three Clauses. In Clause 3 the words "India" and "Burma" were omitted, and the words "or under Our Jurisdiction jointly with another power" were added. Also in the same Clause further references to India, Indian States and Burma were omitted. In Clause 4, recommendations in the case of a member of the Commonwealth, other than the United Kingdom, were to be made by the appropriate Minister of State for the particular Commonwealth country, and for members of the armed forces of the United Kingdom by the Secretary of State for Defence. In Clause 13 provision was made for the cancelling and annulling of any award in Commonwealth countries, other than the United Kingdom, on the recommendation of the appropriate Minister of State of that country. The third, dated 19th May 1965, and published in the *London Gazette* of 15th June 1965, added the following Clauses:

"*Fourteenthly:* It is ordained that every living recipient of the George Cross, who falls to be in this matter a responsibility of the United Kingdom Government, shall from the first day of April, one thousand nine hundred and sixty-five, be entitled to a special pension of one hundred pounds a year, for life, and that subsequently such recipients of the George Cross shall be entitled to the special pension from the date of the act by which the Decoration has been gained, and for life.

Fifteenthly: It is ordained that should a recipient of the George Cross die before he has received a total of fifty pounds in respect of the special pension of one hundred

9. The original Warrant is in P.R.O. PREM 2/108.

pounds a year which is payable to holders of the George Cross by the United Kingdom Government, there should be credited to his estate a sum equal to the balance needed to complete fifty pounds. It is also ordained that when the George Cross is awarded posthumously and the matter is a responsibility of the United Kingdom Government, the sum of fifty pounds should be credited to the estate of the deceased recipient of the award.

Sixteenthly: It is ordained that, subject to such exceptions as We, Our Heirs and Successors may ordain, a citizen of a Member Country of the Commonwealth Overseas to whom the George Cross may be awarded, shall receive such special pension as may be provided from the revenues of that Country under regulations made by the said Country."

By 1971 it was thought that, since no Albert or Edward Medals had been awarded – except posthumously – since 1948, the general public were no longer as conscious as they were of their significance and status. This had the effect of depriving surviving holders of those Medals of the recognition which was their undoubted due[10]. Accordingly, by Royal Warrants of 15th December 1971[11], which came into effect from 21st October of that year, the existing Albert and Edward Medal Warrants were revoked; recipients of those medals who were living on that day were deemed to be persons who had been awarded not the Medal, but the George Cross[12]; and accordingly the Medals might[13] be exchanged for the George Cross. For details of the Victoria Cross and George Cross Association see p.290.

DESCRIPTION

Ribbon Blue. Originally $1\frac{1}{4}$ inches wide but increased to $1\frac{1}{2}$ inches by the Royal Warrant of 8th May 1941.

Suspension By a straight silver bar, slotted for the ribbon, with ring lug below, made in one piece. The front of the bar is ornamented with laurels, and the reverse is plain. The Cross and bar are joined by a small silver ring which passes through the ring lugs of both components.

Obverse (Fig.A)[14] While the design was not altered, the representation of St. George and the Dragon was made in higher relief from about 1944[15].

Reverse Plain, except for the naming (see below).

Bar None has been awarded yet. According to the Royal Mint Report for 1941[16], bars for subsequent acts of gallantry are to be as for the suspender bar without the ribbon lug.

Naming The reverse of the Cross is very attractively engraved with the name of the recipient, rank and Service, or description, if appropriate, and the date of the notification in the *London Gazette*. The full names are engraved in upright capital letters, the initial letter of each name being larger than those following. Service recipients below commissioned rank usually have their serial number included, those for the Royal Navy following the surname. The last line of the inscription gives the date of the *London Gazette* in which the award is published and not, as in the case of the Victoria Cross (q.v.), the date of the act. The day of the month (e.g. 4th) is usually followed by "st", "nd", etc., and precedes the month and year; a comma follows the month, although in later awards this is sometimes omitted. Where the Cross has been exchanged for either the Albert Medal or the Edward Medal the year of the act appears instead of the date of the *London Gazette* announcement.

Copies and Fakes Royal Mint specimens exist, one of which was in the former Royal United Service Institution Museum and was quite plain on the reverse. One type of copy exists which is stamped as such on the reverse of the upper arm. The arms are about $\frac{1}{16}$ inch longer than the genuine issue, and the ends are slightly bevelled on the reverse. The central design is in shallower relief, as are the cyphers in the angles of the Cross; the rose at the bottom of the centre circle is replaced by a dot; the suspender bar appears to be cast, and the laurels

10. See *Hansard* (House of Commons) for 21st October 1971, column 189.

11. See *L.G.*, 6th January 1972. There were separate Warrants for each Medal.

12. This is a curious drafting device in comparison with the eleventh clause of the George Cross Warrant.

13. The wording regarding exchanges, unlike that relating to the Empire Gallantry Medal, is permissive.

14. The Cross was designed by Mr Percy Metcalfe, C.V.O., R.D.I. (see *The Times* of 22nd November 1940). Drawings of a number of suggested designs are in P.R.O. MINT 24/324.

15. *Annual Report of the Deputy Master and Comptroller of the Royal Mint (1944)*, p.185.

16. *Ibid* (1941), p.98.

are poorly finished. Both ring lugs are larger than they should be and the connecting link is of thinner gauge metal. A copy is illustrated by Joslin in his first edition (see Bibliography). A few very convincing copies were made in Glasgow in hall-marked silver. A rather leaden-looking cast copy, stamped "COPY" on the reverse, first appeared in 1972. The size is almost exactly right and the definition is good. However, the flat surfaces are poorly finished.

VERIFICATIONS AND CITATIONS

All awards are notified in the *London Gazette*[17]. Until December 1941 the names are indexed under the award heading in the "State Intelligence" section of the appropriate quarterly index. Thereafter this section gives only the page numbers on which awards are to be found, and the names appear in a comprehensive nominal section headed "Honours, Decorations and Medals". In the case of Army awards, the recipient's home town is normally given. Almost all awards are accompanied by citations except for some made to Service personnel during and shortly after the end of the Second World War. Lists of surviving recipients are recorded in *Whitaker's Almanack* up to and including the issue of 1960[18] and of all recipients to 1976 in *Hamilton's Coin & Medal Despatch* (No. 1 of 1980) published by A. D. Hamilton & Co. Ltd. of Glasgow. Some additional details can be found in Bisset, and Smyth (see Bibliography). The original recommendations for some civilians in 1940 and 1941 are preserved in the Public Record Office in the series PREM 2/105 and 110, while copies of many recommendations for members of the three Services between 1941 and 1946 are in the series AIR 2 (Code 30). Details of awards to officers and men of the Merchant Navy to 1950 sponsored by the Marine Department of the Board of Trade are in the series MT 9 (Code 6).

NUMBERS AWARDED

Excluding exchanges of the E.G.M., A.M. and E.M. (q.v.) and the award to the Island of Malta in 1942, in the period from 1940 to 1979 inclusive 151 awards have been made as follows:

	U.K.	Australia	Canada	India	New Zealand	Others
Navy	23	4	—	—	—	—
Army including F.A.N.Y.	35	4	3	8	2	—
Air Force	19	—	4	—	—	—
Merchant Navy	5	—	—	—	—	—
Civilian – Police Forces	8	2	—	—	—	1
Fire Services	3	—	—	—	—	1
Others	24	1	—	—	—	4
Totals	117	11	7	8	2	6

Of these 106 were gazetted before 1947. Four awards have been made to women i.e. to Mrs. Odette M. C. Sansom, M.B.E.[19], and Violette, Madame Szabo[20], both of the Women's Transport Service (F.A.N.Y.), to Assistant-Section Officer Nora Inayat-Khan, W.A.A.F.[21], and to Miss B. J. Harrison, Stewardess, British Overseas Airways Corporation[22].

ILLUSTRATIVE AWARD

Bombardier H. H. Reed was awarded the George Cross while serving in a detachment of the 2nd Maritime Anti-Aircraft Battery, Royal Artillery, aboard s.s. *Cormount*. On 20th/21st June 1941 this ship was sailing in convoy from Blyth to London. The convoy was attacked by E-Boats and aircraft, and an air-launched torpedo made a direct hit on s.s. *Cormount* under the navigating bridge amidships. Reed's citation[23] tells part of what followed:

"The KING has been graciously pleased to award the GEORGE CROSS to:
Henry Herbert Reed (deceased), Gunner

17. The first awards were gazetted on 30th September 1940 being to Thomas Hopper Alderson, Detachment Leader, Rescue Parties, Bridlington and to Lieutenant Robert Davies and Sapper George Cameron Wylie, both of the Royal Engineers.

18. This also includes those E.G.M. holders who exchanged the E.G.M. for the G.C. In such cases the year of exchange is also given, quite a number having taken place in 1947.

19. *L.G.*, 20th August 1946.

20. *L.G.*, 17th December 1946; posthumous award.

21. *L.G.*, 5th April 1949; posthumous award.

22. *L.G.*, 8th August 1969; posthumous award.

23. *L.G.*, 23rd September 1941. The original is in P.R.O. PREM 2/110.

The ship was attacked by an enemy aircraft with cannon, machine-guns and bombs. She replied at once with her defensive armament and the men at the guns went on firing despite the hail of bullets and cannon shells.

Gunner Reed behaved with the utmost gallantry. He was badly wounded but when the Master asked how he was, he said he would carry on. The Chief Officer was also badly wounded. Reed carried him from the bridge down two ladders to the deck below and placed him in a shelter near a life boat. Gunner Reed then died. It was afterwards found that his stomach had been ripped open by machine-gun bullets.

By his gallant and utterly selfless action Gunner Reed saved the life of the Chief Officer."[24]

Reed's body was landed at Harwich and the ship, although badly damaged, reached Ipswich. On the actual George Cross Reed is incorrectly described as belonging to the Merchant Navy. The Gazette entry merely describes him as "Gunner" and it is probable that the incorrect descriptions were due to Reed's somewhat unusual role of a soldier serving aboard a merchant ship. In fact, he enlisted in the Royal Engineers (T.A.) in 1938 and transferred to the Royal Artillery in 1940 in which he was still serving at the time of his death. Reed was also awarded posthumously Lloyd's War Medal for Bravery at Sea, the 1939/45 Star and War Medal.

24. The Chief Officer was appointed a Member of the Civil Division of the Order of the British Empire for his gallantry on this occasion, the award appearing in the same *L.G.* as that to Reed.

Chapter 21

The George Medal

Fig.A: The George Medal, obverse, George VI issue, first type.

ORIGIN AND DEVELOPMENT

For the circumstances leading to the institution of the George Cross and the George Medal see Chapter 20. The Royal Warrant relating to the George Medal was published in the *London Gazette* of 31st January 1941 as follows:

"GEORGE R.I.

GEORGE THE SIXTH, by the Grace of God, of Great Britain, Ireland and the British Dominions beyond the Seas, King, Defender of the Faith, Emperor of India, to all to whom these Presents shall come,

GREETING!

WHEREAS We have taken into Our Royal consideration the many Acts of great bravery performed both by male and by female persons especially during the present war:

And whereas We are desirous of honouring those who perform such deeds:

We do by these Presents for Us, Our Heirs and Successors institute and create a new Medal.

First: It is ordained that the Medal shall be designated and styled "The George Medal".

Secondly: It is ordained that the Medal shall be circular in form and in silver, that it shall bear on the obverse the Crowned Effigy of the Sovereign, and on the reverse a representation of St. George slaying the Dragon on the coast of England, the design being circumscribed by the words "The George Medal".

Thirdly: It is ordained that the persons eligible for the Medal shall be

(1) Our faithful subjects and persons under Our protection in civil life, male and female, of Our United Kingdom of Great Britain and Northern Ireland, India, Burma, Our Colonies, and of Territories under Our Suzerainty, Protection or Jurisdiction;

(2) Persons of any rank in the Naval, Military or Air Forces of Our United Kingdom of Great Britain and Northern Ireland, of India, of Burma, of Our Colonies, and of Territories under Our Suzerainty, Protection or Jurisdiction, including the Home Guard and in India members of Frontier Corps and Military Police and members of Indian States' Forces and in Burma members of the Burma Frontier Force and Military Police, and including also the Military Nursing Services and the Women's Auxiliary Services;

(3) Our faithful subjects and persons under Our protection in civil life, male and female, within, and members of the Naval, Military and Air Forces belonging to, any other part of Our Dominions, Our Government whereof has signified its desire that the Medal should be awarded under the provisions of this Our Warrant, and any Territory being administered by Us in such Government.

The Medal is intended primarily for civilians and award in Our military services is to be confined to actions for which purely military Honours are not normally granted.

Fourthly: It is ordained that awards shall be made only on a recommendation to Us, for civilians by Our Prime Minister and First Lord of the Treasury, and for Officers and members of Our Naval, Military or Air Forces, as described in the previous Clause of this Our Warrant, only on a recommendation by Our First Lord of the Admiralty, Our Secretary of State for War or Our Secretary of State for Air, as the case may be.

Fifthly: It is ordained that the Medal shall be awarded only for acts of great bravery.

Sixthly: It is ordained that foreign persons shall be eligible for the award of the Medal and that awards to such persons not included under the Third Clause of this Our warrant shall be made only on a recommendation to Us for civilians by Our Secretary of State for Foreign Affairs and for Officers and members of foreign military Forces, by Our First Lord of the Admiralty, Our Secretary of State for War or Our Secretary of State for Air, as the case may be.

Seventhly: It is ordained that the Medal shall be worn by recipients on the left breast suspended from a ribbon one-and-a-quarter inches in width, of red, with five equidistant narrow vertical stripes of blue, and that it shall be worn immediately after the King's Police and Fire Services Medal, for gallantry.

Provided that when the Medal is worn by a woman, it may be worn on the left shoulder, suspended from a ribbon of the same width and colour, fashioned into a bow.

Eighthly: It is ordained that the award of the Medal shall entitle the recipient, on all occasions when the use of such letters is customary to have placed after his or her names the letters "G.M.".

Ninthly: It is ordained that an action which is worthy of recognition by the award of the Medal, but is performed by one upon whom the Medal has been conferred, may be recorded by the award of a Bar to be attached to the ribbon by which the Medal is suspended, that for each such additional award an additional Bar shall be added, and that for each Bar awarded a silver rosette shall be added to the ribbon when worn alone.

Tenthly: It is ordained that the names of all upon whom We may be pleased to confer or present the Medal, or a Bar to the Medal, shall be published in the *London Gazette*, and that a Register of such names shall be kept in the Central Chancery of the Orders of Knighthood.

Eleventhly: It is ordained that reproductions of the Medal, known as a Miniature Medal, which may be worn on certain occasions by those to whom the Medal is awarded shall be half the size of the George Medal.

Twelfthly: It is ordained that it shall be competent for Us, Our Heirs and Successors by an Order under Our Sign Manual and on a recommendation to that effect by or through Our Prime Minister and First Lord of the Treasury, Our First Lord of the Admiralty, Our Secretary of State for War, or Our Secretary of State for Air, as the case may be, to cancel and annul the award to any person of the George Medal and that thereupon the name of such person in the Register shall be erased; provided that it shall be competent for Us, Our Heirs and Successors to restore the Medal so forfeited when such recommendation has been withdrawn.

Lastly: We reserve to Ourself, Our Heirs and Successors, full power of annulling, altering, abrogating, augmenting, interpreting, or dispensing with these rules and ordinances, or any part thereof, by a notification under Our Sign Manual.

Given at Our Court at St. James's, the twenty-fourth of September, one thousand nine hundred and forty, in the fourth year of Our Reign.

By His Majesty's Command,
Winston S. Churchill."

This Warrant was amended twice[1]. The first Warrant, dated 17th October 1942 and published in the *London Gazette* of 3rd November 1942, amended the 3rd, 4th and 12th Clauses so that condominion awards, and direct submissions in the case of any of the Dominions were now permitted. In Clause 3(1) and (2) the words "or under Our Jurisdiction jointly with another power" were to be inserted after "Jurisdiction" in both sub-Clauses. In Clause 4, after "Secretary of State for Air" was to be added "respectively, or in the case of any of Our Dominions the Government whereof shall so desire, on a recommendation by the appropriate Minister of State for the said Dominion". Clause 12 was to be amended by inserting after "Secretary of State for Air" the words "or in the case of any of Our Dominions, the Government whereof shall desire to submit a recommendation, by the appropriate Minister of State for the said Dominion".

The second Warrant, dated 9th April 1964 and published in the *London Gazette* of 26th May 1964, affected the 3rd, 4th, 7th and 12th Clauses. In Clause 3 the words "India" and "Burma" were omitted. In Clauses 4 and 12 the "Secretary of State for Defence" was designated in place of the three Service Ministers, and in Clause 7 it was ordered that the G.M. should be worn immediately after the C.G.M.[2].

1. Similar amendments were made for the George Cross (op. cit.).

2. It is shown in this position in the list published in *L.G.*, 11th February 1947, at p.697 (see Appendix 4).

*Fig.B: The George Medal, obverse,
George VI issue, second type.*

*Fig.C: The George Medal, obverse,
Elizabeth II issue, first type.*

3. See P.R.O. MINT 20/1811.

4. *E.g.*, the award to A. McL. Reid in *L.G.*, 1st May 1956, is of this type.

5. *E.g.*, the award to Major W. C. Harrison, Royal Army Ordnance Corps, in *L.G.*, 7th August 1959, is of this type.

6. See *The Times* of 22nd November 1940 and P.R.O. MINT 24/324 which, *inter alia*, contains reproductions of the bookplate and designs for the bar.

7. The first list of awards appeared in *L.G.*, 30th September 1940, there being 14 recipients, of whom three were women.

By a Warrant of 30th November 1977 and published in the *London Gazette* of 5th December 1977 the three previous Warrants were replaced. The new Warrant made changes in the former Clauses 3, 4, 6 and 12 to take account of certain constitutional changes including, *inter alia*, provision for award to citizens of Commonwealth countries of which Her Majesty is not Queen; and in Clause 5 to provide for posthumous awards.

DESCRIPTION

Ribbon Red, 1¼ inches wide, with five equidistant narrow vertical blue stripes.

Suspension By a silver ring approximately ⅗ inch in diameter.

Obverse There are four obverses as follows:

1. George VI first type (Fig.A) The red cardboard boxes for some war-time issues of the medal were made by G. Ryder & Co. Ltd. of London, E.C.1[3].
2. George VI second type (Fig.B) By a Royal Proclamation of 22nd June 1948 the King's style and titles were altered and a new obverse introduced accordingly.
3. Elizabeth II first type (Fig.C) This type was still being issued in 1956[4].
4. Elizabeth II second type (Fig.D) This type was being issued at least by 1959[5].

Reverse (Fig.E) The same reverse has been used throughout. It was modelled and adapted by Mr. George Kruger Gray, C.B.E., A.R.C.A., F.S.A., after a book-plate designed by Mr. Stephen Gooden, C.B.E., R.A., for the Royal Library, Windsor[6].

Bar (Fig.F) Silver, with "slip-on" fitting; the year of award is engraved on the reverse.

Naming The majority of medals for both reigns are engraved in upright capital letters, usually with serifs, and in slightly varying styles. However, some Army awards gazetted during 1944/45 were impressed in rather smaller capital letters, without serifs. Awards to civilians bear the full names, and a 1941 issue has been seen with the place and date of the act for which it was awarded engraved at either side of the names. Awards to Servicemen normally have the first name and surname in full, other names being represented by initials. However, such awards have been seen with the names given in full, or with all but the surname as initials. The Service number usually appears for those recipients below commissioned rank, although two Elizabeth II issues to Army officers have been found where the personal number in parentheses is also given. For Service recipients the rank is often abbreviated, and with Army awards the Regiment or Corps usually appears.

Copies and Fakes For recent copies see the Note on p.xx.

VERIFICATIONS AND CITATIONS

All awards to British and Commonwealth subjects appear in the *London Gazette*[7]. Awards to foreigners are not gazetted, but their names are registered at the Central Chancery of the Orders of Knighthood. In the *London Gazette* until December 1941 names are indexed under the award heading in the "State Intelligence" section of the appropriate quarterly index, but thereafter they are consolidated into a comprehensive quarterly nominal list headed "Honours, Decorations and Medals". The medal heading is retained in the "State Intelligence" section which merely lists pages upon which awards are to be found. The page references are sometimes corrupt, or show medals as bars or *vice versa*. From 1941 the recipient's home town is often given in the case of Service awards and in rare cases the full address appears. This practice ceased after the end of the Second World War.

Fig.D: The George Medal, obverse, Elizabeth II issue, second type.

Fig.E: The George Medal, reverse.

Fig.F: Bar to the George Medal.

Normally awards to civilians are accompanied by citations. During the Second World War some citations appear for Navy and Air Force recipients, but none has been found for the Army. However, from 1951 awards to Servicemen are usually accompanied by citations, those in respect of service in Northern Ireland being a notable exception. A list of all recipients to 1976 appears in *Hamilton's Coin & Medal Despatch* (No.1 of 1980) published by A. D. Hamilton & Co. Ltd. of Glasgow. Fevyer (see Bibliography) reproduces all *London Gazette* entries announcing awards to December 1945, and provides a nominal index. Details of some awards to naval personnel in the Second World War are to be found in the Public Record Office series ADM 1 (Code 85) while the original recommendations for some civilians are in PREM 2/105 and 110. Copies of many recommendations for all ranks of the three Services between 1941 and 1946 are in the series AIR 2 (Code 30). Details of awards to officers and men of the Merchant Navy to 1950 which were sponsored by the Marine Department of the Board of Trade are in the series MT 9 (Code 6).

NUMBERS AWARDED

The figures given below have been arrived at by counting all the awards appearing in the *London Gazette*. The total number of medals gazetted to 31st December 1979 is 1,978 which includes 50 to women; there were 25 first bars. Honorary awards are not gazetted and therefore are excluded from our figures.

In the following table the Service heading includes awards to members of Dominion, Colonial, etc., Forces; the heading "Navy" includes awards to the Royal Marines; and "Army" includes awards to the Home Guard:

Period	Civilian	Navy	Army	Air Force	Merchant Navy	Total	First Bars
1940–45 ...	724	134	332	154	43	1387	20
1946–48 ...	15	2	32	15	—	64	—
1949–52 ...	91	4	17[8]	12	2	126	—
1953–79 ...	247	23	106	20	5	401	5
Totals:	1077	163	487	201	50	1978	25

The following have been awarded first bars:

London Gazette for Bar

Temporary Lieutenant (E) W. Bailey, D.S.C., R.N.V.R. ... ... 15th May 1945

Able Seaman W. H. Bevan, R.N., P/SSX. 12136 ... ... 9th June 1942

Temporary Lieutenant J. Bridge, R.N.V.R. ... ... 28th October 1941

Acting Lieutenant G. J. Cliff, R.A.N.V.R. 24th November 1942

Lieutenant M. A. Clinton, R.E. ... ... 17th August 1943

Lieutenant G. D. Cook, R.C.N.V.R. ... 10th February 1942

Constable G. E. Dorsett, Metropolitan Police ... ... 23rd June 1959

Temporary Lieutenant B. H. W. Fenwick, R.N.V.R. ... ... 9th June 1942

Temporary Lieutenant F. R. B. Fortt, R.N.V.R. ... ... 9th June 1942

Captain (Temporary Major) L. Gerhold, R.E. ... ... 17th August 1943

Temporary Acting Lieutenant Commander J. L. Harries, R.C.N.V.R. ... 15th May 1945

G. Henderson, Senior Assistant Adviser, High Commission for Aden and the Protectorate of South Arabia ... ... 3rd January 1964

Superintendent I. S. McW. Henderson, Kenya Police Force ... ... 27th September 1955

8. Including awards to Privates E. D. W. Read (acting lance-corporal), R Munday and J. V. Bagge, all of the Dorsetshire Regiment, in substitution for commendations in 1940, see *L.G.*s, 17th December 1940, 14th January 1949 and 8th February 1949. Munday's medal has the George VI second type obverse.

Captain (Temporary Major) J. P. Hudson,
M.B.E., R.E.   ...   .   15th September 1944
Temporary Lieutenant D. J. P. O'Hagan,
R.C.N.V.R.   ...   .   9th June 1942
Lieutenant H. D. Reid, R.A.N.V.R.   ...   9th June 1942
Temporary Lieutenant C. Rowlands,
R.N.V.R.   ...   .   17th November 1942
Superintendent B. E. Ruck, Kenya Police
Force   ...   .   27th September 1955
Lieutenant G. H. O. Rundle, R.C.N.
Reserve   ...   .   14th June 1945
Detective Sergeant J. J. Ryan, Queens-
land Police Force   ...   .   22nd October 1963
G. S. Sewell, Maintenance Engineer,
Shell-Mex and B.P. Ltd.   ...   .   7th July 1941
Lieutenant H. R. Syme, R.A.N.V.R.   ...   9th June 1942
Temporary Lieutenant H. E. Wadsley,
R.N.V.R.   ...   .   28th April 1942
Temporary Acting Lieutenant Com-
mander J. K. Woodrow, R.N.V.R.   ...   26th June 1945
Temporary Lieutenant (E) E. D. Woolley,
R.N.V.R.   ...   .   16th June 1942

ILLUSTRATIVE AWARD

Charles Ernest Burridge and Francis Richard Cox, gasholder repairers to the South Metropolitan Gas Company, were each awarded the George Medal in the *London Gazette* of 3rd December 1940 at p.6,910. Their citation reads as follows:

> "In blackout conditions these two men on their own initiative ascended a large Gas-holder for 90ft. and dealt with a hole made by a time bomb which had penetrated the crown of the holder. The hole on examination proved to be twenty-one inches in diameter, and gas was issuing under pressure.
>
> By their prompt action only a small amount of gas was lost, and a more serious danger was possibly averted. The task was undertaken of their own free will, without thought of danger from falling shrapnel, and with hostile planes bombing in the vicinity.
>
> In addition to the danger from the unexploded bomb, there was a further risk owing to the poisonous nature of the unburnt escaping gas, and the possibility of the gas becoming ignited."

Cox's medal is engraved with his full names in serif capital letters.

Chapter 22

The Indian Distinguished Service Medal

Fig.A: Brooch Bar of the Indian Distinguished Service Medal.

Fig.B: The Indian Distinguished Service Medal, obverse, Edward VII issue.

ORIGIN AND DEVELOPMENT

The Indian Distinguished Service Medal was instituted by a Royal Warrant of 25th June 1907 (see *London Gazette*, 28th June 1907, p.4,429), as follows:

"EDWARD, R. & I.

EDWARD, by the Grace of God, of the United Kingdom of Great Britain and Ireland and of the British Dominions beyond the Seas King, Defender of the Faith, Emperor of India, to all to whom these presents shall come, Greeting!

Whereas We have taken into Our Royal consideration that the means of adequately rewarding the distinguished services of Indian commissioned and non-commissioned officers and men of Our Indian Regular Forces, including the Reserve of the Indian Army, Border Militia and Levies, and Military Police and Imperial Service Troops when employed under the orders of Our Government of India, who have distinguished themselves in peace or on active service are limited:

Now, for the purpose of attaining an end so desirable as that of rewarding individual instances of such distinguished service, We have instituted and created, and do by these presents for Us, Our heirs and successors, institute and create a new Indian Military decoration to be distinguished as hereinafter described, which We are desirous should be highly prized by Our Indian commissioned and non-commissioned officers and men, and We are graciously pleased to make, ordain, and establish the following rule and ordinance for the government of the same which shall henceforth be inviolably observed and kept.

Firstly. – It is ordained that the decoration shall henceforth be styled and designated the "Indian Distinguished Service Medal".

Secondly. – It is ordained that the decoration shall be a silver medal of the same size as a war medal, having thereon Our effigy. On the reverse side a laurel wreath with the words "For distinguished service" in relief thereon.

Thirdly. – It is ordained that the medal shall be worn suspended from the left breast immediately on the right of all war medals, by a red ribbon 1¼ inches wide, of the colour of the ribbon of the Order of British India, edged with blue, three-eighths of an inch wide, of the colour of the ribbon of the Indian Order of Merit.

Fourthly. – It is ordained that the regulations regarding the forfeiture of war medals shall apply to the medal hereby created.

Fifthly. – It is ordained that the power of conferring the medal upon an individual, or of depriving an individual to whom the medal has been granted of such medal, as provided in Article 4, shall be exercised on Our behalf by the Governor-General of India with the same force as if exercised by Us; and the name of an individual so granted the medal or deprived of the medal shall be published in the Official *Gazette of India*.

Given at Our Court at Saint James's, this twenty-fifth day of June, one thousand nine hundred and seven, in the seventh year of Our Reign.

By His Majesty's Command,
John Morley."

By a Royal Warrant of 13th June 1917 (see *London Gazette*, 6th July 1917, p.6,710) eligibility for the medal was extended to non-combatants attached to forces in the field, and a bar for subsequent acts was instituted. By Indian Army Order No. 1294 of 12th November 1918 a certificate, giving details of the award, was to be given to the next-of-kin of recipients who did not survive for the presentation of the medal.

In 1929 the award was extended to Indian warrant officers, petty officers and men of the Royal Indian Marine[1]. In 1938[2] the 5th Ordinance of the original Warrant was amended by deleting reference to the Governor-General and by substituting the Viceroy. Eligibility was further extended in 1940[3] to include Indian warrant officers and men of the Indian Air Force. A consolidating Royal Warrant was approved in 1942[4] which incorporated the previous Warrants although the Ordinance dealing with eligibility was drafted more widely[5], and also authorised recipients to use the letters "I.D.S.M." after their names. This Warrant also formalised the wearing of a silver rose on the ribbon, when the ribbon was worn alone, to denote the award of a bar[6]. At a meeting on 14th September 1943 of the Committee on the Grant of Honours, Decorations and Medals in Time of War[7] it was proposed that the M.M. should be extended to other ranks of the Indian Army and to N.C.O.s and men of the Indian Air Force; that the I.D.S.M. should be regarded as on the same level as the D.C.M. and awards of the former reduced; and that Viceroy's commissioned officers should be excluded from the award of the I.D.S.M. Eligibility was extended in 1944[8] to the Hong Kong and Singapore Royal Artillery[9]. The medal has not been awarded since the India Independence Act of 1947 came into force.

The order of wearing the Indian Distinguished Service Medal has varied. In Army Order No. 246 of August 1912 it was shown following the Edward Medal in a group of gallantry awards which at that time followed Polar medals. In 1921[10] it was shown as following the Air Force Medal; and in 1941[11] the King's Police and Fire Services Medal for Gallantry, the George Medal and the Edward Medal were placed above it. In 1947[12] it was shown in its present position following the King's African Rifles D.C.M. (see also Appendix 4).

DESCRIPTION[13]

Ribbon Dark blue (as for the Indian Order of Merit), 1¼ inches wide, with a central crimson stripe (as for the Order of British India), ½ inch wide.

Brooch Bar (Fig.A) This silver laurelled bar was fitted with a pin and catch at the back possibly because the medal could be awarded for peace-time gallantry when it might be worn alone. However, it is by no means certain when the brooch bar was introduced. It is not mentioned in the Royal Mint Report for 1907[14] nor in the Royal Mint Catalogue published in 1910 (see Bibliography) although it has been found with some Edward VII I.D.S.M.s. The first reference to it that we have traced appears in the Calcutta Mint Report for 1932/33[15] which notes that 50 I.D.S.M.s complete with fittings, brooches and cases were supplied to the Army Department. The Report for 1935/36[16] implies that 21 brooches were supplied separately and in addition to the 70 I.D.S.M.s struck that year. Photographs of six recipients taken c.1937 show three, whose awards were made in 1917, 1932 and 1935 respectively, wearing the brooch bar while three others, whose awards were made in 1918, 1919 and 1932, do not display it. The Report for 1937/38[17] mentions the supply of 25 I.D.S.M.s with brooches. It has been found with some Second World War awards.

Suspension The ornate scroll suspender swivelled until about 1943 at least[18]. Both flange and pin, and claw type fittings were used to secure the suspender to the piece. The illustration in the Royal Mint Report for 1907 shows the flange and pin fitting[19].

Obverse There are four obverses, as follows:

  1. Edward VII (Fig.B).
  2. George V first type (Fig.C) This obverse was first issued from about 1911.
  3. George V second type (Fig.D) According to records at the Royal Mint a master tool with the new crowned effigy of the King and with a Latin inscription was sent to India on 28th July 1931. This is mentioned in the

1. Royal Warrant of 13th September 1929 (see *L.G.*, 20th September 1929, p.6,035). This was apparently a regularising Warrant because six such awards were made in the First World War. At least 10 were made in the Second World War.

2. Royal Warrant of 24th June 1938 (see *L.G.*, 1st July 1938, p.4,238).

3. Royal Warrant of 16th February 1940 (see *L.G.*, 8th March 1940, p.1,395).

4. Royal Warrant of 27th February 1942 (see *L.G.*, 3rd March 1942, p.1,015).

5. Members of the Indian States Forces were, however, specified separately.

6. The rose was authorised in Indian Army Order No.494 of 11th June 1918.

7. See P.R.O. AIR 2/6409.

8. Royal Warrant of 6th March 1944 (see *L.G.*, 28th March 1944, p.1,450).

9. No such awards seem to have been made in the Second World War. However, two were made in the First World War.

10. *L.G.*, 22nd April 1921, p.3,184.

11. *L.G.*, 22nd April 1941, p.2,286.

12. *L.G.*, 11th February 1947, p.697.

13. According to the Royal Mint Catalogue the obverse and reverse were designed and engraved by G. W. de Saulles.

14. *Annual Report of the Deputy Master and Comptroller of the Royal Mint (1907)*, p.15.

15. *Reports on the Administration of the Mints at Calcutta and Bombay for the year 1932/33*, p.15.

16. *Ibid* (1935/36), p.25.

17. *Ibid* (1937/38), p.23.

18. *E.g.*, the medal awarded to Jemadar Azimullah, 14th/12th Frontier Force Rifles (*L.G.*, 4th November 1943).

19. *Annual Report of the Deputy Master and Comptroller of the Royal Mint (1907)*, p.15.

Fig.C: The Indian Distinguished Service Medal, obverse, George V issue, first type.

20. *Reports on the Administration of the Mints at Calcutta and Bombay for the year 1932/33*, p.14.

21. According to records at the Royal Mint, for the Indian Long Service and Good Conduct Medal the previous effigy had been discontinued by July 1933.

22. *Reports on the Administration of the Mints at Calcutta and Bombay, 1937/38*, p.23. By Indian Army Order No. 241 of March 1938, medals awarded on or after 11th May 1937 were to be held in abeyance until the new issue was available. Where immediate presentation was desirable, the previous issue could be used and later exchanged for the new issue.

23. *Reports on the Administration of the Mints at Calcutta and Bombay for the year 1921/22*, p.13.

24. *Ibid* (1925/26), p.15.

25. Thus Hudson and Shakespeare both give citations, Gibbs, Merewether and Smith give brief details, and Chaldecott quotes only the authorities for the awards (see Bibliography). *The Government of India List of Honors* (see Bibliography) gives, *inter alia*, all awards of the I.D.S.M. made between August 1914 and August 1921. Details are confined to the personal particulars of the recipient, together with the theatre of war or force in which the award was gained. No authorities are given.

26. For services prior to the fall of Singapore in 1942. Some corrections to awards already made were gazetted outside the first period mentioned above.

27. In general, military awards appear in Part 1 and the system of indexing in that Part is described here. However, some awards appear in the *Gazette of India Extraordinary* which has its own pagination and a much simpler index.

Calcutta Mint Report for 1932/33[20] in connection, *inter alia*, with the I.D.S.M. According to the Report, which ends at 31st March 1933, work on preparing the resulting dies had not then been completed but it seems likely that the new obverse was brought into use shortly afterwards for all or some of the 21 awards made in that year[21].

4. George VI (Fig.E) According to the Calcutta Mint Report for 1937/38[22] work on the new obverse die was progressing and it seems likely that the new issue appeared in 1938.

Reverse (Fig.F) This has remained constant since the medal was first struck.

Bar (Fig.G) The bar for subsequent acts of gallantry was authorised in 1917 (see above) and the pattern, which is the same as that used with the D.C.M., M.M., etc., remained the same during the existence of the medal.

Naming Details of the recipient are either engraved or impressed on the edge of the medal and include the rank, full names and regiment. The regimental number usually appears, and the rank and regiment are frequently abbreviated. The engraving was carried out in India, various styles of cursive script or capital letters being employed. Medals which are impressed have small capital letters without serifs. Although minor variations occur, the style of impressing corresponds with that used on the D.C.M. and M.M. The Calcutta Mint Report for 1921/22[23] mentions that war medals had been impressed by machine at the Mint since September 1921, instead of the hand impressing previously performed by a contractor. However, from mid-May 1925 impressing was again being done by contractor[24]. Probably some impressing was also carried out under arrangements made by the Royal Mint.

Copies and Fakes For recent copies see the Note on p.xx.

VERIFICATION AND CITATIONS

Occasionally some details appear in regimental and other histories[25], otherwise recourse may be made to the following:

Quarterly Indian Army List Details of serving and pensioned recipients appear in these Lists from July 1907 to January 1931 inclusive. Until July 1922 they are given with the January and July Lists, but thereafter with the January Lists only. Details given include the regimental number, rank, names, unit, and date and authority for the award.

London Gazette The only awards appearing are those gazetted between 18th February 1915 and 25th February 1918, and between 29th November 1940 and 25th September 1947 when the last awards were made[26]. It is by no means certain that all awards made during these periods are gazetted. For the first of the two periods they appear under the medal heading in the "State Intelligence" portion of the indices. Until and including the index for the third quarter of 1916 the recipient's last name is given first; thereafter, including the second period mentioned, names are indexed under the first name. For the second period names are indexed under the medal heading as previously described until January 1942 when they appear in a comprehensive nominal section headed "Honours, Decorations and Medals". The medal heading in the "State Intelligence" section is, however, retained but this merely gives pages upon which awards are to be found. No citations are given.

Gazette of India We have found no citations for the I.D.S.M. in the Gazette although announcements of awards usually give the theatre or other circumstances in which the award was made. The Gazette indices are complicated, being divided into a number of separately indexed parts[27]. Several major changes have been found in the method of indexing. Even within the broad framework of the revised systems minor variations occur and what follows can only be taken as a guide:

Fig. D: The Indian Distinguished Service Medal, obverse, George V issue, second type.

Fig. E: The Indian Distinguished Service Medal, obverse, George VI issue.

1907–1916 Awards appear in the Gazette in the form of Army Department Notifications and Government General Orders[28]. The "Nominal Index to Government General Orders (Army Department)" is a comprehensive index to all promotions, awards and similar announcements, natives being indexed under the first name. The "Subject Index to Government General Orders (Army Department)", under the sub-heading "Rewards", lists authorities for the awards. Both indices give only the number of the Notification or Order and it is therefore necessary to trace the numerical sequence through the Gazettes to find it.

1917–1938 During this period the layout of the indices is simpler. The Index itself is provided with a list of contents which shows the pages of the Index upon which awards are given, under the sub-heading "Decorations . . ." in the "Military" (later "Defence") Section. The page of the Index thus found gives under the medal heading the names of recipients, the Gazette pages, and later, the authority. The Index heading "Miscellaneous Orders and Notifications" gives the pages upon which, *inter alia*, awards are to be found. This system was, in turn, altered. Under the Civil Section of the list of contents, the sub-heading "Decorations . . ." gives the pages of the Index upon which the medal heading is found[29]. This medal heading merely lists the pages of the Gazette where awards are published in the form of announcements from the Office of the Private Secretary to the Viceroy.

1939–1947 We have been unable to find any Gazette indices for this period. However, awards continued to be published in the form of announcements from the Office of the Private Secretary to the Viceroy. In addition to the Service details of the recipient, the later Gazette entries also show his religion and home. In the absence of indices it is possible to trace awards in the *Gazette of India* by finding the corresponding *London Gazette* entry which usually appears at about the same time[30]. However, all awards appearing in the *Gazette of India* may not be repeated in the *London Gazette*. Some of the *Gazette of India* entries are repeated, without citations, in Indian Army Orders.

NUMBERS AWARDED

Until 1941 the following figures have been taken from Bullock (see Bibliography)[31], thereafter they have been extracted from the *London Gazette*[32]. The exact figures for both World Wars are difficult to assess because awards continued to be made, in some cases, long after the end of hostilities. We have attempted to show the numbers in relation to the various types of obverse but the figures are necessarily approximate.

Awards published	Medals	First Bars	Corresponding changes
1907–1910	140	—	Edward VII issue.
1911–July 1914	39	—	First type George V issue.
August 1914–May 1920	3174	23[33]	First World War; first type George V issue
June 1920–1932	592	14	First type George V issue.
1933–1937	139	2	Second type George V issue; approximate dates only (see above).
1938–1939	32	—	George VI issue.
1940–1946	1149	10	Second World War; George VI issue.
1947	6	—	Late awards, Second World War; George VI issue.

No second or subsequent bars were awarded.

For operations in the period from August 1914 to August 1921 *The Government of India List of Honors* gives the names of 3,565 recipients; bars are indicated by mere repetition of the name. An analysis of these awards is as follows:

Aden Field Force	68
Africa, East	254
West	5
Assam/Burma Frontier	20
Black Sea	3
Dardanelles/Gallipoli	88
Egyptian Expeditionary Force ...	456

28. The first awards appear in Army Department Notification No. 586 of 28th June 1907.

29. Under the sub-heading "Indian Army".

30. The first awards in this period appeared in *L.G.*, 29th November 1940, and the last in *L.G.*, 25th September 1947.

31. Bullock bases his figures on the *Gazette of India* and the official statistics (see Bibliography).

32. It is by no means certain that, during the Second World War, all awards appear in the *London Gazette* and it is for this reason that our figures should be treated with reserve.

33. Bullock gives 25, which seems to be a misprint.

Fig.F: The Indian Distinguished Service Medal, reverse.

Fig.G: Bar to the Indian Distinguished Service Medal.

France 646	
Kachin Hills 10	
Kohat Kurram Force 1	
Mekran Force 4	
Mesopotamia 1476	(including 96 for Kut-el-Amara)
Muscat 1	
North West Frontier 143	(including 32 for Baluchistan Force)
Persia 112	
Prisoner of War (escape as) 2	
Salonika 21	
Singapore (mutiny of 5th Light Infantry) 1	
Somaliland 5	
Transcaspia 28	
Turkey 3	
Waziristan 208	
Not given 10	

It will be appreciated that these figures include campaigns ended by the Armistice e.g. in France; those where there were operations, not necessarily against the same enemy, both before and after the Armistice e.g. in Mesopotamia; and those where operations were begun after the Armistice e.g. on the Black Sea coast. Moreover since the Warrant did not restrict awards to gallantry in the face of the enemy, it does not follow that all awards were in respect of services in action although clearly the vast majority were; in any case, the distinction is sometimes difficult to draw.

ILLUSTRATIVE AWARD

Sowar Bishan Singh, 19th Lancers (Fane's Horse) was awarded the I.D.S.M. in Army Department Notification No. 2185 of 20th September 1918 which was published in the *Gazette of India* for the following day[34] at p.1,506. No citation is given and the award does not appear in the *London Gazette*. However, Hudson gives the citation as follows:

> "On 4th February, 1918, near Hargicourt. For great gallantry and devotion to duty in carrying messages from the support to the front line during an intense enemy bombardment, thus keeping up communications at a critical time."

Bishan Singh last appears as a recipient of the I.D.S.M. in Indian Army List for July 1922.

Chapter 23

The Indian Meritorious Service Medal, 1917–1925

ORIGIN AND DEVELOPMENT

Medals for Meritorious Service, and for Long Service and Good Conduct, were instituted in 1888 for the Native Army of India[1]. The conditions of award were, in both cases, similar to those obtaining for the corresponding medals in the British Army. In so far as the Indian Meritorious Service Medal is concerned it was restricted to non-commissioned ranks equivalent to sergeant, i.e. dafadar (cavalry) and havildar (other arms and services), and above. The medal was accompanied by an annuity which was limited to one for each regiment of cavalry and infantry, or their equivalents; further grants were made when vacancies occurred by death, promotion[2], reduction to the ranks, or discharge to pension[3]. Unlike its British equivalent for which no minimum length of service was prescribed, dafadars and havildars were not eligible until they had completed 18 years' service with the colours, and fulfilled certain criteria as to conduct. Moreover, although the British M.S.M. could be awarded for "distinguished or meritorious service", the I.M.S.M. was for "meritorious service". Hence it seems likely that it was not considered as a medium for rewarding gallantry, especially as a minimum length of qualifying service was prescribed.

During the First World War a need had arisen for a military award for gallantry other than in action for services which did not reach the standard required for the existing awards, and for which all "other ranks" would be eligible. This was met by extending the conditions of award of the British M.S.M. for which Indian native soldiers were not eligible[4]. Accordingly, a similar extension was made to the conditions of award of the I.M.S.M. which was notified in Indian Army Order No.74 of 15th January 1917, as follows:

> **"Rewards – Meritorious Service Medal.** It is notified for information that the Government of India have sanctioned the award of Meritorious Service Medals without limit to Indian troops under commissioned rank (i.e. non-commissioned officers and men) for distinctly meritorious service or devotion to duty not necessarily in the presence of the enemy, in any theatre of war since August 1914.
>
> 2. Under this concession, any Indian soldier under commissioned rank, irrespective of period of service, will be eligible for the Meritorious Service Medal. The award of the medal will not, however, carry with it the annuity which usually accompanies the medal, but recipients of the medal will be eligible for consideration for the annuity if they eventually qualify under paragraph 995, Army Regulations, India, Volume 1."

These instructions were amplified by Indian Army Order No.324 of 2nd April 1917 in which the grant of the I.M.S.M. without annuity was to be limited to:

> "(i) Devotion to duty in a theatre of War.
>
> (ii) Gallant conduct in the performance of Military duty or in saving or attempting to save the life of an officer or soldier, otherwise than in action."

It was not to be granted for "devoted or gallant conduct in action"[5]. Subsequently, the I.M.S.M. without gratuity was extended to Indian ranks of the Supply and Transport Corps (excluding Indian officers) and to the Army Bearer Corps[6]; to Imperial Service Troops including Imperial Service Transport and Dhoolie Bearers[7]; to the Malay States Guides[8]; and to combatant ranks of military forces of Allied States whose status corresponded to that of an Indian warrant officer, non-commissioned officer, or soldier[9].

1. Indian Army Circular of January 1888, Clause 15, which in turn was superseded by that of July 1888, Clause 115. Corresponding medals had been instituted for Europeans of the H.E.I.C. Armies in 1848. These continued to be issued until 1873 to Europeans serving with native troops. Thereafter the British pattern was prescribed.

2. To commissioned rank. The medal was retained but the annuity ceased.

3. Since it was held desirable that the annuity "should be held chiefly by men on the active list" Commanding Officers were enjoined not to recommend men, except in very special cases, who were about to be transferred to the pension establishment. In the British Army annuities were paid from an annual Vote, vacancies being limited to promotion, misconduct or death. In consequence awards were often made to men who had already been pensioned for many years.

4. British W.O.s and N.C.O.s of Departmental and non-Departmental Sections of the Indian Army Unattached List and Assistant Surgeons of Warrant rank of the Indian Subordinate Medical Department were eligible, see Indian Army Orders Nos.447 and 448 of 7th May 1917.

5. The Order repeats, almost *verbatim*, the War Office instructions of 11th December 1916 regarding the British M.S.M., see Chapter 29.

6. Indian Army Order No.673 of 18th June 1917.

7. Indian Army Order No.1085 of 1st October 1917.

8. *Gazette of India* of 27th October 1917.

9. *Gazette of India* of 8th February 1919. Honorary awards were made to 40 men of the Nepalese Contingent in the *Gazette of India Extraordinary* of 5th February 1919.

On 13th August 1920 the following announcement appeared in the *London Gazette* and on 23rd October 1920 was repeated in the *Gazette of India*:

"His Majesty the KING has been graciously pleased to approve the institution of a bar to be worn with the Meritorious Service Medal awarded to Indian Troops the bar to be identical with that sanctioned for the British Meritorious Service Medal, and to be awarded under similar conditions."

By this time, however, two bars had already been awarded (see *post*) and the announcement seems to have been intended to regularise the matter. Indeed, during the next five years announcements appeared in the *Gazette of India* cancelling second medals awarded to 10 men at various dates between 1919 and 1921 and substituting bars. Clearly matters had become muddled because eight of these second medals were awarded after the *London Gazette* announcement, and seven after it was repeated in the *Gazette of India*. Moreover, the bar was to be awarded under "similar conditions" to that for the British M.S.M. which, whatever had happened in practice, were restricted to gallantry. As with the British M.S.M., in some cases the *Gazette* notices are not specific and it is impossible to say whether all the bars were awarded for gallantry.

Examination of the announcements of awards in the *Gazette of India* reveals a confusing variety of wording. These include "meritorious service and devotion to duty"[10]; "valuable services and devotion to duty"[11]; "good work and devotion to duty"[12]; "meritorious service"[13]; and "devotion to duty"[14]. These may be contrasted with the announcements of the British M.S.M. where "valuable services" was preferred to "devotion to duty" which rarely appeared. Announcement of some awards was made in conjunction with that of the I.O.M. and I.D.S.M. and here other combinations of wording was used e.g. "gallantry and devotion to duty"[15]; and "gallantry or devotion to duty"[16]. In view of the large number of I.M.S.M.s awarded in these *Gazettes* it must be that some were for gallantry but, due to the way in which the *Gazette* notices were framed, it is impossible to isolate them. However, one group of four awards is headed "for gallantry and devotion to duty" while four individual awards were for "gallant conduct otherwise than in action", and details are given in "Numbers Awarded", see *post*. In passing it should be noted that copies of the War Office instructions of 11th December 1916, 1st August 1918 and 10th August 1918[17] were sent to the Indian authorities and no doubt a measure of consistency was achieved especially where British and Indian troops served under a joint commander. The original Order had restricted awards to services performed in a theatre of war. However, in 1920[18] a number of awards were made for services in India and, no doubt, followed the modification made to the conditions of award of the British M.S.M. for a limited period in 1918/19 whereby the restriction to services performed in a theatre of war was waived.

The last awards of the I.M.S.M. without annuity appeared in the *Gazette of India* for 19th July 1924 and were in respect of "gallantry and distinguished conduct" with the Waziristan Force[19]. The next year a bar was substituted for a second medal awarded in 1920. It may be that, like its British counterpart and for similar reasons, the I.M.S.M. reverted to its original function as an award only with annuity in 1928 and that the absence of intervening non-annuity awards can be accounted for by lack of opportunity for recommendations. Since, however, we have been unable to trace any Order or correspondence to account for its disappearance as an award without annuity the matter is speculative.

There was at least one forfeiture of the medal without annuity on conviction by court martial[20], and 10 awards to members of the Indian Postal and Telegraph Departments were cancelled, presumably because civilians were not eligible[21].

In the order of wearing the I.M.S.M. originally followed the Indian Long Service and Good Conduct Medal for the Native Army which, in its turn, followed the Royal Marine M.S.M. In 1936[22] the Royal West African Frontier Force and the King's African Rifles Long Service and Good Conduct Medals were interposed

10. E.g. *Gazette of India* 4th August 1917; 19th January 1919; 19th April 1919; 3rd April 1920; 11th March 1922.

11. *Ibid* 18th August 1917.

12. *Ibid* 8th December 1918.

13. E.g. *Ibid* 26th November 1918; 8th March 1919; 10th July 1920; 26th February 1921; 25th March 1922.

14. *Ibid* 1st March 1919.

15. E.g. *Ibid* 23rd June 1917; 29th June 1918; 27th August 1921.

16. E.g. *Ibid* 13th July 1918; 8th March 1919; 17th April 1920; 5th February 1921.

17. See Chapter 29.

18. *Gazette of India* 17th April 1920; 1st May 1920; 12th June 1920. These may not be the first, earlier *Gazettes* not always being specific.

19. Together with awards of the O.B.I. and I.D.S.M. This is yet a further variant of announcement which first appears in 1922. Any attempt to interpret it in relation to the I.M.S.M. seems fruitless.

20. Rifleman Sete Thapa, 1st Battalion, 1st Gurkha Rifles; award, *Gazette of India* 27th November 1920; forfeiture, *ibid* 11th December 1926.

21. Awards, *Gazette of India* 15th March 1919; cancellations, *ibid* 29th January 1921.

22. *L.G.*, 24th April 1936.

Fig.A: The Indian Meritorious Service Medal, obverse.

Fig.B: The Indian Meritorious Service Medal, reverse.

Fig.C: Bar to the Indian Meritorious Service Medal.

between the two Indian medals, and in 1964[23] the Royal Sierra Leone Military Forces Long Service and Good Conduct Medal was placed between the two African ones.

DESCRIPTION

Ribbon As for the contemporary British M.S.M. The addition of the outer white edges was notified in Indian Army Order No.692 of 2nd October 1916, and of the central white stripe in Indian Army Order No.52 of 15th January 1918.

Suspension Swivelling, scroll bar suspender.

Obverse (Fig.A)

Reverse (Fig.B)

Bar (Fig.C)

Naming As for the I.D.S.M.

VERIFICATIONS AND CITATIONS

Awards of the medal without annuity appear in the *Gazette of India*[24]. Conversely, those with annuity appear in Indian Army Orders. The majority of awards without annuity appear in Part 1 of the *Gazette* although in 1919, 1920 and 1921 some appear in the *Gazette Extraordinary* which has separate pagination and a separate bi-annual index. In the period concerned, the Index to Part 1 is provided with a list of contents which, under the sub-heading "Decorations . . ." in the Military Section, shows the pages of the Index upon which recipients of awards are listed. The page of the Index thus found gives the names of recipients of military awards (which, from 1918, are grouped under the appropriate award) with the *Gazette* page number (and, from 1918, the number of the Government General Order or Army Department Notification). The sub-heading "Miscellaneous Orders and Notifications" gives the page numbers on which awards are to be found. This is a thoroughly unreliable section which, apart from eccentric internal indexing, frequently muddles awards of the M.S.M. and the I.M.S.M. The Index to the *Gazette Extraordinary* is simpler in that, under the heading "Army Department", only the *Gazette* pages on which awards are to be found are given. In consequence, if a recipient cannot be traced in the nominal indices to Part 1, it is necessary to search for him in every relevant *Gazette Extraordinary*. Fortunately there are only 425 such recipients. No citations are given in either part of the *Gazette* but, commencing in 1919, the theatre usually appears.

The Government of India List of Honors (see Bibliography) gives all awards gazetted between 1917 and 1921. The majority of 1922 awards are also included but, for some reason, those gazetted in March and May of that year are omitted. In the *List* details are confined to the personal particulars of the recipient together with the theatre in which, or the Force with which, the award was gained. There are a number of repeated names which do not necessarily indicate the award of a bar, and a few recipients of the medal with annuity.

NUMBERS AWARDED

1917–1922 After adjustments for duplication, either due to the award of bars or to inadvertence, the *Government of India List of Honors* contains 5,787 names of men awarded the I.M.S.M. These correspond with awards in theatres or with various Forces as follows:

Aden Field Force	152
Baluchistan	22
Black Sea, British Army of ...	33
Constantinople	1
Dardanelles/Gallipoli	36
East Africa	381
Egyptian Expeditionary Force	2,627

23. *L.G.*, 27th October 1964.

24. The first three awards also appear in *L.G.*, 26th April 1917 (repeated in the *Gazette of India* 23rd June 1917). This is an isolated case.

France	... ...	423	
Hospital ships	... ...	5	
India	... ...	769	
Mesopotamia	... ...	1,031	(including 91 for Kut-el-Amara)
North West Frontier	... ...	16	
Persia	... ...	122	(including 37 for Bushire, and 20 with British Military Mission, Meshed)
Salonika, British Force	...	56	
Somaliland	... ...	18	
Waziristan	... ...	48	
Not given	... ...	47	

Our count of the *Gazette of India* entries for the same period reveals 5,746 first awards, excluding 40 honorary awards to the Nepalese Contingent[25], two to the Muscat Levy Corps[26] and 44 for the Waziristan Force[27] which, in the case of the last two, for some reason were omitted from the *List of Honors*. The relatively small discrepancy between the totals may be accounted for by duplications which we have missed and by the undoubted inclusion of a few annuity awards in the *List of Honors*. In passing it should be mentioned that the official statistics (see Bibliography) which are said to be to 31st May 1920 give a total of 1,837 awards and two bars. The former figure is impossible to reconcile with the *Gazette* entries but does, however, indicate that the compiler stopped short, probably in January 1920.

1923 and 1924 Awards gazetted for these years are as follows:

Gallant conduct	... ...	1	(see below)
Iraq	... ...	5	
Mesopotamian Expeditionary Force	1	
Rasmak Field Force	... ...	4	
Waziristan Force	... ...	15	

Gallantry Awards Due to the confusing wording of the *Gazette of India* notices it has not been possible to isolate awards of the medal for gallantry, except for the following:

1. For gallantry and devotion to duty with the Mesopotamian Expeditionary Force in the *Gazette* of 27th August 1921:

2070 Naik Ghulam Nabi[28]
6518 Lance Naik Ghulam Rasul
2235 Lance Naik Arjun Singh
2570 Lance Naik Rajah
} 1st King George's Own Sappers and Miners

2. For gallant conduct otherwise than in action:

1727 Havildar Arjan Singh, 2nd/34th Sikh Pioneers, *Gazette* 15th November 1919 (Bushire).

19397 Driver Baldeo Singh, Royal Field Artillery, *Gazette* 14th February 1920.

19494 Driver Alla Rakka, Royal Field Artillery, *Gazette* 11th September 1920 (Black Sea)

132 Sepoy Ram Singh, 1st/17th Dogra Regiment, *Gazette* 28th July 1923.

Bars In the following list of 13 recipients, the numerical dates given are those of the *Gazette of India*, the letter *E* being added for the *Gazette Extraordinary*. Where the *Gazette* notice is specific i.e. where the award can be related to "gallantry and devotion to duty" or "meritorious service and devotion to duty", the key words are included. "E.E.F." and "M.E.F." signify the Egyptian and Mesopotamian Expeditionary Forces respectively[29].

198 Sapper Fazal Ahmad, 3rd Sappers and Miners; medal 17.8.18 (M.E.F.); bar 3.6.18 *E*, meritorious service (M.E.F.)

1677 Naik Lehna Singh, 1st King George's Own Sappers and Miners; medal 1.1.18 *E*, meritorious service (M.E.F.); bar 25.10.19 (E.E.F.)

5250 Acting Havildar Umdi, 3rd Sappers and Miners; medal 1.5.20 (India); bar 6.11.20, gallantry (Waziristan Force).

25. *Gazette of India Extraordinary* 5th February 1919.
26. *Gazette of India* 11th March 1922.
27. *Ibid* 25th March and 6th May 1922.
28. Award cancelled and bar substituted, see "Bars".
29. Where the *Gazette* notice does not give the theatre or Force this has been taken from the *List of Honors*.

1410 1st Class Sub-Assistant Surgeon Vyasam Venkataramayya, Indian Subordinate Medical Department; medal 1.1.18 *E*, meritorious service (M.E.F.); bar 22.1.21, gallantry (M.E.F.); 2nd medal 3.6.19 *E* cancelled.

1807 Havildar Parmodh Singh, 37th Dogras; medal 26.10.18, meritorious service (France); bar 26.2.21, gallantry (M.E.F.); 2nd medal for meritorious service 14.8.20 cancelled.

4495 Havildar Bahadur Ali, 2nd/127th Queen Mary's Own Baluch Light Infantry; medal 4.5.18, meritorious service (E.E.F.); bar 26.2.21, gallantry (E.E.F.); 2nd medal for meritorious service 27.11.20 cancelled.

922 Naik Fateh Muhammad, 2nd/127th Queen Mary's Own Baluch Light Infantry; medal 4.5.18, meritorious service (E.E.F.); bar 26.2.21, gallantry (E.E.F.); 2nd medal for meritorious service 27.11.20 cancelled.

307 Havildar Mirza Khan, 1st/127th Queen Mary's Own Baluch Light Infantry; medal 4.5.18, meritorious service (East Africa); bar 16.7.21, gallantry (E.E.F.); 2nd medal for meritorious service 27.11.20 cancelled.

4047 Havildar Khamal Khan, 1st/127th Queen Mary's Own Baluch Light Infantry; medal 4.5.18, meritorious service (East Africa); bar 16.7.21, gallantry (E.E.F.); 2nd medal for meritorious service 27.11.20 cancelled.

298 Havildar Mohan Singh, 2nd/23rd Sikh Pioneers; medal 27.11.20, meritorious service (E.E.F.); bar 22.4.22, gallantry (Baluchistan Force); 2nd medal 1.1.20 *E* cancelled.

4363½ Havildar Fazal Dad Khan, 59th Scinde Rifles (Frontier Force); award of medal not traced; bar 28.7.23, meritorious service (E.E.F.); 2nd medal for meritorious service 27.11.20 cancelled.

8725 Lance Naik Chaynjay, Army Bearer Corps; medal 20.7.18 (France); bar 15.3.24, gallantry (E.E.F.); 2nd medal for meritorious service 27.11.20 cancelled.

2070 Naik Ghulam Nabi, 8th Field Company, 1st King George's Own Sappers and Miners; medal 10.7.20, meritorious service (M.E.F.); bar 17.10.25, gallantry (M.E.F.); 2nd medal 27.8.21 cancelled.

ILLUSTRATIVE AWARD

The only details of any awards which we have been able to find are those contained in *The Story of the 97th Deccan Infantry* by Major W. C. Kirkwood, O.B.E. (Hyderabad-Deccan, Government Central Press, 1929) at p.155 where No.429 Sepoy Mahtab Beg and No.7 Sepoy Khaderu are each recorded as having received the I.M.S.M. "for gallant conduct in rescuing a drowning man on 2–10–18." The awards appeared with eight others of the I.M.S.M. in the *Gazette of India* of 15th February 1919 where the men's names are rendered as "Mehtab Beg" and "Kadhera" respectively. This illustrates the difficulty sometimes encountered in finding men in the *Gazette* indices where the names are rendered differently in different sources. The awards appeared with others of the M.C., I.O.M. and I.D.S.M. the announcement being that they were for "gallantry and devotion to duty in the field" and, in consequence, there was nothing to show that any of the I.M.S.M. awards were for gallantry. According to the *List of Honors* the two I.M.S.M. awards were gained in the Mesopotamian Expeditionary Force.

Chapter 24

The Indian Order of Merit (Military and Civil Divisions)

ORIGIN AND DEVELOPMENT

The Military Division of the Indian Order of Merit was instituted in 1837 by the Honourable East India Company. In one sense it is the oldest official British gallantry award for general issue, although it was not until 1860 that the H.E.I.C. forces were transferred to the Crown[1]. According to the correspondence reproduced in Mayo (see Bibliography), in 1834[2] the Governor-General proposed to the Court of Directors that two military orders should be sanctioned for the native portion of the Company's Army, one as a reward to commissioned officers for "long, faithful and honourable service", and the other to all ranks for "conspicuous gallantry in the field". The former was to be styled "The Order of British India"[3], and the latter "The Order of Merit". The reasons[4] advanced for the proposals included the need to strengthen the attachment of native soldiers to the Government; to provide distinctions which did not depend upon seniority; to improve the condition of native soldiers *vis-a-vis* their compatriots in civil administration; and to provide a means of rewarding native officers[5]. It was also pointed out that similar rewards had been found necessary in all armies[6]. It was not until 1837 that the Court gave its sanction to these proposals[7], making some modifications regarding the O.B.I., and accepting those for the I.O.M. However, awards for the latter were to be for prospective acts of gallantry only, although one exception to this rule was allowed[8]. The rules and regulations for the O.B.I. and the I.O.M. were published in the General Order by the Governor-General of India, No. 94, of 1st May 1837[9]. Omitting the particulars regarding the O.B.I., the Order reads as follows:

> "ORDER OF MERIT
>
> The object of this institution is to afford personal reward for personal bravery, without reference to any claims founded on mere length of service and general good conduct.
>
> The Order is to consist of three classes; the two junior to be distinguished by a badge of silver, and the senior by a badge of gold, in the shape of a military laurelled star, bearing in its centre the inscription: "The Reward of Valour".
>
> This badge is to be worn on the left breast, pendant from a dark blue ribbon with red edge.
>
> Third Class
>
> Is to be obtained by any conspicuous act of individual gallantry on the part of any native officer or soldier[10] in the field, or in the attack or defence of fortified places, without distinction of rank or grade.
>
> Second Class
>
> Is to be obtained by those who already possess the third, and for similar services.
>
> First Class
>
> Is to be obtained, in like manner, only by those who already possess the third and second classes.
>
> Admission to each of these classes is to be obtained upon application to the Governor-General of India in Council, with whom alone competency of conferring the Order rests.
>
> The original recommendation must particularly specify the act of gallantry for which the soldier is supposed to have claims for this high distinction; and the preparatory steps to obtaining it are to be as follows:

1. Even then it was only in 1939 that the Crown made Ordinances for the Order (see below). The intervening position is far from clear. Thus the Civil Division was instituted in 1902 by a resolution of the Governor-General in Council, approved by the Secretary of State for India (see below).

2. Letter of 24th October 1834. A number of purely regimental awards in recognition of individual acts of gallantry had hitherto been made in both the British and H.E.I.C. Armies. Frequently, such awards were in the form of medals but, in the British Army, their origin was unofficial, the cost being met by subscription among the officers of the regiment, or from regimental funds. Some rewards and distinctions seem to have been made officially to native officers of the Bombay and Madras Presidency Armies before 1837. Mayo cites some cases where special medals were struck to reward individual natives of the Company's Armies.

3. Since this was not a gallantry award it is outside the scope of the present work.

4. Summarised here only; the reasons given are prolix and it is far from clear whether some attached to the proposed O.B.I. only.

5. Of course, various awards were open to European officers, e.g., the Order of the Bath. Nothing was available to European other ranks of the Company's Army until the institution of the Victoria Cross (q.v.).

6. Yet for other ranks in the Queen's service the D.C.M. (q.v.) was not instituted until 1854.

7. Letter of 1st February 1837; they also dealt with proposals made in 1835 regarding the equalisation of pay among native officers and men of the three Presidencies, and increases in pay for long service.

8. To Havildar Chookalingum of the Madras Sappers and Miners for bravery during the insurrection in Coorg.

9. Certain financial details had been published in G.O.G.G. No. 83 of 17th April 1837 but these are omitted to avoid repetition.

10. In 1879 Eurasians were made eligible, see the Communication from the Secretary of State for India to the Governor-General of India in Council, No. 51 Military, of 20th February 1879.

After an action, in which particular acts of gallantry have been performed which may be considered as entitling a soldier to the "Order of Merit", a representation of the circumstances is to be made, through the Commanding Officer of the regiment, by the Captain or Officer commanding the Troop or Company, to the general officer commanding the Division, who will order a Court composed of European and Native Officers, and consisting of one field officer, two captains and two subadars (the proceedings to be conducted by an officer of the Judge-Advocate-General's Department, if available), before which the individual recommended will be brought, when witnesses will be called and examined as to what they saw the soldier perform in the action referred to.

Should there be any failure of proof, the claim is not to be allowed; but on the other hand, should the particular gallantry of the soldier recommended for the distinction appear to have been conspicuous and undoubted, the report of the Court will be forwarded in Bengal, through His Excellency the Commander-in-Chief in India, and at each of the other Presidencies, through the Commander-in-Chief and local Government, to the Governor-General of India in Council, who has nevertheless the power of rejecting the claim, for reasons to be recorded at the time.

A record in each case of the particular act of gallantry for which the Star has been conferred will be kept in the Office of the Secretary to the Government of India in the Military Department, and a Certificate from that functionary, detailing the grant of the Order, and its concomitant advantages, will be given to each individual on his admission to, or advancement in it.

Admission into the Order of Merit will confer on a member an additional allowance, equal in the third class to one-third, in the second to two-thirds, and in the first to the entire of the ordinary pay of his rank, over and above that pay or the pension he may be entitled to on retirement.

The widow of a member will be entitled to receive the pension conferred by the Order upon her husband, for three years after the date of his decease; and in the case of a plurality of wives, the first married is to have the preference.

No claims founded on acts of gallantry antecedent to the date of this General Order shall be considered admissible under any pretence whatsoever.

Wm. Casement, Colonel,
Secretary to the Government of India,
Military Department."

By at least 1876[11], the additional allowance based on thirds of the ordinary pay had been abolished, and fixed allowances according to the rank of the recipient and to the class of the Order conferred, had been substituted. These allowances were varied from time to time[12].

In 1902 the Civil Division of the Order was instituted, the announcement[13] being in the following terms:

"In order to provide for the suitable recognition and reward of conspicuous acts of gallantry performed by Natives of India, whether servants of Government or not, in aid or support of public authority or safety, the Governor General in Council, with the assent of His Majesty's Secretary of State for India in Council, has resolved to institute a Second or Civil Division of the Order of Merit. The rules for admission to this Division, which have received the approval of the Secretary of State, are hereby published for general information. The new decoration will be conferred only for acts of gallantry performed after the institution of the Order.

Rules for admission to the Civil Division of the Order of Merit

1. The "Order of Merit" (Civil Division) consists of three classes, and is conferred on Natives of India, whether servants of Government or not, as a reward for personal bravery shown in aid or support of the public authority or safety. The insignia are, for the first class, gold; for the second, silver with a gold wreath; and for the third, silver only; to be worn on the left breast, pendant from a dark-red ribbon with blue edges.

2. Admission to the third class is obtained by any conspicuous act of individual gallantry; admission to the second class can be obtained only by members of the third class, and for a similar act of gallantry; and, in like manner, the Order of the first class is conferred only on members of the second class. In recommending persons for admission to the Order, the act of gallantry must be particularly specified, and the

11. See the *Pay Code for India*, Volume 2 (Native Troops), 1876, paragraph 379.

12. *E.g.*, Indian Army Order No. 294 of 1916.

13. Government of India Home Department Notification No. 1,324 – Public, published in the *Gazette of India* of 3rd May 1902 at p.326. It will be noted that the award was confined to acts in respect of *public* authority or safety.

statements of eye-witnesses to the deed must be attached. It is of the highest importance, in view of maintaining the value and prestige of the Order, that the greatest discretion shall be used in submitting recommendations; as it is very desirable that the distinction should only be granted for conduct which can clearly be defined as an act of *conspicuous* gallantry.

3. Admission to each class of the Order rests with the Government of India alone; and, when the act of gallantry has taken place in India, recommendations for the reward will be forwarded through the District Officers to the Local Government, for submission to the Government of India.

4. A record in each case of the particular act of gallantry for which the Order has been conferred is kept in the office of the Secretary to the Government in the Home Department; and a certificate signed by him, declaring the grant of the Order, will be given to each individual on his admission to, or advancement in it.

5. District Officers are required to report immediately to the Local Government, for communication to the Government of India in the Home Department, any casualty by death amongst individuals admitted to the Order which may occur *previous* to the receipt of the decoration.

6. The following are the rules for the disposal of the insignia of the Civil Division of the "Order of Merit" on the decease or promotion of members:

In cases of advancement to a superior class of the Civil Division of the "Order of Merit", the inferior badge is to be forwarded, through the prescribed channel, to the Secretary to the Government of India in the Home Department, Calcutta. The insignia of the Order are, however, allowed to remain in the possession of the family of a deceased member.

7. Whenever a servant of the Government, being a member of the Order, is dismissed the service, and whenever any member of the Order is convicted of any such offence, or subjected by a Criminal Court to any such order, as implies, in the opinion of the Local Government, a defect of character which unfits him to be a member of the Order, a full report of the circumstances shall be transmitted to the Government of India in the Home Department together with an expression of the Local Government's opinion; and it shall, thereupon, be open to the Government of India to direct the dismissal of any such member from the Order and to require the surrender of his decoration.

8. As a rule the conferment of the Order of Merit in the Civil Division will not be accompanied by any grant of money; but the Government of India reserve the right of making such a grant, in addition to conferring the Order, in special cases."

In 1903 the designation of both Divisions was altered[14] from the "Order of Merit" to the "Indian Order of Merit"; this was to distinguish it from the (Imperial) Order of Merit which had been instituted in 1902 as a reward for exceptionally distinguished officers and civilians. Also in 1903 the Rules for the Civil Division were slightly amended[15] to make provision for the method of submission of recommendations in respect of military personnel[16].

In 1911 recipients of the Order in either Division were permitted to use the letters "I.O.M." after their names[17]. The same year the regulations regarding military widows' pensions were altered[18] so that pensions were to continue until death or remarriage and not for the maximum of three years as heretofore. In 1912 this provision was made retrospective to include widows who had not remarried but had discontinued to draw the pension under the three-year rule[19]. Following the extension of eligibility for the Victoria Cross to Indian officers and men[20], it was decided to abolish the 1st Class of the Military Division of the Order, and to re-number the remaining classes 1st and 2nd Class respectively. The alteration was published as Army Department Notification No.757 in the *Gazette of India* for 3rd August 1912 at p.808 as follows:

"In consequence of the extension of the Decoration of the Victoria Cross to Indian Officers, Non-commissioned Officers and Men of the Indian Army, the present 1st Class of the Military Division of the Indian Order of Merit, with the allowances thereto, is abolished, and the existing 2nd and 3rd Classes of the Order, with their attendant allowances, are renamed 1st and 2nd Class respectively.

14. Government General Order No. 344 of 17th April 1903.

15. Home Department Notification No. 2,528 – Public, of 2nd July 1903.

16. By this date two awards of the 3rd Class of the Civil Division had already been made to Native soldiers and the amendment seems merely to have been directed to regularising the method of submitting recommendations for military personnel by directing that they should be forwarded through the usual military channels.

17. Army Department Notification No. 107 of 10th February 1911.

18. Foreign Department Notification No. 253-C of 12th December 1911.

19. Army Department Notification No. 666 of 5th July 1912.

20. Royal Warrant of 21st October 1911.

These changes, which have effect from the 12th December 1911, will not affect the interests of incumbents who were admitted *Army Department Notification No.666 dated the 5th July 1912. to the Order with effect from a date prior thereto, nor will they prejudice claims* to the continuance or restoration of the allowance, of widows whose deceased husbands were members of the Order previous to that date.

General Orders Nos.83, dated 17th April 1837, and 94, dated 1st May 1837, by the Right Hon'ble the Governor-General in Council, relating to the institution, rules and regulations of the Order, are hereby modified to the extent set forth above."

By a Royal Warrant of 25th August 1939[21] the Crown itself made provision for both Divisions of the Order and, *inter alia*, reduced the Civil Division to a single Class[22]. The new Ordinances were as follows:

"First. It is ordained that the Order shall be named "The Indian Order of Merit" and shall be divided into a Civil Division and a Military Division.

Secondly. It is ordained that the Civil Division of the Order shall consist of one Class and that appointment to it may be made only by Our Viceroy. Any of Our subjects of Indian origin or any subject of a Ruler of an Indian State may be appointed to the Order for any act of conspicuous personal bravery in aid of public authority or the safety of others.

Thirdly. It is ordained that the Insignia of the Civil Division of the Order shall be a Badge consisting of an eight pointed star 1-inch in diameter composed of rays, with in the centre a circular ground of dark blue enamel surrounded by a laurel wreath. On the enamel ground there shall be the Royal Cypher surmounted by a Crown encircled with the words "For Bravery". The Badge shall be of silver and the laurel wreath and the design in the centre shall be of gold. The Badge shall be worn on the left breast pendant from a dark red Ribbon with blue edges.

Fourthly. It is ordained that the Military Division of the Order shall consist of two Classes and that appointments to it may be made only by Our Viceroy on the recommendation of the Commander-in-Chief of Our Forces in India. Viceroy's Commissioned Officers, Indian Warrant Officers and Indian other ranks in Our Armed Forces (including Frontier Corps and Military Police) or any members of Indian States' Forces may be appointed to the Second Class for any act of conspicuous gallantry performed in connection with their duties. Appointments to the First Class shall be made only from members of the Second Class for any similar act performed by them.

Fifthly. It is ordained that the Insignia of the Military Division of the Order shall be a Badge consisting of an eight pointed silver star $1\frac{1}{2}$ inch in diameter, with in the centre two crossed swords around which shall be inscribed the words "Reward of Gallantry", all on a circular ground of dark blue enamel and surrounded by a laurel wreath. In the Badge of the First Class the laurel wreath and the design in the centre shall be of gold. In the Badge of the Second Class the laurel wreath and the design in the centre shall be of silver. The Badge shall be worn on the left breast pendant from a dark blue Ribbon with red edges.

Sixthly. It is ordained that Our Viceroy may cancel and annul the appointment to the Order of any member and that thereupon the said member shall be required to surrender his Insignia, provided that Our Viceroy may subsequently abrogate any such cancellation and annulment.

Seventhly. It is ordained that the members of the Order may use the letters "I.O.M." after their names.

Eighthly. It is ordained that it shall be competent for Our Viceroy for the time being to make Regulations to carry out the purposes of this Warrant."

It seems that the words "Our Armed Forces" in the 4th Ordinance were intended to include the Royal Indian Navy[23] and Indian Air Force although the matter was clarified in an amending Royal Warrant of 20th December 1944 (see *post*). At a meeting on 14th September 1943 of the Committee on the Grant of Honours, Decorations and Medals in Time of War[24], it was agreed that the I.O.M. and the I.D.S.M. should be regarded as higher category awards and that the number of awards of both should be reduced. In future the Military Division of the I.O.M.

21. See *L.G.*, 26th September 1939, p.6,510.

22. The Civil Division seems to have fallen into abeyance after 1922 (except for an isolated award in 1933) due, possibly, to the institution of the E.G.M. (q.v.). Even after the revival as a single Class no awards were made until 1942.

23. 2nd Class awards were made in *L.G.*, 2nd February 1943 at p.605 (repeated, with citations, in the *Gazette of India*, 6th February 1943 at p.173) to Acting Petty Officer Mohamed Ibrahim and Able Seaman Ragunath Sohae of H.M.I.S. *Bengal* for an action against Japanese raiders on 11th November 1942.

24. See P.R.O. AIR 2/6409.

would be awarded only in very rare cases where outstanding leadership was the predominating factor. On 21st August 1944 the Committee considered proposals by the Secretary of State for India, the Viceroy, and the Commander-in-Chief, India that, so as to bring the Order into line with other gallantry awards, the two Classes should be reduced to one and that a bar for subsequent acts should be introduced. It was further proposed that the new badge (which in the event was identical with the previous 1st Class badge) should be issued to all those who had been appointed to the 2nd Class since 15th February 1944, and that surviving members of the 1st Class should receive a bar for wear with their original badge, and a silver emblem for wear on the ribbon when the ribbon was worn alone. These proposals were approved by the King on 13th September 1944 and were embodied in Army Instruction (India) No.380 of 10th October 1944. This Instruction modified the proposals to the extent that the new badge was to be issued to those appointed to the Order for *acts* performed on or after 15th February 1944. However, with three exceptions[25], all appointments notified in the *Gazette of India* from including 14th October 1944 are not assigned to a Class. Whatever the true position regarding retrospective operation from 15th February 1944 it is clear that it would have been simpler administratively to issue the new badge in cases of appointment made from that date[26], rather than for acts performed on or after it. An amending Royal Warrant of 20th December 1944[27] made the necessary alterations, but without prescribing for retrospection, as follows:

> "For the Fourth and Fifth Ordinances[28] the following shall be substituted, the existing Ordinances "Sixthly", "Seventhly" and "Eighthly", being renumbered "Seventhly", "Eighthly" and "Ninthly".
>
> Fourthly. It is ordained that the Military Division of the Order shall consist of one class and that appointments to it may be made only by Our Viceroy on the recommendation of the Commander-in-Chief of Our Forces in India. Viceroy's Commissioned Officers of Our Armed Forces (including Frontier and Irregular Corps and Military Police) or Indian Warrant Officers of Our Royal Indian Navy and Our Indian Air Force (in the air) or Officers of equivalent rank of Indian States' Forces and Our Hong Kong-Singapore Royal Artillery may be appointed to the Order for any act of conspicuous gallantry performed in connection with their duties. In very rare cases where outstanding leadership is the feature, Indian Other Ranks of Our Armed Forces (including Indian Other Ranks of Frontier and Irregular Corps and Military Police), or Petty Officers, Ratings and Aircraftsmen of Our Royal Indian Navy and Our Indian Air Force (on the ground), or Indian Other Ranks of Indian States' Forces, and of Our Hong Kong-Singapore Royal Artillery may also be appointed to the Order.
>
> Fifthly. It is ordained that anyone who after having performed services for which this Order is awarded, subsequently performs an approved act of gallantry which, if he had not received the Order, would have entitled him to it, shall be awarded a Bar to be attached to the riband by which the badge is suspended, and for every additional such act an additional Bar may be added.
>
> Sixthly. It is ordained that the Insignia of the Military Division of the Order shall be a badge consisting of an eight-pointed silver star one and a half inches in diameter, within the centre two crossed swords around which shall be inscribed the words "Reward for Gallantry"[29], all on a circular ground of dark blue enamel and surrounded by a laurel wreath. The laurel wreath and the design in the centre shall be of gold. The badge shall be worn on the left breast pendant from a dark blue ribbon with red edges. For every Bar awarded a silver Rose shall be added to the ribbon when worn alone."

It seems, from the wording of the 4th Ordinance, that henceforth the Order was to be regarded primarily as an award for native officers and that the appointment of other ranks was to be altogether exceptional. Only one award was made to the Hong Kong and Singapore Royal Artillery[30].

The following year the badge of the Military Division was redesigned, the operative part of the Royal Warrant of 5th September 1945[31] being in these terms:

25. Gazetted without citation as 2nd Class on 7th July 1945.

26. Between 15th February 1944 and 13th October 1944, 65 Second Class appointments appeared in the *Gazette of India*.

27. See *L.G.*, 29th December 1944, p.5963. Between 1919 and 1944 only six promotions to the 1st Class had been made.

28. Of the Royal Warrant of 25th August 1939.

29. Actual specimens show "Reward of Gallantry"; see under "Description" below.

30. A posthumous single Class award to Jemadar Ali Mohd in *L.G.*, 4th April 1946, p.1,672 (defence of Hong Kong, 1941). A number of awards of the D.C.M., I.D.S.M. and M.M. were made to this Corps.

31. See *L.G.*, 14th September 1945, p.4,591.

163

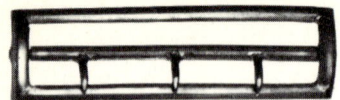

Fig. A: The Indian Order of Merit (Military Division), type of ribbon buckle, 1837–1945.

Fig. B: The Indian Order of Merit (Military Division), obverse, 1837–1912.

32. Actual specimens show "Reward of Gallantry"; see under "Description" below.

33. *Sic.* This seems to have been a misprint for "ground".

34. For services prior to the fall of Singapore in 1942.

35. *L.G.*, 11th February 1947, p.697.

36. *L.G.*, 22nd April 1921, p.3,184.

37. *L.G.*, 22nd November 1929, p.7,529 and subsequent lists given in Appendix 4.

38. See, for instance, a photograph (*c.*1937) in the possession of the Army Museums Ogilby Trust of Subadar Major Natha Singh, 22nd Mountain Battery (I.O.M. awarded in 1917).

39. Later the stars were supplied by the Calcutta Mint (see, for instance, the *Report on the Administration of the Mints at Calcutta and Bombay*, for 1934/35 at p.11, which mentions the supply of ten 2nd Class stars to the Army Department).

40. Royal Warrant of 21st October 1911.

41. Army Department Notification No. 757 of 3rd August 1912, effective from 12th December 1911, and quoted above.

"For the Sixth Ordinance the following shall be substituted:

Sixthly. It is ordained that the Insignia of the Military Division of the Order shall be a Badge consisting of an eight-pointed silver star one and seven tenths inches in diameter with in the centre two crossed swords around which shall be inscribed "Reward for Gallantry"[32] on a circular crown[33] of dark blue enamel and surrounded by a laurel wreath surmounted by a crown. The laurel wreath including the crown and the design in the centre shall be of gold. The Badge shall be worn on the left breast pendant from a dark blue Ribbon with red edges. For every Bar awarded a silver Rose shall be added to the Ribbon when worn alone."

The last awards of the Military Division appear in the *London Gazette* of 25th September 1947 at p.4,517[34].

Originally the Military Division was worn between the Order of British India and the Kaiser-i-Hind Medal. In the 1947 and later lists showing the order of wearing orders, medals and decorations, which are published in the *London Gazette*, it is shown following the M.B.E.[35]. Until 1921[36] the lists show the Civil Division after the S.G.M. in a group of gallantry awards which then followed Polar Medals, but from 1929[37] it is shown in the position indicated in Appendix 4.

DESCRIPTION – MILITARY DIVISION

Ribbon Dark blue, 1½ inches wide with red edges. Usually a three-prong buckle was worn on the ribbon[38] (Fig.A) until the 1945 pattern star was introduced. The buckle was gold for the original 1st Class star, and silver for the remainder.

1837–1912 (Fig.B) The correspondence leading to the pattern of the first stars adopted is given in Mayo (see Bibliography). We have seen one undoubtedly genuine 3rd Class issue with the spelling "Valour". On this the letters "ou" seem somewhat smaller than the remainder, and rather cramped. In the absence of any accompanying campaign medals it is difficult to date the piece although other characteristics suggest that it was a later issue. In addition, Taprell Dorling's 1916 Edition (see Bibliography) has a line drawing of the star with spelling "Valour". The stars are 1½ inches or fractionally more in diameter across the points, with a dark blue enamel centre, as follows:

> *1st Class* – gold star, laurel wreath and design on centre ground. As with the Order of British India, some apparently genuine issues have been seen in silver gilt.

> *2nd Class* – silver star, gold laurel wreath and design on centre ground.

> *3rd Class* – silver star, laurel wreath and design on centre ground. One issue has been seen, made by J. S. Hunt, with the London hall-mark for 1858[39].

Suspension By rings and link from a specially-made suspender. The components are gold for the 1st Class, and silver for the remainder. Some suspenders are made of thicker metal than others, and the shape of the curved portion varies.

Reverse Plain, except for the Class and designation of the Order engraved in script. Some stars have details of the recipient engraved on the reverse. Possibly this was done unofficially. Some later issues have the centre mount screwed in, the retaining nut being flush with the reverse.

Bars Only one was awarded. This was dated "18th June 1888" and was to the 1st Class Order awarded to Subadar Kishanbir Nagarkoti, 5th Gurkha Rifles (see below).

1912–1939 (Fig.C) In 1911 eligibility for the Victoria Cross was extended to Indian officers and men[40]. Accordingly the 1st Class star of the Order was abolished, the remainder being renumbered 1st and 2nd Class respectively[41]. Except for the Class number on the reverse, the design of these two stars remained the same although, probably during the First World War, a rather clumsier version appeared, illustrated here, which was made in this country mainly for award to

Fig.C: The Indian Order of Merit (Military Division), obverse, 1912–1939.

Indian troops serving in France and Flanders. In this the star is fractionally wider and deeper; the laurel leaves form a continuous circle; the centre design is somewhat larger; the connecting link is omitted from the suspender, and the ribbon slot made wider. The reverse is concave, and the Class and designation of the Order engraved in upright capital letters. One of these stars has been seen bearing the name of J. W. Benson Ltd., Ludgate Hill, London, engraved on the reverse.

1939–1945 (Fig.D). In 1939[42] the words on the obverse were changed to "Reward of Gallantry"[43] although there is some doubt as to whether the altered inscription was introduced earlier. In 1944[44] the Military Division was further reduced to a single Class, the star being of the existing 1st Class pattern. A bar was also authorised but, in fact, no award was made.

1945–1947 (Figs.E and F). In 1945[45] the design of the star was altered by modernising the swords, increasing the diameter of the star across the points to $1\frac{7}{10}$ inches, and adding a crown above the laurel wreath. The star was to be in silver, the crown, laurel wreath and central design being in gold. In this pattern the reverse is plain, while the crown and laurel wreath are struck flat in one piece and kept in place by the central design which is retained by a screw and nut, the latter being flush with the reverse. A brooch bar fitted with a pin and catch replaced the three-prong ribbon brooch hitherto worn and a cruder die-struck suspender appeared[46].

Copies and Fakes Copies are sometimes mentioned in old sale catalogues[47]. A miniature of the 1945/47 pattern star has been seen with the inscription "Reward of Gallantry" but with the crown, laurel wreath and central design in silver instead of gold. A second award bar appeared on this miniature being in silver with two horizontal flutings, and a crown in the centre.

DESCRIPTION – CIVIL DIVISION

(For coloured illustration, see Plate 3)

Ribbon Dark red $1\frac{3}{8}$ inches wide with blue edges[48].

1902–1939 3rd Class[49] of the Order (Fig.G). The star is $1\frac{3}{16}$ inches in diameter, and the reverse is plain except for the nut retaining the centre of the obverse. The suspender is in smaller scale but similar to that of the contemporary Military Division of the Order except for the cross piece below the ribbon bar. About 1910 a GRI cypher appeared.

1939–1947 The Royal Warrant of 25th August 1939 (see above) reduced the Civil Division to a single Class, and the star to one inch in diameter (Fig.H). The laurel wreath and centre design are in gold and the star in silver, as for the original 2nd Class of the Order. We have seen a miniature of the single Class with the cruder suspender, and crown above the laurel wreath, as for the 1945/47 star of the Military Division. This miniature had the GRI cypher in upright capital letters.

VERIFICATIONS AND CITATIONS

Army Lists Two series of Lists published in India are useful for verifying awards and for tracing the appropriate authority which, in turn, may reveal a citation. These are:

Presidency Quarterly Army Lists Varying details are given in the three Presidency Lists. In Bengal, recipients are listed from January 1883. For the first year, only effectives are given but thereafter the Lists contain those on the Pension Establishment as well. In Bombay, recipients appear from at least April 1860, but effectives only are listed. In Madras, both categories of recipient are given from at least March 1861. In all three Lists the details given vary slightly in content and layout, but include the Class of award, rank, name and corps; Bengal and Madras quote

42. Royal Warrant of 25th August 1939 (see above).

43. The altered wording may have been due to the word "Valour" appearing on the Victoria Cross.

44. Royal Warrant of 20th December 1944 (see above). This Warrant gave the wording in the centre as "Reward for Gallantry" instead of "Reward of Gallantry"; this may have been a misprint since no issues with the former wording have been seen.

45. Royal Warrant of 5th September 1945 (see above), which again gives the inscription as "Reward for Gallantry".

46. Not all the changes in design are mentioned in the Warrant.

47. It may be that the reverses of these were entirely plain. Alternatively, the cataloguer may have thought that the stars should have borne a recipient's name.

48. The ribbon of the decoration awarded in 1909 to the Maharajah of Burdwan has these colours reversed. The colours we give are those prescribed on institution in 1902 and by the Royal Warrant of 1939.

49. In fact no appointments to the 1st and 2nd Classes were ever made. The stars were to be distinguished in gold and silver as for the Military Division.

Fig.D: The Indian Order of Merit (Military Division), obverse, 1939–1945.

the appropriate General Order while Bombay gives the date of admission only, being in fact the date of the act for which the award was made.

Quarterly Indian Army Lists Details of serving and pensioned recipients appear from January 1890 until January 1943 inclusive. Until July 1904 they are given quarterly; thereafter they are given with the January and July Lists only, and from January 1923 with the January Lists only. Details include the regimental number (where appropriate), rank, names, corps and date and authority for the award; where applicable, subsequent promotions within the Order are also given. Some Military awards are shown incorrectly as Civil awards between January 1915 and January 1924, and other inconsistencies and misprints have been found.

London Gazette Until 1915 awards are not indexed. However, occasionally some details are given in the published despatches from commanders in the field[50]. Other than these, the only awards appearing are those gazetted between 1st January 1915 and 25th February 1918, and 29th November 1940 and 25th September 1947[51]. It is by no means certain that all the awards actually made in these two periods appear in the Gazette. The only citations are those given in the Gazette of 1st January 1915. For the first of the two periods names appear under the medal heading in the "State Intelligence" portion of the indices. Until and including the index for the third quarter of 1916 the recipient's last name is given first; thereafter, including the second period mentioned, names are indexed under the first name. For the second period the medal heading in the "State Intelligence" portion gives only the pages upon which awards are to be found[52]. Until December 1941 names are indexed under the section headed "Civil Appointments and Promotions" and thereafter under "Honours, Decorations and Medals". In 1943/44 the recipient's regiment is occasionally omitted from the Gazette entry.

Gazette of India The Gazette indices are complicated, being divided into a number of parts. Several major changes have been found in the system of indexing[53]. Even within the broad framework of the revised systems, minor variations occur, and what follows can only be taken as a guide.

Until 1916 Awards of the Military Division appear in the form of Government General Orders or, later, Army Department Notifications. In the earlier Gazettes the names of recipients are found in the "Alphabetical Index" which is a comprehensive nominal list of all civil and military promotions, awards and similar announcements. Natives are indexed under the first name, the Gazette page reference being given. Later, awards also appear in the Index to Government General Orders and Notifications (Military Department) where again page references are given. This system was then altered, names appearing in the "Nominal Index to Government General Orders (Army Department)", under the sub-heading "Rewards". Both these indices give only the number of the Order (or Notification) and it is therefore necessary to trace the numerical sequence through the Gazettes to find it. Except for "block" awards, citations are usually given.

As far as the Civil Division is concerned, names appear in the "Alphabetical Index" and, from 1908, also in the indices to the Home Department (Public or Political) or Foreign (later Foreign and Political) Department Notifications. Here, however, page references are given, the actual announcements being accompanied by citations of varying length. The acts of gallantry for which appointments to the Civil Division of military and para-military personnel were made include the disarming of a lunatic soldier, actions against bandits, etc.; for civilian recipients the quelling of a jail riot and the arrest of a dangerous criminal may be instanced.

From 1917 the layout of the indices is simplified. The Index itself is provided with a list of contents which shows the pages of the Index upon which awards are given. For Civil[54] and Military[55] awards these are found under the sub-heading "Decorations . . ." The page of the Index thus found gives under the Order heading the names of recipients, the Gazette page and later, the authority (for military awards). Citations are usually given. Some duplicated announcements, being repeats of *London Gazette* entries have been found. The Index heading "Miscellaneous Orders and Notifications" gives the pages upon which, *inter alia*, awards are to be found. This system

50. See, for instance, Major-General Wilcock's despatch regarding the operations of the Bazar Field Force between 13th February and 2nd March 1908 (*London Gazette*, 22nd May 1908 at p.3,747 et seq.) where recommendations and citations are given without being indexed.

51. Some corrections to awards already made appear outside these dates.

52. Except for the first quarter of 1941 where only one name is given.

53. In general, military awards appear in Part 1 and the system of indexing in that Part is described here. However, some awards appear in the *Gazette of India Extraordinary* which has its own pagination and a much simpler index.

54. Under the main heading "Civil".

55. Under the main heading "Military" (later "Defence").

Fig.E: The Indian Order of Merit
(Military Division), brooch bar,
1945–1947.

Fig.F: The Indian Order of Merit
(Military Division), obverse,
1945–1947.

56. Under the sub-heading "Indian Army".

57. The last list of recipients was published in the Indian Army List of January 1943.

58. The second book also gives details of foreign decorations, and citations for the Victoria Cross and Military Cross awarded to Indian soldiers. Hypher does not give details of awards of the Civil Division to soldiers.

59. Thus Chaldecott, Hudson and Shakespear give some citations, while Gibbs, Merewether and Smith, and Willcocks give brief details (see Bibliography).

60. G.G.O. No. 60 of 1858 is a nominal roll of certain Native Regiments forming part of the Lucknow Garrison, every native soldier of which received the Order of Merit. Hypher, however, only lists those men who were awarded the Order (presumably for individual acts of gallantry during the siege) before the decision was made to award it to every native soldier of the Garrison.

61. We have included Havildar Chookalingum, Madras Sappers and Miners (see above), whom Hypher omits.

62. We have excluded from this figure the 29 men whose names are of British origin. Presumably these were men of mixed parentage (mostly bandsmen) who were not at the time eligible for the Order (see above).

was, in turn, altered. Under the main heading "Civil" in the list of contents, the sub-heading "Decorations ..." gives the pages of the Index upon which the Order heading is to be found[56]. This heading merely lists the pages of the Gazette where awards are published in the form of announcements from the Office of the Private Secretary to the Viceroy. Citations continue to be given. In some cases we have been unable to trace the awards given in the Quarterly Indian Army List to a corresponding entry in the Gazette.

1939–1947 We have been unable to find any Gazette indices for this period. However, awards continued to be published in the form of Notifications from the Office of the Private Secretary to the Viceroy. Most awards carry citations and where these appear they are extremely detailed and make fine reading. In addition to the Service details of the recipient, the later Gazette entries give his religion and home. In the absence of indices, it is possible to trace awards either by the authority given in the Indian Army Lists[57], or by finding the corresponding *London Gazette* entry which usually appears about the same time as that in the *Gazette of India*; however, all awards appearing in the *Gazette of India* from 1941 may not be repeated in the *London Gazette*, and there may be other awards which appear in neither. Awards of the Civil Division continue to appear as Notifications as described above.

Other Sources (Military Division) The two books by Hypher (see Bibliography) give the authority and, where one exists, the citations for awards made between 1837 and 1925[58]. As is frequently found with such compilations, there are a number of misprints and ambiguities, and there may be omissions. Nevertheless, Hypher's work is an invaluable source of information and, subject to the reservations mentioned, has been used as the basis for calculating the numbers awarded (see below). Both books were published in India in 1925 and 1927, and are now very rare. *The Government of India List of Honors* (see Bibliography) gives, *inter alia*, all awards made between August 1914 and August 1921. Details are confined to the personal particulars and corps of the recipient, together with the theatre or force in which the award was gained. The Class of award and authority are not given. Regimental and other histories sometimes provide citations, or some details[59]. Some Second World War awards are repeated, without citations, in Indian Army Orders.

Other Sources (Civil Division) Surviving recipients occasionally appear in the Indian Provincial Civil Lists. Thus for 1935/36 the Bombay List shows one recipient, while that for the United Provinces for the same period shows three.

NUMBERS AWARDED (MILITARY DIVISION)

1837–1914 (excluding the First World War) The table given below has been calculated mainly from Hypher. However, on detailed examination we found that Hypher had misread the G.G.O. relating to the Lucknow Garrison and thereby omitted a number of awards[60]. Although we have supplied the deficiency, it is by no means certain that Hypher did not miss other awards, and therefore what follows can only be taken as a guide:

	1st Class	2nd Class	3rd Class
1837–1910 (excluding the Indian Mutiny)	7	41	1,396[61]
Indian Mutiny (given by Hypher) ...	35	89	1,097
Indian Mutiny (omitted by Hypher) ...	—	—	247[62]
Totals	42	130	2,740

| 1911–1914 (excluding the First World War and after reduction to two Classes) ... ... | — | 6 | |

Several factors need to be taken into account in relation to these figures. Thus the number of Indian Mutiny awards is relatively high in proportion to the remainder for the period under review and, in part, can be accounted for by G.G.O. No. 1544 of 8th December 1857 which authorised the appointment to the Order of every

63. They were also allowed to count three years' additional service (c.f. the additional two years' service allowed to count for the Waterloo campaign). Recipients are listed in G.G.O.s, Nos. 60, 97, 167 and 599 of 1858, and Nos. 566, 567, 997 and 1,525 of 1859. There may be others. The original defenders also received six months' "batta" (roughly, field allowance).

64. *E.g.*, Sepoy Deoram Doobee, 73rd Native Infantry, was specially admitted to the 1st Class in G.G.O. No. 599 of 1858.

65. *E.g.*, Naib Ressaldar Shadil Khan, 3rd Sikh Cavalry, was advanced from the 3rd to the 1st Class in G.G.O. No. 1,057 of 1859.

66. *E.g.*, Subadar, Sirdar Bahadur, Hedayut Ali, Bengal Police Battalion, was appointed, apparently direct, to the 1st Class for "repeated acts of gallantry on several occasions" in G.G.O. No. 1,708 of 1858.

67. *E.g.*, Subadar-Major Mir Akbar Khan, Khyber Rifles, was appointed to the 3rd Class for six separate acts of gallantry in G.G.O. No. 123 of 1889.

68. *E.g.*, Subadar Rampersaud of the 2nd Company, 8th Battalion, Bengal Artillery, was promoted to the 2nd Class by Division Orders of 15th October 1858, the appointment being confirmed in G.G.O. No. 60 of 1858. His initial appointment may have appeared only as a Division Order.

69. *E.g.*, G.G.O. No. 134 of 1898 lists 21 men of the 36th (Sikh) Regiment of Bengal Infantry who would have received the 3rd Class had they survived and whose widows received the pension.

70. Royal Warrant of 20th December 1944 quoted above.

71. He was appointed to the 3rd Class in G.G.O. No. 89 of 1879, being promoted to the 2nd Class in G.G.O. No. 1,260 of 1879, and to the 1st Class in G.G.O. No. 251 of 1880.

72. G.G.O. No. 637 of 1889.

73. Thus in G.O. No. 1,716 of 1922 the 2nd Class was awarded to Subadar Najib Ullah Khan, 46th Punjabis, for services with the Egyptian Expeditionary Force.

74. We have compiled these figures from the details given in Hypher to 1925 and thereafter we have counted the entries in the *Gazette of India*.

Native Officer, N.C.O. and soldier of the Lucknow Garrison[63]. Moreover, we have shown all appointments to the 2nd and 3rd Classes irrespective of whether they were overtaken by subsequent promotions. This is because some of the earlier appointments seem to have been made direct to the 1st or 2nd Class[64], or from the 3rd to the 1st Class[65]. In some such cases there was possibly a notional and unpublished appointment to the lower Classes[66] although instances do occur of appointments to the 3rd Class for several acts of gallantry[67]. Alternatively an initial appointment may not appear as a G.G.O.[68] In a number of cases recipients did not survive the act for which the decoration was awarded and, although it seems that the Order itself was not actually issued to the next-of-kin, the widow was admitted to the appropriate pension[69]. Such awards have been included in the totals.

Although provision for a bar to the Order was not made until 1944[70], a special case occurred in 1888. Subadar Kishanbir Nagarkoti, of the 5th Gurkha Rifles, had been successively promoted to the 1st Class for acts of gallantry during the Second Afghan War[71]. For an act of gallantry on the North West Frontier he was awarded a special gold bar to his 1st Class Order inscribed "18th June 1888"[72].

First World War For this period we calculate from the details given by Hypher that 21 First Class and 1,023 Second Class appointments were made. However, the official statistics (see Bibliography) give 21 First Class and 984 Second Class appointments. A few late awards were made after May 1920 when the official statistics end[73], but these do not account for the entire discrepancy. A number of duplicated names have been found in Hypher and, although these have been discounted in our calculation, there may be others which, due to variations in transliterating Indian names, would be difficult to detect. At all events, the discrepancy between the totals for the Second Class is sufficiently small as to be of little significance. All promotions to the First Class seem to have been from the Second Class. Posthumous awards with, as applicable, pensions awarded to widows have been included in our figures.

August 1914 to August 1921 For this period *The Government of India List of Honors* gives the names of 1,126 recipients which, from internal evidence, are those published between G.O. No.1,141 of 1914 and G.O. No.353 of 1922 inclusive. In most cases the *List* merely shows promotions to the 1st Class by repeating the name. An analysis of the awards is as follows:

Aden Field Force	…	…	…	…	18	
Africa, East	…	…	…	…	65	
Black Sea	…	…	…	…	7	
Dardanelles/Gallipoli	…,	…,	…		39	
Egyptian Expeditionary Force			…		148	
France	…	…	…	…	…	243	
Kachin Hills	…	…	…	…	1	
Mesopotamia		…	…	…	…	434	(including 12 for Kut-el-Amara)
Muscat	…	…	…	…	…	2	
North West Frontier		…	…	…	47	(including 6 for Baluchistan Force)
Persia	…	…	…	…	…	21	
Salonika	…	…	…	…	…	6	
Transcaspia	…	…	…	…	4	
Waziristan	…	…	…	…	…	88	
Not given	…	…	…	…	3	

It will be appreciated that these figures include campaigns ended by the Armistice e.g. in France; those where there were operations, not necessarily against the same enemy, both before and after the Armistice e.g. in Mesopotamia; and those where operations were begun after the Armistice e.g. on the Black Sea coast.

1919–1940 During this period, excluding both World Wars, five First Class and 225 Second Class awards were made[74].

Fig. G: The Indian Order of Merit (Civil Division), obverse, Edward VII issue.

Fig. H: Indian Order of Merit (Civil Division), 1939–1947.

75. Royal Warrant of 20th December 1944 (see above).

Second World War The awards in the *London Gazette* total:

First Class	2
Second Class	332
Single Class	30
Total	364

However, there may be other awards which appear in the *Gazette of India* but which are not repeated in the *London Gazette*. The Order was reduced to a single Class in 1944[75] yet all the 1945 and some 1946 appointments in the *London Gazette* are given as Second Class. However, appointments to the single Class first appear in the *Gazette of India* on 14th October 1944. On the assumption that the *Gazette of India* represents the true position and that issues of the single Class were made in respect of appointments gazetted from 15th February 1944, the figure for the Second Class should be reduced by 160 and this added to the single Class.

The final pattern star was not authorised until nearly a year after the reduction to a single Class, and issues of the final pattern could be as few as 35 although the position is far from clear.

NUMBERS AWARDED (CIVIL DIVISION)

During the existence of the three Classes, 39 initial appointments were made, the first being in 1902 and the last in 1933. There were no promotions. One award was forfeited (see No. 22 below). From 1939, on the reduction of the Civil Division to a single Class, ten further appointments were made, the first being in 1942 and the last in 1947. The following roll gives the description of the recipient as gazetted, the date of the act, a brief description of the circumstances, and the date of the *Gazette of India* announcing the award:

1. Sheikh Adam Sheikh Ibrahim, Serang of Karachi Port Trust Vessel *Jumbo*; 16.6.02; saved over 300 persons from two villages imperilled by a cyclone and in danger of being swept away by the sea; 18.10.02.

2. Havildar Kishen Singh, Derajat Mountain Battery; 6.5.02; disarmed a gunner who had fired a carbine at a comrade and who was in the act of reloading; 15.11.02.

3. Lance-Naick Jagat Singh, 4th Punjab Infantry; 31.10.02; apprehended a thief although wounded by the man and his accomplices; 28.2.03.

4. Dafadar Kamrudin Hidayatali, Kathiawar Agency Police; 6.03; bravery in an encounter with a desperate gang of Miana dakoits holding a strong natural position with arms of precision; 2.1.04.

5. Constable Fatteh Khan, Peshawar Police; 9.6.04; arrested a fanatic armed with a knife and pistol who had stabbed a police constable and was attacking unarmed soldiers; 3.9.04.

6. Constable Fakir Mohamed, Burma Police; 23.4.04; arrested an armed and desperate European named Dennis Hayes; 10.12.04.

7. Sepoy Haidar Khan, 93rd Burma Infantry; 30.6.04; arrested a drunken man who, armed with a "dah", had already wounded a police officer attempting to disarm him; 28.1.05.

8. Private Shaikh Rahiman IV, 117th Mahrattas; 26.12.04; captured an escaped murderer who, armed with a loaded rifle, had already wounded him; 3.6.05.

9 & 10. Police Sergeants Ahmad Khan and Pyara Ram, North West Frontier Province Police; 27.2.05; captured an armed and desperate murderer; 29.7.05.

11. Recruit Naiz Ali, 13th Duke of Connaught's Lancers, 20.10.05; apprehended a Sowar of the 22nd Cavalry who had run amok with a sword and killed a Jemadar's son; 10.3.06.

12. Driver Naick Changhatta, 21st Kohat Mountain Battery; 23.11.05; overpowered, while unarmed, another driver drugged with "bhang" who

had run amok with a sword with which he had grievously wounded a comrade; 10.3.06.

13. Constable Maung Po Cho, Pegu District Police Force; 19.4.06; arrested a dangerous criminal; 15.9.06.

14. Lance-Daffadar Malak, Zhob Levy Corps; 29.9.06; conspicuous bravery on the occasion of an attack made by raiders on a party of cavalry escorting mail; 22.6.07.

15. Constable San U Kaing, Akyab District Police Force; 4.5.07; secured the arrest of an armed and dangerous criminal; 11.1.08.

16. Havildar Ghani Shah, North Waziristan Militia; 26.8.07; arrested a sepoy who had run amok and had already killed one sepoy, wounded another, and was about to shoot a third; 21.3.08.

17. Constable Mansab Ali, Civil Police, Pilibhit District; 27.1.08; arrested an armed and dangerous criminal who had wounded him twice with a revolver; 11.7.08.

18. Sowar Muhammad Shah, Kohat Border Military Police; 25.11.07; single handed, forced his way through some 20 or 25 raiders who were robbing two women and an old man, and raised a large party in pursuit; at great risk to himself he warned local posts and as a result two raiders were killed and three wounded; further raiding in the area ceased; 15.8.08.

19. The Honourable Maharaja Dhiraj Bijay Chand Mahtab Bahadur of Burdwan; 7.11.08; interposed himself between Sir Andrew Frazer, the Lieutenant Governor of Bengal, and a would-be assassin; 2.1.09.

20 & 21. Jemadar Nur Shah, Kohat Border Military Police, and Sub-Inspector Mehr Dass, Teri Police Station; 28.2.09; conspicuous bravery and resource during an encounter with 11 Khattak outlaws who had committed many dacoities, murders and abductions; 26.6.09.

22. Subedar Kawan Khan, South Waziristan Militia; 7.6.09; arrested a sepoy who had run amok with a loaded rifle and who had already shot and killed a man; 28.8.09; dismissed from the Order, 17.2.23[76].

23. Khan Muhammad Zafar Khan, Extra Assistant Commissioner, Punjab; 12.3.96; saved the life of Mr. H. A. Casson, Indian Civil Service, Political Officer, Bannu, from a murderous attack by a Pathan fanatic armed with a knife-pistol[77]; on three occasions in 1910 prevented injury to others from attacks and incidents; 27.5.11.

24. Jemadar Sultan Mahmud Khan, 34th Poona Horse; 18.8.11; captured one and shot dead another of a gang of outlaws who had murdered three people; 23.3.12.

25. Chirag Din, fitter at the Ferozepore Arsenal; 30.8.06; assisted in extinguishing a fire close to a gunpowder store which, had it exploded, would have detonated the main magazine[78]; 25.5.12.

26 & 27. Havildar Abdul Hakim and Naick Gulzar Khan, Mekran Levy Corps; 11.3.13; defended the camp of Mr. J. W. Dunn, Temporary Engineer, Karachi Extension Railway Survey, against a band of Baharloo raiders; 16.8.13.

28 – 30. Jemadar Mauladad, Naick Jahangir and Sepoy Karim Khan, Frontier Constabulary; 12.4.14; pursued and killed a native who had shot and killed three British officers and three Indian soldiers; 19.9.14.

31 & 32. Risaldar Moghal Baz Khan, Extra Assistant Commissioner, Tank, and Muhammad Nawaz Khan, Naib Tahsildar, Jandola; 26.6.13; rounded up and killed a notorious outlaw; 12.12.14.

33. Havildar Mitung Tang, Burma Military Police attached 1/10th Gurkha Rifles; 10.7.16; disarmed a rifleman who had run amok with a kukri; 30.12.16.

34. Inspector of Police Khan Sahib Hazrat Shah; 10.16; arrested an armed murderer who had shot dead a constable; 2.6.17.

35. Risaldar Khan Sahib Ghulam Nabi; 25.6.16; gallantry during an encounter with outlaws; 2.6.17.

76. The Gazette notice announcing the dismissal says "Kawan Khan has been found guilty of actively aiding and abetting a raid on the Kohat Cantonment and although he has been given every opportunity of appearing and standing his trial he has failed to appear. He is reported to have fled to Afghan territory".

77. This act took place some 15 years before the award and the notice makes reference to the circumstances being only recently brought to the notice of the Governor-General.

78. Two Albert Medals in gold and 11 in bronze were awarded for the Ferozepore explosion, in the *London Gazette* of 26th September 1911.

36. Driver Pooran, Bharatpur Imperial Service Transport Corps; 5.11.19; although wounded, apprehended one of a gang of Pathans stealing sheep; 14.8.20.

37. Jemadar Sharifullah Khan, Bhambo Battalion Burma Military Police; 23.3.22; led an attack against raiders from China in the Northern Shan States; 15.7.22.

38. Mr. L. J. V. Towers, Deputy Jailor, Central Jail, Cannanore; 12.21; quelled a riot among Mapilla prisoners; 18.11.22.

39. Sub-Assistant Surgeon Haralu of Assam; date of act not given; bravery in the capture of Gaidiliu, Naga leader and priestess of a rebellious movement in the North Kachin Hills, Assam; 1.4.33.

40. Lala Bansi Lal, stenographer, Dunlop Rubber Company, Lahore; date and details of act not given[79]; 21.2.42.

41. Wadero Ali Mohammed Khan Palejo, Zamindar, Taluka Sujawal, Karachi District; 29.6.42; arrested an escaped murderer; 15.5.43.

42. Maha Singh, Watchman, Watch and Ward Department, Bombay, Baroda and Central India Railway; 19.5.42; arrested a murderer who had wounded him and killed his companion; 12.6.43.

43. Wadero Ghulam Rasul Bhai Phul, Zamindar, Village Phul, Taluka Larkana, Sind; 24.6.41; intercepted and apprehended a party of dacoits; 4.9.43.

44. Sitaram Shivram, Train Examiner, Great Indian Peninsula Railway; 2.8.43; extinguished a fire in a petrol wagon; 12.2.44.

45. Pandit Kedar Nath, son of Pandit Basebo, Hathras, District Aligarh, United Provinces; date and details of act not given; 5.5.45.

46. Darshan Singh Muccadam, Fire Brigade, Ordnance Factory, Khamaria, Jubbulpore, Central Provinces and Berar; 23.3.45; assisted in extinguishing a fire in an ammunition sub-depot; 26.1.46.

47. Appa Arjun, Packer, Karachi General Post Office; 10.5.46; although wounded, attempted to recover a bag of money snatched by bandits; 7.9.46.

48. Sardar Kundan Singh; 26.5.46; organised a party for and effected the arrest of two of a band of five armed murderers; 14.12.46.

49. Sahibzada Abdul Quadir; 28.10.46; disarmed a would-be assassin who had stabbed a visiting notable; 15.3.47.

ILLUSTRATIVE AWARDS

Military Division Rifleman Mungal Joysee, 2nd Goorkha Regiment, was appointed to the 3rd Class of the Order for an act of gallantry during the Second Afghan War. His citation is given in G.O. No. 639 of 19th November 1880[80] as follows:

"... in attacking, with two other men of the regiment, a number of ghazis, who had posted themselves in a court-yard in the village of Sahibdad, killing some and driving the others out, himself receiving a severe wound in the conflict."

The two other men mentioned in the citation, Riflemen Wazeer Singh Nagarkoti and Mukkereah Rana of the same Regiment, were also appointed to the 3rd Class. Although the attack on Sahibdad is mentioned by Shakespear in Volume 1 at p.82, no individual details are given. Mungal Joysee last appears as an effective in the Bengal Army List for October 1885 and, from subsequent Lists, does not seem to have transferred to the pension establishment. He also received the India General Service Medal, 1854, with bars for the North West Frontier and Looshai, the medal for the Second Afghan War with bars for Kabul and Kandahar, and the Kabul to Kandahar Star.

Civil Division The Honourable the Maharaja Dhiraj Bijay Chand Mahtab Bahadur of Burdwan was appointed to the 3rd Class of the Order for an act of gallantry in 1908. His citation appears in the *Gazette of India*[81] as follows:

79. This was for capturing an armed murderer in October 1941, see the *Lahore Tribune* of 22nd October 1941.

80. See *Gazette of India* for 20th November 1880.

81. See *Gazette of India* for 2nd January 1909.

"... for conspicuous courage displayed by him at the Overtoun Hall on the 7th November 1908, in connexion with the attempt upon the life of Sir Andrew Frazer, the Lieutenant-Governor of Bengal. On Sir Andrew Frazer's entering the Hall a young Bengali stepped towards him and presenting a revolver at him, pulled the trigger, but the weapon fortunately missed fire. The Maharaja Dhiraj of Burdwan at once flung himself between Sir Andrew Frazer and the would-be murderer. The latter was seized by Mr. B. R. Barber, the General Secretary of the Young Men's Christian Association in Calcutta, but succeeded in again directing the revolver towards the Lieutenant-Governor and a second time fired the weapon without result. If it had not missed fire, the bullet would in all probability have struck the Maharaja who had courageously interposed himself between Sir Andrew Frazer and his assailant and was effectually shielding him from danger."

The Maharaja had an important political career in India. He was created a K.C.I.E. in 1909, a K.C.S.I. in 1911, and a G.C.S.I. in 1924[82]. A small photograph of him, wearing his orders and medals, appears in *The Historical Record of the Imperial Visit to India 1911* (1914).

82. For further details see *Who was Who.*

172

Fig.A: The Indian Police Medal, obverse, George V issue.

Chapter 25

The Indian Police Medal

ORIGIN AND DEVELOPMENT

The Indian Police Medal was instituted in 1932 and went some way to fulfilling the need to reward members of the Indian Police Forces and Fire Brigades which had not been achieved by the King's Police Medal (q.v.) since the latter had been limited to 50 awards a year for services in India. The Royal Warrant instituting the Indian Police Medal was dated 23rd February 1932[1], and read as follows:

> **"GEORGE R.I.**
> George the Fifth, by the Grace of God, of Great Britain, Ireland and the British Dominions beyond the Seas, King, Defender of the Faith, Emperor of India.
>
> To all to whom these presents shall come:
>
> GREETING:
>
> WHEREAS We have taken into Our Royal consideration the good services rendered by Members of the Police Forces and of Fire Brigades within Our Indian Empire:
>
> AND WHEREAS We are desirous of making further provision for distinguishing meritorious services rendered by them:
>
> We do by these presents for Us, Our Heirs and Successors, institute and create a new Medal to be awarded by Our Viceroy and Governor-General of India for the time being on Our behalf for distinguished conduct.
>
> *First:* It is ordained that the Medal shall be designated and styled "The Indian Police Medal."
>
> *Secondly:* It is ordained that the Indian Police Medal shall consist of a circular Medal of bronze with Our Effigy on the obverse, and on the reverse a wreath surmounted by a Crown and shall bear on the rim the name of the person to whom the Medal is awarded.
>
> *Thirdly:* It is ordained that the Medal shall be awarded only to those members of a recognised Police Force or of a properly organised Fire Brigade within Our Indian Empire who have performed services of conspicuous merit.
>
> *Fourthly:* It is ordained that the names of those to whom this Medal may be awarded shall be published in the *Gazette of India*, and that a Register of such names shall be kept in the Office of the Home Department of the Government of India.
>
> *Fifthly:* It is ordained that each Medal shall be suspended from the left breast, and the riband, of an inch and three-eighths in width, shall be dark blue with a narrow silver stripe on either side and a crimson stripe in the centre.
>
> *Sixthly:* It is ordained that any distinguished conduct which is worthy of recognition by the award of the Indian Police Medal, but is performed by one upon whom the Decoration has already been conferred, may be recorded by a Bar attached to the riband by which the Medal is suspended; and for every such additional award an additional bar may be added.
>
> *Seventhly:* It is ordained that the number of medals awarded in any one year (excluding Bars) shall not exceed 200.
>
> *Eighthly:* It is ordained that it shall be competent for Our Viceroy and Governor-General of India for the time being to cancel and annul the award to any person of the above Decoration, and that thereupon the name of such person in the Register shall be erased, but that it shall be competent for Our said Viceroy and Governor-General to restore any Decoration which may have been so forfeited. And every person to whom the said Decoration is awarded shall, before receiving the same, enter into an agreement to return the medal if his name shall be erased as aforesaid.

1. Published in the *Gazette of India* of 28th May 1932.

Ninthly: It is ordained that it shall be competent for our Viceroy and Governor-General of India for the time being to make regulations to carry out the purposes of this Warrant.

Given at Our Court at St. James's the twenty-third day of February, One thousand nine hundred and thirty-two, in the twenty-second year of Our Reign.

By His Majesty's Command,
SAMUEL HOARE."

The instituting Royal Warrant was amended three times. Firstly, by a Royal Warrant dated 24th June 1938[2] which substituted the words "Our Viceroy" for "Our Viceroy and Governor-General of India" in the preamble, and in the 8th and 9th Clauses; replaced in the 4th Clause the words "in the office of the Home Department of the Government of India" by "such person as Our Viceroy may direct"; and in the 6th Clause provided that a small rose should be added to the ribbon when worn alone by those who had been awarded a bar to the medal. Secondly, an amending Warrant of 25th November 1942[3] ordained that the number of medals (excluding bars) awarded in any one year should not ordinarily exceed 200, but if the Viceroy considered that special circumstances justified the award of medals in excess of that number, the number should then not exceed 250. Finally, the third amending Warrant was dated 20th December 1944[4], the 2nd and 5th Clauses being replaced as follows:

"Secondly. – It is ordained that the Indian Police Medal shall consist of a circular medal of bronze with Our effigy on the obverse, and shall bear on the reverse a wreath surmounted by a crown, and the words "For Gallantry" or "For Meritorious Service" as the case may be, and on the rim the name of the person to whom the medal is awarded.

Fifthly. – It is ordained that each medal shall be suspended from the left breast, and the riband, of an inch and three-eighths in width, shall be dark blue with a narrow silver stripe on either side and a crimson stripe in the centre; and in the case of awards for acts of conspicuous gallantry, each of the blue portions of the riband shall contain a thin silver line down the middle."

The Regulations referred to in the 9th Clause of the original Warrant were published in the *Gazette of India* at the same time as the Warrant and were as follows:

"Regulations relating to the award of the Indian Police Medal.

(*a*) The Medal will be open to all ranks of the Police, civil and military, and to the members of properly organised Fire Brigades, both in British India and in the Indian States.

(*b*) It will be awarded by the Viceroy and Governor-General on the recommendation of the Local Government, or of the administration of the State.

(*c*) Each recommendation will state the name and rank of the person recommended, the Police Force or Fire Brigade of which he is or was a member, and particulars of the action or service for which the grant of the Medal is recommended.

(*d*) The Medal will be awarded –

  (i) for conspicuous gallantry. Awards for gallantry will be made as soon as possible after the event occasioning the grant;

  (ii) for valuable services characterised by resource and devotion to duty, including prolonged service of ability and merit. Such awards will be made once annually on the 1st of January from the list of recommendations which should reach the Government of India in the Home Department not later than the 1st of October in each year.

(*e*) When awarded for gallantry the Medal will carry a monetary allowance at half the rates sanctioned for the award of the King's Police Medal for gallantry.

(*f*) The number of Medals to be awarded each year will not exceed 200. The recommendations received from any one source will be considered with due regard to the number of recommendations which have been or are likely to be received from other sources.

2. Published in the *Gazette of India* of 16th July 1938.

3. Published in the *Gazette of India* of 9th January 1943 (see also the *London Gazette* of 1st December 1942).

4. Published in the *Gazette of India* of 20th January 1945 (see also the *London Gazette* of 29th December 1944).

Fig.B: The Indian Police Medal, obverse, George VI issue.

Fig.C: The Indian Police Medal, reverse, 1932–1944.

5. Published in the *Gazette of India* of 14th December 1940.

6. Published in the *Gazette of India* of 3rd June 1944.

7. It is shown in this position in the order of wearing published in the *London Gazette* of 22nd April 1941 (see also Appendix 4).

8. See the Indian Independence Act of 1947.

9. See the *Gazette of India* of 12th June 1948. It was not continued in Pakistan.

10. As, indeed, it always had been for this medal.

11. See the *Gazette of India* of 10th March 1951.

12. Royal Warrant of 20th December 1944 (see above).

(*g*) The Medal shall be worn next to and immediately after the British Empire Medal (for gallantry).

(*h*) The award of the Medal will not be a bar to the subsequent award of the King's Police Medal.

H. W. EMERSON,

Secy. to the Govt. of India."

These Regulations were reprinted in the *Gazette of India* of 16th July 1938 following the amending Royal Warrant then promulgated. Basically they were the same as the original Regulations but with minor changes in (*b*) and (*d*)(ii) due to the amendment caused through altering "Viceroy and Governor-General" to "Viceroy". The Regulations were further amended on 12th December 1940[5] where in Regulation (*d*)(ii) provision was made for bi-annual awards (i.e. in the New Year's Day Honours List and in the Birthday Honours List); and in Regulations (*e*) and (*h*) the title King's Police and Fire Services Medal replaced the original title. The Regulations were amended in 1944[6]: in Regulation (*f*) the first sentence was deleted, and in (*g*) it was to read as follows:

> "The Medal for gallantry shall be worn next to and immediately after the Indian Order of Merit (Civil)[7] and the Medal for Meritorious Service next to and immediately after the King's Police and Fire Services Medal for Distinguished Service".

It will be noted that this Regulation anticipated the Royal Warrant of 20th December 1944 (see above) when the medal itself was changed, having either "For Gallantry" or "For Meritorious Service" on the reverse. Prior to this the medal had "For Distinguished Conduct" on the reverse irrespective of whether it was awarded for gallantry or for meritorious service.

Following the creation of the Dominion of India on 15th August 1947[8], the medal continued to be awarded. Effect to this decision was given in a Royal Warrant of 1st May 1948[9] which also amended and consolidated the previous Warrants. The principal alterations were that "Our Dominion of India" replaced "Our Indian Empire" in the preamble and the 3rd Clause; the sovereign's effigy in the 2nd Clause was described as "crowned"[10]; "Our Governor-General" replaced "Our Viceroy" in the preamble and the 4th, 8th and 9th Clauses; and the numbers in the 7th Clause were reduced to 175 and 200 respectively. At the same time the Regulations were consolidated and amended, "Our Indian Empire" and "Our Viceroy" being replaced as indicated above, while Regulation (*b*) was altered to read:

> "It will be awarded by the Governor-General on the recommendation of a Provincial Government or the Government of an Indian State or of a Union of States or Administration approved by the Prime Minister of India."

On 26th January 1950 the Dominion of India became a Republic and the medal was accordingly replaced by the Republic's "Police Medal"[11].

DESCRIPTION

Ribbon Until 20th December 1944[12] this was 1⅜ inches wide and dark blue, with a narrow silver stripe at either side, and a crimson stripe down the centre. Thereafter, awards of the medal for gallantry had a thin silver stripe down the middle of the two blue stripes, the original ribbon being continued for awards of the medal for meritorious service.

Suspension By a straight non-swivelling bronze suspender.

Obverse There were two types:

1. George V (Fig.A).
2. George VI (Fig.B) We have been unable to discover if the second type obverse was issued between 1948 and 1950.

Reverse There were three types, with inscriptions as follows:

Fig.D: The Indian Police Medal, reverse, 1945–1950.

Fig.E: Bar to the Indian Police Medal.

1. "For Distinguished Conduct" (Fig.C), used on awards for both gallantry and meritorious service until about 1945.
2. "For Gallantry" (Fig.D), used from about 1945[12].
3. "For Meritorious Service", used from about 1945[12].

Bar (Fig.E) Bronze, with laurel design, and fixed to the ribbon by two large prongs inserted through the ribbon and then bent sideways. This was similar in design to that used from 1934 with the King's Police Medal (q.v.)[13].

Naming Awards have been seen engraved in small italic script, including the initials, surname (or Indian names), rank and Force.

Copies and Fakes None has been seen. Some official specimens are in existence.

VERIFICATIONS AND CITATIONS

All gallantry awards[14] appear in the *Gazette of India* and most of the notices are accompanied by citations; they also appear in the Indian local Gazettes (e.g. *The Calcutta Gazette*). We have found indices for the *Gazette of India* only up to and including 1938. The indices are provided with a list of contents which, in the Civil Section of Part 1, under the heading "Decorations, Honours and Medals – Civil" give page references to the Index[15]. The page of the Index thus found in turn gives the Gazette pages upon which awards appear[16]. Names are not given in the Index and these can be found only from the actual announcements. For the period 1939–1950, despite the absence of indices, awards can be found readily among the announcements from the Office of the Private Secretary to the Viceroy and later, the Governor-General, which appear on the first pages of individual Gazettes.

NUMBERS AWARDED

We have obtained the following numbers of gallantry awards by counting the actual Gazette entries. Only in 1932 (128) and 1942 (109) does the total number of gallantry awards exceed 100. There were no awards to women. It is emphasized that the figures below are not the total number of medals awarded, but only those awarded for gallantry; others were awarded for meritorious service which are not included in our figures. Although the same medal was awarded to members of fire brigades, we have separated these awards from those to the police. In addition, we show awards to Europeans in parentheses since these are also included in the adjoining figures:

	Medals				First bars			
	Police		Fire		Police		Fire	
1932–1936	381	(20)	5	(3)	1		—	
1937–1944	473	(30)	5	(3)	14	(3)	—	
1945–1947	138	(8)	5	(3)	3	(1)	1	(1)
1948–1950	81		—		2		—	
	1,073	(58)	15	(9)	20	(4)	1	(1)
Totals	1,088	(67)			21	(5)		

Recipients of first bars[17] were as follows:

	Gazette of India
Inspector Sardar Harnam Singh	8th December 1934
Constable Mulki Ram	17th September 1938
Subedar Major Manavazhi Madhava Menon ...	20th May 1939
Assistant Sub-Inspector Sardar Bahadur ...	4th May 1940
Sergeant T. M. Farmer	11th May 1940
Sub-Inspector Sher Azam Khan	18th May 1940
Inspector H. C. Tyler	7th September 1940
Superintendent J. P. Morton	7th September 1940
Inspector Tanjore V. A. V. Ayyar	21st November 1942
Sub-Inspector Narayanaswami P. T. P. Nityanandam	21st November 1942

13. See the *Annual Report of the Deputy Master and Comptroller of the Royal Mint (1935/36)*, p.55.

14. Meritorious service awards do not seem to be given in the *Gazette of India*, except in 1944 and 1945; they are published in the *Gazette of India Extraordinary*. They appear, often with citations, in the Indian local Gazettes.

15. Except for the first half of 1938 when, for some reason, references are omitted.

16. Except in 1932 where the reference is under "Home Department – Police" in the "Miscellaneous Notifications and Orders" section.

17. The bars listed are for gallantry; some of these recipients were awarded their medals for meritorious service. In the case of Sergeant S. C. Wintle the opposite occurred. Wintle received his medal for gallantry in the *Gazette of India* of 19th November 1932; he received a bar for meritorious service in the *Gazette of India Extraordinary* of 1st January 1934. Inspector M. R. Ry Voleti Narayanamurti Pantulu was awarded the medal for meritorious service in the *Gazette of India Extraordinary* of 2nd January 1933, and a bar, also for meritorious service, in the *Gazette of India Extraordinary* of 1st January 1935. These are the only two meritorious service bars we have found.

Deputy Superintendent Chaudhri Jagram Singh	... ...	... 23rd January 1943

Deputy Superintendent Chaudhri Jagram
Singh   ... ... 23rd January 1943
Inspector Nattamai Muthu Konar Solamalai
Konar   ... ... 7th August 1943
Sub-Inspector Nur Badshah   ... ... 27th May 1944
Inspector Pandit Tara Chand Sharma   ... ... 30th September 1944
Sub-Inspector Munshi Muhammad Yaqub   ... 7th October 1944
Inspector Mohamed Saleh Mirzakhan
Dahraj   ... ... 29th June 1946
Superintendent H. T. Hewson   ... ... 29th June 1946
District Officer P. S. Bampton (Calcutta Fire
Brigade)   ... ... 29th June 1946
Inspector A. F. Kinchin   ... ... 14th September 1946
Deputy Superintendent Mallavarapu Louru
Thomas   ... ... 24th July 1948
Superintendent Shri S. A. Thomas   ... ... 29th October 1949

ILLUSTRATIVE AWARD

Head Constable Meher Shah was awarded the Indian Police Medal for gallantry in the *Gazette of India* of 9th March 1946 where his citation reads as follows:

> "On the 19th December 1945, Head Constable Meher Shah accompanied the officer-in-charge of Jagatdal Police Station, 24-Parganas, during the latter's investigation of a dacoity case. While the Sub-Inspector was engaged in the investigation, the complaint[18] of the case, who had become mentally deranged, suddenly and unexpectedly made a murderous attack on him with a "Dao"[19]. The assailant was about to deal another blow, which might well have proved fatal, but Head Constable Meher Shah with great presence of mind and at considerable risk to himself felled the assailant with a lathi[20], disarmed him and took him into custody. His courageous action was thus instrumental in saving the life of his superior officer."

18. Possibly a misprint for "complainant".
19. A native knife.
20. *I.e.*, staff.

Chapter 26

The King's (later Queen's) Medal for Bravery (South Africa)

Fig.A: The King's Medal for Bravery (South Africa), obverse, George VI issue.

ORIGIN AND DEVELOPMENT

This rare medal, known sometimes as "The Woltemade Medal" was instituted in 1939 as a reward for gallantry in life-saving performed, originally, within the Union of South Africa or territories under the control of the Union. The instituting Royal Warrant[1] reads as follows:

> "GEORGE THE SIXTH, BY THE GRACE OF GOD, OF GREAT BRITAIN, IRELAND AND THE BRITISH DOMINIONS BEYOND THE SEAS, KING, DEFENDER OF THE FAITH, EMPEROR OF INDIA, ACTING FOR OUR UNION OF SOUTH AFRICA.

> To All and Singular to whom these Presents shall come, Greeting!

> WHEREAS we have taken into Our Royal consideration the many heroic acts performed by those of Our faithful subjects and others within Our Union of South Africa, or in Territories belonging to or administered by the Union, who endanger their own lives in saving or endeavouring to save the lives of others;

> AND WHEREAS we are desirous of distinguishing such heroic acts by some mark of Our Royal Favour;

> We do by these Presents for Us, Our Heirs and Successors, institute a new Medal to be awarded for such acts of heroism, in accordance with the following rules—

> 1. The medal shall be styled "The King's Medal for Bravery".

> 2. The King's Medal for Bravery shall consist of a circular Medal of Silver, or of Gold when it is awarded for acts of such great and exceptional gallantry as to merit a special degree of recognition, and shall, on the obverse, bear the Effigy of the Reigning Sovereign and as circumscription His style followed by the words "Rex et Imperator", and, on the reverse, a design depicting the rescue, on horseback, by Wolraad Woltemade in the year 1773, of persons in danger of drowning as the result of a shipwreck in Table Bay, with the words "For Bravery" and "Vir Dapperheid" as circumscription, and, on the rim, the name of the person to whom the Medal is awarded.

> 3. The Medal shall only be awarded to those of Our faithful subjects and others, within Our Union of South Africa, or in Territories belonging to or administered by the Union, who have endangered their own lives in saving or endeavouring to save the lives of others in Our said Union or in Territories belonging to or administered by the same.

> 4. The Medal shall be awarded on a recommendation to Us by Our Ministers of State for Our Union of South Africa.

> 5. The names of those upon whom We may be pleased to confer this Decoration shall be published in the Government Gazette and also, in the case of persons resident in any Territory belonging to or administered by the Union, in the Official Gazette, if any, of such Territory, and a Register thereof shall be kept in the Office of Our Prime Minister for Our Union of South Africa. Such Register shall show the full name of the person holding the Medal, and particulars of the action for which the Medal has been awarded.

> 6. The Medal shall be worn suspended from the left breast, and the riband, of an inch and three-quarters in width, shall be royal blue with a narrow orange stripe on either side; provided that when the Medal is awarded to a woman it shall be

1. See the *Union of South Africa Government Gazette* of 25th August 1939.

178

worn on the left shoulder, suspended from a riband of the same width and colour fashioned in a bow.

7. Any act of bravery which is worthy of recognition by the award of the King's Medal for Bravery, but has been performed by anyone upon whom the Decoration has already been conferred, may, on a recommendation to Us by Our Ministers of State for Our Union of South Africa, be recorded by a Bar attached to the riband by which the Medal is suspended; and for every such additional act an additional Bar may be added.

8. It shall be competent for Us, by an Order under Our Sign Manual, on a recommendation to that effect by Our Ministers of State for Our Union of South Africa, to cancel the award to any person of the above Decoration, whereupon such person's name shall be erased from the Register. It shall be competent for Us to restore any Decoration which may have been so forfeited, whenever such recommendation shall have been withdrawn. Every person to whom the said Decoration is awarded shall, before receiving the same, enter into an agreement to return the Medal if his or her name be erased as aforesaid.

9. The Governor-General may make regulations for giving effect to the provisions of this Our Royal Warrant.

Given at Our Court at St. James on this twenty-third day of June, One thousand Nine Hundred and Thirty-nine, in the Third Year of Our Reign.

Countersigned and sealed according to law at Pretoria on the twentieth day of July, One thousand Nine Hundred and Thirty-nine.

J. B. M. Hertzog."

This Warrant was, in turn, amended by three others. The first, dated 18th February 1947[2], provided for a miniature medal to be worn on certain occasions; the medal was to be $\frac{3}{4}$ inch in diameter and the ribbon $\frac{5}{8}$ inch wide. The second, dated 24th October 1949[3], extended the award to acts outside the Union and the territories belonging to or administered by it, when performed by:

(1) citizens of the Union; or

(2) other persons saving or endeavouring to save the lives of Union citizens.

The final amending Warrant was dated 17th October 1950[4] and, following the discontinuance of the title "Emperor of India", provided that the words "et Imperator" should be omitted from the obverse of the medal (see below). A consolidating Royal Warrant of 15th December 1952[5] incorporated the previous amendments and provided for the alternative style "Queen's Medal for Bravery" and for the corresponding change in the obverse of the medal (see below).

The Regulations made under Clause 9 of the Warrant were as follows:

"1. The qualifications for the grant of the Medal shall be as follows—

Gallantry performed in the face of imminent and obvious peril by those who endanger their own lives in saving or endeavouring to save the lives of others.

2. In an estimation of the risks incurred, due regard shall be had to the duties and responsibilities of the individual concerned.

3. Upon an award being made the Medal shall be presented by the Governor-General or his Deputy for the time being, or by a person designated by him."

In 1952 the Louw Wepener decoration was instituted as a reward for gallantry in saving or endeavouring to save life by members of the Defence Forces of the Union and thus for all practical purposes the Queen's Medal became a purely civilian award. In any case, the last award was made in 1953 (see below). By a Warrant of the State President of the Republic of South Africa of 25th May 1970[6] "The Woltemade Decoration for Bravery" was instituted, the conditions of award being similar to those of the consolidating Royal Warrant of 15th December 1952 which the President's Warrant abrogated. As before, the decoration is to be in gold or silver depending upon the degree of bravery exhibited, and the ribbon remains unchanged[7]. The design of the obverse is that used for the reverse of the Queen's Medal, while the reverse bears the crest of the coat of arms of the Republic. Originally the decoration was to be $1\frac{1}{2}$ inches in diameter but by a War-

2. *Ibid*, 7th March 1947.

3. *Ibid*, 18th November 1949.

4. *Ibid*, 29th December 1950.

5. *Ibid*, 27th February 1953.

6. See the *Republic of South Africa Government Gazette* of 29th May 1970.

7. In the Royal Warrant "royal blue with a narrow orange stripe on either side", and in the President's Warrant "blue silk ribbon, one and three-quarter inches wide, with a narrow orange stripe on either side."

Fig.B: The Queen's Medal for Bravery (South Africa), obverse, Elizabeth II issue.

Fig.C: The King's (Queen's) Medal for Bravery (South Africa), reverse.

8. See the *Republic of South Africa Government Gazette* of 26th November 1971.

9. Information kindly provided by the Secretary to the Prime Minister of the Republic of South Africa.

10. Photographs of three designs for the reverse are in P.R.O. MINT 24/285. One is of Miss Joubert's design as finally adopted, while another is similar but shows two men in the water and a floating spar. The third depicts a man carrying an injured boy.

rant of 11th November 1971[8] this was reduced by one eighth of an inch. The name of the recipient and date of award are to be inscribed on the edge of the decoration, and on the reverse of any bar awarded which may be in gold or silver.

DESCRIPTION

Ribbon Dark blue, 1¾ inches wide, with narrow orange borders.

Suspension By an oval swivelling ring of the appropriate metal, approximately ¾ inch at its widest.

Obverse Two obverses have been used as follows:

> 1. George VI (Fig.A) This appeared on the first 35 awards, including the one issued in gold which was to F. C. Drake (see No. 14 below). The Royal Warrant of 17th October 1950 provided for the omission of the words "et Imperator" from the inscription but no awards with this obverse were made[9].

> 2. Elizabeth II (Fig.B) This appeared only on the last award made which was presented to L. R. Nilsen (see No. 36 below) on 13th December 1954[9].

Reverse (Fig.C) As the result of a public competition, a design by Miss R. H. Joubert was accepted[10]. This was based on the events of 17th June 1773 when the anchor cables of the *Jonge Thomas*, lying in the roadstead of Table Bay, parted in a gale, the ship being driven ashore near the mouth of the Salt River. Wolraad Woltemade, an old man and a servant of the Dutch East India Company, seeing the plight of the sailors in the stricken ship, rode his horse into the sea to help them. Seven times he made the perilous journey, bringing two survivors ashore each time. When he attempted the eighth, this gallant man and his horse, overladen with panic-stricken sailors, perished amid the waves.

Bar None has been awarded, nor was a design made.

Naming The recipient's name is engraved in upright capital letters on the edge of the medal. The medals were struck and named at the South African Mint.

Copies and Fakes A few unnamed specimens are on display in South African museums, e.g. the South African Mint Museum and the South African National War Museum. For recent copies see the Note on p.xx.

NUMBERS AWARDED; VERIFICATIONS AND CITATIONS

Only 35 silver and one gold medal (to F. C. Drake, No. 14 below) have been awarded. All awards were published, without citation, in the *Union of South Africa Government Gazette*. The Register of recipients is kept in the Office of the Prime Minister of South Africa. The following roll gives the description of the recipient as gazetted; the date of the Gazette; and a brief description of the circumstances of the award:

> 1. Mr. William Tweeddale Dalling; 29th December 1939; tried to save a native in a rockburst, Rose Deep Mine.

> 2. Mr. Dennis Nourse, BSc.; 9th August 1940; saved a man from a shark, Warner Beach, Natal.

> 3. Mr. Robert John Moubray; 31st January 1941; jumped down a fifty-foot waterfall near Tzaneen to save a friend,. who had fallen and struck his head, from drowning in the pool below.

> 4 & 5. Mr. Michael Adriaan van den Berg and Native Givana (son of Ziqwayini); 4th April 1941; saved an injured miner despite ignited dynamite fuses, Venterspost Gold Mine.

> 6. Hendrik Snell; 28th August 1942; this coloured man tried to save the pilot in a crashed and burning aircraft at Lansdowne Road, Cape Town.

> 7. Lieutenant Arnold Edward Rabe, S.A.A.F.; 30th July 1943; saved a pupil-pilot from a burning aircraft.

8. Temporary Flight Sergeant Martin Wilson Taylor Bellingham Brady, S.A.A.F.; 17th December 1943; saved a pilot from a burning aircraft, Youngsfield, Cape Town.

9. No. 328871 V, Pupil Pilot Daniel Nicholaas de Jong, S.A.A.F.; 4th February 1944; saved his instructor from a burning aircraft, Standerton.

10. No. 206268 V, Temporary Second Lieutenant Geoffrey Turner Fowles, S.A.A.F.; 4th February 1944; saved a pilot from a burning aircraft, Pietersburg.

11. No. 101470, Air Mechanic Rudolph Daniel Botes, S.A.A.F.; 4th February 1944; attempted to save the crew of a burning aircraft, Wingfield, Cape Town.

12. Native Mpotu; 6th April 1944; saved a miner in the face of exploding dynamite, Venterspost.

13. No. 189506 V, Air Corporal Joseph Pick Faul, S.A.A.F.; 21st April 1944; tried to save a man overcome by fumes in the fuel tank of a Catalina aircraft.

14. Master Francis C. Drake; 8th September 1944 (award in gold); Drake was only 14 when he rescued a child from a deep well, into which it had fallen, at Parys, Orange Free State; Drake also received the Royal Humane Society's bronze medal and later, the Stanhope Gold Medal, the policy at the time being that the latter was awarded for the best bronze medal case awarded during the year[11].

15 to 21. Temporary Captain H. S. Fisher, Temporary Captain A. L. H. Warner, Temporary Lieutenant H. I. Solomon, Temporary Warrant Officer II H. C. Bruyns, War Substantive Warrant Officer II L. Murcia, Temporary Staff Sergeant P. F. du Plessis, and War Substantive Sergeant C. Pentz, all of the Union Defence Forces; 14th September 1945; bravery on the occasion of an explosion at the Grand Magazine, Pretoria.

22. No. 62971 Lance-Corporal Peter Seholi, Union Defence Forces; 7th December 1945; rescued two men gassed in a sewer at Maitland, Cape Town.

23 to 25. No. 151623 (VE) Sergeant I. M. Ferreira, No. 43345 (V) Sergeant N. J. Bronkhorst, and No. 173210 (V) Temporary Corporal W. S. Breet, all of the Union Defence Forces; 8th February and 21st June 1946; bravery on the occasion of an explosion at the Grand Magazine, Pretoria.

26 to 32. Marthinus Jacobus Theron, John Bassett Hall, Edward George Clark, Erle Snider Snyder, Andries Sehlogo, Frederick Nel, Amos Mpye; 15th February 1946; bravery on the occasion of an explosion at the Grand Magazine, Pretoria, the last three named being natives.

33. No. 68139 Able Seaman H. S. J. Adlam, S.A.N.F. (V); 12th April 1946; saved a native from the sea and sharks at Durban.

34. Peter Thomas Lewis; 23rd January 1948; saved a child from the path of a railway engine at Pretoria.

35. Jack Jacobus Hart; 22nd October 1948; Hart was only 14 when he saved a child from a burning hut in a Johannesburg garden.

36. Mr. Lauritz Richard Nilsen; 27th March 1953; saved a friend with whom he was swimming and whose leg had been bitten off by a shark at Winkle Spruit, Natal.

It is interesting to note that 17 medals (Nos. 15–21 and 23–32 above), being almost half the total number awarded, were given in respect of bravery on the occasion of an explosion at the Grand Magazine, South African Mint, Pretoria, which occurred on 1st March 1945. At that time a section of the Mint was operating as a wartime munitions factory.

ILLUSTRATIVE AWARD

The memorandum of facts which accompanied the submission to King George VI, recommending Mr. P. T. Lewis (No. 34 above) for the medal in silver, was as follows[9]:

11. For further details see *Africana Notes and News*, Volume 19, No. 3, September 1970. Drake's medals are now in the Africana Museum, Johannesburg.

"On the morning of the 3rd April, 1947, two railway engines, coupled together, were proceeding towards the Mitchell Street level crossing, Pretoria, at about twenty miles per hour.

On hearing a sequence of short blasts, Peter Thomas Lewis, a Signal Fitter, who was working at a point some 30 yards from the crossing, looked up and saw a small child standing a short distance from the approaching engines and within approximately a foot from the track.

Realising that the child's life was in immediate danger, Lewis dashed forward and after negotiating the signal wires running parallel to the track and a cattle grid of metal tubing inlaced with barbed wire, dived towards the child, seized it in his arms and rolled clear of the oncoming engines at a time when they were no more than a foot away. Moreover, had Lewis stumbled when crossing the cattle grid, he would have been in grave danger of losing his life.

The promptitude with which Lewis accepted the risk of death or grave personal injury in the rescue of the child sets a fine example of bravery in the face of imminent danger."

Chapter 27

The King's Medal for Courage in the Cause of Freedom

ORIGIN AND DEVELOPMENT

At the end of the First World War the services of certain foreigners had been recognised by the award of "The Allied Subjects' Medal" (q.v.) which, however, was confined to services rendered in respect of British prisoners-of-war. The circumstances of the Second World War were such that a medal of similarly restricted scope would have been quite inadequate. Since, however, it was not considered desirable to make a large number of honorary appointments of Allied civilians to the Order of the British Empire, or of honorary awards of the B.E.M., it was decided to institute two special medals for award to foreigners who had furthered the interests of the Commonwealth in the Allied cause during the War, either by acts of courage, or by service, as appropriate. Originally the medals had been conceived as awards for civilians only. However, as a result of discussions early in 1945 it was decided that the medal for courage should be available to members of foreign armed forces in respect of special services, e.g. clandestine operations, which were outside the scope of normal military duties[1]. The two medals were designated respectively "The King's Medal for Courage in the Cause of Freedom" and "The King's Medal for Service in the Cause of Freedom", and were instituted by Royal Warrants dated 23rd August 1945[2]. The Warrant for the former was as follows:

> "GEORGE R.I.
>
> GEORGE THE SIXTH, by the Grace of God, of Great Britain, Ireland and the British Dominions beyond the Seas, King, Defender of the Faith, Emperor of India, to all to whom these Presents shall come,
>
> GREETING!
>
> WHEREAS We have taken into Our Royal consideration the many Acts of courage performed by foreign persons, both male and female, in furtherance of the interests of the British Commonwealth in the Allied cause, during the war,
>
> And whereas We are desirous of honouring certain of those who perform or who have performed such deeds:
>
> We do by these Presents for Us, Our Heirs and Successors institute and create a new Medal.
>
> *First:* It is ordained that the Medal shall be designated and styled "The King's Medal for Courage in the Cause of Freedom".
>
> *Secondly:* It is ordained that the Medal shall be circular in form, but that the preparation of a design and the manufacture of the Medal shall be postponed for the time being.
>
> *Thirdly:* It is ordained that the Medal is intended to be worn by recipients on the left breast suspended from a ribbon one-and-a-quarter inches in width, of white, with broad red stripes at each edge and at the centre two narrow blue stripes separated by a narrow white stripe.
>
> It is also ordained that when awards are made the ribbon shall be issued to recipients.
>
> *Fourthly:* It is ordained that the persons eligible for the Medal shall be civilians of foreign nationality, male or female, upon whom We may think fit to confer the honour.

1. Summarised from material in P.R.O. AIR 2/9288.
2. See *L.G.*, 28th August 1945.

Fig.A: The King's Medal for Courage in the Cause of Freedom, obverse.

Fig.B: The King's Medal for Courage in the Cause of Freedom, reverse.

3. *Annual Report of the Deputy Master and Comptroller of the Royal Mint* (1946), pp.9 and 21. The reverse of the Medal for Service was designed and modelled by Mr. T. H. Paget.

4. For 7th August 1947 (47 Medals for Courage).

5. For 1st September 1947 (34 Medals for Courage); 1st April 1948 (2 cancellations); and 2nd August 1948 (3 Medals for Courage).

6. For 15th February 1953 (11 Medals for Courage and 171 for Service). The announcement is to the effect that the awards were made by the Queen for services during the Second World War.

7. Published by Hurst and Blackett, London, 1956.

8. Under reference AIR 2/8742, 9288 and 9294.

9. These figures were provided by courtesy of the Secretary, The Central Chancery of the Orders of Knighthood.

10. *Annual Report of the Deputy Master and Comptroller of the Royal Mint*, (1947), p.27

11. See P.R.O. AIR 2/9288.

It is also ordained that foreign persons in military service, male or female, shall be eligible for the Medal provided that they are recommended for special services outside the scope of normal military duties.

Fifthly: It is ordained that awards shall be made only on a recommendation to Us, for civilians by Our Secretary of State for Foreign Affairs, and for Officers and members of foreign military forces by Our First Lord of the Admiralty, Our Secretary of State for War, or Our Secretary of State for Air, as the case may be, or, in the case of any of Our Dominions, the Government whereof shall so desire, by the appropriate Minister of State for the said Dominion.

Sixthly: It is ordained that the Medal shall be awarded only for acts of courage entailing risk to life or for service entailing dangerous work in hazardous circumstances, in furtherance of the Allied cause during the war, and shall be granted without distinction of status or rank.

Seventhly: It is ordained that the names of those upon whom We may be pleased to confer or bestow the Medal, shall be recorded in a Register in Our Treasury.

Eighthly: It is ordained that it shall be competent for Us, Our Heirs and Successors by an Order under Our Sign Manual and on a recommendation to that effect by or through Our Secretary of State for Foreign Affairs, Our First Lord of the Admiralty, Our Secretary of State for War, or Our Secretary of State for Air, as may be appropriate, or, in the case of any of Our Dominions, the Government whereof shall so desire, the appropriate Minister of State for the said Dominion, to cancel and annul the award to any person of the King's Medal for Courage in the Cause of Freedom and that thereupon the name of such person in the Register shall be erased; provided that it shall be competent for Us, Our Heirs and Successors to restore the award so forfeited when such recommendation has been withdrawn.

Lastly: We reserve to Ourself, Our Heirs and Successors, full power of annulling, altering, abrogating, augmenting, interpreting, or dispensing with these rules and ordinances, or any part thereof, by a notification under Our Sign Manual.

Given at Our Court at St. James's, the twenty-third day of August, one thousand nine hundred and forty-five, in the ninth year of Our Reign.

By His Majesty's Command,
C. R. Attlee."

DESCRIPTION

Ribbon White $1\frac{1}{4}$ inch wide, edged with red stripes $\frac{1}{4}$ inch wide; in the centre two dark blue stripes each $\frac{1}{10}$ inch wide, and $\frac{1}{16}$ inch apart.

Suspension By a non-swivelling ring.

Obverse (Fig.A)

Reverse (Fig.B) The reverse was designed and modelled by Mr. W. M. Gardner[3].

Naming The medals were issued unnamed.

VERIFICATIONS AND CITATIONS

Awards do not appear in the *London Gazette*. A number of awards, without citations, appear in the Government Gazettes of North Borneo[4], Sarawak[5] and the Sudan[6]. The citation for *Capitaine* Michel Hardivillier is reproduced in *Secret Weapons – Secret Agents* by Jaques Bergier ("Verne")[7], and for Herr Thorkil Hansen in the catalogue of Glendining and Company's auction sale of 21st May 1970. Details for the awards of some medals, both for Courage and for Service, are preserved in the Public Record Office[8].

NUMBERS AWARDED

Approximately 3,200 Medals for Courage and 2,490 for Service were awarded[9]. The first issues of both Medals were made in 1947[10].

ILLUSTRATIVE AWARD

Capitaine André du Puy Montbrun, of the French Army, was awarded the Medal for Courage in 1945, the recommendation[11] for which being as follows:

"Captain du Puy Montbrun belonged to an intelligence organisation in France, and was responsible for maintaining efficient liaison between the headquarters of the *reseau* and the heads of the various sectors.

During a period of two years, he regularly carried out several times each month clandestine missions which involved travelling long distances under extremely difficult and dangerous conditions.

He was ordered to England for training in the organisation of air-landing and parachute operations, was arrested on the way but escaped and successfully accomplished his journey.

Captain du Puy Montbrun carried out his hazardous activities until the liberation of France, and exhibited throughout a high degree of courage, determination and devotion to duty."

Chapter 28

The King's Police Medal;
The King's Police and Fire
Services Medal;
The Queen's Police Medal

ORIGIN AND DEVELOPMENT

During the early years of this century a need arose whereby gallantry, and distinguished service, in the police forces and fire brigades of the Empire should be recognised by the award of a specific medal. Hitherto, in Great Britain such services had been rewarded by commendations[1] or by monetary awards[2] or by the Albert Medal or various unofficial medals[3]. While it is true that the Constabulary Medal (Ireland) (q.v.) had been in existence since 1842 and that a few Indian police officers had been appointed to the Civil Division of the Indian Order of Merit (q.v.) since its institution in 1902, there was no medal of general application. Moreover, appointments to the Imperial Service Order were restricted to civil servants. Accordingly, in 1909 the King's Police Medal, which was also available to personnel of fire brigades, was instituted by Royal Warrant[4], in the following terms:

Fig. A: The King's Police Medal,
obverse, Edward VII issue.

"EDWARD, R. & I.

Edward the Seventh, by the Grace of God, of the United Kingdom of Great Britain and Ireland and of the British Dominions beyond the Seas King, Defender of the Faith, Emperor of India, to all to whom these Presents shall come: Greeting!

Whereas We have taken into Our Royal consideration the good services which are rendered by officers of the Constabulary Forces and by persons serving in Fire Brigades within Our Dominions and in Territories under Our Protection or Jurisdiction and the heroic acts of courage and instances of conspicuous devotion to duty of such persons which are from time to time brought to Our notice:

And whereas We are desirous of distinguishing such meritorious conduct by some mark of Our Royal favour:

We do by these Presents for Us, Our Heirs and Successors, institute and create a new Medal to be awarded for such acts of courage and conspicuous devotion to duty.

Firstly. – It is ordained that the Medal shall be designated and styled "The King's Police Medal."

Secondly. – It is ordained that the King's Police Medal shall consist of a circular Medal of Silver with Our Effigy on the obverse, and on the reverse a design emblematic of Protection from danger, and shall bear on the rim the name of the person to whom the Medal is awarded.

Thirdly. – It is ordained that the Medal shall only be awarded to those of Our Faithful Subjects and others who being members of a recognized Police Force or of a properly organized Fire Brigade within Our Dominions or in Territories under Our Protection or Jurisdiction, have performed acts of exceptional courage and skill or have exhibited conspicuous devotion to duty; and that such award shall be made only on a recommendation to Us by Our Principal Secretary of State for the Home Department.

Fourthly. – It is ordained that the names of those upon whom We may be pleased to confer this Decoration shall be published in the London Gazette, and that a Register thereof shall be kept in the Office of Our Principal Secretary of State for the Home Department.

1. *E.g.*, by judges, the Director of Public Prosecutions, Chief Constables, civic bodies, etc.

2. *E.g.*, from the Bow Street Police Court Reward Fund.

3. *E.g.*, those of the Royal Humane Society, the Liverpool Shipwreck and Humane Society, the London County Council, etc.

4. See the *London Gazette* of 9th July 1909.

Such Register shall show the name and rank of the person holding the Medal, the Police Force or Fire Brigade of which he is or was a member, and particulars of the action for which the Medal has been awarded.

Fifthly. – It is ordained that each Medal shall be suspended from the left breast, and the riband, of an inch and three eighths in width, shall be dark blue with a narrow silver stripe on either side.

Sixthly. – It is ordained that any act of gallantry which is worthy of recognition by the award of the King's Police Medal, but is performed by one upon whom the Decoration has already been conferred, may, on a recommendation to Us by Our Principal Secretary of State for the Home Department, be recorded by a Bar attached to the riband by which the Medal is suspended; and for every such additional act an additional Bar may be added.

Seventhly. – In order to make such provision as shall effectually preserve pure this honourable Decoration, it is ordained that if any person on whom the Decoration is conferred be guilty of any crime or disgraceful conduct which in Our judgement disqualifies him for the same, this Medal shall, by an especial Warrant under Our Royal Sign Manual, be forfeited, and his name shall be forthwith erased from the Register of those upon whom the said Decoration shall have been conferred. And every person to whom the said Medal is given shall before receiving the same enter into an agreement to return the same, if his name shall be so erased as aforesaid under this regulation. It is hereby further declared that We, Our Heirs and Successors, shall be the sole judges of the circumstances demanding such forfeiture.

Given at Our Court at *Saint James's*, the seventh day of *July*, one thousand nine hundred and nine, in the ninth year of Our Reign.

By His Majesty's Command.
H. J. Gladstone."

The instituting Warrant was amended five times as follows:

3rd October 1916[5] In future the ribbon was to have a third silver stripe running down the centre.

1st October 1930[6] The original forfeiture clause was abrogated by the substitution of a new clause. This widened the power available in ordering forfeiture by omitting reference to "crime or disgraceful conduct", and made provision for restoration should this be subsequently recommended. This followed a recommendation by the Interdepartmental Rewards Committee that all awards for gallantry, except in cases of extreme infamy, should be regarded as irrevocable; hence it was unnecessary to limit the power, as had been done before, by prescribing for particular circumstances.

12th December 1933[7] The 2nd, 3rd, 5th and 6th Clauses were abrogated by substitution. In future the reverse of the medal was to bear, in addition to the original design, the words "For Gallantry" or "For Distinguished Service" as appropriate, and the "gallantry" ribbon was introduced (see below). It was the King's idea that the medal itself should show the services for which it was being awarded[8]. The amended 2nd Clause provided for "Our Effigy" on the obverse, as had the instituting Warrant; this was presumably to regularise the change in obverse which had taken place on the death of King Edward VII. In addition, a silver rose emblem, denoting the award of a bar, was to be added to the ribbon when the latter was worn alone[9].

25th May 1936[10] The 3rd Clause was again abrogated by substitution. The new Clause extended the instituting Warrant, as amended, to the police and fire brigades of those self-governing Dominions whose Governments wished to adopt it[11].

15th December 1936[12] The 2nd and 3rd Clauses were again abrogated by substitution. The obverse of the medal was to bear "the effigy of the Sovereign", thus obviating further amendments for each succession.

A Warrant of 14th March 1938[13] made further provision for the Police Forces and Fire Brigades within the Dominion of Canada. Awards, forfeitures and restorations were to be made only on the recommendation of a Canadian Minister of State; awards were to be published in the *Canada Gazette*; and the Register was to be kept in the Office of one of the Canadian Ministers of State. The Regulations made by virtue of the Warrant provided that awards were not, except in very special circumstances, to exceed twelve annually.

5. See *L.G.*, 10th October 1916.
6. See *L.G.*, 10th October 1930.
7. See *L.G.*, 29th December 1933.
8. See P.R.O. MINT 20/1290.
9. An announcement to this effect was made in the *London Gazette* of 18th August 1922.
10. See *L.G.*, 5th June 1936.
11. A change brought about by the Statute of Westminster, 1931.
12. See *L.G.*, 29th December 1936.
13. See the *Canada Gazette* of 17th September 1938. Canadian awards were not thereafter published in the *London Gazette* except for one award in 1949 and three in 1951. Unlike the South African K.P.M. (see below) that for Canada was of the "Home" pattern.

In 1940 the original and amending "Home" Warrants were revised and incorporated into one dated 20th August 1940[14]. The only major change was that the medal in future was to be known as "The King's Police and Fire Services Medal", and "members of a recognised Police or Fire Service " were to be eligible[15]. The Warrant also made provision for the issue of Regulations by the Home Secretary although, in fact, this had been done since 1909 (see below). In regard to bars, the original Warrant of 1909, the amending Warrant of 1933 and the consolidating Warrant of 1940 all specified that gallantry was a condition precedent to the award of a bar. Four such awards in the *London Gazette* are not specified as for gallantry although other evidence shows them to be so[16].

The first Regulations were published at the same time as the instituting Warrant, and were as follows:

"The following Regulations shall be observed in recommending His Majesty to grant the King's Police Medal:

1. A list of the names of officers of recognized Police Forces, or of properly constituted Fire Brigades, who are recommended for the Medal, shall be submitted once in each year to His Majesty by the Secretary of State for the Home Department.

Provided that a recommendation may be made at any time when His Majesty so commands.

2. A list of officers recommended by the Secretary of State for the Colonies and the Secretary of State for India shall be forwarded to the Home Office in the month of October in each year.

3. Each list shall contain the name and rank of each person recommended, the Police Force or Fire Brigade of which he is or was a member, and particulars of the action or service for which the grant of the Medal is recommended.

4. The number of Medals awarded in any one year shall not exceed one hundred and twenty, of which at the most forty shall be awarded for service in the United Kingdom of Great Britain and Ireland, the Channel Islands, and the Isle of Man, thirty for service in His Majesty's Dominions beyond the Seas, and fifty for service in the Empire of India.

5. In very special circumstances, which, in His Majesty's opinion, would justify an exceptional grant, His Majesty may award Medals exceeding the above number.

6. The qualifications for the grant of the Medal shall be as follows:

(*a*) Conspicuous gallantry in saving life and property, or in preventing crime or arresting criminals; the risks incurred to be estimated with due regard to the obligations and duties of the officer concerned.

(*b*) A specially distinguished record in administrative or detective service.

(*c*) Success in organizing Police Forces or Fire Brigades or Departments, or in maintaining their organization under special difficulties.

(*d*) Special services in dealing with serious or widespread outbreaks of crime or public disorder, or of fire.

(*e*) Valuable political and secret services.

(*f*) Special services to Royalty and Heads of States.

(*g*) Prolonged service; but only when distinguished by very exceptional ability and merit.

H. J. Gladstone.

Whitehall,
    July 7, 1909."

The major changes in these Regulations were as follows:

1st October 1930 The words "or other police service of conspicuous merit" were added to Regulation 6(*b*).

12th December 1933 "The Secretary of State for Dominion Affairs" was added to Regulation 2, and in Regulation 4 the apportionment of medals within the Empire, including the United Kingdom, was abandoned although the overall number available of 120 remained the same.

14. See *L.G.*, 6th September 1940.

15. Thus making provision, *inter alia*, for the National Fire Service.

16. These were to Commissioner of Police Sir Patrick Aloysius Kelly, C.I.E., Bombay (*London Gazette*, 1st January 1931; citation, *Bombay Government Gazette*, 8th January 1931); District Superintendent U Maung Gale, Burma Police (*London Gazette*, 1st January 1932; citation, *Burma Gazette*, 9th January 1932); Deputy Commissioer of Police F. D. Bartley, C.B.E., Bengal (*London Gazette*, 1st January 1933; citation, *Calcutta Gazette*, 12th January 1933); and Deputy Commissioner P. Norton Jones, O.B.E., Calcutta (*London Gazette*, 12th November 1946; citation, *Gazette of India*, 23rd November 1946).

On 20th August 1940 revised Regulations were issued in conformity with the consolidating Warrant. These provided, *inter alia*, for the submission of recommendations annually in May and December except that, in special circumstances, a recommendation could be made at any time for an immediate award; and that the limit of 120 medals available in any one year could be exceeded if the King considered that circumstances so justified. On 30th June 1945 the Regulations were again revised in which recommendations for gallantry were to be made as soon as possible after the act concerned, and in special circumstances recommendations for awards on other grounds could be made at any time for an immediate award.

As with the Albert Medal (q.v.) and the Edward Medal (q.v.) it was later decided that the medal for gallantry should only be awarded posthumously, the last awards to surviving recipients being in 1950.

In 1954 separate medals were instituted for police forces and fire services[17], the former being known as "The Queen's Police Medal" and the latter as "The Queen's Fire Service Medal" (q.v.). The Warrant for the Queen's Police Medal was as follows:

"ELIZABETH R.

ELIZABETH THE SECOND, by the Grace of God of the United Kingdom of Great Britain and Northern Ireland and of Our other Realms and Territories QUEEN, Head of the Commonwealth, Defender of the Faith, To all to whom these Presents shall come,
Greeting!

WHEREAS His late Majesty King Edward the Seventh in consideration of the good services rendered by officers of the Constabulary Forces and by persons serving in fire brigades within His Dominions and in Territories under His Protection or Jurisdiction and the heroic acts of courage and instances of conspicuous devotion to duty of such persons, and being desirous of distinguishing such meritorious conduct by some mark of His Royal Favour did by Warrant under His Royal Sign Manual dated the 7th July, 1909, institute a new Medal to be awarded for such services as aforesaid:

AND WHEREAS We are desirous of having separate Medals for members of police forces and for members of fire services We are graciously pleased to make, ordain, and establish the following Statutes for the governance of the Decoration to be awarded to members of police forces:

"*Firstly*—It is ordained that the Medal shall be designated and styled 'The Queen's Police Medal'.

Secondly—It is ordained that the Medal shall consist of a circular Medal of Silver with the effigy of the Sovereign on the obverse, and shall bear on the reverse a design emblematic of protection from danger and the words 'For Gallantry' or 'For Distinguished Police Service' as the case may be, and on the rim the name of the person to whom the Medal has been awarded.

Thirdly—It is ordained that the Medal shall be awarded only to those of Our Faithful Subjects and Others who have either performed acts of exceptional courage and skill at the cost of their lives, or exhibited conspicuous devotion to duty, as members of a recognised police force within Our United Kingdom of Great Britain and Northern Ireland, Our Channel Islands, Our Island of Man, any of Our Colonies or any territory under Our protection or jurisdiction not being administered by Us in Our Government in any other part of Our Commonwealth, or within any other part of Our Commonwealth Our Government whereof has signified its desire that the Medal should be awarded under the provisions of this Our Warrant to members of any such force within such part, or within any territory under Our protection or jurisdiction being administered by Us in such Government, or as members of a British civil police force established outside the United Kingdom under the authority of the Police (Overseas Service) Act, 1945; and that such award shall be made only on a recommendation to Us by Our Secretary of State for the Home Department, or, in the case of a Member country of Our Commonwealth other than Our United Kingdom of Great

17. See the *London Gazette* of 4th June 1954 where both Warrants are published.

189

Britain and Northern Ireland the Government whereof shall so desire, by the appropriate Minister of State for that country.

Fourthly— It is ordained that the names of those upon whom We may be pleased to confer this Decoration shall be published in the London Gazette, and that a Register thereof shall be kept in the Office of Our Secretary of State for the Home Department, or, in the case of a Member country of Our Commonwealth other than Our United Kingdom of Great Britain and Northern Ireland the Government whereof shall so desire, of the appropriate Minister of State for that country. Such Register shall show the name and rank of the person holding the Medal, the police force of which that person is or was a member and the circumstances in which the Medal has been awarded.

Fifthly—It is ordained that the Medal shall be suspended from the left breast, and the riband, of an inch and three eighths in width, shall be dark blue with a narrow silver stripe on either side and a similar silver stripe in the middle; and in the case of awards for acts of exceptional courage each silver stripe of the riband shall contain a thin red line down the middle.

Sixthly—It is ordained that any act of gallantry worthy of recognition by the award of The Queen's Police Medal which is performed by one upon whom the Decoration or either of its predecessors (namely The King's Police Medal and The King's Police and Fire Services Medal) has already been conferred may, on a recommendation to Us by Our Secretary of State for the Home Department, or, in the case of a Member country of Our Commonwealth other than Our United Kingdom of Great Britain and Northern Ireland the Government whereof shall so desire, the appropriate Minister of State for that country, be recorded by a Bar attached to the riband by which the Medal is suspended.

Seventhly—It is ordained that it shall be competent for Us, Our Heirs and Successors by an Order under Our Sign Manual, and on a recommendation to that effect by Our Secretary of State for the Home Department, or, in the case of a Member country of Our Commonwealth other than Our United Kingdom of Great Britain and Northern Ireland the Government whereof shall so desire, the appropriate Minister of State for that country, to cancel and annul the award to any person of the above Decoration or either of its predecessors and that thereupon the name of that person in the Register shall be erased. Provided that it shall be competent for Us, Our Heirs and Successors to restore any Decoration which may have been so forfeited when such recommendation has been withdrawn. And every person to whom the Decoration is awarded for distinguished service shall, before receiving the same, enter into an agreement to return the Medal if his or her name shall be erased as aforesaid.

Eighthly—It is ordained that Our Secretary of State for the Home Department or, in the case of a Member country of Our Commonwealth other than Our United Kingdom of Great Britain and Northern Ireland the Government whereof shall so desire, the appropriate Minister of State for that country, may make Regulations for the carrying into effect of this Our Royal Warrant.

All previous Warrants issued in this behalf are hereby revoked except in so far as they are already revoked.

GIVEN at Our Court at Saint James's the Nineteenth day of May 1954; in the Third Year of Our Reign.

By Her Majesty's Command
David Maxwell Fyfe."

18. Presumably for distinguished service.

19. *I.e.*, the King's Police Medal and the King's Police and Fire Services Medal. The Warrant implies that these were different medals. This is not so; the consolidating Warrant of 1940 merely amends the 1909 instituting Warrant by substituting new provisions.

20. See *Hansard* (House of Commons) for 22nd July 1969, column 346.

21. See *L.G.*, 22nd October 1971.

It will be noted that the medal was to bear the Sovereign's effigy on the obverse, and on the reverse the original design with the words "For Gallantry" or "For Distinguished Police Service" as appropriate. The ribbons were unchanged. The medal for gallantry was only to be awarded posthumously. A bar for gallantry could be awarded to anyone who had already received the Queen's Police Medal[18], or either of its predecessors[19]. To the end of 1979, 34 posthumous medals for gallantry have been awarded under this Warrant. In 1969 the Queen approved of the use by recipients of the post-nominal letters "K.P.M.", "K.P.F.S.M." or "Q.P.M." as appropriate[20], and a consequent amendment was made by Royal Warrant on 8th October 1971[21]; by the same Warrant recommendations and regulations were to be made by the Secretary of State for Scotland.

Fig.B: The King's Police Medal, obverse, George V issue, first type.

Fig.C: The King's Police Medal, obverse, George V issue, second type.

On 28th May 1954 Regulations were made for the Medal, as follows:

"1. Unless Her Majesty otherwise directs, lists of the names of members of recognised police forces who are recommended for the Medal on any ground other than that of conspicuous gallantry shall be submitted by the Secretary of State for the Home Department in the months of May and December in each year.

2. The names of those recommended by other Departments for inclusion in any such list shall be forwarded to the Home Office not later than one month prior to the date on which the award is to be made.

3. Recommendations for awards on the ground of conspicuous gallantry shall be made as soon as possible after the occasion on which the conspicuous gallantry was shown; and in special circumstances recommendations for awards on other grounds may be made at any time for an immediate award.

4. All recommendations shall state the name and rank of the person recommended, the name of the police force of which that person is or was a member, and particulars of the gallantry or service for which the grant of the Medal is recommended.

5. The qualifications for the grant of the Medal shall be as follows:

    (*a*) Conspicuous gallantry in saving life and property, or in preventing crime or arresting criminals, the risks incurred being estimated with due regard to the obligations and duties of the deceased officer.

    (*b*) A specially distinguished record in administrative or detective service, or other police service of conspicuous merit.

    (*c*) Success in organising police forces, or in maintaining their organisation under special difficulties.

    (*d*) Special services in dealing with serious or widespread outbreaks of crime or public disorder, or fire.

    (*e*) Valuable political and secret services.

    (*f*) Special services to Royalty and Heads of States.

    (*g*) Prolonged service; but only when distinguished by very exceptional ability and merit.

6. The King's Police and Fire Service Medal Regulations made on 30th June, 1945 are hereby revoked."

The order of wearing the medal has varied. In Army Order No. 246 of August 1912 it was shown following the Indian Distinguished Service Medal in a group of medals which, at that time, came after the Polar medals. In 1941[22] the medal for gallantry followed the Air Force Medal, and in 1947[23] it followed the George Medal (see also Appendix 4).

DESCRIPTION

Ribbon Dark blue, 1⅜ inches wide, with a narrow silver stripe at either side. In 1916 a central silver stripe was added[24], and from 1933 gallantry awards were distinguished by a thin red line running down the centre of each of the three silver stripes[25].

Suspension By a silver ring which, in the case of Edward VII issues only, was oval. With the Edward VII and some first type George V issues the ring swivelled, but was fixed for the remaining issues.

Obverse Six types are known as follows:

1. Edward VII (Fig.A).

2. George V first type (Fig.B) This was introduced in 1911[26].

3. George V second type (Fig.C) This was introduced in 1931[27].

4. George VI first type (Fig.D) This was introduced in 1938[28].

5. George VI second type (Fig.E) This was introduced in about 1949.

6. Elizabeth II second type (Fig.F) We have been unable to discover if the first type obverse appeared on any of the gallantry awards; distinguished service awards with the first type obverse were issued.

22. See *L.G.*, 22nd April 1941.

23. See *L.G.*, 11th February 1947.

24. Royal Warrant of 3rd October 1916.

25. Royal Warrant of 12th December 1933.

26. *Annual Report of the Deputy Master and Comptroller of the Royal Mint (1911)*, p.50.

27. *Ibid* (1931), p.43.

28. *Ibid* (1938), p.45.

Fig.D: The King's Police Medal, obverse, George VI issue, first type.

Fig.E: The King's Police Medal, obverse, George VI issue, second type.

Reverse There are four types as follows:

1. With no wording in the exergue (Fig.G). This type was designed by Gilbert Bayes and remodelled by him in 1933[29].
2. With the words "For Gallantry" in the exergue (Fig.H). This type was introduced in 1934[29].
3. With the words "For Distinguished Service" in the exergue. This type was introduced in 1934[29].
4. With the circumscription "For Distinguished Police Service"[30].

Bar (Figs.I and J) Originally a silver dated bar was used which bore the date "1st January" followed by the year of award. In 1934[31] the dated bar was changed to one with a laurel design. Both were fixed to the ribbon by two large prongs inserted through the ribbon and then bent sideways.

Naming Medals are engraved in serif capital letters with the recipient's name (first names are sometimes given in full and sometimes by initials), rank, and service or force.

South Africa A King's Police Medal peculiar to South Africa was instituted by Royal Warrant dated 24th September 1937[32], the conditions of award being similar to those described above. The design of the medal was also similar except that the obverse bore the legend "Georgivs VI Rex et Imperator", while the reverses were bilingual. The gallantry medal had the circumscription "For Bravery" and "Vir Dapperheid" (Fig.K), and that "For Distinguished Service" also had "Vir Voortreflike Diens". In both cases the shield bore the words "Om my volk te beskerm" and "To guard my people". The instituting Warrant was extended to the Police Force of South West Africa by an amending Warrant dated 5th August 1938[33], and the words "Et Imperator" were omitted from the obverse of the medal by a further amending Warrant dated 17th October 1950[34]. A consolidating and amending Warrant dated 15th December 1952[35] provided, *inter alia*, for the Queen's effigy on the obverse of the medal and for a corresponding change in title. Awards were not published in the *London Gazette* but appeared in the *Union Gazette*[36]. From information kindly placed at our disposal by Dr. Felix Machanik we are able to summarise the awards as follows:

		Gallantry	Distinguished Service
1937–49	...	10	13
1950–52	...	—	1
1953–60	...	20	3

Copies and Fakes For recent copies see the Note on p.xx.

VERIFICATIONS AND CITATIONS

All awards under the "home" Warrant are published in the *London Gazette*, and include South African awards made before, but not after, the institution in 1937 of a special medal for the Union[37] (see above).

1909–1930 Until 1911, the heading "Police Medal" in the "State Intelligence" portion of the Gazette quarterly indices gives the pages upon which awards are to be found. From the first quarter of 1911 names are given under this heading which, from the first quarter of 1915 is then indexed as "King's Police Medal". Only very rarely is there any indication that the award is for gallantry although it seems reasonable to suppose that the majority of awards to junior ranks are for gallantry. The entries give the rank, names and force concerned, and sometimes the recipient's serial number.

1931 onwards Gallantry and distinguished service awards are specified as such in the Gazette notices although there are a few where no distinction is made and the

29. See P.R.O. MINT 20/1290 and the *Annual Reports of the Deputy Master and Comptroller of the Royal Mint* (*1910*), p.15, (*1933*), p.16 and (*1934*), p.50.

30. Royal Warrant of 19th May 1954.

31. *Annual Report of the Deputy Master and Comptroller of the Royal Mint* (*1934*), p.49.

32. *Union of South Africa Government Gazette*, 19th November 1937.

33. *Ibid*, 9th September 1938.

34. *Ibid*, 29th December 1950.

35. *Ibid*, 27th February 1953.

36. The medal has now been superseded by various police decorations instituted by the Republic in 1963, and augmented in 1978.

37. Between 1909 and 1931 there were 20 South African awards for distinguished service and 20 for gallantry, with one further award for gallantry each in 1932 and 1933.

Fig.F: The Queen's Police Medal, obverse, Elizabeth II issue.

nature of the award is open to doubt. From the first quarter of 1942 the medal heading (which becomes "Queen's Police Medal" in the second quarter of 1954) gives only the pages upon which awards are to be found, the names being relegated to a comprehensive nominal index headed "Honours, Decorations and Medals". Occasionally, page references under the medal heading have been found to be corrupt, or incomplete in that not all the references are given.

Citations Until 1961 no citations appear in the *London Gazette* although on very rare occasions some indication of the nature of the award is given[38]. However, many Home Office files are preserved in the Public Record Office in the series HO 45 which contain material up to 1946 in respect of recommendations (not all of which were approved) for members of home and overseas police forces and fire brigades. The files contain recommendations either for gallantry or distinguished service, correspondence regarding presentations, receipts and undertakings to return the medal if forfeited, etc. The Colonial Office series also contains similar documents, either in the Chief Clerk's correspondence (CO 523), or in that for individual Colonies. Other than these, the best sources for details are in *The Police Review, The Police Chronicle*, or in the local Press at the time an award was published, or at the time of the incident giving rise to the award. For officers of the Indian and Burma Police and Fire Brigades citations appear in the *Gazette of India* and *Burma Gazette* respectively at about the same time as the corresponding entry in the *London Gazette*.

NUMBERS AWARDED

Medals 1909–1930 Until 1931 the majority of notices in the *London Gazette* do not differentiate between awards for gallantry and those for distinguished service. While it is generally safe to assume that awards to junior ranks were for gallantry it is less certain with senior officers. For this period, therefore, we cannot separate accurately awards for distinguished service from those for gallantry and the following figures[39] combine both classes of award:

London Gazettes	United Kingdom	India & Burma	Dominions	Colonies	
1909–10 ...	38	50	2	5	(including Fire Services – U.K., 3)
1911–30 ...	745	882	103	165	(including Fire Services – U.K., 81; Indian, 7; Dominions, 18; Colonies, 3)

Medals 1931–1979 From 1931 the *London Gazette* notices specify whether awards are for gallantry or distinguished service although there are occasional lapses, particularly in 1931 and 1932. The following awards were gazetted:

London Gazettes	United Kingdom	India & Burma	Dominions	Colonies	
1931–32 ...	24	74	13	11	(including Fire Services – U.K., 1)
1933 ...	12	30	2	5	
1934–37 ...	60	79	10	21	(including Fire Services – U.K., 2)
1938–48 ...	168[40]	198[41]	61[42]	48	(including Fire Services – U.K., 13; Indian, 3; Dominions, 8; Colonies, 3; also including 7 Indian awards not specified as for gallantry or for distinguished service[43])
1949–50 ...	15	12[44]	7[42]	11	(including Fire Services – U.K., 1; Indian, 1; Colonies, 2; also including 2 Colonial awards not specified as for gallantry or for distinguished service[45])

38. Thus the citation for the Albert Medal to Sub-Divisional Inspector F. Wright in the *London Gazette* of 3rd May 1918 includes details of the King's Police Medals awarded to Constables R. Melton and J. Christmas, all of the Metropolitan Police.

39. Found by counting the *London Gazette* entries. Wilson and McEwen (see Bibliography) give a table of awards, without separating gallantry from distinguished service, for various periods between 1909 and 1938. Because we have selected different periods it is difficult to reconcile the two sets of figures.

40. Including Woman Police Sergeant A. M. Watts, Metropolitan Police (*L.G.*, 2nd September 1947), being the only gallantry award so far made to a woman.

41. Including three awards in *L.G.*, 14th November 1947, which are omitted from the Gazette index.

42. Including the following awards which only appeared in *The Canada Gazette*: 1939–48, 30 police and 7 fire service; 1949–50, 1 police; 1951–52, 3 police. A roll of these recipients appears in *The Journal of the Orders and Medals Research Society*, Volume 13 at p.124 et seq.

43. Although, in fact, for gallantry; see the *Gazette of India* for 16th and 28th November 1946.

44. On 26th January 1950 the Dominion of India, created in 1947, became a Republic and the medal was replaced in India by the President's Police and Fire Services Medal; see the *Gazette of India*, 10th March 1951.

45. Although, in fact, for gallantry; see the *Tanganyika Gazette* for 11th July 1950.

Fig. G: The King's Police Medal, reverse, 1909–1933.

London Gazettes	United Kingdom	India & Burma	Dominions	Colonies	
1951–52 ...	—	—	4[42]	2	(all posthumous; including an award to Chief Fire Officer A. A. Indoe, H.M. Dockyard, Gibraltar[46])
1953–79 ...	17	—	11	9	(all posthumous; citations given in most cases from 1961)

There were no gallantry awards in 1957, 1958, 1962, 1967, 1968, 1977 and 1979.

The corresponding overall figures for distinguished service awards are:

London Gazettes	
1931–32 ...	105
1933 ...	41
1934–37 ...	143
1938–48 ...	693
1949–52 ...	249
1953–79 ...	1,935

of which 26 were to women police officers.

Bars As with medals, until 1931 the Gazette notices did not show that awards were for gallantry although, according to the Royal Warrants, this could only be so. Until 1934 (see above) a dated bar was used. We have found the following awards in the *London Gazette.*

London Gazettes	United Kingdom	India & Burma	Colonies	
1914–34[47]	4	30[48]	1	(including 1 U.K. Fire Service)
1934–79[49]	1	17	1[50]	(including Indian Police, 1 second bar; and 1 Indian Fire Service)

The only second bar awarded was to F. W. O'Gorman of the Indian Police, Bombay, whose rank is not given in the *London Gazette* of 1st January 1936[51]. The first bar awarded was to Constable W. C. George of the Kincardineshire Constabulary in the *London Gazette* of 1st January 1914, and the two Fire Services' bars were to Sergeant J. Jones of the Wigan Borough Police Fire Brigade in the *London Gazette* of 1st January 1927, and to N. Coombs, Officer Commanding Fire Services, Bombay, in the *London Gazette* of 9th February 1945. The last bar awarded was to Inspector Mehta Ishar Das, Rawalpindi District Police, in the *London Gazette* of 14th November 1947; this award is not noted in the Gazette index.

ILLUSTRATIVE AWARDS

United Kingdom Chief Inspector L. Elwell and Police Constable S. H. Jackson were each awarded the King's Police and Fire Services Medal for gallantry in the *London Gazette* of 6th August 1948. Their joint citation appears in the *Hertfordshire Mercury* of 13th August 1948 and in both the *Police Chronicle* and *Police Review* for the same day, and reads as follows:

"On the afternoon of the 14th November, 1947, information was received that a boy, aged 14½ years, armed with a loaded rifle, had held up a motorist on the Welwyn-Hertford road, and fired several shots at a passing van in the same district. Police cars were directed to the area, one being in charge of Chief Inspector Elwell and another driven by P. C. Jackson.

Chief Inspector Elwell first sighted the boy in a field, alighted from his car, and shouted to him when he was 30 to 50 yards away. The boy fired a shot at the Chief Inspector, the bullet striking the side of the car a few inches away from where he was standing. At this point Constable Jackson arrived on the scene, climbed over a fence surrounding the field, and ran towards the boy, the Chief Inspector also approaching from his position. The boy immediately fired at the Constable, who avoided being hit

46. In *L.G.*, 20th November 1951.

47. The last dated bars were for 1st January 1934.

48. Three recipients are gazetted twice as receiving medals. In fact, according to the Home Office Register, the second medal was a bar. The *London Gazette* references for these awards are as follows: Head Constable Daim Khan, Burma Police – 1st January 1913 and 1st January 1916; Superintendent E. C. Handyside, North West Frontier Province Police – 3rd January 1911 and 1st January 1918; Superintendent F. Young, United Provinces Police – 1st January 1914 and 1st January 1921

49. The first bar awarded with the laurel design was to Superintendent M. F. Cleary, Chittagong, in the *London Gazette* of 8th May 1934. The correspondence regarding this change in the pattern of the bar is to be found in the Public Record Office under reference HO 45/19487.

50. To Inspector J. H. H. Clarke, Jamaica Constabulary, in the *London Gazette* of 1st February 1937; his medal was awarded for distinguished service in the *London Gazette* of 1st January 1936.

51. His first bar was awarded in the *London Gazette* of 1st January 1930 where his rank is given as Superintendent. In the Bombay Civil List for 1937 he is again shown as a Superintendent.

194

Fig.H: The King's (Queen's) Police Medal, for Gallantry, reverse, from 1934.

Fig.I: Dated bar to the King's Police Medal, for gallantry.

Fig.J: Laurelled bar to the King's (Queen's) Police Medal, for gallantry.

Fig.K: The King's Police Medal, for gallantry (South Africa), reverse.

by dropping to the ground. In an attempt to get away from the officers the boy then climbed a railway embankment and fired at them again. The Constable pursued the boy along the embankment with the Chief Inspector close behind. As the boy reached the mouth of a railway tunnel the Constable approached him and tried to reason with him, but without success.

When the Constable was within 25 yards of him the boy shouted that he had "gone crazy", raised the rifle, and took aim at the officer, who rushed towards him. The boy pulled the trigger but fortunately no bullet was discharged. As the boy attempted to re-load the weapon the Constable reached him, succeeded in wresting the rifle from him, and arrested him. He was found to have in his possession 210 rounds of live .22 ammunition.

It ultimately transpired that the boy had killed a man, wounded another, and shot at a woman cyclist. He appeared at Hertford Assizes on 17th February, 1948, was found guilty of murder and ordered to be detained during His Majesty's pleasure.

Both police officers showed bravery and devotion to duty of a high order, with complete disregard for their own personal safety."

P.C. Jackson's medal is of the first type George VI issue; he also received the Defence, and the Police Long Service and Good Conduct Medals (the latter as a sergeant).

Indian Police Sub-Inspector Mohamed Rafiq Khan and Foot Constable Sher Ali of the North West Frontier Province Police were each awarded the King's Police Medal in the *London Gazette* of 1st January 1913. The awards were repeated in the *Gazette of India* of 4th January 1913 where the citations are given successively, as follows:

"In September 1910, this officer was informed that a notorious outlaw, with two companions, was lying up in the hills near Rustam. The Sub-Inspector, taking with him six constables and a few villagers, went in search. The outlaws were found in a strong position behind rocks. A spirited action followed, for all the outlaws were armed to the teeth. In the end two were killed and a third wounded. Throughout the affair Sub-Inspector Mohamed Rafiq Khan led his men with great gallantry."

"This constable was prominent throughout the affair detailed above. By his courage and resource he saved the life of a villager who was on the point of being shot by one of the outlaws."

Sher Ali's medal has the George V first type obverse, and the pre-1934 reverse. The suspender swivels, and the medal is engraved with his full names, abbreviated rank and force. The Home Office papers regarding the 1913 awards of the King's Police Medal are preserved in the Public Record Office under reference HO 45/10999/217900. These include 50 recommendations made by the Government of India which, in the case of the two officers mentioned above, are almost identical with the published citations. The papers also include a covering submission by the Home Secretary (endorsed as approved by King George V), and a letter from Messrs. Elkington and Co. Ltd., of London, showing that they engraved at least some of the medals awarded. Most of the corresponding receipts for this particular batch of Indian awards, which are combined with an undertaking to return the medal if forfeited, are also to be found in the Public Record Office under reference HO 45/10941/231274. These show that Mohamed Rafiq's medal was presented to him by the Chief Commissioner of the North West Frontier Province, the form being dated 15th May 1913, while Sher Ali's medal was presented by the Inspector-General of the North West Frontier Province Police, the form being dated 17th May 1913.

Chapter 29

The Meritorious Service Medal for the Army, 1916–1928

1. See Chapter 12 where the early history of the M.S.M. appears in more detail. Because the 1854 D.C.M. Warrant applied only to the Army, the Royal Marine M.S.M. continued to be awarded for gallantry in action.

2. For example, it was awarded in 1883 to Sergeant T. Danvers, King's Royal Rifle Corps, for gallantry in assisting the police in an affray in Dublin on 25th November 1882 (see the M.S.M. Register, P.R.O. WO 101/2), and to Colour Sergeant H. J. Harrold, York and Lancaster Regiment, and Sergeant J. Allen, King's Royal Rifle Corps, for gallantry when the troopship R.M.I.S. *Warren Hastings* ran ashore on the Island of Réunion on 14th January 1897 (see Army Orders Nos. 40 of April and 143 of October 1897). According to the M.S.M. Register each of these three men received an annuity of £10. For other instances see Chapter 12 above.

3. The standard required to merit any particular award was, of course, another matter, that for the Albert Medal being particularly high. Moreover, to complicate matters further, between 1858 and 1881 the V.C. could be awarded for gallantry not in the face of the enemy.

4. See the Royal Warrant for the Pay, &c., of the Army 1906, para. 1242.

5. The first award under this provision was to Staff Sergeant L. L. Woodell, R.A.M.C., for services during operations in February 1906 in the Munshi Country, Northern Nigeria, see *L.G.*, 18th September 1906 and P.R.O. WO 101/2. No awards under this provision seem to have been made in the First World War.

6. See Army Order No. 352 of October 1916, and P.R.O. WO 32/4958 and 4960.

7. In a number of cases annuities were awarded subsequently, see for example Army Orders Nos. 10 of January 1933, 122 of July 1933, 103 of June 1945 and 34 of February 1946. Instances are known of the erroneous issue of a second M.S.M. with the annuity.

8. See P.R.O. WO 32/4957. The reason given was that when the original proposals were made, the necessity for a bar had not been determined.

9. See Army Order No. 400 of December 1916.

ORIGIN AND DEVELOPMENT

From its institution in 1845 until 1916 the Meritorious Service Medal had been a reward for soldiers above the rank of corporal. Until the Distinguished Conduct Medal was instituted in 1854 it was awarded, together with an annuity, either for meritorious service (in which length of service was a factor), or for gallantry[1]. Thereafter, as far as "other ranks" were concerned, the D.C.M. and, shortly afterwards, the V.C. became the awards for gallantry in action although, on rare occasions, the M.S.M. seems to have been awarded for gallantry not in the face of the enemy[2]. Here, however, its use was limited since it was necessary for the intended recipient to have attained the required rank, and for sufficient money to remain unappropriated in the annuity fund. Moreover, matters were complicated by the existence of various other medals e.g. the Sea Gallantry Medal (from 1854), the Albert Medal (from 1866), as well as those awarded by a number of private bodies, and it is doubtful if any consistent principles were applied in deciding for what a man should be recommended[3]. In 1906 the conditions of award of the M.S.M. were modified, somewhat indirectly, by the Pay Warrant of that year[4] which provided that the medal could also be awarded to a soldier above the rank of corporal who had been "mentioned in despatches for valuable and meritorious service during a campaign."[5] Such men, if they did not receive an annuity, would be awarded a gratuity of £20 on discharge. By Royal Warrants of 31st August 1906 and 12th July 1911 a limited number of M.S.M.s, without annuity, were made available to Yeomen of the Guard, and to Yeomen Warders of the Tower respectively.

Thus matters stood until the First World War. By 1916, however, a need had arisen for a military award for gallantry other than in action where the services performed did not reach the standard required, *inter alia*, for the Albert Medal, and for which all "other ranks" would be eligible. Accordingly, by a Royal Warrant of 4th October 1916[6], eligibility for the M.S.M. was extended to "warrant officers, non-commissioned officers and men, who render valuable and meritorious service". Such recipients, however, were not entitled to a gratuity or to an annuity but, if above the rank of corporal, could be registered for consideration for the latter[7]. The first awards (448 in all) under this Warrant were gazetted on 18th October 1916 the announcement containing a curious Note to the effect that those marked with an asterisk (who totalled 60) had been gazetted in error as awards of the M.M. on 14th September 1916. There is, moreover, other evidence to suggest that the provisions of the Warrant were not considered sufficiently thoroughly because, exactly one week after it was made, in a letter from the War Office to Sir Frederick Ponsonby, Keeper of the Privy Purse, the King was asked to approve the institution of a bar to the M.S.M.[8] On 13th October Ponsonby replied to the effect that the King agreed to the institution of the bar; it was to be awarded for specific acts of gallantry "under peace conditions", and not for extra periods of meritorious service; it was, in fact, to be awarded under exceptional circumstances. Accordingly, on 23rd November 1916 a bar to the M.S.M. was instituted by Royal Warrant[9], the operative part of which was as follows:

"It is OUR WILL AND PLEASURE and We do hereby ordain that anyone who, after having performed services for which the Meritorious Service Medal is awarded, subsequently performs an approved act of gallantry, not necessarily on active service, in the performance of military duty or in saving, or attempting to save, the life of an officer or soldier which, if he had not received the Meritorious Service Medal, would have entitled him to it, shall be awarded a bar to be attached to the riband by which the medal is suspended, and for every additional such act an additional bar may be awarded."

Since the Warrant extending the scope of the medal made no specific reference to gallantry, while that instituting the bar to it did, some clarification was necessary. This was attempted on 11th December 1916 in instructions[10] sent by the War Office to all theatre commanders that the grant of the medal under the October Warrant should be limited to:

"1. Devotion to duty in the theatre of war.
2. Gallant conduct in the performance of military duty or in saving or attempting to save the life of an officer or soldier, otherwise than in action."[11]

It was not to be granted for "devoted or gallant conduct in action." When reporting awards commanders were to say if the services merited an additional pension of 6d. per day should the soldier eventually be discharged with a pension. The bar was to be granted for a second act of gallantry, or for such an act when the soldier already had the medal "for long and meritorious service". It was to be limited to specific acts of gallantry and was to be granted in exceptional cases only: Indian native soldiers were not eligible for the M.S.M.[12] Even these instructions were, in part, *ultra vires* since they purported to restrict award of the bar to those who had already received the medal for gallantry, or who had received it with annuity i.e. "for long and meritorious service". The Warrant instituting the bar, however, prescribed that anyone who had received the medal should receive a bar in the circumstances provided for. Clearly, therefore, "anyone" included those who had received the medal under the Warrant of October 1916, a class excluded by implication in the War Office instructions. Nor was this all. On 3rd January 1917 it was thought necessary to make a further Royal Warrant[13] "extending" the medal to "warrant officers, non-commissioned officers and men who are duly recommended for the grant (of the M.S.M.) in respect of gallant conduct in the performance of military duty otherwise than in action against the enemy, or in saving or attempting to save the life of an officer or soldier, or for devotion to duty in a theatre of war", and making consequential amendments to the Pay Warrant. It will be noticed that the words used in this Warrant are similar to those used in that instituting the bar; hence the new Warrant may have been thought necessary as a formal measure to remove doubts as to whether the medal itself could be awarded for gallantry. Even then it is difficult to see why an alternative of "devotion to duty in a theatre of war" was necessary since "valuable and meritorious service" in the 1916 Warrant (which had not been revoked) was capable of the widest interpretation. In practice, the vast majority of apparently non-gallantry awards were gazetted for "valuable services" and only rarely did "devotion to duty" appear[14]. The position regarding the first three bars awarded is even more curious. The announcements regarding Sergeant J. Orr, Royal Army Medical Corps[15] and Sergeant A. Shenton, Manchester Regiment[16] merely state the award of the bar, while that for Regimental Quartermaster Sergeant J. Elliott, of the Yeomanry[17], specifies that it is for "valuable services". It will be remembered that the King directed that the bar was to be awarded only for gallantry, and not for extra periods of meritorious service. This is reflected in the Warrant instituting the bar which restricted award to acts of gallantry in the performance of military duty (a formula used in the announcements of all awards following the first three), or gallantry in life saving. In the event, however, records in the Ministry of Defence (Army Department) show that the bars to Orr and Shenton were indeed awarded for gallantry. No record of the circumstances giving rise to the award of Elliott's bar seems to have survived.

10. See P.R.O. WO 32/5400. Theatre commanders were authorised to award the medal, and the bar, and had power to delegate award to corps commanders. It is interesting to note that awards of the Army M.S.M., like those of the D.C.M. and M.M., were made to seaman of the R.N. Division and to men of the Royal Marines.

11. It was thus a reward for gallantry anywhere whether in a theatre of war or not.

12. British W.O.s and N.C.O.s of Departmental and non-Departmental Sections of the Indian Army Unattached List and Assistant Surgeons of Warrant rank of the Indian Subordinate Medical Department were eligible, see Indian Army Orders Nos. 447 and 448 of 7th May 1917. The Indian M.S.M. (soon to be extended like its British counterpart) existed for Indian native soldiers. Strangely enough, the medal issued to Sergeant R. G. Bruce, Indian Unattached List (*L.G.*, 3rd June 1918) was of the latter pattern.

13. See Army Order No. 45 of February 1917.

14. e.g. ". . . on the occasion of the sinking or damage by enemy action to Hospital Ships, Transports and Store Ships" (*L.G.*, 6th September 1918); ". . . during an epidemic in a Prisoners of War Camp, Germany" (*L.G.*29th September 1919); ". . . and valuable services rendered while prisoners or war or interned . . ." (*L.G.*, 30th January 1920).

15. M.S.M. for valuable services *L.G.*, 11th November 1916; bar *L.G.*, 13th February 1917.

16. M.S.M. for gallantry *L.G.*, 26th May 1917 (in York and Lancaster Regiment); bar *L.G.*, 19th November 1917 (in Manchester Regiment).

17. M.S.M. (services not stated) *L.G.*, 27th June 1918; bar *L.G.*, 29th August 1918. Elliot's regiment is not given in either announcement. It was, in fact, The Northumberland Hussars.

In June and July 1918 the conditions of award of the D.S.O., M.C. and D.C.M. were considered at a conference at the War Office. The conference recommended that the three decorations concerned should be regarded primarily as distinctions for services in action (including air raids, bombardments etc. producing conditions equivalent to actual combat); and that some emblem should be adopted to distinguish future "immediate" awards from those conferred through the medium of "Honours Gazettes". Only the former recommendation was accepted by the Army Council and this was notified generally on 1st August 1918[18]. At the same time the situation regarding the M.S.M. was investigated and it was discovered that in France, while it had been given as an immediate award for gallantry not in the face of the enemy, in the case of the half-yearly Honours Gazettes, when awarded for devotion to duty, no account had been taken of whether the duty was performed under fire[19]. In view of the clear restrictions recently imposed upon the award of the D.C.M., and because it was evident that the conditions for award of the M.S.M. laid down in December 1916 had not been uniformly interpreted and applied, it was necessary for further instructions to be issued. Accordingly, on 10th August 1918 these were sent out by the War Office[20]. Assuming that no question of award of the D.C.M. arose and that it was necessary merely to determine whether the M.M. or the M.S.M. should be awarded, it was laid down that:

> (a) the M.M. was to be given as an "immediate" award for a specific act of gallantry in action, or for continuous gallantry during a specified period of active operations. In other words, it was to be an award for gallantry in action.

> (b) the M.S.M. was to be awarded for services in the field as a reward for meritorious service and devotion to duty other than in (a) above. Where the elements of gallantry in (a) existed the services should be recognised by the M.M.

The instructions recognised that, having regard to the depth of the zone which in modern war might be fire swept or under fire, it did not appear possible to lay down any rule in regard to the M.S.M. based on such expressions as "in action" or "under fire" but expressed the hope that the conditions prescribed would meet all cases and be easy of application.

By a War Office letter of 7th September 1918 a limited number of M.S.M.s without annuity were made available for "valuable and meritorious service" not in a theatre of war[21]. This provision was cancelled by a War Office letter of 11th November 1919 and no further recommendations were accepted[22].

By a Royal Warrant of 6th November 1920[23] the previous Warrants relating to the M.S.M. were consolidated. By the 2nd Clause the medal with annuity was confined to soldiers above the rank of corporal who, subject to recommendation for "good, faithful, valuable and meritorious service", satisfied certain criteria as to length of service, conduct etc. The 3rd and 4th Clauses provided that:

Thirdly.—It is ordained—

(a) That the Meritorious Service Medal may be awarded to Warrant Officers Classes I and II, non-commissioned officers and men of Our Military Forces who are duly recommended for the medal by a Commander-in-Chief for gallant conduct in the performance of military duty (not necessarily on active service) or in saving or attempting to save the life of an officer or soldier, or for devotion to duty in a theatre of war;

(b) That a Commander-in-Chief when recommending a soldier of Our Military Forces for the Meritorious Service Medal (or for a bar to the same under (e) of this clause) for gallant conduct shall record his opinion whether the case merits the grant of an additional pension—6d. a day for Europeans, and 3d. a day for Non-Europeans—should the soldier be discharged with a pension;

(c) That the additional pension referred to in (b) of this clause may be awarded if the services are duly recommended by a Commander-in-Chief, and deemed to merit the additional pension; provided that this additional pension has not been previously awarded to the soldier;

18. See P.R.O. WO 32/5232 and WO 32/5400.

19. Indeed, in a letter of 29th July 1918 from the Military Secretary to the Commander-in-Chief, British Armies in France, to the War Office it was said that of the 4,500 M.S.M.s awarded in the last Birthday Gazette (apparently that of 17th June which contained 4,402 awards), 75% were for devotion to duty under fire and that it was too late to make alterations, see P.R.O. WO 32/5400. Conversely, the M.S.M. awarded to Sergeant (A/C.S.M.) C. J. Sharp, R.E., in *L.G.*, 1st January 1918 was cancelled, and the D.C.M. substituted in *L.G.*, 8th March 1918. The reason for this is not apparent.

20. See P.R.O. WO 32/5400. A copy of the December 1916 instructions was sent with the new instructions.

21. It is important to note that the M.S.M. had been and continued to be available for gallantry whether in a theatre of war or not. Ten awards were made for the Faversham munitions factory explosion in 1916, see P.R.O. HO 45/11175/321436 and *L.G.*, 12th March 1917. Two of the recipients, Corporal C. T. Harris, R.E., and Acting Bombardier A. F. Edwards, R.F.A., also received the Edward Medal later, see Chapter 19.

22. See P.R.O. WO 32/5399.

23. See *L.G.*, 19th November 1920. Oddly enough, this Warrant made no mention of awards without annuity to Yeomen of the Guard or to Yeomen Warders of the Tower but this omission was made good in the revised Royal Warrant of 5th February 1931 which was published in *L.G.*, 30th March 1931.

(*d*) That in no circumstances shall the award of the Meritorious Service Medal for gallant conduct or devotion to duty carry with it any claim to the annuity granted under the second clause of this Our Royal Warrant;

(*e*) That should a soldier of any of Our Military Forces who has been awarded the Meritorious Service Medal (either with or without annuity) subsequently perform an approved act of gallantry (not necessarily on active service), in the performance of military duty or in saving or attempting to save the life of an officer or soldier, which, had he not already received the Meritorious Service Medal, would have rendered him eligible for it, may be awarded a Bar; and for every additional such act of gallantry an additional bar may be awarded;

(*f*) That any soldier of Our Regular Army who is granted the Meritorious Service Medal for gallant conduct or devotion to duty in accordance with the conditions laid down in this clause of this Our Royal Warrant shall, if subsequently recommended and approved for an annuity in accordance with the second clause of this Our Royal Warrant, receive the annuity only. In such case he will receive the annuity as well as any additional pension which may have been awarded him under (*c*) of this clause;

(*g*) That soldiers of an Allied or Associated Army, of ranks equivalent to those of Our Military Forces specified in (*a*) of this clause, who have been associated in operations with Our Military Forces, shall be eligible for the award of the Meritorious Service Medal, but no annuity or additional pension shall accompany such awards; and

(*h*) That a Register of the Recipients of the Meritorious Service Medal (and bars) awarded under this clause shall be kept in the office of Our Principal Secretary of State for War, but such Register shall be separate and distinct from the Register referred to under (*d*) of the second clause of this Our Royal Warrant.

Fourthly.—It is ordained that the names of those upon whom We may be pleased to confer the Meritorious Service Medal without annuity under the third clause of this Our Royal Warrant, shall be published in the *London Gazette*.

With the reduction of the Armies following the end of the First World War the number of awards of the M.S.M. without annuity fell considerably. Thus in 1919 no less than 15,773 awards for valuable etc. services and 142 for gallantry had been made[24] but in 1921 the corresponding numbers were 57 and 7 respectively. Moreover, the institution of the Medal of the Order of the British Empire on 4th June 1917[25], and its supersession on 29th December 1922 by Medals of the Order for Gallantry, and for Meritorious Service afforded a medium for reward which rendered the M.S.M. redundant, at least for gallantry[26].

In February 1925 the War Office made certain proposals regarding awards of the Medals of the Order which were circulated by the Permanent Secretary of the Treasury to the Admiralty and to the Air Ministry[27]. The proposals included a provision that the M.S.M. should cease to be awarded for gallantry, but that it should be retained as a reward without annuity for valuable services, and as an award with annuity as it had always been. The view of the Admiralty was that it would be better to abolish the M.S.M. altogether except as an award with annuity for soldiers. The matter was discussed at an inter-Departmental conference on 23rd July 1926 and eventually the Admiralty view was adopted. However, the matter was shelved until the Ponsonby Committee on Honours and Awards had reported. In the meanwhile awards continued to be made in the Army[28] and it was not until 20th June 1928 that the matter was submitted to the King[29] who approved a joint proposal by the First Lord of the Admiralty and the Secretary of State for War that the extensions made during the War for the Army, and immediately after the War to the Navy, should be cancelled, and the M.S.M. should revert to its original limited function as an award with annuity for soldiers above the rank of corporal in the Army and in the Royal Marines. Accordingly, by a Royal Warrant of 7th September 1928[30], the 3rd and 4th Clauses of the 1920 M.S.M. Warrant were revoked.

Dress Regulations for the Army 1900 show the M.S.M. in the order of precedence of wearing immediately before the Army Long Service and Good Conduct

24. The vast majority of these were for services rendered before the Armistice.

25. Reconstituted into civil and military divisions on 27th December 1918.

26. The Report of the Munro Committee dated 24th May 1922 on "Honours and Rewards in War" had recommended the abolition of the M.S.M. except for award with annuity to old soldiers, see the quotation in P.R.O. AIR 2/60 (minute of 4th August 1928).

27. See P.R.O. ADM 116/2483.

28. The last for valuable services being to Sergeant H. J. Edwards, D.C.M., Norfolk Regiment, in *L.G.*, 28th May 1926 (operations in Iraq between September and November 1924) and the last for gallantry being to Sub-Conductor G. E. Turner and Staff Sergeant M. B. Matheson, both of the Indian Army Ordnance Corps, in *L.G.*, 27th May 1927 (Ferozepore Arsenal 6th April 1926). A further award was gazetted on 13th April 1928 to Acting Battery Sergeant Major A. H. Frame, M.M., Canadian Field Artillery. However, the notice, which does not specify whether the award was for gallantry or for valuable services, merely publishes the King's approval to an award made in 1919 by the General Officer Commanding-in-Chief, North Russian Expeditionary Force.

29. See P.R.O. ADM 116/2483.

30. See *L.G.*, 21st September 1928.

Fig.A: The Meritorious Service Medal for the Army, obverse.

Fig.B: The Meritorious Service Medal for the Army, reverse.

Fig.C: The Meritorious Service Medal for the Army, bar.

Medal. However, in an amendment to the Dress Regulations of 1911 made by Army Order No. 246 of August 1912, the M.S.M. was to follow the Naval Long Service and Good Conduct Medal which, in turn, followed its Army counterpart. In 1979 it was ordered to take precedence over the Army Long Service and Good Conduct Medal.

DESCRIPTION

Ribbon Originally this was crimson, as was that of the ribbon of the Army L.S. and G.C. Medal, and could easily be mistaken for that of the V.C. Accordingly, by Army Order No. 183 of June 1916 the ribbons of both medals were altered to crimson with white edges. By Army Order No. 238 of July 1917 a central white stripe was added to the ribbon of the M.S.M. to distinguish it from the L.S. and G.C. Medal. By Army Order No. 172 of April 1921 a small silver rose was to be added to the ribbon, when this was worn alone, to denote the award of a bar. The ribbon is $1\frac{1}{4}$ inches wide.

Suspension Scroll bar suspender. Until about 1926 the suspender was made to swivel; thereafter it was fixed.

Obverse (Fig.A)

Reverse (Fig.B)

Bar (Fig.C)

Naming Impressed in sans-serif capital letters with number[31], rank, initials, name and regiment or corps.

Copies and Fakes None has been seen.

VERIFICATIONS AND CITATIONS

All awards (except honorary awards to foreigners) were published in the *London Gazette*. Awards made for gallantry appear with a statement to the effect that they are for "gallantry in the performance of military duty". The majority of the remainder are for "valuable services"; some, however, are for "devotion to duty" (see above) while a relative few merely recite the fact of award without particularising the services. The theatre in which the award was gained is frequently given and, in the case of awards to British personnel, from *L.G.* 17th September 1917 the recipient's home town. Names are indexed, without differentiation as to the services, under the medal heading in the "State Intelligence" portion of the quarterly indices. The only citations appearing are for gallantry and are in respect of the following:

Sergeant J. Beresford, 3rd Bn. King's Royal Rifle Corps, *L.G.*, 18th February 1921 (Bar – Waziristan)

Private A. W. W. Biddlecombe, 2nd Bn. Dorsetshire Regiment, *L.G.*, 15th March 1921 (India)

Private (Acting Sergeant) T. J. Coleman, Royal Army Service Corps, *L.G.*, 11th July 1924 (Bar – Constantinople)

Lance-Corporal E. J. Dickinson, Royal Corps of Signals, *L.G.*, 15th February 1927 (Waziristan)

2nd Corporal (Acting Sergeant) W. Gallagher, Royal Army Ordnance Corps, *L.G.*, 15th March 1921 (Mesopotamia)

Private F. W. G. Gollop, 2nd Bn. Dorsetshire Regiment, *L.G.*, 15th March 1921 (India)

Private (Acting Lance-Sergeant) W. J. Jewell, Royal Army Ordnance Corps, *L.G.*, 15th March 1921 (Mesopotamia)

Signalman G. H. Jones, Royal Corps of Signals, *L.G.*, 11th July 1924 (Thrace)

Private T. E. Jones, Royal Army Service Corps, *L.G.*, 29th July 1921 (Egypt)

Staff Sergeant J. McCann, Royal Artillery attached Supply and Transport Corps, *L.G.*, 27th September 1920 (Mesopotamia)

31. The number is omitted on awards of the M.S.M. with annuity.

Sapper A. McCulloch, 8th Bn. Canadian Railway Troops, *L.G.*, 13th July 1920 (France)

Staff Sergeant M. B. Matheson, Indian Army Ordnance Corps, *L.G.*, 27th May 1927 (India)

Lance-Corporal (Acting Sergeant) J. Stonehouse, Royal Engineers, *L.G.*, 28th September 1921 (Mesopotamia)

Sub-Conductor G. E. Turner, Indian Army Ordnance Corps, *L.G.*, 27th May 1927 (India)

Private (Acting Sergeant) J. M. Wyper, 1st Bn. Highland Light Infantry, *L.G.*, 13th July 1920 (India)

1st Class Ganger Yen Teng Fen, 130th Chinese Labour Company, *L.G.*, 13th July 1920 (France)

Many of the original First World War recommendations for men of the R.F.C. serving in France and Belgium are to be found in the Honours and Awards files in the Public Record Office series AIR 1. In general it is easier to trace a recommendation through the files of HQ R.F.C./R.A.F. rather than through formation/unit files which, in any case, have not all been preserved. Sainsbury (see Bibliography) lists all recipients of the medal for gallantry and devotion to duty and reproduces citations for 71 of the former, most of which have not hitherto been published. Johnson and Pickford (see also Bibliography) in their own limited spheres reproduce some citations for valuable services.

NUMBERS AWARDED

Except for honorary awards to foreigners, the following figures have been obtained by counting the entries in the *London Gazette*. Some of the citations for valuable services reproduced by Johnson and Pickford (see above) contain elements of gallantry e.g. bringing up supplies under fire over long periods in action, and no doubt the same applies to those noted in the *Gazette* as being for devotion to duty. In consequence the line between awards for gallantry and those ostensibly for other services is difficult to draw. The figures for honorary awards have been obtained from the lists published by the War Office dated between 23rd September 1918 (No. 28) and 4th November 1920 (No. 68). All such awards appear to be for valuable services. However, we have been unable to find lists Nos. 42, 46, 47 and 52 and the summary is therefore incomplete to the extent of any awards in the missing lists.

Medals for Gallantry

	1917	1918	1919	1920	1921	1924	1927	Totals
United Kingdom	128	100[32]	117[33]	5	6	1	1	358
Australia	14	10	4	—	—	—	—	28
British West Indies	—	—	2	—	—	—	—	2
Canada	3	5	14	2	1	—	—	25
Chinese Labour Corps[34]	—	—	3	4	—	—	—	7
East African Forces	1	4	2	—	—	—	—	7
Indian Army	—	—	—	—	—	—	2	2
New Zealand	3	1	—	—	—	—	—	4
South African Forces	1	—	—	—	—	—	—	1
West African Forces	1	—	—	—	—	—	—	1
Totals	151	120[35]	142	11	7	1	3	435

Medals for Devotion to Duty

	1918[36]	1919	1920[38]	1922[39]	Totals
United Kingdom	28	6[37]	109	3	146
Australia	—	2[37]	3	—	5
Canada	—	—	9	—	9
East African Forces	—	2	—	—	2
Totals	28	10	121	3	162

32. Including awards to two men of the R.A.F. – 1st Cl. AM. J. I. Hardy (*L.G.*, 6th August 1918) and Flight Sergeant E. J. O'Shea (*L.G.*, 29th August 1918).

33. Including an award to Able Seaman F. Rise, Drake Bn., R.N. Division (*L.G.*, 17th June 1919), and to Sergeant B. L. Steed, R.M. (*L.G.*, 20th August 1919).

34. Europeans 2, Chinese 5.

35. Including awards in *L.G.*, 27th June 1918 without description to Regimental Quartermaster Sergeant J. Elliott, Yeomanry (Northumberland Hussars) and Corporal A. Ashburn, Canadian Force which, according to records in the Ministry of Defence (Army Department), are for gallantry.

36. On the occasion of the sinking or damage by enemy action of Hospital Ships, Transports and Store Ships, *L.G.*, 6th July 1918.

37. During an epidemic in a prisoners of war camp, Germany, *L.G.*, 29th September 1919 (UK 1, Australia 2); exceptional devotion in the performance of military duties, *L.G.*, 28th November 1919 (UK 5).

38. In Siberia, *L.G.*, 3rd January 1920 (UK 4, Canada 4); and valuable services rendered whilst prisoners of war or interned, *L.G.*, 30th January 1920 (UK 104, Australia 3, Canada 5); exceptional devotion in the performance of military duty, *L.G.*, 11th February 1920 (UK 1).

39. And valuable services rendered whilst prisoners of war (Eastern Anatolia), *L.G.*, 29th March 1922.

Medals for services not described

United Kingdom	38
Australia	6
Canada	2
Total	46

See *L.G.s* 15th February 1917; 8th March, 11th April and 4th September 1918; and 13th April 1928 (Canada 1 late award see footnote 28). Of the awards gazetted without description on 27th June 1918, two were republished as being for gallantry in *L.G.*, 16th August 1918, while the other two (Ashburn and Elliott, see footnote 35) are known to be for gallantry. All four are included in the gallantry figures for 1918, but excluded here.

Medals for Valuable Services

	1916	1917	1918	1919	1920	1921	1922[40]	1923	1924	1925	1926	1927	1928	Totals
United Kingdom	613	1,530	5,218	13,428	638	42	19	21	13	8	1	—	—	21,531
Australia	11	39	403	711	3	1	—	—	—	—	—	—	—	1,168
Canada	23	41	355	906	9	—	—	—	—	—	—	—	—	1,334
East African Forces	—	16	53	91	1	—	—	—	—	—	—	—	—	161
Indian Army	—	157	52	229	50	13	2	7	5	—	—	—	—	515
New Zealand	3	12	95	226	—	—	—	—	—	—	—	—	—	336
South African Forces	—	10	139	153	1	—	—	—	—	—	—	—	—	303
West African Forces	—	—	—	1	—	—	—	—	—	—	—	—	—	1
Miscellaneous	—	—	—	18	—	1	—	—	—	—	—	—	—	19
Totals	650	1,805	6,315	15,763	702	57	21	28	18	8	1	—	—	25,368
Grand Totals	650	1,956	6,506	15,915	834	64	24	28	19	8	1	3	1	26,011

Honorary Awards to Foreigners

	1918	1919	1920	Totals
Belgium	14	49	15	78
France	130	243	87	460
Greece	—	6	—	6
Italy	10	4	24	38
Portugal	—	4	—	4
Rumania	—	—	56	56
Serbia	1	—	1	2
USA	3	26	6	35
Totals	158	332	189	679

Bars The following were awarded first bars:

Sergeant J. Beresford, 3rd Bn. King's Royal Rifle Corps – medal[41] *L.G.*, 14th May 1920; bar *L.G.*, 18th February 1921 (citation)

Corporal T. J. Carmody, Australian Flying Corps – medal[42] *L.G.*, 21st August 1917; bar *L.G.*, 17th June 1919[43].

Private (Acting Sergeant) T. J. Coleman, Royal Army Service Corps – medal[41] *L.G.*, 16th October 1919; bar *L.G.*, 11th July 1924 (citation)

Corporal J. Coxon, Military Mounted Police – medal[41] *L.G.*, 18th January 1919; bar *L.G.*, 20th October 1919.

Regimental Quartermaster Sergeant J. Elliott, Northumberland Hussars – medal[44] *L.G.*, 27th June 1918; bar *L.G.*, 29th August 1918.

Sergeant J. Orr, Royal Army Service Corps – medal[41] *L.G.*, 11th November 1916; bar *L.G.*, 13th February 1917.

Sergeant A. Shenton, York and Lancaster Regiment – medal[42] *L.G.*, 26th May 1917; bar *L.G.*, 19th November 1917 (in Manchester Regiment).

40. The 7 awards in *L.G.*, 8th May 1922 at p.3616 for valuable services in North and North East Persia, 1917–21, are not indexed.

41. Medal for valuable services.

42. Medal for gallantry.

43. The recommendation for Carmody's bar is in P.R.O. AIR 1/1598 (204/83/40)

44. Services for medal not described in *L.G.*; in fact for gallantry.

ILLUSTRATIVE AWARD

Lance-Corporal (Acting Sergeant) J. Stonehouse, Royal Engineers, was awarded the M.S.M. for gallantry at Mosul, Mesopotamia, on 28th June 1920. Notice of the award appeared in the *London Gazette* of 28th September 1921 together with the following citation:

"For gallant conduct and devotion to duty on the occasion of a fire amongst motor lorries at Mosul on the 28th June, 1920. Although arriving late at the scene of the fire, this N.C.O. immediately became conspicuous by his disregard of danger and for his leading of the sappers. He immediately started to look round for new points from which the fire could be attacked. On several occasions he endeavoured to get into the back of one of the lorries to remove tins of petrol and other inflammable material which had not, up till that time, caught fire, but on each occasion he was driven back by the excessive heat. By his courage and example he was responsible for getting the fire in this lorry under control."

The notice gives Stonehouse's home as Folkestone.

Chapter 30

The Meritorious
Service Medal for
The Royal Air Force,
1918–1928

ORIGIN AND DEVELOPMENT

Shortly before the formation of the Royal Air Force on 1st April 1918 a committee was constituted to advise the King whether a special decoration was needed for the new Service, and whether there should be a uniform colour for the ribbon of the Victoria Cross in substitution for the different ribbons (navy, blue; army, red) then worn with that decoration. The committee was composed of the following:

Colonel Sir Douglas Dawson, Comptroller, Lord Chamberlain's Department (Chairman)
Rear-Admiral A. F. Everett, Naval Secretary to the First Sea Lord
Lieutenant-General Sir F. J. Davies, Military Secretary to the Secretary of State for War
Rear-Admiral Mark (E. F.) Kerr, representing the Service shortly to be formed[1]
H. Farnham Burke, Norroy King of Arms

and, in a draft report[2], which was approved by the Board of Admiralty on 21st March 1918, recommended that there should be only one colour for the V.C. ribbon and that it should be red; that a decoration should be instituted for officers and warrant officers of the air force, corresponding to the Distinguished Service Cross and the Military Cross in the other two Services; and that the naval Conspicuous Gallantry Medal and Distinguished Service Medal, and the army Meritorious Service Medal and Long Service and Good Conduct Medal should be extended to the new Service. Eventually, however, only the first recommendation was accepted in its entirety and, in so far as gallantry was concerned, a range of four flying awards was devised. In a letter of 6th May 1918 from Sir Frederick Ponsonby, Keeper of the Privy Purse, to Commodore Sir Geoffrey Paine at the Air Ministry, the King approved the proposal that the new decorations should be "brought out" on his birthday[3]. Accordingly, this was done and the first awards of the Distinguished Flying Cross, the Air Force Cross, the Distinguished Flying Medal and the Air Force Medal were made in the *London Gazette* of 3rd June 1918. Since the new decorations were for gallantry in operational (D.F.C. and D.F.M.) or non-operational (A.F.C. and A.F.M.) flying only, it was evidently thought necessary to have a reward for men below commissioned rank who performed valuable non-flying services in the field. The same *Gazette*, therefore, also announced awards of the M.S.M. to men of the R.A.F. On 9th June 1918, in reply to an enquiry from Sir Douglas Dawson, the Air Ministry told him that no annuity or gratuity accompanied the medal; such questions could be dealt with after the War when the future establishment of the Service would be settled. Moreover, no Warrant for the medal had been prepared because of difficulty in agreeing with the other two Services financial provisions regarding transferees to the R.A.F.[4] Shortly afterwards the following announcement appeared in the *Gazette* of 26th June 1918:

1. Soon to become a Major-General in the R.A.F. According to *Who's Who*, Kerr wrote the memorandum on 10th October 1917 which persuaded the Cabinet to form the R.A.F.

2. See P.R.O. ADM 116/1744.

3. See P.R.O. AIR 2/59.

4. See P.R.O. AIR 2/60. No Warrant was ever made.

"His Majesty the KING has approved of the adoption of the Medal for Meritorious Service by the Royal Air Force, for the recognition of valuable services rendered in the Field by Warrant Officers, Non-Commissioned Officers and Men, as distinct from actual flying service, and the first announcement of awards of this Medal was published in the London Gazette dated 3rd June, 1918."

It is difficult to see what precisely was intended by this announcement. It might have been intended that the R.A.F. should receive the same pattern medal as the Army (which, in the event, it did not) but under a new Warrant or, perhaps less likely that the army Warrants should apply in so far as they were not inconsistent with the requirements of the new Service. In view of what was to follow it is unlikely that much detailed consideration was given in the first place (other than inter-Service wrangling about financial liability), and that matters were dealt with on the basis of expediency as they arose[5].

As indicated in the announcement, the first awards were gazetted on 3rd June 1918. These totalled 104 and, together with the new flying awards in the same *Gazette*, were described as being for "distinguished service". This formula was used in the announcement of all subsequent awards of the Air Force M.S.M. except for five gazetted on 2nd July 1918, two of which were for "Services rendered in a Theatre of War" and three[6] for "meritorious service and devotion to duty on the occasion of an outbreak of fire in a Government Establishment". While the "adopting" announcement spoke only of "valuable services" this is likely to have been interpreted so as to include gallantry because, whatever the *Gazette* notices mean, at least two such awards were made (see below). The announcement also provided that the medal was to be awarded for valuable services "in the Field". This also is capable of wide interpretation and an attempt at closer definition was made in the instructions[7] accompanying Air Ministry Monthly Order No. 746 of 1st August 1918 (which prescribed the procedure in submitting recommendations for the next New Year's Honours List). According to the instructions the medal was not available for services in the air, nor for services ashore in the United Kingdom; it could be awarded for services in "H.M. warships afloat out of harbour", or for services abroad on land or sea. In so far as the medal was not to be awarded for services ashore in the United Kingdom it is not clear whether the instructions represented a change of policy. Indeed, it is uncertain to what extent they were implemented since awards were gazetted on 3rd June 1919 for services apparently at Newhaven, and at Fishguard. However, whatever the explanation, all post-War awards were for services in operational theatres.

On 24th August 1918 the Air Ministry wrote to the Royal Mint asking if 500 M.S.M.s could be supplied for the R.A.F. and, if not, whether a die could be borrowed for use by a sub-contractor[8]. On 28th August the Mint replied saying that the work could be done and that it was understood that the medals would be of the same pattern as the military M.S.M. On 14th October the Air Ministry ordered 250 M.S.M.s of the pattern "similar to that in use in the Army". On 26th October a message was received at the Mint to the effect that Sir Cecil Harcourt Smith, the Director of the Victoria and Albert Museum and who evidently had been consulted in the matter[9], was not happy about the military effigy on the medals ordered, and was making enquiries at the Palace. Accordingly, although the medals were packed and ready for despatch, the Mint held them pending further instructions. Clearly there was a lack of communication somewhere between the parties involved because on 13th December the Air Ministry wrote to the Mint asking when the medals ordered on 14th October would be ready as by then 357 had been awarded. This letter produced a telephone call between the Mint and the Air Ministry the result being that on 18th December Brigadier-General R. H. More, Director of Air Personal Services at the Air Ministry, wrote to Sir Frederick Ponsonby asking if the medals should have the King's effigy in R.A.F. uniform. Ponsonby replied by return saying that the King thought that the

5. In passing it should be noticed that the army Long Service and Good Conduct Medal was not extended to the R.A.F. as the Dawson Committee had recommended. Instead, a corresponding medal for the R.A.F. was instituted by a Royal Warrant of 1st July 1919.

6. To Corporal M. J. Horne and 1st Class Airman E. L. Spike, both of the Australian Flying Corps, and to 1st Class Airman W. H. Howard of the R.A.F. This was for the incident at Stamford, Lincolnshire for which two United States' airmen received honorary awards of the M.S.M., see "Numbers Awarded" below.

7. See P.R.O. AIR 1/1650 (204/95/12).

8. See P.R.O. AIR 2/148, and MINT 20/615.

9. Later he was consulted about the design of the Allied Subjects' Medal.

medals should have his effigy in that uniform and, on 20th December, the Air Ministry sent a copy of Ponsonby's letter to the Mint. On 2nd January 1919 the Mint, in conjunction with the Air Ministry, commissioned Mr. Bertram Mackennal, A.R.A.[10], to produce a plaster cast, using the head which he had designed for the King's coinage, to which was to be added details of the R.A.F. uniform taken from a lay model. When the cast was completed it was sent by the Mint to the Air Ministry and, on 23rd January, Brigadier-General F. L. Festing at the Air Ministry sent it to Ponsonby. Having discussed the matter with the King, on 28th January Ponsonby replied to the effect that the R.A.F. uniform might undergo much alteration in the next two or three years, and (evidently referring to the cast) that it was difficult to see how the ribbon of a grand cross, or the collar of an order, could be worn unsupported on the shoulders; in view of these considerations, the King preferred the classical (i.e. coinage) head to be used. The production of medals with the coinage head was thereupon put in hand and 500 were despatched on 11th February following[11]. In the meantime the Air Ministry had been considering how the medals were to be named and, on 14th October 1918, wrote to Garrard & Company; Elkington & Company; and Spink & Son inviting tenders for the work of engraving the medals. In the event, the contract was awarded to Spink & Son[12]. After the design of the obverse of the medal had been settled, on 27th June 1919 the Air Council approved a ribbon having two equal stripes of red and blue, separated by a narrow white one. This was submitted to the King who objected that the design was too like that of the Mercantile Marine War Medal, and that when the green of the latter and the blue of the former had faded there would be practically no difference between the two. Accordingly, the Air Council thought again and a further pattern, to which white edges were added, was submitted to and approved by the King on 25th August following[13].

By the end of 1919 all awards for the First World War had been made. However, operations had begun e.g. in Afghanistan, or were continuing e.g. in Russia, and further awards for services in various theatres were made until 1924. In the meanwhile, the institution of the Medals of the Order of the British Empire for Gallantry, and for Meritorious Service, on 29th December 1922 had rendered the M.S.M. redundant, at least for gallantry. Even before this the Munro Committee on "Honours and Awards in War" in its Report of 24th May 1922 had recommended the abolition of the M.S.M. except as an award, with annuity, for old soldiers[14], and work on the preparation of a Royal Warrant for the Air Force M.S.M. was suspended[15]. However, it was thought proper to preserve some rights of transferees from the Army and Royal Marines and in Air Ministry Weekly Order No. 637 of 4th September 1924 the regulations relating to the award of the Air Force M.S.M. with annuity were finally settled. The medal and annuity were limited to men who had previously served in the Army or Royal Marines and who had re-engaged, prior to their transfer to the R.A.F., to complete time for pension. Provided that they qualified by rank and service such men were to be placed on the Army or Royal Marine Register, as appropriate, for consideration for the grant of the medal and annuity from Air Force funds[16]. In February 1925 the War Office made certain proposals regarding awards of the Medals of the Order of the British Empire which the Permanent Secretary to the Treasury circulated to both the Admiralty and the War Office[17]. The proposals included a provision that the M.S.M. should cease to be awarded for gallantry, but that it should be retained as a reward, without annuity, for valuable services, and as an award with annuity as it always had been. The view of the Admiralty was that it would be better to abolish the M.S.M. altogether except as an award with annuity for soldiers. The matter was discussed at an inter-Departmental conference on 23rd July 1926 and eventually the Admiralty view was adopted. However, the question was shelved until the Ponsonby Committee on Honours and Awards had reported. Eventually, in Air Ministry Weekly Order No. 400 of 7th June 1928 it was announced, *inter alia*, that the Royal Air Force Meritorious Service Medal had ceased to exist as a separate award, save in so far as it remained issuable with annuity to trans-

10. A well known sculptor who was responsible, *inter alia*, for the memorial tomb of King Edward VII at St. George's Chapel, Windsor.

11. See P.R.O. MINT 16/4.

12. See P.R.O. AIR 2/148.

13. See *ibid* which contains the Submissions.

14. At the time of the Report the original Medal of the Order (instituted on 4th June 1917) was still in existence and had been awarded both for gallantry and for meritorious service.

15. See the quotation in P.R.O. AIR 2/60 (minute of 4th August 1928).

16. This seems to have been the result of a compromise reached after a long wrangle between the finance branches of the three Services concerned, see P.R.O. AIR 2/243. Apparently it was intended that the men would work their way up the Register concerned, as if the annuity was to be paid from the fund to which it related, but when the vacancy occurred, the medal would be provided by the Air Ministry, and the annuity found from Air Force funds.

17. See P.R.O. ADM 116/2483.

Fig.A: The Meritorious Service Medal for The Royal Air Force, obverse.

Fig.B: The Meritorious Service Medal for The Royal Air Force, reverse.

18. See *ibid* where there is a sideswipe against the Air Ministry.

19. Possibly with provision for annuities for non-transferees as well.

20. See *L.G.*, 22nd November 1929, p.7,529. It was shown after the Royal Marine M.S.M. but before the R.A.F. Long Service and Good Conduct Medal (instituted on 1st January 1919 and hence a later award).

21. See P.R.O. AIR 2/148.

ferees from the Army and the Royal Marines. How this decision was reached is not clear. It was in advance of the King's approval to the Submission of 20th June 1928 made jointly by the First Lord of the Admiralty and the Secretary of State for War in respect of the military and naval M.S.M.s (op. cit.) and there is some indication that the Air Ministry had been making difficulties, at least as far as the recommendations of the Munro Committee were concerned[18]. It may be, however, that since complete agreement eventually had been reached in the matter and because there had been no Royal Warrant instituting the Air Force M.S.M., that award could be abolished as informally as it had been "adopted".

As with the naval M.S.M. it is difficult to say whether the "adopting" announcement authorised the limited appropriation by the R.A.F. of what had been a military award, or whether it created an exclusively Air Force M.S.M. The doubts arising from the initial announcement itself have been discussed above. Certain factors, however, tend to show that, whatever the original intention, it was to be regarded as a separate award. Thus it had a different obverse, and, unlike its naval counterpart, a different ribbon. Moreover, it is clear that until the Munro Committee reported it had been intended to make a separate Royal Warrant[19], while the Air Ministry Order abolishing it except as an award with annuity refers to it as a separate award. Finally, again unlike the naval M.S.M., it was accorded a separate order of precedence in wearing although this did not occur until later[20]. All in all it is probably convenient to treat the Air Force M.S.M. as a separate award since any attempt to strike a balance between the conflicting factors summarised above would merely be academic.

The M.S.M. was re-introduced into the R.A.F. from 1st December 1977 as a reward for airmen and airwomen of the rank of substantive sergeant or above who hold the L.S. and G.C. medal and who have completed 27 years qualifying service (23 years where service is terminated due to disability or redundancy). Candidates must have rendered "good, faithful, valuable and meritorious service, with irreproachable character and conduct", and their conduct must have been assessed as "exemplary" since the date of award of the L.S. and G.C. medal. No more than 70 awards may be made annually. The medal and ribbon are as for the Army M.S.M. and it takes precedence over the R.A.F. L.S. and G.C. Medal.

DESCRIPTION

Ribbon 1¼ inches wide, dark blue and red with white edges and a central white stripe.

Suspension Swivelling, scroll bar suspender.

Obverse (Fig.A).

Reverse (Fig.B).

Bar No bars were awarded.

Naming The original contract was awarded to Spink & Son (see above), and the naming was carried out in large, seriffed capital letters. By 24th December 1919 Spink had named 749 medals[21]. By 1921 the medals were being impressed in thin sans-serif capital letters.

Copies and Fakes None has been found.

VERIFICATIONS AND CITATIONS

All awards appear in the *London Gazette*, the names being indexed (together with Army, and later, Navy recipients) under the medal heading in the "State Intelligence" portion of the quarterly indices. In 1918 and 1919 the recipient's home town is usually given and, for just over half the awards, the theatre in which the award was gained. Thereafter only the theatre is given. With the possible exception of three of the awards gazetted on 2nd July 1918 (see above) the entries do not indicate what awards were made for gallantry. There are no citations.

Details of many awards are preserved in the Public Record Office in the series AIR 1 which contains the First World War recommendations for men of the R.A.F. serving in France and Belgium. The recommendations (not all of which gave rise to awards) are contained in the Honours and Awards files in the series. In them we have found only two awards which were for specific acts of gallantry[22] although a number are on the borderline by including reference to prolonged periods under fire (e.g. by observation balloon ground staff). Where only the date of award is known it is preferable to search for the recommendation in the files of HQ R.A.F. which are arranged according to date; where the formation or unit is known the corresponding files may be consulted first although not all have been preserved. The majority of original Submissions to the King are to be found in the series AIR 30; in these only the M.S.M.s for Mesopotamia 1920 have citations[23].

NUMBERS AWARDED

The following summary of the *London Gazette* entries totals 872 excluding cancellations. Where the entry does not give the theatre of operations for which the award was made, this has been obtained from the Ministry of Defence (Air Force Department).

1918	116	(Adriatic 3; Africa, East 1; Canada 1; Egypt 11; France 81; Italy 8; Russia 4; Salonika 4; United Kingdom 3 – outbreak of fire, see above).
1919	634	(Aegean 11; Dunkirk 33; Egypt 76; Flanders 6; France and Independent Air Force 395; India 4; Italy 17; Mediterranean 7; Mesopotamia 25; Paris 4; Russia, North 30; Russia, South 6; Salonika 10; Vendôme 2; United Kingdom 8).
1920	79	(Afghanistan 3; Baltic 5; Kurdistan 10; Mesopotamia 1; North West Frontier 5; Somaliland 10; Russia 45).
1921	22	(Mesopotamia 17; Waziristan 5).
1922	8	(Iraq).
1924	13	(Iraq 4; Kurdistan 8; Waziristan 1).

In addition, honorary awards to foreigners were made in the Air Ministry Lists of 19th July and 10th December 1919 as follows:

France	7
Greece	4
Italy	1
Slavo-British Aviation Corps ...	1
U.S.A.	4

Of these 4 were for gallantry to:

Sergeants M. E. Dudley and H. E. Lewis, 11th American Aero Squadron "for gallant conduct and devotion to duty on 23rd March, 1918, at Stamford, Northamptonshire." (sic.) (19th July 1919)[24].

Acting Corporal L. E. Meckel, 163rd American Aero Squadron "for gallant conduct and devotion to duty on 12th June, 1918, at Narborough, Norfolk." (19th July 1919).

Seaman Mechanist (Stoker) Vittorio Policisto, late Italian Royal Navy "for gallant conduct on 26th July, 1919, at Albenga, Italy, in rescuing a British aviator who was in imminent danger of drowning." (10th December 1919).

22. *I.e.* to Air Mechanic 1st Class L. Betteridge (see "Illustrative Award"), and to A.C.1. J. W. Coultas (*L.G.*, 3rd June 1919) for gallantry when an observation balloon broke loose, see P.R.O. AIR 1/1511 (204/58/12). There may be others.

23. See P.R.O. AIR 30/46. The awards were gazetted on 28th October 1921.

24. This was for the outbreak of fire at a Government Establishment for which awards were made to men of the Australian Flying Corps and the R.A.F., see above.

ILLUSTRATIVE AWARD

Air Mechanic 1st Class Leonard Betteridge was awarded the M.S.M. in the *London Gazette* of 3rd December 1918. No other details are given except that the award was for services in France, and that his home was at Monmouth. The original recommendation is, however, preserved in the Public Record Office[25] and was made on 11th August 1918 by the Officer commanding 9th Wing R.A.F. in the following terms:

> "On the night 26/27th July 1918 at 12.40a.m. this Airman's Lorry, which was loaded with 300 gallons of petrol, 16 gallons of B.B. Oil, and 30lbs of grease caught fire (burst into flames and completely destroyed the lorry[26]).
>
> At the time of the outbreak the lorry was parked close to houses billetted with troops, a Farm-house inhabited by French Civilians, and outhouses stacked with hay. The above mentioned airman, seeing that the fire could not be put out and would certainly set the adjacent buildings on fire, immediately turned the petrol on, started up the engine, and drove the lorry about 200 yards away into open country.
>
> By his prompt and courageous action, this Airman, undoubtedly averted a dangerous fire, which would probably have caused loss of life to both troops and civilians."

25. See P.R.O. AIR 1/1033 (204/5/1434) which is the Honours and Awards file of H.Q., R.A.F. for the period 1st April 1918 to 31st August 1918. The corresponding file of 9th Wing (204/208/19) is not in the P.R.O. series. There is no Submission for Betteridge in P.R.O. AIR 30/34 (Submissions to the King 1918).

26. The words given here in parentheses have been added in ink to the original typescript recommendation.

Chapter 31

The Meritorious Service Medal for The Royal Navy, 1919–1928

ORIGIN AND DEVELOPMENT

Although the M.S.M. had been instituted for the Army in 1845 as an award, with annuity, for sergeants[1] no corresponding award was established for 1st class petty officers of the Fleet. The reason for this is probably that, at the time, captains of ships engaged and rated seamen locally for the duration of a commission, which usually lasted three years, and hence there was no concept of continuous service. Matters were otherwise in the Royal Marines into which men were enlisted for a fixed period. Accordingly, by an Order in Council of 15th January 1849, a Royal Marine M.S.M. was instituted for award to sergeants under conditions similar to those established for the Army[2]. At the same time it was decided to make some provision for petty officers of the Fleet to whom a limited number of gratuities (£7 for a 1st class petty officer; £5 for a 2nd class petty officer) might be awarded on a ship being paid off[3]. It was not until four years later that provision was made, *inter alia*, for the central recruitment of men and the introduction of continuous service engagements and, by then, the time for instituting a naval M.S.M. may have been thought past.

Thus matters stood until almost the end of the First World War. In May and June 1918 doubt had been expressed at the Admiralty as to whether some recent awards of the D.S.M. had come strictly within the terms of the instrument creating that medal which spoke of services "in action" and "under fire". Accordingly, it was decided that future recommendations for the medal would be confined to services in the presence of the enemy, including the known presence of mines[4]. It so happened that, in circulating fresh instructions regarding the Army M.S.M. on 10th August 1918 (see Chapter 29), the War Office sent a "complimentary" copy to the Admiralty[5]. This evidently caused the Admiralty to consider whether the scope of the existing naval awards was adequate. Accordingly, on 11th October 1918, the Admiralty wrote to the War Office to the effect that the Lords Commissioners had under consideration the desirability of adopting some form of reward for "cases of arduous and meritorious service both afloat and ashore, and acts of specific gallantry, not in the actual presence of the enemy, which cannot appropriately be rewarded by the D.S.M.", and asking if the Army Council would have any objection to the Navy adopting the M.S.M. and ribbon for such service, or for acts of gallantry[6]. It was proposed that the medal should be limited to chief petty officers and below in the Royal Navy, to warrant officers and below in the Royal Marines, and to others holding corresponding positions in the Naval Service (including the Women's Royal Naval Service)—

> "(i) For arduous and specially meritorious service either afloat or ashore not in action with the enemy;
> (ii) For a specific act of gallantry in the performance of his or her duty when not in the presence of the enemy."

A bar was to be awarded to a recipient who performed a second act of gallantry, or such an act "performed by a Petty Officer or man who has already obtained the medal for long and meritorious service." The latter provision was quite

1. This term included non-commissioned ranks above sergeant there being, at the time, no warrant officers in the Army.

2. Admiralty Circular No. 47 of 16th January 1849.

3. Order in Council of 15th January 1849 and Admiralty Circular No. 46 of 16th January 1849. The gratuity was not to be awarded if the petty officer concerned was recommended for the Long Service and Good Conduct Medal to which a gratuity already attached. Good conduct badges were also introduced which attracted an increase in pay.

4. See P.R.O. ADM 116/1744.

5. Attaching a copy of the December 1916 instructions which do not seem to have been copied to the Admiralty when they were first issued.

6. See P.R.O. WO 32/4968.

extraordinary since there was no Naval M.S.M. for long and meritorious service, nor by the terms of the letter was it suggested that there should be[7]. Indeed, it seems to have been taken almost *verbatim* from the War Office letter of 11th December 1916 (see Chapter 29) which itself was, in part, *ultra vires* the Warrant which it purported to explain. The Admiralty letter went on to say that, for the purposes of the M.S.M., it was intended that (i) above should include service in waters where submarines were known to be operating or mines to have been laid, while in (ii) gallantry in air raids should be considered "not in the face of the enemy". Moreover, the M.S.M. and not the D.S.M. would be regarded as the appropriate award in cases of minesweeping on known minefields and minelaying in enemy waters, but where the service was of a particularly hazardous nature the D.S.M. would be given. Subject to the latter exception the D.S.M. for service at sea would be restricted to cases where the man had distinguished himself in action between his own vessel and a hostile ship, submarine or aircraft. The War Office did not reply immediately but on 21st October asked the Air Ministry if members of the Women's Royal Air Force were eligible for the (R.A.F.) M.S.M. The answer to this was that ". . . we have not made the women eligible and we have never contemplated doing so."[8] On 29th October 1918 the War Office replied to the Admiralty that there was no objection to the adoption of the M.S.M. by the Navy for award to sailors, marines and "others holding corresponding positions in the Naval Service", provided that the latter were eligible for naval gallantry distinctions, but that the Army Council could not agree with the proposal to award the M.S.M., if adopted from the Army, to members of the W.R.N.S[9]. In the event, matters were resolved by an Order in Council of 14th January 1919 as follows:

"AT THE COURT AT BUCKINGHAM PALACE,
The 14th day of January, 1919.
PRESENT,
THE KING'S MOST EXCELLENT MAJESTY
IN COUNCIL.

WHEREAS there was this day read at the Board a Memorial from the Right Honourable the Lords Commissioners of the Admiralty, dated the 2nd day of January, 1919, in the words following, viz.—

"Whereas by the Royal Warrant of the 19th December, 1845, a silver medal, entitled 'The Meritorious Service Medal', was created to be awarded to Sergeants who rendered distinguished or meritorious service, and by the Royal Warrant of the 10th June, 1884, was extended to all soldiers above the rank of Corporal, and by Your Majesty's Royal Warrant of the 4th October, 1916, was extended to Non-Commissioned Officers below the rank of Sergeant and to Men for valuable and meritorious service:

"And whereas by Your Majesty's Royal Warrant of the 3rd January, 1917, it is ordained that the Meritorious Service Medal may be awarded to Warrant Officers, Non-Commissioned Officers and Men who are duly recommended for the grant in respect of gallant conduct in the performance of military duty otherwise than in action against the enemy, or in saving or attempting to save the life of an officer or soldier, or for devotion to duty in a theatre of war:

"And whereas Your Majesty was graciously pleased by Your Majesty's Order in Council dated the 14th October, 1914, to establish a silver Medal, known as the Distinguished Service Medal, for such Chief Petty Officers, Petty Officers and Men of the Royal Navy, and Non-Commissioned Officers and Men of the Royal Marines, and all other persons holding corresponding positions in Your Majesty's service afloat as may at any time show themselves to the fore in action, and set an example of bravery and resource under fire, but without performing acts of such pre-eminent bravery as would render them eligible for the Conspicuous Gallantry Medal.

"And whereas we are of opinion that it would be desirable that a medal should be awarded to the above classes of Your Majesty's Navy in numerous instances of bravery or devotion to duty not in the presence of the enemy, which cannot be rewarded by the award of the Conspicuous Gallantry Medal or the Distinguished Service Medal:

7. Of course, it would have been remotely possible for, say, a transferee to the Royal Navy to have the Army or Royal Marine M.S.M. with annuity i.e. "for long and meritorious service". Moreover, the Army M.S.M. had already been awarded, but without annuity, to sailors of the R.N. Division under the war-time extensions. But the whole tenor of the Admiralty letter is that these possibilities were not considered. In the event the Order in Council instituting the M.S.M. for the Navy made no reference to a bar.

8. P.R.O. WO 32/4968, letter of 23rd October.

9. The course ultimately adopted was to award the Medal of the Order of the British Empire to them, see *L.G.*, 9th May 1919 in which 22 Medals of the Order were awarded to members of the W.R.N.S.

"We beg leave humbly to recommend that Your Majesty may be graciously pleased, by Your Order in Council, to ordain that the Meritorious Service Medal but without annuity or additional pension, may be awarded to Chief Petty Officers, Petty Officers, Men and Boys of the Royal Navy and to Warrant Officers, Non-Commissioned Officers and Men of the Royal Marines and others holding corresponding positions in the Naval Service, who may be considered deserving of award for arduous and specially meritorious service either afloat or ashore not in action with the enemy, or for a specific act of gallantry in the performance of his duty when not in the presence of the enemy, provided always that nothing in the foregoing provisions shall be deemed to apply to the Annuity Fund placed at our disposal for distribution, in annuities not exceeding £20, under the terms of Article 1193 of the Regulations for the government of Your Majesty's Naval Service as rewards for distinguished or meritorious service rendered by Sergeants, Royal Marines."

HIS MAJESTY, having taken the said Memorial into consideration, was pleased, by and with the advice of His Privy Council, to approve of what is therein proposed.

AND the Right Honourable the Lords Commissioners of the Admiralty are to give the necessary directions herein accordingly.

Almeric FitzRoy."

The first 93 awards made under the Order in Council appeared in the *London Gazette* of 15th February 1919. Of these, 56 were for services performed between 1917 and the Armistice (e.g. in minelaying vessels; in destroyers; in cruisers employed on escort, convoy and patrol duties; etc.), while for the remainder the services were described as "miscellaneous". During the remainder of that year a further 834 medals were gazetted. In a large number of cases the services were not specified in the *Gazette* notification but, where they were, the entries show that services both before and after the Armistice (e.g. in Russia; with the Mine Clearance Force; etc.[10]) were recognised.

On 18th March 1919 the Admiralty placed an order with the Royal Mint for 100 army pattern M.S.M.s, and a further order for 200 on 9th April following. These were despatched on 26th April and 10th May respectively[11]. The Accountant General of the Navy then wrote to the Commissions and Warrants Branch at the Admiralty enclosing one of the medals and asking if it was intended that the Admiralty should issue exactly the same medal as the Army. The Branch minuted that the medal, which had been adopted to meet a long-felt requirement, had been chosen to avoid the institution of a new medal; the desirability of depicting the King in naval uniform when the medal was awarded to ratings was recognised, and it was suggested that the King's pleasure in the matter should be taken[12]. After further discussion at the Admiralty, in which it emerged that in practical terms the problem could be solved by the use of the obverse die of the Naval Long Service and Good Conduct Medal, on 22nd May the matter was referred to Sir Frederick Ponsonby, Keeper of the Privy Purse, who replied that the King's approval had been given for the medal to bear the effigy in naval uniform. Accordingly, on 2nd June the Admiralty ordered 500 M.S.M.s of the naval pattern, and arrangements were made to return the army ones already issued. As a result of telephone calls between the Mint and the Admiralty on 20th and 21st June it was decided that the medals should have the scroll type suspender as used with the army M.S.M. and not the bar type used with most medals bearing the naval effigy.

During 1920 a further 87 awards were gazetted, 72 of which were for services in Russia or in the Baltic or Caspian Seas[13]. Thereafter only six more were gazetted (five of which are known to be for gallantry), the last three being in 1923 (see below). In the meanwhile, the institution of the Medals of the Order of the British Empire for Gallantry, and for Meritorious Service, on 29th December 1922 had rendered the M.S.M. redundant, at least for gallantry[14]. In February 1925 the War Office made certain proposals regarding awards of the Medals of the Order which the Permanent Secretary to the Treasury circulated to both the Admiralty and to the Air Ministry[15]. The proposals included a provision that the M.S.M. should

10. See *L. G.s*, 17th October 1919 and 11th November 1919.

11. See P.R.O. MINT 16/4.

12. See P.R.O. ADM 1/8562/175.

13. Of the remainder, 3 were among the Final Honours of the Mine Clearance Force; 7 were for "Miscellaneous Services"; and the services for 5 were not given.

14. The Report of the Munro Committee dated 24th May 1922 on "Honours and Rewards in War" had recommended the abolition of the M.S.M. except for award with annuity to old soldiers, see the quotation in P.R.O. AIR 2/60 (minute of 4th August 1928). At the time of the Report the original Medal of the Order (instituted on 4th June 1917) was still in existence and had been awarded both for gallantry and for meritorious service.

15. See P.R.O. ADM 116/2483.

cease to be awarded for gallantry, but that it should be retained as a reward, without annuity, for valuable services, and as an award with annuity as it always had been. The view of the Admiralty was that it would be better to abolish the M.S.M. altogether except as an award with annuity for soldiers. The matter was discussed at an inter-Departmental conference on 23rd July 1926 and eventually the Admiralty view was adopted. However, the matter was shelved until the Ponsonby Committee on Honours and Awards had reported and it was not until 20th June 1928 that a joint proposal by the First Lord of the Admiralty and the Secretary of State for War was submitted to the King that the extensions made during the War for the Army, and immediately after the War to the Navy, should be cancelled and that the M.S.M. should revert to its original limited function as an award with annuity for soldiers above the rank of corporal in the Army and in the Royal Marines[16]. The King's approval having been obtained, the instituting Order in Council was revoked by an Order in Council of 1st November 1928.

In retrospect it is difficult to say whether the instituting Order in Council authorised the limited adoption by the Navy of what had been a military award, or whether it created an exclusively Naval M.S.M.[17] On one hand, the Admiralty letter of 11th October 1918, and the War Office reply thereto, was written on the basis of adoption. In addition, the resulting Order in Council spoke of the M.S.M. in the sense that it was an existing medal[18] and, in the preamble, put the C.G.M. and D.S.M. in a context not dissimilar from that given the D.C.M. and M.M. in the War Office instructions of 10th August 1918. Moreover, the submission of 1928 that the M.S.M. should revert to its original exclusive function as an award with annuity for sergeants and above in the Army and Royal Marines was made jointly by the First Lord of the Admiralty and the Secretary of State for War. Finally, unlike the M.S.M. for the R.A.F., the naval M.S.M. was never given a separate precedence in the order of wearing orders, decorations and medals[19]. On the other hand, the conditions of award, notably when not for gallantry, were different. Thus for the Navy "arduous and specially meritorious service" was required; while for the Army "valuable and meritorious service" (Royal Warrant of 4th October 1916) or "devotion to duty in a theatre of war" (Royal Warrant of 3rd January 1917) were prescribed. Further, for the Navy a special obverse was eventually decided upon, only the reverse and the ribbon being common to both medals. All in all it is probably convenient to treat the Army and Navy M.S.M.s as separate awards since any attempt to strike a balance between the conflicting factors summarised above is merely academic.

The M.S.M. was re-introduced into the Royal Navy from 1st December 1977[20] as a reward for men and women of the substantive rank of petty officer (or its equivalent) and above who hold the L.S. and G.C. Medal and who have completed 27 years qualifying service (23 years where service is terminated due to disability or redundancy). Candidates must have performed "good, faithful, valuable and meritorious service" with unbroken VG (i.e. very good) conduct. No more than 59 awards may be made annually. The medal and ribbon are as for the Army M.S.M. When re-introduced the medal was to be worn after the Naval L.S. and G.C. Medal. In 1979 this was altered so that the M.S.M. precedes the L.S. and G.C. Medal.

DESCRIPTION

Ribbon As for the Army.

Suspension Swivelling, scroll bar suspender.

Obverse (Fig.A) Between 2nd June 1919 and 14th April 1920 the Admiralty ordered 1,270 medals with the naval effigy[21]. This exceeds the total gazetted by 250. Clearly, however, some stock-in-hand was necessary for replacements and future awards. Moreover, the last order was placed long before the last awards were made, or the medal itself abolished.

16. See *ibid.*

17. A similar problem arises in regard to the M.S.M. for the R.A.F.

18. Hence, on this argument, it would be unnecessary to mention the bar.

19. Its omission could, of course, have been an oversight.

20. The M.S.M. for the Royal Marines was discontinued in 1951. They are eligible for the re-introduced M.S.M.

21. See P.R.O. MINT 16/4. The orders were on 2nd June 1919 (500); 9th July 1919 (500); 5th March 1920 (250); and 14th April 1920 (20).

Fig.B: The Meritorious Service Medal for The Royal Navy, obverse.

Reverse (Fig.B).

Bar No bars were awarded.

Naming As for the contemporary Distinguished Service Medal. In most cases the inscription is more informative than the *London Gazette* entry. On some medals the inscription includes "WAR SERVICES" or "SERVICES DURING THE WAR" instead of a year, or a specific date.

Copies and Fakes None has been found.

VERIFICATIONS AND CITATIONS

All awards appear in the *London Gazette*, the names being indexed (together with Army and Air Force recipients) under the medal heading in the "State Intelligence" section of the quarterly indices. In just under half the entries no indication of the services is given. Of the remainder, the information is limited to a general heading e.g. ". . . Services in Destroyers of the Grand Fleet Flotillas between 1st July and 11th November 1918"[22]; ". . . awards approved for men of the Royal Naval Transport Service"[23]; ". . . services in the Baltic in 1919"[24]. Except for the last five awards made (see "Numbers Awarded" below) the *Gazette* entries do not indicate which, if any, awards were made for gallantry. With the exception of the material used for the "Illustrative Award" we have found no sources for citations of any awards. Surviving recipients are listed in the Navy Lists for April, July and October 1919 and January 1920. The names are listed in an incomprehensible order and include recipients of some awards made for services with the Army.

NUMBERS AWARDED

The following, totalling 1,020, has been obtained by counting the *London Gazette* entries[25], cancellations being excluded:

1919 ... 927 (pre- and post- Armistice awards; where some details are given, the latter are for mine clearance, or for services in Russia or adjacent waters)

1920 ... 87 (where details are given awards are for mine clearance, or for services in Russia or adjacent waters).

1921 ... 2 (*L.G.*, 12th July 1921 – Leading Stoker W. J. Parish – no details given; *L.G.*, 18th November 1921 – Chief Petty Officer A. Cocks – ". . . in recognition of the courage and promptitude displayed by him when a saluting gun on H.M.S. "Hawkins" misfired on 19th August, 1921").

1922 ... 1 (*L.G.*, 22nd July 1922 – Able Seaman S.Le Marinel – ". . . in recognition of his presence of mind and plucky action in dealing with a bomb at Shanghai").

1923 ... 3 (see "Illustrative Awards").

In addition, honorary awards (which were not gazetted) were made to 5 French and 6 Greek seamen in 1919/20.

ILLUSTRATIVE AWARDS

In the *London Gazette* of 30th November 1923 three sick berth ratings received the M.S.M. ". . . in recognition of their gallant services on the occasion, in September last, of the destruction by earthquake and fire of the R.N. Sick Quarters, Yokohama". The recommendations were made by Surgeon Commander W. P. Hingston, R.N.[26] (who was appointed a C.B. for his services on the same occasion), as follows:

"1. Acting Sick Berth Petty Officer ALFRED GILBERT RICHARDS (O.N. M. 2553)

Assisted me in the recovery of my wife's body. Mainly due to his efforts that it was found and recovered before the fire reached us.

22. See *L.G.*, 17th March 1919.
23. See *L.G.*, 4th July 1919.
24. See *L.G.*, 12th November 1920.
25. For the numbers awarded in each *Gazette* see the *Journal of the Orders and Medals Research Society*, Volume 12, p.208.
26. See P.R.O. ADM 1/8668/176 which contain the case papers on the earthquake of 1st September 1923. Photographs of, *inter alia*, the devastation in the Hospital area are included.

He kept everyone at their stations and supervised the carrying out of rescue work under my orders.

He never left his post until he had seen the uninjured and injured removed to a place of safety, and assisting to carry the last case, Mr. Edward Coutts, to the edge of the Bluff and helping him down the rope, although himself injured, and the flames all around him.

He was suffering from a sprained right ankle, severe bruising and contusions of the back and arms, caused by being buried in the fallen buildings.

He assisted in dressing and nursing the wounded until his injuries rendered him incapable.

He thus upheld the highest traditions of bravery and gallantry in the Royal Navy.

2. Leading Sick Berth Attendant CHARLES VICTOR EYLES (O.N. M. 5178)

Assisted the Matron and Staff Nurse at the General Hospital to recover the patients from the ruins. This completed, he returned and reported himself to me. He then carried out my orders until the R.N. Hospital grounds were untenable.

He then assisted in the transport of the injured to R.M.S. "AUSTRALIA", and worked with great self-sacrifice in that ship attending to the sick.

At all times, day and night, he readily responded to any call continuously made upon him, and took a major share in the heavy work of provisioning R.M.S. "AUSTRALIA" from R.M.S. "CANADA". His behaviour was most gallant.

3. Sick Berth Attendant WILLIAM BILTON (O.N. M. 18103)

After having been rescued from the debris, he assisted me in carrying coils of rope[27] to the assigned places. Was most helpful and cheerful at all times. Remained at his post until R.N. Hospital was untenable.

Assisted in transporting casualties to R.M.S. "AUSTRALIA".

Worked incessantly for the care and nursing of patients, and also helped in the provisioning "R.M.S. "AUSTRALIA" from the "CANADA" bearing a major share of the heavy work. His conduct was exemplary."

27. Between 400 and 500 members of the local British community had assembled on the Hospital lawn. The ropes were required to lower them to safety over a cliff onto reclaimed land.

215

Fig.A: The Military Cross, obverse, George V issue.

Chapter 32

The Military Cross

ORIGIN AND DEVELOPMENT

Until the outbreak of the First World War the normal distinctions available to the Army for gallantry in action were the V.C., D.S.O., and D.C.M. The C.S.C. had been introduced in 1901 for Warrant Officers and subordinate officers of the Fleet and in 1914, under the amended title of D.S.C., had been extended to all officers of the Royal Navy and Royal Marines under the rank of Lieutenant-Commander or its equivalent[1]. In the late autumn of 1914 consideration was given to the provision of a similar decoration for junior officers and warrant officers of the Army. The King's initial views were that its design should be similar to that of the D.S.C. but with a red and white ribbon (if that did not clash with an existing one), the general principle being that the D.S.O., D.S.C. and D.C.M. should be given for the same services but awarded acording to rank[2]; it was out of the question that the Army should have a separate D.S.C.[3] In due course, however, the King accepted that the Army should be consulted about the design of the decoration and, at the suggestion of Lord Kitchener (the Secretary of State for War), that it should be called "The Military Cross". A design was submitted to and approved, with small modifications, by the King on 18th December 1914. The King was strongly opposed to the Cross being struck in iron or black metal (as had been suggested by Lord Kitchener) which would "copy the Germans", and was of the opinion that it should be made of silver[4]. The ribbon was designed by the King and Lord Kitchener and they experienced some difficulty in finding a pattern which had not already been taken up[5]. Accordingly, the Military Cross was instituted by a Royal Warrant of 28th December 1914[6] in the following terms:

"GEORGE, R.I.

GEORGE THE FIFTH by the Grace of God of the United Kingdom of Great Britain and Ireland, and of the British Dominions beyond the Seas King, Defender of the Faith, Emperor of India, To all to whom these Presents shall come Greeting; Whereas We have taken into Our Royal consideration the distinguished services in time of War of Officers of certain ranks in Our Army; And whereas We are desirous of signifying Our appreciation of such services by a mark of Our Royal favour We do by these Presents for Us, Our heirs and successors institute and create a Cross to be awarded to Officers whose distinguished and meritorious services have been brought to Our notice.

Firstly: It is ordained that the Cross shall be designated "The Military Cross".

Secondly: It is ordained that The Military Cross shall consist of a Cross of Silver having on each arm Our Imperial Crown and bearing in the centre the letters G.R.I.

Thirdly: It is ordained that no person shall be eligible for this Decoration nor be nominated thereto unless he is a Captain, a Commissioned Officer of a lower grade, or a Warrant Officer in Our Army, or Our Indian or Colonial Military Forces, and that The Military Cross shall be awarded only to Officers of the above ranks on a recommendation to Us by Our Principal Secretary of State for War.

Fourthly: It is ordained that Foreign Officers of an equivalent rank to those above mentioned, who have been associated in Military operations with Our Army, or Our Indian or Colonial Military Forces shall be eligible for the Honorary award of The Military Cross.

Fifthly: It is ordained that the names of those upon whom We may be pleased to confer this Decoration shall be published in the *London Gazette*, and that a Register thereof shall be kept in the Office of Our Principal Secretary of State for War.

1. See Chapter 16, The Distinguished Service Cross.

2. The King had apparently overlooked the fact that, by this time, the D.S.C. was for officers below the rank of Lieutenant-Commander whose services did not reach the standard required for the D.S.O.

3. See P.R.O. WO 32/5388. What follows is taken from that source although, from internal evidence, it does not contain a record of all that transpired.

4. The Cross was, accordingly, made in silver at the Royal Mint, a specimen being submitted to the King on 12th February 1915.

5. Kitchener's original suggestion had been that the ribbon should be white with a red stripe.

6. See *L.G.*, 1st January 1915.

Sixthly: It is ordained that The Military Cross shall be worn immediately after all Orders and before all Decorations and Medals (the Victoria Cross alone excepted), and shall be worn on the left breast pendent from a ribbon of one inch and three eighths in width, which shall be in colour white with a purple stripe.

Seventhly: It is ordained that The Military Cross shall not confer any individual precedence, and shall not entitle the recipient to any addition after his name as part of his description or title.

Eighthly: It is ordained that any person whom by an especial Warrant under Our Royal Sign Manual We declare to have forfeited The Military Cross shall return the said Decoration to the Office of Our Principal Secretary of State for War, and that his name shall be erased from the Register of those upon whom the said Decoration shall have been conferred.

Lastly: We reserve to Ourself, Our heirs and successors full power of annulling, altering, abrogating, augmenting, interpreting or dispensing with these Regulations, or any part thereof, by a notification under Our Royal Sign Manual.

Given at Our Court at St. James's, this 28th day of December, one thousand nine hundred and fourteen, in the fifth year of Our Reign.

By His Majesty's Command,
KITCHENER."

The seventh Clause is significant in that a recipient was not entitled to use the letters "M.C." after his name. This restriction as to the use of the letters referred to the time-honoured custom which permitted a recipient of the V.C. or of an Order of Chivalry to add the appropriate letters after his name, a practice which had been followed in official documents and correspondence and in the Order in Council of 1901 instituting the C.S.C. (q.v.). The restriction did not find favour in the Army and was later withdrawn (see below).

The first M.C.s were gazetted on 1st January 1915 when 99 officers and warrant officers received the award[7]. In 1916 the rank of warrant officer was divided into Classes I and II and the Warrant amended accordingly[8]. Later the same year a revised Royal Warrant was approved[9] which omitted the word "honorary" when describing awards to foreign officers; introduced a bar or bars for additional services; and permitted the use of the distinctive letters. Army Order No. 290 of August 1916 authorised a silver rose emblem for wear on the ribbon, when this was worn alone, to denote the award of a bar. It is interesting to note that the institution of the bar was proposed by General Sir Douglas Haigh in a letter of 21st May 1916 addressed to Lord Kitchener. In his letter Haig pointed out that the D.S.O. was a difficult award for a junior officer to win because of the high standard required, and of its restriction (apparently in practice) to officers who held the rank at least of captain for a certain period. In consequence, repeated acts of gallantry by junior officers went unrewarded[10]. In September 1916 the King decided that, for the duration of the War, officers and ratings of the Royal Naval Division and officers and men of the Royal Marines, serving in France, should be eligible for military decorations and medals. In consequence, a number of M.C.s were awarded to naval officers. Following discussion between the Admiralty and the War Office it was agreed that an officer or rating already holding a naval decoration or medal should, if occasion arose for a further award, be recommended through naval channels for a bar to it instead of a military decoration or medal[11].

Because the wording of the original Warrant had been that the M.C. could be granted for "distinguished and meritorious services" a number of awards had been made in 1915–16 for services behind the line under circumstances which could not be regarded as under fire. There had been strong feeling in the Army that the M.C. should only be awarded for gallantry under fire and accordingly, on 1st January 1917, orders were given to all commanders in the field that the M.C. (as well as the D.S.O. and D.C.M.) should as far as possible be restricted to the "Fighting Services". These were defined as the fighting personnel of brigades, divisions, corps and army troops, together with certain ancillary services associ-

7. These included some to the Royal Flying Corps, one jemadar and four subadars of the Indian Army, and 27 warrant officers of the British Army.

8. Royal Warrant, 31st May 1916; see *L.G.*, 9th June 1916.

9. Royal Warrant, 23rd August 1916; see *L.G.*, 26th August 1916.

10. See P.R.O. WO 32/5390.

11. See P.R.O. ADM 116/1744.

Fig.B: The Military Cross, obverse, George VI issue, first type.

12. Royal Warrant, 25th June 1917; see *L.G.*, 3rd July 1917.

13. See P.R.O. WO 32/5232 and 32/5400.

14. Royal Warrant, 6th November 1920; see *L.G.*, 19th November 1920.

15. Royal Warrant, 5th February 1931; see *L.G.*, 20th March 1931.

16. In fact, the King had approved this provision in August 1918 (effective from 1st April of that year) and a number of awards were then made, see P.R.O. WO 32/4968 and AIR 2/60. His approval was notified in a War Office telegram of 6th September 1918, see P.R.O. AIR 1/1169 (204/5/2593).

17. Royal Warrant, 21st August 1939; see Army Order No. 144 of August 1939.

18. Royal Warrant, 14th April 1943; see Army Order No. 71 of April 1943.

19. Royal Warrant, 24th September 1953; see Army Order No. 113 of September 1953.

20. See Army Order No. 22 of March 1964.

21. The first awards were made in *L.G.*, 10th January 1917.

22. To Temporary Chaplain R. S. Hook, R.N.V.R. (attached R.M. Commandos) in *L.G.*, 22nd January 1946.

23. The first awards were made in *L.G.*, 1st January 1915.

24. See P.R.O. WO 32/5388.

25. *Annual Report of the Deputy Master and Comptroller of the Royal Mint (1937)*, p.53.

26. *Ibid* (1948), p.22. The award to 2nd Lieutenant J. C. Dunton, The Green Howards (*L.G.*, 10th October 1952) was of this type.

ated in battle with these formations. In June 1917 the award was extended to acting and temporary majors not above the substantive rank of captain[12]. During September 1917 proposals were under consideration as to whether there should be two classes of the D.S.O. and M.C., Class I to be for "Fighting Services" and Class II to be for "non-Fighting Services", each to be distinguished by a different ribbon or by an emblem worn on the ribbon. These proposals were not supported by the Army Council, and no further action was taken at that stage. They were again considered at a conference at the War Office in June and July 1918. The conference recommended that the D.S.O., M.C. and D.C.M. should be regarded primarily as distinctions for services in action with the enemy including air raids, bombardments etc. producing conditions equivalent to actual combat; and that some emblem should be adopted to distinguish future "immediate" awards of those decorations from awards conferred through the medium of "Honours Gazettes". Only the former recommendation was accepted by the Army Council and it was notified generally on 1st August 1918; in fact, it had little practical result since the instructions of 1st January 1917 had already largely confined award of the distinctions concerned to services in action[13].

In 1920 a revised Royal Warrant[14] provided that the M.C. was to be a reward for "gallant and distinguished services in action"; gave details of certain pecuniary awards for other ranks, and defined the conditions for forfeiture and restoration in certain eventualities. A further revised Royal Warrant published in 1931[15] extended the M.C. to officers and warrant officers of "Our Air Forces" for gallant and distinguished services in action on the ground[16] and also authorised a miniature version of the Cross to be worn on occasions when miniature medals are worn. It also drew the forfeiture clause rather more widely by omitting reference to specific acts of misconduct and making the power to order forfeiture completely discretionary. This followed a recommendation by the Interdepartmental Rewards Committee that all awards for gallantry, except in cases of extreme infamy, should be regarded as irrevocable; hence it was unnecessary to limit the power, as had been done before, by prescribing for particular circumstances. The 1931 Warrant was amended in 1939 to make provision for the short-lived rank of Warrant Officer, 3rd Class[17], and in 1943 was further amended to include the Home Guard and to alter the procedure by which Dominion recommendations were to be made[18]. In 1953 eligibility for the M.C. was extended to substantive majors by an amending Warrant[19] which also made minor alterations due to constitutional changes in the Commonwealth. By a Royal Warrant of 24th March 1964 the functions performed by the Secretary of State for War in regard to the M.C. were transferred, *inter alia*, to the Secretary of State for Defence[20].

The M.C. has been awarded to officers and warrant officers of Colonial, Dominion, Commonwealth and foreign countries, as well as to those of the Indian Army. A number of Royal Navy officers received it during the First World War[21], although apparently only one such award was made in the Second World War[22]. Awards have also been made to the Royal Flying Corps[23] and to the Royal Air Force.

DESCRIPTION

Ribbon White, $1\frac{3}{8}$ inches wide, with a $\frac{1}{2}$ inch central purple stripe.

Suspension By a small oval ring from a plain flat suspender.

Obverse The Cross was designed by E. C. Collings, Herald Painter to King George V[24]. There are four obverses as follows:

1. George V (Fig.A) This appears on all issues until 1937, including those awarded during the short reign of Edward VIII.

2. George VI first type (Fig.B) This was first struck in 1937[25].

3. George VI second type (Fig.C) This was first struck in 1948[26], although a Cross dated 1948 is known which has the previous obverse.

Fig.C: The Military Cross, obverse, George VI issue, second type.

Fig.D: The Military Cross, obverse, Elizabeth II issue.

Fig.E: Bar to the Military Cross.

4. Elizabeth II (Fig.D) This was issued from about 1953[27].

Reverse Until about 1938[28] this was plain but thereafter and until at least 1957[29] the year of the award was engraved at the bottom of the lower arm. An Elizabeth II issue has been seen with "1964" engraved in the centre of the reverse.

Bar (Fig.E) The design of the bar has remained the same since institution; from about 1938 the reverse is engraved with the year of the award.

Naming The Cross is issued unnamed although the reverse is sometimes found unofficially engraved with varying details of the recipient.

Copies and Fakes Copies of all four issues exist. All are fractionally smaller and rather thinner than the originals; the arches of the crowns are sometimes too steep and close to the ends of the arms of the Cross; the cyphers and crowns are not well finished; the ribbon bar is narrower; and the suspender link is of smaller gauge. On the George VI copies the top crown is not square below the suspender link and the reverse of the lower arm on these and the Elizabeth II copy is without a year date. Occasionally copies are found named and/or dated, and sometimes in a group of renamed or partly renamed medals. For recent copies see the Note on p.xx.

VERIFICATIONS AND CITATIONS

All awards can be verified from the *London Gazette* except for some made to foreigners. During the First World War many of the early awards and those given for services over a period do not have citations. The first citations appear in the *London Gazette* of 18th February 1915; this is, however, a "mixed" Gazette, the majority of awards published in it being without citations. The names of recipients appear under the "Military Cross" heading in the "State Intelligence" section of the quarterly indices of the Gazette. Frequently the award and citation are separated and it is then necessary to search in later indices to find the citation. A comparison of the citations reproduced in Johnson (see Bibliography) with the corresponding entries in the *London Gazette* disclose that the citations submitted were considerably edited before publication in the Gazette. From 1918 onwards some awards are accompanied by the name of the theatre in which the services were performed and this practice continued with most of those gazetted between the Wars. Since 1921 no citations have been published except for some to the R.A.F. during the Second World War and a number for recent operations, e.g. in the Congo and Vietnam. No citations have been published since 1968. Many of the original First World War recommendations for members of the R.F.C. and R.A.F. serving in France and Belgium are preserved in the Honours and Awards files in the Public Record Office series AIR 1. Where only the date of award is known it is preferable to search for the recommendation in the files of H.Q. R.F.C./R.A.F. which are arranged according to date; where the formation or unit is known the corresponding files may be consulted first although not all have been preserved. With the earlier Second World War awards the theatre is sometimes omitted, possibly on grounds of security, but after a short time it reappeared and is now always given. In January 1942 the Gazette indices were altered and the names of recipients consolidated into a comprehensive quarterly list headed "Honours, Decorations and Medals". A "Military Cross" heading was however retained in the "State Intelligence" section which merely lists the pages on which awards are to be found. The latter was often badly done and some references are corrupt or omitted altogether. Moreover, on occasion references appear under the wrong medal heading although the nominal indices seem reliable. There is at least one instance of a bar being gazetted before the Cross[30]. A few errors occur in the 1920–1939 indices. In January 1942 some awards were accompanied by the full address of the recipient. The next month this was reduced to the appropriate home town, but even then this was not always given. This practice ceased after the end of the Second World War. Where no citation is given in the *London Gazette*, on occasion some details can be found in unit or formation histories, or in War Office

27. *Ibid* (1953), p.33.
28. The award to Captain R. C. Cottrell-Hill, The Border Regiment (*L.G.*, 15th July 1938) has the year impressed in rather small figures.
29. *E.g.*, the award to Major O. J. Mirylees, The Royal Leicestershire Regiment (*L.G.*, 28th May 1957).
30. Captain W. Scott-Plummer, R.H.A.; bar to M.C. in *L.G.*, 30th December 1941; M.C. in *L.G.*, 24th February 1942.

press releases. Extracts from the latter frequently found their way into local news-papers. Until April 1920 lists of surviving recipients appear in the Supplement to the Monthly Army List published in January, April, July and October.

NUMBERS AWARDED

First World War The official statistics (see Bibliography) cover the period from August 1914 to May 1920 and thus extend beyond the campaigns against the Central Powers. The figures given are:

	Services in the Field	Services in connection with the War
M.C.	37,081	23
– 1st bars	2,983	1
– 2nd bars	168	1
– 3rd bars	4	—

Those for services in connection with the War include awards for the Easter Rising, air raids, etc. For the period 1914–1918 Wingate (see Bibliography) gives the totals as 37,031 Crosses with 2,952 first bars, 167 second bars and four third bars. These last were awarded to:

	London Gazette for Third Bar
Captain P. Bentley, 5th Battalion, Yorkshire Light Infantry, T.F.	1st February 1919
Lieutenant H. A. Gilkes, 21st Battalion, London Regiment	1st February 1919
Temporary Captain C. G. Timms, Royal Army Medical Corps	1st February 1919
Acting Captain F. V. Wallington, Royal Field Artillery	16th September 1918

At least 140 naval officers of the Royal Naval Division[31] were awarded the M.C.; of these, 8 received one bar, and 1 received two bars. It is interesting to note that the D.C.M. awarded in the *London Gazette* of 19th August 1916 to Company Sergeant Major W. Bell, Royal Lancaster Regiment, was cancelled and replaced by the M.C. in the *London Gazette* of 26th September 1916.

781 Warrant Officers received the M.C., of whom three were awarded first bars in that rank[32].

We have traced a number of honorary awards to foreigners sponsored by the War Office, and later by the Air Ministry. Some War Office awards were published in *L.G.*, 16th November 1915; thereafter they appeared in printed lists dated between May 1916 and 4th November 1920. The first four lists were unnumbered, the remainder being numbered from 3 to 68 of which we have been unable to find nos. 23, 42, 46, 47 and 52. The Air Ministry list is dated 10th December 1919. The following summary, in which all are War Office awards except where noted, is therefore incomplete to the extent of any in the missing War Office lists:

Arab Army	12	
Belgium	232	(1 Air Ministry)
China	3	
Czechoslovakia	60	
France	1,425	(75 in *L.G.* 16th November 1915; 7 Air Ministry; plus 1 first bar)
Greece	65	
Italy	575	(4 Air Ministry)
Japan	34	
Montenegro	2	
Portugal	37	

31. See the roll in *The Journal of the Orders and Medals Research Society*, Vol.19, p.241 *et seq.*

32. *I.e.* to Sergeant Majors P. Coulter, Cheshire Regiment (*L.G.s*, 3rd June 1918 and 8th March 1919), F. W. Hatt, Royal Dublin Fusiliers (*L.G.s*, 1st January 1917 and 16th September 1918), and T. Sordy, Durham Light Infantry (*L.G.s*, 4th June 1917 and 16th September 1918).

Roumania	... ...	69	
Russia	... ...	6	
Serbia	... ...	68	(plus 1 first bar)
Slavo-British Aviation Corps	... ...	1	(Air Ministry)
U.S.A.	... ...	320	(plus 4 first bars)

Total: 2,909

By Royal Warrants of 12th September 1916 and 12th February 1920 the M.C. was conferred on the cities of Verdun[33] and Ypres[34].

1920–1939 From June 1920 to December 1939 the following 349 M.C.s were gazetted:

1920 ... 80 (1 Aden; 21 Afghan War 1919; 4 Black Sea; 1 India (R.A.F.); 18 late awards (1 R.N.V.R.); 6 Mesopotamia; 4 Somaliland; 2 South Russia; 23 Waziristan)

1921 ... 85 (5 Black Sea; 1 late award; 44 Mesopotamia/Iraq; 3 minor operations in Indian Empire and adjacent territories; 1 Palestine; 1 Siberia; 1 South Persia; 29 Waziristan)

1922 ... 9 (1 Black Sea; 1 Kurdistan; 1 Southern and Western Dafur; 6 Waziristan)

1923 ... 10 (1 Egypt; 1 Malabar; 1 Razmak; 7 Waziristan)

1924 ... 7 (2 Kurdistan; 5 Waziristan)

1925 ... 6 (1 Khartoum; 3 Kurdistan (2 R.A.F.); 1 Waziristan; 1 theatre not given (? India))

1926 ... 5 (Kurdistan, 1 R.A.F.)

1927 ... 1 (Iraq)

1928 ... 3 (1 China, March 1927; 2 Iraq)

1930 ... 3 (North West Frontier)

1932 ... 12 (8 Burma; 3 North West Frontier; 1 restored award)

1933 ... 5 (1 Chitral; 3 Northern Kurdistan (1 R.A.F.); 1 North West Frontier)

1934 ... 2 (North West Frontier)

1935 ... 6 (1 Burma; 4 North West Frontier; 1 restored award)

1936 ... 22 (1 Abyssinia – Addis Ababa; 4 North West Frontier; 17 Palestine (4 R.A.F.)

1937 ... 28 (7 North West Frontier; 3 Palestine; 18 Waziristan)

1938 ... 25 (6 North West Frontier; 16 Palestine; 3 Waziristan)

1939 ... 40 (2 North West Frontier; 28 Palestine; 3 Waziristan; 7 theatre not given (? Palestine)

In addition the following 31 first bars were gazetted:

1920 ... 5 (2 Afghan War 1919; 1 late award; 1 Somaliland; 1 Waziristan)

1921 ... 15 (6 Mesopotamia; 1 Palestine; 8 Waziristan)

1923 ... 1 (Waziristan)

1925 ... 3 (2 Khartoum; 1 theatre not given (? India)

1932 ... 2 (Chitral and North West Frontier)

1933 ... 1 (Chitral)

1935 ... 1 (Burma)

1937 ... 1 (Waziristan)

1938 ... 2 (Palestine)

Second World War Wingate gives the total awarded between 1939 and 1945 as 10,386 Crosses with 482 first bars and 24 second bars. All awards gazetted in 1946 appear to be for the Second World War except for 38 M.C.s (including one to the Royal Air Force) and 1 first bar which were for South East Asia. However, in a number of cases the *Gazette* announcement contains no identifying details. 59 army warrant officers received the M.C., as did one officer of the Royal Navy[35]. The following 81 Air Force awards were gazetted:

Royal Air Force	... ...	65	(including 6 to the R.A.F. Regiment; 1 for South East Asia; excluding 1 first bar[36])
Royal Australian Air Force	... ...	7	
Royal Canadian Air Force	... ...	5	
Royal New Zealand Air Force	... ...	2	
South African Air Force	... ...	2	

33. See P.R.O. WO 32/4570 and *The Times* of 15th September 1916, p.5
34. See P.R.O. WO 32/4571 and *The Times* of 20th May 1920, p.14.
35. Temporary Chaplain R. S. Hook, R.N.V.R. (attached R.M. Commandos), *L.G.*, 22nd January 1946.
36. Flight Lieutenant F. E. E. Yeo-Thomas, *L.G.* 16th May 1944 who was later also awarded the G.C.

The R.A.F. awards include that to Flying Officer G. A. Cork for an action at sea in April 1941 when on passage between Alexandria and Crete[37]. 438 honorary M.C.s and 3 first bars were awarded to foreigners as follows:

Belgium	35
China	3
Czechoslovakia	7
Free French Forces	135 (including 2 air force)
Greece	9
Netherlands	8
Norway	19 (and 3 first bars)
Poland	62
U.S.A.	160

1947–1979 A summary of the 643 Crosses and 20 first bars gazetted during this period is as follows:

Theatre	London Gazettes	Crosses	First bars
Arabian Peninsula	1949–1976	47 (6 R.A.F.)	1
Borneo	1963–1967	46	3
Brunei	1963	2	1
Congo	1961–1962	6	—
Cyprus	1957–1959	5	—
Kenya	1955–1956	11	—
Korea	1950–1954	182	7
Late awards	1947	79 (1 R.A.F.)	1
Malaya	1949–1959	137	14
Malaysia	1965–1966	2	—
Near East	1957	5	1
Northern Ireland	1972–1979	38	—
Palestine	1948	11	—
South East Asia	1947	8	1
Vietnam	1965–1972	64	1

Between 1949 and 1952 inclusive 165 Crosses and nine first bars were gazetted, and between 1953 and 1979, 380 Crosses and 19 first bars.

ILLUSTRATIVE AWARD

Company Sergeant Major Joseph Barwick, 1st Battalion, Scots Guards, was awarded the Military Cross in the *London Gazette* of 18th February 1915 at p.1,691 where the entry appears without citation. However, full details of Barwick's heroism together with two reconstructed illustrations are given in Volume 1 of *Deeds that Thrill the Empire* (see Bibliography). The narrative is too long for reproduction here, and describes several acts of gallantry. On 26th October 1914 near Gheluvelt, Barwick was engaged in sniping from a damaged cottage. The Germans broke through on the right of his battalion and, seeing this, Barwick ran back in full view of the enemy, and under fire, to warn his company commander. He then volunteered to go back to battalion headquarters for reinforcements, and made the journey there and back under heavy fire. As a result of this the break-through was held. During the heavy fighting between 2nd and 10th November following he commanded the remnants of his company with great gallantry, all the officers having become casualties. On the latter day he sustained no less than 13 shrapnel wounds, none of which however was serious. Barwick also received the 1914 Star with bar, the British War and Victory Medals, the Long Service and Good Conduct Medal[38], and the Meritorious Service Medal[39]. His Military Cross is unofficially engraved "3218 Sgt. Maj. J. Barwick (1st Scots Guards) European War 1914". When seen, the British War Medal, Long Service and Good Conduct Medal and Meritorious Service Medal were missing from his group.

37. See the citation in *L.G.*, 22nd July 1941.

38. Awarded in Army Order No. 130 of April 1919.

39. Awarded for valuable services in connection with the War in *L.G.*, 22nd February 1919.

Chapter 33

The Military Medal

Fig.A: The Military Medal, obverse, George V issue, first type.

ORIGIN AND DEVELOPMENT

By a Royal Warrant of 25th March 1916[1] the Military Medal was instituted in the following terms:

"GEORGE R.I.

GEORGE THE FIFTH, by the Grace of God of the United Kingdom of Great Britain and Ireland and of the British Dominions beyond the Seas King, Defender of the Faith, Emperor of India, To all to whom these Presents shall come Greeting: WHEREAS WE are desirous of signifying Our appreciation of acts of gallantry and devotion to duty performed by non-commissioned officers and men of Our Army in the Field We do by these Presents for Us Our heirs and successors institute and create a silver medal to be awarded to non-commissioned officers and men for individual or associated acts of bravery on the recommendation of a Commander-in-Chief in the Field:

Firstly: It is ordained that the medal shall be designated "The Military Medal".

Secondly: It is ordained that the Military Medal shall bear on the obverse the Royal Effigy, and on the reverse the words "For bravery in the Field", encircled by a wreath surmounted by the Royal Cipher and a Crown.

Thirdly: It is ordained that the names of those upon whom We may be pleased to confer the Military Medal shall be published in the *London Gazette*, and that a Register thereof shall be kept in the Office of Our Principal Secretary of State for War.

Fourthly: It is ordained that the Military Medal shall be worn immediately before all war medals and shall be worn on the left breast pendent from a ribbon of one inch and one quarter in width, which shall be in colour dark blue having in the centre three white and two crimson stripes alternating.

Lastly: It is ordained that in cases where non-commissioned officers and men who have been awarded the Military Medal shall be recommended by a Commander-in-Chief in the Field for further acts of bravery, a Bar may be added to the medal already conferred.

Given at Our Court at Saint James's this Twenty-fifth day of March, 1916, in the Sixth Year of Our Reign.

By His Majesty's Command,
KITCHENER."

On 3rd April 1916 a preliminary announcement regarding the new award was made in a circular by the Military Secretary to the Commander-in-Chief, France. This was followed on the 23rd of that month by a circular to the effect, *inter alia*, that recommendations might be retrospective. This evidently reflected instructions issued by the War Office and would account for the first two awards made under the Warrant being for the action of 16th December 1914 at the Hartlepools[2] and, for instance, for other awards known to have been made for services in 1915 in Gallipoli. A further circular of 27th May 1916 contained instructions to the effect that no retrospective cases for the period up to 1st June 1916 would be considered after 1st July 1916, and that posthumous awards would not be made[3].

By a Royal Warrant of 21st June 1916 (see *London Gazette* of 27th June 1916) eligibility for the M.M. was extended to women, whether British subjects or foreign, for "bravery and devotion under fire". The effect of this was that, while the medal could only be awarded to men of the British Army serving in the field, women civilians of any nationality could receive it, although both classes had to be recommended by a Commander-in-Chief in the field. No doubt the wider provision for women was due to the somewhat ill-defined position they then occupied

1. See *L.G.*, 5th April 1916.

2. To Sergeant F. W. Mallin and Acting Bombardier J. J. Hope, R.G.A., see *L.G.*, 7th April 1916. Hope's name was gazetted as "Pope".

3. For these circulars see P.R.O. AIR 1/993 (204/5/1216) and 1/1918 (204/233/4).

when serving with the Forces in one capacity or another. The first awards to such women were gazetted on 1st September 1916[4], and in 1917 the provisions of the amended Warrant were invoked in their widest sense when awards were made to two civilian ladies, Miss Louisa Nolan and Miss Florence Ada Williams, for their services to wounded British soldiers under fire during the Easter Rising of 1916[5].

Army Order No. 290 of August 1916 authorised a silver rose emblem for wear on the ribbon, when this was worn alone, to denote the award of a bar. In September 1916 the King decided that for the duration of the War officers and ratings of the Royal Naval Division and officers and men of the Royal Marines, serving in France, should be eligible for military decorations and medals. In consequence a number of M.M.s were awarded to ratings[6]. Following discussion between the Admiralty and the War Office it was agreed that an officer or rating already holding a naval decoration should, if occasion arose for a further award, be recommended through naval channels for a bar to it instead of a military decoration or medal[7].

In 1918 all servicemen who had received the D.C.M. and M.M. were authorised to use the appropriate letters after their names[8] and, in the case of the M.M., this was later extended to women of the Military Nursing Service[9]. Just before the end of the War, 1st and 2nd Class Warrant Officers were made eligible for the medal[10] and a number of such awards were then made. In 1919 a revised Royal Warrant was made[11] which cancelled the three previous ones, and which extended the use of the letters "M.M." to all who had received the medal, in addition to introducing provisions for forfeiture and restoration. In turn, this Warrant was replaced by another signed the following year[12] which, *inter alia*, removed some latent ambiguities. Thus, until the 1919 Warrant there had been no mention of a bar for women, nor was it clear whether any class of recipient could receive more than one bar although, in fact, this had already been done. The 1920 Warrant removed such doubts by providing that a bar or *bars* could be awarded for subsequent acts of bravery. In addition, the Warrant made the M.M. available to other ranks of "any of Our Military Forces" and to equivalent ranks of Allied or "Associated" Armies[13]. Yet a further consolidating Warrant was signed in 1931 which included a new provision that it could be given to other ranks of "Our Air Forces" for services performed on the ground[14]. It also drew the forfeiture clause rather more widely by omitting reference to specific acts of misconduct and making the power to order forfeiture completely discretionary. This followed a recommendation by the Inter-departmental Rewards Committee that all awards for gallantry, except in cases of extreme infamy, should be regarded as irrevocable; hence it was unnecessary to limit the power, as had been done before, by prescribing for particular circumstances. In 1939 this Warrant was amended[15] to make provision for the short-lived rank of Warrant Officer, Class 3. At a meeting on 14th September 1943 of the Committee on the Grant of Honours, Decorations and Medals in Time of War[16] it was agreed that the M.M. should be extended to other ranks of the Indian Army and to N.C.O.s and men of the Indian Air Force; that the I.D.S.M. should be regarded as on the same level as the D.C.M. and awards of the former reduced; and that Viceroy's commissioned officers should be excluded from award of the I.D.S.M.

By a Royal Warrant of 24th March 1964[17] the functions of the Secretary of State for War in regard to the M.M. were transferred, *inter alia*, to the Secretary of State for Defence.

DESCRIPTION

Ribbon Dark blue, 1¼ inches wide, with three white and two crimson stripes, each ⅛ inch wide, down the centre.

Suspension Ornate scroll bar suspender. Those issued or re-issued with the flange and pin fitting from about 1926 do not swivel. Recent Elizabeth II issues have a fitting similar to that used, for example, on the Burma Gallantry Medal.

4. To women of the Munro Motor Ambulance, Queen Alexandra's Imperial Military Nursing Service, and the Territorial Force Nursing Service. Nurses and other women serving with the Army were not eligible for the M.C. because they were not officers, although some were treated as such. However, any woman could receive the M.M., hence the awards, see P.R.O. WO 32/4966.

5. See *L.G.*, 24th January 1917.

6. In fact some M.M.s had already been awarded to men of the Royal Marines. No awards were made to ratings of the Royal Navy in the Second World War.

7. See P.R.O. ADM 116/1744.

8. Army Order No. 13 of January 1918.

9. Army Order No. 53 of February 1918.

10. Royal Warrant of 1st August 1918; see *L.G.*, 16th August 1918.

11. Royal Warrant of 24th March 1919; see Army Order No. 127 of April 1919.

12. Royal Warrant of 30th October 1920; see *L.G.*, 19th November 1920.

13. The first such awards were made in 1916, see *post*.

14. In fact, the King had approved this provision in August 1918 (effective from 1st April of that year) and a number of awards were then made, see P.R.O. WO 32/4968 and AIR 2/60. His approval was notified in a War Office telegram of 6th September 1918, see P.R.O. AIR 1/1169 (204/5/2593).

15. Royal Warrant of 21st August 1939; see Army Order No. 144 of August 1939.

16. See P.R.O. AIR 2/6409.

17. See Army Order No. 22 of March 1964.

Fig.B: The Military Medal, obverse, George V issue, second type.

Fig.C: The Military Medal, obverse, George VI issue, first type.

Obverse There are six obverses, as follows:

1. George V first type (Fig.A) This appears on all issues before 1930. The King's effigy was prepared by Bertram MacKennal, M.V.O., A.R.A.[18]
2. George V second type (Fig.B) This was introduced in 1930[19], and was also used on those awarded during the short reign of Edward VIII.
3. George VI first type (Fig.C) This was issued from 1938[20].
4. George VI second type (Fig.D) By a Royal Proclamation of 22nd June 1948 the King's style and titles were altered. Not all subsequent issues were of the second type although at least by 1951 it seems to have been in general use.
5. Elizabeth II first type (Fig.E) This type dates from about 1953[21], and was still being issued as late as 1958[22].
6. Elizabeth II second type (Fig.F).

Reverse There are four reverses as follows:

1. George V (Fig.G) This appears with obverses 1 and 2. It was approved by the King on 1st March 1916[23].
2. George VI first type (Fig.H) This was introduced in 1938 and at the same time as obverse 3 above. Until 1943–44 the background is slightly convex and requires careful examination to detect. Thereafter the background is flat although some overlapping of the two variants has been found, due possibly to the year of striking the actual piece.
3. George VI second type (Fig.I) This appears with obverse 4.
4. Elizabeth II (Fig.J) This appears with obverses 5 and 6.

Bar (Fig.K) According to the Royal Mint register of medals ordered between 1916 and 1941[24], on 9th September 1916 five dated bars (including two with the same date, and one with a date already appearing on a D.C.M. bar) were ordered for recipients of the M.M., and a further 11 were ordered on 28th September following (two with the same date; two with dates already ordered; and one with a date already appearing on a D.C.M. bar). Issues were made on 6th October and 6th November respectively. A further order was made for two bars already struck on 20th October but this was not executed. It seems likely, therefore, that about this time – as with the D.C.M. bar – the pattern of bar for both medals was under discussion and it was decided that due to the cost of preparing individual dies, a standard pattern should be adopted. This evidently led to the introduction of the familiar laurelled bar 500 of which, ostensibly for the D.C.M., were ordered on 4th December 1916. This pattern has remained in use ever since[25]. This bar is not fixed to the suspender but worn loose on the ribbon.

Naming Almost all issues are impressed in plain capital letters, without serifs, the First World War issues and those made shortly after having fractionally larger letters and figures. However, some medals awarded to men serving in or with the Indian Army in the Second World War are engraved in plain capital letters. The regimental or equivalent number appears where applicable, followed by the rank, initials, surname and unit of the recipient. Rank and unit are abbreviated in various forms, the First World War abbreviations usually being longer. On First World War medals the rank is normally separated from the first initial by a colon and the battalion etc. number usually precedes the unit. Many of the early awards are impressed with details which follow closely those given in the Gazette entry. From 1918, if the recipient had another award, e.g., the D.C.M., the appropriate letters frequently follow the surname. This, however, is not invariably so, especially when the M.M. recommendation was submitted before the other award was approved. Re-issues are named in the style current when the re-issue was made, although a George VI first type known re-issue to the R.A.F. has been found with details engraved in capital letters. It seems that the First World War awards to foreign troops were issued unnamed.

18. Originally for the Army L.S. & G.C. medal, see *Annual Report of the Deputy Master and Comptroller of the Royal Mint (1911)*, p.15.

19. *Annual Report of the Deputy Master and Comptroller of the Royal Mint (1930)*, p.45.

20. *Ibid* (1938), p.45. The new reverse was adopted at the same time.

21. *Ibid* (1953), p.33.

22. *E.g.*, the medal awarded to Fusilier R. Sanders, Royal Welch Fusiliers (*L.G.*, 18th November 1958)

23. See P.R.O. MINT 20/572 and WO 32/4960.

24. See P.R.O. MINT 16/4.

25. It is first mentioned in the *Annual Report of the Deputy Master and Comptroller of the Royal Mint. (1917)*, p.24.

Fig.D: The Military Medal, obverse, George VI issue, second type.

Fig.E: The Military Medal, obverse, Elizabeth II issue, first type.

Copies and Fakes Copies of both types of the George V issue and the first type George VI issue exist. All are well made although the second type George V copy is thin and has a rather pitted obverse and reverse. The George VI copies are somewhat larger and thicker than the originals, the designer's initials are missing from the base of the bust, and the suspender is rather larger and deeper. A few re-named medals are to be found but, in general, the M.M. does not seem to have been subject to much, if any, deliberate faking. For recent copies see the Note on p.xx.

VERIFICATIONS AND CITATIONS

All awards can be verified in the *London Gazette* except, apparently, those made to foreign troops. Until January 1942 they were listed separately under the medal heading in the "State Intelligence" section of the appropriate quarterly index. Thereafter they are consolidated in a comprehensive quarterly nominal list headed "Honours, Decorations and Medals", although the medal heading has been retained in the "State Intelligence" section. This merely lists pages on which awards are to be found but occasionally page numbers are omitted or the references given are corrupt. The 1942 and subsequent nominal lists seem to be accurate.

From September 1917 the recipient's home town was added to the Gazette details, but the practice ceased soon after the end of the War. It was resumed in June 1941 but not followed consistently. Towards the end of the First World War the theatre in which the medal was gained was sometimes added. This was also done fairly consistently with awards made between the Wars. With the earlier Second World War awards the theatre was omitted, possibly on the grounds of security, but after a short while it reappeared in the majority of cases, and is now always given.

Very few citations have been gazetted. 77 of the 127 First World War awards gazetted to women are accompanied by citations, and there is what seems to be an isolated case in that of Private A. T. C. Stagg, R.A.F.[26]. A small number were gazetted between 1920 and 1923; some appear with awards to the R.A.F. in the Second World War, and a number have been published since the end of the War in respect of recent operations, e.g. in Aden and Vietnam. None, however, has been published since 1968. Details sometimes appear in War Office press releases and extracts from these are frequently to be found in local newspapers. On rare occasions what purports to be an extract from unit orders giving the citation is found with the medal but this is virtually impossible to verify. In the vast majority of cases recourse must be made to unit or formation histories where details occasionally may be found. Leslie (see Bibliography) gives biographical details and photographs of many women awarded the M.M. in the First World War[27]. Many of the original First World War recommendations for men of the R.F.C. and R.A.F. serving in France and Belgium are preserved in the Honours and Awards files in the Public Record Office series AIR 1. Where only the date of award is known it is preferable to search for the recommendation in the files of HQ R.F.C./R.A.F. which are arranged according to date; where the formation or unit is known the corresponding files may be consulted first although not all have been preserved.

NUMBERS AWARDED

First World War The official statistics (see Bibliography) cover the period from August 1914 to May 1920 and thus extend beyond the campaigns against the Central Powers. The figures given are:

						Services in the Field	Services in connection with the War
M.M.	...	...	...	...	...	115,577	12
– 1st bars		...	...	...	...	5,796	—
– 2nd bars	...	...	...	...	...	180	—
– 3rd bars	...	...	...	...	...	1	—

26. See *L.G.*, 31st May 1918.

27. The recommendations for Baroness E. B. de T'Serclaes and Miss M. L. C. G. Chisholm, both of the British Royal Red Cross Society (*L.G.*, 19th November 1917) are in P.R.O. AIR 1/1589 (204/82/78) which is the Honours and Awards file of 4th Brigade R.F.C. for the period August to November 1917. Baroness T'Serclaes was English and married a Belgian. Her M.M. also appears in the War Office list of awards to foreigners dated 1st March 1918.

Fig. F: The Military Medal, obverse, Elizabeth II issue, second type.

Fig. G: The Military Medal, reverse, George V issue.

Those for services in connection with the War include awards for the Easter Rising, air raids and coastal bombardments. For the period 1916–1918 Wingate (see Bibliography) gives the totals as 115,429, with 5,784 first bars, 180 second bars and one third bar[28]. 127 medals were gazetted to women most of whom were members of various nursing organisations.

According to Sparrow and MacBean-Ross (see Bibliography), up to 13th June 1918 the Royal Naval Division had received 555 medals, 23 first bars and one second bar, although these figures probably include awards to non-naval personnel. For the whole War about 570 medals were awarded to petty officers and ratings of the Royal Navy. 167 medals and 2 bars were awarded to men of the Royal Flying Corps; 92 medals to men of the Royal Air Force and 6 medals to men of the Australian Flying Corps[29]. Occasionally groups of medals are found which contain two M.M.s; with one exception, the cases so far discovered show a single Gazette entry, and it seems likely therefore that the man concerned was either issued by mistake with two medals or, for one reason or another, had a re-issue. The exception concerns James William Newton, who was awarded the M.M. during the First World War while serving in the Northumberland Fusiliers[30]. After the War Newton joined the Territorial Army and was embodied in 1939. He was posted to the Black Watch and was captured by the Germans in May 1940, remaining a prisoner until the end of the War. He was awarded a second M.M. for gallantry in 1940 after the end of the War[31]. The double award seems only explicable on the grounds that when the second recommendation was submitted the existence of the first award was overlooked[32]. A few double awards were gazetted during the First World War, but in the cases so far investigated the second entry was later corrected to the award of a bar.

We have traced a number of honorary awards to foreigners which were sponsored by the War Office and which, as far as the M.M. is concerned, appeared in printed lists published between 30th October 1916 and 6th October 1920. Of these we have been unable to find lists nos. 23, 42, 46, 47 and 52 of this series which ends with no. 68. The following summary is therefore incomplete to the extent of any awards in the missing lists:

Belgium	442	(including Baroness E. B. de T'Serclaes[33]; excluding 1 first bar)
Czechoslovakia	320	
France	2,472	(including 1 nurse and 5 women civilians some of whom may have been nurses; excluding 1 first bar)
Greece	140	
Italy	1,320	
Japan	68	
Portugal	76	
Rumania	259	
Russia	7	
Serbia	171	
U.S.A.	413	(including 2 nurses)
Total:	5,688	

1920–1939 From June 1920 to December 1939, 311 medals were gazetted, as follows:

1920 ...	61	(47 late awards; 8 Mesopotamia; 4 North West Frontier; 2 Waziristan)
1921 ...	51	(21 late awards; 2 Black Sea; 27 Mesopotamia; 1 Waziristan)
1922 ...	5	(2 late awards; 3 Waziristan)
1923 ...	18	(3 late awards; 5 Malabar; 10 Waziristan)
1924 ...	3	(2 late awards; 1 Kurdistan)
1925 ...	6	(4 Khartoum; 2 Kurdistan, both R.A.F.)
1927 ...	2	(Iraq and Sudan)
1928 ...	2	(Iraq, R.A.F.)

28. This was awarded to Corporal E. A. Corey, 55th Australian Infantry Battalion, in *L.G.* 17th June 1919.

29. These air force figures are to inclusive *L.G.*, 6th December 1919.

30. *L.G.*, 24th January 1919.

31. *L.G.*, 14th February 1946.

32. See Chapter 17 for details of the award of two D.S.M.s under similar circumstances.

33. This award was also gazetted, see footnote 27.

Fig. H: The Military Medal, reverse, George VI issue, first type.

Fig. I: The Military Medal, reverse, George VI issue, second type.

1930 ... 1 (North West Frontier)
1931 ... 2 (North West Frontier)
1932 ... 6 (2 Burma; 4 North West Frontier)
1935 ... 2 (North West Frontier)
1936 ... 40 (8 North West Frontier; 32 Palestine including 1 R.A.F.)
1937 ... 23 (12 North West Frontier; 5 Palestine including 1 R.A.F.; 6 Waziristan)
1938 ... 28 (7 North West Frontier; 20 Palestine including 1 R.A.F.; 1 Waziristan)
1939 ... 61 (4 North West Frontier including 1 R.A.F.; 50 Palestine including 1 R.A.F.; 6 not stated but probably Palestine; 1 Waziristan)

In addition, one first bar was awarded in 1922 (North Russia 1920), and three first bars in 1924 (2 late awards; 1 Kurdistan). Due to the ambiguous wording used in the *Gazettes* it is difficult to say whether all late awards relate to the First World War.

Second World War Wingate gives the total awarded between 1939 and 1945 as 15,225 medals with 164 first bars and two second bars. However, our count of bars in the *London Gazette* to the end of 1946 is 177 first bars and one second bar[34]. All awards gazetted in 1946 appear to be for the Second World War except 26 (including three to Royal Air Force) which were for South East Asia. However, in a number of cases the *Gazette* announcement contains no identifying details. The following 129 air force awards were gazetted:

Royal Air Force ... ... 119 (including 1 cancelled in *L.G.*, 4th June 1946, no reason being given; 6 to W.A.A.F.; 14 to R.A.F. Regiment; 3 for South East Asia)

Royal Australian Air Force 5
Royal Candian Air Force 1
Royal New Zealand Air Force ... 4

The following members of the Women's Auxiliary Air Force received the M.M.:

	London Gazette
Acting Corporal A. J. Hearn	10th January 1941
Corporal E. C. Henderson	5th November 1940
Sergeant J. E. Mortimer	5th November 1940
Corporal J. M. G. Robins	20th December 1940
Sergeant H. E. Turner	5th November 1940
Acting Sergeant J. M. Youle	10th January 1941

At least five awards were made for engagements at sea, all being in respect of anti-aircraft defence. These were to Lance-Corporal G. P. Vane, Royal Engineers, for services aboard the anti-aircraft paddle-steamer HMS *Royal Eagle* during the evacuation from Dunkirk[35]; to Gunner F. J. Carus, Royal Artillery, for the defence of the tanker *Helka* off Tobruk[36]; to A.C.1. F. Wilson[37] and Sergeant A. Kinnaird[38], both of the R.A.F., for the defence of high speed launches; and to A.C.1. G. A. Cottrill for the defence of a transport[39].

660 honorary awards to foreigners, which were not gazetted, were made as follows:

Belgium	...	...	...	...	...	24
Czechoslovakia		...	...	...	...	18
Free French Forces	...	...	...	...	185 (including 1 marine)
Greece	...	...	...	...	...	24
Netherlands	...	...	...	...	...	9
Norway	...	...	...	...	...	23
Poland	...	...	...	...	...	63
U.S.A.	...	...	...	...	...	310
U.S.S.R.	...	...	...	...	...	4

1947–1979 A summary of the 932 medals and eight first bars gazetted during this period is as follows:

34. To Sergeant F. W. Kite, Royal Tank Regiment, in *L.G.*, 1st March 1945.

35. *L.G.*, 26th September 1940. At the time of the evacuation Vane was serving in the Royal Engineers but he transferred to the Royal Artillery before his award was gazetted.

36. *L.G.*, 21st October 1941.

37. *L.G.*, 20th December 1940 (citation). Wilson also received the B.E.M. in *L.G.*, 1st October 1946 for gallantry on a high speed launch during the invasion of Hong Kong in December 1941.

38. *L.G.*, 1st September 1946; Kinnaird was appointed an M.B.E. in *L.G.*, 2nd January 1956.

39. *L.G.*, 7th April 1942 (citation).

Fig.J: The Military Medal, reverse, Elizabeth II issue.

Fig.K: Bar to the Military Medal.

Theatre	London Gazettes	Medals	First bars
Arabian Peninsula	1950–1979	53 (2 R.A.F.)	—
Borneo	1964–1967	35	2
Brunei	1963	6	—
Congo	1961	1	—
Cyprus	1958–1959	4	—
Kenya	1955–1957	12	2
Korea	1951–1954	225	1
Late awards[40] (Second World War)	1947–1950	141 (3 R.A.F.)	—
Malaya	1949–1959	267 (4 R.A.F.)	3
Malaysia	1965–1966	3	—
Near East	1957	7	—
Northern Ireland[41]	1972–1979	71	—
Palestine	1948–1949	6	—
Restored award (Second World War)	1948	1	—
South East Asia	1947	12	—
Vietnam	1966–1972	88 (1 R.A.A.F.)	—

Of these, 268 medals and one first bar were gazetted between 1949 and 1952, and 510 medals and seven first bars between 1953 and 1979.

ILLUSTRATIVE AWARD

Sergeant H. C. Bolton received the M.M.[42] while serving with the 20th Battalion, Lancashire Fusiliers, during the First World War.

Barlow (see Bibliography) gives the citation[43] as "During the hours of daylight going across 'No Man's Land' and blowing up a chimney". A fuller account is, however, given by Latter (see Bibliography) as follows:

> "The Military Medal and the Divisional Commanders's congratulations were earned by Sergeant H. C. Bolton of the 20th Battalion (Lieutenant-Colonel E. Vaughan, Manchester Regiment) for a brilliant piece of daylight patrolling near Arras on 20th September (1916). He went out during the afternoon to investigate an old chimney in No Man's Land which had given rise to much suspicion. At a second attempt he succeeded in entering it and found a ladder leading up to a hole made by a shell in the wall about twenty feet from the ground. Iron supports were fastened inside the chimney as if to enable an observer or sniper to sit in comparative comfort while using the hole. There were traces of fresh mud on the rungs of the ladder. The chimney was afterwards suitably dealt with."

Bolton also received a bar to the M.M.[44], Barlow's version of the citation[45] being as follows:

> "During an action he showed great determination and devotion to duty, exposing himself continually in supervising his men and setting a fine example under most trying circumstances. He made several journeys into 'No Man's Land' to bring in wounded who would not have been able to reach our lines."

Latter only mentions this incident briefly, giving the occasion as the attack on the Houthhulst Forest on 22nd/23rd October 1917. Bolton's M.M. is impressed with his number, rank, name and regiment, the battalion number also appearing.

40. The award to Private R. Johnson, Australian Military Forces for services in 1941 in the Middle East published in *L.G.*, 11th February 1949 is repeated with a different army number and a slight variation in spelling the Christian name in *L.G.*, 6th October 1950.

41. Including one award to a woman i.e. Lance-Corporal S. J. Warke, Women's Royal Army Corps, *L.G.*, 18th September 1973.

42. *L.G.*, 9th December 1916, p.12,042.

43. He gives the date of the award as one day earlier than the *L.G.* entry.

44. *L.G.*, 23rd February 1918, p.2,410. Bolton's home is given as London.

45. In giving the citation Barlow quotes the date as 14th November 1917. Since this is neither the date of the act itself nor that of the *L.G.*, it is either a misprint or the date of the theatre award.

Chapter 34

The New Zealand Cross

Fig.A: The New Zealand Cross, obverse.

ORIGIN AND DEVELOPMENT

The New Zealand Cross, a decoration unique to New Zealand and awarded only for services in the Second Maori War of 1860–1872, was instituted as a direct result of the original limited terms of eligibility for the Victoria Cross (q.v.). The first Victoria Cross Warrant, dated 29th January 1856, restricted the award to officers and men of "Our naval and military services"[1] and required that recommendations should be forwarded by Imperial officers. In 1864 Captain Charles Heaphy of the Auckland Militia was recommended for the Victoria Cross by the General Officer Commanding the Forces in New Zealand, but the award was not approved on the ground that locally raised forces did not constitute part of the Imperial Army. Further strong recommendations pointed out that Heaphy had been recommended initially by Lieutenant-Colonel Sir Henry Havelock, himself a Victoria Cross winner during the Indian Mutiny, and by whom he had been placed in command of a detachment of Imperial troops.

Accordingly, by a Royal Warrant of 1st January 1867, the original Victoria Cross Warrant was amended to extend eligibility to members of local forces when serving with Imperial troops under the command of a "general or other officer". The Warrant was retrospective, the preamble making particular reference to operations "undertaken against the Insurgent native tribes of Our Colony of New Zealand" and, shortly afterwards, Heaphy's Victoria Cross was gazetted[2], being the first awarded to a member of a colonial force, as well as being the first to a non-regular serviceman. Later, in 1867, when the Government of New Zealand assumed full responsibility for the suppression of the Maoris, the General Officer Commanding returned to the United Kingdom and the Imperial troops were progressively withdrawn. Although further acts of gallantry were performed by New Zealanders, the Government of the Colony did not forward any recommendations for the Victoria Cross because the local forces were neither serving with Imperial troops nor under the command of an Imperial officer. Since there was now no decoration available to the New Zealand local forces, in a letter of 19th November 1868, Colonel G. S. Whitmore[3] requested that a sum of money should be made available from the Armed Constabulary Reward Fund for the purchase of 20 rosettes and special chevrons[4] for members of the Armed Constabulary who distinguished themselves in action, and to whom a monetary grant of £5 should be made from the same fund. From this modest request the idea gradually developed of the institution of the New Zealand Cross. In his letter Whitmore recommended Constable Henare Kepa Te Ahururu for a monetary reward and in a further letter, dated 14th January 1869, he recommended Constables Benjamin Biddle and Solomon Black for similar rewards which, in due course, they all received. These three men became the first to receive the New Zealand Cross. The Cross itself was instituted by an Order in Council made at Government House, Wellington, on 10th March 1869[5], which read as follows:

"G. F. Bowen, Governor.

ORDER IN COUNCIL

At the Government House, at Wellington, this tenth day of March, 1869. Present -

HIS EXCELLENCY THE GOVERNOR IN COUNCIL

Whereas it is expedient that Regulations should be made for conferring a Decorative Distinction on members of the Militia, Volunteers and Armed Constabulary, who may particularly distinguish themselves by their bravery:

1. The Victoria Cross Warrant of 13th December 1858 extended eligibility to civilian volunteers serving in the Indian Mutiny.

2. *L.G.*, 8th February 1867, p.696.

3. Commandant of the New Zealand Armed Constabulary.

4. Since 1842 chevrons (and medals) had been available for gallantry to members of the (Royal) Irish Constabulary.

5. See *The New Zealand Gazette* for 1869, p.127.

Now, therefore, His Excellency the Governor, with the advice of the Executive Council of New Zealand, and in exercise of all powers and authorities enabling him in this behalf, doth by this present Order institute a Decorative Distinction, to be conferred on members of the Militia, Volunteers or Armed Constabulary, who may particularly distinguish themselves by their bravery in action, or devotion to their duty while on service.

And doth, with the like advice and consent, make and ordain the following regulations under which such Distinction shall be conferred:

Firstly, The decoration shall consist of a Silver Cross, with the name of the Colony and the name of the recipient engraved thereon.

Secondly, It shall be suspended from the left breast by a crimson riband.

Thirdly, Any person upon whom the Distinction has been conferred, who shall afterwards perform any act of bravery which would, had he not been already decorated, have entitled him to the honor, may receive for every such act a silver bar, to be attached to the riband by which the Cross is suspended.

Fourthly, The Distinction shall only be conferred upon those officers or men who, when serving in the presence of the enemy, shall have performed some signal act of valor or devotion to their duty, or who shall have performed any very intrepid action in the public service; and neither rank, nor long service, nor wounds, nor any other circumstance or condition whatever, save merit of conspicuous bravery, shall be held to establish a sufficient claim to the honor.

Fifthly, The Distinction shall be awarded by the Governor only. It shall not be claimed by any individual on his own account, but the claim must be made in favour of the person considered to be entitled to it by the Commanding Officer of the Force or District to which such person belonged, and the Governor shall call for such description and attestation of the act as he may think requisite.

Sixthly, Every person upon whom this Distinction is conferred shall be publicly decorated before the force or body to which he belongs, or with which the act of bravery for which he is to be rewarded shall have been performed; and a Roll shall be kept in which shall be inscribed the names of the recipients, with a brief description of the special act for which the Distinction has in each case been awarded; and every inscription on the Roll shall be published in the Government Gazette.

Seventhly, If any person on whom such Distinction shall have been conferred be convicted of treason, felony, cowardice, or of any infamous or disgraceful offence, his name shall be forthwith erased from the Roll.

Eighthly, Constables and privates decorated with this distinction will take command of other constables or privates on duty, when no officer or non-commissioned officer is present.

FORSTER GORING
Clerk of the Executive Council."

In forwarding the Order to the Secretary of State for the Colonies[6], the Governor-General pointed out the urgent necessity of holding out a distinction available to officers and men of the Colony's forces. However, while appreciating that the Queen alone was the fountain of honour, the decoration was to be a purely local honour analogous to the medals presented by the Royal Geographical Society and the (Royal) Humane Society. Although he would have preferred to refer the matter home in the first instance, he was advised that there should be no delay on the ground that, to be most prized, the awards should be conferred at once. This he had done upon four Europeans and one Maori.

This exercise in sophistry brought forth a despatch[7] from the Secretary of State for the Colonies which was couched in no uncertain terms. He chided the Governor-General for exceeding his authority and pointed out that what had been done was not to be taken as a precedent either in New Zealand or in any other Colony. In future, similar steps must be with the cognisance of the Home Government and with the personal sanction of the Queen. However, in all the circumstances the Queen had ratified the Order in Council.

The title "New Zealand Cross" was not immediately adopted and, in the Order in Council and the two despatches mentioned above, it was merely referred to as a

6. The covering despatch of 2nd July 1869 is reproduced in Mayo (see Bibliography) quoting the *Journal of the House of Representatives of New Zealand*.
7. Dated 2nd October 1869. See also Mayo, op. cit.

"Decorative Distinction". Until the title was settled it was called variously the New Zealand Cross of Valour, Order of Merit, Colonial Order of Merit, Order of the Southern Cross, Cross of New Zealand, Colonial Cross, Southern Cross, and Silver Cross. Even after its title was settled it was sometimes referred to as the New Zealand Cross of Valour, or Order of Valour, the latter part no doubt being added to explain the letter "V" forming part of the suspender.

The New Zealand Cross Endowment Act of 1869 provided for the setting aside of 5,000 acres of land, the revenue from which was to be used to provide pensions for recipients who had become too old or infirm to earn a livelihood. No action was taken until 1875 when land surveys were made, although none was proclaimed a reserve. After lengthy discussions extending over two years, the Act was repealed and in 1877 the Defence Department was instructed to provide from its annual estimates a yearly pension of £10 for each recipient with effect from 1st January following.

A Royal Commission was appointed on 15th September 1873 to examine a number of recommendations following the award of the first seven Crosses[8], and to make recommendations to the Governor for any further awards. Some recommendations were rejected on the ground that the events took place before the institution of the Cross, the Commissioners holding that the Order in Council conferred no retrospective authority[9].

Despite the fact that the Commissioners were required to report to the Governor within ten days and that a number of recommendations were upheld, no further awards were made for almost two years.

In August 1875 the Governor, on a recommendation forwarded from London by General Sir Trevor Chute, late General Officer Commanding the Forces in New Zealand, approved the award of a Cross to Doctor I. E. Featherston for services in 1865–1866 while on the Staff of the Native Contingent (see No. 8 below). This excited discussion in the Legislative Council where some members held that Chute should have recommended Featherston for the Victoria Cross, as he could have done, and that he should not have waited until the New Zealand Cross was instituted some years later. A Special Board of Officers was then set up to review the recommendations of the 1873 Commission. The Board upheld the recommendations of the Commissioners, and added a number originally turned down on the grounds of lack of retrospective authority (Nos. 8–10 below). No doubt Featherston's award had some effect on this change of view.

In 1885 the Premier proposed that the Cross should be extended to cover acts of outstanding bravery in saving human life. To distinguish such awards from the military version it was suggested that the ribbon should be of a different colour and the stars omitted from the Cross. This proposal was rejected because it was found that the medal of the Royal Humane Society of Australia, instituted in 1882, was available for rewarding such acts.

Following some agitation two further awards were made in 1886 (Nos. 20 and 21 below) and another was made in 1898 (No. 22 below). This aroused some criticism and the Cabinet ordered that the Roll should be closed. However, in 1910 a strong movement sought the award for Ensign H. W. Northcroft of the Patea Rangers (as he was in 1866) on whom the 23rd and last Cross was bestowed – nearly 44 years after he had earned it.

No bars to the Cross have been awarded, nor have there been any forfeitures[10]. Although the original Order in Council has never been rescinded it is unlikely that it could be invoked for future awards. Apart from the present availability of the Victoria Cross and George Cross, the various forces upon whose members the Cross could be conferred have all been disbanded, the Armed Constabulary in 1886, and the Militia and Volunteers in 1911.

8. The last of these being gazetted on 8th February 1870.

9. This conclusion is questionable since the first four Crosses were awarded for acts performed before the Order in Council.

10. The first recipient, Constable Henare Kepa Te Ahururu of the Armed Constabulary, deserted but his Cross was not forfeited.

DESCRIPTION (For coloured illustration, see Plate 3)

Origin of the Design On 12th July 1870 a Royal Commission was appointed to design the decoration, and on 27th September following, its recommendations were despatched to the United Kingdom. The Queen's approval was conveyed to the Governor in a despatch dated 27th January 1871[11]. On 7th June 1871 the Colony's Agent-General in London (Doctor I. E. Featherston, who was later awarded the Cross himself) was instructed to have 20 Crosses made, and the work was accordingly entrusted to Messrs. Phillips Bros. and Son of Cockspur Street, London[12]. Doctor Featherston and Colonel Whitmore[13] (who happened to be in London at the time) authorised various modifications to the design suggested by the manufacturers. These included a major change in the shape of the crown and the introduction of a suspender with a V-link which was copied from the Victoria Cross. By the time the New Zealand Government received notification of the design changes, it was too late to do anything as the Crosses had already been struck.

Ribbon Crimson, $1\frac{1}{2}$ inches wide, and identical with that of the Victoria Cross. A gold two or three prong buckle was provided for pinning the decoration on the coat.

Suspension By a frosted flat silver bar, with raised polished edges, to which gold laurel leaves are riveted. The V-piece is made in one with the suspender bar and attached to the crown above the Cross by two gold rings. The reverse of the suspender is plain except for the rivets of the laurel leaves and for Messrs. Phillips's cartouche which was affixed to the first 20 Crosses made in 1871, at which time only seven awards had been authorised. The ribbon lug is slightly wider than the bar of which it forms part.

Obverse (Fig.A) The crown, stars and laurel wreath are of gold, the crown being pinned through a fitting at the top of the Cross, and the wreath by flanges bent over between the arms. The Cross is $1\frac{1}{2}$ inches wide across the limbs.

Reverse Plain except for the raised portions on the arms of the Cross and centre circle, and for details of the recipient (see below).

Bars Although no bars were awarded, the recommendation made to the Queen was that the bar was to be of plain burnished silver inscribed with the date and, if any, the name of the action in which it was awarded.

Naming The recipient's rank, names and unit are engraved in the outer circle of the reverse, and the date of the act in the inner circle[14]. Some awards have the place of the act engraved above the date.

Copies and Fakes The dies of the Cross were left in the hands of Messrs. Phillips who completed an order for five Crosses in 1886, making a total of 25 struck, ostensibly for awards. A few suitably engraved specimens were struck for the Royal Mint and eminent collectors in the United Kingdom, but the dies passed through other hands before they were recovered by the Agent-General in 1908. In the intervening years a number of unauthorised specimens were struck[15], two of which were engraved with the names of Constable Black (No. 2 below) and Trooper Lingard (No. 4 below). These were spurious since they did not have the Phillips's cartouche, and the original awards are known to exist. The dies were returned to New Zealand in 1953 and are deposited at the Dominion Museum, Wellington. An unnamed Cross exists which when seen was accompanied by documents regarding Trooper Rodriquez de Sardinha (No. 18 below). From the documents it appears that de Sardinha lost part of the decoration in 1887, and was issued with a complete replacement in 1889. Although the documents are not specific on the point, it seems likely that the portions he did not lose were the buckle, ribbon and suspender bar which he returned to the New Zealand Government. The Cross referred to here has a genuine buckle and suspender bar but the Cross, which lacks the crown, is very

11. The despatches are reproduced in Mayo quoting the *Journal of the House of Representatives of New Zealand.*

12. Who also made the Albert Medals (q.v.).

13. Whitmore had been a member of the design Commission.

14. No date appears on the awards to Captain F. J. Mace, Taranaki Militia and Private T. Adamson, Corps of Guides; in both cases the name of the recipient's regiment appears in the inner circle.

15. An unnamed Cross was sold in Glendining and Company's sale of 25th September 1963.

crudely made and attached by links direct to the suspender. While the buckle and suspender bar may have been de Sardinha's originals, the Cross itself could not have been, nor is it likely to have been a replacement.

NUMBERS AWARDED: VERIFICATIONS AND CITATIONS

In all 23 awards were made. In the following list[16] recipients are given in the order in which they appear in the official Roll. Ranks, names and units are shown first, followed by the dates and places of the acts, and the references to the *New Zealand Gazette* announcing the award:

1. Constable Henare Kepa Te Ahururu; 1st Division, Armed Constabulary; 7th November 1868; Moturoa; No. 16 of 25th March 1869. He later deserted, but was living at Ruatoki in 1878. Date of death not known.

2. Constable Solomon Black; 1st Division, Armed Constabulary; 8th January 1869; Ngatapa; No. 16 of 25th March 1869. When last heard of he was living in a Glasgow workhouse in 1910 and was then 77 years old.

3. Constable Benjamin Biddle; 1st Division, Armed Constabulary; 8th January 1869; Ngatapa; No. 16 of 25th March 1869. He was the last survivor of the recipients of the N.Z. Cross, and died at Whakatane on 10th March 1933, aged 85 years.

4. Trooper William Lingard; Kai Iwi Cavalry Volunteers; 28th December 1868; Tauranga-ika; No. 31 of 3rd June 1869. Died at Wellington in 1922, aged 77 years.

5. Sergeant George (Rowley) Hill; 1st Division, Armed Constabulary; 10th April 1869; Jerusalem Pa; No. 34 of 26th June 1869. He also fought in the Baltic, Crimea, and Indian Mutiny and was awarded two medals by the Royal Humane Society for saving life, one in 1860 and the other in 1896. Tried unsuccessfully to enlist for the South African War at the age of 63. Died in Auckland on 15th February 1930, aged 93 years.

6. Cornet Angus Smith; Bay of Plenty Cavalry Volunteers; 7th June 1869; Opepe; No. 63 of 6th November 1869. Later promoted to captain; he also fought in the Crimean War. Died at Opotiki on 3rd April 1902, aged 70 years.

7. Sergeant Arthur Wakefield Carkeek; Armed Constabulary; 8th February 1870; Ohinemutu; No. 36 of 7th July 1870. Died at Otaki on 24th May 1897, aged 54 years.

8. Dr. Isaac Earl Featherston; Staff, Native Contingent; 14th January 1866; Otapawa Pa; No. 60 of 28th October 1875. Was a Member of Parliament, 1853–70, and was four times elected Superintendent of Wellington. Appointed Agent-General for New Zealand in London in 1870, where he died on 21st June 1876, aged 63 years.

9. Inspector John Mackintosh Roberts; Armed Constabulary; 7th November 1868; Moturoa; No. 27 of 11th May 1876. Appointed the first Officer Commanding the Permanent Militia, with the rank of Lieutenant-Colonel, when that body was formed in 1887 after the disbandment of the Armed Constabulary. Died at Wanganui on 12th October 1928, aged 88 years.

10. Major Keepa Te Rangihiwinui (Kemp); N.Z. Militia (Native Contingent); 7th November 1868, Moturoa, and 13th March 1869, Otauto; No. 27 of 11th May 1876. Commanded the Wanganui Native Contingent and received a Sword of Honour from Queen Victoria for his services. Died at Wanganui on 15th April 1898, aged 75 years.

11. Major Ropata Wahawaha; Native Contingent; 5th January 1869; Ngatapa; No. 27 of 11th May 1876. A warrior of renown prior to the First Maori War, he led the Ngati-Porou Native Contingent from 1865 to 1871 and received a Sword of Honour from Queen Victoria for his services. He was a member of the Legislative Council from May 1887 until his death at Gisborne on 1st July 1897, aged 90 years.

12. Captain Francis Joseph Mace; Taranaki Militia; 4th June 1863 at Kaitikara River, 11th March 1864 at Kaitake, and 20th October 1865 at Warea; No. 27 of 11th May 1876. Mentioned in despatches eight times. Died at Oakura on 7th August 1927, aged 90 years.

13. Sub-Inspector George Augustus Preece; Armed Constabulary; 5th January 1869; Ngatapa; No. 27 of 11th May 1876. Mentioned in despatches three times and twice received the special thanks of the Government. Tried to enlist during the First World War in 1914 and again in 1918 when he was 73 years old. Died at Palmerston North on 10th July 1925, aged 80 years.

16. Reproduced by permission from *An Encyclopaedia of New Zealand.*

14. Assistant-Surgeon Samuel Walker; Armed Constabulary; 13th March 1869; Otauto; No. 27 of 11th May 1876. Served in 34 engagements against the Maoris. Died at Taupo on 24th December 1880, aged 38 years.

15. Sergeant Christopher Louis Maling; Corps of Guides; 26th February 1868; Tauranga-ika; No. 27 of 11th May 1876. Later rose to the rank of Major. His N.Z. Cross is in the Royal Collection at Windsor Castle. Died in England in February 1917, aged 74 years.

16. Sergeant Richard Shepherd; Armed Constabulary; 13th March 1869; Otauto; No. 27 of 11th May 1876. Also served in the Crimean War and in Burma 1855–57. Died at Auckland on 2nd November 1913, aged 76 years.

17. Sergeant Samuel Austin; Wanganui Volunteer Contingent; 7th January 1866 at Putahi Pa, and 17th October 1866 at Keteonetea; No. 27 of 11th May 1876. Served in the Imperial forces in the First Maori War in 1846–47 and afterwards until 1859. Died at Wanganui on 25th January 1903, aged 74 years.

18. Trooper Antonio Rodriquez de Sardinha; Taranaki Mounted Volunteers; 2nd October 1863 at Poutoko, and 11th March 1864 at Kaitake; No. 27 of 11th May 1876. Twice mentioned in despatches. Died at New Plymouth on 12th May 1905, aged 73 years.

19. Private Thomas Adamson; Corps of Guides; 7th May 1869; Ahikereru; No. 27 of 11th May 1876. Took part in 25 engagements against the Maoris. Died at Wanganui on 29th December 1913, aged 67 years.

20. Lieutenant-Colonel Thomas McDonnell; N.Z. Militia; October 1863 at Paparatu, and 7th January 1866 at Putahi Pa; No. 20 of 1st April 1886. Took part in 40 engagements against the Maoris, many times mentioned in despatches, and wounded four times. Died at Wanganui on 8th November 1899, aged 67 years.

21. Captain Gilbert Mair; N.Z. Militia; 7th February 1870; Rotorua; No. 20 of 1st April 1886. Commanded the Arawa Native Contingent and enjoyed the full rank and status of a chief of the Arawa. Later was native interpreter to the House of Representatives and a Magistrate of the Native Court. Died in the Bay of Plenty on 29th November 1923, aged 80 years.

22. Cornet Harry Charles William Wrigg; Bay of Plenty Cavalry Volunteers; 29th June 1867; Opotiki; No. 18 of 18th March 1898. Died at Auckland on 30th June 1924, aged 82 years.

23. Ensign Henry William Northcroft; Patea Rangers; 2nd October 1866 at Pungarehu, and 5th November 1866 at Tirotiro Moana; No. 67 of 7th July 1910. Fought in 49 engagements against the Maoris. He was appointed Chief Justice and Resident Commissioner of the Cook Islands in 1912. Died in Auckland in December 1923, aged 79 years.

Citations were published in the *New Zealand Gazette*. All except the last two are reproduced in Tancred (see Bibliography). Biographical details and photographs of some recipients are to be found in Cowan (see Bibliography).

ILLUSTRATIVE AWARD

George Hill (No. 5 above) was awarded the New Zealand Cross in the *New Zealand Gazette*, No. 34 of 26th June 1869 at pp. 303–304[17] where his citation reads as follows:

> "On the 10th of April, 1869, Constable (now Sergeant) George Hill, of No. 1 Division, Armed Constabulary, accompanied the Wairoa Natives, who under Ihaka Whanga, proceeded to relieve Mohaka, then being attacked by Te Kooti. A party volunteered to run the gauntlet of the enemy's fire, and to dash into the Jerusalem Pa, then sorely pressed. This was a dangerous service, and it was in a great measure due to the example set by Constable Hill, who led the party, that it was successfully carried out. During the subsequent portion of the siege, Constable Hill animated the defenders by his exertions, and contributed greatly to the repulse of Te Kooti, and his conduct is spoken of with admiration by the Natives themselves."

Hill was born on 6th January 1837 at Dawlish, Devonshire, and first went to sea as a boy serving on coastal coal brigs. In 1851 he joined the Royal Navy and later served in the Baltic and the Crimea[18]. At the outbreak of the Indian Mutiny he was

17. Where it is described as "the Decorative Distinction".

18. For these and other details, see above, Cowan, Seaby's *Coin and Medal Bulletin* for October 1960 at p.414, *The Journal of the Orders and Medals Research Society* for December 1969 at p.127 et seq., and *The Bulletin of the Military Historical Society*, Volume 20, p.83 et seq.

serving in H.M.S. *Shannon* and joined Peel's Naval Brigade, being slightly wounded at the Relief of Lucknow. While serving in the Mediterranean in 1860, with others, he deserted ship and joined Garibaldi's Army. He saw action at Palermo, Capua and in the Straits of Messina and was again wounded. In due course he was taken by a naval picket and returned to his ship, but it appears that his desertion was overlooked since British sympathy for Garibaldi ran high. In 1862 he again deserted, this time in South Africa and wandered far up country before working his way home in a clipper. In 1864 Hill was a member of the crew of the troopship *Empress* which carried Imperial troops to fight in the Second Maori War. While the ship was anchored in Waitemata Harbour he jumped overboard and swam ashore. He joined No. 2 Company, Forest Rangers under Major von Tempsky and later served with No. 1 Company, Hawkes Bay Military Settlers, and with No. 1 Division, Armed Constabulary, with whom he won his Cross. For this exploit he was also promoted Sergeant, but shortly afterwards reverted to the ranks at his own request. In all he fought in 17 engagements against the Maoris. After the War ended he continued in the Armed Constabulary until it was disbanded in 1886 on the formation of the New Zealand Permanent Militia and the New Zealand Police Force. In the original Roll of the Permanent Militia, which he then joined, Hill is shown as No. 92, 3rd Class Torpedoman in the Torpedo Corps. Although his date of discharge is uncertain, it is known that he served for a further ten years in Government service before retiring, and tried – unsuccessfully – to enlist for the South African War at the age of 63. He died on 15th February 1930 aged 93, and is buried at Auckland.

In addition to the New Zealand Cross, Hill received the Baltic Medal; the Crimea Medal with bar "Sebastopol"; the Turkish Crimea Medal; the Indian Mutiny Medal with bars "Lucknow" and "Relief of Lucknow"; the New Zealand Medal; the New Zealand Long and Efficient Service Medal (16 years); the Royal Humane Society's large bronze medal (A.B., H.M.S. *Hannibal*, 17th February 1860)[19]; the Royal Humane Society of Australasia's bronze medal (28th February 1896)[20]; and the New Zealand Maori War Veterans' Medal.

19. For saving the life of a shipmate who had fallen overboard off Corfu.
20. For saving life in Auckland Harbour.

Chapter 35

The Most Excellent Order of the British Empire
1. The Medal of the Order, 1917–1922

ORIGIN AND DEVELOPMENT

By 1917 the First World War had entered its third year and yet no end was in sight. The whole Empire had been mobilised in the war effort and a need had arisen to recognise a wider range of services than had been the case when wars were confined largely to combatants. The difficulty was that the existing awards, except for those for civilian gallantry, were virtually restricted to persons in public service or who held public office and, in consequence, they were ill-suited to the enlargement necessary. Nor was this all. In the Forces there was a requirement, particularly for officers below flag rank and its equivalent, for a reward for services not in action. During the earlier stages of the War this requirement had been met to some extent in the Army by awards of the D.S.O. and M.C. and, in consequence, had led to a good deal of criticism. Various expedients were considered in regard to civilian and military awards but eventually the King decided that the solution lay in the creation of a new Order entitled "The Most Excellent Order of the British Empire" to which persons who had rendered important services to the Empire were to be admitted. The Order was to consist of five classes, and a medal. The decision to introduce five classes was influenced largely by the intention to appoint a large number of foreigners who had assisted the war effort, and by the fact that many foreign orders consisted of five classes. Moreover, women were to be admitted equally with men. This was to be the first time that women of all degrees were to be eligible for full admission to a BritishOrder of Knighthood and the innovation coincided with Parliamentary acceptance of women's suffrage[1]. It was also decided that among the first awards of the medal should be a generous allotment for munitions workers who had displayed courage and devotion to duty under hazardous circumstances. The Order was instituted by Letters Patent of 4th June 1917 which were published in the *London Gazette* of 24th August 1917. The following Statutes dealt with the Medal:

"21. It is ordained that a medal in connection with the said Most Excellent Order shall be awarded to persons, not being members of the five classes of the said Most Excellent Order, whose services to Our Empire would warrant such mark of Our Royal appreciation.

22. It is ordained that the medal of the Most Excellent Order of the British Empire for men and for women shall consist of a circular medal in silver, having on the obverse a representation of Britannia within the circle and motto of the Order and on the reverse Our Royal and Imperial Cypher, and shall be worn on the left side suspended by a ring to a purple riband of one inch and one-sixteenth of an inch in width.

23. It is ordained that it shall be competent for Us, Our heirs and successors by a Warrant under Our Royal Sign Manual to cancel and annul the award of any Medal of the Most Excellent Order of the British Empire, and that thereupon the name of the recipient in the Register shall be erased, but it shall be competent for the Sovereign to restore the medal to any person whose name may have been so erased, when circumstances render it just and expedient so to do."

1. Similar provision for women was made in the statutes of the Order of the Companions of Honour which was instituted at the same time.

237

Fig.A: The Medal of the Most Excellent Order of the British Empire, 1917–1922, obverse.

Fig.B: The Medal of the Most Excellent Order of the British Empire, 1917–1922, reverse.

On 27th December 1918[2] King George V instituted a Military Division of the Order to date from the creation of the Order on 4th June 1917. The Order, and the Medal of the Order, originally had no Divisions, being awarded to both civilians and Service personnel without differentiation. In fact the majority of awards were to civilians. With the institution of the two Divisions the following classes of person were eligible for appointment to the Military Division:

> "All commissioned, warrant and subordinate Officers subject to the Naval Discipline Act or employed under the Order of the Admiralty, and all commissioned and warrant Officers recommended by any Commander-in-Chief in the field or elsewhere, or by the General Officer Commanding, Independent Force, Royal Air Force, or employed under the War Office or Air Ministry, or under the Administrative Headquarters of Dominions or Overseas Forces, or employed under the Ministry of Munitions or the Ministry of National Service on work which, but for the creation of those Departments, would have been performed by the War Office; and all members of the Naval, Army, Dominions, or Overseas Nursing Services, or officials of the Women's Royal Naval Service, Queen Mary's Army Auxiliary Corps, or the Women's Royal Air Force, and such commandants of the Women's Legion or similar organizations as are under contract with or employed by the Admiralty, War Office or Air Ministry.
>
> Persons already appointed to the Order who are qualified for the Military Division will, on the recommendation of the First Lord of the Admiralty, the Secretary of State for War or the Secretary of State for the Royal Air Force, as the case may be, be transferred to the Military Division.
>
> The Insignia for both Military and Civil Divisions will be the same, but the ribbon of the Military Division will be distinguished by a vertical red stripe in the centre of the existing ribbon."

The Medal of the Most Excellent Order of the British Empire was superseded on 29th December 1922 by the institution of the Medal of the Most Excellent Order of the British Empire, for Gallantry, and the Medal of the Most Excellent Order of the British Empire, for Meritorious Service (q.v.).

By an Additional Statute dated 14th March 1941 which was published in the *London Gazette* of 22nd April 1941, it was ordained that the original Medal, i.e. that instituted in 1917 and superseded in 1922, should be known as the British Empire Medal. This also applied to the Medal instituted in 1922 (q.v.).

Originally the 1917 and 1922 Medals were worn immediately after the Indian Order of Merit (Civil Division) but later became separated from it by the insertion of certain gallantry medals instituted after 1922 (see Appendix 4).

DESCRIPTION

Ribbon Originally this was purple and $1\frac{1}{16}$ inches wide. On the creation of the Civil and Military Divisions, the Civil Division retained the original ribbon, while that of the Military Division was distinguished from it by a vertical red stripe in the centre.

Suspension By a silver ring through which the ribbon passed.

Obverse (Fig.A).

Reverse (Fig.B).

Naming The medals were issued unnamed.

Copies and Fakes So far none has been found.

VERIFICATIONS AND CITATIONS

All awards are published in the *London Gazette* and appear under the heading "British Empire Medal", or "British Empire, Most Excellent Order of, Medal" or "British Empire, Medal of the Order of" in the appropriate quarterly "State Intelligence" section of the Indices. Of the total of 2,014 medals gazetted, 1,282 have citations of two or more lines.

2. See *L.G.*, 27th December 1918 at p.15,135. This followed proposals on behalf of the three Services that awards for civil and military services should be distinguished as had been done with the Military and Civil Divisions of the Order of the Bath.

NUMBERS AWARDED

A total of 2,014 were awarded, which can be summarised as follows:

London Gazette			Division not given	Civil Division	Military Division
24th August 1917	...	...	52[3]	—	—
1st January 1918	...	...	367[4]	—	—
3rd June 1918[5]	...	...	218[4]	—	—
1st January 1919	...	...	—	—	5[6]
15th January 1919	...	...	274[4]	—	—
15th February 1919	...	...	—	—	2[7]
17th March 1919	...	...	—	—	3[8]
9th May 1919	...	...	—	—	22[9]
3rd June 1919	...	...	—	—	1[10]
16th September 1919		...	—	—	1
10th October 1919	...		—	—	1[11]
17th October 1919	...	...	—	—	5
23rd January 1920	...	...	—	—	405
2nd March 1920	...	...	—	102[12]	—
7th July 1920[13]	...	...	423[14]	—	—
7th October 1920	...	...	—	46[15]	—
20th October 1920	...	...	—	—	1
23rd November 1920		...	—	—	1
4th February 1921	...	...	—	—	6[16]
18th February 1921	...	...	—	—	4
15th March 1921	...	...	—	—	4
21st April 1921	...	...	—	—	4
1st June 1921	...	...	—	—	18
17th June 1921	...	...	—	—	5
29th July 1921	...	...	—	—	2
9th September 1921		...	—	—	1
28th September 1921		...	—	—	6
11th November 1921		...	—	4[14]	—
20th January 1922	...	...	—	1	—
24th January 1922	...	...	—	2	—
29th March 1922	...	...	—	—	1
1st January 1923	...	...	—	15	12
Totals:			1,334	170	510

Grand Total: 2,014

3. None has a citation.

4. All have citations of two or more lines.

5. Two of these awards were subsequently cancelled, one on 26th March 1920, and the other on 5th May 1925.

6. "For services in connection with the War".

7. "For valuable services whilst prisoner of war in Germany in promoting the welfare of their comrades".

8. "In recognition of their services in rescuing survivors from a torpedoed steamship".

9. All to W.R.N.S.

10. To W.R.A.F.

11. To R.A.F., "for gallant conduct in France".

12. All in recognition of a number of different services in India during the War.

13. No Division given, but the majority to members of different Fire Brigades.

14. All have citations of two or more lines.

15. All to members of the Metropolitan Special Constabulary.

16. "In recognition of valuable services rendered whilst Prisoners at Baku in promoting the welfare of their comrades".

17. Information supplied by the Central Chancery of the Orders of Knighthood.

18. *L.G.*, 17th October 1917, p. 10,680.

19. *L.G.*, 12th December 1917, p.13,028.

Up to March 1941, 801 awards had been made to foreign nationals. This figure includes those who had been awarded the Medal of the Order of the British Empire instituted in 1922. No breakdown of the total figure is available[17].

ILLUSTRATIVE AWARD

Sergeant Edward John Greengrass, 24th (County of London) Battalion, the London Regiment (The Queen's), was awarded the Medal of the Most Excellent Order of the British Empire in the *London Gazette* of 3rd June 1918 "for conspicuous courage and devotion to duty while on special service in Russia and Roumania". He had accompanied Lieutenant-Colonel A. C. Bromhead of the same Regiment on a Special Mission to the Russian Armies in 1916 and 1917, and served from Riga to the Caucasus, and in Roumania. He also received the Russian Medal of St. George, 4th Class, which he was granted unrestricted permission to wear on 17th October 1917[18]. Greengrass also received personally from the Czar a watch bearing the Imperial coat of arms; unfortunately he later lost this in Romania. He also received the M.S.M. for gallantry in Russia[19].

Chapter 36

The Most Excellent Order of the British Empire
2. The Medal of the Order, for Gallantry, 1922–1940

Figs. A and B: The Medal of the Most Excellent Order of the British Empire, for Gallantry, laurel branch for ribbon, and obverse.

ORIGIN AND DEVELOPMENT

The Medal of the Order of the British Empire, for Gallantry, more commonly known as the Empire Gallantry Medal (E.G.M.), was instituted by a Royal Warrant dated 29th December 1922 which was published in the *London Gazette* of the same day. The Royal Warrant is a long one, and provides for "Further amended Statutes of the Order of the British Empire". The Clauses dealing with the E.G.M. are as follows:

"37. It is ordained that a Military and Civil Medal of this Order shall be awarded to persons who perform acts of gallantry warranting such mark of Our Royal appreciation.

38. It is further ordained that a Military and Civil Medal of this Order shall be awarded to persons who render meritorious service warranting such mark of Our Royal appreciation and that such Civil Medal for meritorious service shall not be awarded to Members of or persons eligible for appointment to any of the five classes of Our said Order, and such Military Medal shall only be awarded to persons subordinate to those who are eligible for the Military Division of the various classes of this Order.

39. It is ordained that the medal of the Most Excellent Order of the British Empire for men and for women shall consist of a circular medal in silver, having on the obverse a representation of Britannia within the circle and motto of the Order with, upon the exergue, the words "For Gallantry" or "For Meritorious Service", and on the reverse Our Royal and Imperial Cypher, and shall be worn on the left side suspended from a clasp to a purple riband of one inch and one-sixteenth of an inch in width, with the addition in the case of recipients of the Military Medal of the Order of a vertical red stripe in the centre of the riband of about one-tenth of an inch, and that the clasp shall be ornamented with laurel leaves for gallantry, or with oak leaves for meritorious service, as the case may be.

40. It is ordained that it shall be competent for Us, Our heirs and successors by a Warrant under Our Royal Sign Manual to cancel and annul the award of any Medal of the Most Excellent Order of the British Empire, and that thereupon the name of the recipient in the Register shall be erased, but it shall be competent for the Sovereign to restore the medal to any person whose name may have been so erased when circumstances render it just and expedient so to do."

The Statutes were revised after the death of King George V, two of which, dated 30th July 1937, were as follows:

"XXXVII. It is Ordained that a Military and Civil Medal of this Order shall be awarded to persons who perform acts of gallantry warranting such mark of Our Royal appreciation, and that any person to whom such Medal has been, or may be, awarded may, on all occasions when the use of such letters is customary, place after his or her names the letters "E.G.M." (Empire Gallantry Medal) and that any member of the Order upon whom such Medal has been, or may be, conferred shall be entitled to wear it in addition to the Insignia of the Order. It is also Ordained that a

Post nominal "E.G.M." permitted

Fig.C: The Medal of the Most Excellent Order of the British Empire, for Gallantry (Empire Gallantry Medal), reverse, George V issue.

Fig.D: The Medal of the Most Excellent Order of the British Empire, for Gallantry (Empire Gallantry Medal), reverse, George VI issue.

1. In fact this was introduced in 1933, see *Annual Report of the Deputy Master and Comptroller of the Royal Mint (1933)*, p.44. The emblems were in two sizes, the smaller being for wear when the ribbon alone was worn.

2. See P.R.O. MINT 20/773.

3. Royal Warrant of 30th July 1937; see also the *Annual Report of the Deputy Master and Comptroller of the Royal Mint (1937)*, p.53.

Institution of Bar for further acts of gallantry further act of gallantry deemed worthy of an award of the Medal performed by a person upon whom the Medal has been conferred shall be recorded by a Bar attached to the riband from which the Medal is suspended, and that for every additional such act an additional bar may be awarded.

XXXIX. It is Ordained that the Medal of the Most Excellent Order of the British Empire for men and for women shall consist of a circular medal in silver, having on the obverse a representation of Britannia with the motto of the Order, and, upon the **New reverse to Medal** exergue, the words "For Gallantry", or "For Meritorious Service" and on the reverse the Royal and Imperial Cypher of the Sovereign, and the words "Instituted by King George V", and shall be worn on the left side suspended from a clasp to a rose pink **New riband colour** riband edged with pearl grey of one inch and one quarter in width, with the addition, in the case of recipients of the Military Medal of the Order, of a vertical pearl grey **Institution of Laurel branch on riband** stripe in the centre of the riband of about one-sixteenth of an inch, and that the clasp shall be ornamented with laurel leaves for gallantry, or with oak leaves for meritorious service, as the case may be. And it is further Ordained that the riband of the Medal "For Gallantry" shall be ornamented with a branch of Laurel in silver."

The E.G.M. was superseded by the George Cross (q.v.) in September 1940 and until then it was worn after the Indian Order of Merit (Civil Division). The first E.G.M. to be gazetted was an award of the Civil Division to Albert Waterfield, Park Keeper, Richmond Park, in the *London Gazette* of 1st January 1923, the award being dated 30th December 1922. The last to be gazetted were four awards in the Military Division on 17th September 1940, to Lieutenant E. W. Reynolds, 2nd Lieutenants E. E. Talbot and W. L. Andrews, and Lance-Sergeant W. J. Button, all of the Royal Engineers.

DESCRIPTION

Ribbon Civil Division – purple, $1\frac{1}{16}$ inches wide. Military Division – as for Civil Division but with the addition of a vertical red stripe in the centre about $\frac{1}{10}$ inch wide. On 30th July 1937, by the revised Statutes, the ribbon was changed. The ribbon of the Civil Division was to be $1\frac{1}{4}$ inches wide of rose pink edged with pearl-grey stripes. The Military Division was to be as for the Civil Division but with the addition of a vertical pearl-grey stripe of about $\frac{1}{16}$ inch in the centre.

Laurel Branch (Fig.A) The silver laurel branch mentioned in the 1937 Statute[1] was fixed to the ribbon by two prongs which were pushed through the ribbon and then bent over.

Suspension By a straight clasp ornamented with laurel leaves.

Obverse (Fig.B) This has remained constant. The medal was designed by Langford Jones. A number were struck with the legend "FOR GOD & EMPIRE" but before they were issued it was realised that the motto of the Order was "FOR GOD AND THE EMPIRE". Accordingly, the medals were recalled and melted down. New dies were then made and medals struck with the correct legend[2].

Reverse Two types of reverse were issued:
1. George V (Fig.C).
2. George VI (Fig.D) In 1937 the words "Instituted by King George V" were added, and the cypher altered[3]. A similar alteration was made to the reverse of the Medal for Meritorious Service (q.v.).

Bar Although provided for in the revised Statutes of 30th July 1937, none was awarded.

Naming We have seen two awards, one of the Civil and the other of the Military Division. Both were engraved in serif capital letters with the recipients' full names; the military award had the rank abbreviated: "FLT.CDT.", and had "R.A.F." after the surname.

Copies and Fakes For recent copies see the Note on p.xx. A number of Mint specimens were struck.

VERIFICATIONS AND CITATIONS

All awards are notified in the *London Gazette*, except the four honorary awards; three of the latter are given by Wilson and McEwen (see Bibliography). In the *London Gazette* every award is indexed under the heading "British Empire, Most Excellent Order of ..." in the "State Intelligence" portion of the appropriate quarterly index. Wilson and McEwen give all the citations until 31st December 1938. Smyth (see Bibliography) gives all awards of E.G.M. holders who subsequently exchanged their E.G.M. for the George Cross. Bisset (see Bibliography) gives the majority of the awards.

NUMBERS AWARDED

A total of 130 Empire Gallantry Medals were awarded as follows:

Civil Division	... ...	64
Military Division	... ...	62
Honorary awards	... ...	4

Of the total, four (3 Civil and 1 Military) were posthumous awards made before 3rd September 1939 and therefore, under the terms of the Royal Warrant instituting the George Cross (q.v.), could not be exchanged for that award. There were four posthumous E.G.M.s awarded between the outbreak of the Second World War and the institution of the G.C.; these were exchanged for the G.C. The four honorary awards to foreigners could not be exchanged for the G.C., and the recipients were therefore the only persons permitted to wear the medal after the institution of the G.C. Of the balance (122), 112 have been exchanged for G.C.s and the names are given by Smyth; this leaves 10 E.G.M.s which have not been exchanged. The four honorary awards were to:

Name	Nationality	Date of Act
Camiel Van Hove	Belgian	30th December 1933
Julien T. J. Tanguy	French	19th February 1936
Paul Grieu	French	19th February 1936
Capitaine L. Loussot[4]	French	22nd January 1940

In theory, the E.G.M. was returned to the Central Chancery of the Orders of Knighthood, and at a subsequent investiture the holder was decorated with the George Cross. It is known that some E.G.M.s were not returned, although the recipient did subsequently attend an investiture and was decorated with the G.C.

ILLUSTRATIVE AWARD

Sergeant William George Hand, M.M., 2nd Battalion, Dorsetshire Regiment, was awarded the E.G.M. in the *London Gazette* of 2nd June 1923 "for services rendered in connection with military operations in Malabar, 1921–1922." His obituary in the *Devonshire and Dorset Regimental Journal*, Volume 4, No. 14 of May 1962, amplifies the bald statement in the *London Gazette*, and records:

"After the war he was posted to the 2nd Battalion at Portland and accompanied the Battalion to India. There was much unrest in India at the time and before long the Dorsets found themselves on service again in the Malabar country with a full-scale Moplah rebellion on their hands. On September 24, 1921, near Nilambur, Sgt. Hand's No. 6 Platoon was leading the advance guard, moving along the road through thickly wooded country, when they were ambushed by rebels holding a very strong position. Small arms fire was insufficient to dislodge the enemy and even the temporary withdrawal of the platoon to allow the supporting eighteen-pounder gun of the Royal Artillery to fire on the strong point, had no effect. Sgt. Hand then asked his Company Commander for permission to go forward himself to try and dislodge the rebels with hand grenades. Private (Thomas) Miller (also awarded the E.G.M.), of No. 8 Platoon, asked to be allowed to move on to the other side of the road to catch any enemy who tried to get away after they had been bombed by Sgt. Hand. The ruse was entirely successful and Miller was able to complete the work, bayoneting those of the enemy who had not been killed by grenades."[5]

4. Of the French Mercantile Marine. His citation is in P.R.O. PREM 2/110.

5. Reproduced by permission.

Hand was subsequently invested with the G.C. by King George VI at Buckingham Palace on 3rd February 1942.

In addition to the E.G.M. (later G.C.), Hand was also the recipient of the India General Service Medal, 1908–1935, the Military Medal[6], the 1914–15 Star, the British War and Victory Medals and the Military Long Service and Good Conduct Medal (Regular Army). After his discharge he later joined the War Department Constabulary, and became an Inspector. He received the Defence Medal. He died on 28th October 1961.

6. *L.G.*, 24th January 1919, as a sergeant in the 1st Battalion of the Dorsetshire Regiment.

Chapter 37

The Most Excellent Order of the British Empire
3. The Medal of the Order, For Meritorious Service, from 1922

Fig.A: The Medal of the Most Excellent Order of the British Empire, for Meritorious Service (British Empire Medal), obverse.

ORIGIN AND DEVELOPMENT

This Medal was instituted by the same Royal Warrant, dated 29th December 1922 and published in the *London Gazette* of that day, which instituted the E.G.M. (q.v.).

The Statutes were revised after the death of King George V, two of which, dated 30th July 1937, were as follows:

"XXXVIII. It is further Ordained that a Military and Civil Medal of this Order shall be awarded to persons who render meritorious service warranting such mark of Our Royal appreciation. Such Civil Medal shall not be awarded to Members of any of the five Classes of the Order or to persons eligible for appointment thereto, and such Military Medal shall only be awarded to persons subordinate to those who are eligible for the Military Division of the various Classes of the Order, but a recipient of the Medal, whether Military or Civil, who may subsequently be appointed a Member of one of the five Classes of the Order, may continue to wear the Medal in addition to the Insignia of the Order.

XXXIX. It is Ordained that the Medal of the Most Excellent Order of the British Empire for men and for women shall consist of a circular medal in silver, having on the obverse a representation of Britannia with the motto of the Order, and, upon the *New reverse* exergue, the words "For Gallantry", or "For Meritorious Service" and on the reverse *to Medal* the Royal and Imperial Cypher of the Sovereign, and the words "Instituted by King George V", and shall be worn on the left side suspended from a clasp to a rose pink *New riband* riband edged with pearl grey of one inch and one quarter in width, with the addition, *colour* in the case of recipients of the Military Medal of the Order, of a vertical pearl grey stripe in the centre of the riband of about one-sixteenth of an inch, and that the clasp *Institution* shall be ornamented with laurel leaves for gallantry, or with oak leaves for meri- *of Laurel* torious service, as the case may be. And it is further Ordained that the riband of the *branch on* Medal "For Gallantry" shall be ornamented with a branch of Laurel in silver." *riband*

An Additional Statute dated 14th March 1941 which was published in the *London Gazette* of 22nd April 1941, annulled the 38th and 39th Clauses quoted above[1], and established the following:

"XXXVII. It is Ordained that a Military and Civil Medal of this Order shall be awarded to persons who render meritorious service warranting such mark of Our Royal appreciation. Such Civil Medal shall not be awarded to Members of any of the five Classes of the Order or to such persons eligible for appointment thereto, and such Military Medal shall only be awarded to persons subordinate to those who are eligible for the Military Division of the various Classes of the Order, but a recipient of the Medal, whether Military or Civil, who may subsequently be appointed a Member of one of the five Classes of the Order, may continue to wear the Medal in addition to the *Designated* Insignia of the Order. It is further Ordained that the said Medal, including the Medal *the British* awarded prior to 29th December, 1922, shall be known as "The British Empire *Empire* Medal"."

1. Also the 37th Clause dealing with the Empire Gallantry Medal.

Designated the British Empire Medal

Fig.B: The Medal of the Most Excellent Order of the British Empire, for Meritorious Service (British Empire Medal), reverse, George V issue.

Fig.C: The Medal of the Most Excellent Order of the British Empire, for Meritorious Service (British Empire Medal), reverse, George VI issue, first type.

2. Originally the Medal was worn after the Indian Order of Merit (Civil Division). The Burma Gallantry Medal was later advanced in the official order of wearing and certain other gallantry awards were inserted immediately above the B.E.M., see Appendix 4.

3. See Royal Warrant of 30th July 1937, and the *Annual Report of the Deputy Master and Comptroller of the Royal Mint (1937)*, p.53.

4. See P.R.O. MINT 20/1820.

XXXVIII. It is Ordained that the said Medal for men and for women shall consist of a circular medal in silver, having on the obverse a representation of Britannia with the motto of the Order, and, upon the exergue, the words "For Meritorious Service", and on the reverse the Royal and Imperial Cypher of the Sovereign, and the words "Instituted by King George V", and shall be worn on the left side, immediately after the Burma Gallantry Medal[2], suspended from a clasp ornamented with oak leaves, attached to a rose pink riband edged with pearl grey of one inch and one-quarter in width, with the addition, in the case of recipients of the Military Medal of the Order, of a vertical pearl grey stripe in the centre of the riband about one-sixteenth of an inch: provided that when the Medal is worn by a woman, it may be worn on the left shoulder, suspended from a riband of the same width and colour, fashioned into a bow. It is further Ordained that on occasions when miniature decorations are worn, reproductions of the Medal in miniature may be worn by those to whom the Medal is awarded.

XXXIX. It is Ordained that services or acts deemed worthy of recognition by the award of the Medal, but rendered by a person upon whom the Medal has already been conferred, may be recorded by a Bar or Bars attached, for men, to the riband, and for women, to the centre of the bow, from which the Medal is suspended. It is further Ordained that when the riband is worn alone, the award of a Bar is to be indicated by the placing of a small silver rosette on the riband, a further rosette being added for each bar."

A Statute signed by King George VI, dated 10th June 1942, authorised the use of the post-nominal letters "B.E.M.".

DESCRIPTION

Ribbon For the Civil Division this was purple and $1\frac{1}{16}$ inches wide; for the Military Division it was as for the Civil Division but with the addition of a vertical red stripe in the centre about $\frac{1}{10}$ inch wide. On 30th July 1937, by the revised Statutes, the Civil Division ribbon was changed to rose pink edged with pearl grey stripes and $1\frac{1}{4}$ inches wide; the ribbon of the Military Division was to be as that of the Civil Division but with the addition of a vertical pearl grey stripe in the centre about $\frac{1}{16}$ inch wide.

Suspension By a straight, swivelling suspender ornamented with oak leaves.

Obverse (Fig.A) This has remained constant.

Reverse There are four types of reverse, as follows:

1. George V (Fig.B).
2. George VI first type (Fig.C) This shows the alterations made in 1937, i.e. change in the Royal Cypher and addition of the words "Instituted by King George V"[3].
3. George VI second type (Fig.D) By a Royal Proclamation of 22nd June 1948 the King's style and titles were altered and the Royal Cypher changed accordingly.
4. Elizabeth II (Fig.E).

Bar (Fig.F) This was introduced by the Statute of 14th March 1941, the design being approved by the King soon after[4].

Naming The Medal is always issued named and the particulars of the recipient are engraved in capitals round the edge. Those to Service personnel have their number and unit or Service included. Civil awards usually have the names in full, or the first name and surname in full, other names being indicated by initials; this sometimes occurs in Military awards as well.

Copies and Fakes For recent copies see the Note on p.xx.

VERIFICATIONS AND CITATIONS

All awards are notified in the *London Gazette*, each award being indexed under the heading "British Empire, Most Excellent Order of" in the "State Intelligence" section of the appropriate quarterly index until the end of 1941. From January

Fig.D: The Medal of the Most Excellent Order of the British Empire, for Meritorious Service (British Empire Medal), reverse, George VI issue, second type.

Fig.E: The Medal of the Most Excellent Order of the British Empire, for Meritorious Service (British Empire Medal), reverse, Elizabeth II issue.

Fig.F: Bar to the Medal of the Most Excellent Order of the British Empire.

5. Information supplied by the Central Chancery of the Orders of Knighthood.

6. Including New Year Honours.

7. Including Birthday Honours.

1942 the "State Intelligence" section gives only the pages upon which awards are to be found, but the individual names appear in a comprehensive nominal section headed "Honours, Decorations and Medals". Very few citations are given for awards before the outbreak of the Second World War.

During the Second World War many of the awards to A.R.P. workers, policemen, etc., and the Merchant Navy have very full and graphic citations. Generally speaking citations are found only for gallantry awards, while awards for meritorious service appear only as bare announcements. Awards to foreigners do not seem to have been gazetted. Details of some naval awards are to be found in the Public Record Office series ADM 1 (Code 85) and ADM 116 (Code 85); both series contain a large number of files and it is desirable to know the date of award and, where possible, the action or theatre for which it was awarded, before consulting the indices. Copies of recommendations for all three Services (including those for "non-gallantry" awards) from 1941 are available (subject to the "30-year" rule) in the series AIR 2 (Code 30); again, it is desirable to know at least the date of award before consulting the index. Recommendations for some Merchant Navy seamen are in the series MT 9.

NUMBERS AWARDED

The first awards were gazetted on 1st January 1923, being dated 28th December 1922. From that Gazette to the close of 1939 the following numbers were gazetted:

Year of Gazette			Civil Division	Military Division	Total in Year
1923	...	...	6	2	8
1924	...	...	17	—	17
1925	...	...	11	—	11
1926	...	...	4	—	4
1927	...	...	24	9	33
1928	...	...	16	1	17
1929	...	...	27	14	41
1930	...	...	24	17	41
1931	...	...	27	25	52
1932	...	...	37	21	58
1933	...	...	32	13	45
1934	...	...	27	16	43
1935	...	...	40	17	57
1936	...	...	33	18	51
1937	...	...	73	63	136
1938	...	...	63	45	108
1939	...	...	70	40	110
		Totals:	531	301	832

Up to March 1941, 801 awards had been made to foreigners. This number includes those awarded the Medal of the Order of the British Empire, 1917–1922. No breakdown of the total figure is available[5].

The numbers awarded annually from 1940 are considerably greater than those awarded before. We have therefore selected four years as examples although, due to the length of the Second World War and the unsettled world conditions following, no year can be regarded as typical. Our count shows the following awards in the London Gazette:

Year			First Quarter[6]	Second Quarter[7]	Third Quarter	Fourth Quarter	Total
1944	...	...	1134	1201	177	565	3077
1954	...	...	406	336	16	24	782
1964	...	...	357	339	1	5	702
1974	...	...	393	431	—	4	828

The totals are of the Civil and Military Divisions combined. They do not allow for any cancellations and are therefore approximate within a small margin of error.

The following recipients have been awarded first bars:

Division	Name	London Gazette awarding bar
Civil	A. E. Alcock, Head A.R.P. Warden, Coventry	...12th September 1941
Civil	J. H. Algar, Constable, Mauritius Police Force ...	...20th February 1972[8]
Military	C.P.O. A. Balson, Royal Navy	...20th January 1942[9]
Military	C.P.O. (Clearance Diver) B. E. Bray, R.N.	...15th April 1975[9]
Military	W.O.II R. B. Christison, R.E.	...8th June 1968[8]
Military	Sergeant L. W. G. Coates, R.A.F.V.R.	...12th March 1946[9]
Civil	F. J. Cox, Inspector, Plymouth Special Constabulary ...	...24th April 1942
Military	Driver A. I. Evans, R.A.S.C.	...28th September 1943
Military	Corporal I. W. Foster, R.A.A.S.C.	29th November 1960[8]
Military	P. O. Cook (S) R. C. Fry, D.S.M., R.N.	...21st April 1950
Civil	P. G. Gibbins, Sergeant, Metropolitan Police Force	...17th April 1970[8]
Military	Flight Sergeant A. R. Hall, R.A.F.	...12th June 1965
Civil	N. Jaeger, Leader, A.R.P., Lambeth	...6th June 1941
Military	Sergeant A. Jones, Royal Marines	...28th June 1977
Civil	A. E. Jones, Company Officer, No. 36 (London) Area, National Fire Service	...17th July 1945
Civil	A. Letch, Greaser	...2nd May 1944
Civil	W. Malt, Ploughman, Horden Colliery, South Durham Division, National Coal Board	...17th November 1953
Military	Chief Electrician (A) J. R. Mullender, R.N. ...	...31st December 1976
Military	Acting P. O. J. Paynter, R.N.	...3rd July 1945
Civil	G. A. Plant, Volunteer in charge of Coastguards, Lulworth, Dorset	...19th October 1965[8]
Civil	E. A. Sibbick, Upholsterer, Osborne House	...15th August 1969[9]
Civil	T. M. Skelton, Police Inspector, Liverpool City Police Force	...10th October 1941
Military	Leading Seaman N. L. Smith, R.N.	...17th November 1942
Military	C.P.O. Writer V . N. Smithbone, R.N.	...30th December 1978
Civil	R. W. F. Thompson, Sergeant, Royal Ulster Constabulary	...25th February 1969[8]
Military	Flight Sergeant J. Whitehead, R.A.F.	...3rd June 1971
Civil	G. Whyte, Carpenter, Merchant Navy	...20th July 1943

8. Awarded bar for gallantry, see Chapter 38.

9. In substitution for award of a second B.E.M.

ILLUSTRATIVE AWARD

Apprentice Harry Marshall Fortune, of the s.s. *Ascot* (British Steam Ship Company Ltd.) was awarded the B.E.M. (Civil Division) in the *London Gazette* of 26th June 1945 where his citation reads as follows:

> "The s.s. *Ascot*, sailing alone in the Indian Ocean, was torpedoed by a Japanese submarine. The ship began to sink and the crew got away in the boats and on rafts. The submarine surfaced, shelled the ship and then rammed the boats and rafts, machine-gunning the occupants, of whom all but eight were killed. Seven of the survivors clambered back on to one of the rafts. Two days later another survivor, who was found in one of the boats, was taken aboard the raft and after a further three days, the eight survivors were rescued by a friendly steamer.
>
> Apprentice Fortune showed conspicuous courage and qualities of leadership throughout. In spite of his overwhelming experiences he took charge of the raft and, under his direction, the injured were made as comfortable as possible, an awning was rigged, food and water rationed and life on the raft organised. There is no doubt that it was greatly due to Fortune's courage, resourcefulness and inspiring example that the survivors were eventually brought to safety."

Fortune also received Lloyd's War Medal for Bravery at Sea, and his name is listed by Masters (see Bibliography).

Chapter 38

The Most Excellent Order of the British Empire
4. The Emblem for Gallantry, 1957–1974

Fig.A: Emblem for Gallantry, Most Excellent Order of the British Empire, 1957 to 1974.

ORIGIN AND DEVELOPMENT

Ever since the institution of the Order of the British Empire in 1917 there have been cases where persons were appointed to it, promoted in it, or awarded the B.E.M. for acts of gallantry rather than meritorious service. This was very marked in the Second World War, and especially as far as the Merchant Navy and Civil Defence are concerned. There are hundreds of awards of the B.E.M., and appointments as an O.B.E. or as an M.B.E. in the *London Gazette* showing great and sustained gallantry. Awards were also made to a considerable number of Service personnel working behind the enemy lines, one of the best known being Odette Sansom, later Mrs. Hallowes, G.C., M.B.E. However, it was not until 1957 that gallantry awards in the Order were physically distinguished from meritorious awards when a silver crossed oak leaf emblem was introduced to be worn on the ribbon of the former. The emblem was not retrospective.

By an Additional Statute of 6th December 1957, and notified in modified form in the *London Gazette* of 14th January 1958[1]:

> "It is Ordained that those persons whom we think fit to admit in the future into this Most Excellent Order, in the Military or Civil Division, in recognition of gallantry, and those persons on whom we may think fit to confer the British Empire Medal, in the Military or Civil Division, in recognition of gallantry, shall wear on the riband from which the Badge or Medal is suspended a silver Emblem of two oak leaves, and in the announcement of the conferment of the award it shall be stated that the award has been made for gallantry.
>
> It is further Ordained that, when the riband is worn alone, the silver Emblem is to be worn in miniature; that this classification of certain awards as made for gallantry shall have no effect on the seniority or precedence of members of the various Classes of the Order; that those persons whom we may think fit to admit in the future into this Most Excellent Order in recognition of gallantry shall if promoted from a lower to a higher Class of the Order retain and wear the silver oak leaf Emblem whether the promotion is for gallantry or otherwise, the Emblem being thus worn on the riband of the highest Class to which such persons may be promoted; that those persons upon whom we may think fit to confer the British Empire Medal, in recognition of gallantry, shall if subsequently appointed to the Order continue to wear the silver oak leaf Emblem on the riband of the Medal, and shall wear a silver oak leaf Emblem on a riband of the Order only if appointment to or promotion in the Order was in recognition of gallantry."

Thus if a member of the Order, for gallantry, is later promoted in the Order for meritorious service, the gallantry emblem continues to be worn on the ribbon of the Class to which the member has been promoted. If the recipient of the B.E.M. for gallantry is entitled to wear the oak leaf emblem and is subsequently awarded a bar, the emblem is worn on the ribbon of the medal above the bar. When ribbons alone are worn the gallantry emblem is worn further from the left shoulder than the silver rose denoting the bar[2].

1. As a Note in the "order in which Orders, Decorations and Medals shall be worn".

2. See the *London Gazette* of 27th October 1964 where this rule is given as a note to the order in which Orders, Decorations and Medals should be worn.

In 1968[3] the Queen decided that recipients of the B.E.M. for Gallantry should attend investitures at Buckingham Palace to receive their awards. Hitherto these had been presented regionally by Lords Lieutenant, by Ministers or by General Officers Commanding, etc.

By an additional Statute of 7th December 1971 it was ordained, *inter alia*, that a person promoted from a lower Class in one Division to a higher Class in the other Division of the Order should retain and wear the insignia of the lower Class in addition to that of the higher Class.

With the institution of the Queen's Gallantry Medal (q.v.) on 20th June 1974 awards in the Order for gallantry ceased.

DESCRIPTION
Emblem (Fig.A) It is fixed to the ribbon by two prongs which are bent over after being passed through the ribbon.

VERIFICATIONS AND CITATIONS
All awards are notified in the *London Gazette* under the heading "British Empire, Most Excellent Order of" in the "State Intelligence" section of each quarterly index which gives the pages upon which awards are to be found; some omissions have been discovered in this section. Individual names are given in a comprehensive nominal section headed "Honours, Decorations and Medals". The majority of awards have long citations.

NUMBERS AWARDED
The first gallantry awards under the new Statute were notified in the *London Gazette* of 4th February 1958, there being eight recipients, all in the Civil Division. The following awards have been made each year:

Year	C.B.E. Civ.	C.B.E. Mil.	O.B.E. Civ.	O.B.E. Mil.	M.B.E. Civ.	M.B.E. Mil.	B.E.M. Civ.	B.E.M. Mil.	Total	B.E.M. bars for Gallantry
1958	—	—	1	—	6	3	37	12	59	—
1959	—	—	—	—	2	2	31	6	41	—
1960	—	—	—	—	9	4	58	8	79	1
1961	—	—	1	—	2	—	21	3	27	—
1962	—	—	—	—	4	2	25	5	36	—
1963	—	—	—	1	6	1	48	6	62	—
1964	—	1	—	—	6	1	22	8	38	—
1965	—	—	2	1	4	11	50	14	82	1
1966	—	—	—	—	4	3	47	8	62	—
1967	—	—	—	1	2	6	47	13	69	—
1968	—	—	—	—	3	9	32	9	53	—
1969	—	—	—	—	6	2	51	10	69	1
1970	—	—	1	1	2	2	48	9	63	1
1971	—	—	—	1	6	9	53	23	92	—
1972	—	—	—	—	2	1	18	16	37	1
1973	—	—	—	—	6	2	35	27	70	1
1974	—	—	—	—	3	5	13	12	33	—

ILLUSTRATIVE AWARD
John Thomas Scrimshire, Farm Foreman, Home Farm, Stubton, Newark, Lincolnshire, was awarded the B.E.M. (Civil Division), for Gallantry, in the *London Gazette* of 26th June 1962 where his citation reads as follows:

"An aircraft crashed on a farmhouse completely demolishing it, killing two occupants and two of the aircrew. Mr. Scrimshire was in his house on the opposite side of the road and reached the front door as the aircraft hit the farmhouse thirty yards away. The scene was immediately one of great confusion, the air being full of flying debris from the demolished farmhouse, and fire had broken out. The whole area was

3. *The Times*, 1st March 1968.

saturated with large quantities of jet fuel and the risk of a major explosion was made even greater by the fact that the blazing wreckage had fallen on top of the farm bulk fuel storage tank. Under these most frightening circumstances, and with complete disregard for his own personal safety, Mr. Scrimshire dashed across the road to the scene of the crash. He heard the farm owner calling for help and discovered him about ten feet from the blazing aircraft buried up to his armpits in wreckage. Scrimshire managed to drag him free and carry him to a place of safety where he was screened by a low wall from the danger of an explosion."

Chapter 39

The Queen's Fire Service Medal

Fig.A: The Queen's Fire Service Medal, obverse.

ORIGIN AND DEVELOPMENT

The Queen's Fire Service Medal was instituted by a Royal Warrant dated 19th May 1954 which was reproduced in the *London Gazette* of 4th June 1954 as follows:

"ELIZABETH R.

ELIZABETH THE SECOND, by the Grace of God of the United Kingdom of Great Britain and Northern Ireland and of Our other Realms and Territories QUEEN, Head of the Commonwealth, Defender of the Faith, To all to whom these Presents shall come,

Greeting!

WHEREAS His late Majesty King Edward the Seventh in consideration of the good services rendered by officers of the Constabulary Forces and by persons serving in the fire brigades within His Dominions and in Territories under His Protection or Jurisdiction and the heroic acts of courage and instances of conspicuous devotion to duty of such persons, and being desirous of distinguishing such meritorious conduct by some mark of His Royal Favour did by Warrant under His Royal Sign Manual dated the 7th July, 1909, institute a new Medal to be awarded for such services aforesaid:

AND WHEREAS We are desirous of having separate Medals for members of fire services and for members of police forces We are graciously pleased to make, ordain, and establish the following Statutes for the governance of the Decoration to be awarded to members of fire services:

Firstly – It is ordained that the Medal shall be designated and styled "The Queen's Fire Service Medal".

Secondly – It is ordained that the Medal shall consist of a circular Medal of Silver with the effigy of the Sovereign on the obverse, and shall bear on the reverse a design emblematic of protection from danger and the words "For Gallantry" or "For Distinguished Fire Service" as the case may be, and on the rim the name of the person to whom the Medal has been awarded.

Thirdly – It is ordained that the Medal shall be awarded only to those of Our Faithful Subjects and Others who have either performed acts of exceptional courage and skill at the cost of their lives, or exhibited conspicuous devotion to duty, as members of a recognised fire brigade or service within Our United Kingdom of Great Britain and Northern Ireland, Our Channel Islands, Our Island of Man, any of Our Colonies or any territory under Our protection or jurisdiction not being administered by Us in Our Government in any other part of Our Commonwealth, or within any other part of Our Commonwealth Our Government whereof has signified its desire that the Medal should be awarded under the provisions of this Our Warrant to members of any such brigade or service within such part, or within any territory under Our protection or jurisdiction being administered by Us in such Government; and that such award shall be made only on a recommendation to Us by Our Secretary of State for the Home Department, or, in the case of a Member country of Our Commonwealth other than Our United Kingdom of Great Britain and Northern Ireland the Government whereof shall so desire, by the appropriate Minister of State for that country.

Fourthly – It is ordained that the names of those upon whom We may be pleased to confer this Decoration shall be published in the *London Gazette*, and that a Register thereof shall be kept in the Office of Our Secretary of State for the Home Department, or, in the case of a Member country of Our Commonwealth other than Our United

Kingdom of Great Britain and Northern Ireland the Government whereof shall so desire, of the appropriate Minister of State for that country. Such Register shall show the name and rank of the person holding the Medal, the brigade or service of which that person is or was a member and the circumstances in which the Medal has been awarded.

Fifthly – It is ordained that the Medal shall be suspended from the left breast, and the riband, of an inch and three eighths in width, shall be red with a narrow yellow stripe on either side and a similar yellow stripe in the middle; and in the case of awards for acts of exceptional courage each yellow stripe of the riband shall contain a thin dark blue line down the middle.

Sixthly – It is ordained that any act of gallantry worthy of recognition by the award of The Queen's Fire Service Medal which is performed upon whom the Decoration or either of its predecessors (namely, The King's Police Medal and The King's Police and Fire Services Medal) has already been conferred may, on a recommendation to Us by Our Secretary of State for the Home Department, or, in the case of a Member country of Our Commonwealth other than Our United Kingdom of Great Britain and Northern Ireland the Government whereof shall so desire, the appropriate Minister of State for that country, be recorded by a Bar attached to the riband by which the Medal is suspended.

Seventhly – It is ordained that it shall be competent for Us, Our Heirs and Successors by an Order under Our Sign Manual, and on a recommendation to that effect by Our Secretary of State for the Home Department, or, in the case of a Member country of Our Commonwealth other than Our United Kingdom of Great Britain and Northern Ireland the Government whereof shall so desire, the appropriate Minister of State for that country, to cancel and annul the award to any person of the above Decoration or either of its predecessors and that thereupon the name of that person in the Register shall be erased. Provided that it shall be competent for Us, Our Heirs and Successors to restore any Decoration which may have been so forfeited when such recommendation has been withdrawn. And every person to whom the Decoration is awarded for distinguished service shall, before receiving the same, enter into an agreement to return the Medal if his or her name shall be erased as aforesaid.

Eighthly – It is ordained that Our Secretary of State for the Home Department, or, in the case of a Member country of Our Commonwealth other than Our United Kingdom of Great Britain and Northern Ireland the Government whereof shall so desire, the appropriate Minister of State for that Country, may make Regulations for the carrying into effect of this Our Royal Warrant.

All previous Warrants issued in this behalf are hereby revoked except in so far as they are already revoked.

GIVEN at Our Court at Saint James's the Nineteenth day of May, 1954, in the Third Year of Our Reign.

By Her Majesty' Command.
David Maxwell Fyfe."

On 28th May 1954 Regulations were made for the Medal as follows:

"1. Unless Her Majesty otherwise directs, lists of the names of members of recognised fire brigades or services who are recommended for the Medal on any ground other than that of conspicuous gallantry shall be submitted by the Secretary of State for the Home Department in the months of May and December in each year.

2. The names of those recommended by other Departments for inclusion in any such list shall be forwarded to the Home Office not later than one month prior to the date on which the award is to be made.

3. Recommendations for awards on the ground of conspicuous gallantry shall be made as soon as possible after the occasion on which the conspicuous gallantry was shown; and in special circumstances recommendations for awards on other grounds may be made at any time for an immediate award.

4. All recommendations shall state the name and rank of the person recommended, the name of the fire brigade or service of which that person is or was a member, and particulars of the gallantry or service for which the grant of the Medal is recommended.

Fig.B: The Queen's Fire Service Medal, for gallantry, reverse.

5. The qualifications for the grant of the Medal shall be as follows:

(a) Conspicuous gallantry in saving life and property, the risks incurred being estimated with due regard to the obligations and duties of the deceased person recommended.

(b) A specially distinguished record in the fire service.

(c) Success in organising fire services, or in maintaining their organisation under special difficulties.

(d) Special services in dealing with serious or widespread outbreaks of fire or other serious public catastrophes.

(e) Special services to Royalty and Heads of States.

(f) Prolonged service; but only when distinguished by very exceptional ability and merit."

In 1969 the Queen approved of the use by recipients of the post-nominal letters "Q.F.S.M."[1] and a consequent amendment was made by Royal Warrant on 8th October 1971[2]; by the same Warrant recommendations and regulations were to be made by the Secretary of State for Scotland.

DESCRIPTION

Ribbon Red, 1⅜ inches wide, with a narrow yellow stripe at either side and one in the centre; for gallantry awards a thin dark blue stripe is added to the centre of each yellow stripe.

Suspension By a silver ring approximately ½ inch in diameter.

Obverse (Fig.A).

Reverse (Fig.B) It will be noted that, while there is a special reverse for distinguished service, the gallantry reverse is the same as that for the Queen's Police Medal for gallantry[3].

VERIFICATIONS AND CITATIONS

Awards are published in the *London Gazette*. The pages upon which awards are to be found are given under the medal heading in the quarterly indices, the names and page references to individuals being in the nominal index to "Honours, Decorations and Medals". No citations have been published in the *Gazette*.

NUMBERS AWARDED

No awards have been made for gallantry[4]. Up to 31st December 1979, 422 awards have been made for distinguished service.

1. See *Hansard* (House of Commons) for 22nd July 1969, column 346.

2. See *L.G.*, 22nd October 1971.

3. See the *Annual Report of the Deputy Master and Comptroller of the Royal Mint (1954)*, pp.8 and 27.

4. By Clause 3 of the Warrant, gallantry awards are only made posthumously.

Chapter 40

The Queen's Gallantry Medal

Fig.A: The Queen's Gallantry Medal, obverse.

ORIGIN AND DEVELOPMENT

On 20th June 1974, in a written answer to a question in the House of Commons[1], the Prime Minister (Mr Harold Wilson) announced the institution of the Queen's Gallantry Medal. He explained that recognition of acts of gallantry of a slightly lower degree than that required for the George Cross and George Medal had hitherto been recognised by awards in the Order of the British Empire, the choice of level in that Order depending not upon the degree of gallantry but upon the rank or level of responsibility of the individual concerned. Considerations of rank and level of responsibility were not generally relevant to acts of gallantry and it was confusing and anomalous that they should enter into decisions about awards for gallantry. These considerations had led his predecessor (Mr Edward Heath) to recommend the discontinuance of the use of the Order of the British Empire to recognise gallantry, and the institution of a new award for gallantry to take its place. He had been glad to renew that recommendation, which the Queen had approved, on taking office. In consequence, no further awards for gallantry would be made in the Order of the British Empire, and future acts would be rewarded by the new medal.

The Royal Warrant for the Queen's Gallantry Medal reads as follows[2]:

"ELIZABETH R.

Elizabeth the Second, by the Grace of God of the United Kingdom of Great Britain and Northern Ireland and of Her other Realms and Territories Queen, Head of the Commonwealth, Defender of the Faith, to all to whom these Presents shall come: Greeting!

WHEREAS We have taken into Our Royal consideration the many acts of Bravery performed both by male and female persons.

AND whereas We are desirous of honouring those who perform such deeds:

We do by these Presents, for Us, Our Heirs and Successors institute and create a new Medal.

Firstly: It is ordained that the Medal shall be designated and styled "The Queen's Gallantry Medal".

Secondly: It is ordained that the Medal shall be circular in form and in silver, that it shall bear on the obverse the Crowned Effigy of the Sovereign, and on the reverse a design of laurel leaves and the words "THE QUEEN'S GALLANTRY MEDAL" surmounted by the Crown.

Thirdly: It is ordained that the persons eligible for the Medal shall be:

(i) Our faithful subjects and persons under Our protection in civil life, of Our United Kingdom of Great Britain and Northern Ireland, of Our Dependent Territories and Associated States, or Territories under Our Jurisdiction jointly with another power, or under Our Suzerainty or Protection;

(ii) Persons of any rank in the Naval, Military or Air Forces of Our United Kingdom of Great Britain and Northern Ireland, of Our Dependent Territories and Associated States, or Territories under Our Jurisdiction jointly with another power, or under Our Suzerainty or Protection, and including also the military Nursing Services and the Women's Auxiliary Services:

(iii) Our faithful subjects and persons under Our protection in civil life, within, and members of the Naval, Military or Air Forces belonging to, any Member country of the Commonwealth, other than Our United Kingdom, the Government whereof has signified its desire that the Medal should be awarded under the provisions of this Our Warrant, and any Territory being administered by Us in such Government.

1. See *Hansard* (House of Commons) for that date, column 226.
2. See Command Paper No. 5653 of June 1974.

The Medal is intended primarily for civilians and award in Our military services is to be confined to actions for which purely military Honours are not normally granted.

Fourthly: It is ordained that awards shall be made only on a recommendation to Us, for civilians by Our Prime Minister and First Lord of the Treasury, and for members of Our Naval, Military or Air Forces, only on a recommendation by the Secretary of State for Defence, or, in the case of any Member of the Commonwealth, other than Our United Kingdom, the Government whereof shall so desire, by the appropriate Minister of State for the said Commonwealth country.

Fifthly: It is ordained that this Medal shall be awarded only for exemplary acts of bravery.

Sixthly: It is ordained that foreign persons and citizens of countries within the Commonwealth of which We are not Queen shall be eligible for the award of the Medal and that awards to such persons not included under the Third Clause of this Our warrant shall be made only on a recommendation to Us for civilians by Our Secretary of State for Foreign and Commonwealth Affairs, and for Officers and members of foreign military Forces, by Our Secretary of State for Defence.

Seventhly: It is ordained that the Medal shall be worn by recipients on the left breast suspended from a ribbon one-and-a-quarter inches in width, of dark blue with a central vertical stripe of pearl grey bearing a narrow stripe of rose pink at the centre, and that it shall be worn immediately after the Colonial Police Medal for Gallantry. Provided that when the Medal is worn by a woman, it may be worn on the left shoulder, suspended from a ribbon of the same width and colour, fashioned into a bow.

Eighthly: It is ordained that the award of the Medal shall entitle the recipient, on all occasions when the use of such letters is customary, to have placed after his or her name the letters "Q.G.M.".

Ninthly: It is ordained that an action which is worthy of recognition by the award of the Medal, but is performed by one upon whom the Medal has been conferred, may be recorded by the award of a Bar to be attached to the ribbon by which the Medal is suspended, and that for each such additional award an additional Bar shall be added, and that for each Bar awarded a silver rosette shall be added to the ribbon when worn alone.

Tenthly: It is ordained that the names of all those upon whom We may be pleased to confer or present the Medal, or a Bar to the Medal, shall be published in the London Gazette, and that a Register of such names shall be kept in Our Central Chancery of the Orders of Knighthood.

Eleventhly: It is ordained that reproductions of the Medal, known as a Miniature Medal, which may be worn on certain occasions by those to whom the Medal is awarded, shall be half the size of The Queen's Gallantry Medal.

Twelfthly: It is ordained that it shall be competent for Us, Our Heirs and Successors, by an Order under Our Sign Manual and on a recommendation to that effect by or through Our Prime Minister and First Lord of the Treasury or Our Secretary of State for Defence or, in the case of any Member of the Commonwealth, other than Our United Kingdom, the Government whereof shall so desire, by the appropriate Minister of State for the said Commonwealth country, to cancel and annul the award to any person of The Queen's Gallantry Medal and that thereupon the name of such person in the Register shall be erased: provided that it shall be competent for Us, Our Heirs and Successors to restore the Decoration so forfeited when such recommendation has been withdrawn.

Lastly: We reserve to Ourself, Our Heirs and Successors, full power of annulling, altering, abrogating, augmenting, interpreting, or dispensing with these rules and ordinances, or any part thereof, by a notification under Our Sign Manual.

Given at Our Court at St. James's the Twentieth day of June One thousand Nine hundred and Seventy-four, in the Twenty-third Year of Our Reign.

By Her Majesty's Command,
Harold Wilson."

3. See *L.G.*, 5th December 1977.
4. A similar amendment was made to the George Medal Warrant, see Chapter 21.

By a Royal Warrant of 30th November 1977[3] the 5th Clause was amended by adding at the end the words "and that the Medal may be awarded posthumously."[4]

Fig.B: The Queen's Gallantry Medal, reverse.

Fig.C: The Queen's Gallantry Medal, bar.

DESCRIPTION

Ribbon Dark blue, 1¼ inches wide, with a central stripe of pearl grey having a narrow stripe of rose pink at the centre.

Suspension By a silver ring.

Obverse (Fig.A)

Reverse (Fig.B) The officially issued brooch is also illustrated.

Bar (Fig.C)

Naming Impressed with the names and, when appropriate, the Forces' details of the recipient.

Copies and Fakes None has been seen.

VERIFICATIONS AND CITATIONS

Awards are published in the *London Gazette*. The pages upon which awards are to be found are given under the medal heading in the quarterly indices, the names and page references of individuals being in the nominal index to "Honours, Decorations and Medals". Citations appear except where apparently precluded on grounds of security e.g. for awards in Northern Ireland.

NUMBERS AWARDED

334 medals and 2 first bars have been gazetted as follows:

Year	Police	Other Civilians	Navy	Royal Marines	Army	Air Force	Total	Bars
1974	19	6	—	—	12	—	37	—
1975	29	10	5	5	46	3	98	—
1976	47	20	1	—	6	—	74	2
1977	16	14	6	—	9	—	45	—
1978	17	4	1	3	9	1	35	—
1979	24	4	4	1	12	—	45	—

Of these, 5 medals were awarded to women (3 police, 2 other civilians).

Bars were awarded to:

<table>
<tr><td></td><td>Gazette for Bar</td></tr>
<tr><td>Sergeant F. A. Irvine, Royal Ulster
   Constabulary[5] ... ...</td><td>17th February 1976</td></tr>
<tr><td>Constable R. K. David, Metropolitan
   Police Force[5] ... ...</td><td>7th December 1976</td></tr>
</table>

ILLUSTRATIVE AWARD

The *London Gazette* of 5th December 1977 announced the award of the George Medal to Constable Raymond Peter Kiff, Metropolitan Police, and of the Queen's Gallantry Medal to Peter Anthony Chalk, Engineer, Post Office and Joseph Stephen, Railway Motorman, London Transport Executive, where their combined citation appears as follows:

"On 15th March 1976 at 4.45 p.m. a terrorist bomb exploded in the leading carriage of a Metropolitan Line train injuring a number of passengers.

Following the explosion the train stopped and a man was seen to jump from the damaged coach on to the track and Mr. Stephen, who was the driver of the train, was seen to alight from the driver's cab. Mr. Stephen then moved towards the front of the train where he waved his arms to signal to an oncoming train on another track to stop. As he did this he came face to face with the man who, after altercation, raised a gun and shot Mr. Stephen who fell mortally wounded.

Mr. Chalk was at the station when the explosion occurred, he saw the debris and thought it was a bomb. His immediate thought was for the wounded and he ran through the station and on to the line. He saw some injured and promised to get help. He then went on to the carriage where the explosion had been to see if anyone was trapped. He saw the gunman, who was covered in blood with his clothes torn; when

5. Medal awarded in *L.G.*, 18th March 1975.

he was close to the man he saw he was apparently reloading a gun which was immediately pointed at him. Telling the man that he wanted to help the injured, Mr. Chalk continued to move forward and walked by within three feet of the gun in his effort to reach the wounded; he was shot in the chest when he was about 4 feet past the gunman.

The gunman then seemed undecided which direction to take and it was at this juncture that a Constable arrived nearby in his Panda car. He had heard the explosion and driven immediately to a road which ran parallel with the railway. He saw the man standing near the front of the train and was warned that he was armed and had shot a man; at the same time the gunman fired a shot at the officer which missed. The Constable immediately gave a clear account of the events on his personal radio, then got back into his vehicle and reversed to a point some 50 yards up the road. He again left the car and saw the man walking towards him along the track, the gunman again took deliberate aim and fired at him, but the Constable continued his commentary.

The gunman then made for the nearest station during the course of which he threatened one more person. He then climbed on to the platform, down the exit stairs into the street. Meanwhile Constable Kiff, who had heard the Constable's radio commentary, had arrived at the station and been told the gunman was coming down the track. He cleared the platform, jumped on to track, but failed to find the man. He then heard shots in the vicinity of the booking hall and so ran down the stairs where he saw a man lying on the path, but holding a revolver in both hands. The Constable went to tackle the man who got up and went along the road, still brandishing his weapon. The officer followed the man who kept turning and threatening him so he crossed the road and followed from there. The gunman turned into a factory yard and Constable Kiff ran to the shelter of a van parked opposite the yard entrance from where he saw through the driver's window that although the man was semi-prone on his back he appeared to be aiming at a target within the yard. In view of this, the Constable immediately left the cover of the van and ran towards the gunman's back, jumped on him striking him with his truncheon and at the same time disarming him. After the gunman was arrested it was discovered that he had shot himself in the chest.

In facing this dangerous and armed terrorist in the knowledge that he had already caused a bomb explosion and mortally wounded a man, Constable Kiff displayed gallantry and devotion to duty of a very high order. Mr. Chalk and Mr. Stephen also displayed outstanding gallantry and a complete disregard for their safety when they faced this armed criminal.''

The award to Joseph Stephen was posthumous being the first such award. The medal was presented to his widow by the Queen at an investiture at Buckingham Palace on 7th February 1978.

Chapter 41

The Royal Red Cross

Fig.A: The Royal Red Cross, obverse, Victoria issue.

Fig.B: The Royal Red Cross, obverse, Edward VII issue.

ORIGIN AND DEVELOPMENT

Until the Egyptian campaign of 1882, nurses had not been considered eligible for war medals. However, in that year it was decided that, for their services at Alexandria, Ismailia and in the hospital ship *Carthage*, certain nurses should receive the medal for Egypt. In all 17 awards were made, three being to foreign nurses. As a result of these awards, the question was reconsidered of the grant of the South Africa medal to army nurses and to members of the Stafford House Aid Society who had served in Natal during the Zulu War. In the event, 14 such awards were made although a War Office Committee, which had been appointed to consider claims for the medal, had previously ruled against them. From the general recognition of nursing services rendered during a campaign it was but a short step to the recognition of individual instances of special devotion[1] in nursing sick and wounded and accordingly, by a Royal Warrant of 23rd April 1883[2], the Royal Red Cross was instituted in the following terms:

"VICTORIA, R.

WHEREAS We have been pleased to take into Our consideration the services rendered by certain persons in nursing the sick and wounded of Our Army and Navy, and have resolved specially to recognize individual instances of special devotion in such service; Now, for the purpose of attaining this end, We have instituted, constituted, and created, and by these presents for Us, Our Heirs and Successors, do institute, constitute, and create a decoration, to be designated as hereinafter prescribed; and We are pleased to make, ordain, and establish the following rules and ordinances for the government of the same, which shall from henceforth be inviolably observed and kept:

First. – The decoration shall be styled and designated "The Royal Red Cross," and shall consist of a Cross, enamelled crimson, edged with gold, having on the Arms thereof the words Faith, Hope, Charity, with the date of the institution of the decoration; the centre having thereon Our Effigy.

On the reverse side Our Royal and Imperial Cipher and Crown shall be shown in relief on the centre.

Secondly. – The cross shall be attached to a dark blue riband edged red, of one inch in width, tied in a bow and worn on the left shoulder.

Thirdly. – The decoration may be worn by the Queen Regnant, the Queen Consort, or the Queen Dowager of the United Kingdom of Great Britain and Ireland; and it shall be competent for Us, Our Heirs and Successors, to confer the decoration upon any of the Princesses of the Royal Family of Great Britain and Ireland.

Fourthly. – It shall be competent for Us, Our Heirs and Successors, to confer the decoration upon any ladies, whether subjects or foreign persons, who may be recommended to Our notice by Our Secretary of State for War for special exertions in providing for the nursing, or for attending to, sick and wounded soldiers and sailors.

Fifthly. – It shall be competent for Us, Our Heirs and Successors, to confer this decoration upon any Nursing Sisters, whether subjects or foreign persons, who may be recommended to Our notice by Our Secretary of State for War, or, as the case may be, by the First Lord of the Admiralty through Our said Secretary of State, for special devotion and competency which they may have displayed in their nursing duties with Our Army in the Field, or in Our Naval and Military Hospitals.

Sixthly. – The names of those upon whom We may be pleased to confer the decoration shall be published in the London Gazette, and a registry thereof kept in the office of Our Secretary of State for War.

1. In 1855 the Queen presented Miss Florence Nightingale with a specially designed jewel in recognition of her services during the Crimean War. This award was unique to Miss Nightingale and it is now preserved in the National Army Museum. Mayo (see Bibliography) illustrates it in colour.

2. See *L.G.*, 27th April 1883.

Lastly. – In order to make such additional provision as shall effectually preserve pure this honourable distinction, it is ordained that if any person on whom such distinction shall be conferred shall by her conduct become unworthy of it, her name shall be erased, by an order under Our Sign Manual, from the register of those upon whom the said decoration shall have been conferred.

And it is hereby declared that We, Our Heirs and Successors, shall be the sole judge of the conduct which may require the erasure from the register of the name of the offending person, and that it shall at all times be competent for Us, Our Heirs and Successors, to restore the name if such restoration should be justified by the circumstances of the case.

Given at Our Court at *Osborne*, this twenty-third day of *April*, one thousand eight hundred and eighty-three, in the forty-sixth year of Our Reign.

By Her Majesty's Command,
Hartington."

Two provisions of the Warrant require special notice. Clause 4, although restricted to "ladies", was otherwise drawn very widely indeed; the decoration could be awarded to ladies of any nationality who, despite the limiting wording of the preamble, might be held eligible even if the services rendered were to foreign soldiers or sailors. Clause 5 restricted the award to nursing sisters whose services were in respect of either the Royal Navy, or the Army. As will be seen from what follows, doubts were soon raised as to the interpretation of these Clauses and it was found necessary to amend both in 1884.

The first awards, which totalled 31, were gazetted on 25th May 1883. Six were to Princesses of the Royal Family; three, of which one was to Miss Florence Nightingale, were made under Clause 4; and the remainder were to army or navy nurses, all but one[3] being for services wholly, or in part, abroad in connection with the campaigns in Southern Africa or in Egypt.

In 1884 consideration was given to rewarding four women for their services in the South African War of 1880/81. One, Mrs M. J. W. Armfield, who had nursed casualties in Durban and Pietermaritzburg, was a civilian nurse; two, Mrs A. Fox and Mrs M. Maistre, who had attended the wounded in the action at Bronkhorst Spruit on 20th December 1880[4] and after, were soldiers' wives; while the fourth, whose services had been performed during the siege of Pretoria, was the wife of Lieutenant-Colonel G. F. Gildea, commanding the 1st/21st Royal Scots Fusiliers. Since none were Army nurses they did not come within Clause 5 of the Warrant, while Clause 4 was restricted to "ladies" among whom, by contemporary standards, Mrs Fox and Mrs Maistre would not be counted. However, on 18th March 1884, without citing any particular cases, the Secretary of State for War proposed certain amendments to the Warrant on the grounds that it was unfair to restrict awards to women of a particular social class under Clause 4, or to nursing sisters under Clause 5 because this clause was interpreted to mean only those nursing sisters engaged and remunerated by the War Department or by the Admiralty[5]. The amendments, which the Queen approved, were as follows:

Clause 4 – omit "or for attending to"; add at end "of Our Army and Navy."
Clause 5 – add after "Nursing Sisters" – "or other persons engaged in nursing duties".

These amendments do not seem to have been published[6], but were incorporated into the 1897 Warrant (see below). At all events, the three awards which apparently gave rise to them, and that to Mrs Gildea, were gazetted on 27th May 1884. It is curious that the award to a third woman present at Bronkhorst Spruit, Mrs M. Smith, was not gazetted until 1st August 1905, almost 25 years after the events concerned[7]. Apart from the award to Miss Nightingale, which in any case was in a special category, awards for the Crimean War (of which there were 10) were not gazetted until 1897 and 1898, at least 14 years after the R.R.C. was instituted.

3. Miss E. Wheldon, Nursing Sister, Netley Hospital.

4. For an account of the action see *The Ranger: A Journal for the Connaught Rangers*, Vol. IV, No. 8 for September 1925 at p.162 *et seq.* Mrs Fox was the wife of Sergeant Major G. Fox of the 94th Regiment. Both she and her husband were wounded. After the action the Regimental Colours were hidden from the Boers in the stretcher occupied by Mrs Fox. She died as a result of her wounds at Portsmouth in 1888 and by command of the Queen was buried with full military honours. Mrs Maistre was the wife of Sergeant Henry Maistre, the Orderly Room Clerk of the same Regiment.

5. See P.R.O. WO 32/6276. This file is incomplete but from what survives it is almost certain that these cases brought about the amendments to the Warrant. A recommendation for Mrs Gildea is also in the file but, from internal evidence, it does not seem to be the first.

6. Mayo (see Bibliography) reproduces the amended 1883 Warrant but does not indicate that the amendments have been made.

7. Mrs Smith was the widow of Bandmaster Benjamin Smith of the 94th Regiment who died on 4th July 1880, see muster roll in P.R.O. WO 16/2021. She had been admitted to the Order of St. John of Jerusalem on return home in 1881 and, when the other awards came to be considered, it may have been thought that she had been sufficiently rewarded already. Early in 1881 she had been publicly thanked in Orders by the Officer Commanding Pretoria District, see *The Ranger, op. cit.* Having remarried, her R.R.C. was gazetted in the name of Jeffreys.

In 1897 the Queen wished to confer the decoration on Queen Olga and Princess Sophie of Greece in recognition of their services to the sick and wounded in the Graeco-Turkish War. As it then stood Clause 3 of the Warrant restricted the decoration to the Queen herself[8], and to "Princesses of the Royal Family of Great Britain and Ireland." In consequence, Princess Sophie, who was a grand daughter of Queen Victoria was eligible but Queen Olga was not. Accordingly, to give effect to the Queen's wishes, on 11th December 1897 a new Warrant was signed. This reproduced exactly the wording of the amended 1883 Warrant, save that at the end of Clause 3 the following was added[9]:

> "also upon the Queens or Princesses of Foreign Countries who may have specially exerted themselves in providing for the nursing of the sick and wounded of Foreign Armies and Navies."

The Warrant of 24th July 1902, which we have been unable to trace, probably made provision for the effigy and cypher of King Edward VII to appear on the badge in place of those of his mother[10].

On 8th September 1909 a new Warrant was signed which reproduced all the previous provisions, as amended, save that in Clause 5 the words "through Our said Secretary of State" were omitted. This was to regularise what had always been done, i.e. that submissions in regard to naval nurses were to be made direct to the Sovereign by the First Lord of the Admiralty. In practice, of course, it was necessary for the Admiralty to keep the War Office informed since the Secretary of State for War kept the Register[11].

Following the outbreak of the First World War it was necessary to reconsider the existing provisions. On 14th July 1915 the Military Secretary at the War Office, Major-General Sir F. S. Robb, wrote to Lord Stamfordham, the King's Private Secretary, to the effect that while the number of nurses (over 4,000) serving in the War exceeded anything hitherto known, to award the R.R.C. on a scale commensurate with the numbers employed would lower its prestige; that it had been suggested to Lord Kitchener that the time had come for a new and lower decoration (as had been done by the institution of the M.C. in relation to the D.S.O.); and that Lord Kitchener, who favoured the proposal, suggested the formation of a committee to recommend whether there should be a new decoration, or a 2nd Class of the R.R.C.[12] The King agreed that a committee should consider the matter and accordingly, on 23rd July 1915, the committee held its first meeting, being composed as follows:

Surgeon-General Sir Alfred Keogh – Director General of Army Medical Services,
Sir Reginald Brade – Secretary, the War Office,
Major-General Sir Frederick Robb – Military Secretary, the War Office,
Colonel Sir Douglas Dawson – Comptroller, the Lord Chamberlain's Department,
Lieutenant-Colonel Sir Frederick Ponsonby – Keeper of the Privy Purse,
Miss E. H. Becher[13] – Chief Matron, Queen Alexandra's Imperial Military Nursing Service.

At its second and last meeting on 30th July 1915 the original members were joined by:

Surgeon-Vice-Admiral Sir Arthur May – Director General of the Medical Department of the Royal Navy,
Mr T. C. Macnaughten – a representative from the Colonial Office.

On 28th September 1915, drafts having been circulated previously for agreement to the Departments concerned, the committee's proposals were sent by Robb to Ponsonby for the King's consideration. Summarised, they were as follows:

a. A new and inferior grade of R.R.C. should be established.

b. Awards of the 1st Class should not exceed 2%, and of the 2nd Class 5%, of the total establishment of nurses. Whatever establishment of the two Classes was fixed, distribution should be in proportion to numbers in each Nursing Service.

8. It could be "worn" by the Queen (and the Queen Consort and Queen Dowager) but was to be "conferred" on other persons.

9. See P.R.O. WO 32/6276. This clumsy device for effecting minor amendments was used again in 1909. Neither the 1897 nor the 1909 Warrant referred to predecessors and, on the face of it, each was an instituting Warrant in its own right. However, the 1915 and subsequent Warrants recite predecessors.

10. It may be that this Warrant was merely a repetition of the previous provisions since the effect of a verbatim re-enactment in the new reign would, *inter alia*, automatically alter the badge.

11. See P.R.O. WO 32/9046.

12. See P.R.O. WO 32/3436 from which this and the subsequent events leading to the institution of the 2nd Class, and of the bar, are taken.

13. Who herself had been awarded the R.R.C. in *L.G.*, 27th September 1901, for services in South Africa, and who was to be awarded a bar thereto in *L.G.*, 1st January 1918. She was appointed a G.B.E. in *L.G.*, 3rd June 1918 and was also a Lady of Grace of the Order of St. John of Jerusalem.

c. There should be no restriction in rank for appointment to either Class.

d. Members of the 2nd Class should be eligible for advancement to the 1st Class.

e. Members of the 2nd Class should be known as "Associates" and be entitled to the letters "A.R.R.C." after their names.

f. Ladies who had voluntarily undertaken duties in establishing, running, or assisting in, hospitals or who had performed valuable services in the Red Cross or kindred societies should be eligible for appointment to either Class as honorary members, additional to establishment.

g. The 2nd Class insignia should be of the same form and size as the 1st Class but of frosted silver with a red enamel Maltese Cross superimposed thereon not exceeding half the linear dimensions of the 1st Class insignia. The legend Faith, Hope, Charity was to be engraved on the reverse, together with the year 1883, being that of the institution of the original decoration. The ribbon of the 2nd Class was to be the same as that of the 1st Class.

On 1st October 1915 Ponsonby replied saying that the King thought occasion might arise which would render necessary a larger distribution than the 2% and 5% proposed[14]. On 7th October the proposals were sent to the Prime Minister (H. H. Asquith) for his concurrence, and on 10th November 1915 were embodied in a Royal Warrant[15] the operative part of which was as follows:

"Firstly: The Decoration shall be styled and designated "The Royal Red Cross," and shall be divided into two Classes.

The First Class shall consist of a Cross, enamelled red, edged with gold, having on the arms thereof the words, Faith, Hope, Charity, with the date of the institution of the Decoration; the centre having thereon in relief the Royal and Imperial Effigy. On the reverse thereof the Royal and Imperial Cipher and Crown shall be shown in relief on the centre.

The Second Class shall consist of a Cross which shall be of the same form and size as in the First Class, but shall be of frosted silver and shall have superimposed thereon a Maltese Cross enamelled red not exceeding half its dimensions, the centre having thereon in relief the Royal and Imperial Effigy. The reverse shall have inscribed on the arms thereof the words Faith, Hope, Charity and the date of the institution of the original Decoration, and shall bear in the centre in relief the Royal and Imperial Cipher and Crown.

Secondly: The Cross in either Class shall be attached to a dark blue riband edged red, of one inch in width, tied in a bow and worn on the left shoulder.

Thirdly: The Decoration may be worn by the Queen Regnant, the Queen Consort, or the Queen Dowager of the United Kingdom of Great Britain and Ireland; and it shall be competent for Us, Our Heirs and Successors, to confer the Decoration upon any of the Princesses of the Royal Family of Great Britain and Ireland; also upon the Queens or Princesses of Foreign Countries who may have specially exerted themselves in providing for the nursing of the sick and wounded of Foreign Armies and Navies.

Fourthly: It shall be competent for Us, Our Heirs and Successors, to confer either Class of this Decoration upon any members of the Nursing Services without restriction as to rank, or upon other persons engaged in nursing duties whether subjects or foreign persons, who may be recommended to Our notice by Our Secretary of State for War or by the First Lord of the Admiralty, as the case may be, for special devotion and competency which they may have displayed in their nursing duties with Our Army in the Field, or in Our Naval and Military Hospitals.

Fifthly: The number of awards in the First Class of the Decoration shall not exceed two per cent. of the total establishment of Nurses, and the number of awards in the Second Class of the Decoration shall not exceed five per cent. of the total establishment of Nurses, the allotments to be proportionate to the numbers of each Nursing Service provided nevertheless that it shall be competent for Us, Our Heirs and Successors, to make such additions as, under exceptional circumstances, We may deem fitting.

Sixthly: Recipients of the Second Class of the Decoration shall be eligible for advancement to the First Class as vacancies may arise.

Seventhly: Recipients of the First Class of the Decoration shall be designated Members of the Royal Red Cross, and shall be entitled to the letters R.R.C. following

14. As will be seen below, this suggestion was incorporated in Clause 5 of the new Warrant.

15. See *L.G.*, 16th November 1915.

262

their names. Recipients of the Second Class of the Decoration shall be designated Associates of the Royal Red Cross, and shall be entitled to the letters A.R.R.C. following their names.

Eighthly: It shall be competent for Us, Our Heirs and Successors, to confer either Class of the Decoration upon any ladies, whether subjects or foreign persons, who may be recommended to Our notice by Our Secretary of State for War as having voluntarily undertaken the duties of establishing, conducting or assisting in hospitals for the treatment of sick and wounded soldiers and sailors of Our Army and Navy, or of Our Indian Military Forces or of the Naval and Military Forces of Our Self-governing Dominions beyond the Seas, or as having performed valuable services with the Red Cross or kindred societies at home or abroad, or as having otherwise rendered eminent services in the care of sick and wounded soldiers and sailors of Our Army and Navy; and it is hereby ordained that all persons appointed under this Clause shall be regarded as Honorary Members or Associates, and their appointments shall be additional to the establishment ordained in the Fifth Clause of this Our Royal Warrant.

Ninthly: The names of those upon whom We may be pleased to confer the Decoration shall be published in the London Gazette, and a register thereof kept in the office of Our Secretary of State for War.

Tenthly: In order to make such additional provision as shall effectually preserve pure this honourable distinction, it is ordained that if any person on whom such distinction shall be conferred shall by her conduct become unworthy of it, her name shall be erased, by an order under the Royal Sign Manual, from the register of those upon whom the said Decoration shall have been conferred. And it is hereby declared that We, Our Heirs and Successors, shall be the sole judge of the conduct which may require the erasure from the register of the name of the offending person, and that it shall at all times be competent for Us, Our Heirs and Successors, to restore the name if such restoration should be justified by the circumstances of the case.

Lastly: We reserve to Ourself, Our Heirs and Successors, full power of annulling, altering, abrogating, augmenting, interpreting, or dispensing with these Regulations, or any part thereof, by a notification under the Royal Sign Manual.

By 15th December following a specimen 2nd Class badge had been approved by the King and an initial order for 300 was placed (see further in "Description", *post*). In February 1916 there was correspondence between Brade and Ponsonby regarding the allotment of awards to allied countries. They agreed that France[16] and Russia should each receive 10 First Class and 25 Second Class awards, while Belgium would receive 2 and 5 of these Classes respectively; there was no need to consider Japan, Montenegro and Serbia although some awards would be made later. Both Brade and Ponsonby seem to have overlooked the provisions of the Warrant which restricted awards for services to foreign armies to Queens and Princesses of foreign countries. It is unlikely, however, that any objection would have been sustained in view of the arrangements between the Allies for what amounted to the bulk exchange of awards between them.

As the War progressed, in the nature of things, awards in both Classes increased considerably. These had not been restricted entirely to executive nursing services because, at that time, there was no other form of reward available for administrative services in connection with military and auxiliary hospitals. However, in March 1917 the King decided that both Classes should be reserved solely for actual nursing services[17] and the subsequent creation of the Order of the British Empire in June 1917 afforded a medium of reward for such administrative services.

On 18th October 1917 Ponsonby wrote to Brade telling him that the King wished to institute a bar to the R.R.C. and pointing out that there was no means of rewarding nurses who had received the decoration for services in the South African War. On 24th October Brade replied asking whether the King wished the bar confined to the 1st Class and adding that this would seem to meet the case as holders of the 2nd Class were eligible for advancement to the 1st Class. Ponsonby gave Brade's letter to Dawson who answered it on 26th October saying that the

16. Mlle Eugenie Antoine had been awarded the R.R.C. in *L.G.*, 20th October 1914 for her services to British wounded under shell fire at Vailly-sur-Aisne. Presumably the award was made under Clause 4 of the 1909 Warrant.

17. A decision embodied in the 1920 Warrant (see *post*).

263

King agreed that the bar should be confined to the 1st Class and, perhaps not having considered the possibility before, asked if promotions to the 1st Class would swamp it. Dawson added that he was having a design for the bar prepared (see further in "Description" *post*) and that the King wished the award of a bar to be denoted by a rosette[18]. On 10th December Brade replied. He said that the present ratio of 1st Class to 2nd Class awards was 1:4.5 which was well within the prescribed ratio of 2:5; further, there was no difficulty in keeping numbers within the limits. It was not considered desirable "on other grounds" to institute a bar for the 2nd Class[19], nor that persons should be advanced from the 2nd Class for services similar to those which had merited their appointment to that Class in the first place. If the services were outstanding the individual would be advanced in her profession and become eligible for the 1st Class. Gallantry or devotion (*sic*) could be recognised by the award of the 1st Class[20], or of the M.M.[21] Accordingly, by a Royal Warrant of 15th December 1917[22] a bar was instituted, the operative part of the Warrant being in the following terms:

"... hereby ordain that anyone who, after having rendered services for which the Royal Red Cross Decoration, First Class, is awarded, subsequently renders such approved services as would, if she had not received the said Decoration, have entitled her to the same, shall be awarded a Bar to be attached to the said Decoration."

By a Royal Warrant of 30th April 1918[23] Clause 6 was amended to provide for the return of the 2nd Class badge on advancement to the 1st Class[24] and by Army Order No. 357 of December 1918 a silver rose emblem was to be worn on the ribbon, when the ribbon was worn alone, to denote the award of a bar[25].

By a Royal Warrant of 25th October 1920[26] all the existing provisions were consolidated and, in some cases, varied, the operative part of the Warrant being as follows:

Firstly. – It is ordained (i) that the Decoration shall be styled and designated "The Royal Red Cross," and that it shall be divided into two Classes.

(ii) That the First Class shall consist of a Cross, enamelled red, edged with gold, having on the arms thereof the words, Faith, Hope, Charity, with the date of the institution of the Decoration; the centre having thereon in relief the Royal and Imperial Effigy; and that on the reverse thereof the Royal and Imperial Cipher and Crown shall be shown in relief on the centre; and

(iii) That the Second Class shall consist of a Cross of the same form and size as the First Class, but of frosted silver, with a Maltese Cross enamelled red not exceeding half its dimensions superimposed thereon, the centre having thereon in relief the Royal and Imperial Effigy; and that the reverse shall have inscribed on the arms thereof the words Faith, Hope, Charity and the date of institution of the original Decoration, the centre having thereon in relief the Royal and Imperial Cipher and Crown.

Secondly. – It is ordained that the Cross in either Class shall be attached to a dark blue riband edged red, of one inch in width, tied in a bow and worn on the left shoulder.

Thirdly. – It is ordained that the Decoration may be worn by the Queen Regnant, the Queen Consort, or the Queen Dowager of the United Kingdom of Great Britain and Ireland, and that it shall be competent for Us, Our Heirs and Successors, to confer either Class of the Decoration upon any of the Princesses of the Royal Family of Great Britain and Ireland; also upon the Queens or Princesses of Foreign Countries who may have specially exerted themselves in providing for the nursing of the sick and wounded of Foreign Armies and Navies.

Fourthly. – It is ordained that the First Class of the Decoration may be conferred upon a fully trained Nurse who is a member of one of the officially recognized Nursing Services, and who has shown exceptional devotion and competency in the performance of actual nursing duties with Our Army in the Field, or in Our Naval, Military, or Air Force Hospitals, or in an Auxiliary War Hospital, over a continuous and long period, or who has performed some very exceptional act of bravery and devotion at her post of duty; and whose name has been brought to Our Notice by Our Secretary of State for War, Our First Lord of the Admiralty, or Our Secretary of State of Air.

18. This seems to have been overlooked at the time and provision was not made until Army Order No. 357 of December 1918.

19. Since the King had already agreed that the bar should be confined to the 1st Class it is difficult to see why Brade reverted to the question of one for the 2nd Class. From the minutes on the file in which the correspondence is contained it seems that among the "other grounds" was the view that too many forms of reward produce extravagant recommendations and, perhaps on a more factual level, that the record of the award of a bar in the 2nd Class would be extinguished on promotion to the 1st Class.

20. Clause 5 of the Warrant spoke of "special devotion and competency" which could be held to include gallantry in nursing. Certainly a number of such awards had been made. The 1920 and subsequent Warrants put the matter beyond doubt by including bravery in terms.

21. Women were made eligible for the M.M. by the Royal Warrant of 21st June 1916, see Chapter 33.

22. See *L.G.*, 21st December 1917.

23. See *L.G.*, 17th May 1918.

24. This had been overlooked when the 1915 Warrant was drafted.

25. Curiously enough this provision has not yet found its way into any of the successive R.R.C. Warrants.

26. See *L.G.*, 19th November 1920.

Fifthly. – It is ordained that the Second Class of the Decoration may be conferred upon a fully trained Nurse, or an Assistant Nurse, Probationer, or V.A.D. Nursing Member, who belongs to one of the officially recognized Nursing Services, and who has shown special devotion and competency in the performance of actual nursing duties with Our Army in the Field, or in Our Naval, Military, or Air Force Hospitals, or in an Auxiliary War Hospital, over a continuous and long period, or who has performed some very exceptional act of bravery and devotion at her post of duty; and whose name has been brought to Our Notice by Our Secretary of State for War, Our First Lord of the Admiralty, or Our Secretary of State for Air.

Sixthly. – It is ordained that the number of awards in the First Class of the Decoration shall not exceed two per cent. of the total establishment of Nurses, and that the number of awards in the Second Class of the Decoration shall not exceed five per cent. of the total establishment of Nurses, the allotments to be proportionate to the numbers of each Nursing Service; provided nevertheless that it shall be competent for Us, Our Heirs and Successors, to make such additions as, under exceptional circumstances, We may deem fitting.

Seventhly. – It is ordained that a recipient of the First Class of the Decoration shall not afterwards be awarded the Second Class; that recipients of the Second Class of the Decoration, if trained nurses, shall be eligible for advancement to the First Class as vacancies may arise; and that on such advancement the Second Class Decoration shall be returned to the office of Our Secretary of State for War.

Eighthly. – It is ordained that recipients of the First Class of the Decoration, who are Our Subjects, shall be designated Members of the Royal Red Cross, and shall be entitled to the letters R.R.C. following their names; and that recipients of the Second Class of the Decoration, who are Our Subjects, shall be designated Associates of the Royal Red Cross, and shall be entitled to the letters A.R.R.C. following their names.

Ninthly. – It is ordained (i) that either Class of the Decoration may be conferred upon Ladies (other than those referred to in the 4th and 5th Clauses of this Our Royal Warrant), whether subjects or foreign persons, who may be recommended to Our Notice by Our Secretary of State for War, Our First Lord of the Admiralty, or Our Secretary of State for Air, as having voluntarily undertaken nursing duties, and shown special devotion and competency in the performance of such duties, over a continuous and long period in hospitals which have been specially established for the treatment of sick and wounded personnel of Our Naval, Military or Air Forces – including Our Indian Forces, and the Forces of Our self-governing Dominions beyond the seas: but the First Class of the Decoration shall be conferred only upon a fully trained nurse.

(ii) That any foreign Lady upon whom the First Class of the Decoration is conferred under this Our Royal Warrant shall be regarded as an "Honorary Member," and that such person upon whom the Second Class is conferred, shall be regarded as an "Honorary Associate," and

(iii) That the numbers of each class of the Decoration which may be conferred under this Clause, shall be additional to the Establishment ordained in the Sixth Clause of this Our Royal Warrant.

Tenthly. – It is ordained that if anyone upon whom the First Class of the Decoration has been conferred is subsequently recommended for such approved service as would have rendered her eligible for the Decoration, had she not already received it, she shall be awarded a Bar to be attached to the Decoration.

Eleventhly. – It is ordained that the names of those upon whom We may be pleased to confer the Decoration shall be published in the *London Gazette*, and a register thereof kept in the office of Our Secretary of State for War.

Twelfthly. – In order to make such additional provision as shall effectually preserve pure this honourable distinction, it is ordained—

(1) That if any person upon whom such distinction shall be conferred shall, in the opinion of Our Army Council, Our Board of Admiralty, or Our Air Council, so conduct herself as to become unworthy of it she shall forfeit the Decoration.

(2) That if the recipient of this Decoration is convicted by the Civil Power, or is dealt with under the Probation of Offenders Act, 1907, she shall be liable to a like forfeiture on the recommendation of Our Army Council.

Fig.C: The Royal Red Cross, 1st Class, with bar, obverse, George V issue.

Fig.D: The Royal Red Cross, 1st Class, obverse, George VI issue.

Fig.E: The Royal Red Cross, 1st Class, obverse, Elizabeth II issue.

Fig.F: The Royal Red Cross, reverse, Victoria issue.

Fig.G: The Royal Red Cross, reverse, Edward VII issue.

27. See P.R.O. WO 145/1.

28. See *L.G.*, 20th March 1931.

29. See A.O. No. 224 of December 1942.

30. See A.O. No. 66 of October 1961.

31. See A.O. No. 22 of March 1961.

32. The first awards under the new Warrant were announced in the *London Gazettes* of 31st December 1976 (one R.N.) and 11th June 1977 (one R.N., one R.A.F.).

(3) That the forfeiture shall be carried out under an authority bearing Our Royal Sign Manual; and that the recipient's name shall thereupon be erased from the Register of those upon whom the said Decoration shall have been conferred.

(4) That We, Our Heirs and Successors, shall at all times have power to restore a forfeited Royal Red Cross.

(5) That a notice of forfeiture or of restoration shall in every case be published in the *London Gazette*.

Lastly. – We reserve to Ourself, Our Heirs and Successors, full power of annulling, altering, abrogating, augmenting, interpreting, or dispensing with these Regulations, or any part thereof, by a notification under the Royal Sign Manual."

Clauses 4, 5 and 9 of this Warrant had the effect of limiting awards to services performed in actual nursing. In addition, Clauses 4 and 9 restricted awards of the 1st Class to trained nurses. In so far as the Nursing Services were concerned, exceptional (1st Class) or special (2nd Class) devotion and competency over a continuous and long period were required, or the performance of some very exceptional act of bravery and devotion. Clauses 7 and 8 avoided any doubts which may have arisen under Clauses 6 and 7 of the 1915 Warrant by providing, *inter alia*, that a recipient of the 1st Class could not afterwards be awarded the 2nd Class, and that the post-nominal letters were for use only by subjects of the King. Clause 12 placed forfeiture in the hands of the Army Council, or the Board of Admiralty or the Air Council and not in those of the Sovereign as hitherto.

In 1928 it was discovered that of the 588 nurses still serving, 61 had the 1st Class and 66 the 2nd Class decoration whereas the establishment in accordance with Clause 6 would have been only 11 of the 1st Class and 29 of the 2nd Class. The matter was put to the King who decided that all First World War awards should be regarded as made in exceptional circumstances under the proviso to Clause 6. Moreover, when a nurse left the Service her award should cease to count against the allotment[27].

By a Royal Warrant of 5th February 1931[28] the previous Warrant was superceded. The new Warrant reproduced substantially the terms of the previous Warrant and, in particular, made no alteration in the classes of person eligible; in the standards required; or in the number of awards permitted. However, it introduced a new Clause authorising miniatures of either Class of badge to be worn on certain occasions, and drew the forfeiture Clause rather more widely by omitting reference to civil conviction or to probation, and replaced forfeiture in the hands of the Sovereign subject to its being recommended by the First Lord of the Admiralty or a Principal Secretary of State. This followed a recommendation by the Interdepartmental Rewards Committee that award should be regarded as irrevocable, except in cases of extreme infamy; hence it was unnecessary to provide, as before, for particular circumstances.

An amending Royal Warrant of 17th September 1942[29] provided that recommendations for award or forfeiture might be made direct to the Sovereign by a Minister of State for any Dominion. A further amending Warrant of 30th September 1961[30] removed "Imperial" from the description of the royal effigy, crown and cypher on the badges, and made minor amendments consequent on constitutional changes in the Commonwealth.

By a Royal Warrant of 24th March 1964[31] the functions performed by the Secretary of State for War in regard, *inter alia*, to the R.R.C. were transferred to the Secretary of State for Defence.

A Royal Warrant of 30th December 1976 replaced the previously existing provisions for the decoration. The most important change effected by this Warrant was to make unambiguous provision for awards to men[32]. The tenor of all previous Warrants had been that the decoration was for women only, e.g. it was to be worn by the Queen Regnant, Consort or Dowager; it could be conferred upon Princesses of the Royal Family, or on foreign Queens or Princesses; it was to be

Fig.H: The Royal Red Cross, 1st Class, reverse, George V issue.

Fig.I: The Royal Red Cross, 1st Class, reverse, George VI issue, first type.

Fig.J: The Royal Red Cross, 1st Class, reverse, George VI issue, second type.

Fig.K: The Royal Red Cross, 1st Class, reverse, Elizabeth II issue.

33. None of this explains awards of both classes to certain Italian medical officers in the First World War, see *post*.

34. See A.O. No. 279 of August 1913; considering the terms of the instituting and subsequent Warrants the R.R.C. seems hardly appropriate to the group selected.

35. See P.R.O. WO 32/4966 and WO 32/9024.

36. See *L.G.*, 11th February 1947.

37. See P.R.O. WO 145/1.

38. See *ibid*.

39. See P.R.O. WO 32/9046.

40. See P.R.O. WO 145/1. At a stocktaking on 17th October 1913, 16 badges remained. Between that date and the conversions 2 were issued and therefore a further 5 must have come from somewhere to account for the 19 converted.

41. There is evidence that from time to time badges of deceased members were returned to the War Office. Whether these were used to augment Garrard's stock is not clear.

42. See P.R.O. 145/1.

worn from a ribbon tied in a bow on the left shoulder; from 1920 the qualifications for award in either Class referred to, *inter alia*, "some very exceptional act of bravery or devotion at her post of duty"; from 1916 it had been available to ladies who had undertaken certain voluntary nursing duties; and the forfeiture clause referred to the erasure of "her name"[33]. Under the new Warrant awards to men are to be worn on the left breast; awards to women are to be worn as before "except with coats of a military pattern". The remaining changes made by the Warrant were consequent upon eligibility for men, e.g. the decoration can now be conferred upon "any Member of the Royal Family" (previously Princesses only); "Distinguished Persons of a Foreign Country" (previously Queens and Princesses); "a member of the nursing personnel of the Navies, Armies and Air Forces of Our Realms" (thus making unambiguous provision for male nurses of the Forces).

No order of precedence seems to have been assigned to the R.R.C. until 1913 when *Dress Regulations for the Army, 1911* were amended by placing it the group of long service, meritorious and efficiency awards (which were themselves placed in order of date of institution) between the Royal Marine Meritorious Service Medal and the Indian Long Service and Good Conduct Medal (for Native Army)[34]. However, following the institution of the 2nd Class decoration and towards the end of the First World War the matter was reconsidered[35] and in A.C.I. No. 754 of 5th July 1918 the 1st Class was advanced to follow next after the M.B.E., and the 2nd Class was placed after the A.F.C. In 1947 the I.O.M. (Military Division) and the O.B. (for gallantry) were inserted between the M.B.E. and the R.R.C.[36]. The precedence of the A.R.R.C. has not changed (see also Appendix 4).

DESCRIPTION – 1st CLASS BADGE

(For coloured illustration, see Plate 3)

Ribbon Dark blue, one inch wide, with red edges.

Obverse There have been five types of obverse, which were due to changes in the Sovereign's Effigy, as follows:

1. Victoria (Fig.A) Until 1952 the badges of both Classes were made by Garrard and Company Limited, the Crown Jewellers. 100 of the Victorian type were ordered in 1883; 12 in 1899; 50 in 1900; and 50 in 1901[37]. Probably only the 1883 badges were made of gold, all subsequent badges being silver gilt.

2. Edward VII (Fig.B) 50 badges of the "new pattern" were ordered on 17th February 1903[38]. On 1st July 1909 Garrards submitted an unpriced account for three badges which were for presentation to naval nurses on the 22nd of that month. It is not clear whether the account was in respect of three badges which had just been made, or whether it was merely a record of issues from the stock of the original 50 held by the Company on behalf of the War Office[39]. On 18th August 1914 Garrards were paid for converting six badges, apparently to the George V type, and on 3rd October following for converting a further 13 badges[40]. From the surviving records it is not possible to say if any badges were converted from the Victorian type[41] and accordingly the precise number of Edward VII badges cannot be calculated; probably it lies between 31 and 35.

3. George V (Fig.C) The first order for this type (excluding conversions) was made on 29th September 1914[42].

4. George VI (Fig.D)

5. Elizabeth II (Fig.E)

Reverse There have been six types of reverse, which were due to changes in the Royal cypher, as follows:

1. Victoria (Fig.F)

2. Edward VII (Fig.G)

Fig.L: The Royal Red Cross, 2nd Class, obverse, George V issue.

Fig.M: The Royal Red Cross, 2nd Class, reverse, George V issue.

3. George V (Fig.H)

4. George VI first type (Fig.I) This was introduced in 1938[43]. On this and all subsequent issues the year of award is engraved on the lower arm of the cross.

5. George VI second type (Fig.J) By a Royal Proclamation of 22nd June 1948 the King's style and titles were altered and a new cypher introduced accordingly.

6. Elizabeth II (Fig.K)

Bar (Fig.C) On 8th November 1917 Colonel Sir Douglas Dawson, Comptroller of the Lord Chamberlain's Department, sent to Sir Reginald Brade, the Secretary of the War Office, two designs for the bar. One was of the shape subsequently adopted but, in the design, placed on the bow of the ribbon, while the other was similar but rectangular in shape and linked to the cross in the manner subsequently adopted. In his reply of 12th December Brade expressed a preference for the first of the two designs. The matter was then submitted by Dawson to the King who approved the first design saying, however, that the bar should be placed in the position shown in the second design, i.e. linked to the cross. On 17th December Garrards were requested to prepare a pattern bar which the King approved on 3rd January 1918[44]. The Second World War and later issues have the year of award engraved on the back of the bar.

DESCRIPTION – 2nd CLASS BADGE

(For coloured illustration, see Plate 3)

Ribbon As for 1st Class.

Obverse There have been three types of obverse, which were due to changes in the Sovereign's effigy, as follows:

1. George V (Fig.L) The badge was designed by Sir Henry Farnham Burke, Norroy King of Arms, and approved by the King on 8th November 1915. On 24th November the War Office requested Garrards to prepare a sample badge for submission to the King. Two patterns were prepared. On the first the red enamel was superimposed on the cross (as was prescribed in the Warrant), while on the second it was flush with the surface of the cross and hence less liable to chip. The second pattern was selected by the King and on 15th December an initial order for 300 was placed with Garrards[45].

2. George VI \
3. Elizabeth II $\}$ The design of the badge has remained constant except for changes in the Sovereign's effigy corresponding with those to the 1st Class badge.

Reverse (Fig.M) The design of the reverse has remained constant except for changes in the cypher corresponding with the last four changes to the 1st Class badge. Commencing in 1938 the year of award is engraved in rather cramped figures below "1883" on the lower arm of the cross.

VERIFICATIONS AND CITATIONS

All awards, except for honorary awards to certain foreigners, appear in the *London Gazette*. Until December 1940 names are indexed under the decoration heading in the "State Intelligence" portion of the appropriate quarterly index. Thereafter this section gives only the pages upon which awards are to be found, names being relegated to a comprehensive section headed "Honours, Decorations and Medals". From June 1891 to April 1901 and from February 1914 to September 1922 names are also given in the "Civil Promotions" section of the indices. From October 1888 to October 1908 names of surviving recipients appear in the Quarterly Army Lists, together with the date of award (which usually corresponds with the date of the *L.G.*[46]) and, where appropriate, the theatre in which it

43. See *Annual Report of the Deputy Master and Comptroller of the Royal Mint (1938)*, p.43.

44. See P.R.O. WO 32/3436. On 18th July 1918 Garrards submitted an account for 100 bars at a total cost of £45. The stock can only have been exhausted recently.

45. See *ibid.*

46. Awards in *L.G.*, 27th September 1901 were to bear the date 29th November 1900 (except where stated). The latter date is given in the Army Lists.

47. Published with the Lists of January, April, July and October.

48. See *L.G.*, 17th March 1916 (R.R.C. 2; A.R.R.C. 2).

49. See *L.G.*, 14th June 1917 (R.R.C. 1; A.R.R.C. 2). The same announcement notified the award of the D.S.O. to Major R. T. Meadows, R.A.M.C. and the M.S.M. to four men of the same Corps. The ship was the *Tyndareus*.

50. See *L.G.*, 1st October 1954 (A.R.R.C. 1).

51. *E.g.* South Africa (*L.G.*, 27th September 1901); Palestine (*L.G.*, 12th October 1948); Korea (*L.G.*, 1st July 1953); Cyprus (*L.G.*, 9th February 1960) etc.

52. See *L.G.s*, 1st December 1905 and 6th February 1906 (R.R.C. 4)

53. See *L.G.s*, 8th March, 22nd March, 17th May and 7th June 1929 (R.R.C. 2; A.R.R.C. 2).

54. These were in 1902 (R.R.C. 4); 1916 (R.R.C. 1., A.R.R.C. 3); 1917 (R.R.C. 1, A.R.R.C. 1); 1918 (R.R.C. 2, A.R.R.C. 3); 1919 (A.R.R.C. 3); 1922 (A.R.R.C. 1); 1944 (R.R.C. 1) and 1946 (A.R.R.C. 2). In *L.G.*, 27th September 1901 awards were made to four members of the Army Nursing Service (S. E. Oram, M. Thomas, W. Tulloh and S. E. Webb) in respect of services during the South African War. However, each had already received the R.R.C. for previous services. As there was no provision for award of a second R.R.C., nor at that time for the award of a bar, the awards were cancelled in *L.G.*, 26th June 1902 and each was enrolled as an Honorary Associate of the Grand Priory of the Order of the Hospital of St. John of Jerusalem. In *L.G.*, 1st January 1918 the A.R.R.C. was awarded to Sister F. Harley, Q.A.I.M.N.S. Since this nurse had already been awarded the R.R.C. in *L.G.*, 3rd June 1915 the award of the A.R.R.C. was cancelled in *L.G.*, 19th December 1922. According to the R.R.C. Register Miss M. Huxley, Matron, Dublin University Auxiliary Hospital, declined the A.R.R.C. awarded her in *L.G.*, 24th October 1917 "as she considered her insignificant work prevented her accepting the award" and accordingly this was cancelled in *L.G.*, 18th February 1918.

55. For a list of recipients and details from the R.R.C. Register to *L.G.*, 20th February 1914 see *The Journal of the Orders and Medals Research Society*, Vol. 12, p.138.

56. For a list of recipients of the bar see *ibid*, p.16.

was gained. Similar details appear in the Supplement[47] to the Monthly Army List from April 1900 to April 1920. From December 1899 to January 1920 the names of naval recipients and the date of award appear in the Navy Lists.

Very few citations appear in the *L.G.* although occasionally an element of gallantry can be inferred from the announcement e.g. "for valuable services and devotion to duty on the occasion of the loss of the Hospital Ship 'Anglia' "[48]; "for gallantry and meritorious service on the occasion of the mining of a Hospital Ship"[49]; "in recognition of brave conduct during the fire on H.M.T. Empire Windrush"[50], etc. Other announcements specify the theatre[51], or give some indication of the circumstances from which the award arose e.g. the Dharmsala earthquake[52], devoted service during King George V's illness[53], etc. Very occasionally further details may be gleaned from despatches published in the *Gazette*.

The Register of awards of the decoration to including *L.G.*, 21st June 1918 is preserved in the Public Record Office under reference WO 145/1. The Register gives the names of recipients, the *L.G.* reference and occasionally additional details, e.g. particulars of presentation or disposal of the decoration, a note of the circumstances of the award normally amounting to no more than a very brief extension of the *L.G.* announcement, issue of a replacement decoration etc.

Some Submissions to the King recommending awards in respect of nurses serving with the Royal Air Force between 1918 and 1946 are in the Public Record Office series AIR 30.

Details of some awards appeared in Press Releases from which extracts frequently found their way into local newspapers.

NUMBERS AWARDED

Gazetted Awards The following table summarises awards appearing in the *London Gazette*, account being taken of cancellations[54]:

			R.R.C.[55]	A.R.R.C.	First bars[56]
1883–	1900	… …	106	—	—
1901–	1902	… …	100	—	—
1903–	1913	… …	35	—	—
1914[57]–1920[58]		… …	943	5,079	79
1921–	1939	… …	41	49	1
1940–	1946	… …	381	953	17
1947–	1948	… …	17	47	2
1949–	1952	… …	23	45	1
1953–	1979	… …	157	350[59]	—

First World War honorary awards We have traced a number of honorary awards to foreigners (male and female) which were sponsored by the War Office. As far as the R.R.C. and A.R.R.C. are concerned these appeared in printed lists published between December 1916 and December 1919 of which we have been unable to find those numbered 23, 42, 46 and 47. The following summary is therefore incomplete to the extent of any awards appearing in the missing lists:

	R.R.C.	A.R.R.C.
Belgium	16	32
France	10	36
Italy	12 (including 4 men)	33 (including 10 men)
U.S.A.	19	56
Totals	57	157

The Italian awards to men are curious, all apparently being to medical officers.

57. Two awards were made in 1914 being to Miss E. S. Kelly (*L.G.*, 20th February 1914) for services in India and to Madamoiselle Eugenie Antoine (*L.G.*, 20th October 1914) for gallantry in the First World War, see *post*.

58. The official statistics (see Bibliography) which cover the period from 4th August 1914 to 31st May 1920 give the following analysis of awards – Services in the Field: R.R.C. 456; Bars 39; and A.R.R.C. 1,506 – Services in connection with the War: R.R.C. 465; Bars 37; and A.R.R.C. 3,522.

59. Including 11 awards to men under the 1976 Warrant.

ILLUSTRATIVE AWARDS

1. The first award for services in the First World War was for gallantry and made to a Frenchwoman, Madamoiselle Eugenie Antoine. It was made, apparently, under Clause 5 of the 1883 Warrant and notified in *L.G.*, 20th October 1914 as being "in recognition of her courageous and devoted services to the British wounded in hospital at Vailly-sur-Aisne whilst the village was under shell fire."

2. Staff Nurse Minnie Byrne, Territorial Force Nursing Service, also received the R.R.C. for gallantry, notification of the award appearing in *L.G.*, 29th March 1920 accompanied by the following citation:

> "For gallantry and devotion to duty at the 2nd Northern General Hospital, Leeds, on the 1st January, 1920, when through an unforseen cause a patient's bed was set on fire. With great presence of mind Staff Nurse Byrne endeavoured to smother the flames, and whilst so doing her own clothing was set on fire. She succeeded, nevertheless, in moving her patient to another bed, suffering extensive burns herself meanwhile."

Chapter 42

The Sea Gallantry Medal

*Fig.A: The Board of Trade (large)
Medal for Gallantry in Saving Life,
obverse, Victoria issue.*

*Fig.B: The Board of Trade (large)
Medal for Gallantry in Saving Life,
obverse, Edward VII issue.*

*Fig.C: The Board of Trade (large)
Medal for Saving Life at Sea,
obverse, Victoria issue (the "Humanity" Medal).*

*Fig.D: The Board of Trade (large)
Medals, reverse.*

ORIGIN AND DEVELOPMENT

1. We use the modern title throughout.

2. These provisions were re-enacted in section 677 (e) of the Merchant Shipping Act, 1894, which is still in force.

3. It is thus the earliest official British gallantry medal awarded to civilians but, in this sense, it is important to note that unlike the V.C. (extended to civilian volunteers in 1858 for services in the Mutiny) and A.M. (instituted in 1866) it was not originally intended to be worn.

The origin of the Sea Gallantry Medal[1] is to be found in the Merchant Shipping Act, 1854. It is the only gallantry medal instituted by Act of Parliament. By section 418 of the Act, the Mercantile Marine Fund was to be charged with certain expenses which, in sub-section (5), included those "... for affording assistance towards the preservation of life and property in cases of shipwreck and distress at sea and for rewarding the preservation of life in such cases as the Board of Trade directs"[2]. In pursuance of these powers the Board of Trade decided in 1855 to institute a medal, to be awarded in silver or bronze, for saving life at sea which became known as "The Board of Trade Medal for Saving Life"[3]. The design of the medal was approved by the Prince Consort, and the obverse was to bear a legend which depended upon the circumstances of the award. Where the recipient risked

Fig.E: The Sea Gallantry Medal, obverse, Edward VII first type small issue.

Fig.F: The Sea Gallantry Medal, obverse, Edward VII second type small issue.

4. Occasionally this rule was relaxed in the case of the Foreign Services Medal where the rescue was in harbours or rivers abroad.

5. The Foreign Services Medal (q.v.) was made wearable in 1854.

6. See P.R.O. MT 9/901 (M.3504/1905). The first submissions were made in 1906.

7. *E.g.*, the bronze medal awarded to G. A. Tomlinson in *L.G.*, 4th May 1965, was presented by the Queen at an investiture on 8th July 1965.

8. See P.R.O. MINT 20/200.

9. A bar for the Foreign Services Medal was approved in 1908.

10. See P.R.O. HO 45/17097.

his own life the obverse read "AWARDED BY THE BOARD OF TRADE FOR GALLANTRY IN SAVING LIFE" (the "Gallantry" medal); where he did not the obverse read "AWARDED BY THE BOARD OF TRADE FOR SAVING LIFE AT SEA" (the "Humanity" medal). Thus the "Humanity" medal might be awarded to the master of a vessel which sent out a boat to effect a rescue, "Gallantry" medals being reserved for the boat's crew. In the case of the "Gallantry" medal the class of award depended upon the degree of gallantry displayed, and in the case of the "Humanity" medal upon the extent of the services rendered. In practice the award of a medal for services which did not involve risk of life was infrequent, and the last award of the "Humanity" medal was made in 1893; thereafter, such services were recognised by plate or monetary awards. Two classes of the Albert Medal (q.v.) were instituted in 1867 and thereafter awards of the Board's medal ceased for a time, although the Foreign Services Medal (q.v.) continued to be given.

Although no written decision on the matter can be traced, awards of the Sea Gallantry Medal were resumed in 1876 the standard of gallantry for the silver medal being that which just failed to reach the standard for the Albert Medal.

Since the Sea Gallantry Medal is instituted by Act of Parliament there is no Royal Warrant prescribing the conditions of award, nor are there any published regulations. However, in 1887 the Board of Trade defined the circumstances in which both the S.G.M. and the Foreign Services Medal would be awarded, as follows:

> (1) for rescue of life from shipwreck on the coasts of the United Kingdom, whether the ship be British or foreign.
>
> (2) for rescue of life from British vessels, whether by foreigners or by British subjects.

As a rule shipwreck or distress at sea are conditions precedent to the award[4]. Awards are not given for rescue from drowning unless the person rescued incurred the danger in the course of a sea voyage, nor are they made in cases of accidents to pleasure boats.

In 1903 King Edward VII, who took a great interest in the subject of awards, gave his consent to the proposal that the medal should be reduced in size and made wearable[5], and approved the design of the medal and ribbon (see below). The next year the King ordered that, in common with other gallantry medals awarded by the Crown, it should be worn on the left breast and in 1905 expressed the wish that, in future, recommendations should be submitted to him for approval[6]. Later, the King indicated a desire to bestow medals personally whenever possible and did so for the first time on 22nd July 1909 when a number of medals were presented in respect of incidents which had occurred in 1908–09. This practice has continued[7]. In 1905 the King approved a proposal that the obverse should be altered to read "AWARDED BY THE BRITISH GOVERNMENT FOR GALLANTRY IN SAVING LIFE AT SEA". In view of the size of the medal this would have produced a cramped legend and accordingly "FOR GALLANTRY IN SAVING LIFE AT SEA" was substituted[8]. In 1921 a bar for further acts of gallantry was approved[9] (see below). In November 1936 King George VI approved the use of the post-nominal letters "S.G.M.", and the medal became known as "The Sea Gallantry Medal"[10].

In 1941 the Marine Department of the Board of Trade was transferred to form the nucleus of the Ministry of Shipping (later incorporated in the Ministry of War Transport, Ministry of Transport and Civil Aviation etc.), and recommendations for the award were made to the Sovereign by the Minister responsible for those Departments. Early in 1955 the Marine Department was transferred from the Ministry of Transport back to the Board of Trade (now Department of Trade), and the Secretary of State again has the duty of making and submitting recommendations. Some awards are posthumous.

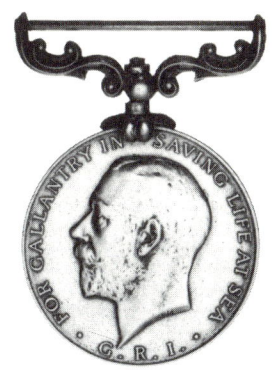

*Fig.G: The Sea Gallantry Medal,
obverse, George V issue.*

*Fig.H: The Sea Gallantry Medal,
obverse, George VI issue, first type.*

The position of wearing the Sea Gallantry Medal has varied. In Army Order No. 196 of October 1905 it was shown following the Order of St. John, the Conspicuous Service Cross and the Albert Medal, while Army Order No. 246 of August 1912 placed it after the Albert Medal in a group of gallantry awards which at that time followed Polar medals. In 1929[11] it was shown following the Air Force Medal, the Indian Distinguished Service Medal and the Constabulary Medal (Ireland), where it has since remained although the I.D.S.M. has itself been moved higher in the order of wearing (see also Appendix 4).

DESCRIPTION

LARGE MEDALS (2.25 inches in diameter)

General According to the Royal Mint Catalogue (see Bibliography) the early medals were engraved and struck by B. Wyon, but in 1857 the work was undertaken by the Royal Mint. The medals were issued in a presentation case and without means of suspension, although occasionally they are found with unofficial suspenders.

Obverse There are three types of obverse as follows:

"Gallantry" Medal

1. Victoria (Fig.A).
2. Edward VII (Fig.B) This was introduced on the accession of the King but was reduced in size in 1904 (see below).

"Humanity" Medal

3. Victoria (Fig.C) This obverse was used when the recipient did not risk his life (see above). It was last used in 1893 when the award was made to Skipper J. Burgoyne of the smack *Catherine McKilvie* of Rothesay[12].

Reverse (Fig.D) This is common to all three medals[13].

Naming Details of the recipient and the circumstances of the award are engraved round the edge of the medal. Some of the orders for individual medals placed by the Board of Trade with the Royal Mint between the years 1859 and 1883 are preserved in the Public Record Office[14]. These orders specify the type of medal required, and how it is to be named, with an indication of which words may be omitted should the inscription be too long. That some words actually were omitted is evidenced by comparison between the orders and surviving medals. In general, medals were to be engraved with the full names of the recipient (middle names being abbreviated if necessary); the name of the ship, preceded by "Wreck of the" (or "Loss", "Abandonment", etc.), and occasionally its type e.g. barque, fishing boat, schooner, etc.; its home port (last given in 1882); the place e.g. "on the rocks near Skerries" (last given in 1876); and the date. Occasionally when the services were to an individual, rather than to a number of persons, a different form of inscription was used e.g. "Robert Peters, rescuing a seaman 16th February 1860 off Holyhead"; similarly, a different form was used when a number of acts was recognised e.g. "Henry Watts, for Saving Life from Drowning on Various Occasions." The type of lettering varies, and is usually in capitals with or without serifs; sometimes a mixture of capitals and script appears.

SMALL MEDALS (introduced in 1904; 1.27 inches in diameter)

Ribbon Light red, $1\frac{1}{4}$ inches wide, with $\frac{1}{8}$ inch white edges. This was first manufactured by Dalton, Barton and Co. Ltd. of London[15].

Suspension By an ornate scroll bar suspender.

Obverse There are six types of obverse as follows:

1. Edward VII first type (Fig.E) This was first struck in 1904[16], the King's approval of the new medal and ribbon being communicated to the Royal Mint on 1st March 1904[15]. The first orders for the medal in 1904 were

11. *L.G.*, 22nd November 1929, p.7,529.

12. See P.R.O. MINT 16/3 which is the Royal Mint register of medals ordered.

13. In 1927 a new reverse was proposed showing a man in a raging sea being thrown a life-belt from a ship, see P.R.O. MINT 24/25. This reverse was not adopted.

14. Under references MINT 16/9 and 16/11. Not all the orders have survived. In addition there are two odd orders for 1857 and one each for 1885 and 1897. No awards were made between 1868 and 1874.

15. See P.R.O. MINT 20/200.

16. *Annual Report of the Deputy Master and Comptroller of the Royal Mint* (1904), p.55.

17. See the Royal Mint register of medals ordered, P.R.O. MINT 16/3.

18. For details of a specific exchange see P.R.O. MT 9/901 in which permission was given in 1904 for T. Sherwin to exchange the large bronze medal presented to him in 1903 for a small one.

19. *Annual Report of the Deputy Master and Comptroller of the Royal Mint (1905)*, p.48.

20. See P.R.O. MINT 20/266.

21. *Annual Report of the Deputy Master and Comptroller of the Royal Mint (1911)*, p.50. In 1913, following consultation between the Board of Trade and the Royal Mint an improved case for the medal was sanctioned; medals were to be fitted with brooches, and a length of spare ribbon put in the case, see P.R.O. MINT 20/501.

22. *Annual Report of the Deputy Master and Comptroller of the Royal Mint (1948)*, p.22.

23. *Annual Report of the Deputy Master and Comptroller of the Royal Mint (1920/21)*, p.30.

24. The silver medal awarded to Private Peter Fisher of the Black Watch gives no indication that he was a soldier. It was awarded for services during a fire at sea aboard H.M.T. *Caronia* in May 1917, see *The Times* of 4th September 1918 at p.5. With later issues, the name of the vessel is omitted. Similarly, the silver medal for Major T. H. Barclay, Surrey Yeomanry (H.M.T. *Transylvania*, 4th May 1917) gives neither his rank nor regiment. The name of the vessel appears on an award dated 1934 but is omitted from one dated 1950.

25. A bronze S.G.M. to So Hau was gazetted, together with an Albert Medal (in bronze) to George Henry White, on 17th November 1925. The next S.G.M. approved was in silver to George Wilson on 4th January 1926, but this does not seem to have been gazetted. Regular notices begin with the silver medal awarded to James Darling and the bronze medal to William Henry White gazetted on 9th April 1926.

26. Not only of the S.G.M. but of the Foreign Services Medal (q.v.), of plate, of money etc. for saving life at sea.

27. The index to these Returns is to be found under "WRECKS. IV. 4" in the "General Alphabetical Index of Bills, Reports, Estimates, Accounts and Papers printed by order of the House of Commons, and the Papers Presented by Command, 1852–1899". Due to a minor alteration in the title of the Returns, those to 1870 are indexed separately.

placed on 5th March[17] and it seems likely that all 1904 awards were of the new pattern. Shortly before this consideration was given to the proposal that recipients of large medals awarded since the accession of the King might be permitted to exchange them for small ones[15], and the Royal Mint register of medals ordered records a number of exchanges, the last being in 1909[18].

2. Edward VII second type (Fig.F). This obverse was introduced in 1905[19] (see above). In a letter from the Royal Mint to the Board of Trade dated 21st September 1905 the revised legend was said to present no objection[20]. According to the register of medals ordered[17] only one medal was ordered in 1905 after the date of that letter but the register does not show whether the resulting issue was of the new or old pattern.

3. George V (Fig.G) This obverse was introduced in 1911[21] and continued until 1935 when the last award of the reign was made.

4. George VI first type (Fig.H) The first award of the reign was made in 1940 when this reverse was used.

5. George VI second type (Fig.I) In 1948 the cypher was altered to "G VI R" in conformity with the Royal Proclamation of 22nd June 1948[22].

6. Elizabeth II (Fig.J) The first award of the reign was made in 1954.

Reverse (Fig.K) This is common to all six medals.

Bar The only bar so far awarded (see below) was struck in 1921[23], the existing die of the bar for the Foreign Services Medal being used. The bar was approximately $\frac{1}{2}$ inch wide, the edges being ornamented with scrolls, and the centre inscribed:

S.S. "URBINO"
6 FEBRUARY 1921

Naming As for the large medals, details of the recipient, the vessel, and the date are engraved round the edge[24]. The text of the inscription is usually shorter than that on the large medal, although some Edward VII issues retain much of the detail given on the large medals. Capital letters of varying styles, with or without serifs, are used.

Copies and Fakes For recent copies see the Note on p.xx.

VERIFICATIONS AND CITATIONS

London Gazette Regular notices first appear in the *Gazette* from 1926[25]. The names of recipients are shown in the "State Intelligence" section of the indices under "Bronze (or "Silver") Medal(s) for Gallantry in Saving Life at Sea". Before 1940 the medal heading appears under "Trade, Board of", but thereafter it appears as a main heading in its own right. From January 1942 the medal heading gives only the pages upon which awards are to be found, names being indexed in a comprehensive nominal list headed "Honours, Decorations and Medals". Before 1941 only abbreviated citations are given but thereafter they appear in full.

Other Sources Citations for awards[26] made between 1856 and 1876 are to be found in the annual Returns of Wrecks which were ordered to be printed by Parliament[27]. Details of awards to 1950 may be found in the P.R.O. series MT 9 which contains the papers of the Marine Department of the Board of Trade[28]. Wilson and McEwen (see Bibliography) reproduce, from official sources, awards made between 1887 and 1935. Before 1922 only the bare details of the recipient, the ship or ships concerned, and the date of the incident are given. Thereafter a full extract from the Board of Trade Register appears[29]. However, before even 1890 Press Notices announcing awards were sent by the Board of Trade to the Central News, the Press Association, the Exchange Telegraph Company and all London daily newspapers (e.g. *The Times*), and it is thus possible to trace details by reference to contemporary sources.

28. Thus MT 9/334 (M. 9123/88) contains statements which led to the award of the silver medal to David Dryburgh who saved three lives when the *Golden Fleece* was wrecked in the Timor Straits on 27th December 1885; a copy of the request to the Royal Mint for a medal, with details of naming; and a press cutting regarding the presentation of the medal at a meeting of the Leith Mercantile Marine Board.

29. The *London Gazette* notices (see above) are much briefer.

Fig. I: The Sea Gallantry Medal, obverse, George VI issue, second type.

30. Including silver medals to Mrs May S. Hectorson who, with others, rescued two men from the sea at Burraness, North Yell (Wreck Return for 1858) and Major F. W. Festing, Royal Marine Artillery, who, with others, rescued three men from a schooner off Hayling Island (Wreck Return for 1865).

31. Three awards were made in 1948 all or some of which could be of the previous type.

32. The last awards in this period were to D.A. McIsaac (silver; posthumous) and M. Caffery (bronze) in *L.G.*, 13th April 1973 (wreck of the *London Valour* off Genoa on 9th April 1970).

33. The only bar to a Foreign Services Medal was that to the silver medal awarded to Jacob Don, a Dutch seaman, see Chapter 43.

34. See the file of orders for the S.G.M. in P.R.O. MINT 16/10.

NUMBERS AWARDED

The overall figures have been provided by courtesy of the Department of Trade and we have edited them according to the varying types of medal issued. However, these can only be taken as a rough guide because it may be that old stock was used up before a new issue commenced. Until 1893, when the last "Humanity" medal was issued, the figures include both the "Gallantry" and "Humanity" medals.

	Silver	Bronze	Remarks
1856	?	?	9 medals issued; classes not known.
1857–1880[30] ...	118	343	
1881–1886 ...	62	120	Board of Trade records missing. Figures calculated from Royal Mint register of medals ordered.
1887–1901 ...	288	263	
1902–1903 ...	11	23	Edward VII large type; some later exchanged for small type.
1904–1905 ...	16	9	Edward VII first small type; not including large medals replaced by small.
1906–1910 ...	54	69	Edward VII second small type.
1911–1936 ...	384	371	George V issue.
1937–1947 ...	7	13	George VI first type.
1948–1951 ...	—	6	George VI second type[31].
1952–1979 ...	19	9	Elizabeth II issue[32].

24 silver and 10 bronze medals were awarded to officers and men of the army between 1911 and 1923.

Bars Only one bar has been awarded[33] which was to Chief Officer James Whiteley. He was awarded the silver medal while serving in S.S. *Colorado* on 20th October 1917, the medal being presented by the King on 23rd March 1918. While serving in S.S. *Urbino* on 6th February 1921 he performed another act of gallantry for which the King approved the award of a bar. This was presented by the Superintendent of the Mercantile Marine Office, Hull, on 12th May 1922. The bar is not mentioned by Wilson and McEwen.

ILLUSTRATIVE AWARDS

Silver Medal On 5th February 1876 the Board of Trade ordered from the Royal Mint a silver medal to be inscribed "Thomas Williams gallantry in saving life on the 30th December 1874"[34]. The medal was to be in a case with the inscription "Board of Trade Medal for Gallantry in Saving Life at Sea, awarded to Thomas Williams 1876". The circumstances giving rise to the award appear in the Board of Trade Return of Wrecks etc. contained in the Parliamentary Papers for 1876, Volume 67 at p.710 as follows:

> "In testimony of his gallantry in saving the life of Captain Stevens of the "Ida C.," who during a fit of insanity threw himself overboard in Puerto Plata Harbour. Williams immediately sprang into the water and succeeded in bringing Captain Stevens to the surface, but when both men were being hoisted on deck, they were attacked by a shark, Williams receiving a severe wound, from which he did not recover for nearly three months."

The Return also shows that Williams was the cook of the brigantine *Ida C.*

Bronze Medal In 1950 Sparehands John Clark and Stanley King were each awarded the S.G.M. in bronze for acts of gallantry while serving in the trawler *Tesla* off Iceland. Their combined citation, which appears in the *London Gazette* of 22nd December 1950 at p.6,393, reads as follows:

> "In rough and bitterly cold weather in a position off Utskalar on the west coast of Iceland, the Skipper of the trawler *Tesla* fell overboard from a ladder owing to a sudden lurch of the vessel, striking the verandah rail and bulwark in his fall. The vessel was manoeuvred round as quickly as possible but it was fifteen minutes before the Skipper was sighted trying to swim towards the ship which was then about 60

Fig.J: The Sea Gallantry Medal, obverse, Elizabeth II issue.

Fig.K: The Sea Gallantry Medal, reverse; small medals.

yards away. He had swallowed a lot of water and after a time realised that he could not get back. Shortly afterwards it was seen that he had lost consciousness.

Without hesitation, Sparehand King, who was wearing his full rig except for sea boots, tied a line round his waist, dived from the verandah rail and began swimming towards the Skipper. However, he was rapidly overcome by the cold and had to be hauled back practically unconscious.

Sparehand Clark, meanwhile, seeing that the unconscious Skipper was in immediate danger of drowning and that King could not reach him, dived overboard without a line. He also was wearing full rig except for sea boots. The distance was now about 15 yards. Clark reached the Skipper, whose face was submerged by this time, and raised his head clear of the water until a lifebuoy on a line was thrown to him. He slipped the buoy over the Skipper's head and remained supporting him until they were both hauled alongside.

The ship was rolling heavily in the beam sea and Clark held the Skipper between his legs and fended off from the ship's side until the crew could reach down and haul both men aboard. Artificial respiration was applied and the Skipper recovered."

King's medal, which has the George VI second type obverse, is named in small engraved serif capital letters "STANLEY KING, 16th MARCH, 1950".

Chapter 43

The Sea Gallantry Medal (Foreign Services)

ORIGIN AND DEVELOPMENT[1]

By 1839 a need had arisen to recognise services to British subjects performed by foreigners and, on 14th March of that year, the Foreign Secretary (Viscount Palmerston) wrote to the Master of the Royal Mint as follows[2]:

"It has frequently happened on occasions when assistance has been afforded by Foreigners to subjects of Her Majesty who have been in danger and distress, in consequence of disasters at Sea or otherwise, that Her Majesty's Government have felt the want of some suitable acknowledgement, other than a pecuniary Reward, to be presented in the name of Her Majesty, or of Her Government, to Foreigners who have particularly distinguished themselves on such occasions; and it has appeared to Her Majesty's Government, that a Medal, having on one side the Head of Her Majesty, and having on the other side a space for a short Inscription commemorative of the service and including the name of the Individual who performed it, and surrounded by some ornamental Device, would in such cases be a suitable acknowlegement.

I have accordingly to request, that you will cause to be prepared, for the consideration and approval of Her Majesty's Government, the model of a Medal which may be fit to be used for this purpose, and which, as a Work of Art, may do credit to the taste and skill of this Country. Such a Medal would be wanted for distribution either in Gold, in Silver, or in Bronze, according to the circumstances of each case; and it appears to me, that the most suitable size would be that of a Gold Piece of the value of about Five or Six Pounds Sterling."

It is clear from this letter and, in particular, the words "or otherwise" that it was intended that the scope of the medal should not be restricted to services at sea. On 19th March the Deputy Master wrote to Benedetto Pistrucci[3] asking him to carry out the work "... in accordance with the instructions conveyed in Lord Palmerston's letter, unless it may appear to you that the mode proposed of putting in the Inscription upon the Reverse, commemorative of the particular service, is impracticable; in which case you will report thereon to the Master of Mint." In the event, Palmerston did not approve Pistrucci's design. Accordingly, in February 1841 William Wyon, Chief Engraver to the Mint, was commissioned to carry out the work and a specimen medal was submitted to and approved by the Queen on 10th September following[4].

In 1848 Brigadier Altieri of the Sardinian Navy received the silver medal for assisting the brigantine *John Cunningham* of Belfast, and the Consul at Cagliari reported that "Some disappointment is felt at its not being made to hang from the breast, the same as the French medals already awarded for similar services, and enquiries have been made if it might be worn, and if so, what is the colour of the riband to which it ought to be attached." To this Palmerston replied on 30th May that "Her Majesty's Government have no objection to Brigadier Altieri wearing the medal lately presented to him on their part. If so worn, it should be suspended by a red riband."[5]

Eventually, the cost of a special reverse for each medal was found to be unwarranted in most cases and accordingly in 1849 two standard reverses were introduced being those "FOR SAVING THE LIFE OF A BRITISH SUBJECT" and "FOR ASSISTING A BRITISH VESSEL IN DISTRESS". The following

1. We gratefully acknowledge the assistance of Major C. E. C. Townsend, T.D., who has supplied us with certain material for this Chapter.

2. See P.R.O. MINT 1/36.

3. An Italian who, being a foreigner, could not hold a permanent appointment. He designed many coins and medals and at one time was Chief Medallist to the Sovereign.

4. See P.R.O. MINT 1/38 (Wyon's letter of 4th April 1842) and MT 9/1578 (18405/1922). At Palmerston's request the obverse was copied from Wyon's effigy of the Queen used on the medal commemmorating her visit to the Guildhall, London, in 1837.

5. Altieri's medal survives and has been fitted with a swivel suspender.

year that "FOR SAVING THE LIVES OF BRITISH SUBJECTS" was approved. In 1854 it was found that the size of the medals was inconvenient and that their expense (at any rate when struck in gold) was considerable. Accordingly they were reduced in size and made wearable by fitting a suspender. Lord Clarendon, who by then had become Foreign Secretary, enquired why the ribbon was red instead of Garter blue and was told that Palmerston had ordered the ribbon to be "crimson, as more cognate to the Order of the Bath than to that of the Garter." In 1858 the reverse "FOR GALLANTRY AND HUMANITY" was introduced with the central legend "FROM THE BRITISH GOVERNMENT" instead of "PRESENTED BY THE BRITISH GOVERNMENT" which appeared on the other standard reverses[6].

With the creation of the Marine Department of the Board of Trade in 1850 the Board commenced making recommendations to the Foreign Office in respect of services at sea, the cost being met, as with medals originating at the Foreign Office, out of the Civil Contingencies Fund. In 1872 the Treasury raised the question of the payment of Wyon's account and, after some characteristic inter-Departmental wrangling, it was decided that, on grounds of economy, in future medals should be struck at the Royal Mint and that the Board should pay for the medals it sponsored out of the Vote for the Relief of Distressed Seamen. This arrangement continued until 1882 when it was agreed that the Board should order medals without consulting the Foreign Office except in rare cases where doubt existed as to the propriety of awarding a medal, in which case the Foreign Office should be asked to decide. It was, however, urged that medals should be sent to the Foreign Office for presentation as was done in regard to other awards to foreigners[7]. Medals continue to be presented under arrangements made by the Foreign Office although sometimes they are presented by the Sovereign at an investiture, the first such occasion being in 1922.

When first instituted the medal was not awarded exclusively for services at sea, nor was peril necessarily an ingredient. Thus, on the one hand it was awarded for endeavouring to save the life of a British subject who had been attacked by lions at the Paris Hippodrome and on the other for providing the site of a British cemetery in Brazil. However, after the Board of Trade began to make recommendations the medal acquired a much more nautical flavour although, until at least 1883, awards for services ashore were being initiated by the Foreign Office[8]. There are no regulations or other instrument prescribing rules for the medal but in 1887 the Board defined the cases in which the S.G.M. and the Foreign Services Medal would be awarded, as follows:

(1) for rescue of life from shipwreck on the coasts of the United Kingdom, whether the ship be British or foreign.

(2) for rescue of life from British vessels, whether by foreigners or British subjects.

As a rule shipwreck or distress at sea are conditions precedent to award although occasionally this has been relaxed in favour of foreigners who save life in harbours or rivers abroad. Awards are not given for rescues from drowning unless the person rescued incurred the danger in the course of a sea voyage, nor are they made in cases of accident to pleasure boats. The two reverses for saving life were reserved for cases in which life was saved without gallantry, while that for assisting a vessel in distress was used where it was possible for the crew to remain aboard, e.g. in towing rescues. The use of these reverses has been discontinued (see under "DESCRIPTION" below) and awards of plate are now made instead. The use of the reverse "FOR GALLANTRY AND HUMANITY" is confined to gallantry, awards on grounds of humanity having been discontinued by 1895. About the same time the Board's practice of awarding gold medals to officers and silver medals to ratings ceased, gold and silver medals being awarded thereafter according to the degree of gallantry displayed.

6. For a time special reverses were struck for particular occasions e.g. "TO THE COMMENDADOR DOMINGOS DA SILVA PORTO FOR SERVICES TO THE CREW OF THE SHIP WILLIAM GIBSON, 1859" (see Hocking, Vol.2, p.199); "FOR GALLANTRY IN DEFENCE OF THE BRITISH LEGATION JULY 6TH 1861" (see Mayo, Vol.2, p.385), etc.

7. See P.R.O. MINT 16/13.

8. The last we have found was to Mr. Ayerst Henham Hooker (gold medal "FOR GALLANTRY AND HUMANITY") in respect of a cholera epidemic in Egypt, see P.R.O. MINT 16/45.

Fig.D: The Foreign Services Medal (small), obverse, Victoria issue.

Fig.E: The Foreign Services Medal (small), obverse, Victoria issue (variant).

Fig.F: The Foreign Services Medal (small), obverse, Edward VII issue.

In 1905 King Edward VII desired that recommendations for all awards should be submitted to him and the practice of submitting recommendations to the Sovereign has been followed ever since[9]. In 1908 a silver bar and the sum of £3 was awarded to Jacob Don, a pilot apprentice in the Netherlands Pilot Cutter No. 11 of Rotterdam, for gallantry in rescuing survivors from the s.s. *Sydney* on 31st August 1908. Don had been awarded a silver medal for a similar act concerning the brigantine *Lothair* on 20th November 1906. At an investiture in 1922 King George V noticed that the ribbon of the S.G.M. and that of the Foreign Services Medal were different; later the same year he directed that the existing S.G.M. ribbon should, in future, be used for both[10].

The most recent awards of the Foreign Services Medal were made in gold in 1968 to First Officer Sigurjon Hanneson and Second Officer Palmi Hlodverson of the Icelandic Coastguard Service vessel *Odinn* who rescued 18 members of the crew of the trawler *Notts County* which went aground in Iceland early that year. The medals were presented by H.M. Ambassador to Iceland at a ceremony aboard the *Odinn* on 16th October 1968. The Commanding Officer of that vessel, Captain Sigurdur Arnason, was appointed an Honorary Officer of the Order of the British Empire and received the badge of the Order on the same occasion.

Fig.A:
The Foreign Services Medal (large), obverse, Victoria issue.

Fig.B:
The Foreign Services Medal (large), specially struck reverse.

Fig.C:
The Foreign Services Medal (large), reverse 5.

DESCRIPTION

LARGE MEDALS (1.78 inches in diameter)

Suspension None, although sometimes fitted privately.

Obverse (Fig.A).

Reverse There are five types of reverse with inscriptions as follows:

1. Individually struck inscription (Fig.B). Medals with such inscriptions continued to be issued on occasion after the introduction of the standard reverses described in 3 to 5 below.

2. VICTORIA REGINA CUDI JUSSIT MDCCCXLI within the oak wreath below the crown. This was used for presentation and specimen medals.

3. FOR SAVING THE LIFE OF A BRITISH SUBJECT. This was introduced in 1849, the design being the same as in Fig.H.

9. See P.R.O. MT 9/901 (M. 3504/1905).

10. See P.R.O. MT 9/1578 (M. 18405/1922).

Fig.G: The Foreign Services Medal (small), obverse, George V issue.

Fig.H: The Foreign Services Medal (small), reverse 1.

Fig.I: The Foreign Services Medal (small), reverse 2.

11. *Annual Report of the Deputy Master and Comptroller of the Royal Mint (1911)*, p.50

12. See P.R.O. MINT 16/3, order no. 1444 of 14th March.

13. *Ibid*, order no. 699 of 15th September.

14. *Ibid*, order no. 592 of 20th July.

15. *Annual Report of the Deputy Master and Comptroller of the Royal Mint (1908)*, p.44.

16. P.R.O. MINT 16/45. There is an odd requisition, and a receipt in MINT 16/43.

17. Between 1883 and 1892 some of *The Times* notices are pasted in the Royal Mint register of medals ordered, P.R.O. MINT 16/3.

4. FOR ASSISTING A BRITISH VESSEL IN DISTRESS. This was introduced in 1849, the design being the same as in Fig.I.

5. FOR SAVING THE LIVES OF BRITISH SUBJECTS (Fig.C). This was introduced in 1850.

Naming Except where details appeared on the reverse itself, the name of the recipient, the date of the services rendered, and the place or other identifying details were engraved on the edge.

SMALL MEDALS (introduced in 1854; 1.27 inches in diameter)

Ribbon To 1922, crimson 1¼ inches wide; thereafter, as for the S.G.M. i.e. light red, 1¼ inches wide including ⅛ inch white edges.

Suspension By an ornate scroll bar suspender.

Obverse There are five types of obverse as follows:

1. Victoria (Figs.D and E). Variations occur in the size of the effigy, and its accompanying star.

2. Edward VII (Fig.F). This was designed by G. W. de Saulles.

3. George V (Fig.G). This was introduced in 1911[11].

4. George VI. The last awards with this obverse were made in 1948.

5. Elizabeth II. The most recent awards with this obverse were made in 1968.

Reverse There are four types of standard obverse although, following their introduction, for a time medals with specially struck inscriptions continued to be issued on occasion. In the following, those numbered 3 and 4 were numbered 4 and 5 respectively in official correspondence:

1. FOR SAVING THE LIFE OF A BRITISH SUBJECT (Fig.H). From the entries in the Royal Mint register of medals ordered it seems likely that the last issue of this reverse was made in 1906[12].

2. FOR ASSISTING A BRITISH VESSEL IN DISTRESS (Fig.I). This seems to have been last issued in 1896[13]. An unnamed Elizabeth II specimen with this reverse is known.

3. FOR SAVING THE LIVES OF BRITISH SUBJECTS (Fig.J). This seems to have been last issued in 1926[14].

4. FOR GALLANTRY AND HUMANITY (Fig.K). This was introduced in 1858 with the central legend "FROM THE BRITISH GOVERNMENT" instead of "PRESENTED BY THE BRITISH GOVERNMENT" which appeared on reverses 1 to 3.

Bar The only bar awarded was struck in silver[15] for Jacob Don (see above). It was approximately ½ inch wide, the edges being ornamented with scrolls, and the centre inscribed:

S.S. "SYDNEY"

31 AUGUST 1908

Naming Impressed or engraved, with the name of the recipient and usually with the date, either in full or as the year only. In the case of awards for services at sea sometimes the name of the ship concerned is added. Some of the requisitions for medals between 1873 and 1883 are preserved in the Public Record Office[16]. Each requisition specifies the type of metal and reverse required (in fact all are for reverse No. 5 i.e. "FOR GALLANTRY AND HUMANITY"); the recipient's names; and the date to be inscribed.

Copies and Fakes None has been found.

VERIFICATIONS AND CITATIONS

Awards are not gazetted but for many years notifications have been circulated in the form of Press Notices. In consequence details may be found frequently in national newspapers, notably *The Times*[17]. Citations or other details for services at sea between 1856 and 1876 are to be found in the annual Returns of Wrecks which

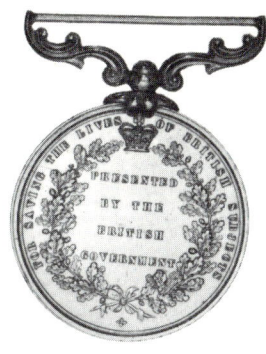

Fig.J: The Foreign Services Medal (small), reverse 3.

Fig.K: The Foreign Services Medal (small), reverse 4.

were ordered to be printed by Parliament[18]. Details of recommendation and presentation of the earlier awards may be found in the Foreign Office records preserved in the Public Record Office, while for services at sea recourse may be made to the series MT 9 which contains the papers of the Marine Department, Board of Trade[19].

NUMBERS AWARDED

Large Medals Until 1854 when the medal was reduced in size and made wearable, 96 gold, 118 silver and 14 bronze medals were awarded for actual services. In addition, 10 gold and 24 bronze presentational or specimen medals were struck.

Small Medals The following table has been based upon annual figures provided by courtesy of the Department of Trade and, in consequence, for the period from 1857 (when that Department's records of the medal begin) to 1877 they do not include awards sponsored by the Foreign Office. The figures for the period from 1878 to 1886 have been found from the Royal Mint register of medals ordered[20]. Thereafter the figures reflect all awards, the Board of Trade having assumed responsibility for the medal in 1882.

			Gold	Silver
1857–1877	...	...	76	331
1878–1886	...	...	76	221
1887–1901	...	...	79	430
1902	...	...	3	30
1903–1909	...	...	5	175
1910	...	...	—	9
1911–1937	...	...	44	569
1938–1952	...	...	—	9
1953–1979[21]	...	...	2	9

Two men are known to have received both a silver and a gold medal. Marcel Marie Labousse and Victor Toussaint were each awarded a silver medal and £2-10s-0d for saving the crew of the sloop *Phantom* which struck on the rocks off the Island of Molène on 28th November 1861[22]. On 17th January 1865 the same two men, with others, rescued the three survivors of the steamship *Columbian* which had foundered near Conquet; for their services both received a gold medal and £10[23]. At least two women have received medals. Thomas Russell and his wife Mary Ellen received, with others, gold medals for services in connection with the rescue of the master of the *Caroline* on 2nd February 1859, the ship having struck on the bar of the port of Boston, Massachusetts, during a severe snowstorm[24]. In 1882 Sister Barbara Erkmann also received a gold medal for services rendered during a cholera epidemic in Egypt[25].

ILLUSTRATIVE AWARDS

Gold Medal On 14th October 1874 the Board of Trade ordered from the Royal Mint a gold medal with reverse No. 5 (i.e. "FOR GALLANTRY AND HUMANITY") for Paul Rivet which was to be dated "1874"[26]. The circumstances giving rise to the award appear in the Board of Trade Return of Wrecks etc. contained in the Parliamentary Papers for 1875, Volume 70 at p.963 as follows:

"The brig "Wanderer", of Banff, bound from Goole to Cette, foundered at sea on November 29th, 1873. The crew took to a boat and endeavoured to reach the coast of France. When close of land their boat capsized, and finding themselves in shallow water, they prepared to make their way ashore, not knowing that between them and the land there ran a branch of the river Authie, which was much swollen by the tide and agitated by the storm. Rivet, having perceived their dangerous position, at great risk, swam across the stream, and by means of a boat which soon afterwards arrived, succeeded in getting the shipwrecked crew ashore. They were then conveyed to the Maritime Hospital at Berck, where they were treated with great kindness. From the effect of his exertions Rivet was confined to his bed for a month. The French Government showed their appreciation of his gallantry by awarding him a gold medal."

The Return shows that Rivet was a fisherman of Berck (a fishing village about 30 miles South of Boulogne) and also that the Physician and Officers of the Maritime Hospital received the thanks of Her Majesty's Government. The date of the services rendered is given as 30th November 1873.

Silver Medal On 16th July 1885 the Board of Trade ordered a silver medal with reverse No. 4 (i.e. "FOR SAVING THE LIVES OF BRITISH SUBJECTS") for A.M. Gratcheff[27]. The circumstances giving rise to the award are described in *The Times* for 1st August 1885 at p.12 as follows:

> "The Board of Trade have awarded a silver medal to Afunasi Michailoff Gratchoff (*sic.*), Master of a Russian fishing boat, and a gratuity to each of his crew of four men, in recognition of their humane services to six seamen of the British steamship *James Groves*, whom they rescued in an exhausted condition from the ship's boat, in which they had been driven down the Sea of Azoff by a sudden gale on May 3 last."

27. See order no. 212 in the Royal Mint register of medals ordered, P.R.O. MINT 16/3.

Chapter 44

The Victoria Cross

Fig.A: The Victoria Cross and bar, obverse.

1. For a fuller treatment of this aspect see *The Evolution of the Victoria Cross* by M. J. Crook, 1975.

2. Horse Guards General Order No. 638 of 15th December 1854 which also authorised the clasps for the Alma and Inkerman. The remaining clasps were authorised later.

3. Crook (*op. cit*) deals at length with these difficulties in his Chapters 2–4.

4. Matters had not entirely stagnated by the institution in August 1855 of the C.G.M. although this, of course, was only available to petty officers and seamen of the Royal Navy and to equivalent ranks of the Royal Marines. No awards for the V.C. were gazetted for just over one year after the Warrant was signed. In the meanwhile, in addition to awards of the D.C.M. and C.G.M., permission was given for a large number of British officers and men to receive French, Sardinian and Turkish decorations. Many Crimean V.C. recipients had another British or foreign decoration – frequently awarded for the same services that won the V.C.

5. See *L.G.*, 5th February 1856, p.410.

ORIGIN AND DEVELOPMENT[1]

In 1854, after almost forty years of peace, Great Britain became involved in a major war against Russia. A considerable deployment of naval and military forces took place whose heroism and suffering quickly caught the imagination of the British public. Within a relatively short time the D.C.M. (q.v.) was instituted, and a campaign medal for the Crimea approved[2]. However the situation remained unsatisfactory, particularly for officers, in that the Order of the Bath was virtually confined to those of field rank (or its equivalent) or above; and, at least in the Army, brevet promotion or a mention in despatches tended to fall to members of the Staff who, in the nature of things, were under the immediate notice of commanders in the field. Nor could it have escaped notice that the junior grades of the Legion of Honour were available to both officers and men of the French forces for gallantry in action and that, by the end of 1854, a number of awards of that decoration had been made for services at the Battle of the Alma. Various suggestions were made both in Parliament and in the Press that there should be some special way of rewarding individual instances of gallantry and the matter engaged the attention of the Government, the Queen and the Prince Consort. On 29th January 1855 the Duke of Newcastle – at that time the Secretary of State for War – announced in the House of Lords that the Queen had been advised "to institute a Cross of Merit which would be open to all ranks of the Army in future", and went on to say that the rules were not "entirely matured, for the subject requires a good deal of consideration". This, indeed, proved to be the case[3] and exactly one year elapsed before the Royal Warrant instituting the Victoria Cross was signed[4]. The preamble envisaged a single decoration available to officers and men alike of both Services but, curiously enough, while making passing reference to the Order of the Bath, made none at all to the existence of the D.C.M. and the C.G.M. The terms of the Warrant were as follows[5]:

"VICTORIA, by the Grace of God of the United Kingdom of Great Britain and Ireland, Queen, Defender of the Faith, &c.

To all to whom these presents shall come, greeting!

WHEREAS We, taking into Our Royal consideration that there exists no means of adequately rewarding the individual gallant services either of officers of the lower grades in Our Naval and Military Service, or of warrant and petty officers, seamen and marines in Our Navy, and non-commissioned officers and soldiers in Our Army; And whereas the Third Class of Our Most Honourable Order of the Bath is limited, except in very rare cases, to the higher ranks of both Services, and the granting of medals, both in Our Navy and Army, is only awarded for long service or meritorious conduct, rather than for bravery in action or distinction before an enemy, such cases alone excepted where a general medal is granted for a particular action or campaign, or a clasp added to the medal for some special engagement, in both of which cases all share equally in the boon, and those who by their valour have particularly signalised themselves remain undistinguished from their comrades; Now, for the purpose of attaining an end so desirable as that of rewarding individual instances of merit and valour, We have instituted and created, and by these presents, for Us, Our Heirs and Successors, institute and create a New Naval and Military Decoration, which We are desirous should be highly prized and eagerly sought after by the officers and men of Our Naval and Military Services, and are graciously pleased to make, ordain, and establish the following rules and ordinances for the government of the same, which shall from henceforth be inviolably observed and kept.

Firstly. – It is ordained, that the distinction shall be styled and designated the "Victoria Cross", and shall consist of a Maltese Cross of Bronze with Our Royal Crest in the centre, and underneath which an escroll bearing this inscription, "For Valour".

Secondly. – It is ordained, that the Cross shall be suspended from the left breast, by a blue riband for the Navy, and by a red riband for the Army.

Thirdly. – It is ordained, that the names of those upon whom We may be pleased to confer the Decoration shall be published in the *London Gazette*, and a registry thereof kept in the office of Our Secretary of State for War.

Fourthly. – It is ordained that anyone who, after having received the Cross, shall again perform an act of bravery, which if he had not received such Cross would have entitled him to it, such further act shall be recorded by a Bar attached to the riband by which the Cross is suspended, and for every additional act of bravery an additional Bar may be added.

Fifthly. – It is ordained, that the Cross shall only be awarded to those officers or men who have served Us in the presence of the enemy, and shall have then performed some signal act of valour, or devotion to their country.

Sixthly. – It is ordained, with a view to place all persons on a perfectly equal footing in relation to eligibility for the Decoration, that neither rank, nor long service, nor wounds, nor any other circumstance or condition whatsoever, save the merit of conspicuous bravery shall be held to establish a sufficient claim to the honour.

Seventhly. – It is ordained that the Decoration may be conferred on the spot where the act to be rewarded by the grant of such Decoration has been performed, under the following circumstances:

I. When the Fleet or Army in which such an act has been performed, is under the eye of a command of an Admiral or General Officer commanding the forces.

II. Where the naval or military force is under the eye and command of an Admiral or Commodore commanding a squadron or detached naval force, or of a General commanding a corps, or division or brigade on a distinct and detached service, when such Admiral, Commodore, or General Officer shall have the power of conferring the Decoration on the spot, subject to confirmation by Us.

Eighthly. – It is ordained, where such act shall not have been performed in sight of a commanding officer as aforesaid, then the claimant for the honour shall prove the act to the satisfaction of the captain or officer commanding his ship, or to the officer commanding the regiment to which the claimant belongs, and such captain or such commanding officer shall report the same through the usual channel to the Admiral or Commodore commanding the force employed on the service, or to the officer commanding the forces in the field, who shall call for such description and attestation of the act as he may think requisite, and on approval shall recommend the grant of the Decoration.

Ninthly. – It is ordained that every person selected for the Cross, under rule seven, shall be publicly decorated before the naval or military force or body to which he belongs, and with which the act of bravery for which he is to be rewarded shall have been performed, and his name shall be recorded in a General Order, together with the cause of his especial distinction.

Tenthly. – It is ordained that every person selected under rule eight shall receive his Decoration as soon as possible, and his name shall likewise appear in a General Order as above required, such General Order to be issued by the naval or military commander of the forces employed on the service.

Eleventhly. – It is ordained that the General Orders above referred to shall from time to time be transmitted to Our Secretary of State for War, to be laid before Us, and shall be by him registered.

Twelfthly. – It is ordained that as cases may arise not falling within the rules above specified, or in which a claim, though well founded, may not have been established on the spot, We will, on the joint submission of Our Secretary of State for War, and of Our Commander-in-chief of Our army, or on that of Our Lord High Admiral or Lords Commissioners of the Admiralty in the case of the Navy, confer the Decoration, but never without conclusive proof of the performance of the act of bravery for which the claim is made.

Thirteenthly. – It is ordained that, in the event of a gallant and daring act having been performed by a squadron, ship's company, a detached body of seamen and marines, not under fifty in number, or by a brigade, regiment, troop, or company, in which the Admiral, General or other officer commanding such forces, may deem that all are equally brave and distinguished, and that no special selection can be made by them, then in such case the Admiral, General, or other officer commanding may direct that for any such body of seamen and marines, or for every troop or company of soldiers, one officer shall be selected by the officers engaged for the Decoration; and in like manner one petty officer or non-commissioned officer shall be selected by the petty officers and non-commissioned officers engaged; and two seamen or private soldiers or marines shall be selected by the seamen, or private soldiers, or marines engaged respectively, for the Decoration; and the names of those selected shall be transmitted by the senior officer in command of the naval force, brigade, regiment, troop, or company, to the Admiral or General Officer commanding, who shall in due manner confer the Decoration as if the acts were done under his own eye.

Fourteenthly. – It is ordained that every warrant officer, petty officer, seaman, or marine, or non-commissioned officer or soldier, who shall have received the Cross, shall, from the date of the act by which the Decoration has been gained, be entitled to a Special Pension of Ten Pounds a year, and each additional Bar conferred under rule four on such warrant or petty officers, or non-commissioned officers or men, shall carry with it an additional pension of Five Pounds per annum.

Fifteenthly. – In order to make such additional provision as shall effectually preserve pure this most honourable distinction, it is ordained, that if any person on whom such distinction shall be conferred, be convicted of treason, cowardice, felony, or of any infamous crime, or if he be accused of any such offence and doth not after a reasonable time surrender himself to be tried for the same, his name shall forthwith be erased from the registry of individuals upon whom the said Decoration shall have been conferred by an especial Warrant under Our Royal Sign Manual, and the pension conferred under rule fourteen shall cease and determine from the date of such Warrant. It is hereby further declared that We, Our Heirs and Successors, shall be the sole judges of the circumstance demanding such expulsion; moreover, We shall at all times have power to restore such persons as may at any time have been expelled both to the enjoyment of the Decoration and Pension.

Given at Our Court at Buckingham Place, this twenty-ninth day of January, in the nineteenth year of Our reign, and in the year of our Lord one thousand eight hundred and fifty-six.

By Her Majesty's Command,
PANMURE."

The first awards were announced in the *London Gazette* of 24th February 1857, and on 26th June following, in Hyde Park, Queen Victoria invested 62 of the 111 Crimean recipients. Correspondence relating to some early recommendations by Commanding Officers is to be found in the Public Record Office[6] together with a number of claims from men who considered themselves entitled to the decoration. It will be noted that Rule 8 provided for claims. The same year the Indian Mutiny broke out and, in due course, gave rise to a further 182 awards. By virtue of Rule 7 (II) a number of these were provisionally conferred by the Commander-in-Chief, India, and later confirmed by the Queen. Where the person concerned died before the award was confirmed, or between gazetting and presentation, the Cross was delivered to his personal representatives. It was also during the Indian Mutiny that the first awards were elected under Rule 13[7]. The last awards elected were in 1918 for the raid on Zeebrugge[8]. A Royal Warrant of 10th August 1858 extended the Victoria Cross to "Non-Military Persons" who had served in the Mutiny as volunteers. Four such awards were gazetted, being to T. H. Kavanagh, Assistant Commissioner[9], R. L. Mangles, Assistant Magistrate[9], W. F. McDonnell, Magistrate[10], all of the Bengal Civil Service, and to G. B. Chicken, a mercantile marine officer serving with the Indian Naval Brigade[11].

So far the Victoria Cross has yet to be won by a woman but it is interesting to note that a gold representation of the decoration, without the wording in the scroll, was presented to Mrs. Webber Harris (wife of the Officer Commanding 104th Bengal

6. Under reference WO 98/2.
7. See *L.G.*, 24th December 1858 for the initial awards under this Rule. There were 29 such awards in the Mutiny, and 46 have been made in all.
8. See *L.G.*, 23rd July 1918; four awards, two each to the Royal Navy and Royal Marines.
9. *L.G.*, 8th July 1859, p.2,629.
10. *L.G.*, 17th February 1860, p.557.
11. *L.G.*, 27th April 1860, p.1,596.

285

Fusiliers) by the officers of the Regiment, for her "indomitable pluck" in nursing the men of the Regiment during a cholera outbreak in September 1859. The outbreak was so bad that 27 men died in one night.

A Royal Warrant of 10th August 1858 provided that the V.C. could be awarded, subject to existing Rules, for "acts of conspicuous courage and bravery under circumstances of extreme danger, such as the occurrence of a fire on board ship, or the foundering of a vessel at sea, or under any other circumstances in which, through the courage and devotion displayed, life or public property might be saved". It is generally stated that six Crosses were awarded under the circumstances provided for[12], the first being to Private T. O'Hea of the Rifle Brigade for extinguishing a fire in an ammunition truck in Canada[13], and the remainder to Assistant Surgeon C.M. Douglas and four men of the 24th Regiment for rescuing some comrades through a dangerous surf at Little Andaman Island[14]. However, Captain A. Scott of the Bengal Staff Corps was awarded the V.C. for going to the assistance of two British officers who were being murderously attacked by coolies on a parade ground at Quetta, and it may be that this award should come within the same category[15]. None of these Crosses would have been accompanied by a corresponding campaign medal. Moreover, there have been other Crosses won in operations for which no campaign medals were issued of which those in Japan in 1864 and South Africa in 1881 may be instanced. From 1881 (see below) the Cross could only be awarded for gallantry in the presence of the enemy.

Rule 15 of the instituting Warrant made provision for erasure of the recipient's name in case of misconduct. In all there have been eight erasures (see below), the first man to be so penalised being E. St. J. Daniel who had won the Cross as a Midshipman, Royal Navy, in the Crimea[16]. Originally it seems to have been accepted that erasure involved the surrender of the Cross and steps were usually taken to retrieve the decoration. However, in 1908 the Treasury Solicitor gave an opinion to the effect erasure did not entail forfeiture of the Cross itself[17]. The case of Gunner J. Collis, R.H.A., is not without interest. Collis was awarded the V.C. for gallantry at Maiwand in 1880[18] during the Second Afghan War. In 1895, more than four years after his discharge from the Army, he was convicted of bigamy, imprisoned, and his name erased. During the First World War he re-enlisted in the Suffolk Regiment and died in London in 1918, being buried with full military honours. After his death, Collis' sister petitioned the King that the erasure should be cancelled and that his name should be replaced on the V.C. Roll. The petition was presented by the Secretary of State for War who, however, was unable to advise the King to issue any special instructions thereto. This decision was somewhat softened by a letter from Lord Stamfordham, the King's Private Secretary, in which he wrote "The King says that most certainly Gunner Collis' name should be inscribed with those of the other V.C.s on the tablets of the R.A. Victoria Cross Memorial"[19].

By a Royal Warrant of 1st January 1867 (see *L.G.*, 25th January 1867, p.429), eligibility was extended to members of local forces serving with Imperial troops under the command of a "general or other officer". The Warrant was retrospective, the preamble making particular reference to operations "undertaken against the Insurgent native tribes of Our Colony of New Zealand". Almost immediately the Cross to Major C. Heaphy of the Auckland Militia was gazetted[20], being the first to a non-regular serviceman. Later, in 1867, when the Government of New Zealand assumed full responsibility for the suppression of the Maoris, the General Officer Commanding returned to the United Kingdom and the Imperial troops were progressively withdrawn. Although further acts of gallantry were performed in New Zealand the Government of the Colony did not forward any recommendations for the V.C. since the local forces were neither serving with Imperial troops nor under command of an Imperial officer. This state of affairs led to the institution of the New Zealand Cross (q.v.).

12. A recommendation was forwarded in respect of Private A. Walsh, 54th Regiment, for gallantry during the fire aboard the *Sarah Sands* troopship at sea on 11th May 1857. Despite the fact that this incident was the very inspiration for the amendment the recommendation was rejected on the ground that the Warrant had no retrospective effect, see P.R.O. WO 32/7345 and 98/2.

13. *L.G.*, 1st January 1867, p.22; a forgery of O'Hea's Cross exists, see the *Bulletin of the Military Historical Society*, Volume 4, p.56.

14. *L.G.*, 17th December 1867, p,6,878. It has been suggested that the rescues were in the face of the enemy since the rescuers were under arrow fire from hostile natives. Whatever the true position was it is clear that the recommendations were put forward on the basis of the 1858 Warrant, see P.R.O. WO 32/7373.

15. *L.G.*, 16th January 1868, p.272.

16. *L.G.*, 24th February 1857, p.652; his surname was corrected in *L.G.*, 13th March 1857, p.979. His name was erased for desertion.

17. See Crook, p.64.

18. *L.G.*, 17th May 1881, p.2,553; his name was erased by Royal Warrant, 18th November 1895.

19. See *The Gunner* for September 1919, p.218, and the *Royal Artillery Institution Leaflet* of November 1920, p.184.

20. *L.G.*, 8th February 1867, p.696.

As mentioned above, a clarifying Royal Warrant of 23rd April 1881 declared that the qualifications for the Cross should be "conspicuous bravery or devotion to the country in the presence of the enemy" and thus, by implication, revoked the 1858 Warrant which had extended the decoration to non-operational circumstances. This latter provision had been much disliked at the War Office and, in fact, had not been invoked since 1867–68 (see above); nor, indeed, had the Warrant been published. In any case it had become a virtual dead letter since the institution and subsequent extension of the Albert Medal (q.v.) Nevertheless, the revised wording, despite defective drafting, had a different purpose. Hitherto the general line taken had been that an act of duty, however bravely performed, was not a sufficient qualification for the Cross. This principle was, of course, easier to state than to apply and accordingly it had been decided to widen the qualification by including gallantry performed in the course of duty[21]. In addition, this Warrant extended eligibility to officers and men of the naval and military auxiliary and reserve forces. A further Royal Warrant of 6th August 1881 extended eligibility to members of the Indian Ecclesiastical Establishments on the ground that, although they did not receive military commissions, if attached to an army in the field they would be required to perform the same duties as military chaplains who were already eligible for the decoration. This Warrant gave rise to the award to the Reverend J. W. Adams of the Bengal Ecclesiastical Department for services during the Second Afghan War[22].

In July 1898 it was decided that the special pension payable to recipients below commissioned rank might be increased in cases of need, at discretion, from £10 up to £50 per annum. The latter figure was later advanced to £75 per annum. It was not until 1959 that the special pension was increased to £100 per annum, and made payable irrespective of rank.

Although the instituting Warrant made no reference to posthumous awards, it had been decided from the very beginning that the Cross would not be given for an act in which the potential recipient was killed, or where he died shortly afterwards. In such cases the announcement in the *London Gazette* was to the effect that had the person concerned survived he would have been recommended for the Victoria Cross. However, in 1900 a Cross was awarded to Lieutenant the Honourable F. H. S. Roberts, K.R.R.C.[23], although he died little more than 24 hours after performing the act for which the award was made. Nearly two years later, in the *London Gazette* of 8th August 1902, King Edward VII approved the issue of six posthumous Crosses, arising from the South African War of 1899–1902, to the personal representatives of the deceased concerned. The question then arose as to what should be done in respect of six similar cases which had been gazetted between 1859 and 1897, and for which no Crosses had been issued. Although a precedent had now been set for the posthumous award of Crosses, for some time the King resisted making these further awards, and it was not until 1907[24] that they were gazetted, and the Crosses transmitted to the personal representatives of the deceased. Thereafter the Crosses of subsequent posthumous recipients were actually presented, specific provision for posthumous awards being written into the consolidating Royal Warrant of 22nd May 1920 (see below).

By a Royal Warrant of 21st October 1911 (see *L.G.*, 12th November 1911, p.9,369), eligibility was extended to native officers and men of the Indian Army who were to receive pensions of 575 and 150 rupees per annum respectively, with a further 150 or 75 rupees for each additional bar. These pensions were to be continued to the recipient's widow until her death or re-marriage. The extension of the V.C. to native ranks of the Indian Army brought about changes in the Indian Order of Merit (q.v.) whereby the original 1st Class of the Order was abolished, the remaining two Classes being re-numbered 1st and 2nd respectively.

In 1916 the miniature for wear on the ribbon in undress was approved (initially it indicated a bar) and in 1918 the crimson ribbon was adopted for all Services (see below).

21. See Crook, Chapter 15.

22. *L.G.*, 26th August 1881, p.4,393.

23. *L.G.*, 2nd February 1900, p.689. His name, together with the other Colenso recipients, is missing from the "State Intelligence" portion of the Index. The *L.G.* entry gives "since deceased".

24. See, for example, *L.G.*s, 27th May 1859, p.2,106, and 15th January 1907, p.325, for the Mutiny award to Private E. Spence, 42nd Regiment. Crook deals with the difficult question of posthumous awards in his Chapter 8.

In 1918 a committee was formed to consider the whole question of the V.C. and in 1919 a new Royal Warrant was approved by the King based upon its recommendations. However, to ensure that it did not have retrospective effect implementation was delayed until the Peace Treaty had been ratified. Accordingly, on 20th May 1920 the Warrant was signed (see *London Gazette*, 18th June 1920, p.6,702) which consolidated, varied and extended the previous provisions. It used simpler wording and made few major changes, although the Rules were re-numbered to incorporate amendments made by previous Warrants. The condition precedent to the award of the Cross was somewhat enlarged as "most conspicuous bravery or some daring or pre-eminent act of valour or self-sacrifice or extreme devotion to duty in the presence of the enemy"; specific provision was made for posthumous awards; and, in addition to officers and men of the Forces of the Empire and the Mercantile Marine[25], women of the Nursing and Hospital Services and civilians of both sexes when serving with the Forces of the Empire were declared eligible. The old Rule 13 which dealt with elected awards was re-numbered 9. In future, where the size of the unit did not exceed 100, one officer, one warrant or non-commissioned officer and one private (or their equivalents) could be selected; where the size of the unit was over 100 but did not exceed 200, one additional private could be selected; where the unit exceeded 200, the number of Crosses would be specially considered; selection would be by secret ballot; and death in action was not to be a bar to selection. Erasures and restorations were to be published in the *London Gazette*[26].

The 1920 Warrant was, in turn, superseded by one dated 5th February 1931 (see *London Gazette*, 20th March 1931, p.1,886). Apart from minor changes in wording, the new Warrant gave official approval for a half-size replica of the decoration to be worn "on certain occasions"[27]; and provided that forfeiture and restoration should be completely discretionary by omitting reference to the conditions precedent hitherto obtaining. This followed a recommendation by the Inter-departmental Rewards Committee that all awards for gallantry, except for cases of extreme infamy, should be regarded as irrevocable; hence it was unnecessary to limit the power, as had been done before, by prescribing for particular circumstances. Four amending Warrants followed. The Warrant of 9th May 1938 (see Army Order No. 134 of July 1938) made separate provision for the Burma Military Forces, Burma having ceased to be part of India the previous year; that of 21st August 1939 (see Army Order No. 144 of August 1939) extended eligibility to the short-lived Army rank of Warrant Officer, Class III; while that of 24th January 1941 (see Army Order No. 8 of January 1941) made all ranks of the newly formed Indian Air Force eligible. The last amending Warrant was dated 31st December 1942 (see Army Order No. 224 of December 1942) and incorporated the following changes by:

(a) extending eligibility to the Home Guard (and similarly constituted forces) as well as the para-military forces of India and Burma;

(b) affirming that members of the Women's Auxiliary Services should be eligible;

(c) providing for direct submissions in the case of the Dominions; and

(d) making the pensions of Indian and Burman recipients subject to local regulations.

No further amendments to the 1931 Warrant were made. With effect from 1st August 1959 pensions paid from British funds were increased to £100 per annum and made payable irrespective of rank[28].

The 1931 Warrant has now been superseded by one dated 30th September 1961 (see Army Order No. 65 of October 1961) which was made necessary by constitutional changes in the Commonwealth. The new Warrant makes no fundamental alterations and affirms that servicemen and women of the Member Countries of the Commonwealth are eligible, subject to the adoption of the Warrant by the Government concerned; incorporates the 1959 pension award; makes special provision for widows of Brigade of Gurkha pensioners[29]; and omits reference to the

25. The latter had to be serving under Naval or Military authority or to become subject to enemy action during the course of their duties.

26. The last erasure was in 1908. There have been no restorations.

27. *E.g.*, with Mess Dress or dinner dress. This Cross is to be distinguished from that worn on the ribbon when the ribbon is worn alone.

28. For over 100 years the pension for United Kingdom recipients was restricted to "other ranks", and limited to £10 per annum, although from 1898 this could be increased in case of hardship.

29. The Brigade of Gurkhas is now part of the British Army and it was necessary to preserve the rights of widows under the Indian regulations.

30. See the Submission in P.R.O. WO 146/1.

31. See the Submission of 9th February 1883 in P.R.O. WO 32/7484; the award was published in *L.G.*, 16th February 1883, p.859.

32. See the Submission of 26th January 1899 in P.R.O. WO 146/1.

33. See the Submission of April 1899 in P.R.O. WO 32/7426; the award was published in *L.G.*, 21st April 189 p.2,545.

34. See the Submission of 4th August 1900 which was cancelled by that of 8th September 1900 in P.R.O. WO 146/1.

35. *L.G.*, 5th October 1900, p.6,126.

36. *L.G.*, 27th September 1901, p.6,317.

37. *L.G.*, 7th October 1902, p.6,341.

38. In *L.G.*, 4th June 1901, p.3,769 where his initial is incorrectly given as "C". In 1909 his name was erased from the V.C. Register, see *post*.

39. *L.G.*, 27th September 1901, p.6,314. O'Moore Creagh (see Bibliography) says that this was for the action at Frederikstad which makes the subsequent cancellation difficult to understand.

40. *L.G.*, 7th January 1902, p.151.

41. *L.G.*, 7th June 1904, p.3,363.

42. *L.G.*, 9th December 1904, p.8,449. See also P.R.O. WO 32/7502.

43. *L.G.*, 9th September 1916, p.8,870.

44. *L.G.*, 22nd September 1916, p.9,306.

45. *L.G.*, 20th October 1916, p.10,213.

46. *L.G.*, 19th April 1901, p.2,700.

47. *L.G.*, 30th August 1901, p.5,737 which also includes the D.S.O. cancellation; see also Crook, p.258.

48. *L.G.*, 16th November 1915, p.11,420.

49. *L.G.*, 15th March 1917, p.2,619 which also includes the D.C.M. cancellation.

50. *L.G.*, 27th January 1944, p.518.

51. *L.G.*, 7th September 1944, p.4,157 which also includes the D.C.M. cancellation; see also Crook, p.225.

52. *L.G.*, 5th September 1916, p.8,704. Robinson belonged to the Worcestershire Regiment.

53. *L.G.*, 3rd September 1940, p.5,385.

54. *L.G.*, 15th November 1940, p.6,569.

55. *L.G.*, 9th September 1916, p.8,869; France; temporary Lieutenant-Colonel attached 8th Battalion, Gloucestershire Regiment.

publication of forfeitures and restorations. By a Royal Warrant of 24th March 1964 (see Army Order No. 22 of March 1964) the functions performed by the Secretary of State for War in regard to the Victoria Cross were transferred, *inter alia*, to the Secretary of State for Defence.

The early photographs reproduced in Wilkins (see Bibliography) suggest that the V.C. was worn much as the recipient fancied, one style being popular where it occupied the central position with other medals grouped round it. However, *Queen's Regulations for the Army*, 1881, which gave a rudimentary order of wearing, laid down that the V.C. was to follow the Order of the Indian Empire (the Companion's badge of which was then worn on the breast), while *Dress Regulations for the Army*, 1900, gave it as following the Royal Victorian Order (instituted 1896). According to de la Bère (see Bibliography), in 1902 King Edward VII ruled that it should precede all decorations placed on the bar brooch worn on the breast. *Dress Regulations for the Army*, 1904, show the V.C. in its present premier position (see also Appendix 4).

There are at least 10 instances of recipients whose V.C. has cancelled another award. Thus on 4th January 1883[30] the Queen approved award of the D.C.M. to Private F. Corbett, King's Royal Rifle Corps, for an act of gallantry in Egypt but this was cancelled shortly afterwards and the V.C. awarded instead[31]; Corporal J. Smith, East Kent Regiment, was awarded the D.C.M. for gallantry on the North West Frontier[32], the V.C. being substituted later[33]; similarly, the D.C.M. awarded to Sergeant H. Engleheart, 10th Hussars, for an act in South Africa[34] was cancelled and replaced by the V.C.[35]; Private W. House, Royal Berkshire Regiment, received the D.C.M. for the same campaign[36], the V.C. being substituted subsequently[37]; Private G. Ravenhill, Royal Scots Fusiliers, was awarded the V.C. for Colenso[38] and later the D.C.M.[39] which in turn was cancelled due to the previous award[40]; Lieutenant H. A. Carter, Indian Army, was awarded the D.S.O. for the action near Jidballi, Somaliland in 1903[41] but, following a further report in the matter, the V.C. was substituted[42]; Private W. Jackson, 17th Battalion, Australian Infantry, was awarded both the V.C.[43] and the D.C.M.[44] for the same act near Armentières, the latter award being cancelled shortly afterwards[45]; Captain H. N. Schofield, R.F.A., received the D.S.O. for Colenso[46] which in turn was replaced by the V.C.[47]; Corporal J. E. Grimshaw, Lancashire Fusiliers, was awarded the D.C.M. for gallantry at Gallipoli[48] but was subsequently selected by his comrades to receive the V.C.[49]; and Company Sergeant Major P. H. Wright, Coldstream Guards, received the D.C.M. for an action near Salerno[50] which, at the instance of the King, was replaced by the V.C.[51].

The V.C. has been won three times in the United Kingdom – by Captain W. L. Robinson, R.F.C., at Cuffley, Hertfordshire[52], for bringing down the first Zeppelin over these Islands; posthumously by Leading Seaman J. F. Mantle, R.N., during an air attack on his ship in Portland Harbour[53]; and by Flight Lieutenant J. B. Nicolson, R.A.F., who displayed outstanding valour in air combat over Southampton[54] although badly wounded and with his aircraft on fire.

The Victoria Cross has been won by a number of men of foreign origin, of whom Captain A. Carton de Wiart, 4th Dragoon Guards[55] (Belgian), Major A. F. E. V. S. Lassen, Commandos[56] (Danish), Corporal F. C. Schiess, Natal Native Contingent[57] (Swiss) and Sergeant Major C. Wooden, 17th Lancers[58] (German) may be mentioned.

56. *L.G.*, 7th September 1945, p.4,469; action at Lake Commachio, Italy; posthumous award.

57. *L.G.*, 29th November 1879, p.7,148; Rorke's Drift; his true Christian names seem to have been Christian Ferdinand, see the

Bulletin of the Military Historical Society, Volume XI, p.41.

58. *L.G.*, 26th October 1858, p.4,575; Balaklava.

Fig.B: The Victoria Cross and bar, reverse.

59. *L.G.*, 13th August 1861, p.3,363; Taku Forts.

60. *L.G.*, 15th September 1916, p.9,085; Jutland; posthumous award.

61. *L.G.*, 18th June 1858, p.2,959; Indian Mutiny.

62. *L.G.*, 24th December 1858, p.5,516; Indian Mutiny; later Field-Marshal the Rt. Hon. the Earl Roberts, V.C., K.G., K.P., G.C.B., O.M., G.C.S.I., G.C.I.E., V.D.

63. *L.G.*, 2nd February 1900, p.689; Colenso; Roberts' award was possibly posthumous.

64. *L.G.*, 26th October, 1916, p.10,393; France; posthumous award.

65. *L.G.*, 21st October 1859, p.3,792; Indian Mutiny.

66. *L.G.*, 15th January 1904, p.331; Somaliland.

67. *L.G.*, 17th March 1919, p.3,590; Zeebrugge; posthumous award.

68. *L.G.*, 25th November 1916, p.11,525; France; posthumous award.

69. *L.G.*, 21st October 1859, p.3,792; Indian Mutiny.

70. *L.G.*, 24th December 1858, p.5,516; Indian Mutiny; with the award to J. E. Gough (mentioned above) the Gough family have thus won three Victoria Crosses.

71. *L.G.*, 17th May 1881, p.2,553; Second Afghan War.

72. *L.G.*, 26th October 1874, p.5,113; Ashantee War.

73. *L.G.*, 18th November 1915, p.11,448; France; posthumous award.

74. *L.G.*, 20th November 1942, p.5,023; Western Desert.

75. *L.G.*, 13th May 1943, p.2,141; Western Desert.

76. *L.G.*, 12th September 1946, p.4,573; Far East.

The youngest recipients seem to have been Hospital Apprentice A. Fitzgibbon, Indian Medical Establishment[59], who was 15 years 3 months of age when he won his Cross; and Boy, 1st Class, J. T. Cornwell, R.N.[60], who was 16 years 4 months. The oldest seems to have been Captain W. Raynor, Bengal Veteran Establishment[61], who was about 69.

There are three cases of both father and son receiving the Victoria Cross:

    (1) Lieutenant F. S. Roberts, Bengal Artillery[62]
        Lieutenant the Honourable F. H. S. Roberts, K.R.R.C.[63]

    (2) Captain W. N. Congreve, Rifle Brigade[63]
        Brevet-Major W. La T. Congreve, D.S.O, M.C., Rifle Brigade[64]

    (3) Major C. J. S. Gough, 5th Bengal European Cavalry[65]
        Brevet-Major J. E. Gough, Rifle Brigade[66]

There are four known cases of awards to brothers:

    (1) Lieutenant Commander G. N. Bradford, R.N.[67]
        Lieutenant-Colonel R. B. Bradford, M.C., Durham Light Infantry[68]

    (2) Major C. J. S. Gough, 5th Bengal European Cavalry[69]
        Lieutenant H. H. Gough, 1st Bengal European Light Cavalry[70]

    (3) Captain E. H. Sartorius, 59th Regiment[71]
        Major R. W. Sartorius, C.M.G., 6th Bengal Cavalry[72]

    (4) 2nd Lieutenant A. B. Turner, Royal Berkshire Regiment[73]
        Lieutenant-Colonel V. B. Turner, Rifle Brigade[74]

A unique instance occurs in the case of the brothers Seagrim, one of whom received the Victoria Cross, and the other the George Cross. Lieutenant-Colonel D. A. Seagrim, The Green Howards, was awarded the V.C. in 1943[75], and Major H. Seagrim, D.S.O., M.B.E., 19th Hyderabad Regiment, the G.C. in 1946[76]. Both awards were posthumous.

Re-unions of recipients, many of whom came from distant countries, were held in London in 1920 and 1929. The Victoria Cross Association was formed from surviving recipients in 1956, and in 1961 it was enlarged to admit recipients of the George Cross, the Association being renamed accordingly. Re-unions of recipients were held biennially under the auspices of the Association between 1956 and 1978. The re-union which would have been held in 1980 was postponed to 1981 to coincide with the Silver Jubilee of the Association.

DESCRIPTION

General Ever since its institution the Cross has been supplied by the well-known London jewellers, Messrs. Hancocks and Co., now of Burlington Gardens, London W.1. The Cross and suspender are first cast in gunmetal and then chased and finished by hand; from 1914 to 1950 a die-cast suspender was used. The metal is taken from guns captured from the Russians in the Crimean War although during and after the First World War it is fairly certain that metal from captured Chinese guns was used for a short period. The components of the decoration are then treated chemically to obtain the uniform dark brown finish which is darker on some issues than on others. The Cross is 1.375 inches wide and, together with the suspender bar and link, weighs about 0.87 ounces troy, although chasing and finishing may cause slight variation in these figures. Crook attributes the design of the Cross to H. H. Armstead who at the time of its inception was working for Hancocks; and illustrates both a preliminary design and the original specimen approved by the Queen.

Ribbon Crimson (described as "red" in the Warrants), $1\frac{1}{2}$ inches wide. Originally the ribbon was dark blue for the Royal Navy and crimson for the Army. Shortly before the Royal Air Force was formed on 1st April 1918 a committee was constituted under the chairmanship of Colonel Sir Douglas Dawson, Comptroller, Lord Chamberlain's Department, to advise the King whether a special decoration was needed for the new Service and whether there should be

77. See P.R.O. ADM 116/1744 which contains a draft of the committee's recommendations annexed to the Board of Admiralty's minutes of 12th March 1918.

78. See Army Order No. 290 of September 1916.

79. See Army Order No. 114 of April 1917. The provisions regarding miniatures and the modified ribbon were incorporated into the consolidating Royal Warrant of 22nd May 1920 (see above).

80. E.g., the Cross awarded to Private F. Whirlpool, 3rd Bombay European Regiment (L.G., 21st October 1859, p.3,793) bears the dates 3rd April and 2nd May 1858. In such cases it is sometimes contended that the man concerned should have received the V.C. and bar. This ignores the provision of the Royal Warrants that, to be eligible for a bar, the recipient must already have received the V.C.

81. The pattern was decided in 1915 by the Military Secretary at the War Office, apparently without reference to the King, on a bar being awarded to Captain A. Martin-Leake, R.A.M.C., see P.R.O. WO 32/4992.

82. These positions are reversed in the case of Farrier Sergeant-Major W. J. Hardman, New Zealand Mounted Rifles. It seems that Hardman was presented with an unengraved Cross in 1902, the Cross intended for him not then being available. He kept the unengraved Cross and, apparently, later had it engraved himself (the Cross intended for him being returned to the War Office), see the *Journal of the Orders and Medals Research Society*, May 1962, p.114. The Cross awarded to Lieutenant A. S. Heathcote, 60th Rifles (L.G., 20th January 1860, p.178) has no date in the centre of the reverse. His citation speaks of "highly gallant and daring conduct at Delhi, throughout the siege, from June to September 1857, during which he was wounded . . ." and, because no specific dates of gallantry are given in the citation, it may have been thought proper to leave the centre of the reverse blank. The reverse of the Cross awarded to Flight Lieutenant J. B. Nicholson, R.A.F. (see also footnote 54) bears the date 10th November 1940 which is the date the recommendation was submitted to the King (see P.R.O. AIR 30/157 (139)).

83. See L.G., 15th January 1907 for six such cases, two being for the Indian Mutiny.

a uniform colour for the ribbon of the V.C. The committee recommended, *inter alia*, that what had been the Army ribbon should be adopted by all recipients, and this proposal was approved by the King[77]. When the ribbon is worn alone a miniature of the Cross is pinned to it, a bar being indicated by a second miniature worn beside the first. When first approved in 1916, a single miniature indicated the award of a bar[78]; from 1917 the single miniature was to be worn by Army first recipients (and after the introduction of the unified ribbon in 1918 by all recipients), bars being indicated by additional miniatures[79].

Suspension By a straight bar, slotted for the ribbon, with a V-lug below, made in one piece. The front of the bar is ornamented with laurels (the die-cast bars having the leaves set more closely together), and the reverse engraved with details of the recipient. The Cross and suspender bar are joined by a small link which passes through the lugs of both components. On earlier issues the link is completely circular and the inside bottom of the V-lug slightly recessed to accommodate it. Later the link was made oval and the lug not recessed.

Obverse (Fig.A) In reality the Cross is not a Maltese Cross, as it is described in the Royal Warrants, but is closer to a cross patté.

Reverse (Fig.B) The date (or dates[80]), of the act of gallantry is engraved in the centre circle (see below).

Bars (Figs.A and B) This is based on the suspender bar but without the V-lug, ribbon and frame above[81]. The reverse is engraved with details of the recipient and the date or dates of the act.

Naming Details of the recipient are engraved in capital letters on the reverse of the suspender bar, and the date or dates of the act of gallantry in the centre circle of the reverse of the Cross[82]. The style of engraving varies although, generally speaking, the use of serifs seems to have been discontinued during the South African War. However, King Edward VII having approved posthumous issues (see above), some comparatively modern Crosses exist which were awarded for services performed many years before[83]. Sometimes the inscription is engraved through the dark brown finish, revealing the bright colour of the metal beneath and making the inscription stand out more clearly, and sometimes the inscription is engraved before the decoration is chemically treated, in which case the inscription is of the same colour as the decoration itself. The latter practice seems to have been more general before the South African War although thereafter no particular pattern is apparent.

The details on the suspender bar include the rank, name and regiment, or other description of the recipient. Abbreviations are used, according to the length of the inscription, and during the First World War the practice of adding the regimental or equivalent number in the case of recipients below commissioned rank was introduced. Occasionally the recipient's full (or abbreviated) first names appear. The First World War and later inscriptions tend to be fuller than those appearing previously. The details on the reverse of the Cross give the date or dates of the act concerned, the month usually being abbreviated.

Re-issues Occasionally a recipient has been issued with a replacement which, in itself, cannot readily be detected, although suspicion may be aroused if the accompanying medals are themselves replacement issues. Messrs. Hancocks are able to say if a replacement has been issued.

Copies and Fakes Various types of copy exist, some cast examples being very well made indeed. However, due to the cooling of metal in the mould, they are slightly smaller than the genuine Crosses and not of the correct weight. Nevertheless Messrs. Hancocks do not consider the weight of great importance as the thickness of the decoration can vary, especially with early issues. Some copies are struck from dies which, together with some of those cast, are poorly finished and of too light a colour. On one type of copy the sides of the suspender bar are not straight but have a curved excrescence either side of the ribbon slot, while another type has V-shaped niches at either end of the ribbon slot. Recently a particularly well-made copy has appeared on the market; in this, however, the inner diameter of the centre circle of the reverse is 14mm which is too wide and hence relatively easily recognisable. Some copies have been faked by the addition of details of actual recipients although usually the engraving is of poor quality. Messrs. Hancocks can almost invariably state whether a Cross is genuine or not.

VERIFICATIONS AND CITATIONS

All awards can be verified from the *London Gazette* where, until 1941, names are listed under "Victoria Cross" in the "State Intelligence" section of the indices. With occasional omissions, names also appear in the "Civil Promotions" (later "Civil Appointments and Promotions") section. From 1942 the "State Intelligence" section gives only the pages upon which awards are to be found, names being included in a comprehensive nominal index headed "Honours, Decorations and Medals".

Citations invariably appear[84] except for some elected awards and what appears to be the isolated case of Lieutenant A. W. S. Agar, R.N.[85]. The account of various actions against enemy submarines for which awards had been made to Naval personnel in 1917 were not published until the following year[86] when the need for security had passed. A list of First World War Army awards giving the names, regiment, theatre, date of deed and *London Gazette* reference is published in the *London Gazette* of 31st March 1919 at p.4,153 et seq. Montgomery (see Bibliography) gives the official recommendations in respect of 50 of these recipients, the recommendations generally being longer than the gazetted citations. Details of the awards for Zeebrugge and Ostend in April and May 1918 are preserved in the Public Record Office in ADM 116/1811. For flying personnel the series AIR 1 contains the First World War recommendations for the R.F.C. and R.A.F. serving in France and Belgium[87]; AIR 2 (Code 30) contains those for the Second World War[88]; and AIR 30 contains the Submissions to the King from 1918 to 1945. Citations for First World War army awards appear in Army Orders. During the Second World War details of awards appeared in Press Releases from which extracts often were made in local newspapers.

A large number of books on the Victoria Cross have been published which, quite naturally, deal mainly with the recipients themselves rather than with ancillary matters. Of these the books by Crook, Gordon Roe, O'Moore Creagh, Parry, Smyth, Stewart, Turner and Wilkins (see Bibliography) may be mentioned, and in which additional or background details of recipients may be found. In particular, O'Moore Creagh provides all *London Gazette* entries and many portraits of recipients down to 1920. Wilkins, *inter alia*, gives portraits of recipients to 1903, and Stewart all *London Gazette* entries to 1921. Gordon Roe and Turner deal with the Second World War awards, and the former provides many illustrations of recipients. Smyth gives an excellent general account until 1963 and deals with additional matters (e.g. The V.C. and G.C. Association; re-unions, etc.) which are not readily available elsewhere. Many interesting details are to be found in local newspapers at the time an award was published, or, for instance, when a recipient died. Mention must be made of the immensely detailed biographical material compiled by Canon W. M. Lummis, M.C., which is now in the safekeeping of the Military Historical Society at the Duke of York's Headquarters, Chelsea. This lifetime's work consists of separate manuscript files for each recipient, containing both published and unpublished biographical information, copies of photographs, etc.

An interesting gallery of Victoria Cross incidents was painted by the Chevalier L. W. Desanges. These were exhibited in London in the 1870s and excited a good deal of comment in *The Times*. The recipients sat for their portraits so that their

84. In 1965 General Sir Lewis Halliday, V.C., K.C.B., held that the citation for his award in *L.G.*, 1st January 1901 (at p.3) was incorrect, see *The Times* of 1st September 1965. No alteration was made since the Ministry of Defence decided that the citation was made in accordance with the best information available from the men on the spot (see *The Daily Telegraph*, of 2nd September 1965). This apparently isolated case seems to be no ground for doubting the accuracy of other published citations which, in any case, are not easy to compose, reflect infinitely varying literary styles and represent an amalgamation of witnesses' reports.

85. *L.G.*, 22nd August 1919, p.10,631. An account of Agar's act of gallantry is given, however, by Boyle (see Bibliography).

86. *L.G.*, 20th November 1918, p.13,693 et seq.

87. See the Honours and Awards files in this series. Where only the date of award is known it is preferable to search for the recommendation in the files of H.Q. R.F.C./R.A.F. which are arranged according to date; where the formation or unit is known the corresponding files may be consulted first although not all have been preserved.

88. The numerical sequence of the AIR 2 references does not reflect the strict chronology of the various files and it is necessary to consult the whole index to the Code when searching.

89. Who himself was awarded the Victoria Cross in the Crimea as Captain R. J. Lindsay, Scots Fusilier Guards.

90. Messrs. Gale and Polden Ltd. made a series of picture postcards of these.

91. For example, in the First World War many officers were attached to the R.F.C. and are shown in the Army List both in their regimental and in the R.F.C. lists. The case of the pre-1873 regimental surgeons is even more complicated.

92. Including one forfeited award.

93. Including five elected awards.

94. Including two elected awards.

95. Including 27 elected awards and six forfeitures.

96. Including six elected awards, and bars to Lieutenant A. Martin-Leake and Captain N. G. Chavasse, M.C., both of the R.A.M.C.

97. Including one award to 10th Gurkha Rifles which are now part of the British Army. Previous awards to the Gurkha Rifles have been included in the figures for the Indian Army.

98. Excluding eight recipients attached R.F.C./R.A.F.

99. Including the bar to Captain C. H. Upham, New Zealand Military Forces.

100. Including one award to the Indian Navy, one to the Bengal Ecclesiastical Department, six elected awards, and one forfeiture. For this period Smyth gives 101 awards for the H.E.I.C. Forces/Indian Army, and reduces the British Army total accordingly. The allocation of the actual numbers is controversial.

101. Awarded for the Indian Mutiny under the 1858 Royal Warrant. The award to the Reverend J. W. Adams under the 1881 Royal Warrant is included in the figure for the Indian Army.

102. Awarded in 1921 for the First World War. No award was made to the British Unknown Warrior who, however, received the United States' Congressional Medal of Honor. Reports of the ceremonies at Arlington Cemetery and in Westminster Abbey appear in *The Times* of 18th October and 12th November 1921 respectively.

103. Including two awards for the North West Frontier of India in 1915, and five for Russia in 1919.

104. Four Korea; one Sarawak; four Vietnam.

105. *L.G.*, 13th May 1902, p.3,176.

106. *L.G.*, 18th February 1915, p.1,700.

107. *L.G.*, 26th October 1916, p.10,394.

108. *L.G.*, 14th September 1917, p.9,531.

109. *L.G.*, 14th October 1941, p.5,935.

110. *L.G.*, 26th September 1945, p.4,779.

features were correct, whatever criticism may have been made of the pictures themselves. Lord Wantage[89] purchased 46 of them which he presented to the town of Wantage[90], but in about 1920 they were dispersed on permanent loan to various Officers' Messes, Regimental Museums, etc. Not all the pictures were purchased by Lord Wantage and the remainder found their way into the possession of various owners, both public and private. Many were shown at the V.C. Centenary Exhibition of 1956 and some at the Indian Army Exhibition of 1962.

NUMBERS AWARDED

In all, 1,349 Crosses and three bars have been awarded. However, difficulty arises when analysing the figures in tabular form. Thus a recipient may have been attached to a different regiment when he won his Cross and the award could be attributed to either regiment[91]. Moreover this difficulty extends beyond the British Army and overlaps into the H.E.I.C. Forces, the Indian Army and Commonwealth Forces. Even the question of what is a posthumous award is not free from doubt. While it is clear that a person who is killed performing the deed which wins him the Cross is a posthumous "recipient", it is less easy to decide when he dies later of wounds incurred during the deed, or dies from whatever cause before the recommendation is initiated by his Commanding Officer, or forwarded by the appropriate commander. The figure usually given for posthumous awards is 293 Crosses and one bar, only 14 such awards being made before 1914, and we accept this as approximately correct, although some individual cases are arguable. For all these reasons, therefore, probably no analysis is entirely satisfactory, and what follows is merely one interpretation of the figures.

	1856–1913	1914–1919	1920–1938	1939–1945	1946–1979	Total
R.N., R.N.R., R.N.V.R., and R.N.A.S.	39[92]	46[93]	—	22	—	107
Royal Marines	4	5[94]	—	1	—	10
British Army	348[95]	415[96]	1	61	5[97]	830
R.F.C. and R.A.F.	—	9[98]	—	22	—	31
Australian Forces	5	63	—	19	4	91
Canadian Forces	4	62	—	13	—	79
New Zealand Forces	2	10	—	9[99]	—	21
Newfoundland	—	1	—	—	—	1
South African Forces	21	4	—	3	—	28
Fiji Military Forces	—	—	—	1	—	1
King's African Rifles	—	—	—	1	—	1
H.E.I.C. Forces and Indian Army	95[100]	18	4	30	—	147
Civilians	4[101]	—	—	—	—	4
United States Unknown Warrior	—	—	1[102]	—	—	1
Totals	522	633[103]	6	182	9[104]	1,352

Bars The three recipients of bars are as follows:

A. *Martin-Leake* Cross awarded as Surgeon Captain, South African Constabulary, for the action at Vlakfontein, South Africa, 8th February 1902[105]; bar awarded as Lieutenant, R.A.M.C., for services near Zonnebeke, Belgium, 29th October–8th November 1914[106].

N. G. *Chavasse* Cross awarded as Captain, R.A.M.C., for services at Guillemont, France, 9th August 1916[107]; bar at Wieltje, Belgium, 31st July–2nd August 1917[108], being a posthumous award.

C. H. *Upham* Cross awarded as 2nd Lieutenant, 20th Battalion, New Zealand Military Forces, for services at Maleme, Crete, 22nd–30th May 1941[109]; bar at El Ruweisat Ridge, Western Desert, 14th/15th July 1942[110].

Erasures There have been eight erasures as follows:

	London Gazette awarding V.C.	*Royal Warrant ordering forfeiture*
Bambrick, V. Private, 60th Regiment	24th December 1858, p.5,513 (Indian Mutiny)	3rd December 1863
Collis, J. Gunner, R.H.A.	16th May 1881, p.2,553 (Second Afghan War)	18th November 1895
Corbett, F. Private, K.R.R.C.	16th February 1883, p.859 (Egypt 1882)	30th July 1884
Daniel, E. St.J. Midshipman, R.N.	24th February 1857, p.652 (Crimea)	4th September 1861
Lane, T. Private, 67th Regiment	13th August 1861, p.3,363 (China)	7th April 1881
McGuire, J. Sergeant, 1st Bengal European Fusiliers	24th December 1858, p.5,519 (Indian Mutiny)	22nd December 1862
Murphy, M. Private, Military Train	27th May 1859, p.2,106 (Indian Mutiny)	5th March 1872
Ravenhill, G. Private, Royal Scots Fusiliers	4th June 1901, p.3,769 (South Africa)	24th August 1908

Under the provisions of the Royal Warrant existing at the time, none of the erasures was gazetted. There were no restorations.

ILLUSTRATIVE AWARD

Sergeant[111] Daniel Cambridge, 8th Company, 11th Battalion, Royal Artillery, was awarded the Victoria Cross for services performed before Sebastopol during the Crimean War. The *London Gazette* of 23rd June 1857 at p.2,165 announced the award, giving the citation as follows:

> "For having volunteered for the spiking party at the assault on the Redan, 8th September, 1855, and continuing therewith, after being severely wounded; and for having, in the after part of the same day, gone out in front of the advanced trench, under a heavy fire, to bring in a wounded man, in performing which service, he was himself severely wounded a second time."

But this is not the full story. In the Library of the Royal Artillery Institution there is a manuscript book[112] which contains a copy of the original citation sent to the Adjutant-General of the Forces on 19th December 1856. This is somewhat fuller than the published version and relates that Cambridge was first wounded in the leg but refused to retire although recommended (*sic*) to do so. The citation adds that it was in front of the advanced trench in the Quarries that he was severely wounded a second time, being shot through the jaw. Lieutenant-Colonel H. F. Strange (commanding his Company) and Captain G. Davis (who commanded the spiking party and also received the V.C.) are given as recommending the award. A letter from Cambridge himself which was written in 1868 is also preserved in the Institution[113]. In this he says that in fact he was wounded three times, the last occasion being the wound to the jaw[114], and "by the assistance of several doctors I have at present got 185 bits of bone out of my jaw. And I can assure you that I suffer very much from my head, I may say all over". As noted above, Cambridge's recommendation for the Cross was forwarded on 19th December 1856. This may have been unknown to him since, from a copy letter preserved in the Ministry of Defence (Army Department), it appears that he wrote to Lord

111. This is the rank given in the *London Gazette* and on Cambridge's Cross. In fact, Cambridge was a Bombardier when he won his Cross and, according to his record of service, preserved in the Public Record Office (WO 10/2231) he was not promoted Sergeant until 21st April 1856.

112. Catalogue number MS C1/171E.

113. Catalogue number MS 118.

114. In *L.G.*, 26th September 1855, he is listed as severely wounded.

115. The Secretary of State for War.

116. This is not an isolated case, see above.

117. *House of Commons Papers 1857 (Session2)*, Volume 27, p.215, and Royal Artillery General Regimental Order of 17th July 1857; where possible, the medals were to be presented on parade "and with every formality which may tend to impress upon the Recipients, and their Comrades, the value of the decoration".

118. Awarded, with a gratuity of £10, in the Royal Artillery Regimental Order of 16th July 1861.

119. *The Standard*, 10th September 1897.

120. *The Daily Mail*, 22nd and 30th October 1899.

121. Parry and O'Moore Creagh both say that a duplicate was issued, apparently basing their information on the auctioneer's suggestion.

122. *The Daily Telegraph*, 14th July 1906.

123. After passing through a number of collections, they are now in the possession of the Royal Artillery.

124. For further details of Cambridge's career and of his medals, see the *Journal of the Society for Army Historical Research*, Volume 42, p.59 et seq.

Panmure[115] soliciting the award himself[116]. From the acknowledgement sent to Cambridge it seems that the original letter had been accompanied by enclosures, which may have been reports from witnesses. Unfortunately the letter and enclosures are no longer available but a further copy letter shows that they were forwarded to the Commander-in-Chief on 1st May 1857. In due course the award was gazetted and Cambridge received the Cross from Queen Victoria at the first V.C. investiture in Hyde Park on 26th June 1857. Soon afterwards Cambridge received the Sardinian *Al Valore Militare*, the citation for which[117], although to some extent covering the action at the Redan, is rather wider and reads as follows:

> "Served in the trenches throughout the whole of the siege of Sebastopol. Formed one of the spiking party on the 8th September, 1855, on which occasion he was severely wounded. Was noted for his cool and intrepid conduct under fire. This non-commissioned officer has received the Victoria Cross."

It is interesting to note that on this medal his rank is given correctly as Bombardier, while on the V.C. it appears as Sergeant.

On 27th June 1871 Cambridge was pensioned as a Master-Gunner after almost exactly 32 years' service, and in the same year became a Yeoman of the Guard. Wilkins shows him in the latter uniform wearing his medals. In the upper row Cambridge wears first his Long Service and Good Conduct Medal[118], followed by the British Crimean medal (with bars Inkerman and Sebastopol) and the Turkish Crimean medal; in the lower row he wears first the *Al Valore Militare* and, lastly, the V.C. He died at Plumstead in 1882 aged 62 years, and in 1897 his medals were auctioned[119]. Two years later a second Cross and a single British Crimean medal, purporting to be his, were offered for sale by the same auctioneers. Due to representations made by the purchaser of the original medals, the latter were withdrawn, the auctioneers admitting that there was some doubt about the authenticity of the second Cross but suggesting that a duplicate could have been issued[120]. In fact no record exists of such a duplicate[121]. In due course the purchaser of the original (and genuine) medals bought the second Cross privately, but later this was stolen from him. It found its way into the possession of a pawnbroker; legal proceedings were taken[122]; and an order was made restoring the second Cross to the original purchaser who, in the meantime, had sold the genuine medals[123]. In 1962 the second Cross was traced and submitted to Messrs. Hancocks who found it to be a fake[124].

Appendix 1

Mentions in Despatches

ORIGIN AND DEVELOPMENT

The practice of mentioning subordinates in despatches from commanders at sea, or in the field, is of long standing. Originally it was a device for bringing the services of deserving officers to the attention of higher authority, but was largely confined to formation and unit commanders, and to senior staff officers. It seems that Sir Charles Napier was the first to make mention of men below commissioned rank and a number of European and native other ranks are named in annexures to his despatch of 2nd March 1843 regarding the Scinde Campaign[1]. In the period following the Crimean War many such instances formed the basis for the award of medals, notably the D.C.M[2]. The actual form of mention varied from a mere list of names to a description of the individual services performed. Where the latter was the basis for an award, or of promotion in rank[3], it sometimes took the form of what now would be regarded as a citation. Many officers and men were mentioned in the various South African War despatches. Every recipient of the D.S.O. and C.S.C. was mentioned[4] and almost every recipient of the D.C.M., although few were accompanied by a citation. In 1902, following a recommendation by the Interdepartmental Rewards Committee, it was decided that publication in the *London Gazette* was essential to constitute a mention[5].

A very large number of mentions were made during the First World War (see below) and it became increasingly difficult, except in the case of small operations, to describe the services performed. For this reason the vast majority of military despatches merely gave lists of names, although naval despatches tended to be more informative. While it cannot be said that the percentage of mentions received by military personnel (about 2.3% of the total number of troops under arms) depreciated the value of the distinction, it became evident that it was losing favour in the eyes of the recipients. The main causes were:

1. The custom of the French and Belgian Armies to award a Croix de Guerre in respect of a "citation" in the orders of certain commands.

2. The "service" ribbons adopted during the War by France, Belgium and Italy which were, in fact, the equivalents of the British "Service Chevrons".

3. The natural desire of the recipient to wear some specific proof of recognition of his services.

4. To a lesser degree, the unofficial introduction of Corps and Divisional gallantry certificates[6], when the individual services did not attain the standard required for a decoration. Such services did not necessarily also gain a mention in despatches but nevertheless received a degree of local recognition.

Accordingly in 1919 King George V approved of a special certificate to be given to all persons mentioned in First World War despatches[7] in the Services, the Indian, Dominion, and Egyptian Forces, as well as certain recognised societies and organisations[8], and other civilians of both sexes serving with the Forces. Even then this was not thought to be entirely satisfactory and in 1920 it was decided that a multiple-leaved bronze oak leaf should be worn on the ribbon of the Victory Medal, by all those entitled to that medal, to denote a First World War mention[9]. Only one emblem was to be worn irrespective of the number of times an individual had been mentioned.

1. *L.G.*, 9th May 1843. Some of the natives received the I.O.M.

2. The majority of despatches are reproduced in the *London Gazette* and/or the *Gazette of India*.

3. A device frequently used in the Royal Navy.

4. This was originally a condition precedent to the award of the D.S.O. and C.S.C./D.S.C.

5. See P.R.O. WO 32/8315.

6. A practice revived in the Second World War.

7. For the Army this was announced in Army Order No. 166 of May 1919, similar orders being made in the other Services. Certificates were also awarded in the Second World War, and subsequently. In describing the evolution of the mention in despatches, we have quoted Army authorities to avoid duplication of references.

8. *E.g.,* the Y.M.C.A. and Y.W.C.A., the British Red Cross Society, etc.

9. Army Order No. 3 of January 1920. Later, permission was given for those mentioned for services between 12th November 1918 and 10th August 1920 to wear the emblem on the ribbon of the Victory Medal. The implication is that, at the time, those not entitled to the Victory Medal did not wear the emblem. This rule was altered in Army Order No. 109 of September 1947 (see below).

Mentions continued to be made between the Wars. According to the headings of lists published in the *London Gazette*, from the outbreak of the Second World War and thereafter, all mentions have been approved by the Sovereign. Some of these are classified as immediate, or as posthumous, awards[10]. Indeed, Army Order No.109 of September 1947 stated that mentions in despatches and commendations had been formalised as State awards and were subject to forfeiture[11] as with certain other awards.

In August 1943 King George VI approved of a single-leaved bronze oak leaf of a different pattern from that previously authorised, being awarded to members of the Services who had been mentioned in despatches, or who had received Civil[12] or Military commendations published in the *London Gazette*, for service in the Second World War[13]. Until the institution of the War Medal 1939–45 the emblem was worn after the ribbons of any other medals awarded, or if there were none, where a single ribbon would have been worn.

Army Order No.109 of September 1947 (which is difficult to interpret)[14] made certain innovations, and modified the existing rules regarding the wearing of emblems as follows:

1. *Multiple-leaved emblem* The first type emblem was also to be worn by those mentioned in despatches for operations between 12th November 1918 and 10th August 1920 (or which began before the latter date), on the ribbon of the appropriate campaign medal[15] if they were not eligible for the Victory Medal (on which otherwise it would be worn). If the recipient was not eligible for such medals, the emblem was to be worn after any medal ribbons.

2. *Single-leaved emblem* The second type emblem was to be worn on the ribbon of the appropriate campaign medal for those mentioned after 10th August 1920; for the Second World War it was to be worn on the ribbon of the War Medal. Only one emblem was to be worn on any one ribbon; if a person had been mentioned for services which on a campaign medal were recognised by the first type emblem and was again mentioned for services which otherwise would be represented by the second type emblem on the same ribbon, he was to wear the former only[16]. If the recipient was not eligible for the appropriate campaign medal, he was to wear the emblem after any other medal ribbons. The emblem was also to be worn to denote a commendation for brave conduct or for valuable service in the air in respect of service in the Armed Forces. Where the commendation was for service in the Armed Forces (or Merchant Navy) during the Second World War it was to be worn on the ribbon of the War Medal; where it was for service qualifying for a general service medal it was to be worn on the ribbon of that medal; where it was for service not qualifying for the War Medal or a general service medal it was to be worn after any other medal ribbons.

Emblems worn with the medal itself were to be fixed to the centre of the ribbon at an angle of 60 degrees from the inside edge of the ribbon, with the leaves pointing upwards. When ribbons alone were worn the emblem was to be fixed horizontally across the ribbon, with the stalk furthest from the shoulder.

A mention in despatches is now normally awarded only for gallantry or distinguished service in operations against the enemy. In cases of gallantry, it is awarded where the services do not reach the standard required for a gallantry decoration. Formerly it was also awarded posthumously in cases where the otherwise appropriate decoration or medal could not be awarded posthumously.

DESCRIPTION

Multiple-leaved emblem (Figs. A and B) This was issued in two sizes. The larger is approximately 1⅜ inches long, and ⅜ inch at its widest, being for wear when the medal itself is worn; the smaller is approximately 1 inch long, and ¼ inch at its widest, being for wear when the ribbon alone is worn. Both issues are secured to the ribbon by "bend over" pins fixed to the back of the emblem, although some strikes have holes for sewing to the ribbon or coat. Various strikes of these emblems exist, some having more clearly defined detail than others. Small replicas of the emblem are made for wear with miniature medals.

10. It seems that an immediate award was given when the services performed did not merit the award of a gallantry decoration. A relatively large number of posthumous awards were made in the Second World War, no doubt where the services would not have merited a gallantry decoration, or which otherwise would have merited such a decoration but which, however, could not be awarded posthumously.

11. Some unexplained cancellations appear in the *London Gazette* during the Second World War which may have been unconnected with forfeiture, e.g., a name gazetted twice, or in error.

12. This was, of course, before the silver commendation emblem had been approved. Army Order No.109 of September 1947 (see above) altered this rule by making the mention in despatches emblem applicable only in respect of commendations earned in the Armed Forces. Second World War Merchant Navy commendations are, however, denoted by the mention in despatches emblem.

13. Army Order No.18 of February 1944 gave details for the Army. Members of the Home Guard, the Voluntary Aid Detachments and nursing officers were also eligible. Army Order No.58 of April 1945 extended the award to members of the Army Cadet Force (when in military uniform) and to British and foreign civilians as well as to foreign military personnel who had received a military commendation.

14. Rules for wearing the mention in despatches or commendation emblems were first published in the *London Gazette* during 1947 as an addition to the list showing the approved order of wearing orders, decorations and medals (see Appendix 4). These rules which have been repeated in subsequent lists, are less detailed than the Army Order summarised here.

15. The operations are specified in detail in the Army Order. If the recipient had earned the campaign medal for other service, and had not earned it for the operation in which he was mentioned, the emblem was to be worn after the other medal ribbons.

16. This would occur, for instance, in the case of a person awarded the India General Service Medal 1908–1935 who was mentioned for operations, say, in Afghanistan 1919 and again in Waziristan 1921–1924.

Fig.A: Emblem for Mention in Despatches between 1914 and 1920; large size.

Fig.B: Emblem for Mention in Despatches between 1914 and 1920; small size.

Fig.C: Emblem for Mention in Despatches from 1920; large size.

Fig.D: Emblem for Mention in Despatches from 1920; small size.

17. A brooch fitting on the back of the leaf has also been seen.

18. Authorised in Army Order No. 44 of March 1950.

19. After the creation of the Ministry. Occasionally, members of one Service are mentioned in a despatch dealing in the main with members of another.

20. In the Second World War, Dominion headings were added to cover awards to Dominion Forces.

21. Between July 1971 and June 1973 no page numbers are given under this or any other heading although individuals continue to appear in the nominal index.

22. A rare book *South African War 1899–1902 – Mentioned in Despatches* published by the *Army and Navy Gazette* in 1902 gives almost all the naval and military awards and mentions in that War. The book was reprinted in 1971.

Single-leaved emblem (Figs. C and D) This was first issued in one size only, being approximately ¾ inch long and ⁵⁄₁₆ inch at its widest. It was to be sewn on to the garment on which it was worn through a hole at the end of the leaf and by looping cotton over the stalk[17]. Subsequently it has been issued for wear on the ribbon when the latter is worn alone. For wear on a ribbon from which a medal is suspended a larger variety is issued which is approximately 1⅛ inches long and ⅜ inch at its widest, and with "bend over" pins at the back. Different strikes of these emblems exist, variations in depth of colour and detail being particularly noticeable. Small replicas of the emblem are made for wear with miniature medals[18].

VERIFICATIONS AND CITATIONS

Where naval or military despatches were published in the *London Gazette* no index to the names mentioned was provided until the last quarter of 1916. Before this it is necessary to trace the appropriate despatch and search for the name; this can be tedious because mention may be found almost anywhere in the despatch although a later practice was to relegate names to the end of the despatch, or to an annexure which was not necessarily published at the same time as the despatch itself. From the last quarter of 1916 to the last quarter of 1941 names appear under the headings "Admiralty", "Air Ministry"[19] and "War Office" in the "State Intelligence" portion of the quarterly indices. Thereafter and until the last quarter of 1960 these headings[20] give only the pages on which awards are to be found, the names being given in a comprehensive nominal section headed "Mentions in Despatches and Commendations". From January 1961 to June 1971 the page numbers are to be found, without differentiation, under the heading "Queen's Commendations"[21], and from July 1973 under "Mentions in Despatches". The nominal section continues to appear as before. In so far as citations are concerned, naval despatches in general tend to be more informative than those relating to the Army. Even so many military despatches prior to the South African War of 1899–1902 contain a good deal of individual material, although usually more can be found in regard to officers than to other ranks.

Before the introduction of officers' confidential reports a mention in despatches was one way of bringing deserving services to notice and, as such, was much coveted. Indeed, such mentions were frequently couched in general terms and, only where appropriate, mentioned instances of gallantry. The South African War despatches contain many mere lists of names. However, some lists are published with gallantry citations (one example is given below) and are sometimes annotated to the effect that the person concerned had been awarded or recommended for the V.C., D.S.O. or D.C.M., or had been promoted or noted for promotion. Examples[22] are to be found in:

Buller's Despatch of 16th December 1899 (*London Gazette*, 26th January 1900, p.506).

Buller's Despatch of 30th March 1900 (*London Gazette*, 8th February 1901, p.938 *et seq.*).

Kitchener's Despatch of 8th May 1901 (*London Gazette*, 9th July 1901, p.4,547 *et seq.*).

Kitchener's Despatch of 8th July 1901 (*London Gazette*, 20th August 1901, p.5,481 *et seq.*).

Kitchener's Despatch of 8th October 1901 (*London Gazette*, 3rd December 1901, p.8,544 *et seq.*).

Kitchener's Despatch of 8th November 1901 (*London Gazette*, 17th January 1902, p.373 *et seq.*).

Kitchener's Despatch of 8th March 1902 (*London Gazette*, 25th April 1902, p.2,765 *et seq.*).

In these despatches the names of officers are sometimes separated from those of the men and, apart from unit groupings, no particular order of presentation is apparent. In the First World War individual mentions are rare, except in the smaller despatches, although naval despatches (as in the Second World War where actual citations are sometimes given) continue to be generally more informative. The lists gazetted in the Second World War and thereafter usually give the theatre of operations (the naval lists sometimes give the action or other details) but do not refer to a particular despatch; this was probably because from the outbreak of the Second World War the Sovereign's approval was sought for all mentions. Recommendations for, or other details regarding naval mentions in both World Wars are to be found in the Public Record Office series ADM 1 (Code 85) and ADM 116 (Code 85); both series contain a large number of files and it is necessary to know the date of award and, where possible, the action or theatre of operations for which it was made, before consulting the indices. Many First World War recommendations for members of the R.N.A.S., R.F.C. and R.A.F. serving in France and Belgium are to be found in the Honours and Awards files in the series AIR 1. Where only the date of award is known it is preferable to search for the recommendation (which was frequently in the form of a citation) in the files of H.Q. R.F.C./R.A.F. which are arranged according to date; where the formation or unit is known the corresponding files may be consulted first although not all have survived.

NUMBERS AWARDED

Due to the long period and many despatches involved, as well as to the varying types of service attracting mention it is not easy to assess the numbers awarded. However, it is probably fair to say that the South African War 1899–1902 and both World Wars provide the largest single blocks. For the First World War the Official Statistics (see Bibliography) show that 141,082 military mentions were gazetted between 1914 and 1920. Of these only 1,038 were special mentions not for service in the field (e.g. those performed at Home and in India, and for anti-aircraft service in the U.K.). In addition, between 1917 and 1920 a large number of officers, other ranks and civilians were brought to notice by the Secretary of State for War for valuable services in connection with the War; their names were communicated to the Press but were not gazetted. No comparable figures for the Second World War have been published. However, we have counted those gazetted in 1942 and find approximately 12,270 mentions were made. Due to the varying operations which have taken place since the War no years can be taken as typical. Thus in 1952, 879 were gazetted (4 for operational minesweeping, bomb and mine disposal, 379 for Malaya, 496 for Korea); in 1962, none; and in 1972, 150 (48 for Vietnam, 102 for Northern Ireland)[23].

The greatest number of mentions made of any one individual seems to have been of Field-Marshal Earl Roberts who is shown in the Army List for January 1914 as being mentioned 20 times in despatches published in the *London Gazette;* however *Who was Who* gives him as being mentioned 23 times in despatches before the campaign in Afghanistan[24].

The longest gap between a first and last mention seems to have been gained by Colonel Sir Edward Thackeray, V.C., who was first mentioned in General Sir Archdale Wilson's Despatch as one of the engineer officers accompanying the columns assaulting Delhi during the Indian Mutiny[25], and lastly in a despatch from General the Earl of Cavan for his services with the British Royal Red Cross Society in Italy during the First World War[26].

ILLUSTRATIVE AWARDS

General Buller's Despatch of 30th March 1900[27] mentioned Gunner C. Colton, 66th Battery, R.F.A., in connection with the Battle of Colenso, as follows:

23. The page references given in the "State Intelligence" portion of the indices are sometimes unreliable and the figures for the four years quoted cannot be guaranteed.

24. The discrepancy may be due to omissions from the Army List of *L.G.* entries, as well as the omission of the reference to local despatches.

25. *L.G.,* 15th December 1857, p.4,449, as a Lieutenant, Bengal Engineers. This is claimed as a mention in the Quarterly Army Lists as, indeed, literally it was. While there is no reference to his services it should be added that he was later awarded the Victoria Cross for extinguishing a fire in the Delhi Magazine enclosure.

26. *L.G.,* 5th June 1919, p.7,213, where his rank is given as General.

27. *L.G.,* 8th February 1901, p.938.

"Conspicuous bravery in continuing to perform his duties as No.5 of his gun until ammunition was exhausted, though shot through the ankle very early in the day – recommended for the D.C.M."

In due course Colton received the D.C.M.[28], the Queen's South Africa Medal with five bars, the King's South Africa Medal, the 1914 Star, the British War and Victory Medals.

For the mention leading to the award of the K.A.R. D.C.M. to Lance-Corporal Stima during the First World War see page 89.

The despatch dated 15th February 1920 from the Governor and Commander-in-Chief of the Somaliland Protectorate[29] regarding the operations against the Mullah Mohammed bin Abdullah Hassan (the "Mad Mullah") mentioned Group Captain R. Gordon, R.A.F., and Captain G. G. P. Hewett, R.N., in the following terms:

"23. The good work of the Officers of the Royal Navy and the Royal Air Force will no doubt obtain recognition through their own service channel, but I desire to bring to Your Lordship's notice the conspicuous service rendered to the Protectorate by Group-Captain R. Gordon, C.M.G., D.S.O., at request of Air Ministry, and the valuable work performed by Captain G. G. P. Hewett, Royal Navy, H.M.S. *Odin*."

Gordon was appointed a C.B. for these services[30].

Able Seaman E. W. Cunningham, R.N., was posthumously mentioned in despatches in 1942 while serving in a motor gun boat which engaged the enemy in the Straits of Dover. The *London Gazette* entry reads as follows[31]:

"For great fortitude in action against the Enemy. Able Seaman Cunningham fought his gun, with outstanding skill and devotion until he fell, mortally wounded, at his post."

28. *L.G.*, 19th April 1901, p.2,707. Colton's D.C.M. was sent out to South Africa in August 1901 for presentation.
29. *L.G.*, 1st November 1920, p.10,597.
30. *L.G.*, 12th July 1920, p.7,421.
31. *L.G.*, 13th October 1942, p.4,448.

The King's (later Queen's) Commendation for Brave Conduct

Fig.A: King's Commendation for Brave Conduct; original plastic badge.

Fig.B: King's (later Queen's) Commendation for Brave Conduct; emblem for civil commendation.

1. See, for example, *L.G.*, 22nd December 1916, p.12,559, for some Mercantile Marine commendations.

2. *I.e.*, in non-operational theatres, or in operational theatres not in the face of the enemy.

3. See the minutes of the meeting on 3rd October 1940 of the Committee on the Grant of Honours, Decorations and Medals in Time of War in P.R.O. PREM 2/104.

4. Drawings of the various designs for the badge and for the oak leaf are in P.R.O. MINT 24/333.

5. At p.8,327. These were in respect of seven officers and men of the Merchant Navy, serving in the S.S. *Mopan*, the S.S. *Lochgoil* and the S.S. *Goodwood*, group citations being given.

6. Occasionally the page numbers are corrupt or omitted altogether. Later separate Dominion headings were introduced to cover awards to the Dominion Forces.

ORIGIN AND DEVELOPMENT

Although some civilians had been commended for "good service" in the First World War[1], it was not until 1939 that commendations were made consistently, the award corresponding roughly to a "civilian" mention in despatches. While the first such awards were made for gallantry (see below) it is by no means certain that all commendations were made on this basis although, at all events, this soon became the practice. In this connection it is worth noting that some commendations were made in respect of Civil Defence units and not individuals. It was soon found that occasions arose where Servicemen performed acts of gallantry for which a mention in despatches (see Appendix 1) or other award was not appropriate[2] and, in this sense, the concept of official commendation soon lost its purely civilian aspect. Moreover, in 1942 the first awards of a special commendation "for valuable service in the air" were made to civilians and Servicemen alike (see Appendix 3), and commendations were placed on the same footing as other recognised awards.

Commendations earned in the Services, or in the Merchant Navy during the Second World War, are denoted by the mention in despatches emblem and the rules for wearing that emblem apply (see Appendix 1). For civilian awards the emblem is worn on the appropriate medal or, if no medal has been awarded, on the coat after any other medals or ribbons; if none have been awarded the emblem is worn in the position where a single ribbon or medal would be worn. Certificates accompany the award of a commendation. For civilians these are signed by the Prime Minister[3] and for Servicemen by the appropriate Service Minister.

DESCRIPTION

From about 1943 a plastic badge (Fig.A) was issued to denote a civil commendation. The badge is gold coloured, the voided portion within the wreath being red. Later this was replaced by a silver oak leaf (Fig.B) which is similar to the miniature version worn on the ribbon of the Empire Gallantry Medal (q.v.) between 1933 and 1940[4]. The first issues were made with two prongs at the back for fixing to the ribbon or to the coat, but are now made with a brooch fitting.

VERIFICATIONS AND CITATIONS

The first commendations for the Second World War appear in the *London Gazette* of 15th December 1939[5]. Until the last quarter of 1941 names are listed, with some omissions, under the following mutually exclusive headings in the "State Intelligence" portion of the Gazette indices: "Admiralty", "Air Ministry", "Civil Defence", "Commendations", "Merchant Navy" and "War Office". Thereafter and until the first quarter of 1947 these headings give only the pages upon which awards are to be found[6], the names themselves being relegated to a comprehensive nominal section headed "Mentions in Despatches and Commendations". Throughout the whole of the period 1939–1947 specified above the names or page numbers given under the headings of the Service Departments also include references to persons mentioned in despatches and it is only the actual Gazette notice which will show whether the award is a mention or commendation. Beginning with the index for the second quarter of 1947 commendations[7] are indexed separately for the first time as "King's Commendations" in the "State Intelligence", becoming "Queen's Commendations" in the second quarter of 1952[8].

During the Second World War some citations are given in respect of civilian and Merchant Navy commendations, occasionally being introduced as part of the narrative describing the award of a decoration or medal to another person concerned in the same action, or as a brief note of the individual circumstances. Later citations of varying lengths are given in respect of almost all commendations.

NUMBERS AWARDED

No overall figures have been published and therefore we have selected four years as examples although, due to the length of the Second World War and the unsettled world conditions following, no year can be regarded as typical. Moreover, the page references given in the "State Intelligence" portion of the Gazette indices are sometimes faulty and our figures therefore cannot be guaranteed. Nevertheless, the following table (which includes Commonwealth awards) may be taken as a reasonable guide:

Year	Air Force	Army	Civil Defence	Civilian	Merchant Navy	Navy	Total
1942	32	69	141	64	475	56	837
1952	5	16	—	84	—	—	105
1962	2	8	—	37	—	1	48
1972	3	5	—	58	—	—	66

We show the wartime Merchant Navy figures separately because such commendations were then denoted by the mention in despatches emblem (q.v.).

ILLUSTRATIVE AWARD

Sergeant K. Johansson, 1st Prince of Wales's Own Regiment of Yorkshire, was commended in 1962[9], his citation reading as follows:

> "For courage when confronted by an armed civilian attempting to obtain ammunition. Although held up at pistol point for an hour, Sergeant Johansson did not comply with the man's demands and by his presence of mind ensured his apprehension."

7. Page numbers only are given, the comprehensive nominal section appearing as before. Occasionally the heading has been inadvertently omitted from the index.

8. From the first quarter of 1948 to the first quarter of 1950 commendations for valuable service in the air are indexed separately, but thereafter they are indexed under the general heading. From January 1961 to June 1973 mentions in despatches are also indexed, without differentiation, under "Queen's Commendations".

9. *L.G.*, 30th January 1962, p.789.

The King's (later Queen's) Commendation for Valuable Service in the Air

Fig.A: King's (later Queen's) Commendation for Valuable Service in the Air; civil badge.

ORIGIN AND DEVELOPMENT

This form of award was instituted during the Second World War in recogntion of meritorious service in the air, or of gallantry not reaching the standard required for the Air Force Cross or the Air Force Medal (q.v.). The first awards were made in 1942.

In the Services, the mention in despatches emblem is worn to denote a military commendation for valuable service in the air and the rules regarding that emblem apply (see Appendix 1). The special badge denoting a civil commendation is worn on the coat immediately below any medals or medal ribbons or, in civil air line uniform, on the panel of the left breast pocket.

A certificate, signed by the appropriate Minister, accompanies commendation.

DESCRIPTION

The silver badge (Fig.A) was designed by Mr. Percy Metcalf, C.V.O., R.D.I., and it was approved by King George VI on 10th September 1945.

VERIFICATIONS AND CITATIONS

The first Service commendations appear in the *London Gazette* of 1st January 1942, the page references being found under the heading "Air Ministry" in the "State Intelligence" portion of the Gazette quarterly index, while the actual names are relegated to a comprehensive nominal section headed "Mentions in Despatches and Commendations". Thereafter the "Air Ministry" heading gives the page numbers upon which both mentions in despatches and commendations are to be found and it is necessary to turn to the actual page to find which type of award is indicated. The first civil commendations appear in the *London Gazette* of 11th June 1942[1], the page references being found under "Commendations, miscellaneous", and the names in the nominal section. Beginning with the first quarter of 1948 a special heading "King's Commendations for Valuable Service in the Air" was introduced which again gave only the page numbers. These, however, were for both military and civil commendations. The names appeared in the nominal section as before. Beginning with the second quarter of 1950 awards are indexed as "King's Commendations"[2] and it is necessary to refer to the actual Gazette notice to determine whether a commendation for brave conduct, or for valuable service in the air, is intended. Very few citations appear.

NUMBERS AWARDED

No overall figures have been published and therefore we have selected four years as examples, although due to the length of the Second World War and the unsettled world conditions following, no year can be regarded as typical. Moreover, the page references given in the "State Intelligence" portion of the Gazette indices are sometimes faulty and our figures therefore cannot be guaranteed. Nevertheless, the following table (which includes Commonwealth awards), may be taken as a reasonable guide:

1. At p.2,506. Awards to British Overseas Airways Corporation, Royal Air Force Ferry Command, etc.

2. "Queen's Commendations" from the second quarter of 1952. The comprehensive nominal section continued as before which, on occasion, has been found to be incomplete. From January 1961 to June 1973 mentions in despatches are also indexed, without differentiation, under the same heading.

Year	Air Forces	Civilian	Navy	Army	Total
1942	11	4	—	—	15
1952	60	42	1	—	103
1962	67	9	—	—	76
1972	36	10	—	1	47

ILLUSTRATIVE AWARD

Flight Lieutenant D. C. Kwong, Hong Kong Auxiliary Air Force, was commended in 1962[3], his citation reading as follows:

> "For outstanding skill, courage and determination as pilot of a helicopter which rescued an injured climber in hazardous flying conditions."

This officer also received the A.F.C. in *L.G.*, 21st December 1965 for an helicopter rescue.

3. *LG.*, 22nd May 1962, p.4,123.

The Order of Wearing Orders, Decorations and Medals

It was not until the second half of the 19th century that medals came to be awarded in significant numbers and, in consequence, for question of relative precedence to arise. Indeed, for many years following the Crimean War recipients seem to have worn their medals much as they pleased and many of the portraits reproduced in Wilkins (see Bibliography) show highly individual and even bizarre methods of wear. The Army Enlistment Act of 1870 introduced the short service system into the British Army and hence, despite the increased number of campaign medals being awarded, until the First World War a soldier with more than, say, four medals was a comparative rarity. On the other hand, officers tended to serve longer and, at least for the senior ranks, a wider range of awards was open to them. In due course it became necessary for the sake of uniformity to prescribe an order[1] for wearing the various distinctions available. Initially, the Services issued their own regulations on the subject, but these were unco-ordinated and incomplete. However, King Edward VII was much interested in the matter and it was during his reign that attempts were made to lay down rules applicable to the Services and to civilians alike.

Lists of the approved order of wearing began to be published at irregular intervals in the *London Gazette*, beginning in 1921. Prior to this, lists were to be found in various official, semi-official and unofficial publications[2] which, indeed, continued to be published. The early lists are comparatively straightforward, due to the fewer awards then available although, despite this, contemporary sources do not always agree with each other. With the introduction of new awards the lists became longer, individual placings in the precedence changed, and many complications ensued.

In the following table we give the present order of wearing to which we have added footnotes only in respect of the decorations described in this work, or where some other explanation is necessary. We have based the notes largely on the lists given in the *London Gazette* although we have drawn on earlier sources where possible[3]. Even then this is by no means the full story and, to obtain the correct order at any one time, it is necessary to consult contemporary sources. Since the lists[4] in the *London Gazette* are not easy to find through the indices, the references are as follows:

> 22nd April 1921, p.3,184
> 7th November 1922, p.7,871
> 22nd November 1929, p.7,529
> 24th April 1936, p.2,621
> 22nd April 1941, p.2,286
> 11th February 1947, p.697
> 12th July 1949, p.3,403
> 27th July 1951, p.4,033
> 15th May 1954, p.3,537
> 19th April 1955, p.2,259
> 14th January 1958, p.363
> 28th April 1961, p.3,147
> 27th October 1964, p.9,121

1. To be distinguished from the precedence conferred by the statutes of various Orders upon the members thereof.

2. *E.g.*, the various editions of *Dress Regulations for the Army* (official), *Dress Worn at His Majesty's Court* (semi-official), and *Whitaker's Almanack* (unofficial).

3. These are from the Army sources since they are readily accessible and provide a fairly close dating for changes. The Army Orders we quote are amendments to Dress Regulations.

4. From 1947 onwards the lists also give rules for wearing the Mention in Despatches and Commendation Emblems (see Appendices 1–3).

5. *Victoria Cross* The early photographs reproduced in Wilkins suggest that the V.C. was worn much as the recipient fancied, one style being popular where it occupied the central position with other medals grouped round it. However, Queen's Regulations for the Army, 1881, which gave a rudimentary order of wearing, laid down that the V.C. was to follow the Order of the Indian Empire (the Companion's badge of which was then worn on the breast), while Dress Regulations for the Army, 1900, gave it as following the Royal Victorian Order (instituted in 1896). According to de la Bère (see Bibliography), in 1902 King Edward VII ruled that it should precede all decorations placed on the bar brooch worn on the breast. Dress Regulations for the Army, 1904, show the V.C. in its present premier position.

6. *Order of the British Empire* Appointments to and promotions for gallantry in the Order after 14th January 1958 are so described and a silver oak leaf emblem is worn on the ribbon. A person appointed to the Order for gallantry after that date and subsequently promoted, whether for gallanty or not, retains and wears the oak leaf emblem. This does not apply to the holder of the B.E.M. for gallantry unless he was appointed to the Order for gallantry in which case he wears the emblem on both ribbons, otherwise he continues to wear it on the ribbon of the B.E.M. only. By an additional Statute of 7th December 1971 it was ordained, *inter alia*, that a person promoted from a lower Class in one Division to a higher Class in the other Division of the Order should retain and wear the insignia of the lower Class in addition to that of the higher Class.

7. *Distinguished Service Order* The instituting Royal Warrant of 1888 gave precedence after the Order of the Indian Empire although, in the order of wearing, the V.C. then came between the two. An amending Royal Warrant of 1902 gave precedence after the Royal Victorian Order, this provision in turn being amended by one of the following year which gave precedence after the 4th Class of that Order. The consolidating Royal Warrant of 1918 placed the D.S.O. after the C.B.E.

8. *Indian Order of Merit (Military)* Originally worn after the Order of British India, its present position is shown in *L.G.* 1947.

9. *Order of Burma* Shown only in *L.G.*s 1941 and 1947. In the former it followed the Kaisar-i-Hind Medal. The Order was instituted as a reward for good service by a Royal Warrant of 10th May 1940, and extended to acts of gallantry by a Royal Warrant of 11th September 1945. No gallantry awards seem to have been made.

10. *Various* In Army Order No. 196 of October 1905, the C.S.C., A.M. and S.G.M. were shown following the Order of St. John, but in Army Order No. 246 of August 1912 the C.S.C. was shown following the C.G.M. The latter authority gave the following after Polar Medals: Constabulary Medal (Ireland), Albert Medal, Board of Trade Medal for Saving Life at Sea, Indian Order of Merit (Civil), Edward Medal, Indian Distinguished Service Medal, King's Police Medal. Army Council Instruction No. 754 of July 1918 showed the D.S.C. and A.M. in their present positions. *L.G.* 1921 showed the I.D.S.M. as next after the A.F.M. and in *L.G.* 1929 the remaining five medals were shown as following the I.D.S.M. *L.G.* 1941 placed the King's Police Medal, the G.M. and E.M. in that order between the A.F.M. and I.D.S.M. *L.G.* 1947 gave the present order.

In the footnotes these are referred to merely by the year of publication, e.g., "*L.G.*, 1929". Except for the New Zealand Cross we have shown various obsolete decorations in their last recorded positions; even this is not free from difficulty as, for example, with the E.G.M. which is shown after the I.O.M. (Civil) although it was originally worn in the same position as the B.E.M. for Meritorious Service which, due to the inter-position of various Police Medals for gallantry, now appears lower in the list. We have been unable to find any official placing for the New Zealand Cross although a case could be made out for it to follow immediately after the Victoria Cross; however, the matter is now entirely academic.

In the following list it will be appreciated that when the miniature or ribbon of a higher class of a junior order is worn with that of a lower class of a senior order, the higher class miniature or ribbon is worn first, e.g., the K.B.E. will come before the C.B., and the G.C.M.G. before the K.C.B. The small silver rose, denoting the award of a bar to certain decorations or gallantry medals when ribbons alone are worn, was first sanctioned in 1916 (see the *Journal of the Orders and Medals Research Society* for June 1968 at p.43 et seq., where the material in the Public Record Office File WO 32/5394 is summarised).

Victoria Cross (V.C.)[5]
George Cross (G.C.)
Order of the Garter (K.G.)
Order of the Thistle (K.T.)
Order of St. Patrick (K.P.)
Order of the Bath (G.C.B., K.C.B. and D.C.B., and C.B.)
Order of Merit (O.M.; ranks next after G.C.B.)
Order of the Star of India (G.C.S.I., K.C.S.I. and C.S.I.)
Order of St. Michael and St. George (G.C.M.G., K.C.M.G. and D.C.M.G., and C.M.G.)
Order of the Indian Empire (G.C.I.E., K.C.I.E. and C.I.E.)
Order of the Crown of India (C.I.)
Royal Victorian Order (G.C.V.O., K.C.V.O. and D.C.V.O., and C.V.O.)
Order of the British Empire (G.B.E., K.B.E. and D.B.E., and C.B.E.)[6]
Order of the Companions of Honour (C.H.; ranks next after G.B.E.)
Distinguished Service Order (D.S.O.)[7]
Royal Victorian Order (M.V.O.; Class IV)
Order of the British Empire (O.B.E.)[6]
Queen's Service Order (Q.S.O.)
Imperial Service Order (I.S.O.)
Royal Victorian Order (M.V.O.; Class V)
Order of the British Empire (M.B.E.)[6]
Indian Order of Merit (Military)[3]Order of Burma (for gallantry) (O.B.)[9]
Royal Red Cross (Class I; R.R.C.)
Distinguished (formerly Conspicuous) Service Cross (D.S.C.)[10]
Military Cross (M.C.)
Distinguished Flying Cross (D.F.C.)
Air Force Cross (A.F.C.)
Royal Red Cross (Class II; A.R.R.C.)
Order of British India (O.B.I.)
Kaisar-i-Hind Medal
Order of Burma (for good service) (O.B.)[9]
Order of St. John
Albert Medal (A.M.)[10]
Union of South Africa King's (Queen's) Medal for Bravery, in gold
Distinguished Conduct Medal (D.C.M.)[11]
Conspicuous Gallantry Medal (C.G.M.)[11]
George Medal (G.M.)[12]
King's (Queen's) Police Medal, for Gallantry (K.P.M., K.P.F.S.M., Q.P.M.)[10]
Queen's Fire Service Medal, for Gallantry (Q.F.S.M.)
Edward Medal (E.M.)[10]
Royal West African Frontier Force Distinguished Conduct Medal (D.C.M.)[13]

King's African Rifles Distinguished Conduct Medal (D.C.M.)[13]
Indian Distinguished Service Medal (I.D.S.M.)[10]
Burma Gallantry Medal (B.G.M.)[14]
Union of South Africa King's (Queen's) Medal for Bravery, in silver
Distinguished Service Medal (D.S.M.)
Military Medal (M.M.)
Distinguished Flying Medal (D.F.M.)
Air Force Medal (A.F.M.)
Constabulary Medal (Ireland)[10]
Board of Trade Medal for Saving Life at Sea (S.G.M.)[10]
Indian Order of Merit (Civil) (I.O.M.)[10]
Empire Gallantry Medal (E.G.M.)[15]
Indian Police Medal for Gallantry[16]
Burma Police Medal for Gallantry[17]
Ceylon Police Medal for Gallantry
Sierra Leone Police Medal for Gallantry
Sierra Leone Fire Brigades Medal for Gallantry
Colonial Police Medal for Gallantry[18]
Queen's Gallantry Medal (Q.G.M)
Queen's Service Medal (Q.S.M.)
Uganda Services Medal (if awarded for gallantry)
British Empire Medal (B.E.M.)[19]
Canada Medal (C.M. or M. du C.)
Life Saving Medal of the Order of St. John[20]
King's (Queen's) Police Medal for Distinguished Service (K.P.M., K.P.F.S.M., Q.P.M.)
Queen's Fire Service Medal for Distinguished Service (Q.F.S.M.)
Queen's Medal for Chiefs
War Medals (in order of date of campaign)
Polar Medals (in order of date)
Royal Victorian Medal (in gold, silver or bronze)
Imperial Service Medal
Police Medals for Meritorious Service
Uganda Services Medal (if awarded for meritorious service)
Badge of Honour
Jubilee, Coronation and Durbar Medals[21]
King George V Long and Faithful Service Medal
King George VI Long and Faithful Service Medal
Queen Elizabeth II Long and Faithful Service Medal
Efficiency and Long Service Decorations and Medals, Medals for Champion Shots, Independence, etc., Medals
Other Commonwealth Orders, Decorations and Medals (instituted since 1949, otherwise than by the Sovereign) and awards by the States of Malaysia and the State of Brunei
Foreign Orders (in order of date of award)
Foreign Decorations (in order of date of award)
Foreign Medals (in order of date of award)

11. *Distinguished Conduct Medal and Conspicuous Gallantry Medal* To judge by early photographs no order of wearing for the D.C.M. or the C.G.M. originally seems to have been prescribed. The earliest mention of the D.C.M. is in Queen's Regulations for the Army, 1881, which laid down that it was to be worn immediately after the appropriate war medal. In the Admiralty Uniform Regulations of 1879 (see Bibliography), which incorporated the regulations as to the wearing of medals etc. made on 28th August 1877, British decorations were to precede British medals and, within this arrangement, were to be worn in the order of date of award. No specific mention of the C.G.M. was made and, indeed, it is arguable whether, at that time, it was classified as a decoration or as a medal. In the latter event it might have been worn, like the D.C.M., after the appropriate war medal. Army Order No. 181 of July 1902 gave the D.C.M. precedence of all war medals while Army Order No. 196 of October 1905 shows it following the C.G.M. which, in turn, then followed Jubilee, etc., medals. Army Order No. 246 of August 1912 showed the D.C.M. and C.G.M. in their present relative positions. Lance Sergeant J. E. Preston, Royal Marine Light Infantry, received both the D.C.M. and C.G.M. for gallantry in China in 1900; this is a unique combination. The C.G.M. (Flying) is worn in the same relative position as the Naval C.G.M.

12. *George Medal* In *L.G.* 1941 the G.M. is shown following the King's Police and Fire Service Medal for Gallantry which, at that time, in turn followed the A.F.M. Its present position is shown in *L.G.* 1947.

13. *R.W.A.F.F. and K.A.R. Distinguished Conduct Medals* In *L.G.*s 1936 and 1941 these were shown following the D.S.M.; *L.G.* 1947 shows the present order.

14. *Burma Gallantry Medal* Shown only in *L.G.*s 1941 and 1947. In the former it followed the Colonial Police Medal for Gallantry and in the latter the I.D.S.M.

15. *Empire Gallantry Medal* This last appeared in the *L.G.* lists in 1936.

16. *Indian Police Medal for Gallantry* First appears in *L.G.* 1936 following the E.G.M. With the conversion of the latter into the G.C. and the alteration in the position of the King's Police and Fire Service Medal for Gallantry, and the Edward Medal (see footnote 6 above), its present position is shown in *L.G.* 1941.

17. *Burma Police Medal for Gallantry* Appears only in *L.G.*s 1941 and 1947.

18. *Colonial Police Medal for Gallantry* With *L.G.* 1961 the holder of the Colonial Police Medal for Meritorious Service who is subsequently awarded a bar for gallantry wears the Meritorious Service Medal and gallantry bar, and the Meritorious Service ribbon and rose emblem, in the order assigned to the Colonial Police Medal for Gallantry.

19. *British Empire Medal* Formerly the Medal of the Order of the British Empire for Meritorious Service, and also includes the Medal of the Order awarded before 29th December 1922. A holder of the Medal for gallantry granted since 14th January 1958, if subsequently appointed to the Order, continues to wear the emblem on the ribbon of the Medal and wears the emblem on the ribbon of the Order only if appointed to the Order for gallantry. On the ribbon of the Medal the emblem is worn above any bar which may have been awarded. When ribbons alone are worn the gallantry emblem is worn further from the left shoulder than any silver rose emblem denoting the award of a bar.

20. *Life Saving Medal of the Order of St. John* Last appears in *L.G.* 1947.

21. *Jubilee etc. Medals* The position of these medals varied. A.C.I. No. 754 of July 1918 showed them following the Albert Medal while A.C.I. No. 1230 of November 1918 moved them to follow the King's Police Medal as it then stood (see footnote 6 above).

Appendix 5

Post-Nominal Letters

1. V.C.	29. C.V.O.	55. I.D.S.M.
2. G.C.	30. C.B.E.	56. B.G.M.
3. K.G.[1]	31. D.S.O.	57. D.S.M.
4. K.T.[1]	32. M.V.O.[4]	58. M.M.
5. K.P.	33. O.B.E.	59. D.F.M.
6. G.C.B.[2]	34. Q.S.O.	60. A.F.M.
7. O.M.	35. I.S.O.	61. S.G.M.
8. G.C.S.I.[3]	M.V.O.[5]	I.O.M.[14]
9. G.C.M.G.[2]	37. I.O.M.[6]	62. E.G.M.[15]
10. G.C.I.E.[3]	38. O.B.[7]	63. C.P.M.[7]
11. C.I.	39. R.R.C.	64. Q.G.M.
12. G.C.V.O.[2]	40. D.S.C.	65. Q.S.M.
13. G.B.E.[2]	41. M.C.	66. B.E.M.
14. C.H.	42. D.F.C.	67. C.M. or M.du C.
15. K.C.B.	43. A.F.C.	K.P.M.[8]
16. D.C.B.	44. A.R.R.C.	K.P.F.S.M.[8]
17. K.C.S.I.	45. O.B.I.	Q.P.M.[8]
18. K.C.M.G.	O.B.[8]	Q.F.S.M.[8]
19. D.C.M.G.	46. A.M.[9]	68. M.S.M.[16]
20. K.C.I.E.	47. D.C.M.	69. E.R.D.[17]
21. K.C.V.O.	48. C.G.M.[10]	70. V.D.[18]
22. D.C.V.O.	49. G.M.	71. T.D.[19]
23. K.B.E.	50. K.P.M.[11]	72. E.D.[20]
24. D.B.E.	51. K.P.F.S.M.[11]	73. R.D.
25. C.B.	52. Q.P.M.[12]	74. V.R.D.
26. C.S.I.	53. Q.F.S.M.[12]	75. C.D.
27. C.M.G.	54. E.M.	
28. C.I.E.	D.C.M.[13]	

1. Not used for Ladies of the Order of the Garter or of the Thistle.
2. Used also by Dames Grand Cross.
3. Used also by Dames Grand Commander.
4. When of the 4th Class.
5. When of the 5th Class.
6. When in the Military Division.
7. When for Gallantry.
8. When for Distinguished or Good Service.
9. Medals in Gold no longer awarded; Albert Medal now only awarded posthumously.
10. Used both for the naval medal and for the flying medal.
11. When for Gallantry.
12. When for Gallantry; posthumous only.
13. If for Royal West African Frontier Force or the King's African Rifles.
14. When in the Civil Division.
15. Now usable only in reference to unexchangeable honorary awards before the creation of the George Cross in 1940.
16. Post-nominal letters customarily used when awarded for naval service before 20th June 1928.
17. Emergency Reserve Decoration (Army).
18. Denotes the Volunteer Officers' Decoration (1892–1908); V.D. for India and the Colonies (1894–1930), and the Colonial Auxiliary Forces Officers' Decoration (1899–1930).
19. Denotes both the T.D. (1908–1930), the Efficiency Decoration (instituted 1930) if awarded to an officer of the (Home) Auxiliary Military Forces, and the T.A.V.R. Decoration (instituted 1969).
20. Denotes the Efficiency Decoration when awarded to an officer of Commonwealth or Colonial Auxiliary Forces.
21. Widely denoted however as V.A. in quasi-official references.

Note that the post-nominal letters G.M.B., G.M.S.I., G.M.M.G., G.M.I.E., G.M.V.O. and G.M.B.E., indicating the Great Master of the Order of the Bath, and Grand Masters of the Orders of the Star of India, St. Michael and St. George, Indian Empire, Victorian Order and British Empire, though used, are not officially authorized.

Decorations which do not carry authorized post-nominal letters are:

1. Royal Victorian Chain.
2. Royal Order of Victoria and Albert[21].
3. Kaisar-i-Hind Medal next after the O.B.I.
4. Order of St. John next after the Order of Burma (for good service).
5. Union of South Africa King's (or Queen's) Medal for Bravery in Gold, next after the A.M.
6. Union of South Africa King's (or Queen's) Medal for Bravery in Silver, next after the B.G.M.
7. Constabulary Medal (Ireland).
8, 9, 10 and 11, India, Burma, Ceylon and Sierra Leone Police Medals for Gallantry, in that order next after the E.G.M.
12. Sierra Leone Fire Brigade Medal for Gallantry, next after the Sierra Leone Police Medal for Gallantry.

13. Uganda Services Medal (if for Gallantry), next after the Colonial Police Medal for Gallantry.
14. Life Saving Medal of the Order of St. John, next after the Canada Medal.
15. Royal Victorian Medal (in Gold, Silver or Bronze), next after Polar Medals.
16. Imperial Service Medal, next after the Royal Victorian Medal.
17. Police Medals for Meritorious Service (other than King's/Queen's medals and C.P.M.), next after the Imperial Service Medal.
18. Uganda Services Medal (if for meritorious service), next after Police Medals above.

The following post-nominal letters were previously used:

K.B.   indicated Knighthood of the Order of the Bath prior to its division into three classes in 1815.

G.C.H. indicated membership of one of the three classes – Knights Grand Cross,
K.C.H. Knights Commander or Knights – of "The Order of the Guelphs" conferred from and 1815 to 1837 during the Union of the Crowns of Hanover and the United
K.H. Kingdom.

K.S.I. Knights of the Most Excellent Order of the Star of India. This designation was used between 1861 and 1866 before the Order was enlarged into three classes.

C.S.C. Conspicuous Service Cross (instituted in 1901); redesignated D.S.C. in 1914.

Index to Recipients Mentioned in the Text

Note: Following the recipient's name in parentheses is the award mentioned in the text. Other awards to which the recipient was entitled are omitted. Conventional post-nominal abbreviations are used except where none has been authorised, in which case the following appear:

In the case of the Dominion and Colonial D.C.M., the C.G.M. (Flying), the Indian Order or Merit (Civil Division) and the Sea Gallantry Medal (Foreign Services) an asterisk is added to the authorised abbreviation. For simplicity, non-European names are indexed under the recipient's first name.

311

Seagrim, D.A. (V.C.) 290
Seagrim, H. (G.C.) 290
Seale, M.D. (D.F.C.) 98
Sears, F.J. (D.C.M.) 77
Seggie, W. (D.C.M.) 65 *(footnote)*
Sehlogo, A. (K.M.B.) 181
Seholi, P. (K.M.B.) 181
Sepulchre, O. (A.S.M.) 29
Sete Thapa (I.M.S.M.) 155 *(footnote)*
Sewell, G.S. (G.M.) 148
Seymour, G. (D.C.M.) 65 *(footnote)*
Shadil Khan (I.O.M.) 168 *(footnote)*
Shaik Mohiden (A.M.) 21 *(footnote)*
Shaikh Rahiman IV (I.O.M.*)
    169 *(footnote)*
Sharifullah Khan (I.O.M.*) 171
Sharp, C.J. (M.S.M./D.C.M.)
    198 *(footnote)*
Sheehan, C. (D.C.M.) 74 *(footnote)*
Sheikh Adam Sheikh Ibrahim (I.O.M.*)
    169
Shenton, A. (M.S.M.) 197, 202
Shepheard, J. (C.G.M.) 44
Shepherd, B.G.E. (D.S.M.) 115 *(footnote)*
Shepherd, R. (N.Z.C.) 235
Sher Azam Khan (I.P.M.) 176
Sher Ali (K.P.M.) 195
Sherratt, F.W. (A.F.M.) 14 *(footnote)*
Sherwin, T. (S.G.M.) 274 *(footnote)*
Shiers, W.H. (A.F.M.) 14
Shingleton, D. (D.C.M.) 67 *(footnote)*
Shorter, J. (D.S.M.) 116
Shri S.A. Thomas (I.P.M.) 177
Sibbick, E.A. (B.E.M.) 247
Silkstone, G.H. (E.M.) 134, 135 *(footnote)*
Sindall, K. (C.P.M.) 42
Sitaram Shivram (I.O.M.*) 171
Skelton, T.M. (B.E.M.) 247
Smallie, J. (D.C.M.) 67
Smith, A. (N.Z.C.) 234
Smith, F. (E.M.) 134 *(footnote)*,
    135 *(footnote)*
Smith, G. (D.C.M.) 77
Smith, H. (A.M.) 23
Smith, H.P.R. (A.F.C.) 10
Smith, J. (D.C.M.) 67 *(footnote)*
Smith, J. (V.C.) 289
Smith, M. (R.R.C.) 260
Smith, N.L. (B.E.M.) 247
Smith, R.M. (D.F.C.) 96
Smith, W. (A.M.) 23
Smith, W.G.G.D. (D.F.C.) 98
Smithbone, V.N. (B.E.M.) 247
Smits de Savoye (A.S.M.) 30
Snell, H. (K.M.B.) 180
Snyder, E.S. (K.M.B.) 181
So Hau (S.G.M.) 274 *(footnote)*
Soles, G.H. (D.C.M.) 82
Solomon, H.I. (K.M.B.) 181
Sophie, Princess (R.R.C.) 261
Sordy, T. (M.C.) 220 *(footnote)*
Spence, E. (V.C.) 287 *(footnote)*
Spencer, J. (D.C.M.) 74 *(footnote)*
Spike, E.L. (M.S.M.) 205 *(footnote)*
Spitteler, T.M. (B.P.M.) 38 *(footnote)*
Stagg, A.T.C. (M.M.) 226
Stanley, C.B. (B.P.M.) 38 *(footnote)*

Stapleton, E. (C.M.I.) 60
Stebbings, J.M. (E.M.) 135 and *footnote*
Steed, B.L. (M.S.M.) 201 *(footnote)*
Stephen, J. (Q.G.M.) 257
Stewart, A.J. (A.M.) 21
Stima (D.C.M.*) 89, 300
Stonehouse, J. (M.S.M.) 201, 202
Stonier, J. (A.F.C.) 10
Strawbridge, R.A. (D.F.M.) 103
Stroud, A.E. (E.M.) 134 *(footnote)*
Struthers, J.G. (D.S.C.) 110
Sturdy, G.H. (D.S.M.) 118
Sullivan, J. (A.M.) 20 *(footnote)*
Sullivan, J. (C.G.M.) 45
Sultan Mahmud Khan (I.O.M.*) 170
Supple, C. (C.M.I.) 58
Sutton, A.H. (D.C.M.) 78
Syme, H.R. (G.M.) 148
Szabo, V. (G.C.) 142

Tadman, J.F. (C.G.M.) 49
Tait, J.B. (D.S.O.) 128
Talbot, F.E. (E.G.M.) 241
Tanguy, J.T.J. (E.G.M.) 242
Tanjore, V.A.V.Ayyar (I.P.M.) 176
Taylor, J. (C.G.M.) 44, 45
Thackeray, E.T. (M.i.D.) 299
Theron, M.J. (K.M.B.) 181
Thomas, M. (R.R.C.) 269 *(footnote)*
Thomas, R.H. (D.F.C.) 98
Thompson, R.W.F. (B.E.M.) 247
Thomson, A.C. (D.S.C.) 110
Thorne, J.H. (E.M.) 134, 135 *(footnote)*
Thorne, P.D. (A.F.C.) 10
Timms, C.G. (M.C.) 220
Timour Mehmet (C.P.M.) 41 *(footnote)*
Titlestad, S. (D.C.M.*) 89
Tomlinson, G.A. (S.G.M.) 272 *(footnote)*
Topley, T.A. (D.S.M.) 116
Topp, G. (? M.S.M.) 70
Topp, R.L. (A.F.C.) 10
Toussaint, V. (S.G.M.*) 281
Towers, L.J.V. (I.O.M.*) 171
Trant, T. (C.M.I.) 56, 58
Trewavas, J. (C.G.M.) 45
Tsang Wing (C.P.M.) 42
Tuckett, F.R. (C.M.I.) 57 *(footnotes)*
Tulloch, W. (R.R.C.) 269 *(footnote)*
Turnbull, L.W. (C.G.M.*) 52
Turner, A.B. (V.C.) 290
Turner, E. (C.G.M.) 48
Turner, G.E. (M.S.M.) 199 *(footnote)*, 201
Turner, H.E. (M.M.) 228
Turner, V.B. (V.C.) 290
Tyler, H.C. (I.P.M.) 176

U Maung Gale (K.P.M.) 188 *(footnote)*
Ulyett, H. (M.S.M.) 63
Umdi (I.M.S.M.) 157
Upham, C.H. (V.C.) 293

Van den Berg, C. (K.M.B.) 180
Van Hove, C. (E.G.M.) 242
Van Kul (B.G.M.) 34
Vane, G.P. (M.M.) 228
Veladi Sammai (A.M.) 21 *(footnote)*,
    135 *(footnote)*

Verdier, A.E.L. (D.F.M.) 104 *(footnote)*
Vercoe, F. (D.C.M.) 82
Vinnicombe, W. (D.C.M.) 71
Vinters, T. (E.M.) 135
Voelcker, F.W. (D.S.O./O.B.E)
    128 *(footnote)*
Vuylsteke, J. (D.F.M.) 104
Vyasam Venkataramayya (I.M.S.M.) 158

Wadero Ali Mohammed Khan Palejo
    (I.O.M.*) 171
Wadero Ghulam Rasul Bhai Phul
    (I.O.M.*) 171
Wadsley, H.E. (G.M.) 148
Wadsworth, H.H. (A.M.) 21 *(footnote)*
Wagner, C. (A.M.) 21
Wagstaff, T. (E.M.) 135, 136
Walker, C. (D.C.M.) 67 *(footnote)*
Walker, F.J. (D.S.O.) 128
Walker, S. (N.Z.C.) 235
Wallington, F.V. (M.C.) 220
Walsh, M. (D.C.M.) 69 *(footnote)*
Ward, A.H. (D.F.M.) 14
Wardle, T.F.J.L. (C.S.C.) 110
Warke, S.J. (M.M.) 229
Warner, A.L.H. (K.M.B.) 181
Waterfield, A. (E.G.M.) 241
Watkins, W.J. (G.M.) 19 *(footnote)*
Watson, E.R.H. (D.S.C.) 111
Watts, A.M. (K.P.F.S.M.) 193 *(footnote)*
Watts, H. (S.G.M.) 273
Watts, J. (D.C.M.) 71 *(footnote)*
Wazeer Singh Nagarkoti (I.O.M.) 171
Webb, S.E. (R.R.C.) 269 *(footnote)*
Weiner, F.E. (A.S.M.) 30
Welsby, J. (E.M.) 135 and *footnote*
West, F. (D.C.M.) 77
Western, D. (A.M.) 22
Wheatley, F. (D.C.M.) 66 *(footnote)*
Whelan, J. (D.C.M.) 71 *(footnote)*,
    80 *(footnote)*
Wheldon, E. (R.R.C.) 260 *(footnote)*
Whirlpool, F. (V.C.) 291 *(footnote)*
Whistler, H.A. (D.F.C.) 96
Whistler, T.A. (A.M.) 21
White, A.P. (D.S.M.) 117
White, G.H. (A.M.) 274 *(footnote)*
White, J. (D.C.M.) 67 *(footnote)*
White, P. (D.C.M.) 66 *(footnote)*
White, S.G. (D.S.M.) 114
White, S.P.R. (D.S.C.) 110
White, T.E. (C.G.M.*) 52
White, W.H. (S.G.M.) 274 *(footnote)*
Whitehead, J. (B.E.M.) 247
Whiteley, J. (S.G.M.) 275
Whitlock, S.G. (D.S.M.) 117
Whyte, G. (B.E.M.) 247
Wilkinson, C.E. (D.S.C.) 110
Williams, C. (D.C.M.) 71 *(footnote)*
Williams, F. (D.S.O./D.C.M.) 125
Williams, F.A. (M.M.) 224
Williams, G. (A.M.) 21 *(footnote)*
Williams, G. (D.C.M.*) 88 *(footnote)*
Williams, T. (S.G.M.) 275
Williams, W. (E.M.) 133 *(footnote)*
Willis, W. (C.M.I.) 59
Wilson, F. (M.M.) 228

Notes

Notes